The Charnock Discourses

by Stephen Charnock

Edited by Anthony Uyl

Devoted Publishing

Woodstock, Ontario, 2017

The Charnock Discourses
by Stephen Charnock (1628-1680)
Edited by Anthony Uyl

Originally Published in 1864

The text of The Charnock Discourses is all in the Public Domain. This edition is published by Devoted Publishing a division of 2165467 Ontario Inc.

What kind of philosophies do you have?
Let us know!

Contact us at: devotedpub@hotmail.com
Visit our shop on Facebook: @DevotedPublishing

Published in Woodstock, Ontario, Canada 2017

For bulk educational rates, please contact us at the above email address.

ISBN: 978-1-77356-029-8

Table of Contents

A Discourse of God's being the Author of Reconciliation

And all things are of God, who hath reconciled us to himself by Jesus Christ, and hath given to us the ministry of reconciliation; to wit, that God was in Christ, reconciling the world unto himself.--2 Cor. 5:18,19.

These words are small in bulk, but great in mystery, it is the heads of the gospel in a nut-shell; the most sparkling diamond in the whole golden ring of Scripture. It comprehends the counsels of eternity and the transactions of time. A wonder in heaven, God bringing forth a man-child to be a propitiation for sin, which was the Jews' stumbling-block and the Gentiles' scoff. 1 Cor. i. 23, 24; but wherein the wisdom and grace of God's counsel in heaven, and the power of his actions on earth, clearly shine forth in the face of Jesus Christ. The Jacob's ladder, the upper part fixed in heaven, and the lower foot standing upon the earth. Angels descended on that; God descends to man by this in acts of wisdom and grace, and man ascends to God in acts of faith and love.

If there be any mystery in Christianity more admirable than another, it is this of reconciliation. If any mystery in this mystery, it is the various and incomprehensible engagement of the Father in it, in and through Christ. If anything in Scripture sets forth this mystery in a few words like a picture in a little medal, it is this which I have read, wherein the apostle gives us a short but full and clear account of the doctrine of reconciliation, which is the substantial part of the gospel.

There is a double reconciliation here and in the following verse expressed.

First, Fundamental; at the death of Christ, whereby it was obtained. This is the ground of God's laying aside his anger; this is reconciliatio legalis or de jure.

Secondly, Actual or particular, when it is complied with by faith. This regards the application of it, when God does actually lay aside his enmity, and imputes sin no more to the person. Which consists of two parts.

1. The proclamation of this: ver. 20, 'We pray you in Christ s stead, be ye reconciled to God,' declaring God's willingness to take men into favour. This is the declaration of reconciliation de jure, or the right of reconcilement. The gospel contains the articles of peace, and the counsels and methods of God about it. It is the copy of God's heart from eternity.

2. Particular acceptance, which is on our part an acceptance of the terms of reconcilement, on God's part an acceptance of us into his favour, and a non-imputation of our sins to us, which the apostle calls, Rom. v. 11, the receiving the atonement; this is the accepting the atonement, the ground of reconciliation on man's part, and the application on God's part.

The first, viz., the proclamation of it to us, is God's promise to us, the other is the performance; the one is God's gracious favour to us, the other is God's gracious act in us. Christ is the cause of both these reconciliations: of the fundamental reconciliation by his death, of our actual reconciliation by his life; the one by himself in person, the other by his deputy the Spirit.

God. God is taken here by some* "ousiodos", for the whole trinity, Christ, "oikonomikos", as mediator.

Others, and more likely, understand by God the Father, to whom reconciliation is ascribed per modum appropriationis, as he is the fountain of the divinity, as the fathers use to call him. As the Father is the principal person wronged, and declaring his anger against us, the reconciliation is principally made to him; in which sense we are said to have 'access to the Father,' Eph. ii. 18, through Christ, and by the Spirit. The Son brings us to the Father, and the Spirit directs us to the Son. Christ takes away God's enmity to us, and the Spirit takes away our enmity to God. As the first creation is appropriated to the Father, so is the second also. The apostle having described the new state of things, ver. 17, tells us, ver: 18, that 'all things are of God, who has reconciled us to himself by Jesus Christ;' that this new state is of God, who is no less the creator of the second state than of the first. Adam, the common head of God's appointment, by his falling, overthrew himself and his posterity; God therefore appoints another head to reduce men again to himself. What is here called reconciling, is called, Eph. i. 10, 'gathering together in one,' "anakephalaiosasthai". God would gather them together to himself under one head, as they had been separated from him under one head.

God was in Christ. Some make this expression to signify no more than by Christ, ver. 18; or for

Christ's sake: Eph. iv. 34, 'As God for Christ's sake has forgiven you.'

But the expression notes something more than for Christ's sake. In actual pardon, Christ, is the moving cause by his intercession, as well as the meritorious cause by his propitiation: 1 John ii. 2, 'If any man sin, we have an advocate with the Father, Jesus Christ the righteous, who is a propitiation,' &c. But the first purpose of reconciliation, and the appointing Christ as the medium for it, had no moving cause but the infinite compassion of God to his fallen creature. Christ was not the moving cause of this, though he be the meritorious cause of all the effects of it, and laid the foundation of an actual reconciliation by being the centre of the agreement between the justice and mercy of God. God's anger was appeased by the death of Christ, but God was the first author of this propitiation, appointing this method of restoring the creature, and this person, or Jesus, to do it.

God was in Christ. It may be meant of the Trinity: the Father was in Christ constituting and directing, the Son was in Christ by personal union, the Spirit was in Christ gifting him for this work of reconciliation; but I would rather understand it of the Father.

Being in Christ is not meant,

1. Of that essential inness or oneness whereby the Father and the Son are one in essence. Or as a father of the flesh and his son are said to be of the same nature, disposition, and likeness, whereby we say the father lives in the son, in the lineaments and temper of the son, whereby he resembles the father. It is true, the father and the son have the same nature, the same perfections and divine excellencies; so the Father is in the Son without any respect to reconciliation. He is so in the Son in creation also; he is so also one with the Spirit. But this notes some singular manner of inness in Christ, which is not in the third person, or in any else.

2. Nor in regard of that affection the Father bears to Christ. He is indeed in a peculiar manner in Christ in regard of love, more than in all believers besides. He loved him as the head, believers as the members. This is common to believers with Christ, though not in the same degree.

3. But it notes some peculiar manner of operation in Christ as mediator. Redemption was not the work only of the Son; the Son wrought it, the Father directed it; the Son paid the price, the Father appointed him to do so, received it of him, accepted it from him, and accounted it to others through him, which is that we are bound to believe, as Christ tells the Jews, John x. 38, 'that you may know and believe that the Father is in me, and I in him,' John xiv. 20, 'I am in my Father.' The Father is in Christ by way of direction, support, and influence, and Christ in the Father by way of observance, obedience, and dependence. As the world was in Christ as in their surety and head, satisfying God, so God is in Christ as in his ambassador, making peace with the world. All things that Christ acted and managed in this work are to be referred to God as the prime author.

The world. The world properly signifies the frame of heaven and earth, and all creatures therein, joined together by an exact harmony, order, and dependence upon one another; but in the Scripture is chiefly understood of mankind, the top of the lower world and end of its creation. It is frequent in all writers to put the place for the inhabitants; and it is taken for the most part for the corrupted world, the world fallen under sin and wrath, and opposing God: John i. 10, 'The world knew him not.' And when God takes some out of the world, he calls them not by the name of the world, but his church. And those that he brings out of this sinful condition, he is said to bring 'out of the world" John xv. 19, and to choose 'out of the world,' John xvii. 6. The world is fundamentally reconciled, there being a foundation laid for the world to be at peace with God, if they accept of the terms upon which this amity is to be obtained; or all ages of the world, those before the coming of Christ in the flesh as well as those after, 1 John ii. 2.

Reconciling. The greatest controversy lies in this word, whether by it be meant God's reconciliation to us, or our laying down our enmity against God. Socinus and his followers say God was not angry with man, he was reconciled before, but that this place is meant of affection towards God, because it is said we are reconciled to God, and not God to us.

But learned men have cleared this. The phrase in heathen authors of men's being reconciled to their gods, is always understood for appeasing the anger of their gods, and escaping those dreadful judgments either actually inflicted or certainly threatened from heaven. By reconciliation of us to God in this place cannot be meant our conversion, or any act of ours.

1. Because the reconciliation here spoken of was the matter of the apostles' discourses and sermons, and the great argument they used to convert the world to God. If, then, that sense were true, it would be an impertinent argument, unworthy of those that Christ called out to be the first messengers and heralds of this redemption. The sense of their discourse would run thus: God has already converted you, therefore be converted to him; as it is nonsense to exhort a man to do that very act which he has already done.

2. This reconciliation does formally consist in the non-imputation of sin to men. Now this is God's act, not the creature's. 'Not imputing sin' and 'forgiving sin' are the same thing, Rom. iv. 7, 8, therefore the reconciliation itself is an act of God. If God were to be brought into our favour as a person offending, we should be said rather not to impute God's supposed offences to him, and not to charge

him with that which was the ground of our hatred of him.

The apostle tells us that God does not impute the trespasses of the world to them emphatically, as Grotius observes, but he does to another whom he had made sin for them: ver. 21, 'For he has made him to be sin for us, who knew no sin.' And the apostles were sent about the world to testify this benefit, that men might give credit to God, and turn to him.

And upon the declaration of this doctrine, that God had in Christ laid aside his anger for their sins, and having punished another for then, would not punish them if they embraced by faith what was proposed to them, they besought men that they would lay aside their enmity against God, as he declared himself willing to lay aside his enmity against them, and had testified this by sending his own Son to bear their punishment.

There is a like place with this: Rom. v. 6, 10, 'if, when eve were enemies, we were reconciled to God by the death of his Son, much more, being reconciled, we shall be saved by his life.' If Christ died for sinners to make an atonement for them, it was then to procure God's well-pleasedness with them, because they had offended him. But if he died to bring God in favour with us, then his death was an atonement for God, and to expiate God's offences, who never was, nor can be, guilty of any towards his creature.

But it is evident the reconciliation there mentioned, as well as in the text, was antecedent to conversion, and therefore is not the same with the conversion of the creature.

1. Because otherwise the apostle's argument would have little validity in it, for it proceeds a majori, 'much more, being reconciled by his death, we shall be saved.' If God were so infinitely kind to us as to turn away his anger from us by the death of his Son when we were yet enemies, how much more tender will he be of us since he has taken us into favour, and we are actually converted to him!

2. The effect of this reconciliation is a saving from wrath by the blood of Christ: ver. 9, 'Much more, being justified by his blood, we shall be saved from wrath through him.' Therefore this reconciliation must be by appeasing that wrath under which we should otherwise have fallen.

And the effect of it is to have peace with God: ver. 1, 'We have peace with God;' whereas, if it were meant of God's being brought into our favour, it should have been said, God has peace with us, and that God has access to us.

3. Justification is the effect and consequent of this reconciliation. And this Crellius confesses, Justificatio est effectus reconciliationis. But this is the act of God, Rom. iv. 5, Rom. viii. 33.

4. Reconciliation is here attributed to the death of Christ as a distinct cause from that of conversion: Rom. v. 10, 'If, when we were enemies, we were reconciled to God by the death of his Son;' that is the reconciliatio impetrata, which in the second expression of our actual or applied reconciliation is ascribed to the life of Christ or intercession, that being the end for which he lives in heaven, Heb. vii. 25.

5. We are said to 'receive the atonement,' Rom. v. 11, which is the same with 'receiving forgiveness of sins,' Acts x. 43. But to receive conversion is a phrase not at all used in Scripture. When a man turns to the east, no man says he receives turning to the east. Besides, if it were meant of bringing God into our favour, it were more proper to say God received the atonement, and not we.

6. If by reconciliations were meant our bending our hearts to love God, there could not be any sufficient reason rendered why the sanctification of the heart should be laid down by the apostle as the end of this reconciliation, as it is Col. i. 22, 'Yet now has he reconciled, in the body of his flesh through death, to present you holy and unreprovable in his sight.' For nothing can be both medium and finis sui ipsius, its own end and means too.

By reconciliation is meant the whole work of redemption. The Scripture has various terms for our recovery by Christ, which all amount to one thing, but imply the variety of our misery by sin, and the full proportion of the remedy to all our capacities in that misery. Our fall put us under various relations; our Saviour has cut those knots, and tied new ones of a contrary nature. It is called reconciliation as it respects us as enemies, salvation as it respects us in a state of damnation, propitiation as we are guilty, redemption as captives, and bound over to punishment. Reconciliation, justification, and adoption differ thus: in reconciliatio, God is considered as the supreme Lord and the injured party, and man is considered as an enemy that has wronged him; in justification, God is considered as a judge, and man as guilty; in adoption, God is considered as a father, and man as an alien. Reconciliation makes us friends, justification makes us righteous, adoption makes us heirs.

This verse then represents to us the doctrine of redemption under the term of reconciliation. In it we have,

I. The principal author and spring of this reconciliation, God.

II. The immediate efficient or the meritorious cause of it, Christ.

III. The subjects, God and the world: 'the world to himself.'

IV. The form of this reconciliation, or the fruit of it: 'not imputing their trespasses unto them,' not charging them with their crimes.

V. The instrumental cause of actual reconcilement, the ministry of the word.

The observations we may take notice of are these:ó

First, Reconciliation by Christ is the foundation of the regeneration of nature: ver. 17, 18, 'All things are become new, and all things are of God, who has reconciled us to himself by Jesus Christ.' The design of God was to reduce us to happiness, which was not to be done without the satisfaction of his justice. Christ by his death satisfies that; in his life is a model of our sanctification. God is first the God of peace before he be the God of sanctification: 1 Thes. v. 23, 'and the very God of peace sanctify you wholly.' The destruction of the enmity of our nature was founded upon the removing the enmity in God. There had been no sanctification of our natures had there not been a redemption of our persons, no more than for devils, who remain unholy because they remain unreconciled. Besides, since God has been at peace with us he will sanctify us, that the actual peace may be preserved by the weeding out the remainders of the enmity in our natures. It is as he is a God of peace that he conquers any of our spiritual enemies. He will never engage in the bruising Satan under our feet till he be our reconciled God in Christ: Rom. vi. 20, 'the God of peace shall bruise Satan under your feet.'

Secondly, God does not act principally as a Creator, but as a reconcilable God ever since the first promise All blessings flow from him as standing in that relation. All his providences in keeping up the world, the fruitful showers, the enjoyments of the sons of men in the world, are upon the account of the Mediator, wherein he has declared himself a reconciling God. He acts towards the world as a reconciling God, towards believers as reconciled. He is reconcilable as long as he is inviting and keeps men alive in a state of probation. But he is not reconciled but to those that accept of the way of reconciliation which he has wrought in his Son, and according to the methods whereby he wrought it. The relation of a Creator cannot cease while there is any creature; but if God should act towards the world only as Creator, the dissolution of the world had been long ago, because the law of the creation had been transgressed. But he acts as a 'faithful Creator', 1 Pet. iv. 19, as a Creator according to the promise of the new covenant, which his faithfulness respects.

Thirdly, And that which I only intend, is this,

I. Doctrine. God is the great spring and author of our recovery. Or God was principally engaged in the whole undertaking and effecting of our redemption and reconciliation by Christ. God was the first mover in those acts whereby the first foundation-stone was laid and the building reared. All was begun by his order, and managed by his direction and influence: 2 Cor. v. 18, 'All things are of God, who has reconciled,' i. e. all things are of God in this reconciling act. The whole Trinity is concerned in it. Each person acts a distinct part. The glory of contriving is appropriated to the Father, as he that made the first motion, counselled Christ to undertake it, sent him in the fullness of time, and bruised him upon the cross, making his soul an offering for sin. The glory of effecting it is ascribed to the second person, both in the satisfactory part to the justice of God, and also in the victorious part, the conquest of Satan. The glory of working the conditions upon which it is enjoyed, and the applying it, is attributed wholly to the Spirit. The story of the creation seems to intimate some other work to be done in the world by God besides that work of creation which God the Father made at that time: Gen. ii. 2, 'And on the seventh day God ended the work which he had made, and rested from all his work which he had made;' and ver. 3, 'and rested from all the work which God created and made;' thrice repeated, He rested from that work which he had made, he made no more of that kind and nature. But a rest he could not find; he rested from it, but not in it; there was a work of a nobler strain behind to be made by him for his rest. He foresaw how soon he should be disturbed by the entrance of sin; and though he rested from making any more creatures of that sort, yet he had works of grace to make afterwards, more wonderful than those of nature. He had a further display to make of his gracious perfections, which could not be deciphered on the face of that creation; but a work there was remaining wherein he intended to bring forth the glory of his divine excellency which yet lay hid. This is the highest draught of divine wisdom and goodness; therefore if the Father created all things wherein his wisdom and goodness appears in a shadowy manner, drawn with fainter colours, he should have no less hand in this, wherein his wisdom was to appear without a veil, in its full lustre and eternally durable colours, when this material world shall pass away: Eph. iii. 10, 'A mighty variety of wisdom,' "polupoikilos sophia", which delights the Creator and amazes the creature! He would no less have a hand in the second creation of all things by Christ than he had in the first, since a greater glory was to redound to him as reconciling than as creating, by how much it is more excellent to give man a happy being than to give man a bare being. God is therefore said to be the 'head of Christ,' 1 Cor. xi. 3, as Christ is the head of man. As man was made to declare the glory of Christ, so is Christ formed to declare the glory of God. As all influences the members receive in point of direction and motion are from the head, so all the influences Christ had were from God, as the head directing and moving him. As the head counsels what the members act, so God counsels what Christ acts. God brings forth this Mediator as his divine image, and diffuses all his perfections in and through him before the eyes of men, and thought it a work too worthy to be contrived by any but himself, and transacted be any but his Son. God only sent him to make it, and called him back to himself as soon as ever he had finished it.

We shall consider,

1. What reconciliation is, and wherein the nature of it consists.
2. That God the Father is and must be the prime cause of this.
3. Wherein the agency of the Father appears, and by what acts it is manifested in this transaction.
4. The use.

1. *First, What reconciliation is*

(1.) Reconciliation implies that there was a former friendship. There were once good terms between God and man, there was a time wherein they lovingly met and conversed together. Man loved God and was beloved by him, till he left his first love and broke out into rebellion against him. God pronounced all his creatures 'good,' and man at the last 'very good,' with an emphasis. A God of infinite goodness could not hate his creature, which was an extract of his own image. Man had the law of God engraved upon his heart, and therefore could not in that state hate God, while he was guided by that law of righteousness and exact goodness in himself. Thus was man God's favourite above all creatures of the lower world, styled his son, Luke iii. 38; but how quickly did he prove a parricide, and a quarrel was commenced between God and him! Now, reconciliation is piecing up of a broken amity, and a reglutination of those affections which were disjoined. And the miracle of this reconciliation made by God in Christ excels the former friendship; that might be broken off, as we find by woeful experience it was. This as to some acts and fruits may be interrupted, not abolished; as the beams of the sun may be clouded, but the influence of the sun cannot be eclipsed. Then God and man were not so closely united but they might be parted; now God and the believer are so affectionately knit that they cannot be separated.

(2.) Reconciliation implies an enmity and hatred, or at least a disgust on one or both sides. Adam was created in a state of God's favour, but not long after his creation he apostatised to corruption; by his creation a child of God's love, by his corruption a child of God's wrath. While he stood, he was the possessor of paradise and heir of heaven; when he fell, God seals a lease of ejectment, and man becomes an heir of hell; he turns rebel, and joins with Satan, God's greatest enemy. God took the forfeiture of his possession, turns him out of house and home, and hinders his re-entrance by a flaming sword turning every way to keep his fingers off from the tree of life, Gen. iii. 24, or hope of felicity upon the former score. Man invaded God's right of sovereignty, and God, of a sovereign Father, becomes a punishing judge. Man falls into sin, and wrath falls upon man; sin separated between God and him, and unsheathed the flaming sword. Thus are heaven and earth at variance. The hatred is mutual: God hates men, not as his creatures, but sinners; man hates God, not as God, but as sovereign and judge. Man turned off God from being his Lord, and God turned off man from being his favourite; man vents his serpentine poison against God, God pours out his wrathful anger on man. On man's part this enmity is by sin; on the part of God (1.) from the righteousness of his nature, since he cannot behold iniquity without indignation, Hab. i. 13. As he cannot but love goodness, so he cannot but hate iniquity, Ps. v. 5, 6. He hates and abhors all the workers of iniquity. He hates the sins of his saints, though not their persons; he hates the persons of wicked men, not primarily, but for their sin. (2.) From the righteousness of his law made against sin, whereby he cannot but according to his veracity punish it. His curses must be executed, his law vindicated, and his justice satisfied; truth and fidelity to his law, his nature, his justice engages him. Since there is nothing of the life of God in us naturally, there can be nothing of the love of God to us; for what affection can the Deity have to brutishness, and infinite purity to loathsomeness? Now, there having been such an enmity, man is properly said to be reconciled. Good angels cannot properly be said to be reconciled, because there was no difference between God and them. It is a question, because believers are said to be reconciled, and reconciliation implying a former hatred, Whether God hated believers before their conversion? In answer to this,

[1.] To say God hated them fully before, and loves them now, would argue a mutability in God, which the apostle excludes: James i. 17, he is 'the Father of lights,' who is so far from having any real change, that he has not 'a shadow' of it. If he did not love his elect before Christ died for them, and loves them afterwards, then there is a change in his will; for to love them is nothing else but to will eternal life to them, and for God to hate any is not to will eternal life to be their inheritance. If God did so hate his elect before Christ's death as to will that they should not inherit eternal life at all, and after Christ's death did will that they should, his will would then be inconsistent and changeable. If God chose them from eternity, he loved them from eternity; if he chose them in Christ as their Head, Eph. i. 4, he loved them in Christ as their Head, he could not choose them to eternal life in those methods without loving them. As he loved Christ the Head before he died for those that were to be his members, so he loved those that were to be his members before they were actually engrafted in him. As he loved Christ as Mediator before he was actually sacrificed, so he loved his chosen ones before they were actually reconciled. When Christ came to reconcile, he came to do God's will; and when any soul is actually reconciled, it is not a change in God's will, but the performance of God's eternal will.

[2.] There is a change in the creature, but that does not imply a change in God. It is not a new will in God, but a new state in the creature. The creation adds no new relation or accident, but a change and effect in the creature. And as the schools generally determine, it is one thing mutare voluntatem, another thing velle mutationem; as a master commands a servant this work one day, another work another day, the master changes not his will, but wills a change in his work, or as some illustrate it, as a physician prescribes his patient one sort of physic one day, another kind of physic the next, the physician does not change his will, but will a change. As a man has a mind to adopt a poor child to be his son, affection is the ground of this resolution; but he lets him for a while run about in rags, and seems to take no notice of his misery, yet at length takes him, and clothes him, and adopts him. There is a change in the state of this child, but not in the affection, the original of it. There was a change in the prodigal when he returned, but not in the father when he embraced him: "My son which was lost is found,' it was a new finding of the son, but not a new affection in the father.

Well, but how may God be said to love or hate believers before their actual reconciliation, since he is the author of it?

[1.] God loves them with a love of purpose. God loves them with a love of purpose or election, but till grace be wrought, not with a love of acceptation, we are within the love of his purpose as we are designed to be the servants of Christ, not within the love of his acceptation till we are actually the servants of Christ: Rom. xiv. 18, 'serves Christ,' and is 'acceptable to God.' They are alienated from God while in a state of nature, and not accepted by God till in a state of grace. There is in God a love of good will and a love of delight, amor benevolentiae, seu "eudokias", amor complacentiee seu "euarestias". The love of good will is love in the root, the love of delight is love in the flower. The love of good will looks upon us afar off, the love of delight inns itself in us, draws near to us. By peace with God we have access to God, by his love of delight he has access to us. God wills well to them before grace, but is not well pleased with them till grace. Christ is the effect of his love of benevolence and compassion to relieve us, which love ordered Christ as the means, John iii. 16; but Christ is the cause of that love of friendship wherewith God loves us. A king has a kindness for a prisoner in his bolts, and sends some to clothe him; but he has no delight in him to think him fit for his embraces, till he be delivered, both from his fetters and his filthiness. An elect person is not simply beloved before his actual reconciliation, because he has no gracious quality which may be the object of that love. Neither is he simply hated, for if so, how could he have any gracious habits infused into him whereby he may be made the object of delight? It cannot be denied but that God intends to bestow supernatural gifts upon those he has chosen, else wherein does his love consist? And it cannot be conceived how a simple hatred can consist with such an intention. He loves them to make them his friends, and after reconciliation he loves them as his friends. It is love in God to make an object for his love. God loves an object qualified with grace, therefore to qualify an object so as to make it lovely, argues love in God to that object he so qualifies; love in intention before the qualification. Hatred could never be the foundation and cause of that qualification; sea, the gift of Christ, which is the effect, does suppose the love of God which is the cause. God indeed was angry with all mankind, but it was an anger mixed with love; he was angry, but yet willing to be appeased. A pregnant example of this, which may give us an understanding of it, we have from the mouth of God himself: Job xiii. 7, 8, 'My wrath is kindled against thee' (speaking to Eliphaz), 'and against thy two friends. Therefore take unto you now seven bullocks and seven rams, and go to my servant Job, and offer up for yourselves a burnt-offering.' There is a cloud upon God's face, but his mercy as the sun peeps out behind the cloud, as he acquaints them with his anger, so he shows them the way to pacify it. Though his wrath was kindled, yet he is not so ready to inflame it as he is to have it quenched by the means he prescribes them, wherein Job was a type of Christ, whose sacrifice Gold only accepts as well as appoints. There is no love of complacency either in the persons or services of any, but as considered in Christ the reconciler satisfying the justice of God. When an elect person is engrafted in Christ, that love which was bubbling in the fountain from eternity flows out in the streams.[2.] God does hate his elect in some sense before their actual reconciliation. God was placable before Christ, appeased by Christ. But till there be such conditions which God has appointed in the creature, he has no interest in this reconciliation of God; and whatsoever person he be in whom the condition is not found, he remains under the wrath of God, and therefore is in some sense under God's hatred.

First, God does not hate their persons, nor any natural or moral good in them. Not indeed the person of any creature, for as persons they are his own work. The creation was good in God's eye at the first framing, and whatsoever of goodness remains is still affected by an unchangeable Being, for infinite and unbounded goodness cannot hate that which is good either naturally or morally. Christ loved that morality he saw in the young man. God loves their moral qualities, and they are the common gifts of his Spirit, and qualities wherewith he has endowed them; as their primitive natures were good, so what approaches nearest to that nature has some tincture of goodness, and therefore has some amiableness in the eye of God. But he took no pleasure in them, neither in their persons nor services, as acceptable to him, without the Son of his love.

Secondly, God hates their sins. Sin is always odious to God, let the person be what it will. God

9

never hated, nor ever could, the person of Christ, yet he hated and testified in the highest measure his hatred of those iniquities he stood charged with as one surety. The father could not but hate the practices of a prodigal, though he loved his person. God loves nothing but himself, and other things as they are like himself, and in order to himself; therefore God must needs hate whatsoever is contrary to his immaculate purity, and different from his image. He hates the sins of believers, though pardoned and mortified; though his mercy pardons them, his holiness can never love them; though the punishment be removed from the person, yet the nature and sinfulness is not taken from the sin. Much more does God hate the sins of his unconverted elect, which are neither pardoned nor mortified. If he hates sin in its weakness, much more in its strength. He hates their sins objectively, that is the object of, and the only object of, his hatred; their persons terminative, as the effects of his wrath do terminate in their persons. Though sin is the object of God's hatred, as being a contrariety to his holy law, yet it is not the object of his wrath, but the person sinning; actions are not immediately punished, neither can, but the persons so acting. In that respect God may be said to hate the persons of men, and of his elect before conversion, as the effects of his wrath do terminate in them.

Thirdly, God hates their state. Though God loves morality in men, yet that does not include the acceptation of their persons, or of their moral acts, or any love to their state. Though Christ loved the young man's morality, yet he could not love his state, since it was at some distance from the kingdom of heaven, though not so great a distance from it. The elect before their conversion are in a state of enmity, a state of darkness, a state of ignorance, and a state of slavery; and that state is odious to God, and makes them incapable, while in that state, to 'inherit the kingdom of God.' 1 Cor. vi. 9-11, 'Such were some of you,' such sinners, and in such a state of sin that could not inherit the kingdom of God. A man that has a love to a beggarly child, and does intend to adopt him, he loves his person, but hates his present state of nastiness and beggary; and when he does actually adopt him, changes his state, his relation, and divests him of his filthiness. The state of the elect before actual reconciliation is odious, because it is a state of alienation from God; whatsoever grows up from the root of the old Adam cannot be delightful to him.

Fourthly, God hates them as to the withholding the effects of his love. We call the effects of God's grace grace, and the effects of God's wrath wrath. So God may be said to hate an elect person before his conversion, because, being in that state a child of wrath, the wrath of God abides on him, and the curses of the law are in force against him. As God is said to repent, when he withholds those judgments and effects of his anger which he had threatened against a nation, so God may be said to be angry and to hate, when he pours out vials of wrath, and also when he withholds the fruits and proper effects of love.

(3.) Proposition as a caution. Though God be the prime author of this reconciliation, yet no man is actually reconciled to God till he does comply with those conditions whereupon God offers it. 'God was in Christ' when he was 'reconciling the world;' we must be in Christ if we be reconciled to God: he in a way of direction, we in a way of dependency. Till a man does believe, though God has been reconciling the world in Christ, yet he is not under the actual peace with God, though under the offers of this peace. 'The wrath of God abides' on him, as well as the offers of peace are proposed to him, otherwise what need had the apostle to beseech men to be reconciled to God, upon the account that he was in Christ reconciling the world to himself, if there were not something to be done by us in order to it: ver. 20, 'We pray you in Christ's stead, be ye reconciled to God.' To what purpose should we be exhorted to lay down our arms, discard our enmity, offer up our weapons, if nothing were to be done on our parts. It is true, God is in Christ 'reconciling the world, not imputing their trespasses unto them.' But to whom? To all the world without any distinction? Though the offers are made to all, yet while men accept not of them, sin will be imputed to the unbelieving world. Shall we think God will recede from his anger till we recede from our sins? What rebels can be said to be reconciled to their prince till they observe the conditions in his proclamation? Christ cannot present men friends till by faith they are united to him; for though there be an accomplishment of the general reconciliation in the death of Christ, yet there is no benefit accruing to us till full union by faith. Much less can man be said to be reconciled from eternity; the apostle cuts off that conceit: Col. i. 21, 'Yet now has he reconciled,' now, not before. If it were from eternity, the Colossians were never enemies to God, if always reconciled, the apostle speaks a falsehood, for to be enemies and friends at the same time implies a contradiction, to be reconciled from eternity, and yet but now, are inconsistent. Alas! we come into the world with the badge of God's wrath upon us, and our backs turned upon God. The first thing we do is to kick against him. Reconciliation in the decree is from eternity; but we cannot more properly be said to be reconciled from eternity because of that, than to be created and born from eternity, because decreed to come upon the stage of the world in time. Reconciliation in the purchase is temporary; we were reconciled meritoriously at the time of Christ's death, but no more actually reconciled than we can be said to be born when Adam was created, because we were in him as a cause. Reconciliation particular and actual is temporary; we have then God appeased towards us, when we can by faith hold upon his Son upon the cross, and with a hearty sincere faith plead the wounds made in Christ's sides, the sorrows in his soul as a propitiation for sin, an atonement of God's own appointment. It is not sin but the sinner is reconciled. 'God will hold an eternal antipathy to sin, as sin does to God; God will never be pacified towards sin, though he will towards the sinner. He is in Christ reconciling the world, not sin in the world, to himself; let none, therefore, build false conceits upon this doctrine. We must distinguish between reconciliation designed by God, obtained by Christ, owned by the gospel, received by the soul.

(4.) This reconciliation on God's part in and by Christ is very congruous for the honour of God, and absolutely necessary for us.

[1.] For the honour of God.

First, For the honour of his wisdom. Had not a mediator been appointed, mankind had been destroyed at the beginning of his sin, God had lost the glory of his present works, and his wisdom would seem to lie under a disparagement in publishing a rest from his works and pronouncing them good, when the very same day (as some think) they should be sullied with an universal spot, and the choicest part of the lower creation turned back upon God, and all the other creatures employed to base and unworthy ends, below their creation and contrary to the honour of their Creator. Without the appointment of a reconciler, the honour of God in creation had been impaired, the creation had been in vain. No creatures could have attained the true end of their creation, since man, whom they were designed to serve, had apostatised from the service of his and their Creator; they could not be employed by him in that state for the service they were ultimately intended for.

Secondly, For the honour of his truth and justice. Since God had decreed and enacted that whosoever sinned should die, God must either, upon man's sin, destroy him to preserve his truth and justice, or neglect his own law, and turn it upside down for the discovery of his mercy. These things were impossible to the nature of God; he must be true to himself, just to his law. If justice then should destroy, what way was there to discover his mercy? If God should restore man to his friendship without any consideration, where would be the honour of his justice, the firmness of his truth in his threatening? The wisdom of God finds a way for the honour of both, whereby he preserves the righteousness of his law and the counsel of his mercy, not by changing the sentence against sin, but the person, and laying that upon his Son as our surety, which we by the rigour of the law were to endure in our own persons, whereby justice was satisfied with the punishment due to the sinner, and mercy was satisfied with the merit due to our Saviour.

[2.] Necessary for us. Necessary since all men had breathed in the contagion of Adam, had his corrupt blood, and the poison of the old serpent diffused in their veins; and being thus enemies to God, became subject to wrath and the eternal malediction of the law. Necessary at the very first defection; had there not been an advocate to interpose, we cannot conceive how, according to the methods of the established law, God could have borne one moment with the world. There was as much necessity for some extraordinary remedy against the biting of the old serpent as against the bitings of the fiery ones in the wilderness, which could not be cured by any natural means. They must have inevitably perished under their venom, and man under his. If we come to God in ourselves, what are we but as criminals before a judge, stubble before fire? God is infinitely good, i. e. infinitely contrary to evil; and if to evil, then to us, who think, speak, act nothing but evil. The justice of God upon man's sin required that man should endure an infinite punishment; and because he could not endure a punishment intensely infinite, by reason of the limitedness of his nature, as a finite creature, therefore he was to endure a punishment extensively infinite in regard of duration, whereof he was capable by reason of the immortality of his soul. Since things stood thus, the fallen creature could not be restored to felicity till some way were found out to restore the amity, with a full satisfaction to both, that God might, without any dishonour to himself and his law, rejoice in his creature, that the creature might with a firm security rejoice again in God. The will of God is an evidence of the necessity of it. Why did God ordain it if it had not been necessary? The natural inclination and will of Christ as man was contrary to it; for he in the flesh desired this cup might pass from him. How, then, should the infinite wisdom of God, the infinite affection to his Son, put him upon that which was so ignominious, and the infinite wisdom of the Son consent to such an event, without an apparent necessity?

2. Second thing. That God the Father must needs be, and is, the author of this reconciliation

1. That God must needs be the author of this work. Reconciliation in all the parts and degrees of it, in all the model and frame of it, is his act. The first invention of this way, the first proposition, the last execution and acceptation, owns him for the author. To him we must needs owe the contrivance, declaration, and accomplishment. If God be the first cause in all things, he is the first cause in the highest of his works. Nothing comes to pass in time but what was decreed in eternity, If anything were done which he did not first know, he were not infinitely wise; if anything were done which he did not first will, positively or permissively, he were not infinitely supreme and powerful. All things are

wrought by his counsel, which is the act of his understanding; all things are wrought by his will, which is the act of his sovereignty, Eph. i. 11. By God in Scripture sometimes is meant the Father, by way of eminency, because he is the fountain of the Deity: Eph. i. 3, 'Blessed be the God and Father of our Lord Jesus Christ.'

(1.) No creature could be the original author of this work.

[1.] All human nature could not first invent it. The whole wisdom of Moses and the Jewish nation in the wilderness could not find a remedy against the bitings of the fiery serpents, which indeed were so venomous that they were absolutely mortal. And if they were the presteres, as the Greeks call them, which word signifies the same that the Hebrew does, burning serpents, no remedy was found against their venom for many ages after. In the time of the Romans' flourishing, the poison suddenly inflamed the blood, puffed up the skin, disfigured the countenance, deprived them of the shape of men, with the benefit of life; an exact representation of the misery of man by the fall. No remedy could be found in nature against this evil in the figure, no more can any against the evil represented by it; neither the languishing law of nature, nor the sickly philosophy of the heathens, could ever find a cure. The reconciliation of God to man was too stupendous a work for the joint wit and wisdom of man to arrive at. Man was so plunged in the sink of lapsed nature, that he knew not how to desire it; so amiable were his dreams of happiness in his rebellion, that he had no mind to cherish any thoughts of it. He was so furious in his unjust war against God, that he had no will to accept of any such motion. The world was filled with all unrighteousness, and men were 'haters of God,' Rom. i. 29, 30. By all their wisdom they knew him not, 1 Cor. i. 21. No mind to know God, no will to be at peace with him. Had the wisdom of the world been sensible of their deplorable condition, could it have contrived a way for the glorifying his mercy without invading the rights of his justice, they might have dreamt of a pardon from his mercy as the supreme governor. But how would the contentment of his justice, as eminent a perfection in God as that of his mercy, and the stability of his truth in his threatening, have insuperably puzzled them? The difficulty lay not upon the point of mercy; every day's sun, and every seasonable shower were rich discoveries of this. But there was no direction in the other case, to be read in the whole manuscript of nature. The heavens declare the glory of God as creator, not as reconciler; they discovered his glory, not any way of entrance into it. Had they had thoughts of accomplishing it by a surety between God and them, where could they have pitched upon one worthy of God's acceptance? If they could have found out and proposed one, what tie was there upon God to accept any other offer for the offenders but to exact it of their own persons? What man could have thought of such an extensive love as the reconciliation, not of one or two particular men, but of the world, by so strange a means as the death of God's own Son? We read, indeed, of some one or two of the heathen philosophers that declared an impossibility of the world's reformation without God's taking flesh, but none imagined anything of the death of the Son of God; no, not the Jews, but here and there one of their rabbis, long before his coming. Oh the immense grace of God, to discover that to us in his gospel, which all the wisdom of fallen nature might have fruitlessly studied to eternity! As no man can frame an universal law, accommodated to the several states and tempers of all the men in the world, and to those notions of fit and just in the minds of men, but God, who knows what he has engraved upon men's minds; so none but God can know how to find a way of redemption that may answer the glory of all his attributes, and the pressing urgency of men's necessities.

[2.] But might not the unblemished wisdom of angels, out of pity to mankind, have found out a way of reconcilement? They knew much more of God than man; they knew the wonders of his goodness, yet had seen many of their own order drop into hell under his wrath. They might know that the devils, a stronger nature, could not satisfy God for their offence, much less man, the weaker nature. They would never have stood gazing upon it with astonishment when it was revealed, had it been so obvious to their clear and comprehensive reasons. The greatest learning they have in it is by the church: Eph. iii. 10, 'To the intent that now, unto the principalities and powers in heavenly places, might be made known, by the church, the manifold wisdom of God.' Objectively, not efficienter. It was a mystery hid in God, and only in him; not an angel seems to have had any thoughts of it till the revelation of it was made to the church. Now, not before; all the angels in heaven were ignorant of it, and probably understood not the meaning of the first promise in paradise till the coming of Christ in the flesh. Yea, after the revelation, those intelligent spirits have not a perfect knowledge of the whole scope of the gospel state, for, 1 Peter i. 12, they 'desire to look into' those things they could never be inventors of, or consulters in, that which they did not understand. Well, then, angels and men may admire it when revealed, but not before imagine it; they may applaud it, but never contrive it. Which of them could presume to nourish such a thought, that the Father should call out his eternal Son to be a temporary sufferer, to veil his divinity with the rags of an afflicted humanity? What, then, was impossible to the approved wisdom of men and angels, must only be ascribed to the wisdom and grace of God.

(2.) God the Father must needs be the principal in this business.

[1.] The order of the Trinity requires it. There is an order in the operation as well as the subsistence of the three persons. As the Son is from the Father in order of subsistence, so the actions of the Son are from the Father in order of motion and direction. The Son is sent by the Father, not only as man, but as God; for the Spirit, that has only a divine nature, is said to be sent by the Father and the Son. The persons are all equal: Philip. ii. 6, Christ 'thought it no robbery to be equal with God,' yet one operation is appropriated to the Father, another to the Son, another to the Holy Ghost, in regard of order; and the Father, as he is the fountain of the Deity, is the fountain of all divine operation. As the sun is the fountain of its beams, so it is the fountain of all the operation of its beams. All things are of the Father, by the Son. He 'created all things by Jesus Christ,' Eph. iii. 9. He reconciled us unto himself by Christ, 2 Cor. v. 18. All things of the Father as the fountain, by the Son as the medium. There is a priority of order in the divine paternity upon the account of generation, and this order is observed in the divine institutions. Baptism is first in the name of the Father, then of the Son, then of the Holy Ghost, Mat. xxviii. 19. Now, it is most congruous, that as the Father was the original of our Saviour's person, so he should be of his office; as he was God of his substance, so he should be mediator of his will, the Father first sets the copy, after which the Son writes. John v. 19, 'The Son can do nothing of himself, but what he sees the Father do, for what things soever he does, those also does the Son likewise.' All operations begin first from the Father; this place the ancient fathers understood of Christ as the second person, not as mediator. If the first motion come from Christ, the order of working in the Trinity would be inverted; the Father would then do what he sees the Son do; the Son would be the director, the preceder, and the Father the follower; the Son would go before in proposal, and the Father follow after in consent. God would not then be the God of order in heaven. Besides, the love of the Father would not then be the principal cause of our redemption, upon which the Scripture everywhere places it, but the love of the Son. Nay, if the authority of constituting the mediator were not in the Father by way of order, there could be little or no testimony of his love since the fall of man. To imagine, therefore, any other root of our redemption, is to contradict the order in the trinity. But this is agreeable to our conceptions of things, as far as we can apprehend such mysteries. The Father from himself, Christ from the Father, the Spirit from both, so the Father contrives this, and is pleased with it, as being the most exact model of his love, wisdom, and justice, and the highest act of love he could show to his Son. The Son consents to it, and is pleased with it, as being the highest act of love he could show to his Father, and to men, in being their reconciler, and to angels in being their head. The Spirit is pleased with gifting him, as being the greatest demonstration of his power to gift Christ for so great a work, therefore the Spirit is said to 'rest upon him,' Isa. xi. 2. Not only noting the continuance of the Spirit on him, but the satisfaction the Spirit should have in his employment, as much in gifting Christ for it, as Christ in undertaking and managing the work.

[2.] If the Father were not principal in it, the undertaking a reconciliation could not of itself be valid.

First, There had been an injury to the Father in undertaking it without his full consent at least. The Father is the principal party injured, and was therefore to be consulted with in that which concerned his own right. He is also the governor of the world. It is not convenient that a public work should be undertaken in a nation without the consent of the chief magistrate, who may else make it frustrate. When princes of equal dignity are at war, none undertakes the composing of the quarrel, till both parties accept of the mediation. But here is the supreme Lord of the world and ungrateful rebels at variance; the chief governor unjustly wronged. Now, every man would judge it a presumption for any to offer terms of peace to his enemies, and undertake the satisfaction of himself without his own consent in the case.

Secondly, The Father could only by right appoint the terms upon which, and the way whereby, this reconciliation should be made. The Father being the law-maker could only dispense with his law, and judge that satisfaction was fit for the vindication of it. The law ran in that strain, that the party sinning should die. Had the letter of the law been exacted, every man had been a stranger to salvation; the right, therefore, of waiving the letter of the law, while he maintained the reason and substance of it, belonged to the Father. As the supreme Governor, too, he could only transfer the punishment from the offending party to another that was willing to stand under the penalty in his stead. Since creation is appropriated to the Father, and sin entered upon the world immediately after the creation, it was God as a creator was principally injured. The first sin struck more immediately at the Father, as creator; unbelief at the second person, the Redeemer; and a despitefull contempt of Christ, after the manifestation of him by the Spirit, and the motions pressing upon men, is called the sin against the Holy Ghost. Christ intimates this when he says, 'They have both hated me and my Father;' i. e. me now, as well as my Father before. Non they show a particular hatred to me by unbelief, as well as they have done to my Father formerly by idolatry. The Father, therefore, only had the right to appoint the way of reconciliation according to his good pleasure; since he was chiefly dishonoured, he is fittest to prescribe the method which he judges most convenient for the restitution of his honour. As all his attributes were wronged by sin, so it was fit all his attributes should be glorified in reconciliation of his enemies. It was not fit that glory he is so jealous of should be entrusted in any hands but by his own will; and his prescribing all the ways of vindicating and illustrating it, and the glorifying of himself, was his end in appointing Christ to this work: Isa. xlix. 3, 'Thou art my servant, O Israel, in whom I will be glorified;' and the glory of God seems to be a name whereby Christ is called: Isa. lx. 1, 'The glory of the Lord is risen upon thee.' Since, therefore, a greater glory was his end in redemption than barely in creation, he had as much a right to be principal in the miracle of restoration as in that of creation.

Thirdly, The Father was not obliged, nor could be obliged by any to entertain any thoughts of a reconciliation. He might, without any prejudice to his goodness, have demolished this defiled world, and by his power reared another wherein to show forth the glory of his immense perfections; he might have made good the law upon the person of every sinner, much less was he bound to accept of any surety; he might have exacted the satisfaction at the hands of the criminal before he would have been reconciled. Being sovereign, it was at his liberty whether he would be appeased or no towards rebels. If he was willing to be appeased, he might have chosen whether he would have admitted of any surety to stand in their place. When Reuben offered Jacob his two sons as a pledge for Benjamin, Gen. xlii. 37, Jacob was not bound to receive this offer, but at his liberty whether he would take them or no. Nor was Naboth bound to part with his vineyard for a better than his own upon Ahab's offer, 1 Kings xxi. 2, 3. No man is bound to part with his propriety in his goods, or his right over his prisoner; but if a price be agreed upon, he is then bound by the rules of commutative justice to set the prisoner at liberty.

Fourthly, Therefore if the Son of God himself had been incarnate, and died for the world without the Father's call and mission, the Father was not obliged to accept it as the price of our redemption. For all things without a call are of themselves invalid, and depend only upon the will of the person to whom they are related for their acceptation. God's institution confers validity upon any things. Could the brazen serpent ever have cured the bitings of the fiery ones had not God fixed it as a remedy?

Three things go to the establishing the reconciliation: 1. The dignity of the person reconciling; 2. The valuableness of the satisfaction he offers; 3. The call of the person injured, or the acceptation of it.

The two first makes the merit sufficient, the third only makes it accepted. Had Christ endured all the torments of the cross, the acceptation of him for us might not have been, had not the Father's constitution of him for that purpose preceded his undertaking. Though the death of Christ had an intrinsic value, and therefore was in itself acceptable, yet the consent of the Father only made it accepted; he 'made us accepted' in Christ, Eph. i. 6; therefore our acceptation depends first upon the acceptation of Christ. The strength, therefore, of it in Scripture is put upon God's well-pleasedness with him, 'This is my beloved Son, in whom I am well pleased.' And upon God's call of him, Eph. i. 9, it was his will, the 'good pleasure of his will', and 'purposed in himself;' it rose up in his own heart and mind. Though the satisfaction of Christ derives not its virtue of meriting from the grace of God, yet it derives its acceptation from the grace of God. The grace of God, and the merit of Christ, relate to one another as the cause and the effect, the antecedent and the consequent. The merit of Christ is the cause of our actual favour with God, but the merit of Christ is not the first spring of it; for it is subordinate to the general grace of God, which orders it as a means of that reconciliation which he purposed in himself. In short, it is like this case: when a man desires the goods of another, and offers him as much as they are worth, and more, though what he offers has an intrinsic value to compensate the possessor for those goods, whether the person accept of that offer or no, yet the acceptation of it depends purely upon his will, and the sum has no validity to purchase what is desired without the will of the present possessor.

First, If the Father had been obliged to receive any satisfaction, it must be from the person offending. No obligation can be conceived incumbent upon him to receive it from a person wholly innocent, though it were of infinite value, because none can transfer over the right of another but he whose right it is.

Secondly, Had not the Father fully agreed to this, I do not see how Christ could have made a compensation by his sufferings. Had he assumed a body, and laid down that body, and courted death, had that been justifiable without a call? The humanity of Christ was a creature, and therefore obliged by the law of nature, as creatures are, to preserve itself. All men are bound to do so, unless God calls them to lay down their lives, who is the supreme Lord of life and death. Suppose our Saviour might have laid down his life intentionally as a compensation for us, what could he have undergone in his humanity but a temporal death? Was it not more we were to suffer? Was not the wrath of God due to our souls? The soul was the chief offender, the soul then ought to be the principal sufferer. If God therefore had not appointed Christ for those ends, the wrath of God could not have been inflicted upon the soul of Christ, for who should have inflicted it? Had it been just with God to have loaded a person with his wrath, who was innocent from any actual or imputed crime both in his own person and transferred from others? His mere bodily sufferings could not have been a recompense for the sin of the soul. The order of things fairly lies thus: man being unable to satisfy God for himself, nor any creature being sufficient to satisfy God for them, the Father calls the Son to take upon him the human nature, and by satisfying his justice for sin, restore us to happiness. The Father's call, and his own voluntary consent, make him capable of having our sins transferred upon him, and bearing them in his own body on the tree. And Christ lays it upon the commandment received from his Father, together with his own free consent: John x. 18, 'I have power to lay down my life, and I have power to take it again. This commandment have I received from my Father.' He had an authority to lay down his life, he had also a promise of restoration of it by his resurrection. And to this end he had received, not only an invitation, but a command, which gave him full authority to die, and a ground also to plead the validity of it, for the ends designed by it. Therefore had he not received such a command, he had had no authority to lay down his life; no more than Abraham had authority to sacrifice Isaac of his own head, neither could he have challenged any acceptance of it for man at the hands of God.

Thirdly, The Scripture does ground the merit of Christ upon the grace of God. It is called the 'gift of God,' and 'the gift by grace, which by Christ has abounded to many,' Rom. v. 16, 16, &c. Some bring this place to prove the absolute efficiency of Christ's merit, had he laid down his life without the appointment of the Father, because, as the sin of Adam had demerit enough to condemn the world, so the righteousness of Christ had merit enough to save the world. But the question is, whence this merit did arise? It did arise personally from Christ himself and the dignity of his person; but as to the acceptation, from the Father, which the apostle resolves in this place in telling us; it is the grace of God, and the gift of God, because if Christ's death had a natural power of merit without any precursory agreement between the Father and the Son, it could not be said then to be the grace of God, for God could not but in a way of justice accept it. There is a double merit, absolute, and ex pacto or covenanted merit, óabsolute when any good is done to a person, which in the very deed itself obliges him for whose good it is done to the benefactor which does it, as generation and education are the acts whereby parents merit of their children. So that, whether children will or no, upon that very account that they are begotten and brought up they owe everything to their parents so creation being the work of God, the good of the creature, for that very cause every creature, especially rational, is obliged to God, and God by this act does merit all adoration, obedience, and respect from his creature. Covenanted merit is a work done which does not in its own nature oblige, but by virtue of some preceding compact and agreement between the person meriting and that person of whom he does merit. As when a king proposes a reward to those that run a race, let men run never so well, they have no right to demand a reward but upon such a declaration of the prince; and supposing that edict and declaration, he that runs has a right to the reward promised and appointed by the king, but no right to a reward in general. The whole right does rise, not from the race simply considered, but as it respects the declaration and order of the prince. If we speak of a covenant merit, Christ did fully merit at the hands of God eternal salvation, for he fully performed what was agreed upon; but if we speak of absolute merit, neither Christ nor any creature could merit anything at the hands of God, or render God obliged to them by a natural right, no more than any man that runs a race can oblige a king by his swiftness. As the merit of Christ regards us, it is absolute, for Christ by his very undertaking (supposing he had not had any agreement with the Father) to deliver us, and appease the wrath of God against us, he had absolutely merited of us all love and observance, yea, though he had failed in it; but he had not merited of God anything for us, by any undoubted right, but as it respects that agreement between the Father and the Son. Ps. xvi. 2, 'My goodness extends not unto thee, but to the saints which are in the earth.' Christ did not add anything to God, whereby he might absolutely merit of him; but to the saints he did, whereby they are for ever obliged to him. Christ did not merit anything for us at the hands of God but as mediator, and to this office he was predestinated by God, and therefore he merited nothing but by that decree. What he did was from the office of mediator or priest; and because he was so, therefore he merited. As when any officers are appointed by the king, whatsoever they act by virtue of their office has its foundation in, and force from, the royal authority. His faithfulness whereby he merited has its validity from the appointment of him in his offices by God, who, Heb. iii. 2, was 'faithful to him that appointed him.' There had been no honour accruing to him, and consequently nothing challenged by him, unless he had been called of God: Heb. v. 4, 'No man takes this honour unto himself but he that is called of God.' Christ himself owns the Father to be the foundation and stability of all the salvation he wrought: Ps. lxxxix. 27, 'He shall cry unto me, Thou art my Father, my God, and the rock of my salvation; also I will make him my first-born, higher than the kings of the earth.' This is taken from 2 Sam. vii. 14, and cited, Heb. i. 6, as belonging to Christ, to prove his dignity above the angels. 'The rock of my salvation,' the strength and foundation of the salvation I have wrought for men, or alluding to the rock from whence the waters flowed to the Israelites in the wilderness; either way our Saviour owns his Father as the stability of it. This salvation, i.e. not personal but mediatory salvation.

Thirdly, As it could not have been valid had not the Father been principal in it, so it must needs be principally from him, because it had not been for his honour that it should principally have come from another hand. It was not expedient that we should be redeemed by any but God, both as to the medium of our redemption and the grand author and contriver of it. As God created us for happiness, so we by our own fault revolted from him. To be restored to that happiness from which we fell is a greater good than simply to be created, because it is more deplorable to lie under the intolerable vengeance of an infinite God, than to lie in the depth of nothing. Since therefore man's happiness does consist in a blessed immortality, how much more would man be obliged to him who restores him to his lost happiness, than to him who created him in a state wherein he might fall to imperfection and misery! Being God has given us life, if another should bring us to a better life, without his interesting himself in it, how much more of tender melting bowels would he discover in conferring upon us that which is more magnificent! And we should be indebted to him for the greater, to the former for the less. If it were so honourable a thing for his goodness to create us by himself, it is no less honourable to interest himself in our restoration. It had been no honour to him to have his work restored to beauty and perfection by any other skill and directions rather than his own. It is as much for the honour of the Father to appoint a head for the restoring world, as he did a head for the increase of it. By that one man which he appointed, the root of mankind, a blot came upon the world; it were not honourable for him to have another head stand up for reinvesting man in a nobler happiness without his appointment.

Considering that in this work there is a discovery of the dearest love and profoundest wisdom, therefore the Father, the principal person in the Deity, must needs be the principal author and director, otherwise the principal glory of these perfections would not belong to the principal person.

Love. If the first motion came not from him, it would represent him a hard master, negligent of the good of his creature, without bowels, and only won by the importunities of his Son to have pity towards us. It would represent him only with thunders and the Son with bowels; the greatest honour would redound to the Son, and the Son would deserve more honour than the Father, whereas the honour upon the account of mediation is equally due to both: John v. 23, 'That all men should honour the Son, even as they honour the Father.' The Father is to be honoured for the greatness of his love, in committing his right of judging to the Son. As the Son is to be honoured for undertaking, so the Father is to be honoured for sending him. 'He that honours not the Son, honours not the Father which has sent him.' The sending Christ is the ground of the honour due to the Father in the work of redemption. If the Father were not then the chief author, the honour of this love of Christ would not redound to him; it would not be 'to the praise of the glory of his grace,' as Eph. i. 6, but to the praise of the glory of the grace of the Son. Herein is the love of the Father, that he was placable, desirous to be at peace, orders his Son to procure it upon such honourable terms for himself, and secure in the issue for the creature, that he might communicate his goodness through a mediation to the polluted and rebellious world. The love of the Father in this dispensation is as great in moving it, as the love of Christ was in consenting. Abraham's willingness to sacrifice his son was a type of this. Christ's death was prefigured in Isaac, the Father's willingness represented in Abraham.

Wisdom. As goodness was the motive of this reconciliation, so wisdom was the director. The Father would not be principal in the greatest and highest notes of wisdom that ever sounded in the ears of men; the highest act of wisdom would originally flow from the Son, not from the Father. In this business he is known to be the only wise God, which attribute Paul celebrates with an emphasis: 1 Tim. i. 17, 'Now unto the King eternal, &c., the only wise God, be honour and glory for ever and ever,' after he had spoken of salvation by Christ. No less than the wisdom of God could invent it. A punishment was due to lapsed man, that justice might not be defrauded; an infinite punishment the creature could not bear; the honour of God could not be fully vindicated in that way. Man justly owed a satisfaction, but could not pay it; nor without that satisfaction could be acquitted by justice from the obligation to an eternal curse. What but infinite wisdom could contrive a way for man's deliverance, whereby justice might have the highest right, and mercy the greatest applause; that the enmity between God and the creature might be totally demolished, never to break out again; the security of the creature established never to be unravelled any more! The wisdom of God must then be the arbitrator in this great affair, to compose all seeming contradictions, and appoint means fully proportioned to the ends intended. His love would not leave the world to perish, nor his justice leave sin without punishment. The one did not consist with his merciful goodness, nor the other with the honour of his law and the immutability of his sentence. There is a way therefore found in the treasures of his wisdom to procure peace to the sinner with honour to himself; to reconcile the sinner without impunity for the sin; to satisfy both the cries of his justice and the yearnings of his bowels: the one in the punishment of sin in a surety, the other in pardoning sin in our persons. That God might be appeased, and that man might have wherewith to appease him, there is given to the human nature a new man, greater than a man, which might satisfy for man, and have that in himself which might exceed all the debt man owed to God. This is such a manifold wisdom which must spring from the Father, and to whom the honour of it is due, as being the eternal purpose which he purposed in Jesus Christ our Lord, Eph. iii. 10, 11. This being therefore the highest act of wisdom, must originally arise from the Father, the principal person in the Deity, the fountain of all decrees, and therefore of those wherein the choicest wisdom of the Deity sparkles. How could it be the praise of the glory of his grace, Eph. i. 6, if he had not concerned himself in the whole undertaking? It is hereby that title of the Father of Glory belongs to him, as he is the God of our Lord Jesus Christ as Mediator, Eph. i. 17; herein shines the glory of his paternity.

2. God the Father is the principal author of this reconciliation.

(1.) The particular style God assumes in the New Testament manifests it. A title not known in the Old Testament, often in the New, Eph. i. 3, Eph. iii. 14, 1 Pet. i. 3. In the Old Testament he was called the God of Israel; and immediately before the discovery of Christ in the flesh, Zacharias blesses him under that tide: Luke i. 68, 'Blessed be the Lord God of Israel, for he has visited and redeemed his people.' And God in a solemn manner entitles himself 'the Lord God of their fathers, the God of Abraham, the God of Isaac, the God of Jacob.' This was to be his name for ever, and his memorial to all generations, Exod. iii. 15, because he was a God settling his covenant with them, and promising the Messiah out of their loins; therefore when he was to deliver the Israelites from the Egyptian bondage according to his promise to Abraham, he entitles himself thus, that their fathers might respect him in that promise, and among them he was chiefly known by this title, and that of 'their God that brought them out of the land of Egypt,' and sometimes 'the Lord which created heaven and earth.' But when the mystery of redemption, hid in God from ages and generations, was drawn out of his treasury, he appears upon the stage in another garb, with a new title, when the spiritual redemption, whereof all their other deliverances were as types, was wrought. He declares himself in a new style as 'the God and Father of our Lord Jesus Christ,' because the seed promised, upon which account he was called the God of Abraham, was now come, and the covenant of redemption was fully settled with him and in him; and so he is called the God of Christ, Eph. i. 17. [1.] Not in regard of the divine nature, for so Christ is God equal with the Father, Philip. ii. 6; but in regard of his human nature, as he was a creature, and subject to God as a creature. [2.] In regard of his mediatory office, in which respect he is his Father's ambassador, sent with a commission, acting according to instructions received from him. In this regard he often owns that he acted by his Father's authority, that his Father was greater than himself. [3.] In regard of the covenant between them: in this respect chiefly he is said to be the God of our Lord Jesus Christ, as he is said to be the God in a special manner to Abraham, Gen. xvii. 7, as being in covenant with him. Christ was in covenant with God several ways: under the legal covenant, having subjected himself to it, and covenanted to fulfil the conditions of it; in the covenant of redemption, wherein it was promised him to have a seed, and to be the mediator and foundation of the covenant of grace, the confirmer of it by his death, and interpreter of it, and advocate for the fulfilling the terms of it, though he was not properly in that under the covenant of grace himself. And as he is thus the God and Father of our Lord Jesus Christ, he is the 'Father of mercies,' and 'God of all comfort to us,' 2 Cor. i. 3. And as he stands in this relation, all spiritual blessings flow from him to us, Eph. i. 3; he is therefore the principal person to be considered in the work of reconciliation, not only as the party to whom we are reconciled, but the party by whom the whole plot and model of our reconciliation was laid, which is effected by the Son, and applied by the Spirit.

(2.) All the spiritual blessings we have by Christ spring from the Father. Surely, then, reconciliation and redemption, which are none of the meanest blessings, indeed the visible foundation of all the rest, arising immediately from election, the secret foundation, and which are indeed the end which electing love aimed at, these are the corner stone upon which all the rest are built. What communications could we have from a God implacable? a God not reconciled? Therefore to God the Father the apostle ascribes all: Eph. i. 8, 'blessed be the God and Father of our Lord Jesus Christ, who has blessed us with all spiritual blessings in heavenly places in Christ.' If all, then this; none are excepted, pardon of sin, endowment with righteousness, adoption of sons, infusions of grace, participation of the divine nature; whatsoever blessings deserve the title of spiritual own the Father as the first fountain. He adds, 'in heavenly places,' as our translation, or 'heavenly things,' as others; both amount to the same, all the blessings which respect our heavenly state. The Father was the authoritative actor in all that Christ did: John xiv. 10, 'The Father that dwells in me, he does the works.' As the power of a prince resides in the ambassador for the performance of those actions to which he is designed. Whatsoever Christ purchased of the Father, he purchased by the will of the Father, that he might communicate himself to us with honour to all his glorious perfections. The Old Testament also ascribes this to the principal person in the Deity: Hosea i. 7, 'I will save them by the Lord their God,' or Jehovah their God; or, as the Chaldee, 'I will redeem them by the word of the Lord.' He is therefore frequently called 'the God of peace,' because he is full of thoughts of peace, and is the fountain of our peace in Christ; as he is called the God of holiness, because there is nothing he thinks, nothing he does, nothing he speaks, but is holy, and is the fountain of all holiness to his creatures. All that which we have by Christ is said to be 'the mystery of his will, purposed in himself, according to his good pleasure,' Eph i. 9. What was the object of this purpose? All those spiritual blessings the apostle had numbered up before, which he resolved himself to complete and communicate to us by Christ. As all the motions in the world depend upon the motion of the primum mobile, so all our blessings upon the motion of God's love. In the communication of those blessings the Father has a particular hand; it is not said only that Christ is 'made to us wisdom, righteousness, sanctification, and redemption,' but made all those to us of God, 2 Cor. i. 80. And the apostle distinguishes the Father from the Son by this character, 'The Father, of whom are all things; and one Lord Jesus Christ, by whom are all things,' 1 Cor. viii. 6. The Father is the first cause, first mover, first contriver of all spiritual mercies for us: 'of him are all things.' Christ, the only means appointed by the Father to work those things for us, and communicate them to us; therefore it is said, 'by him are all things.' Therefore the whole work of redemption is often in the Old Testament called God's salvation, and in the New Testament called 'the will of the Father;' and Christ all along owns it: 'As my Father has commanded me, so I do.' Even those blessings which follow upon the death of Christ are the issues of the grace of God; 'the riches of his grace' is the first cause of forgiveness, Eph. i. 7; the freeness of his grace, of our justification: Rom. iii. 24, 'Being justified freely by his grace through the redemption that is in Christ.' Yet those are the meritorious fruits of Christ's death, much more are the counsels, contrivances, and resolves about this, the acts of his free grace.

(3.) The order and foundation of election discovers it. God chose men in Christ, Eph. i. 4, which election is there ascribed to the Father. This was an act of love in the Father, which in no wise falls under the merit of Christ. Some things Christ merited, as our reconciliation, justification, &c.; some things were purely the acts of God's love, without any merit of Christ, as election, and the incarnation of Christ, Christ did not merit election, for he was the first fruit of it; nor God's purpose of reconciliation, nor his own mission into the world. Election, then, being the proper act of the Father, all those means which were ordered for the accomplishing the ends of election are of the Father's appointment, for under election does fall both the manner and order of that which is to be done, therefore Christ also, who is the only means of our redemption; and Christ himself tells us that the love of the Father did precede his mission, John iii. 16; it did therefore precede his designation. And Peter expressly asserts it: 1 Peter i. 19, 20, 'Who verily was foreordained before the foundation of the world, but was made manifest in these last times for you.' For you relates not only to the manifestation in the latter times, but to the foreordination of him before the foundation of the world. Christ was first elected as head and mediator, and as the cornerstone to bear up the whole building; for the act of the Father's election in Christ supposes him first chosen to this mediatory work, and to be the head of the elect part of the world. After this election of Christ, others were predestinated to be conformed to this image of his: Rom. viii. 29, 'Whom he did foreknow, he also did predestinate to be conformed to the image of his Son, that he might be the first-born among many brethren;' i. e. to Christ as mediator, and taking human nature; not to Christ barely considered as God, for, as God, Christ is nowhere said to be the first-born among many brethren. This conformity being specially intended in election, Christ was in the intention of the Father the first exemplar and copy of it. One foot of the compass of grace stood in Christ as the centre, while the other walked about the circumference, pointing out one here and another there, to draw a line, as it were, between every one of those points and Christ. The Father, then, being the prime cause of the election of some out of the mass of mankind, was the prime cause of the election of Christ to bring them to the enjoyment of that to which they were elected. It is likely that God, in founding an everlasting kingdom, should consult about the members before he did about the head. Christ was registered at the top of the book of election, and his members after him. It is called, therefore, 'the book of the Lamb;' Christ was the title and chief subject-matter of the book. He was first chosen as the well-head of grace and glory, then others chosen on whom, from, and through him those should be conferred; for he has chosen us in him, that we should be holy, therefore he chose Christ as the spring to convey this holiness to his elect. The elect were given by the Father to Christ as mediator. Christ therefore was set up as mediator by the Father's pleasure; his office was settled by the Father before the gift was bestowed upon him.

(4.) The creation of the world, which is ascribed to the Father, was principally intended by him for this end: 'All things were created by him and for him,' Col. iii. 16. Christ was the means whereby God created all things, and the end for which they were created, that he might be head of the elect kingdom which God intended to establish by him, and discover the perfections of God in an illustrious manner, and therefore God willed Christ then as the head of all his works. It was from eternity decreed by God to create a world, to communicate himself to his creature, and to have a number of elect to praise him; therefore he resolved to create man, and endue him with such faculties, yet mutable. He knew that everything would work if it were created in this or that state and condition. He knew the devil would be envious of man's happiness; he knew what temptation would assault man, and the full strength of that temptation, to what degree it would arise, and that man would sink under his temptation, apostatise from him, engulf himself and the whole human race in misery, and give him thereby an occasion to lay open his wisdom, goodness, mercy, and justice; for God sees all things distinctly in their true causes, and therefore cannot but know the event of them. Upon this foreknowledge God appointed a remedy for man, wherein to manifest his perfections in a transcendent manner. And indeed God willed the creation, and upon that the permission of sin, that he might take occasion from thence to communicate himself to man in the most excellent manner; for he that works wisely does not only work from foreknowledge, but from a previous intention; as when God would make Joseph a prince in Egypt, and use to that end the envy and ill-will of his brothers, it is not to be thought that God only, after the foresight of their sin, did will to make Joseph a prince, but, on the contrary, he would advance Joseph to a prince-like state; and therefore did permit his brothers' sin, to use their evil to a good end. We find all the providences of God concurring since the foundation of the world, to the bringing forth Christ the head of it; therefore, the first will of God in the creation was the advancement of his Son, and founding an everlasting kingdom under him, because in all wise disposals of things, even by men, the execution of things answers the intention, and those things which are last in execution are first in intention. And the Scripture does clearly evidence this, for it speaks of 'a promise of eternal life given to those that believe before the world began,' Titus i. 1. He does not say the decree, but the promise. This promise was then made by the Father to Christ, for the constituting this mediatory kingdom; he is therefore, by this promise, settled by the Father as head of the creation, and the author of reconciliation; for it is made to him as the head of the believing world, and as the feoffee in that for them, for it concerns eternal life. To us, says he, i. e. to those that believe; and this promise was nothing else but that word which is now manifested through preaching, ver. 3. The whole gospel is built upon this promise, and is nothing else but the manifestation and result of that negotiation between them before the beginning of the world. The gospel is nothing else but this piece of gold beaten into lead. We cannot rightly understand the gospel till we understand this transaction, because the gospel is nothing else but the explication of this first promise of God to Christ. Now these great acts of election and creation being the acts principally of the Father, and done for the glory of Christ, and the completing under him an eternal kingdom, it will follow, that the Father was also principal in all the designs of Christ, and in what he did. All things are for the elect, the elect for Christ, Christ for God. The glory of God stands at the top, as the chief end of all: 1 Cor. iii. 22, 23, 'All are yours, you are Christ's, and Christ is God's'. They were all created for Christ as the immediate end, for God as the ultimate end, and therefore now ruled and governed by Christ; and at last the kingdom shall be delivered up to the Father, that God may be all in all, 1 Cor. xv. 24.

(5.) All the thoughts of God in all ages of the world were about this concern. Christ owns this in his acknowledgement to God: Ps. xl. 6, 'Many, O Lord my God, are thy wonderful works which thou hast done, and thy thoughts to us-ward; they cannot be reckoned up in order unto thee: if I would declare and speak of them, they are more than can be numbered.' Some observe that this psalm has wholly a respect to Christ, by reason of the different placing the words of the title; the name of David in the Hebrew being put before the word psalm, "ledawid mizmor", and rather to be rendered, 'To the chief musician, concerning David, a psalm,' i. e. the antitype of David, Christ being called David, Hos. iii. 5, Jer. xxx. 9. He that speaks of the innumerable thoughts or consultations of God about this, is the same person that speaks, ver. 6-8; which words are applied to Christ, Heb. x. 6-7, and those verses seem to tell us what those counsels of God which appear so admirable were, viz. about redemption by Christ. To this result did they all come, that 'Sacrifice thou wouldst not, but a body hast thou prepared me.' The infinite numberless thoughts of God centre in this one thing, of making Christ the foundation of the reconciliation intended, and exalting him thereupon. All the thoughts of God discovered to us in the Scripture refer to this; the spirit of prophecy seems to be given chiefly for the publication of this. This God spake by the mouth of all his holy prophets ever since the world began, concerning the sufferings of Christ: Acts iii. 18, 'Those things which God before had showed by the mouth of all his prophets, that Christ should suffer, he has fulfilled.' Concerning also his exaltation, and the completing of his kingdom, it was spoken 'by the mouth of all the holy prophets since the world began,' ver. 21. This thing run so in the mind of God, that he would have all the mouths of all his prophets filled with it; and when prophecy began first to breathe in the world, it was to declare this grace of God. Not a signal prophecy revealed since the foundation of the world, but there was something of Christ in it. 'The testimony of Jesus is the spirit of prophecy,' Rev. xix. 10. The prophetic Spirit which was from the beginning of the world, was a witness of Christ, what God had appointed him to do; not one prophet is excepted, Luke i. 70, Acts x. 43. And therefore the Spirit is sometimes more large in those stories or passages which were types or declarations of Christ, than in other things; as in Abel's death by Cain, when nothing is spoken of the death of the other children of Adam. How lively and largely is the story of Joseph, a type of Christ in his sufferings and advancement, represented; David's flights, and his ascent to the crown; Solomon's temple, the particular description and punctual delineation of the Jewish ceremonies, all relating to this; the story of Jonah upon record, when many other prophecies were lost, chiefly as a type of his death in the belly of the whale, and of his resurrection in being cast out upon dry land, after three days' lying in the pit. The law and the prophets appear two distinct things at the first sight, as Moses and Elias at Christ's transfiguration appeared distinct from Christ, Mat. xvii. 8, 8; but when the cloud was removed, none but Christ was seen. So law and prophets centre in him, and his reconciling expiatory death; they, as it were, disappear, and Christ appears to be the full sum and scope of them, when we lay our eyes nearer to the divine mystery. His whole undertaking was enclosed in the types, and represented by the prophets. God has discovered that all his counsels and thoughts from the beginning of the world were about this, and whenever he sent any prophetic message, it was a witness of Christ, or had some relation to him. This may give us an item how we should read the prophets with an eye to Christ, that our thoughts in reading may agree with God's thoughts in declaring. So that I think, from these put together, it appears that the Father is the principal author of our redemption; that the original of God's favour to lapsed men must spring from his own natural grace and goodness, that the death of Christ did not first dispose God to have mercy on us. The Father's love preceded the gift, and therefore preceded his resolution concerning the gift. The Scripture makes Christ's death everywhere the effect of God's love; what is the effect is not the moving cause; his first workings of mercy to us were not raised up by the death of the Redeemer.

3. Third thing. Wherein the agency of the Father in this affair does appear

'God was in Christ reconciling the world.'

1. As choosing and appointing Christ. In which respect he is called, Isa. xiii. 1, 'the Elect of God,' the servant whom he has chosen, Isa. xliii. 10, said to be appointed by him, Heb. iii. 2. He was foreordained in the decree, designed in the promise, prefigured in the types, predicted by the prophets. Our Redeemer came forth of the womb of a decree from eternity, before he came out of the womb of the virgin in time; he was hid in the will of God before he was made manifest in the flesh of a Redeemer; he was a lamb slain in decree before he was slain upon the cross; he was possessed by God in the beginning, or the beginning of his way, Prov. viii. 22, 23, 31, the head of his works, and set up from everlasting to have his delights among the sons of men. The Father's appointment of Christ is not to be understood of an appointment to his Sonship, for so he was from eternity begotten; but to his mediatorship. As he was from eternity the Son of God by generation, so he was from eternity the Mediator between God and man by constitution. The one is natural, the other arbitrary. As he was the Son, he was only God; as Mediator, God and man. His being a Son is in order of nature before his being a Mediator; his being a Son is from God's nature, his being a Mediator is from God's will. Believers are said to be begotten sons according to his will, but Christ is a begotten Son according to his nature, and Mediator according to his will. Christ is a name of charge and office, not of nature. He had been a Son had be never been a Mediator, or stepped in for the rescue of the world. All therefore that Christ did is comprehended in one word, doing the will of God: Heb. x. 7, 'I come to do thy will, O God.' There was an antecedent act of will in God before there was a subsequent act of will in Christ in order of nature. It is called therefore the wisdom of God in regard of contrivance, Eph. iii. 10; his purpose in regard of the immutability and peremptoriness of his will, :Eph. i. 9; the pleasure of the Lord, Isa. liii. 10, in regard of the delight he took both in the contrivance and resolution, both in the act of his head and heart.

(1.) He was appointed by the Father to this end, viz. of redemption. God set him up as a screen between the injured Deity and the offending creature. It is the scope of the author of the epistle to the Hebrews to manifest that Christ was designed to be an high priest, to offer sacrifice for men. He was designed to be a sacrifice, because all other revere insufficient, Ps. xl. 6, 7 and he submits to be a sacrifice, for to that purpose he had a body to do the will of God in. This was God's aim in his first choice; he was to be the foundation of the covenant for his people, to bring the prisoners from prison, and those that sit in darkness out of the prison-house, Isa. xiii. 1, 6, 7; he intended him as a propitiation for sin: Rom. iii. 25, 'Whom God has set forth to be a propitiation,' "proetheto", purposed (the same word is translated, Eph. i. 9, purposed), ver. 25, 26; 'to declare, I say, his righteousness at this time that he may be just, and the justifier of them that believe in Jesus.' "Hilasterion", alluding to the propitiatory under the law, a type of Christ. He purposed him in his eternal decree to this end, he shadowed him in the mercy-seat under the law, and afterwards exposed him to public view, to declare his righteousness in the remission of sin. And because it seems incredible, which a wounded conscience especially will hardly believe, the apostle repeats it again. One would think that justice should lay aside its demands against the sinner rather than feed on so rich a sacrifice. But God did, notwithstanding his near relation to him, single him out in his eternal council from angels and men, intended him in the "hilasterion", and all the types of the law, and brought him upon the stage in time to declare his justice to be as ready to be appeased and save upon that account, as before it was to damn. He is therefore called the Lamb of God, John i. 29 (in allusion to the lambs separated for the daily sacrifice), to be offered up to God for the taking away the sins of the world. It was with respect to the will of God in this first appointment that he delivered up himself, Gal. i. 4. :He 'gave himself for our sins according to the will of God,' whereby is meant the Father in the Deity. In the very ordaining him, the Father respected our glory: 1 Cor. ii. 7, 'Hidden wisdom which was ordained for our glory.' This hidden wisdom is Christ crucified, as appears in the next verse. Christ as reconciling by his suffering is the wisdom of God, hidden with him, not known to the world for many ages. Had God had a mind to remain an enemy, he had dealt with mankind after that covenant of works which they had transgressed, and never had deputed a mediator to stand between himself and them, to administer things according to the tenor of another covenant. It was highly represented, Exod. xxiv. 8, when Moses sprinkled the blood of the sacrifice upon the people, calling it the blood of the covenant. At the end of this action Moses and Aaron, with his sons and the seventy elders, saw the God of Israel in a human shape: ver. 10, 'There was under his feet as it were a paved work of sapphire, and as it were the body of heaven in its clearness.' The sapphire, some tell us, was an emblem of the kingly and priestly office. Such a representation there was when he appeared as a man to Ezekiel, chap. i. 26. Immediately after this typical representation of him in the sprinkling the blood of the covenant, he appeared to them in a human form, as the great intended antitype of that type they had been immediately before celebrating. As the Spirit is appointed to a peculiar office to sanctify, and therefore is called a 'Spirit of holiness,' and the end of his mission is to sanctify, Rom. i. 4, so the appointment of Christ was to an office of high priest and reconciler, and therefore whatsoever he did and suffered belonged to that office by peculiar designation. He was appointed to be a 'witness to the people, Isa. lv. 4, 5, a witness of the transcendent love of God, to bring men to God, that the nations which knew him not might run unto him.

(2.) God appointed him to every office in order to this redemption, to every degree and circumstance: as a priest, to appease his wrath; a prophet, to declare his mercy; a king, to bring men to the terms of reconciliation. He was appointed a priest for ever, that we might draw nigh to God, Heb. vii. 17, 19; God designed him as a prophet, from whom we might receive his lively oracles, Acts vii. 37, 38; God set him up as a king, that those might be blessed that put their trust in him, Ps. ii. 6, 12. The very circumstances were appointed by God: that be should be born of a virgin; the place where, Bethlehem; of the Jewish race; of the royal line of David, and that when it was decayed and sunk to poverty and misery, 'a rod out of the stem of Jesse,' Isa. xi. 1, a 'root out of a dry ground,' Isa. liii. 2; and the Jews never questioned the royalty of Christ's extraction. The time of his coming was fixed in Jacob's prophecy about the time of the fall of the Jewish government, Gen. xlix. 10, before the ruin of the second temple, Mall iii. 1, after seventy weeks of years from the time of Daniel's prophecy. What was figured in God's opening Adam's side to form a spouse; in the death of righteous Abel by the hands of his brother Cain; in Isaac, under the edge of the knife upon mount Moriah, and raised to be a blessing to the world; in Joseph in the pit and prison, and afterwards on the throne, to deliver the church from famine; in the paschal lamb, killed to save the sprinkled houses with its blood from the destroying angel, were really fulfilled in him; all the circumstances were appointed with a particular designation of the end of them. The manner of his death was foretold by David: Ps. xxii. 16, 'They have pierced my hands and my feet.' The manner of his crucifixion, his burial, resurrection, and prosperity afterwards, the blessing of men by him, justification by the knowledge of him, were deciphered by Isaiah, chap. liii., above seven hundred years before his coming, so exactly, as it that prophecy had rather been a Gospel written after his death, since the events answered so punctually to each prediction. He was promised as a 'Prince of peace,' Isa. ix. 6, one that should make no noise, appear with no pomp and grandeur, Zech. ix. 10, send forth the prisoners out of the pit, ver. 11; be 'the peace' himself, Micah. v. 5; as a king destroy the empire of the devil, pour the waters of grace upon the world, Ezek. xxxvi., take away iniquity, make reconciliation for sin, bring in everlasting righteousness, Dan. ix. 24.

(3.) It was a settled, firm, and irreversible constitution. It was not only a counsel, wherein wisdom pitched upon it as absolutely the best means for the creation's standing; but determinate, wherein it was unalterable: Acts ii. 23, 'Delivered by the determinate counsel and foreknowledge of God.' Counsel and foreknowledge are joined, to show that there was the highest reason and most resolute will; not a casual thing or contingency, but an immutable decree for his reconciling death, fixed after the wisest counsel. And therefore, in this appointment to this office, God took an oath, and thereby constituted Christ an irrevocable priest, 'after the order of Melchisedec,' Heb. vii. 21, to bless his people with peace, which oath must refer to the first appointment of Christ to this office, in order to the making him a surety of a better testament, ver. 22; better, for the preservation of the honour of God and happiness of man. It was such a constitution that admitted not of the least alteration or repentance in God; an oath which was not taken for the creation of the world, or the settling of the Aaronical priesthood. By this oath he declares this constitution to be irreversible. In this regard he is said to be sealed by God, to skew the perpetuity of this constitution, as the seal to the book, Rev. v. 1, skews the irreversible certainty of God's decrees. And therefore his appearance before his incarnation in his glory, as well as after his ascension, was with a rainbow encircling him, Ezek. i. 28, Rev. iv. 8; a sign of an everlasting covenant that God would no more bring a destroying deluge upon the world, Gen. ix. 16. The apostle seems to intimate as though this decree and constitution was the standard of all God's other actions; the point in which they should all centre, or the rule which they should be squared by; for as all our sins met on Christ, Isa. liii. 6, so all God's counsels met in him, Eph. i. 9. The rule must be perpetual, since all God's works were to be regulated by this counsel. Speaking of this mystery of his will, which he had purposed in himself, to gather in one all things in Christ, he repeats again, ver. 11, this purpose of him 'who works all things according to the counsel of his own will.' All things took birth from this counsel, and were for the perfecting this will.

(4.) God chose him to this work with an high delight, as one fully fit for the work, in whom he could confide. He 'put no trust in his saints,' Job xv. 15, for they were in their own nature defectible. Where a man cannot trust his concerns, he can have no pleasure. The Son of God's undertaking to be the head of the elect, and satisfy for them, was that the Father could only place his confidence in. This was that which could only be acceptable to him. He calls him his elect: Isa. xlii. 1, "bechiri", 'Behold my servant whom I uphold, my Elect in whom my soul delights.' My tried elect; the word signifies, one chosen after serious consideration and trial. God found none so fit among all the legions of angels, none that could so completely answer his design for reconciliation; but upon a full examination of the whole affair he found him exactly fit for it, and therefore brings him in with a Behold, a note of admiration, as one he could rest in; for so the word "etmach" signifies, as well as to uphold. Upon this trial, and upon this confidence, his soul, as it follows, delighted in him. He knew he would be faithful, and able to perfect it; some therefore refer Heb. i. 9, 'Thou hast loved righteousness, &c., therefore God has anointed thee,' &c., to the first constitution of Christ. God rested upon the holiness of his nature; and that Isa. xlix. 1, 'From the bowels of my mother has he made mention of my name,' expresses (in the judgment of some) the great joy of God in this mediator. He had my name, as I was constituted mediator, continually in his mouth. It was his pleasure to be always thinking and speaking of it; or it may note the familiar converse between the Father and the Son, concerning this work of redemption. We speak and think much of that wherein we have the greatest pleasure; and those words, Prov. viii. 30, 31, 'I was daily his delight, rejoicing in the habitable parts of the earth,' intimate that the Son was the daily delight of the Father, as he had placed his mediatory delights among the sons of men, as the Father saw all things exactly settled and governed by the Son, according to his mind and counsel. And therefore, when this suretyship of Christ is mentioned, God is pleased to express himself with a pleasing admiration: Jer. xxx. 21, 'Their governor shall proceed out of the midst of them, and I will cause him to draw near, and he shall approach unto me: for who is this that engages his heart to approach unto me? says the Lord;' showing the delight of his soul in his own choice, and his Son's acceptance, in the greatness of his person, and the heartiness of his undertaking. The word "arav" signifies to pawn, or be a surety. We many times express our joy in a mode of admiration; so is God pleased to descend to our capacities in expressing his. What is the ground of it? Ver. 22, the everlastingness of the covenant: 'And you shall be my people, and I will be your God.' How may we approach to God with the pleas of Christ in our mouths, since the Father had so mighty a delight in him?

(5.) The Father had a particular love to Christ in this appointment, and highly loved him for his acceptance of it. If he loved his Son's consent to it, he loved his own proposal of it: John xvii. 24, 'Thou hast loved me before the foundation of the world;' which, according to the best interpreters, respects Christ's person as mediator, rather than his naked deity. The Father loved Christ as mediator in the first designment, that in him he might love his elect. Our Saviour prays as mediator; the love therefore which he uses as an argument, was the love of the Father to him as mediator. The Father's love to him as the second person in the Trinity, had not been an argument congruous for that petition of his people's seeing his glory; for the love of the Father to him in that regard, did not necessarily infer a love to any creature; but his love to him as mediator and head does infer his love to all his members, and was a suitable argument wherewith to press him for a glorifying his whole body. Certainly if God loved Christ because he did 'lay down his life for his sheep,' John x. 17, there must be an high degree of love to him, because he answered the Father's appointment of him from eternity, by a voluntary consent. As the act of suffering, so the first undertaking, draws out the Father's love. The Father loved him before as his natural Son, he now loves him as the universal head. The Father's loving him for complying with this appointment, manifests the height of his love to all his members, for whose sake, next to his own glory, he constituted him in his mediatory office. Some think that the well-pleasedness of the Father with Christ for this work was one part of the glory of Christ; no doubt it was, after his performance of it, and is his glory now in heaven. If so, I would thus understand John xvii. 5, 'Glorify me with thy own self, with that glory which I had with thee before the world was;' i. e. testify thyself well-pleased with my mediation, which was the glory I had with thee as mediator before the world was. The glory of his deity was not impaired; that was not therefore the glory he prays for. It is a glorifying him with his own self. What is it, then, but the high affection the Father bore to him; for what glory can we conceive to come from the Father to the Son, as mediator, before the world was, but this? The argument he uses evidences it. Ver. 6, 'I have manifested thy name,' i. e., I have actually done that, in the undertaking whereof, O Father, thou were so highly pleased. And ver. 4, 'I have glorified thee on the earth, and finished the work thou gave me to do.' I have glorified thee by witnessing that thou art a God placable, full of love, reconciling the world, therefore glorify me. As the glory Christ brought to God relates to the business of redemption, so the glory he requests of God, which he had before, more likely relates, not to the glory of his deity, but his glory as mediator, which is God's mighty pleasure with it, acceptation of his willingness to perform it, and great affection he bore to him thereupon. The glory of his deity was not a subject to be prayed for; the glory which he was by covenant to have after his death and resurrection in his human nature, was a glory in decree, and by compact, but not actually possessed before his ascension. But the acceptation of him, and high pleasure in him, as undertaking to be our surety, was a glory he really had with the Father before the world was. Nor does this sense weaken the proof from hence of the deity of Christ; for if he were in being before the world was, he was no creature. How comfortably may we take up the same argument in our mouths as Christ did here, since the love he bore to Christ, as mediator, before the world was, did redound to every member of his sons which was to be in time!

(6.) God does glory in this contrivance and appointment. With what daring expressions to all creatures does God challenge the honour of founding this covenant of love and peace wholly to himself! No creature did so much as put in his opinion in this counsel, or contribute anything to it, but he would go away with the whole glory himself: Isa. xiv. 21, 'Tell ye, and bring them near; yea, let them take counsel together: who has declared this from ancient time? who has told it from that time? have not I the Lord? and there is no God besides me; a just God, and a Saviour.' There is no contriver, no declarer of this but myself. It is not meant of the deliverance from Babylon, as some interpret it, which is evinced by the following verses, to the end of the chapter; as also verse 17, where it is called an 'everlasting salvation,' which shall admit of no shame and confusion, world without end; a salvation that shall last as long as eternity endures. Well might all the attributes of God glory. How surprising is his love, that the Holy of holies should so love sinners, the sovereign Monarch justly jealous of his glory, furious rebels, and unprofitable slaves, as to appoint his Son for the reconciler and saviour. What motives could there be but misery to draw out the bowels of his love! What attractives in ungrateful creatures lying in their blood! What arguments could be in our thoughts to plead with God for so admirable a design! Justice and mercy are comprehended as the great things he glories in; 'just God, and a Saviour.' Wisdom might glory in the contrivance, and goodness in the appointment of one so strong to be a sacrifice for propitiation; to be himself a just Judge, and yet a tender Saviour (for the Father is called Saviour as well as the Son, Titus iii. 4; 'the kindness of God our Saviour,' distinguished from Christ our Saviour, ver. 6). He finds a way to have a valuable satisfaction of his justice, wherein should be bound up an eternal security to the sinner: a great priest for our guilt, and a beautiful pattern for our imitation; justice should triumph in the punishment, mercy in the redemption, the creature in the fruits redounding from both. How much was his sovereignty glorified in it, which he seems also to aim at: 'I am a God, and there is none besides me.' His sovereignty was manifest over all the creation, men and angels were his absolute vassals, there was nothing wanting to declare the highest pitch of it, when his own Son became a servant; the Lord of all things became lower than angels, and as low as the meanest man. Who shall stand out against his pleasure, since the Son, equal with him, stood not out against his Father's will? God does this of himself, of his own grace; by himself, his own wisdom; for himself, his own glory,

2. God the Father solemnly called him: John x. 86, 'Say you of him whom the Father has sanctified and sent into the world, Thou blasphemes? because I said, I am the Son of God?' Our Saviour mentions a double act of the Father towards him, separation and mission, a dedication of Christ to his mediatorship, and then his actual mission. This call is expressed, Isa. xlix. 1, 'The Cord has called me from the womb,' which does not imply, says Calvin, that he was but then called, when he came out of the womb of the virgin, or that the prophet does define the beginning of time; but it is as much as if he had said, Before I came out of the womb, God called me, and separated me to this office. As Paul speaks of his separation from the womb, Gal. i. 5, yet he was chosen before the foundation of the world; and Jeremiah was known before he was formed in the belly, and sanctified and ordained a prophet before he came out of the womb, Jer. i. 6; so that in this place the prophet introduces Christ speaking of his call to this office after it was formed in the eternal counsel of God. In regard of this call by God, and his acceptance of it, he is the same yesterday that he was today, and will be for ever. His call to the mediatorship was of a higher date than the types of the law, for before Abraham was, he was, in the call to and actual exercise of his mediatory function, it was an argument to prove his former assertion, that Abraham saw his day, and rejoiced in the sight of it, which would be of no strength if he were not then known as mediator, by whom God was to be reconciled to man. It is I am, to show the constant relation he had to this office: 'Before Abraham was, I am,' mediator, affirming himself here to be the Messiah, according to the Jews' usual speech, that the law and the Messiah were before the creation of the world. The words used to express the call of Christ are of a greater signification than the word used for the call of Aaron, Heb. v. 4, kaloumenos", as if you should in an ordinary way call a man to you, or call him by his name; but ver. 10, speaking of the call of Christ, it is a word of more weighty signification, "prosagoreutheis", solemnly called and pronounced a high priest.

(1.) God called him to it as an honour: Heb. v. 4, 'No man takes this honour unto himself, but he that is called of God, as was Aaron. So also Christ glorified not himself to be made an high priest; but he that said unto him, Thou art my Son, today have I begotten thee.' Christ glorified not himself to be made a high priest, but he, i. e. the Father, glorified him, and bestowed an honour upon him when he called him. The Father thought it an honour at the time of the call, not that there could be any addition of honour to the person of Christ as God, or as though he had been defective in honour in being the Son of God and not the mediator, but as the mediatory or priestly office is an excellent office and honourable employment. Supposing the incarnation of Christ designed, the mediatory office was the highest honour could be conferred upon him. What greater glory can there be than to be placed in such a sphere, wherein he may honour the Creator more than all besides! Can there be a greater honour, next to being the Son of God, than to compensate the injuries God had suffered, and repair the ruins under which the creature had fallen; to restore God's honour to him without blemish, yea, with a greater brightness; like a bloody sun in the evening, rising fairer and fresher the next day; and happiness to man without a flaw; to give God ground to look upon his works with pleasure, and man a foundation to look upon God with delight? The honour appears to consist in being the 'author of eternal salvation,' as it follows, ver. 9. Though this honour was to cost him dear, yet he was recompensed in the ends of it, the high satisfaction of God and reparation of the creatures. In which sense 'his reward' is said to be 'with him,' as well as 'his work before him,' Isa. xl. 10, 11. How is his work his reward? 'He shall feed his flock like a shepherd, and gather the lambs with his arm;' he shall restore God's chosen ones into his fold. What greater glory than to be a reconciling mediator, through whose hands all the communications between God and man were to pass! Nay, the very calling him to death, and proposing it to him for such high ends, seems to be a greater honour than his innocence barely considered, or his exaltation afterwards: Heb. ii. 9, 'But we see Jesus, who was made a little lower than the angels for the suffering of death, crowned with glory and honour; that he by the grace of God might taste death for every man.' It would be worth consideration whether this glory and honour be not meant of the honour of his office, as his being lower than the angels is meant of his state of humiliation in the world; and understanding it so, the words lie very fair before us. If it were understood of his glory after his sufferings, why should it be added immediately after, 'that he should taste death for every man'? That was not the end of his exaltation after his death, but his exaltation was the reward of that. But the sense runs cleverly thus: But we see Jesus, who in his state in the world was lower than the angels, yet in regard of his office and design had a crown of honour and glory above them all, in that by the grace of God he was set apart to taste death for every man; and by the pursuit of the apostle's discourse, speaking of his perfection by suffering for the destruction of the devil, who had brought death upon mankind, and the making reconciliation for the sins of the people, the office itself in which he was placed for those great ends may be well said to be a crown of honour and glory. It was an honourable office in a state of humiliation, as David's line was an honourable line in a state of poverty. It was in his death he discovered his virtues, victories, and triumph. In his death he blazoned out all the perfections of his Father; he illustrated his mercy, and showed how dear the souls of men were to him. He displayed his holiness, and manifested how odious the sins of men were to him. What would Christ have been (supposing the union of the second person to the humanity) if he had not died? He had not been made perfect, as the apostle intimates (ver. 10, 'to make the Captain of their salvation perfect through suffering') without suffering. He was called by God to suffering, that he might be perfect as mediator, that the justice of God might as it were quench its thirst in his blood, and the mercy of God rise out of that sea of blood, like a rich morning sun; and perfect also as a pattern, for in that his humility, charity, patience appeared in the highest manner to the sons of men for their imitation. God called him to it as an honour, and placed the very honour of it in the very suffering that death, as well as in acting afterwards upon that foundation as high priest for reconciling man. It is inconsistent with the immense goodness of God, to bind his creature to anything but what is highly conducing to the honour and happiness of his creature. Much less does it consist with the goodness of God, and that infinite affection he bore to his Son, to call him to that which was not an honour in itself. But this honour of high priest God calls him to, is an honour next to that of his sonship, which those words intimate, Heb. v. 5, but 'thou hast said to him, Thou art my Son, today have I begotten thee,' as if it were a new begetting him. If it be then an honour in the account of God for Christ to die for such worthy ends, it is not less an honour to him to exercise that office, which is so honourable in itself, which is an high ground of faith and confidence in him, in all our approaches to him, wherein we do engage him in glorious acts and worthy of him.

2. God counselled him upon this call to undertake it with large proffers: Ps. xvi. 7, 'I will bless the Lord who has given me counsel.' It was the same person that blesses God for this counsel, who says, ver. 8, that he had 'set the Lord always before him;' which words are expressly said by Peter to be spoken by David concerning him, i.e. Christ: Acts ii. 25, 'I foresaw the Lord always before my face, for he is on my right hand;' and so cites it to the end of the psalm. Christ does bless God for this counsel, and set this counsel of God always before him, which I have spoken of in reference to Christ blessing God for it, before upon another occasion. I now cite it to evidence that there was a counsel of God to Christ about this affair. What was that he was counselled unto? To his sufferings, which are intimated in the following verse; upon the assurance, that his flesh should rest in hope, and that his soul should not be left in hell or the grave, the state of the dead, and the assurance of the fullness of joy and pleasure which he should have upon the account of this mediation for evermore. If the Father were the first mover, that motion was not without an advice to Christ to concern himself as mediator, and declaring how agreeable it would be to him; upon which account, what Christ did and suffered was not only out of a bare obedience, but an affectionate obedience: John xiv. 81, 'That the world may know that I love the Father.' Therefore, Ps. xl. 8, it is said, 'God's law was within his heart,' or within his bowels. It proceeded out of a tenderness of affection to satisfy his Father, who was desirous of reconciling man to him. For in Christ's undertaking, it could not be love to the Father, unless the effect of it, which was reconciliation of man, had been declared by his Father to be a thing highly pleasing to him, which declaration was as a counselling Christ to this work. The Father counsels the creation of man: Gen. i. 26, 'Let us make man;' no less was the counsel about redemption the Father's counsel, Let us so make man. The Father counselled him to be the head and knot of the whole creation, whereby he might rest in it with a full complacency; the Son clasped about the Father with love and joy, the Father enfolds Christ in the glorious bosom of his counsel; the Son embraces the Father with the arms of an affectionate

compliance: a mighty harmony! The one in proposing, the other in complying, that the glory of God, and the felicity of the creature, might be completed in an eternal marriage. The truth is, the manner of the eternal decrees and counsels of God, are to us finite creatures incomprehensible; but the Scripture lowers itself in expressions suitable to our conceptions. As God is, in his word, represented to us with eyes and ears and human members, in a way of condescension to our capacities, upon the same account are the transactions of God, by such ways of expression, brought down to our apprehensions. Add to this, Zech. vi. 12, 13, 'The counsel of peace shall be between them both.' Some make this counsel of peace to be between the two offices, the royal and priestly, both in conjunction and not interfering one with another, as sometimes they did in the Jewish state. Others, between the two persons, the Lord, and the man that is called the Branch. The will of the Father and the Son, as they are one essence, is one; as they are two persons, there is the counsel of both. Counsels seem to belong rather to persons than offices.

3. God gives Christ a particular command concerning our reconciliation and redemption. God purposing the redemption of man, the uniting his elect under one head, designing the person, proposing to him the affair, to be managed in a body; our mediator, accepting of this constitution, receives a command to die: John x. 18, 'This commandment have I received of my Father,' i.e. to lay down his life. Sometimes it is called the will of his Father. The will of God is called a law, Ps. xl., and the sufferings of Christ are called obedience: Philip. ii. 8, 'He became obedient unto the death of the cross.' He was obedient in all things, things antecedent to the cross, and to the last point. It could not be obedience to the law as a creature, because he never transgressed it; and being innocent, and under the covenant of works, he had not disobeyed, if he had not suffered, because, according to that covenant of works, he was not bound to suffer; for being without sin he might have pleaded his right; besides, God would never command any thing against his own covenant. It must, therefore, be obedience to some other precept, concerning his mediatory sufferings. And Rom. v. 19, 'As by one man's disobedience many were made sinners, so by the obedience of one shall many be made righteous.' The obedience of Christ is opposed to the disobedience of Adam; therefore, as the disobedience of Adam was a proper disobedience, opposite to a plain precept, so the obedience of Christ was a proper obedience, conformable to some precept. A congruous reason may be rendered for this command, because, as men were destroyed by disobedience, so they should be repaired by obedience; and because a work done in obedience is more perfect in itself and acceptable to God, for his authority and sovereignty, the righteousness, holiness, and equity of his law is solemnly owned thereby. Some question whether the command laid upon Christ, as mediator, was a particular precept, or only a revealing of his incarnation and death as a necessary means for the redemption of man, because he had decreed to accept no other satisfaction. Some think this latter, and that, upon God's revealing his mind, there presently did arise in Christ an obligation to undertake this. It is more likely that this affair is expressed to us under the notion of a call, counsel, command, to show the ardency of the Father's affection for man's recovery, in an honourable way, to himself; because the Scripture places redemption in the Father's love and grace, as the fountain, and in Christ's love to his Father as well as to us, as has been before noted. There was the declaration of the will of the Father, which was the rule of Christ's acting, as the will of God is the rule of the Spirit's intercession in us: Rom. viii. 27, 'According to God;' or as our translators have it, 'according to the will of God.' A rule seems to be set for the Spirit's acting when he was sent, and a rule set for Christ's acting when he was called. The Spirit had a rule set, for he was to glorify Christ, John xvi. 14, and act upon that foundation. This does not weaken the voluntariness of Christ in his undertaking, who was ready to comply with the call, 'and made himself of no reputation, when he became obedient to the death of the cross.' When this command was given, is not so clear; but as the promise was made before the world began, Titus i. 2, so might the precept be given, before the world began, to Christ, considered as mediator; for precepts many times accompany promises. The divine nature, which undertook the mediatory office, was not in itself capable of a command or a promise.

Use of these two heads.

1. First, How adorable then is the depth of God's wisdom, and the vehemence of his kindness, to have a remedy ready to apply for the cure of fallen nature! God had a salve lying by him for the sore, and provided himself with a remedy for defeating the designs of Satan. When he came to make a process against Adam for his disobedience, and pronounce that death which he had merited, he like a merciful Father declared this appointment of one that should suffer indignities from Satan, and delivered man from the death he had deserved. When he came to expel Adam out of his forfeited paradise, he assures him of one that should open the gates of the heavenly paradise to him. He appoints his recovery, as well as charges him with his crime; and though he barred the garden against him by a flaming sword, he promises to re-admit him by the 'seed of the woman,' Gen. iii. 15, in whose blood that sword would lose both its edge and flame, its cutting and scorching quality. Oh the miracles of divine love! The law saw us guilty, insolently taking up arms against him, plunging ourselves into those crimes he had prohibited, loathing those virtues he had commanded, guilty of millions of sins, meriting millions of deaths, and the wrath of God, the quintessence of hell. Yet how did his bowels work within him, and

never ceased till he had found a way infinitely satisfactory to himself, and infallibly safe for his creature, whereby his injured attributes are righted, and our offending souls rendered capable of the happiness they had made themselves unworthy of! He did this, and did it himself, by a decree incapable of any alteration, standing like a firm pillar to support man's happiness; the everlasting fountain of his love and joy were opened at the very thoughts of this admirable design. He clasped about the mediator with the dearest affections never to be withdrawn, counselled, commanded, would not grow cool, and faint in the concern. He drew out of the depths of his infinite wisdom such a model which makes angels gaze, and believing sinners fall down to the dust in an humble admiration. He has appointed the heir of all things to be a servant for rebels, the Lord of glory to be a man of sorrows, to pay his life, more worth than the lives of all the angels, as a ransom for us; appointed him to shed his blood, to preserve ours, and singled him out to feel the sword of his wrath in his own heart, that we might feel the effusions of his healing balm in ours. Oh wonderful goodness, to appoint and call out purity to suffer for impurity, and the innocent for the criminal!

2. Raise pleas in prayer from these considerations. You address yourselves to the Father of the Lord Jesus Christ; represent to him his eternal design, the mark of his love, the centre of his delight. Desire of him that Jesus, with all his glories, with all his graces. Argue with him, whether he has not as much joy to see the fruits of his Son's death, to confer them upon his lost and sensible creatures, as to call him out for so great a purpose. Spread before him his eternal counsels, open the book of his resolves about Christ, read every syllable before him; let your soaring admirations, and your ardent petitions, keep pace together. How infinitely will the Father be pleased with such arguments, drawn from his own eternal thoughts of redemption. If he appointed a mediator for you when you were rebellions, he will not deny that mediator to you, when you are earnest and humble suppliants. His delight will be as much to bestow him upon them that seek him, as it was to consecrate him for men, when he knew they would spurn against him. He has the same thoughts of reconciling mercy, and nothing that he has done in order to this does he yet repent of; he has sworn when he called his Son, and will not repent: 'Thou art a priest for ever after the order of Melchisedec.' Make use therefore of him as supports of faith, and arguments in prayer.

3. The Father enters into terms of agreement with the Son about the work and methods of redemption, which is expressed by divines by the term of a covenant.

A covenant is an agreement of two or more persons, in some common end pleasing to them both, upon certain articles and conditions voluntarily consented to by both, and to be performed by each party with solemn obligations. So that in it there are two persons, mutual proposals and conditions, mutual consent, terminating in one and the same end. Now this covenant between the Father and the Son was a transaction between them concerning man's recovery, consisting of articles to be performed by both parties; something to be performed by Christ to the Father, something to be performed by the Father to Christ; something the Father required of him, something the Father promised to him. Some make this covenant to be rather God's purpose and decree concerning Christ's incarnation and, passion, and success of his suffering, and the issue thereupon, and therefore improperly called a covenant. I do not stand upon the term, though it seems to be best represented to our conceptions under the notion of a covenant. And the Scripture delivers it to us under the form of a treaty and debate, Isa. xlix. Though the Father, Son, and Spirit have but one will essentially, yet in this affair they are distinctly considered as two Persons treating and agreeing in one point upon certain conditions; or, as there was a new habitude of will in the Father and the Son towards each other, that is not in them essentially, and it is called new, as being in God freely, not naturally. Such a covenant is acknowledged by most. Arminius confesses it to be pretty clear from Isa. liii. 10, 'When thou shalt make his soul an offering for sin he shall see his seed, he shall prolong his days,' in his oration de sacerdotio Christi. And some of the greatest Jesuits, as Suarez, Tirinus on Isa. liii. 10, which is much. For, asserting this covenant, the doctrines of election, efficacious grace, and perseverance of that seed, are established.

That there is such a covenant, I shall offer some considerations.

1. As there was a covenant made with the first Adam for himself and his posterity, so it is very likely there was a covenant made with the second Adam, for himself and those which were chosen in him. Though this covenant of redemption be not the same with the covenant of grace, yet something in this covenant of redemption did concern the seed of Christ. Upon the account of this covenant, God is the God of Christ, Ps. lxxxix. 26, xl. 8, and Rev. iii. 12; you have Christ calling God his God, no less than four times in that verse. He is a surety of the covenant of grace; there was then some other previous treaty whereby Christ entered into terms of suretyship.

2. Christ is said to be faithful, Heb. iii. 2. As obedience implies a precept, so faithfulness implies a trust, and a promise whereby a man has obliged himself to perform that trust, according to the direction given him; and Christ is said to trust God, Heb. ii. 13. As a precept is a formal object of obedience, so a promise is a formal object of trust; as he had a command, so he had a promise, both which imply a covenant.

3. Christ's prayer does in various parts manifest this; he does not only entreat and petition, but he

challenges something as due to him, upon the account of what he had done; in John xvii., he seems to run altogether upon a covenant strain, which must suppose some agreement and promise on the Father's part. God had not else been obliged to accept what he had done, nor could our Saviour have challenged it at the hands of God. A claim implies a promise preceding, annexed to a condition to be done by the party to whom the promise is made, which being performed, gives a right to demand the reward. And hence, perhaps, it is that he calls God 'righteous Father,' appealing therein to the faithfulness of God in this business. And, indeed, the mediatory covenant seems to me, by that John xvii., to be the ground upon which Christ builds his whole intercession; that being a transcript of it, and the pleas there being drawn by a strong compact.

4. This treaty is distinctly evidenced, Isa. xlix. 3-6, from which chapter to the end of that prophecy, there seems to be a continued discourse concerning Christ. Christ directs his discourse to the Gentiles, acquainting them with the manner of this treaty: ver. 1, 'Listen, O isles, unto me; and hearken, ye people, from far.'

(1.) God calls out Christ by the name of Israel: ver. 3, 'and said unto me,' i. e. the Lord, 'Thou art my servant, O Israel, in whom I will be glorified;' the name of the body being given to the head, as the name of the head is given to the body. The church in union with Christ the head is called Christ, 1 Cor. xii. 12, which some think also to be the meaning of Gal. iii. 16. The promises were made to Abraham and his seed; 'not to seeds, as of many, but as of one, and thy seed which is Christ,' Christ mystical. I will be glorified in thee, as the head of the Jews, to prepare them a spiritual people for me.

(2.) Christ thinks this too low: ver. 4, 'Then I said,' i.e. he whose mouth God had made a sharp sword, 'I have laboured in vain, I have spent my strength for nought; yet surely my judgment is with the Lord, and my work is with my God.' A small income for so great pains and cost. What, shall I glorify thee only in Israel? It is but a little glory thou wilt get from so small a handful that will believe in me among them, however, I refer myself to thee, O Father, and will stand to thy judgment. It is a glorious thing to be the Redeemer of Israel, yet it seems to be too narrow a field for me to run my race in. Judge of the greatness of my pains; and though I shall be in thy eye, though Israel be not gathered, yet consider whether so great an undertaking will not require a greater reward than a few Israelites. Thou shalt, O Father, be glorified in me, but I foresee that few of the Jews will embrace my doctrine; I shall spend my strength, prayers, and blood for nought, "hevel tohu", the word used to express the chaos before it was formed into a world. It will be as a thing without form, a very little part of a new creation. Christ was at first God's angel to Israel, and before his coming in the flesh had no other nations, but as some sprinklings of them were proselyted to the Jews; and therefore the Gentiles are said, Isa. lv. 5, to be a people that he knew not, i.e. that he did not actually possess as his peculiar, in that manner as he ruled in Israel, though the providential government of all nations was committed to him. But after his exaltation in his human nature, he had the possession of them. Therefore

(3.) Christ then declares God's enlarging his terms: ver. 5, 'My God shall be my strength;' which words some take by themselves, as the beginnings of God's further grant. My God was my strength, he added courage to me by enlarging his gift, which is expressed, ver. 6, 'And he said, It is a light thing that thou should be my servant, to raise up the tribes of Jacob, and to restore the preserved of Israel; I will also give thee for a light to the Gentiles, that thou may be my salvation unto the end of the earth.' The word also represents as it were a former sticking in the Jews. It is too low a thing to take flesh, sweat, labour, and die for one nation; thou shalt spread thy tents to the end of the earth, and have the Gentiles for thy possession. When God saw me ready for so high a work, he did in his treaty extend the bounds of my power and advantage further. He said the limits of Israel were too narrow, the gain of Israel too light a recompense for so great a labour. God is brought in here proposing; Christ grieving at the narrowness of it, yet complying with it. God making a second proposal, wherein Christ does acquiesce; and no further debate is mentioned, after the Gentiles were cast into his lap. Whereupon some make a double decree, or at least two parts of the decree of salvation: 1, for the conversion of the Jews; 2, a decree for the conversion of the Gentiles.

5. The notion of a treaty and covenant is suitable to our conceptions, and gives us a distinct account of the methods of redemption; and also of the ground of the salvation of the fathers, who died before the coming of the Redeemer in the flesh. In order of conception, the first resolution was this, that man should be redeemed; the second, by what ways and means this redemption should be wrought; and how to make it sure, that there may be no revolt again. The second person is pitched upon for this undertaking. We must then conceive his voluntary consent to this, and also some terms upon which he undertakes it, which is necessary to every action according to the rules of wisdom. Had not this way of redemption been settled and stated, the fathers before and under the lay could not have been saved; for they were saved by faith. Faith could not be without a promise; a promise could not be without a previous ascertaining the method of redemption. Had Christ only consented to it at the time of his coming into the world, there had been no ground of any promise before, because the consent of the Redeemer had till that time been uncertain; but the promise supposes his consent positively given, before the promise was made. Again, the covenant of grace is as ancient as the first promise of the seed

of the woman. And since the grace the patriarchs had was communicated by virtue of a covenant of grace, it implies that there was an agreement between the Father and the Sour for it is by this agreement the covenant of grace is established. Faith in a mediator, the condition of that covenant, supposes the settlement of the mediator. We cannot suppose how anything could be bestowed upon men by virtue of a covenant of grace, before the Redeemer had actually merited, without this agreement; for whatsoever was bestowed, was given upon the account of that merit to be wrought in time, therefore at least a promise of so meriting must precede; as articles of agreement are made among men, before the sealing of writings and payment of the money, by virtue of which articles there is some kind of right converted. Upon the account of this agreement, the Spirit was given to some particular men, but to very few, and in a less measure, for it was not congruous that there should be as great an effusion of the Spirit before the actual payment required for it, as after. How this could be without a designation of the person of Christ to this work of redemption, and a voluntary undertaking on his part, and how there could be this designing and appointing him to it, and his accepting of it, without some terms in the nature of a covenant between the Father and the Son, cannot so distinctly and easily be conceived by us. But such a notion as this makes the whole work more obvious to our weak understandings.

For a close of this part, I shall direct you to Ps. lxxxix. throughout, where this covenant is very plainly mentioned; and the whole contexture of the psalm discovers the design of it to be, to set forth some higher person than David; and seems to be too magnificent and lofty for an earthly prince. As ver 2, 'Mercy shall be built up for ever, thy faithfulness shalt thou establish in the very heavens.' But how was it established in the heavens? Ver. 8, in making a covenant with his chosen, and swearing to David his servant: 'Thy seed will I establish for ever, and build up thy throne to all generations.' Here indeed was faithfulness established in heaven. This will be more remarkable if the notion of a learned man of our own be true, that this psalm was penned in the time of the Israelites' bondage in Egypt, by Ethan, the son of Zerah, and grandchild of Judah, the son of Jacob, who is mentioned 1 Chron. ii. 6; therefore called Ethan the Ezraite, or of Zerah, who was the son of Judah. Though there is mention made of Ethan in the time of David, 1 Chron. xv. 17, 19, and though David be often mentioned in the psalm, yet, says he, that was done prophetically. Howsoever it is, the psalm is understood of Christ by most of our interpreters. And Christ is several times called David in the prophets, who lived after the time of David. Why might not David be prophetically mentioned many years before his birth, as well as Cyrus was by the prophet Isaiah, some years before his? Some make this covenant of redemption the same with the covenant of grace. But they seem to be two distinct covenants

1. The parties are distinct. In the one, the Father and the Son are the parties covenanting. In the covenant of grace, God and man. In the mediatory covenant, there were two persons equal. In the covenant of grace there is a superior, God; and an inferior, man.

2. The conditions are different. Death, and satisfaction for sin thereby, was the condition of the covenant of redemption. Faith is the condition in the covenant of grace; death required on Christ's part, faith required on man's part. The giving Christ a seed, and eternal life to that seed, is the condition on God's part to Christ, the giving eternal life only to the party believing, is the condition on God's part in the other. So that the reward in that covenant is larger than the reward promised to us in the covenant of grace. In the covenant of grace, the condition runs thus, 'Believe in the Lord Jesus Christ, and thou shalt be saved.' In the covenant of redemption the condition runs thus, 'Make thy soul an offering for sin, and thou shalt see a seed.' The promises of God to Christ, or rather God absolutely considered in that covenant, was the object of Christ's faith; God in Christ is the object of our faith in the covenant of grace. Believing in Christ could be no condition in the covenant of redemption, as it is in the covenant of grace. Christ must be then the object of his own faith, not his Father's.

3. The time of making these covenants is different. The covenant of grace was made in time, after man had broke the covenant of works; the covenant of redemption was made from eternity. 'I was set up from everlasting, from the beginning, or ever the earth was; when there were no depths, I was brought forth, while as yet he had not made the earth, nor the fields, nor the highest part of the dust of the world; (set up as mediator) rejoicing in the habitable parts of the earth,' Prov. viii. 24, 25, 31. He rejoiced in angels, the chief parts of his creation, as God; in the habitable parts of the earth, as mediator. The revelation of the covenant of redemption was in time, but the stipulation was from eternity; the Father and Son being actually in being, and so stipulators. The decree of making a covenant of grace was from eternity, but not the actual covenant, because there was no soul to covenant with; as the decree of creating the world was in time, but the actual creation at the beginning of time. The covenant of redemption is expressed, Isa. liii., whence we can no more conclude, that it was but then made, than we may say, that Christ suffered then, because his sufferings are spoken of there as already undergone. It was made when some were given to Christ, and therefore must be as ancient as election, which was before the foundation of the world.

4. Christ is the mediator of the covenant of grace, Heb. xii. 24, but not the mediator of the covenant of redemption, but a party. He was the surety of the covenant of grace, Heb. vii. 22. The covenant of redemption had no surety; the Father and the Son trusted one another upon the agreement.

The covenant of grace is confirmed by the blood of Christ; but we cannot say that the covenant of redemption was confirmed properly by that blood, any more than as the shedding of his blood was a necessary article in that covenant.

5. Christ performed his part in the covenant of redemption; and by virtue of this mediatory covenant, performed the covenant of works; but he did confirm, not perform, the covenant of grace.

6. By the covenant of redemption, Christ could challenge his reward upon his own account; but by the covenant of grace, believers have a right to the reward only upon the account of Christ. There is an intrinsic worth in the obedience of Christ whereby he merited, for there was a proportion between it, in regard of the dignity of his person and the infiniteness of God; but there is no intrinsic worth in that grace which is the condition of the covenant of grace, to merit anything. There was a condition of a valuable consideration required of Christ, but the condition required of us has no valuable proportion to the greatness of the reward. The reward was of debt to him, because what he performed was by his own strength; of grace to us, because what we perform is by the strength of another. And though the exaltation of Christ is called a free gift, 'He has given him a name above every name,' "echarisato", Philip. ii. 9, that is in respect of the whole economy of the mission of Christ, and the manifestation of him, which is an act of God's free grace to us. And in his exaltation he is considered as appearing for us, and receiving from the Father all for our good; and because it was an act of free grace to us, to unite the second person in the Trinity to our flesh.

7. The mediatory covenant respects others in Christ, as well as Christ himself, viz. his seed, and the giving them a glory. In the covenant of grace, the promise respects only the particular person that believes; it regards none else but the particular person answering the terms of that covenant. No person can challenge any right upon another's believing, but must believe himself, if he will be within the compass of the covenant. But Christ, upon the performance of the condition of the mediatory covenant, could challenge not only for himself, but for others, and all that were to be his seed, and were to believe on him to the end of the world, John xvii. 20, 24, because that covenant respected not only himself, but others, upon those conditions he was to perform; for the redemption, justification, and happiness of believers are promised to Christ upon the condition of dying, Isa. liii. 11. All the seed of Christ are in the covenant of redemption before they are regenerate, but not actually in the covenant of grace, and under the influence of the special benefits of it, till they are regenerate; as all mankind were in the loins of Adam, but not guilty of his pollution till their natural generation.

8. If the covenant of grace and that of redemption were the same, then Christ should be both the testator and a party. Christ is the testator of the covenant of grace, Heb. ix. 16, 17. A testator makes not a will to bequeath legacies to himself.

So that these two covenants are distinct; they agree in the common nature of a covenant, that there are conditions to be performed, and privileges thereupon to be enjoyed. But the conditions and privileges are distinct. They agree in this, that the salvation of the seed is promised in both covenants: it is promised to the believer upon his faith; it is promised to Christ in behalf of the seed upon his suffering; and, further, the covenant of redemption is the foundation of the covenant of grace. In the covenant of grace, Christ, or God in Christ, is the object of faith. Christ had not been the object of faith, had not such an agreement between the Father and the Son preceded. How is Christ the object of faith, but as dying? What force had his death had, without some compact between the Father as the principal party wronged, and the Redeemer as the person satisfying? The everlastingness of the covenant of grace depends upon the perpetuity of the covenant of redemption: Ps. lxxxix. 28, 29, 'My covenant shall stand fast with him; his seed will I make to endure for ever.' This covenant between the Father and the Son must be broken, before the covenant of God can fail to a believer. Upon this account Christ is said to be 'given for a covenant to the people,' Isa. xlii. 6; a covenant to the people, i. e. to bring the people into covenant with me; as being the foundation of the covenant of grace, upon which account he is called the peace, Eph. ii. 17; as being the foundation and cause of peace between God and man. And all the promises as established by his death are yea and amen in him: they receive their validity from his death, and his death receives its validity from the covenant of redemption. He thereby performing what was required on his part, settled the covenant of grace between God and us for ever unrepealable, and it had not its full settlement but in the establishment of this. Upon the account of this covenant, the right of Christ as a testator bequeathing the inheritance is grounded, for he could not as a testator bequeath what he had no right unto. His testament was made by him, not as God, but as mediator by means of his death, Heb. ix. 15, 16. Therefore, as mediator, he had a right, which cannot well be supposed without some precedent agreement between the Father and the Son, because the right originally resided in the Father. And this covenant of redemption is the ground of our hope and faith: Titus i. 2, 'In hope of eternal life, which was promised before the world began.' The hope believers have of eternal life springs up originally from that promise made by the Father to the Son before the foundation of the world; for the promises of the covenant of grace were included in this covenant of redemption; and to be made good when Christ made the conditions on his part in that covenant good. In this agreement, then, God was in Christ reconciling the world.

(1.) The Father covenants with Christ, that he should undertake for man as a common head; to free men from that dreadful condition, wherein God foresaw from eternity they would fall upon their creation. Hence he is called the second Adam, as being a public person; and as Adam had fallen off from righteousness to the love of iniquity, and violated the law of God, so the second Adam, as a head of many fellows, was to 'love righteousness, and hate iniquity,' Heb. i. 9, i. e. vindicate the honour of God, laid prostrate by sin, and restore the righteousness of the law. This being rendered there the ground of his advancement by God as his God, a God in covenant with him, implies that it was the main article insisted on, and a condition in the covenant which Christ was to perform. Man was a criminal debtor, the debt must be paid; Christ by agreement puts himself in the sinner's stead, to pay this debt, submit to the revenging arm of justice, and thereby release the prisoner: Gal. iv. 4, 5, 'He was made under the law, to redeem them that were under the law;' as we were under the law, so was Christ to bear the curse of the law for us, that whatsoever power the law had over us in regard of its precepts, Christ was to obey, in regard of its curses he was to undergo, and thus undertaking for us, he was to endure the shock of his Father's wrath, which we sinners are liable to: and, therefore, he is brought in, offering himself as a surety in our stead Ps. xl. 7, 'Lo, I come to do thy will, O my God;' thy covenant-will, as thou art my God; which will was our sanctification by the 'offering of his body,' Heb. x. 10. Referring to ver. 7, and as being instead of us the principal debtors, he calls our sins his own (ver. 13, 'mine iniquities have taken hold of me'); as he was our surety, the debt which a surety engages to pay being legally his own debt, though he did not personally incur it by any crime of his own, or receipt of that for which he stands indebted.

(2.) In order to this, another condition necessarily consequent upon the other was, that he was to take a body. This debt could not be paid, nor the articles of the covenant be performed, but in the human nature, the divine being impassible. He was therefore to have a passible nature, a nature capable of, and prepared for suffering, Heb. x. 5; a body to suffer that which was represented by these legal sacrifices wherein God took no pleasure, ver. 6. He was to have a body of flesh, surrounded with the infirmities of our fallen nature, sin only excepted; whereupon Christ does freely comply, 'I come to do thy will, O my God;' I am come to take such a body, which by thy will is allotted to me.

(3.) In this body he was to pay a service and obedience to his Father. After this agreement, whatsoever Christ did in the body falls under the term of obedience to the mediatory law prescribed him. Hence he is called God's servant, Isa. xiii. 1, and 'took upon him the form of a servant,' Philip. ii. 7; not as servants were formerly bought with a price, and passed wholly into the right and dominion of another, but a servant who, by covenant and agreement, undertakes an employment by the order of another; for he was such a servant, that he was also Lord, Heb. iii. 6, Heb. i. 2. This is expressed, Isa. 1. 5, 'The Lord God has opened mine ear, and I was not rebellious.' God constituted him his servant by the opening his ear, according to the Jewish custom of boring the ear, and he was not in any thing rebellious, he was to do whatsoever was commanded him to do; and, therefore, all the time of his life before his death, he acted an obedience to his Father, and did nothing but by his Father's command and order: John xiv. 31, 'As the Father has given me commandment, so I do.' He stipulated to take upon him the 'form of a servant,' Philip. ii. 6, 7, which seems to refer to this agreement; and after that, 'was made in the likeness of men,' referring to his incarnation; as a man is said to take upon him such a task, when he has covenanted to do it.

(4.) In this body he was to die at last; and, therefore, his dying is said to be obedience: Philip. ii. 8, 'He became obedient to death, even the death of the cross;' his dying, and dying so ignominiously upon the cross, was obedience; which implies a command and order to die, and to die such a death, otherwise it had not been obedience, though it might be termed affection. This was the chief article of the covenant: Isa. liii. 10, 'When thou shalt make his soul an offering for sin, he shall see his seed.' "Tasim" is then the third person, and being feminine, agrees well with "nefesh", a feminine noun. Other translations read it, If he shall make his soul an offering for sin; or, rather, according to others, and according to grammar, If his soul shall make an offering for sin. In this death he was to respect the satisfaction of God's justice; for it was not a bare offering, but an offering for sin. God, in imposing this article, respected this chiefly, as this was the main end of sending him to be an "hilasmios": 1 John iv. 10, 'God has sent his Son to be the propitiation for our sins.' So it was the main end of this article of dying, which Christ was to respect in his dying; for the regarding the end of any service or command is a principal ingredient in obedience; by virtue of which covenant and command thereupon, there was an ought upon Christ: Luke xxiv. 26, 'Ought not Christ to have suffered those things?' And a command, John x. 18, 'I have power to lay down my life; I have,' "ksousian", 'authority, for I have received a command from my Father.' Hence his death is said to be determined: Luke xxii. 22, 'The Son of man goes as it was determined.' In the first giving himself to God, he gave himself as a ransom, to be testified and brought forth upon the stage in time, wherein his mediatory office chiefly consisted, 1 Tim. ii. 5, 6. And methinks Christ does intimate this laying down his life for his sheep to be the effect of this mutual agreement between the Father and himself: John x. 15, 'As the Father knows me, even so know I the Father, and I lay down my life for the sheep.' It was the effect of their knowledge of one another, not a bare knowledge, for that might have been without Christ's dying; but an intimate conjunction of mind, an approbation on both parts. This mind, to take upon him the form of a servant, was in Christ, Philip. ii. 5, and therefore this mind was in his Father, for their minds could not be different; there was a mutual knowledge and agreement in the whole affair, and from this knowledge one of another, did arise the laying down of his life. God required this sacrifice of Christ, exclusively of all others, in the first treaty, as to any satisfaction: Heb. x. 5-7, 'Sacrifice and burnt-offering thou wouldst not; in them thou had no pleasure; then said I, Lo, I come.' He pronounced them utterly useless for the satisfaction of justice, though fit to prefigure the grand sacrifice he intended. And that voice of Christ upon the cross, 'It is finished,' John xix. 30, seems to refer to this agreement. I am come to a period on my part, the article on my part is completed, there remain no more deaths for me to suffer. This seems to be a necessary article, very congruous to the wisdom of God, as he is creator, governor, and the end of all things: Heb. ii. 10, 'It became him for whom are all things, and by whom are all things, in bringing many sons to glory, to make the captain of their salvation perfect through sufferings.' It became him as a wise Creator, as a wise Governor, as he is the end of all things, to insist upon the sufferings of Christ as the fittest means for the attaining the end he aimed at; for hereby his justice and mercy are glorified. In the performance, Christ was very exact in every punctilio: 'As they were skewed by the mouths of the prophets, he so fulfilled them,' Acts iii. 18; and God showed them by the mouth of the prophets as they were determined and agreed upon. The ancient Jews had some prospect of this covenant. One of their writers. says, God treated with the Messiah: Righteous Messiah, those who are hid with thee, are such whose sins in time shall bring thee into grief; thy ears shall hear reproaches, thy tongue cleave to the roof of thy mouth, thou shalt be wearied with sorrow. The Messiah answered, Lord of the world, I joyfully take them upon me, and charge myself with their torments, but upon this condition, that thou shalt quicken the dead in their days. God, says the rabbi, granted him this, and from that time the Messiah charged himself with all kind of torments; as it is written, Isa. liii., 'He was afflicted.' So that the death of Christ was not by a fortuitous reencounter of things, nor merely by the violence of the Jewish rage, nor from any inability in his Father or himself to hinder so strange an event, but it was the issue of a previous agreement, flowing from infinite love, managed by incomparable wisdom, disposing things to so great an end.

(5.) In regard of what Christ was to do and suffer, the Father makes excellent promises to him. [1.] Promises of assistance. [2.] Of a seed. [3.] Of glory.

[1.] Promises of assistance.

First, Promises of a fitness for it. He had the promise of the Spirit to this purpose: Isa. xi. 1-3, 'The Spirit of the Lord shall rest upon him, the Spirit of wisdom, understanding, counsel, might, knowledge, and of the fear of the Lord;' to distribute all his gifts to him, in a fullness of measure, in a fullness of duration. All the gifts of the Spirit should reside in him, as in a proper habitation, perpetually; as the Deity dwelt in the humanity, and was never to forsake it. The human nature being a creature, could not beautify and enrich itself with needful gifts; this promise of the Spirit was therefore necessary, his humanity could not else have performed the work it was designed for. So that the habitual holiness residing in the humanity of Christ, was a fruit of this eternal covenant. Though the divine nature of Christ by virtue of its union, might sanctify the human nature, yet the Spirit is promised him, because it is the proper office of the Holy Ghost to confer those gifts which are necessary for any undertaking in the world; and the personal operations of the Trinity do not interfere. It also might be, because every person in the Trinity might evidently have a distinct hand in our redemption.

Secondly, Promises of protection in it. Upon this one stone there were to be seven eyes, Zech. iii. 10. Seven eyes upon one stone, a special care of him, and counsel about him. Seven notes multitude; eyes note intention. Providence is signified by eyes in Scripture; a special providence shall be exercised towards Christ in the whole management of his office, and defence of his kingdom; hence, he does acknowledge that he was under the choice care of God: Luke ii. 49, 'Wist you not that I am about my Father's business?' "en tois tou patros", among those things my leather takes care of; 'why sought you me?' Do you not know that I am the choicest jewel of my Father, and that he has his eye upon me; as one of the cabinet rarities of my Father? God promised to hide him in the shadow of his hand, preserve him as a shaft in his quiver, in the midst of the rage and fury of his enemies. He does solemnly promise his omnipotence, all his creating and governing power, to hold his hand in his being for a covenant of the people, and a light of the Gentiles, till he had brought 'the prisoners from the prison, and them that sit in darkness out of the prison-house,' Isa. xiii. 5-7. He promises here, in the loftiest expressions, to strengthen him so, that he should not be discouraged, but see the blessed effects of his undertaking. He would uphold him tenderly, as a father does his son in his arms, that no hurt may happen to him, and that because he had called him in righteousness; or, as some, our righteousness, to settle an evangelical righteousness in the earth. He is said, therefore, to be made strong by God for himself: Ps. lxxx. 16, 'The Son of man, whom thou hast made strong for thyself,' the King, Messiah, whom thou hast strengthened for thyself; so the Targum. The title of Son of man was by way of eminency given to the Messiah in Daniel, and the title he commonly gave himself in the New Testament. This assistance of Christ was represented by the ark, which had three coverings, together with the table of shewbread representing the

Church, Num. iv. 8, as a type of a special protection to both, whereas other consecrated things had but two coverings.

Thirdly, This assistance was to run through the whole course of his mediation. He was to be assisted in his conflict, and in his success, while his soul was travailing, and while it was triumphing. He should not be discouraged, till he had 'set judgment in the earth,' Isa. xiii. 4. It is a meiosis; he shall be mightily encouraged, till he have wrought a perfect deliverance for his people; and there shall be a supporting hand under him till he has completed the work of redemption. He should stand, and be established, and 'feed in the strength of the Lord,' Mic. v. 4, 'in the majesty of the name of the Lord his God.' He should gather, rule, and save his sheep in the choicest of God's strength, as he was his God, i. e. a God in covenant with him, and had appointed him to be 'the Judge of Israel,' ver. 1, and this, till he should be 'the peace,' ver. 5, not only laying the cornerstone by his death, but the top-stone by his exaltation.

Fourthly, Christ was to plead these promises, and encourage himself in them. He was to plead them: Ps. lxxxix. 26, 'He shall cry unto me, Thou art my Father, my God, and the rock of my salvation.' After the repetition of the promises of strength and assistance, ver. 19-21, &c., he was enjoined to put those covenant promises in suit, and then he should be made the firstborn, higher than the kings of the earth, and his covenant should stand fast with him; as though God promised him the Gentiles for his possession, yet he was to ask it, Ps. ii. 8. In this covenant there was an injunction upon Christ to intercede and plead for himself, and for his people; so that the intercession Christ does manage in heaven for the completing of those promises, which were formerly in that covenant, or depended upon it (as all the promises in the covenant of grace do), is an article in that covenant, and therefore will be kept up till all enemies are made his footstool, and death, which is the last, swallowed up in victory. Christ encouraged himself in those promises; by these God made him hope when he was 'upon his mother's breasts,' Ps. xxii. 9, and he prophetically pleads them, ver. 10, 11, 'I was cast upon thee from the womb: be not far from me, for trouble is near.' It was an high satisfaction to him, that he should not be moved, therefore he set God always before him, Acts ii. 25. In regard of confidence, and supply of strength, his eye was not upon him in one strait or two, but in the whole affair, Ps. xvi. 8, 9; he had a confidence that God would be at his right hand, which signifies to be an helper and fellow-champion in fight for the weakening of his enemies; it being a metaphor taken from conflicts, where he that is at the right hand of his companion does first expose himself to danger, and receiving the enemies' force defends his associate from the blows. The same expression is used of standing by Christ: Ps. cx. 5, 'The Lord at thy right hand shall strike through kings.' How loftily does he express his confidence in it: Isa. l. 8-10, 'The Lord God will help me; therefore have I set my face as a flint, and I know that I shall not be ashamed. The Lord God will help me; who is he that shall condemn me?' and challenges all the power of earth and hell to contend with him, since he had the promise of God to justify him. 'My God shall be my strength,' Isa. xlix. 5, my God in covenant with me. And the apostle brings him in declaring his trust in God: Heb. ii. 13, and 'I will put my trust in him.' And he acknowledges that the preservation of his disciples, and consequently all his people enjoy by him, is through the 'name of his Father,' John xvii. 12. He acknowledges his powerful assistance in every particle of his work. 'I have kept them in thy name.'

[2.] Promises of a seed, as the success of his undertaking. He was first in order to die, and then to see his seed: Isa. liii. 10, 11, 'When his soul shall make an offering for sin, he shall see his seed, he shall see the travail of his soul;' his grief and pain shall not be fruitless. He was to have a flock to guide as a shepherd, members to animate as an head, a spouse to cherish as a husband, children to breed up as a father, subjects to reign over as a king. There was a designation of some to him for those relations at this first agree meet, which he does acknowledge as a donative from his Father: John vi. 6, 'Thine they were, and thou gave them me.' Thine by election and creation, mine by donation and merit; they belonged to Christ as God before, though originally to the Father as the fountain of the Deity; but now to Christ by another tie, as mediator, as jewels to be made up by him; upon the account of which gift by compact, he calls them his sheep before their actual enfolding, John x. 15, 16. The promise made to Abraham of the blessing of the nations in his seed is said to be made to Christ, Gal. iii. 19; 'till the seed should come, to whom the promise was made, which seed is Christ,' ver. 16. And some interpret ver. 17, 'the covenant that was confirmed before of God in Christ,' "eis Christon" for to Christ, as Eph. i. 5, "eis auton" for "heautoi", and Col. i. 20, reconcile all things "eis auton", to himself; but howsoever, the promise to Abraham is certainly grounded upon a promise to Christ, that in him who was Abraham's seed all nations should be blessed; whether that Hos. xiv. 5, 6, be a promise to Christ, who is called Israel, or rather a promise or prophecy concerning the church, of the beauty of Christ's seed as a lily, the firmness as a cedar, and the fruitfulness as an olive.

God promised, 1. A numerous seed. 2. A succession of seed. 3. A duration of seed.

God promised him a numerous seed, like the dew that falls at the dawn of the morning in abundance upon the flowers and plants of the earth, Ps. cx. 3: 'The dew of thy youth, from the womb of the morning.' Micah v. 7, As the dew upon the grass. As the poets call the dew the tears of the morning, so was this the fruit of Christ's tears and blood; they were upon his ascension to flock to him from all quarters of the world. He promised to 'bring his seed from the east, and gather them from the west; he would say to the north, Give up; and to the south, Keep not back; bring my sons from far, and my daughters from the ends of the earth,' Isa. xliii. 5, 6. And Isa. liv. 1, 'More shall be the children of the desolate than the children of the married wife, says the Lord.' The Rachel of our mystical Jacob, that had remained so long barren, should be suddenly mother of a numerous train. Then was our Saviour Israel indeed, one that prevailed with God (as the word signifies) to enlarge the lines of his inheritance to the Gentiles. He was to 'speak peace to the heathens,' Zech. ix. 10. And, according to this article, God enlarged the tents of the church, so that twenty-three years after the publication of the gospel, not only Syria and Arabia, and the bordering provinces on Judea, were full of Christians, but Asia, Italy, Spain, and the chiefest of the western part. And Tacitus says, that in the eleventh year of Nero, which was thirty-one years after Christ's ascension, Rome, the capital city of the world, swarmed with men professing the name of Christ. The death of Christ was to be more fruitful than his life, and being lifted up upon the cross, he was to draw all men after him, and gather a plentiful harvest of all kindreds, tongues, and nations; a mighty generation to be new born to serve him. He was to be cast into the ground, that seed should spring up from him, John xii. 24. He was to be dead in reality, as Isaac in figure, that he might be the everlasting father of many nations. Thus, when he was on his part to be laid low as a root in the earth, by making his soul an offering for sin, God, the husbandman of this vine, promises to bring forth a new set, an abundance of branches sprouting up from him. They should come 'from afar off and build in the temple of the Lord,' Zech. vi. 15. Gentiles as well as Jews should be knit together as lively stones to rise up for a temple to the Lord.

God promises a succession of seed. 'His name shall be continued as long as the sun,' Ps. lxxii. 17, "yinon", filiabitur, his name shall be childed in him, as the name of a man is continued successively in his posterity. It is not only one morning that the rich and plentiful dew shall fall from heaven upon the hearts of men, but successively to the end of the world, as long as this Sun of righteousness shall rise in any horizon, and the day dawn before him. Grace shall be dropped upon the hearts of men for a succession of seed, till in the last generation a period be put to the world. Seed shall be springing up till the last fire seize upon the world, at which time there shall be some caught up into the air to meet him, and a generation among the nations shall be successively blessed in him.

A perpetual seed is promised him. God's covenant shall stand fast with him, and the issue of that is, that his seed will God make to endure for ever, and his throne as the days of heaven, Ps. lxxxix. 28, 29. His seed and throne are coupled together, as if his throne could not stand if his seed did fail. If his subjects should perish, what would he be king of? If his members should consume, what would he be head of? The promise of a perpetual kingdom secures the duration of his seed. This was so considerable an article, that in his plea he insists on it more resolutely, and challenges it with a more vigorous earnestness: John xvii. 24, 'Father, I will that they also whom thou hast given me be with me,' &c., as he had at the first treaty insisted upon the enlarging his inheritance among the Gentiles. He had hitherto been praying only for his own glory, and their preservation and sanctification in the world. He now brings in an also; there was an article for the glory of his seed, as well as for the glory of his person, and the word also signifies that he would be as earnest for them, and insist as much upon the performance of this article which concerned them, as upon that which concerned himself. And the reason rendered signifies thus, 'For thou didst love me from the foundation of the world.' Thou did manifest the love to me as mediator before the foundation of the world, in this promise of a seed, and that they should be perpetually with me to behold my glory; this was the main article which encouraged Christ to this work, wherein the Father manifested his love to him as mediator before the world, and therefore in that rich promise wherein God engages the majesty of his name for the strengthening of him, the perpetuity of his seed is ensured: Micah v. 4, 'He shall stand and feed in the strength of the Lord, in the majesty of the name of the Lord his God, and they shall abide.' Who? Ver. 3, the remnant of his brethren that shall return to the children of Israel, the brethren of that ruler in Israel whose goings forth have been from everlasting, they shall abide. And some thus interpret Isa. liii. 10, 'He shall see his seed, he shall prolong his days,' i. e. those of his seed. They shall be perpetually with him. For it was the pleasure of the Lord in this compact to give them a kingdom (as Christ tells his disciples); and this pleasure of the Lord should prosper in the hands of the mediator. That which God in his wisdom aimed at in his Son's sufferings, he aimed at certainly in the calling him and engaging him by covenant to suffer, and that was the bringing many sons to glory: Heb. ii. 10, 'It became him, in bringing many sons to glory, to make the captain of their salvation perfect through sufferings.' The end and the means were becoming propositions for the wisdom of God to make, and as becoming for the wisdom of God to perform. Since the means have been fully wrought, the end will be perfectly attained. Christ had those promises of eternal life made to him as a common head, and a feoffee in trust for them: Titus i. 2, 'Eternal life was promised before the world began.' Not for himself, who was the eternal Son of God. Could the promise of eternal life to his humanity make him take flesh barely for that? It was promised to him for his seed, for whose redemption he was to lay down his life as a ransom. As God made a covenant with Adam, not as an individual person, but as a nature, he being the representative of mankind, so that if he had stood, his posterity had stood and enjoyed life; so he made a covenant with Christ to give eternal life to those that should believe in him, who are as really in him by regeneration as men are in Adam by natural descent.

To which may be added,

God promised his grace to draw men to him. That this seed should be sure to him, God promises to prepare men for him: to remove the stony heart, mollify their hearts, give them hearts of flesh, conquer their carnal principles and resolutions, and put his Spirit into them, that they might be a fit progeny for Christ. Christ intimates this in that speech 'None can come unto me except the Father, which has sent me, draw him,' John vi. 44. As the Father's sending him was the issue of a compact between them, so the drawing any is a fruit of that compact; for Christ removes this from himself, as an article to be performed on his part, as that which lay solely upon his Father's hands, as belonging to him as much as his own mission, and the particular circumstances of it. And this promise he had, Ps. cx 2, 'That the people should be willing in the day of his power.' God ordered him indeed to call the nations: Isa. lv. 5, 'Thou shalt call a nation which thou know not; and nations that knew not thee shall run unto thee, because of the Lord thy God; for he has glorified thee.' But the vigour which should spirit them to so quick a race to Christ he reserves to himself; they shall run because of the Lord thy God; by his power, as he was the Lord, by his faithfulness, as he was his God in covenant; and the reason rendered is the glorifying him; which is both an engagement to Christ to call those his Father would have him call, and an engagement on the Father to bring the nations to him. The coming in of nations would redound to his honour; and it is likely this is part of the glory Christ prays for, John xvii. 5. He does not particularise what that glory was, but some guess may be made by his falling off from that petition to the praying for his people. The preservation of them and keeping those that had been given to him (which includes the bringing them all in) is part of the glory which was promised to him. And this glorifying of him in his people he begs for at his Father's hand, as being by this covenant to be his act. The coming in of nations to him was a great part of the glory of Christ promised him in this covenant. The conversion of every man by the efficacy of grace, is the fruit of the covenant between the Father and the Son, as God is the Lord God of Christ. And therefore the calling of us by God is said to be according to his own purpose, and that grace, which was given us in Christ before the world was, 2 Tim. i. 9, a promise of grace for us, and of our calling in time, made then. For what is here called the purpose of God is, Titus i. 2, called the promise of God, and intimated as a promise in those words, 'given us in Jesus Christ,' by an agreement with him as our head, as the promise of life upon the covenant of works was given us in Adam as our common head. And so the promise of taking away the heart of stone, and giving an heart of flesh, may be said to be promises made to Christ on the behalf of his seed, not of his person; because, without this taking away the heart of stone, and giving an heart of flesh, it was impossible the nations, or any man, could be blessed in him. Notwithstanding that this efficacious grace is from the Father, and by his Spirit, by the covenant, yet all thus regenerated may well be called the seed of Christ, because the end of the sufferings of Christ was to merit a spirit of grace for those that were given to him; and the Spirit does nothing in forming a seed, but what rises up from the merit of Christ's sufferings. It is the travail of his soul, though the formation of the Spirit. Christ endured the pangs upon the cross for every new creature, though the Spirit brings it forth into the world. So that they are his seed, as springing up from the merit of his death, and being animated by the power of his life; they are Christ's seed by right of purchase, the Spirit's seed in regard of operation; yet as they are the Spirit's seed, they may be called Christ's seed, because the coming of the Spirit in its plentiful effusion for such an end was a fruit of his death and his ascension, John xvi. 7. He was sent by him as the greatest gift of his royalty.

There was something concerned Christ to do in this article of a seed; he was to take a special care of them. There was not only a may, but a must bring: John x. 16, 'Other sheep I have which are not of this fold; them also I must bring, and they shall hear my voice.' He was to call them, and the Father would draw them, and he was to bring them into one fold with the Israelites; and this does arise from this compact, or the mutual knowledge the Father and he had of one another; the mutual agreement, which was the cause of laying down his life, Ver. 15. Knowing, in God, sometimes signifies election, 2 Tim. ii. 19. God had chosen Christ to this end, and Christ had accepted of it to this end. These he was to teach, Isa. viii. 16. Those which he calls children, which the Lord had given, are, ver. 18, called his disciples, among whom he was to seal the law; whom he was to instruct in that knowledge of God which was eternal life, and manifest his name to them, John xvii. 2, 3, 6. And particularly, he was to instruct them in this great doctrine we are now treating of: ver. 7, 'Now they have known, that all things whatsoever thou hast given me are of thee'; which was indeed the manifestation of the name of his Father, which he had spoken of, ver. 5, that all things which I do are by thy appointment, order, and assistance. I have ascribed nothing to myself, but magnified thy love, as the sole fountain of all that I have done; which was necessary, for I doubt many men think the Father to be cruel, and full of hatred to his creatures, and that he was over-persuaded to redemption by the importunities of his Son, as a severe prince might be mollified by the supplications of his heir. It was not so, and Christ was to acquaint men with the true notion of God, and what his thoughts and affections were concerning them, and to show him to be a proper object of faith in this business. He was to use a great tenderness towards them, he was not only to gather the lambs with his arm and power, but to carry them in his bosom, not only to lead them, but gently to lead them; to have a special care of them, Isa. xl. 11. When they were given to him, they were given with some rules and orders how he should manage them, and he was to have his eye not only upon the flock in general, but upon every one in particular, that as any of them were weak, he should use them with more gentleness; take such an one in his bosom, he should have seven eyes upon the weakest, as his Father had upon him the corner-stone. He is therefore said to know his sheep, John x. 14 (every one in particular, as he knows the stars by name); otherwise the foundation of the Lord, this covenant of redemption, which is the foundation of all his proceedings, could not stand sure. The Father knew them in particular when he gave them to Christ, and Christ knew them in particular when he received them from him. It seems also that by this covenant he was to bring every conquering soul to a triumph, and he had power given him to this purpose, John xvii. 2. In the perfection he promises to them that overcome, he seems to refer it all to the covenant with the Father: Rev. iii. 12, he would make them pillars in the temple of his God, write upon them the name of his God, and the name of the city of his God, which is new Jerusalem, which comes down out of heaven from his God; where he mentions God as his God in every reward he promises the victorious souls in the church of Philadelphia, four times in that verse, as I have observed before.

[3.] Promises of a glory upon his suffering. As he was to endure the cross, so he was also to enjoy a crown. The enduring the cross was an article on his part, the bestowing a crown was an article on God's part. It was testified before by the prophets that sufferings should precede, the glory follow, 1 Pet. i. 11. The solemn inauguration into all his offices was after his making reconciliation; making an end of sin, bringing in everlasting righteousness, and thereby shutting up all prophecy and vision, because all the prophecies tended to him, and were accomplished in him, and then as manifesting himself the most holy, he was to be anointed, i.e. fully invested in all the offices of king, priest, and prophet, Dan. ix. 24. The compact runs thus, Do this, suffer death for the vindication of the honour of my law, and thou shalt be a priest and king for ever. He could not, therefore, be solemnly installed till he had performed the condition on his part (for the promise was made to him considered as mediator, or God-man); then it was that he was advanced, for the ground of his exaltation is pitched wholly upon his sufferings: Philip. ii. 9, 'Wherefore God has highly exalted him;' i.e. because he became obedient to the death of the cross. God has given him a name which is above every name; and because he loved righteousness, therefore God, as his God covenanting with him, has anointed him with the oil of gladness above his fellows, Heb. i. 9, therefore he has given him a glory, as a just debt due to the price paid, the sufferings undergone, and the obedience yielded to the mediatory law. Therefore the glory Christ prayed for, which he had before the world was, John xvii. 5, may be understood of that glory which he had in promise to be given to him upon the completing the work he then engaged for. For this covenant was not about giving him his essential kingdom, for that belonged to him by nature, as he was God equal with the Father. But the mediatory kingdom belonged to his office by a particular grant. There were two works of Christ, works of humiliation, which were suffering and dying; which were voluntary, not natural works; no natural tie upon him as the Son of God to undergo them, but a moral tie, after agreement and promise. There are regal works which were conferred on him by his Father, that he should be honoured and adored in the world as mediator, Heb. i. 6, worshipped by all the angels of God, when the glory of his deity should be manifested in the humanity, which had been so long veiled, and had but now and then beamed out; and this full shine of the Deity through the humanity was a new mode of glory acquired by the right of his death.

First, He had a promise of resurrection. As he had a power or authority by command to lay down his life, so he had a power and authority by promise to take it again, John x. 18. His heart was glad, his glory rejoiced, his flesh had hope in his sufferings; the ground of which hope was the assurance from his Father that his soul should not be left in hell, nor his Holy One (one so holy in the undertaking, and so holy in the execution) see corruption, but should be reduced again to the path of life more glorious, and attended with a fullness of joy, Ps. xvi. 10, 11. It is contained in the promise of seeing his seed; for if he were to remain dead, how should he see his seed?

Secondly, A promise of a royal inheritance. The appointing him in the human nature heir of all things (Heb. i. 2, 'Whom he has appointed heir of all things, by whom also he made the worlds'), which is distinguished from that power he had over all things by right of the creation of them, as the person by whom God made the worlds. That power was natural, this by appointment. The inheritance that belonged to Adam, as the head of the lower creation, being forfeited by him, was restored to the human nature of Christ; which Christ was so pleased with in the first grant, that he esteems it a goodly heritage, Ps. xvi. 6, which appointing him head and heir of all things was for the behoof of the church, his spiritual seed: Eph. i. 22, 'The head over all things to the church.'

Thirdly, An extensive power. In heaven as well as earth, Mat. xxviii. 18, not only to judge among many people, and rebuke strong nations, Micah iv. 3, but to be the head of principalities and powers. That every knee in heaven, and under the earth, as well as in the earth, should bow down to him, and every tongue should confess that he is Lord, to the glory of God the Father, who appointed him, Philip. ii. 10,11. A power over all flesh was granted to him, and claimed by him, as a glory given him by promise upon his glorifying of his Father: John xvii. 2, 'Glorify thy Son, as thou hast given him power over all flesh, that he should give eternal life to as many as thou hast given him.' A power over the seed of the serpent, the whole flesh as it stood in opposition to spirit and the interest of the redeemed ones; for it was granted to him as a feoffee in trust for the use and behoof of his seed, and to be exercised by him in subservience to the eternal happiness of his people, the great design and fruit of reconciliation. He had power before his suffering; for as God saved men upon the promise of his suffering, so upon the same promise he committed all power of judgment to him; but the solemn investiture and publication of it was at his resurrection and ascension: Acts ii. 86, 'God has made that same Jesus whom thou have crucified both Lord and Christ.' For the setting him at his right hand in the human nature was a full declaration and confirmation of the right of that power which he had acquired by his death; therefore he prays for his glory, and pleads a deed of gift for it, which was by this agreement, and therefore desires a full investiture of it, as it had been agreed on first to be asked by him, and then given by God: Ps. ii. 8, 'Ask of me.'

Fourthly, A perpetual and royal priesthood, Ps. cx. 4. And indeed all the rights of the firstborn, which were the right of government, and the right of priesthood; by virtue of which he was to perpetuate the virtue of his expiation, and also purify the sons of Levi, and purge then as gold and silver, that they might offer to the Lord an offering in righteousness, Malachi ii. 2.

Fifthly, An universal victory; the propagation of his kingdom in all parts of the world. Isa. xiii. 4, 'The isles shall wait for his law;' the conquest of many hearts by his Spirit, the willingness of people in the day of his power, the subduing some rebellions by the sword of his mouth, others by the sword of his arm, when the Lord at his right hand should strike through kings in the day of his wrath, Ps. cx. 5, 6. At last a conquest of all his enemies, the devil and death, 1 Cor. xv. 26, which was for the benefit of his people. He had conquered the devil and death in his person, he was to have a complete victory over both in his members; so that we see the encouraging promise made him by his Father was the purchase of a seed, and the glory God promised him was in relation to, and for the advantage of, that seed, that the reconciliation to be purchased for them night be completely enjoyed by them. Judge then whether the Father was not signally, in this agreement in Christ, reconciling the world to himself.

We have handled this covenant, let us see what confirmation there was of it. On God's part we find an oath. God swears that Christ should be a priest, Ps. cx. 4; he is therefore called the man of God's right hand in the prayer of the church: Ps. lxxx. 17, 'Let thy hand be upon the man of thy right hand,' whether for the hastening the suffering of Christ, or for his assistance, is uncertain; the man to whom thou hast sworn with thy right hand, so the Targum; the manner of taking oaths being to lift up the right hand: so Ps. lxxxix. 3, 'I have sworn to David my servant,' when he made a covenant with him; though this was spoken to David in the type, 1 Sam. vii., yet, ver. 14, 'I will be his Fathers and he shall be my Son,' is applied to Christ, Heb. i. 5. And he swears by his holiness: Ps. lxxxix. 36, 'Once have I sworn by my holiness, that I will not lie unto David. His seed shall endure for ever, and his throne as the sun before me.' By David I understand Christ; once, i.e. once for all, irrevocably, unchangeable; and that by his holiness, by all that will fit him for a governor and judge of the world, by that holiness which he chiefly aimed to advance by this undertaking of his Son. As I am an holy God, and desire my holiness may be trusted by this undertaking, I will stand to my word, by that holiness which is the beauty of every attribute, without which, neither power, mercy, justice, nor wisdom could be perfections worthy of a God, as they could not be if holiness could not be ascribed to every one of them, holy power, holy mercy, holy justice, and holy wisdom. By his holiness, which comprehends all his attributes, which would fail, should he violate his oath; whereby it appears that this of settling the seed of Christ, was the main article which God intended, which his heart was set upon, since he assures it by the strongest bond of an oath, and an oath by that attribute which was so necessary to the being of the Deity, without which we can have no conception of a God. We may conceive God punishing all men by justice, or pardoning all men by mercy, but we cannot conceive a God without holiness, for then we conceive a God without the highest perfection belonging to the Deity, an ungodded God. Now, by this seed is not meant Christ the seed of David, because that David whom he had found as his servant, ver. 20, must be meant of Christ, by the greatness of the expression which follows after, and it is the seed of this David he will make to endure for ever, ver. 29; 'his seed,' his seed who was the first born. And though the word of the oath is said to be since the law, Heb. vii. 28, that must be in regard of the manifestation of it, or rather in order of nature. For in this covenant God excluded all other sacrifices as insufficient, the order in the decree runs thus: first, the creation of man, covenant of works, &c. The foresight of the violation of that covenant, the insufficiency of other sacrifices for expiation, then the settling this grand sacrifice and high priest by an oath; for the first call of Christ was upon the inability of other sacrifices to afford God any pleasure, Heb. x. 5-7; i. e. the foresight of their inability. It was confirmed also to Abraham by an oath, that the nations should be blessed in his seed: Heb. vi. 17, "emesiteusen" he mediated by an oath, the tenor whereof was, that as Abraham was willing to offer his son in a bloody sacrifice to him, so he would offer up his only Son for Abraham, and all such as should follow his example of faith and obedience.

Use of this.

1. We see the main cause of unbelief and despair. It is the ignorance of the Father's interest in redemption; the ignorance of the transaction between the Father and the Son is the cause of this, John xv. 21, 'because they know not him that sent me.' They consider not that this was the Father's contrivance, that I am sent forth by him, and ordered by him to do what I do. If we had a clear vision of the gospel, and remembered God as intent upon a way of redemption, we should not nourish that which disparages the whole plot. Such souls look upon him as a God of wrath rather than a God of peace, whose hand is more filled with thunders than his heart with love; they regard him as one of a narrow and contracted goodness; that God minded nothing after man's sin but preparing his bow and sharpening his arrows. Hence they have frightful thoughts of God, slavish fears, fretful jealousies, that he will never accomplish their desires though they seek him never so fervently.

2. See the blackness of unbelief. It is as much as lies in a man to make void the end of God, frustrate the covenant of redemption, deprive God of all the glory he was to get by the articles of it, and Christ of the honour of his undertaking, and make the whole covenant insignificant, rejecting the eternal counsel of wisdom, as well as the rejecting John's baptism, Luke vii. 30, was so interpreted. Whosoever does not believe upon the declaration of the gospel does endeavour to deprive Christ of a seed as far as he can. And those that endeavour to keep off others from Christ, endeavour, as far as their power extends, to make God violate his oath. This contrivance of God is the greatest masterpiece of wisdom and love; it was the most becoming thing God ever set about, most agreeable to his mercy and justice. Unbelief does what it can to demolish this fabric of God's erecting, as though the contrivance of his wisdom were a piece of folly, and the beating of his heart only worthy of the spurns of our feet.

3. Salvation is upon the most certain terms to every believer.

(1.) In regard that every believer is the seed of Christ. God has given such to Christ with an absolute will that they should not perish. Christ by covenant was to take care of them; God by covenant was engaged that Christ should see his seed. He confirmed it by oath, that his seed should endure for ever. Shall God be defeated of his will and the design of his everlasting covenant? He committed by covenant the souls of his people to Christ as his charge, John vi. 37-39. Would God put a charge he values into the hands of impotence or unskilfulness. Will Christ be guilty of disaffection to his Father? Can he break the trust reposed in him? Will the Father be guilty of unfaithfulness to Christ? Can there be a violation of articles so solemnly made between them? This seed was to be perfect, Christ was to see the travail of his soul, which will be when he has given Christ a full possession of that trust he acquired for him upon the cross; but they must wait, for it is with his people as with himself. He obtained a right upon the cross for himself and them, but neither he nor they are yet in a full possession of the right he then purchased.

(2.) In regard of the firmness of the covenant between them. The covenant the Father has made with Christ is an obligation wherein he stands bound to Christ, and consequently to every parcel of his seed. Free grace to us made him a promiser to Christ, and his promise made him a debtor to him. Therefore if it be possible that the infinitely true God could be false to a temporary promise, how could he be false to his Son, the Son of his dearest love, the Son that he appointed, called out, and put upon this undertaking! How can he be false to his own counsel, and to a solemn everlasting covenant! His truth is a powerful engagement for performance, especially added to that love which first moved him to make this covenant. The covenant indeed was firm between God and Adam, had Adam stood; but there was not altogether so strong an obligation on God, he never confirmed it by an oath; he never was so much pleased with that, as with this. The greater pleasure any man has in the promise he makes, and the stronger resolution to perform it, the stronger asseverations he backs it with. To what purpose does Christ give us a draught and epitome of this eternal transaction as the ground of his pleas in heaven, but that the joy of believers may be full, that they might have his joy fulfilled in themselves? John xvii. 13, 'These things I speak in the world, that they might have my joy fulfilled in themselves;' that they might have a joy in the consideration of it, as he had in the making this covenant, and performing his part in it. 'These things I speak in the world.' I give them this history of our agreement, this copy of the articles between thee and me, that they may read thy eternal counsel concerning their good, and have a strong consolation, and run to this public record in all cases, spread it before, yea, and plead it with thee. And by virtue of this covenant, though a believer fall into sin (for it is not possible he can run on in a course of sin), God will reduce him. The afflicting them to that end is a condition ensured in this covenant, Ps. lxxxix. 28-32, God will visit them with rods, but not lash them with scorpions; he will afflict them, but not destroy them; whip them, but not damn them; because he will not take away his loving-kindness from his Son, or suffer his faithfulness to fail.

(3.) In regard that Christ has suffered and performed all on his part. Christ has performed his part by making his soul an offering for sin; he must therefore see his seed, and that to satisfaction, Isa. liii. 11, otherwise there would be a breach of covenant and promise on the Father's part. God was to please Christ, as Christ had pleased him; and the pleasure is not mutual unless both be pleased alike. The wafting therefore of every believer through this vale of misery is a debt God owes to Christ, and a satisfaction necessary to make his happiness as mediator complete, and which our Saviour may challenge as a due debt by virtue of compact. Will God ever go back from his word, tear the articles on his part in pieces, and so let the strength and blood of Christ be spent for nought?

(4.) In this covenant God has linked his own glory and the salvation of believers together. For in this covenant, wherein God was to be glorified, Christ was to be his salvation to the ends of the earth, Isa. xlix. 3, 6. As he covenanted with Christ for a glory from him, so by covenant he gave up the Gentiles to him; and thus having settled them together upon one corner stone, the happiness of a believer is as firmly upon that basis established as the honour of God. And therefore what the prophet calls the glory of God, Isa. xl. 5, 'All flesh shall see the glory of God,' Luke expresses by salvation, Luke iii. 6, 'All flesh shall see the salvation of God;' and when God has declared his will for the sending Christ for the redeeming of the prisoners from captivity, Isa. xiii. 5, 6, ver. 8 he says, 'My glory will I not give unto another.' I will entrust no other with redeeming work, which is my glory, but this servant of mine; so that the peace is as firm as God's honour, and can then only cease when God shall cease to love himself, his Son, and his own glory. What greater ground of faith can there be than this, since God's love cannot reach a strain higher than to venture his own glory in the same bottom with a believer's happiness?

4. Fly to this covenant of redemption, as well as to the covenant of grace, since that is the foundation of this. All other considerations of Christ's death, merit, and everything stored up in Christ, can give us little hope, unless we consider this covenant, which supports all the other stones of the building. Fly to it when your souls are in heaviness. Though there may be sometimes clouds upon the face of God, yet consider those compassion in his heart, when he struck this covenant with Christ. He covenanted to bruise his own Son by his wrath, while he promised to support him by his strength, and the sounding of his bowels always kept pace with the blows of his hand. The consideration of this will encourage our faintness, silence our fears, nonplus our scruples, and settle a staggering faith. Is a believer in a storm? Here is an anchor to hold him. Is he sinking? Here is a bough to catch at. Is he pursued by spiritual enemies? Here is a refuge to fly to. Sin cannot so much oblige God's justice to punish, as his oath to Christ obliges him to save a repenting and believing sinner. These two covenants, that of redemption, and the other of grace, are as a Hur and Aaron to hold up the hands of a feeble faith. His love cannot die, as long as his faithfulness remains, nor his peace with the soul perish as long as the covenant with his Son endures. This covenant of redemption is to be pleaded by us, as well as the merit of Christ's death, because the merit of his death is founded upon this compact.

IV. The Father did fit Christ for this great undertaking to make reconciliation. Christ was the vine, John xv. 1, 'I am the vine, and my Father the husbandman,' a vine of the Father's planting, a vine of the Father's dressing. And God planted him a noble vine, in order to the bearing branches. He made him a vine fit to cherish those he should insert in him. He is therefore said to be sanctified by the Father when he is sent into the world: John x. 36, 'Say you of him whom the Father has sanctified and sent into the world,' sanctified in order to his mission, or sanctified at his mission, that the glory of God's reconciling love might be manifest by him; sanctified to do the works of his Father, for which end he was sent into the world, as ver. 37 intimates, 'If I do not the works of my Father, believe me not.' Much of God's secret counsel was spent about him, whence he is called 'a polished shaft in his quiver,' Isa. xlix. 2, 'in the quiver of his secret counsel wherein he was hid.' This promise he had in that agreement between them, that 'the Spirit of the Lord should be put upon him,' Isa. xlii. 1; and for this great end of redemption, as you may read in the following verses in that chapter. And since the end of his undertaking was to glorify God in the work of redemption, the wisest counsels would be employed to furnish Christ for bringing about the highest glory to God and happiness to man.

1. A fitness for so great a task was absolutely necessary. In regard of his office: As he was settled in an office by the Father, so the graces and gifts of the Spirit were necessary to fit the human nature for those great works of the Father which were to be performed in it. The human nature had been unprofitable without an office, and an office had been unsuccessful without graces and gifts for the execution of it. An office of mediator, without capacity, fullness, charity, and goodness, had been useless, and to no purpose. In regard of the greatness of the work he was to do: Sin had blemished the world, turned all creatures from their true end by man's revolt from the service of God, whereby those creatures which were made to serve a loyal subject were forced to serve a rebel. The world then was to be restored, the ruins by sin repaired, the sin removed, and the sinner redeemed. As this required infinite skill for the contrivance, so it required infinite fitness for the execution. The glory of God's design required it, which was to make his attributes most illustrious, and display them more magnificently in the work of redemption than in that of creation; and this being to be done in the human nature (whose fall had necessitated a reparation or destruction) because by that God was dishonoured, in that therefore

the glory of his attributes was to be manifested, it required a mighty fitness for the manifestation of an infinite glory.

2. Christ in regard of his divine nature was infinitely fit, and in regard of the union of that to the human suitably fit. For in regard of his infinite knowledge, he knew the rights of God in the infinite extent of his glory, and what was fit for the reparation of those rights which had been violated, he knew the infinite holiness of his Father, he knew the utmost malice of the inward bowels of sin, which he was to expiate; for he knew all things; for 'the Father loves the Son, and shows him all things that himself does,' John v. 21. As God, he knew what wrong God had sustained in point of honour, and in point of service; and what was necessary to restore the honour to God, and reduce the creature to the service of the Creator. In regard of his infinite holiness therefore, God, who is holy, could be sanctified in his righteousness, Isa. v. 16. In regard of his power, as he was the fittest medium by whom God created the world, Heb. i. 2, so he was the fittest medium by whom God might repair the world, and give a new consistency to it: Col. i. 16, 'He was before all things, and by him all things consist.' He was 'the mighty God, the everlasting Father,' or the Father of the age to come, and therefore 'the prince of peace,' Isa. ix. 6. It was necessary he should be God, as it was necessary he should be man, to make the compensation suitable, because the human nature had committed the trespass; so it was necessary he should be God, to make the compensation sufficient, because God had received the wrong. Two things were requisite: suffering, therefore he must be man; satisfaction by that suffering, therefore he must be God. Two things in justice to be considered: the equity of justice, therefore the nature offending must suffer; the infiniteness of justice, therefore an infinite person must suffer. He therefore being thus infinite, could answer the infiniteness of God's honour in the reparation, and the infiniteness of our debts in the expiation. For as he had a human nature, wherein to merit, so he had a divine nature whereby to make that merit sufficient. No other nature could be fit; the angelical nature was not infinite, and therefore could not pay an infinite price; the human nature was neither infinite nor innocent, and therefore could not satisfy for infinite guilt. He was to stand under the sin of the world, and what creature could ever be fit to bear so vast a burden! As none but an infinite goodness could exercise so great a patience towards the sins of men, so none but an infinite goodness could pay a satisfaction for them. Now, though Christ, as he was the Son of man, 'gave his life a ransom for many,' Mat. xx. 28, yet the value of the redeeming price arose from it, as 'the blood of God,' Acts xx. 28. He gave his life as man, but the purchase was made by him as God. It could not have been for our glory, or purchased a glory for us, unless he who was the Lord of glory had been crucified, 1 Cor. ii. 6, 8; for 'being the express image of God, and upholding all things by the word of his power, he did by himself purge our sins,' Heb. i. 8. So that his shoulders were able to bear the weightiest burden, his strength able to endure the sharpest curses, and his soul able to drink down the bitterest potions. Christ therefore being God, and united to the human nature, was every way fit, as being God and man in one person, that what the human nature could not do by reason of its imbecility as a creature, the divine might; and what the divine nature could not do by reason of its perfection, the human nature might perform: that God's honour might be repaired by an infinite satisfaction, and man reduced to service by the highest motive, viz. the incarnation of his Son, than which God could not afford a greater.

3. The fitness, whether of his divine nature or his human, did originally arise from the Father. The Father, as the fountain of the Deity, did confer on him his natural fitness, by communicating to him the divine nature from eternity by natural generation. He had a natural fitness as the Son of God, and a gracious fitness as the Son of man. The natural fitness was from the Father, for 'as the Father has life in himself, so has he given to the Son to have life in himself,' John v. 26. To have life in himself is the property of God, who is therefore called the living God, and this is given by the Father.

(1.) All the fullness whereby he is fit to reconcile, and accomplish his mediatory work, he is enriched with from the Father: Col. i. 19, 'It pleased the Father that in him should all fullness dwell.' It is true, the word Father is not in the Greek text, but is to be supplied from the discourse of the apostle before, verse 12, where he begins a thanksgiving to the Father. He did not only ordain him to be head of the church, but he fitted him with whatsoever was necessary to constitute him in that office, and enable him for the exercise of it. By this fullness is meant both a fullness of the divinity, as he is the image of God, and a fullness of habitual grace, as he is the first born of every creature, having the rights of the firstborn given to him, as he is the head of the body the church, and the firstborn from the dead. God would have this great mediator filled with all the perfection of the Deity, and all the excellency of grace in his humanity, that he might be in this office of mediation every way acceptable to God, and successful for man; that no fault might be found in him, either by God or man, to stave off the acceptance of the one or the reliance of the other, that so the reconciliation might be in all parts and degrees complete.

(2.) The Father stored up this fullness in Christ with a mighty pleasure. He did not only order the communication of this fullness to him, and the perpetual residence of it in him for his appointed ends, but he did it with a transcendent pleasure, an "eudochia", such a pleasure as he had in his person, as that which answered all his ends, both for his own glory and his creatures' recovery. As he was the treasury of grace for us, so he was the object of God's delight.

(3.) This fullness was lodged in Christ, for the making peace with his Father, and accomplishing all the ends of it. As he assembled all light together and fixed it in the sun, as a natural type of Christ, to convey light and heat thereby to all sublunary bodies, as also to the stars in the firmament, whence both might derive that excellency they have, and so agree in one point and principle, so he has espoused together the divine and human perfections in one person, that thereby he might reconcile all things to himself; by him I say, 'whether they be things in earth or things in heaven,' that both the restoration of the broken peace with men, and the confirmation of the standing peace with angels, might meet in him, and be derived from him as one centre of both. For as it pleased the Father, that in him should all fullness dwell, so it was a pleasure to him that it should perpetually reside in him to this end, that peace might be made, and all the intendments and consequence of it be promoted to a perfect issue; that he having an alliance to God by his divinity, and an alliance to man by his humanity, might stand as a perfect mediator between God and his creature, to make peace and preserve it. For hereby he understood the rights of God to secure them, and the indigences of man to relieve him. He had his humanity fitted to be a sufferer, and his divinity fitted to be a repairer; the one made him possible, the other able, and the holiness of his person made him acceptable. His being in the form of a servant made him obnoxious to suffering, and his being in the form of God made that suffering meritorious of our peace, that in all respects he might become a prince of peace both in heaven and earth.

4. We may note also the constancy of it; it dwells in him. This was the pleasure of the Father, that it should not only be communicated to him to lodge, but dwell in him; not as a private person, but an universal principle; as head of the body, as well as a reconciler, that he might be able to do the works of God, and fill the emptiness of man. God promised to engrave the engravings of this stone, which is ushered in with a repetition of a behold: Zech. iii. 5, 'Behold the stone that I have laid: behold, I will engrave the engravings thereof, says the Lord,' that men might observe it, and the end of it. He would work all habitual grace in him with an indelible character; as the engravings of a stone cannot be razed out without defacing and dissolving some part of the stone at least, sometimes not without breaking the whole. The end of this engraving is expressed in the following words: 'And I will remove the iniquity of that land in one day.' Some understand it also of his death; and I think it may be understood of both his fitness for suffering, and his actual suffering. The end of this sculpture was for the taking away sin, and making reconciliation with God by the expiation of it. So that the graces of the Spirit are not only poured upon his head, as that which may be dried up again, but engraved on him, as noting fixedness and duration. Fullness acquaints us with the abundance of this grace, and dwelling signifies the perpetual residence of it, engraving the deep rootedness, and all for this end of redemption.

This fitness of his human nature was the work of the Father, not immediately, but by his Spirit.

1. He is fitted with a body.

(1.) This was necessary. Man, as constituted of soul and body, had violated the articles of the first covenant; therefore man, as constituted of soul and body, must answer the violations of it. He was therefore to have a body of the same kind with that man that had broken the covenant, whose punishment he was to remove; therefore he was not to be new made from the earth as Adam was, but to descend from him; otherwise he had not been of the same kind, and so could not satisfy for that kind whereof he was not a part. As the obligation descended upon all men from the first man, so it was fit that one descended from him should satisfy that obligation.

(2.) It was also necessary that he should have a mortal body, that he might be nearly related to us in all things (sin excepted), and redeem us by his passion. Blood was to be shed, death was to be endured (for we owed to God our life and blood), the righteousness of God was to be declared, Rom. iii. 25, which could not be but in the offending nature. His life he must lose, thereby to lay a strong foundation for the removing of sin, with a rich manifestation of God's righteousness. Now, to make a body mortal, which was not in itself sinful, was a work only to be wrought by the wisdom of God, whereby to make a salvo for his righteousness, always manifested to his rational creatures. That soul that sins, it shall die. Had not Adam sinned, he had not died. Our Saviour died who never sinned; he was therefore to have such a body whereby our sins might be imputed to him, yet not inherent in him. He was then to have a human nature to suffer our punishment, as well as a divine nature to surmount it. A flesh was necessary to be a sacrifice for sin, as well as the Deity to be a priest. What could he have offered for us, had he not had flesh and blood? Without a body be had been a priest without a sacrifice, without an holy flesh he had been a priest with a sinful sacrifice. He was to have a body to 'bear our sins on a tree,' 1 Peter ii. 24; yet an holy body, that by the offering of that body 'once for all, we might be sanctified,' Heb. x. 10. As God only could, so he did provide him such a body. This he ascribes to God: Heb. x. 5, 'A body hast thou prepared me.' A mortal body, fit to be a sacrifice; a body prepared, after the rejection of all other sacrifices, wherein God could find no pleasure; a body also prepared to be a reconciling sacrifice, such a body wherein he might do the will of God, i. e. the whole will of God, which was to take away sin. It was a body so fitted as to be obedient to the soul, to have no rebellious power in it against reason and command, but to be fully and readily obedient in all its motions to God;

not barely a body, but a body so tempered as to do the service required of it. It was not indeed fit that the body wherein the Deity was to tabernacle, John i. 14, "eskenosen", should be framed by a less wisdom, and slighter order, than the Mosaical tabernacle, which was a shadow of it, which was done by exact order, and by the inspirations of the Spirit, filling the workmen with skill, Exod. xxxi. 2, 3.

(3.) Yet he was to have a holy body, free from any taint of moral imperfection, fit for the service he was devoted to, for which the least speck upon his humanity had rendered him unfit. This could not have been, had he descended from Adam by way of ordinary and natural generation. He had then been a debtor himself, a lamb with blemish, and so wanted a sacrifice for himself. His sacrifice would have been defective, and have needed some other sacrifice to fill up the gaps of it. It was necessary he should descend from Adam in a way of birth, but not in a way of seminal traduction, that he might have the nature of Adam without the spot. Such a knot could not be untied without infinite skill, nor such a way of production be wrought without the infinite power of God.

Therefore,

(1.) The Holy Ghost frames the body of Christ of this seed of the woman, that it might be mortal, and have his heel bruised by the devil, Gen. iii. 15; not of the seed of the man in an ordinary way of generation, that it might be without any taint of sin, sanctifying therefore the seed of the woman in a peculiar manner. Wherefore in relation to his humanity, conception, and birth, he is 'the holy thing,' Luke i. 35; as his body is called the Holy One in the grave: Ps. xvi. 10, 'Thou wilt not suffer thy Holy One to see corruption.' His soul was not in the grave, being separated from the body upon the recommendation of it upon the cross into his Father's hand. And as it was an holy body, so it was a mortal body, called therefore a 'body of flesh,' Col. i. 22. This God had appointed and predicted as an extraordinary thing: Jer. xxxi. 22, 'The Lord has created a new thing in the earth, a woman shall compass a man;' "gibor", a mighty man. By calling it a new thing, he points to a miraculous birth of the Messiah, and the word creating signifies something out of a natural course, next to a mere creation, and God's work as much as creation. A new thing as not being from the old stock; for though his nature was the same with Adam's, yet he had no taint of original sin; because he was not morally in the loins of Adam before his fall (the promise of his incarnation of the seed of the woman being given after the fall), whereby the sin of Adam could not be imputed to him. It was therefore a new thing, and an holy thing according to that new promise after the fall. Though the Spirit was the immediate agent in fitting this body, yet it was by the appointment and power of the Father: Luke i. 85, 'The Holy Ghost shall come upon thee, and the power of the Highest shall overshadow thee;' where by the Highest is understood the Father, the mystery of the Trinity being manifested in the incarnation of the Son of God.

(2.) The Holy Ghost makes the union between the divine and human nature. The overshadowing by the power of the Highest unites the two natures, whereby that 'holy thing' in the virgin's womb should be 'called the Son of God,' Luke i. 35, which could not be without a union of the divine nature to the substance made of the seed of the woman, by this overshadowing; which also is the act of the Father by the Spirit, as being in the 'power of the Highest.' And this is that which is called the gratia unionis, grace of union, which Christ had from God, whereby the Godhead dwelt bodily in him, or personally, Col. ii. 9; the two naturesóthe divine, signified by the Godhead, the human, by that wherein it dweltómaking up one person; "Soma" among the Greeks signifying not a bare body, but a person, as it does also in common speech among us.

The union of the two natures by a particular conjunction, whereby the divine nature dwelt substantially in the human, and was acted by it in all undertakings, was the work of God by his Spirit. This union of both natures was for the making peace: Col. i. 21, 22, 'And you that were sometimes alienated, yet now he has reconciled, in the body of his flesh through death.' Who? Ver. 15: He who was 'the image of the invisible God.' The image of the invisible Deity rendered himself visible in the humanity, to reconcile us to his Father, so that by this union we who are afar off from the Deity are brought near in his humanity; and the gulf of original sin, which consisted in enmity to God, and which hindered the passage of God to man, or man to God, is filled up, taken away, and the work done in and by him. As he was God, he knew the terrors of hell, because he knew all things; but, as God, he could not have experience of them: he was to have a body of flesh to bear them, as well as he was the image of the invisible God to support that body under them. As man, he was fit to endure his wrath; and as God, fit to appease it. As man, he was fit to undergo the sharpness of the curse; and as God, able to remove it. As man, he was capable to obey both the moral and mediatory law; and as God, to transmit the fruit of that obedience to us, which is intimated in these words, 'Yet now has he' (who was the image of the invisible God) 'reconciled, &c. to present you holy, and unblameable and unreprovable in his sight.' Presenting us, as he is the image of God in our nature, free from sin by the washing of his blood, after he had reconciled us through the body of his flesh; the meriting of reconciliation was wrought in his flesh, but arose from his deity.

Thus Christ had a body every way fitted with a holy soul, with a glorious indweller, that he might be every way fit for making peace: a body in all things lily ours, but without impurity, that he might be our kinsman, and become a Goel, a redeemer by right of propinquity; that he might be the suffering head of the human nature, which he could not be without our nature. Had he taken the angelical nature, which was more excellent in itself, and suffered in that, his sufferings would have been esteemed the sufferings of that whole nature, but not of the human nature, because not partaking of it, and so he could not have suffered for it unless he had suffered in it: for since he was to make reconciliation for the sins of the people, 'he took upon him not the nature of angels, but he took on him the seed of Abraham, because it behoved him to he made like unto his brethren, that he might be a merciful and faithful high priest in things pertaining to God, to make this reconciliation,' Heb. ii. 16, 17. We may note, besides the holiness of his body, it was so framed by the appointment of the Father, and the operation of the Holy Ghost, and tempered with such affections, as to do this work with the greatest compassion to the fallen nature of man, that whereas he had a holiness to make him faithful to God, so he had a tenderness in his nature to make him merciful to us for the carrying on this reconciliation and the ends of it to the highest perfection, so that those two natures, thus united by God, made him every way capable and fit to be a reconciler, knowing the justice of God's claim, that he might give to God what he knew to be his due, and feeling the infirmities of our nature, that he might purchase that remedy he knew we wanted. Herein we see the incomparable wisdom and love of the Father, in fitting Christ, so that he might be in him reconciling the world to himself.

(3.) He is filled with his Spirit by the Father, i. e. with all the gifts and graces of the Spirit necessary to this work. That precious ointment, composed of so many sweet and excellent ingredients, wherewith the Levitical high priest was anointed, Exodus xxx., was a type of those excellent graces of the great high priest, whereby he was qualified for the exercise of his offices. As the Spirit espoused the human nature to the divine, so he espoused all his gifts and graces to the human. As the body was conceived by the power of the Holy Ghost, so his soul was beautified and adorned by the graces of the Holy Ghost, whereby he became 'fairer than the children of men, and grace was poured into his lips,' Ps. xlv. 9: 'His going forth is prepared as the morning,' Hos. vi. 3, furnished with all things necessary to work out redemption, and free the world from the wrath of God, as the sun is with light to deliver the world from the darkness of the night.

[1.] The subject of these gifts was the rational soul of Christ. The human nature was only anointed with the Spirit; the divine nature being infinite, could receive no increase of gifts, it having a fullness of perfection by eternal generation. Yet though the divine nature stood in no need of those gifts, it did capacitate the humanity of Christ for greater receipts, by reason of its union with it, than any other mere creature was capable of. We must not think, as some may conceive, that the divine nature was instead of a soul to the body of Christ. He had a real rational soul; for since the whole nature of man was corrupted, both soul and body, the whole nature of man was to be repaired. How could he have suffered in a body, without a soul, the wrath due to our souls as well as bodies? Had he only had a body, he had not taken the human nature; only the meanest and worst part of man, not that which constitutes the man. Unless he had been God and man in one person, his blood could not have been called 'the blood of God;' and unless he had a soul and body, an entire nature, his blood could not have been the blood of man. As he was to have a body prepared, so he was to have a soul proportionately furnished.

[2.] He was abundantly filled with them; he had 'the Spirit not by measure,' John iii. 34; not as light in a room, but as light in the sun; not as water in a vessel where the bounds are visible, but like water in the ocean, where the depths and limits are unknown. In him there was nothing but Spirit and fullness, without limits for quantity, without imperfections for quality; all the treasures, the fountain, not the rivers. There are varieties of gifts, as there are of stars, and the qualities of them, in heaven; and of flowers, and the beauties of them upon earth: what were various in others were entire in him. Others have parcels of those gifts and graces, like Abraham's children by Keturah; but Christ had them entire. As Isaac had an inheritance as the heir of promise, so Christ, as the heir of all things, had the possession of the choicest gifts in the treasuries of his Father. As God had communicated an infinite being to him by eternal generation, so it was convenient to communicate a fullness of graces and gifts to the humanity as far as it was capable to receive and contain it, because it was joined to so excellent a nature as the divine; for though he was made flesh, yet he had 'the glory as of the only begotten Son of God.' It was fit therefore he should be 'full of grace and truth' in that flesh, John i. 14. It was not congruous that the Spirit of God should come into the soul of Christ with half his attendants, but with the greatest majesty, with his whole train of excellencies. Not that the perfections poured out upon his soul by the Spirit of grace and glory were infinite, because those graces were created qualities, and infiniteness can never be ascribed to a creature; and his soul was the subject of them, and that being a creature, was not capable of receiving into it subjectively that which is infinite; but he had them without measure, as to the kinds of gifts; in the mass, not in parcels. As to the degrees of them, others have them in a lower degree, as light in a candle; Christ in the highest degree, as light in the heavens: so that whatsoever pertains to the nature of grace was conferred on Christ, as whatsoever belongs to the nature of light and heat is stored up in the sun. 'All his garments did smell of myrrh, aloes, and cassia,' Ps. xiv. 8. As God has made the sea a treasure of waters, emptied into it from all the rivers of the world, so he has made Christ a mighty ocean of all perfections, in a vaster quantity and richer qualities than any other creature is capable to receive, as the sea is more capacious to receive the perpetual floods than the greatest river in the world. If the whole creation should be reaped, and gleaned, and stored up in one person, it would be but as the drops of a bucket to the fullness of Christ, which the Father has laid up in him.

(4.) These graces were infused into him at once. As the new creature has all its parts framed at once, so the head of all the new creatures was principled at once with them, though in regard of the various exercises of them, they grew up in him by degrees: Luke ii. 40, 'The child grew, and waxed strong in spirit, filled with wisdom,' ver. 52, and shone forth as he increased in age, by new excitations of them by the Spirit of God. Grace came into the soul of Christ, as his soul into his body, or as light into the sun at the creation, not by pieces; but as the soul did not exercise its functions, so his graces did not exert their strength, but by degrees, according to the capacity of his age, and occasional occurrences. The anointing of this Spirit was conferred upon him at his incarnation; when he was made flesh, he was full of grace and truth, John i. 14. Also visibly at his baptism, which was his entrance into the exercise of his office, as a visible token of his Father's acceptation of him, now at his inauguration, Mat. iii. 16, 17; as David, the type, was anointed at Bethlehem, the place of his habitation, by Samuel, and afterwards at Hebron, when he was actually installed king by the tribe of Judah. The first anointing at his incarnation was his furniture for his office, that at his baptism his investiture in his office.

(5.) These gifts and graces of the Spirit were necessary for the human nature. It was necessary that the soul of Christ should exert supernatural acts. There was a necessity of love to God, to spirit him in his mighty difficulties; of faith in God, to suck refreshment from the promises made to him as mediator, when he should arrive at any conflict: these were supernatural acts in themselves, and so were above the bare natural strength of the soul of Christ, and the powers of it. As the soul of Christ did need a natural concourse to natural actions, as other souls do, and needed the gift of miracles for the working of miracles, so he needed a supernatural grace to exert supernatural acts. It is essential to the nature of a creature to depend upon God for all communications. To act independently, and without the influence of another, is a property of God, not to be derived to any creature. The humanity of Christ then being a creature, could not act of itself without the influence of a superior being; the humanity then did not endow itself; grace is not minted by any creature. It did no more inspire itself with grace than it did inspire itself with life. As God was the Father of Christ, so he was the Father of grace to him; the divine nature of Christ gave a personal dignity by union, but conferred not of itself a beauty upon it. Had the divine nature, by virtue of its union, elevated the faculties of Christ's soul, he needed not have grown in wisdom and knowledge; the divine nature, though united to the humanity, did not communicate to it all that it was capable of receiving. This communication was the proper world of the Spirit, according to the order in the operations of the Trinity: hence his human soul knew not the time of the day of judgment, though as God he did. If his divine nature had advanced his rational faculties, it had also stocked him with full comforts, without the mission of an angel to refresh him in the garden, Luke xxii. 43, and why did it not also advance the vegetative power to rear up his body to a full stature?

This elevation was the work of the Spirit. It was necessary he should be thus furnished.

[1.] In regard of the greatness of his task. Gifts are imparted to men suitable to the places wherein they stand for action, and according to the largeness of the vessel. Christ's place was higher, his work harder than any creature's, therefore required a greater measure of gifts than all creatures in heaven and earth put together. Though he was mighty in his person, and fit to have help laid upon him for us, yet he was to be anointed with the holy oil, Ps. lxxxix. 19, 20). Without this fullness of grace the human nature could never have arrived to the perfection of the great undertaking, but would have sunk in the midst of the work.

[2.] In regard he was to be a pattern, as well as the prince of believers. A pattern ought to be the most perfect in the kind. Christ was to be set up as a pattern for believers, both of the Spirit's operation in him, and of their imitation of him. Those who draw pictures look upon the original, that they may work them into a likeness to it. The Spirit of God in the fashioning souls, is to conform them to the image of Christ, Rom. viii. 29. It was fit that the pattern of all the heirs of heaven should be fully exact to the pleasure of God. It being God's end to bestow more upon the creature in this redemption than he did upon it by creation, and that in a more suitable manner, there was as much need of an infinite fitness in the person that was to prepare the way for those communications in an honourable manner to God, and everlastingly comfortable to the creature.

(6.) The Father was the principal cause of this furniture. It was God that 'anointed Jesus of Nazareth with the Holy Ghost,' Acts x. 38, and 'God gives the Spirit not by measure to him,' John iii. 34. It is rendered as a reason why 'he that God has sent' (which is a peculiar and ancient title of Christ) 'speaks the words of God.' This the Father did out of the infinite affection he bore his Son for this work of mediation; ver. 35, 'The Father loves the Son, and has given all things into his hand.' The power he had conferred upon him, giving all things into his hand, did require a fullness of the Spirit to manage that power also, that he might be a person fit to be believed on, and confided in, ver. 30. All this was that he might do the Father's will, speak his words, perform his command of love in the repair of his creature. The Lord anointed him, Isa. lxi. 1, and as a God in covenant with him. God, Heb. i. 9, 'Even thy God,' according to the promise made to him, and with an oil of gladness, a joyful oil, as that which is a pleasure to the Father, makes the countenance of Christ cheerful, as the psalmist speaks of oil in another case, and joyful to the church; because upon this fitness depends its happiness and salvation, its reconciliation, and all the fruits of it. And if "dia toutou", therefore, notes to us the final cause or end of this anointing, viz., that he might love righteousness, and hate iniquity; it acquaints us that the end of this unction was to fit him for this work of redemption with a perfect holiness, without which he could not have restored God's honour, nor appeased his wrath, nor consequently reduced the creature to terms of amity with God. This putting his Spirit upon him was a fruit of that delight God had in him as his servant: Isa. xiii. 1, 'My servant in whom my soul delights, I have put my Spirit upon him.' Which delight is also testified, when the Spirit did visibly descend upon him, that he was 'his beloved Son in whom he was well pleased,' Mat. iii. 16, 17.

The gifts and graces he was endowed with by this Spirit the Father had given him, were

[1.] Habitual holiness. He was infinitely holy in regard of his deity holy by the hypostatical union in his humanity, holy by the residence of the Spirit; a greater holiness than man in innocence or angels in heaven have. The giving the Spirit not by measure to him implies a greater holiness, as well as other abilities in the human nature, than all the angels in heaven ever had, who have the Spirit by measure. The holiness, therefore, of Christ's person incomparably exceeds all the holiness of the angelical nature, which has a limited communication of the Spirit. As the apostle argues for his deity, Heb. i. 5, 'Unto which of the angels said he at any time, Thou art my Son?' so to which of the angels did he at any time give the Spirit not by measure? Though he took upon him the form of a servant, yet he was a righteous servant. There was no original sin in his conception, nor actual sin in his conversation; he was separate from sinners in the manner of his birth and in the actions of his life; he had a purity of nature and a purity of life commensurate to the law, that he might be our paschal lamb without blemish; he was holy in the account of angels, Luke i. 35; holy in the account of devils, Mark i. 24, 'the Holy One of God;' holy in the account of his Father: John viii. 29, 'He always did those things which pleased him.'

This was necessary for his office. It became him and us, as our high priest, to be undefiled, Heb. vii. 26. As it was necessary he should suffer for the satisfaction of God's justice, so it was necessary he should by a purity be fit for so great a task. As reasonable creatures we owe a perfect obedience, as rebellious creatures an eternal punishment; there must, therefore, be an holiness commensurate to the precepts of the law, as well as a passion commensurate to the curses of the law. Upon this holiness of his is our reconciliation grounded: 2 Cor. v. 21, 'For he has made him to be sin for us who knew no sin, that we might be made the righteousness of God in him.' Had he known experimentally the least spot, he could not by his sacrifice have been made the righteousness of God to us; for not only as his servant, but as his 'righteous servant,' he was to 'justify many,' Isa. liii. 11. Hereby he was able to 'appear to take away our sins,' and did do it, because 'in him there was no sin,' 1 John iii. 5, the apostle rendering the latter as the reason of the former. Had he had the least speck, he could not have been a mediator, because he had then been a party in being a sinner; his office could not have been performed, which was to make up the breach, not to make a new one; he had rather polluted than purged us, and fastened our sins rather than took them away. What could he have offered if he had not had flesh and blood? How could he have offered acceptably if there had been any spot upon him in his appearance before the holy justice of his Father? Heb. ix. 14. He had then been a rebel, a prisoner, and had forfeited all that might have been a ransom for us. How could he have made peace with God for us, when by reason of a blemish he could not make peace in his own conscience? An inevitable destruction had been brought upon mankind, which could not have been repaired. His intercession kept up the world from sinking when Adam fell; but whose mediation should have preserved the world had this mediator failed, since God had no other son to employ in so great an affair?

It was necessary in regard of his dignity. The Deity, because of infinite holiness, could not have dwelt in a tainted humanity. Though this habitual grace be given by God, yet it is a connatural property of Christ, God-man, because by the dignity of his person it was due to him. It had been a prodigious and preternatural thing to unite the human nature without the ornaments of grace to the divine, as it had been if the body of Christ had not by reason of the hypostatical union been made immortal and glorious, though those properties of the body do not flow from the union by any physical resultant; for to the humanity by this union there is only communicated esse personale, not essentiale divinae naturae, the personal, not the essential being of the divine nature; and therefore divine operations of grace do not physically follow this union, but as they are due to that nature so united. Had they followed physically this union, the body of Christ could not have been weary, hungry, and subject to the infirmities of our flesh. In regard of the dignity of his person, this holiness was due to him; without it, it had been the greatest disparagement to God to send him, and the greatest prejudice to us; for had there been any spot, the person of Christ had been said to sin, as well as the person of Christ is said to suffer. Since the Father had placed his delight in him, and had promised to uphold him, it could not be that that should enter upon him, which was so contrary to the perpetual delight God had promised to fix in him.

This was the act of the Father, and ascribed to him: John x. 36, 'Say ye of him whom the Father has sanctified and sent into the world.' Some understand it of the sanctification of Christ by eternal generation, receiving, by that, holiness per essentiam, by essence; others by sanctification understand only a separation of him to his office. But it rather seems to be meant of the preparations for the exercise of his office, sanctification and mission being joined together; the Father separated him and anointed him with the Spirit, who, as the Spirit of the fear of the Cord resting upon him, Isa. xi. 2, was the immediate inspirer of him with this internal holiness.

[2.] With wisdom and knowledge. As God, he had an uncreated knowledge, but this could not be communicated to his humanity, because a creature is not capable of anything infinite; and though he was filled with all gifts from his conception, "hupestatikos", personally, yet it does not follow from thence that the soul of Christ should know everything, because this did not belong to the property of that nature. And though he was the head of angels, it will not follow that he should know, as man, what the angels knew; for then he had not stood in need of an angel to strengthen him. And if he were made lower than the angels, it was no disparagement to him, as being in the form of a servant, to be ignorant in some things which the angels knew, which he implies he was in that speech concerning his ignorance of the day of judgement: Mat. xxiv. 36, 'Of that day and hour knows no man, no, not the angels of heaven.' But there was no privative ignorance in Christ, but a negative, which is not sinful; and this kind of ignorance was no more disparagement to Christ than it was, that his soul, which was the soul of God, as well as his blood the blood of God, should be sad to death. But the wisdom he was filled with was the wisdom pertaining to his office of mediator; as he was to reprove, and convince, and smite the earth with the rod of his mouth: Isa. xi. 2-4, 'The Spirit of the Lord shall rest upon him, the Spirit of wisdom and understanding, the Spirit of counsel and might, the Spirit of knowledge and the fear of the Lord'. He had wisdom, i.e. a right judgement of things pertaining to his office, judging of things according to the divine will, counsel and prudence in the direction of his actions, knowledge of all accidents and circumstances which might occur to hinder him from the accomplishment of his work, and might to effect all; which gifts were bestowed upon him by the Spirit. All which gifts did end in this of the fear of the Lord, a reverence and observance of his Father as superior to him in this work of mediation. And therefore it is repeated again, verse 3, 'Shall make him of quick understanding in the fear of the Lord;' an observance of the will of God in that work committed to him. All the gifts he had were to run into this ocean of faithfulness to God. The fear of the Lord in Christ was a reverence of the divine majesty and the divine command; not a fear of separation from the Father by any sin, or a fear of punishment by him for any sin, because he could not sin. Without a reverence of God, he had not been faithful; without wisdom and knowledge, he had not been able. Ignorance could never have managed his work, unfaithfulness could never have accomplished it; the one had made him incapable to attempt it, the other to perfect it; the one had stripped him of all capacity for it, the other of all successfulness in it. The knowledge of the will of God was that whereby he was 'mighty to help', Ps. lxxxix. 19. He had counsel to direct as well as power to effect; he had the gift of wisdom to manage his power to the defeating of his enemies. This was necessary; the human nature had been defective in that which it was designed for, unless it had understood what was fit to be done in order to it. It had not consisted with the wisdom of God to send one about so great a work who did not understand the nature of it, who was not fully instructed how to manage it. This was necessary as well as holiness, without knowledge he could not have been a reasonable and voluntary sacrifice, all voluntary acts being to be founded in reason; and without holiness concurring with it, he could not have been an acceptable sacrifice. This wisdom did fit him to sprinkle many nations: Isa. lii. 13, 15, 'My servant shall deal prudently, he shall be extolled, and be very high; so shall he sprinkle many nations.' "Yashchil", some translate prosper, it signifies both; when any one prospers, it is commonly ascribed to his own prudence and wise management of things. He shall understand what is due to God for the reparation of his honour, what is necessary for men for the relieving their necessities, and so purge many by the blood of his sacrifice. Now this wisdom, and the increase of it, was from the strength of the Spirit in him, and the grace of God upon him, Luke ii. 40. There were constant revelations to him of what was fit to be done by him in the exercise of his office, according as the Father pleased by his Spirit to communicate himself to his humanity.

[3.] The Spirit was given him to fit him with a tenderness to man, and to lead him out to those exercises whereby he might be sensible of the indigences of man. He had not only the law of redeeming love in his head, whereby he had a knowledge of his office, but in his bowels, whereby he was fitted for a tender execution of that office: Ps. xl. 8, 'Thy law is within my heart,' "me'ay", bowels. The Spirit therefore descended upon him in the likeness of a dove, an emblem of meekness and tenderness. And the apostle Peter, Acts x. 3, intimates that the intendment of this unction of him was to fit him for a compassionate converse with man: 'God anointed Jesus with the Holy Ghost, who went about doing good, and healing all that were oppressed of the devil.' He had a tenderness as God, and his humanity is fitted with a tenderness to keep pace with that of the Deity as much as was possible, that the tenderness of both natures might be joined together in one person. And when this Spirit visibly settled on him after his baptism, he led him presently to an exercise whereby he might feel the miseries of man, and from an experience of them, be affected with more tenderness towards him: Mat. iv. 1, 'Then was Jesus led up of the Spirit in the wilderness, to be tempted of the devil.' Then; when? As soon as ever he had the Spirit as a dove lighting upon him, and had heard those encouraging words, Mat. iii. 16, 17, 'This is my beloved Son, in whom I am well pleased.' He was led by this Spirit to be tempted by the evil one, that he might in his humanity be acquainted with the craft and subtilty of that adversary which had overturned the world, brought all the dishonour upon his Father, and sank mankind into their present misery; that he might know the enemy which was threatened in the promise of his incarnation, and experience the subtilties of that serpent which had wrought all those mischiefs he came to redress, and so, as he was to be 'acquainted with grief,' Isa. liii. 3, he might understand the first author of that which occasioned this grief to him. It was by this grace of meekness and humility he was specially fitted to be a second Adam to redeem us, because pride was the sin of the first Adam to destroy us, who, because he would become as high as God who created him, the Redeemer would become lower than man that was created by him; yea, 'a worm and no man,' Ps. xxii. 6; so excellently did the Spirit fit him with a humility proportionable to his undertaking.

[4.] The Spirit was given to him by his Father, to enable him with a mighty power to go through this undertaking. He had a 'Spirit of might,' executive of his wisdom and counsel, Isa. xi. 2, a courage to attempt the most daring difficulties, and endure the fiercest calamities: a power to suffer for the satisfaction of justice, a power to relieve the pressures of our wants, a power to conquer his and our enemies. When he was anointed by God with the Holy Ghost, he was anointed 'with power,' Acts x. 38, "dunamei", not "eksousiai", for the exercise of his office and the doing good. The design of putting the Spirit upon him, was that he might bring forth judgment to the Gentiles, for that immediately follows the promise of the Spirit to him, Isa. xlii. 1. This was his encouragement actually to engage in the exercise of every part of his office: Isa. lx. 1, The Spirit of the Lord God is upon me, because he has anointed me to preach glad tidings to the meek,' &c. The Spirit was upon him in all the acts of his mediation, the Spirit therefore did continually assist him in every exercise; he was not left alone, but 'he that sent him was with him,' John viii. 29. The Father was with him by his Spirit: the Father had promised his assistance. Now, assisting grace is the work of the Holy Ghost. His grace was fed and actuated by the Spirit, and brought forth into exercise. The Spirit led him into temptation, what? only to lead him to the conflict and desert him in it? No, surely, but to actuate those graces wherewith he had filled him against the tempter: 'God was with him,' Acts x. 38, assisting, exciting, actuating him. And the Spirit did assist him, and excite the graces in him to the very last gasp, for 'through the Spirit he offered up himself' Heb. ix. 14, through the virtue of this Spirit sanctifying his human nature, gifting him with strength and wisdom, exciting those eminent graces upon the cross, wherewith he had filled him at his conception, and supporting him with his power while the Father was bruising him. As he lived in this holiness of Spirit, so he died and offered up himself through the strength of it, without spot to God. Through the Spirit, signifies the strength and power of the Spirit, as when we are said 'to mortify the deeds of the body through the Spirit,' Rom. viii. 13, i.e. through the powerful operation of the Spirit. For as the highest graces of Christ, faith, love, and obedience, were to be exercised upon the cross, so the assistance of the Spirit was necessary to the exciting and actuating those graces; for acts of grace being supernatural, a suitable concourse is necessary for the exerting those acts, and this concourse is truly the exciting and assisting grace of the Spirit. The natural powers of the humanity cannot otherwise be helped by the word, but as the "logos" or word does flow in upon it to actuate those powers of the soul. But this influx and motion is common to the Trinity, and therefore it is not from the divine nature, as hypostatically united, but from God as the first cause, and from the Spirit as the person whose office it is to excite grace, and assist it in the exercise. Not that the Spirit did so possess Christ, as that he did not exercise his own faculties in his whole office; but as the Spirit is said to pray in us, Rom. viii. 26, and we said to pray in him, Jude 20. The Spirit quickens our faculties, and by his inspiration excites and assists the act. The Spirit did all along enable Christ with a mighty power; it did first unite his soul to his body, his divine nature to the human, strengthened him in his temptation, stood by him in his passion, and at last united his body to his soul at his resurrection: 1 Pet. iii. 18, 'Quickened by the Spirit', Rom. i. 14, 'Declared to be the Son of God with power, according to the Spirit of holiness, by his resurrection from the dead;' showing himself here in the whole administration a Spirit of holiness, in his conception, conversation, oblation, justification, and resurrection. Upon which account he is said to be 'justified in the Spirit,' in the administration and ordering of the church. For it was 'through the Holy Ghost he gave commandments to the apostles whom he had chosen,' Acts. i. 2, not leaving his human nature till it was made immortal and glorious in heaven, that thereby the redemption and reconciliation might be every way complete. It was to those ends and purposes God gave the Spirit not by measure to him.

[5.] The Spirit was given to him by his Father, not only to fit him for his mediatory undertaking, but thereby to accomplish all the fruits of reconciliation in his seed. As God prepared him a body to lay down as a ransom for us, Mat. xx. 28, so he gave him the Spirit to bestow as a largess on us. He was given to him to be derived from him, as from the fountain, to all believers, whence they are said to be his fellows, Heb. i. 9. As he made himself their fellow, by descending to the fellowship of their nature, so they were to be his fellows by the communications of his Spirit. All men are his fellows in regard of his partaking of human nature, but believers only are his fellows in regard of conformity to the image of God. There is a fullness of merit in him resident in heaven, as a sweet smelling savour before God, and a fullness of grace to distil upon his seed to make them acceptable to God: merit to keep up the amity on his Father's part, and grace to keep up the amity on the believer's part. The graces of the Spirit were given to him, not only as mediator, without which the human nature had not been capable for the work, but as a head, which redound from him upon his members, Col. ii. 19, and convey nourishment to every part. As God assembled light in the sun to fit it for a full fountain of light, to transmit from heaven to the creatures on earth motion, warmth, and influences, whereby the qualities in all bodies are preserved and excited, so has God given the Spirit to Christ, the Sun of righteousness, and stored him with grace and holiness, as a common fountain of gardens, a public head, for the quickening, beautifying, and enriching believers. Without this fullness of light, the sun could not be beneficial to the world, nor answer the end of its creation, so without this fullness of Spirit in Christ, he could not accomplish the fruits and ends of the reconciliation he has made. And therefore, though the Spirit sanctified Adam in innocence, as the third person in the Trinity, and so he breathed an holiness upon Christ, yet he sanctifies believers now in a new habitude, not only as the third person in the Trinity but as the Spirit of Christ, the mediator, sent in his name by the Father, John xiv. 26, as purchased by Christ, upon which account he is called the Spirit of Christ, and Christ is said to send him, John xvi. 7. Because, as mediator, he acquired a right by the merit of his sufferings to dispense this fullness of the Spirit, who now acts as a fruit of Christ's intercession upon believers: John xiv. 16, 'I will pray the Father, and he shall give you another comforter.'

Use of this part.

1. How gross a sin is unbelief, which practically denies the ability of that Saviour, which the Father so richly fitted by his Spirit to the work of reconciliation! It is a charge and imputation upon God, as though he did not furnish him with sufficient abilities. It is a deriving his divinity or humanity, or both. It is all the heresies that ever were started against the person of the Son of God in the mass; they are all practically bundled up in this one single sin. God's anger will most flame when that which cost him the greatest treasures is despised. It is the despising all that is great in God; his riches, his power, his honour: his riches in furnishing him, his power in supporting him, his honour designed by him in both. It is a more sensible contradiction to the Trinity than any sin against the light of nature, because there is a more evident discovery of the Trinity in his mediation; the Father appointing, calling, counselling, ordering; the Spirit furnishing, fitting, exciting, supporting; the Son acting as the subject of all this. It does affront not a man; nor an angel, no, nor only the Son of God himself, but the magnificence of the Father towards him, and the pains of the Spirit on him.

2. How should we be encouraged to faith in this able Saviour! Since he has all the fitness that could delight God, and all the fullness whereby he can pleasure man, he is every way able to satisfy God and save the believer. His ability being so much and so great upon the earth, is not diminished in heaven, no more than his compassions are abated. As he learned a new mode of compassionating men before his departure out of the world, so, since his ascension to heaven, he has received a greater power of assisting men. Before, he had the Spirit to gift himself, now he has the Spirit to send upon his people. He has a fullness of grace, a fitness of gifts, that he may be every way able to help. He had a body to bear our sins, and a divine nature whereby to expiate them, his merit was as infinite as his person. He is an holy high priest, not tainted with any of those evils which he was to expiate in others. He is not only man; then he might have fallen as the first Adam did, and left us in the same, or a worse condition than before: he is not only God, then he could have performed no obedience to the law, as being not concerned in it as a subject, but as the lawgiver; nor could he have offered any satisfaction to God, as being incapable of suffering in the Deity; but God and man, fit to repair the honour of God and the fallen state of the creature. He had an enlarged understanding to know his work, inconceivable power to perform it, and incomparable goodness to be faithful in it. Such wisdom as he was furnished with could not be ignorant of his office, nor is to this day; such power could not be weak, nor will ever languish; such integrity could not be false, nor will ever deceive the comers to him.

3. Admire these infinite compassions of God. Oh marvellous grace! that Christ should be endued with the richest grace by his Father to relieve our poverty, with the highest might to help our weakness, with a powerful assistance to conquer our enemies, with an overflowing fullness to fill up our emptiness, and abundant grace poured into his lips to comfort our dejectedness. God cannot show greater love than to send his Son to make the peace, and unlock his cabinet wherewith to furnish him. An old frame of thankfulness will not fit an evangelical discovery of love. When God tells them, Isa. xiii. 9, 10, of his 'Servant in whom his soul delights,' and upon whom he had put his Spirit for the redemption of man, then he makes this use of exhortation of it, 'Sing unto the Lord a new song.' New love calls for new praise. God might have destroyed us with less cost than he has reconciled us; for our destruction there was no need of his counsel, nor of fitting out his Son, nor opening his treasures; a word would have done it, whereas our reconciliation stood him in much charge. It was performed at the

expense of his grace and Spirit, to furnish his eternal Son to be a sacrifice for our atonement. An inexpressible wonder, that the Father should prepare his Son a mortal body, that our souls might be prepared for an incorruptible glory!

4. God commissioned Christ to this work of reconciliation. He gave him a fullness of authority us well as a fullness of ability. He is therefore said to be sealed, as having his commission under the great seal of heaven: John vi. 27, "Touton gar ho pater esfregisen, o Theos". Sealing notes a special designment of the thing sealed to some special purpose; so the sealing of Christ signifies his separation and authority to exercise his offices, and in particular, of giving meat to the world, which should endure to everlasting life. By virtue of this commission, whatsoever Christ does is valid, for he does it as God's attorney, to whom he has transferred a power to carry on the work of redemption, in which respect he is called God's servant, not by nature, but a servant by office. In this respect he is said to be anointed, Isa. lxi. 1. Anointing was not so much the fitting a person as a declaration of his fitness, and an authorising him to an exercise of his offices. Anointing under the law signified an authority conferred upon a person for government, priesthood, or prophecy. In that place Christ does distinguish his commission from his fitness, and declares himself fit, because he was commissioned. 'The Spirit of the Lord God is upon me;' there is his fitness, 'because, "ya'an", therefore the Lord has anointed me.' It was not agreeable to the divine wisdom to commission any for an office but whom he had furnished with an ability for that office. What was he commissioned for? Not to thunder the law, but to declare the gospel, the gospel of peace to the broken-hearted, to reveal the thoughts of amity which his Father had. Upon this account Christ tells us he did not come of himself, John vii. 28, and in regard of this commission he is called God's angel, Mal. iii. 1, 'messenger;' the word signifies an angel, the 'apostle of our profession,' Heb. iii. 1, because, as he authorised and sent the apostles, so the Father authorised and sent him; 'a messenger, and an interpreter,' John xxxiii. 23. Though this commission was given him at his birth, yet God renewed the declaration of it several times: at his baptism, Mat. iii. 17, 'This is my beloved Son, in whom I am well pleased;' at his transfiguration, Mat. xvii. 5, 'This is my beloved Son, in whom I am well pleased; hear you him.' Christ pleads this commission, as well as the covenant between them: John xvii. 4, 'I have finished the work thou gave me to do,' when he calls it a work given him to do. What work I have done was appointed me, and I have done it by thy authority, and therefore our redemption and security in it depends primarily upon the covenant or federal transaction between the Father and the Son; and next, upon the commission given to Christ, which was indeed but the performance of the first articles on the Father's part. Christ's commission was declared several ways; by the miracles he wrought by his own hand, as well as by the apostles; by the holiness of his life; by the accomplishment of all the predictions of the prophets in his person; by his resurrection from the dead; and by the conversion of the world executed in the most astonishing and divine manner. This commission he had at once, as well as his fitness; but he did successively enter into the exercise of his offices. At first he performed his prophetical, then exercised his priestly a little before his death, at his authoritative prayer, John xvii., where he begins his intercession, the greatest, choicest, and most durable part of his priesthood. His kingly he exercised more especially after his resurrection, in the orders he settled for the church; all power was then more manifestly declared to be given him.

He had then in the whole, the stamp of all God's authority upon him.

(1.) His whole work was prescribed him; which is expressed by the notion of a precept as he was God's servant. The command of a superior is a sufficient commission to a servant to do a work he is ordered to perform; and Christ, in regard of his mediatory office, was inferior to his Father, John xiv. 28. In which respect the Father is said to be greater than he. The command was his commission from God, but miracles were the manifestation of that commission to man. This command implies not any unwillingness in Christ to undertake and perform this work (as though God were necessitated to bend his will thereunto, and to force him by virtue of his obedience to it); but it is rather a law or rule of his acting voluntarily, agreed upon between the Father and the Son, and as heartily embraced by Christ as it was kindly enacted by God for the good of man. In regard of this particular order, his whole mediatory management in the world is called obedience: Philip. ii. 8, 'He became obedient unto death, even the death of the cross.' Obedient to death, even to the utmost and sharpest point; which infers an extension of the command on God's part, and obedience on Christ's part, in all things preceding the cross, and all the circumstances of his reconciling death, doing nothing in his whole state of humiliation but in obedience to his Father's injunctions; which injunctions were so particular, that there is no material thing in the whole life and death of Christ upon record in the New Testament, but is expressed in the mysteries of the law, or the oracles of the prophets in the Old. He did nothing either as man or as mediator, but according to God's order. As he was man, he was observant of the moral law, as being that covenant of works he was to make up the breach of, which he performed in the highest manner upon the cross, manifesting his love to God in laying down his life according to his order, and love to man in giving his life for a ransom for him; and by an act of charity incumbent upon him by the moral law, praying for his persecutors. As he was born under the Jewish administration, he observed God's orders in that: in circumcision, as a federal rite, which he suffered in his flesh; and the Passover, a commemoration of a national deliverance, which he celebrated with his disciples; but not in purifications and sacrifices, which were appointed for atonement, and implied sin in the offerer, which it was not congruous for him to be subject to by reason of the exact purity of his person. But above all, he was an exact observer of the mediatory law, which was a law added over and above to him in that economy, and incumbent upon none else, neither angels nor men. In this he did nothing but by order; he 'did nothing of himself, but what he saw the Father do,' John v. 19, i.e. what he had directions from his Father to perform; for if you understand it of Christ as mediator, he did many things which the Father did not do, but nothing but what the Father did order him to do. And therefore whatsoever Christ did was manifested to him by the Father: ver. 20, 'For the Father loves the Son, and shows him all things that himself does,' &c.; and he had no respect to his own will, did nothing of his own head, but observed exactly the pattern set him by the will of his Father: ver. 30, 'I can of my own self do nothing; I seek not my own will, but the will of the Father which has sent me.' As he was sent by his Father's order, so he was altogether guided by his Father's will, wherewith his own will exactly concurred. Therefore those good works he had done were showed them from his Father, John x. 32, those "kala erga", those comely works; all that tenderness he had showed, either to soul or body, were wrought by his Father's commission and his Father's power. In this respect, as he was polished in regard of fitness, so he was a shaft in regard of motion, Isa. xlix. 2, flying swiftly to the mark whereto the archer designed him. And because he had so exactly observed his commission, he did 'abide in his Father's love,' which he uses as an incentive to his disciples' obedience, both from his own example and the issue of it, John xv. 10.

(2.) God gave him instructions how to manage this work. When any wise man intends an end, and fixes upon the best means for it, he orders every circumstance, time, place, manner, as far as he is able. God intending the mediation and incarnation of Christ, comprehended under that decree the place, manner, and all the circumstances of it in every punctilio. It is so evident that Christ had his instructions from God, that the Socinians fancy an ascension of Christ into heaven after his birth, and before his preaching in the world, to be instructed by God what he should preach; for Paul, say they, ascended into heaven before he was sent to the Gentiles; and if the servant did, why not the master? But this is to argue against the deity of Christ. It is strange that the Scripture, which speaks so particularly of the actions of Christ, of what was done before his preaching, viz. his birth and baptism, should be silent in so remarkable an occurrence, and every evangelist be forgetful of it. It is not credible, that if they had known it, they should be silent in it. But the Scripture plainly denies this pretended ascension: Heb. ix. 12, 24, 'He entered once into the holy place.' In regard of this instruction, God is said to call Christ to his foot, Isa. xii. 2, i.e. taught him, as scholars used to sit at their master's feet: 'Who raised up the righteous man from the east,' "tsedek", righteousness. Some understand it of Abraham, some of Cyrus, both which were raised from the east; but the following expressions are too high to suit either of them. God brought him as the sun from the east, to shine upon a dark and blind world. His work is in this respect said to be before him, Isa. lxii. 11, as having his instructions copied out to him, as ambassadors receive instructions from the prince. His doctrine is therefore said not to be so much his as his Father's, John xvii. 16; it is a transcript of his Father's mind and will: whence Ps. xl. 9, 10, 'I have not hid thy righteousness within my heart, I have declared thy faithfulness and thy salvation, I have not concealed thy loving-kindness and thy truth;' wherein Christ is represented speaking to his Father, and giving an account how he had observed his rule, and how faithful he had been in the declarations of his will; how emphatically is he referring all to God, thy righteousness, thy faithfulness, thy salvation, thy loving-kindness, thy truth. Whatsoever Christ spoke, he heard from the Father; not only as a Son by eternal generation, but as a mediator by an authoritative instruction, he spoke to the world those things which he had heard of the Father, John viii. 26, and every little of his instructions was observed, John xv. 16. He had communicated all things which he had heard of his Father; and whatsoever he did communicate, was revealed to him by his Father. This declaration, which was the chief part of his instructions, was of the name of God, which he pleads he had declared, John xvii. 6, 26, the name of grace and love which is expressed, Exod. xxxiv., his reconciling name. The name of God is said to be in him: Exod. xxiii. 21, 'My name,' i.e. my law and doctrine, as in some places the law of Christ is expounded, his law, Isa. xiii. 4, which is rendered his name, Mat. xii. 21. This was promised, Deut. xviii. 18,19, 'I will raise them a prophet, and will put my words in his mouth, and he shall speak unto them all that I shall command him.' They were God's words in his mouth; God's words which he should speak in God's name. God gave him authority to reveal his will, and commanded men to hear him if then had any mind to eternal happiness. You have the full instructions of the work he was to do and the words he was to speak, Isa. xlix. 8, 9, after the covenant made with him: he was to establish the tottering earth, which was shaken and disordered by sin, he was to be an herald, to proclaim pardon and liberty in favour to the prisoners bound in chains of guilt. God instructs him what he should say: 'That thou may say to the prisoners, Go forth; to them that are in darkness, Show yourselves;' come out of your dungeon, you that are sold under the power of sin, show yourselves, appear before God as a reconciled Father; for I am the covenant of the people, and God's salvation to the ends of the earth.

(3.) Miracles performed by him were a confirmation of the authenticness of his commission. They were miracles of that nature that had not been performed by any prophet before him. The opening the eyes of one that was born blind was an act unheard of in the world, and the raising one that had lain some days putrefying in his grave was not to be paralleled by any of the ancient prophets. And those miracles done by him which were of the same kind with those done by the prophets of old, were done with more ease, and in a way of absolute authority. These were such credentials, that not only Nicodemus acknowledged him upon that account to be 'a teacher sent from God,' John iii. 2, but the devils knew him to be the Messiah, the Son of God, Luke iv. 41. The casting out devils was an unanswerable argument of his authority, since those malicious spirits were too strong to be subject to a created power, or obey his command without a touch of omnipotence to compel them to it; these he dispossesses with authority, as one that had power over them, whence the people began to admire the excellency of his doctrine, because accompanied with such triumphant seals, Mark i. 27. Without a divine commission to fortify his command, his word had been as ridiculous to them as they were malicious against him. The end of all those miracles wrought by him was to testify God's approbation and mission of him. Acts ii. 22, 'Jesus of Nazareth, a man approved of God among you by miracles, wonders, and signs, which God did by him in the midst of you,' "apodedeigmenon". They were demonstrations of his commission, and are called signs which God did by him, as they are called also the works of his Father, John v. 36, which did bear witness of him that the Father had sent him, and challenge from the Jews a belief of him, and he intimates that their unbelief had been excusable if he had not done such works, John x. 37. These miracles were an evident testimony that the Father was in him, because, exceeding the sphere of natural causes, they were products of the creative power which is ascribed in Scripture principally to the Father, and therefore more unanswerable than an audible voice from heaven, which had been more liable to evasions and objections than ocular demonstrations, allowed by the common sense of all spectators, and felt by the subject who received the benefit of them. These being acts of omnipotence, could not be affixed to a falsity. For it would follow that either God were deceived himself, which he cannot be because of his omniscience, or that he would deceive others, which is impossible, because of his truth. And especially when he was solemnly desired to assist him with his omnipotence in the raising Lazarus, to this end, that 'they might believe that he had sent him,' John xi. 42, which he durst never have desired, nor would God ever have granted, had he only pretended an authority; for then he had settled the faith of man upon a false foundation, in overpowering their reason by a supernatural work, to assent to those things which they could not have been induced unto by lower arguments. These were the seals of his patent from heaven; whence, when John sent his disciples to know of him whether he were the Messiah, he gives no other demonstration than that of the supernatural works he had wrought.

(4.) The end of this commission was the reconciliation and redemption of man.

[1.] Satisfaction for our sins: Gal. i. 4, 'Who gave himself for our sins, that he might deliver us from this present evil world, according to the will of God and our Father.' It was the will of God and our Father, that he should give himself for our sins; wherein God acted not only as a just judge, to have the honour of his law maintained; nor only as a sovereign lord, to reduce the creature to obedience; but as a tender father, out of a paternal affection to restore the creature to happiness, 'according to the will of God and our Father.' The apostle lays therefore our atonement upon the will of God whereby Christ was authorised to this work, 'by which will we are sanctified,' Heb. x. 10. By this will of God given in charge, and instructions to Christ, we are atoned and brought into a state of reconciliation, through the offering of the body of Christ once for all. Hence "hilaskesthai", a making reconciliation for the sins of the people, is said to be a thing pertaining to God, wherein Christ expressed his faithfulness to the instructions God gave him as a high priest, Heb. ii. 7.

[2.] Testification of the love of God. Isa. xliii. 10, 11, 'Ye are my witnesses, and my servant whom I have chosen, that you may know and believe me, and understand that I am he, I, even I am the Lord, and besides me there is no Saviour.' To witness the nature and love of God in the salvation he has provided, to evidence that he was the only true God, because the only fountain of salvation to the lost world. He had therefore an account of all from his Father upon whose hearts an impression of this love was to be made, so that he knew them all by name, John x. 3. It was to give us an understanding of God, both of his truth and of his love, 1 John v. 20.

[3.] Final and perfect salvation. It was the will of God not only that he should give himself for our sins, but that he should deliver us from this evil world, i. e. conduct us to heaven, that we might be for ever there without spot or any stain of the evil of the world upon us, Gal. i. 4. Upon this account he had authority, "eksousian", to give eternal life to as many as God had given him, and it was in his instructions not to cast off any that came to him, John vi. 38. Whence the conversion of the Samaritan woman is said to be the will of his Father, John iv. 34, and there is no work of grace upon any soul by the merit of his passion and power of the Spirit, but is by an order of his Father to him for it; and therefore when God shall call for all those that as a right are deposited in his hands, he expects the full performance of his charge, and a resignation of them all to him without the loss of one, John vi. 39. For his commission and instructions extended not only to take away the enmity on God's part by the satisfaction of his justice, but to present them unblameable and unreprovable in the sight of God, that there might be no ground for the breaking out of this enmity again on either side, Col. i. 20, 22. Thus was our Saviour made, by the authority of God, a 'surety of a better testament,' Heb. vii. 22: a surety on man's part, to satisfy the debts which were owing to the justice of God, which he performed as a priest by his death; and a surety on God's part, to secure pardon and peace to believers, that they should be no more under arrest for their debts, which was ensured when all authority and power was given into his hands; so that the commission and instructions were every way extensive for the asserting the honour of God and ensuring the happiness of the creature.

5. The Father actually sends him. Nothing more frequent in the Gospels, especially of John, than Christ's affirming he was sent by the Father: John viii. 42, 'I proceeded forth, and came from God; neither came I of myself, but he sent me.' As he intruded not himself, nor appointed himself, so he did not take his journey, and present himself to the world, till he had his despatch from God; as he had his divine being by communication from the Father, so he had his temporary mission from his Father. His generation is the proper ground of his mission. John vii. 29, 'But I know him: for I am from him, and he has sent me,' though his mission is not the necessary consequent of his eternal generation; his eternal generation did not necessitate his temporal incarnation, no more than the eternal procession of the Spirit from the Father and the Son can necessitate the incarnation of the Spirit. There was in the Father a right of sending prompter relationem originis; and because of Christ's voluntary putting himself into the relation of a mediator. In respect of his being the second person in the Trinity, he is said to be begotten; as mediator and reconciler, he is said to be sent. Generation was an eternal act, mission a temporal; that was natural, this voluntary; the decree of mission was eternal, the act of mission temporal. His being sent does not impair his deity; though sent, he is Jehovah: Zech. ii. 8, 9, 'Thus says the Lord of hosts, After the glory he has sent me: and you shall know that the Lord of hosts has sent me.' The person that says he is sent is Jehovah, and he is sent by Jehovah; and the end of his sending is there expressed, ver. 11 for the conjunction of many nations to the Lord, in that day of his sending and dwelling in the midst of Zion. And when he affirms that he is sent by the Lord,óIsa. xlviii. 16, 'And now the Lord God, and his Spirit, has sent me,'óhe affirms himself to be 'the first and the last', ver. 12, 13, 'Whose hand laid the foundation of the earth, and his right hand spanned the heavens,' when he called unto them to stand up together. His ancient name was sent, which some think is the signification of the word Shiloh, Gen. xlix. 10, which they derive from a word which signifies sending; and Moses speaks of him to God by this title. Exod. iv. 13, 'O my God, send, I pray thee, by the hand thou wilt send;' which anciently was understood of the Messiah, because the patriarchs did in difficult things express their desire of the coming of the Messiah, who was to restore and settle all things in a happy state. Moses knew that God would send him to be a redeemer, and he desires God would send by him. And it is a title appropriate to Christ by John Baptist: John iii. 34, 'He whom God has sent.'

(1.) There is the highest reason to acknowledge him sent of God. That there was such a person in the world, is acknowledged by the very enemies to his person, and owned in human stories as well as divine writ. Since he professed himself to be sent by God, if he were not sent by him, he had been guilty of the greatest falsity; and greatest folly in affirming so. Had he been a mere man, and come without any authority, how comes it to pass, that after his death he prevailed against the laws of the nation, the grandeur and valour of the world, the wisdom and eloquence of men, and against the whole world that resisted his doctrine; that he put to flight the powers of hell, silenced their oracles? How should one crucified as a malefactor be so powerful, after his death, to make such impressions upon the minds of men; to change the whole scene of the world, to assist his followers for many years after in the working of miracles? If God would for a time have left such a wickedness (had it been a false assertion} unrevenged, yet would he never have seconded it by his own power, and nonplussed men into a belief of it! Would he have assisted the heralds of this news even against himself, and his own truth and righteousness? Had this been done by human means, it might have been suspected; but a divine wisdom and art appeared in all. It was not by riches, honours, or the promises of worldly greatness, that this doctrine spread itself over the world, and found such harbour in the minds of men; but by promises of an invisible and future happiness, and assurance of present misery, reproach, poverty, prisons, torments, and death; and by these means his followers increased to a formidable number, against the opposition of princes and learning of the world; and they were more willing and fond to lay down their lives to seal the truth of the doctrine, that Christ was sent of God, than to strike one stroke for the propagation of it, though they wanted not courage for acting, as well as for suffering, had any such commission been granted them. Now if God does rule the world justly and righteously, we must believe that Christ was sent by God for those ends he declared in the time of his life, or we must deny the righteous providence of God, and acknowledge all things to be ordered by chance, or some worse power; we must accuse God of the highest unrighteousness, in bearing witness by a divine power to so great an imposture, whereby millions of souls would be undone, had he not, according to his own declaration, been sent by God.

(2.) God sent him for this end of reconciliation and redemption. He was sent as 'the messenger of the covenant,' Mal iii. 1, to declare the peace, as well as to be the peace, Eph. ii. 14, 17. The thing itself was so incredible, that an injured God should be desirous of reconciliation, and upon such terms as the death of his Son, that it was as needful to be declared by God, as contrived and acted by God. The objections that might have been made against it had such strength, that he only who lay in the bosom of the Father, and knew all his eternal counsels, and was the actor of it in his own person, could reveal the thoughts, purposes, and resolves of his Father concerning it from all eternity, John i. 18.

6. Uses. (1.) We see again here the sad charge against unbelief and disobedience. It is a despising the stamp of all God's authority upon Christ, and tearing his commission; a refusal of one particularly sent, a rejection of the messenger of the covenant, and all the covenant treaties of love and peace. This was the aggravation of the Jews' sin, and is likewise of all the inheritors of that unbelief, to the end of the world; that Christ has an authoritative commission from his Father, and is not received by the rebels; that he speaks in his Father's name, and is not believed by the offender, John v. 43. God was in Christ reconciling the world, as a prince in an ambassador; therefore God and his reconciling offer are despised in the refusal of his commission. It is to God the affront is offered, Christ being the representative of God in the highest and most gracious charge, in the tenderest and most indulgent offers; any slight thoughts of his person, any contempt of his precepts, any disregard of his promises, redounds upon the person authorising him to those ends. He was sent to be heard and obeyed, Mat. xvii. 5, not to be slighted and despised.

(2.) Study Christ's commission in the extent of it. Whatsoever Christ does, he does it by command, and commission from his Father. This will support faith against fears, and hope against despondencies. It will afford us arguments in prayer, when we can open before God the commission he gave to his Son, and back every petition with some clause in it; when we can go to Christ as an officer authorised and instructed, and show him what instructions he had: Isa. lxi. 1-3, 'To bind up the broken-hearted, proclaim liberty to the captives, and the opening of the prison to them that are bound; to give beauty for ashes, the oil of joy for mourning, the garment of praise for the spirit of heaviness, that they may be trees of righteousness.' To bind up the broken-hearted, deliver the captives, open the prisons, change deformity into beauty, and sorrow into joy, a spirit of heaviness into a spirit of praise, a languishing frame into a fruitful growth; all which parts of his commission were owned by him, Luke iv. 18, and observed in his actings in the world. The poor woman pleaded with him for mercy, as he was the Son of David,' Mat. xv. 22; we upon a higher title, as he is the commissioner of God, the apostle of our profession, the messenger of the covenant.

3.) Act faith much upon it. There is little comfort in all that Christ did and suffered, unless we respect him as one sent. Had he come of his own head, we could not with any confidence plead his merit before God. He is sent as his Father's servant, to do service for his Father and his people. Christ must be respected, not only as dying, but as one sent by the Father to such an end. This is the character he gives his disciples' faith in his relation to the Father: John xvii. 8, 'They have believed that thou did send me.' It is this commission Christ pleads in his intercession: 'Let not them that wait upon thee, O Lord God of hosts, be ashamed for my sake; let not those that seek thee be confounded for my sake, O God of Israel because for thy sake I have borne reproach,' Ps. lx. 6, 7. It is Christ's passion prayer. The 9th, 21st, 22rd verses, are applied to Christ in the New Testament. It was by thy order, and for thy honour, I bore this reproach; let not, therefore, any believer be ashamed and confounded. What he desired on earth, he intercedes for in heaven, and upon the same ground. He will not therefore refuse those that come unto God by him, he has an office in heaven for their reception. You come to one who has an obligation and order from his Father to receive you, and has too faithful a disposition, and too compassionate a nature of his own, ever to reject you. It was from the strict observance of his Father's orders, that he did nothing but what was pleasing to God: John viii. 29, 'I do always those things that please him' (a r e s t a) (aresta). 'A r e s t o n (Areston) signifies, some say, an order of a court. Not a work done not a word spoken, but was agreeable to the tenor of his commission, to the copy of his instructions: John xii. 49, 50, 'Whatsoever I speak therefore, even as the Father said unto me, so I speak.' We cannot but please God by believing one that is so exact, by presenting to him what he is so highly pleased with. The command given him by his Father, was the publishing everlasting life. We should then believingly put in plea God's order. This is a stronger ground of support than the principles of sciences, and fallibility of sense, and the totterings of reason.

(4.) Bless God for his love, and for any work in your hearts. The authorising Christ is a piece of love, that could never enter into the heart of any man, unless God had revealed it. It is therefore called a mystery, Eph. iii. 3. The apostle could not consider the will of God and our Father in this work, without interrupting his discourse with a doxology: Gal. i. 4, 5, 'To whom be glory for ever and ever, Amen.' Bless him for any gracious work in any of your hearts. It was by the order of his Father any work was done by him in the world. It is by the same order any work is done by him in your souls. It is Christ's 'meat and drink to do his Father's will' in both. Not a person that finds the qualifications of grace in his heart, but may read his name in the commission of the Father to Christ. As the angels rejoiced in the manifestation of the wisdom and power of God, when the new creation was laid in the incarnation of

Christ, so should we in the mission of the Son of God. 'Glory to God, and peace on earth,' are in conjunction in themselves, and should be in our meditations on it.

7. The Father actually bruises him. In this act is the corner-stone of our reconciliation laid. He bore from his Father our punishment; the punishment of sense in his agonies in the garden, the punishment of loss in the eclipse upon the cross. In the one, he tasted the terrors of hell, in the other, he felt the bitterness of a temporary clouding of heaven. He was 'smitten of God and afflicted,' Isa. liii. 4, percussum Dei, "muchah Elohim". Men that were extremely afflicted, they regarded as smitten by the immediate hand of God. God indeed both loved and punished him in that act, John x. 17: he loved him as our Redeemer, and bruised him as the surety engaging for our debts; he loved him for the glory he was to gain by him, and punished him for the sins he did legally bear upon himself; he loved him as his servant in whom he would be glorified by the punishment of our sins, and the redemption of our souls. It is granted on all hands, that God was the supreme cause and author of Christ's sufferings; but some say, not the immediate executioner with his own hands. For the phrase in Scripture, that God did these or those things, concludes not that he did them with his immediate hand; but that he was the decreer, disposer, and director of them by his just judgment in a holy manner to correct the sins of men, or by his wisdom to make trial of his saints; God using for the executioners men or angels, good or bad, or other inferior creatures, as seems best to his wisdom: Amos iii. 6, 'Shall there be evil in a city, and the Lord has not done it?' where he does not ascribe all evil of punishment to the immediate hand of God, but to the sovereign judgment and power of God, appointing and ordering what should be done.

It is certain, that the grace of God was the cause of his tasting death, Heb. ii. 9. But it is most likely, that the Father did immediately bruise him.

(1.) It seems necessary that the stroke should come immediately from the Father.

[1.] In regard of what he was to suffer. It was more than a bodily death was due by the first sentence against Adam in case of failure on his part. Gen. ii. 17, 'In the day thou eatest thereof, thou shalt surely die,' "mot tamut". All kinds of death; the curse of the law reached further than the case of the body. If nothing more were due to the sinner but the temporal death of the body, it were a light and tolerable punishment. An infinite wrath surely was due both to soul and body for transgressing the precepts of an infinite majesty. The soul being principal in sin, must be the principal in suffering; the soul was the agent, the body but the instrument. The whole nature of man had sinned, and violated the articles of the covenant; the whole nature of man must therefore answer. The soul in us then being the proper subject of sin, the soul of Christ must be the immediate subject of suffering, otherwise he suffered not the penalty due to sin. Not one of those murderers, whose hands reeked with the blood of his body, could reach his invisible soul, and stain their hands immediately with the oppression of his spirit; that was beyond their touch, and was obnoxious only to the Father's stroke. No creature could drop an inward wrath upon his soul. An infinite justice was wronged, an infinite punishment must be suffered. Now none can execute infinite wrath, but an infinite person; what creatures could be sufficient to revenge an infinite offence against an infinite majesty? As every faculty of our souls had been depraved by sin, so must every faculty of the soul be afflicted with sorrow. 'The whole world was guilty before God,' Rom. iii. 19, u p o d i k o V t w J e w (hupodikos toi Theoi), under the judgment of God: 'his wrath abode upon us, John iii. 30. We were 'by nature children of wrath,' Eph. ii. 3. Christ must endure the wrath due to us; it was more than a common death that he was to taste, and did taste, Heb. ii. 9, 14, 15óthat death which the devil had the power of, who labours not only for the death of the body, but for that of the soul; that death which men under a sense of guilt feared, which was not a temporal, but an eternal one. Men feared not a death in sin, but a death for sin; not so much the death of the body, as that of the soul. Such a death which men feared, Christ endured; the penal death of men, not the spiritual death of men; and that in regard of the nature of it, not of the continuance, nor the despairs and moral evils which follow upon it. Such sins as the damned are guilty of, are not essential to the nature of punishment, but arise from the inherent unrighteousness of the person; neither is the eternal duration of the punishment essential to its nature, but arises from the finite nature of the suffering creature which renders a commensurate satisfaction from him impossible. The infinite holiness of Christ's nature was a bar against the sins which are committed by others under that wrath, and the infinite grandeur and dignity of his person was a bar against the eternal duration of that punishment. Now such a death is immediately inflicted by the wrath of God. I cannot see how any creature can inflict that which is infinite.

[2.] In regard of the attributes the Father intended to glorify in the death of Christ. He acted herein as judge, for the manifestation of his vindictive justice; as supreme lawgiver, for the vindication of his holiness; as a governor, for the declaration of his tenderness and kindness towards man: all which attributes were glorified in the highest strain by his being an actor in the death of his beloved Son.

His Justice. His justice had not been so eminent, if Christ had only suffered the death of the body, without impressions of wrath on his soul; nor if God had left him to the strokes of others, without striking him himself. This attribute had been manifested upon the highest creatures, angels in heaven, man upon the earth, and upon the account of the latter had reached both the irrational and inanimate creatures; there wanted nothing to express it to the utmost but this of bruising his Son. God designed the utmost demonstration of this in the death of his Son, Rom. iii. 26. Christ was 'set out as a propitiation, that God might be just;' that God might be just, i. e. that he might be known, and declared in the highest manner to be a righteous God; implying, that all other expressions of it before had been drawn in fainter colours than what he intended here, as if he could not have been known to have an impartial justice without such a way of discovery. He did, therefore, all in this case which an exact justice could require; for to neglect what it requires, is an injury to it, as well as to do what it prohibits. In the creation, he was a God of power and wisdom; in the law, a God of vengeance, which is mounted to the highest point in inflicting wrath upon Christ for man's violation of that law. In extraordinary visible judgments by the hand of God, there are clearer notices of his justice than when the hand of instruments is more sensibly felt in them. 'The heavens' then 'declare his righteousness,' when 'the Lord is Judge himself,' Ps. 50. 6. Abraham's obedience was more eminent by the laying hands upon his own son Isaac himself, according to God's order; so was God's justice in laying his own hand upon Christ, than if it had been committed merely to instruments. Had our Saviour suffered only a bodily death, with those griefs in his soul which are incident to men barely for the death of the body, he had under all that load of sin which was laid upon him suffered less than madly men have done. There was something therefore of wrath dropped into his soul, which was the act of his Father's bruising of him, for the manifestation of his justice, and giving it an unexceptionable satisfaction.

His holiness. God was now upon the highest discovery of his holiness and hatred of sin. Had this punishment been left only to instruments, he had indeed declared his holiness, but in a fainter degree; his hatred of sin had not been so conspicuous, had he not with his own hands poured out a wrath upon him. His end in sending his Son 'in the likeness of sinful flesh' being to make him a sacrifice to 'condemn sin in the flesh,' Rom. viii. 3, his shooting his wrath upon him was a more sensible, high, and full condemnation of sin, than if all the devils in hell, and all their subjects and votaries on earth, had been let loose to buffet him. Herein he showed that sin was odious and abominable to him, that it should not be spared though it were only by imputation upon his Son; and hereby he lays a foundation of greater awe and reverence of his sanctity, and pure indignation upon the hearts of men. Here was the beauty of his holiness, as well as the exactness of his justice; vindicating the honour of his law, displaying the purity of his nature by sheathing his sword with indignation in the bowels of sin, while he pierced the heart of his beloved Son. A prince punishing his own son for some enormous crime by his own hand, would evidence a greater abhorrence of it than if he only exposed him to the hands of executioners.

His love. If God's love appeared more in giving up Christ as a sacrifice than if he had saved the world without the death of his Son, and without any satisfaction,óas appears, John iii. 17, 'God so loved the world that he gave his only begotten Son,' &c., which was a purer strain of love than pardoning sin without a sacrifice,óit may also follow, that since God resolved to signalise his love to us, he would have it reach the highest note, and it could not be screwed up to a higher peg than the sacrificing of his Son for us with his own hand. If there be such an emphasis of love in sending him, there is a stronger emphasis of love in bruising him. 'God so loved the world, that he gave his only begotten Son;' but God so loved the world, that he bruised his only begotten Son, declares a richer magnificence of love, and raises it to a height of glory, in showing what he would do for miserable creatures. He magnifies his kindness, demonstrates how much he values and delights in his elect, and gives an undeniable proof of the treasures of love in his heart for them. His earnestness in shooting his arrows into himself, rather than lose his people, and engraving upon him the marks of his anger, is the highest point his compassion to us could amount unto, and a step beyond the bare offer and mission of him. God would save us as a Judge, with the evidence of his righteousness; as a Lawgiver, in the discovery of his holiness; as a King, in the display of his sovereignty: Isa. xxxiii. 22, 'The Lord is our Judge, the Lord is our Lawgiver, and the Lord is our King; he will save us;' and as a Father too with the clearest and dearest affection.

(2.) God did bruise him: Isa. liii 10, 'Yet it pleased the Lord to bruise him; he has put him to grief: when thou shalt make his soul an offering for sin, he shall see his seed, he shall prolong his days, and the pleasure of the Lord shall prosper in his hands.' This chapter is the history of the cross, and the epitome of the gospel; it is Christ's crucifixion in effigy before he was crucified in person. The double state of Christ, of humiliation and exaltation, are here described. The verse is a prophecy which has something minatory and something consolatory: minatory, 'It pleased the Lord to bruise him,' he speaks of what was future as if it were past, consolatory, 'He shall see his seed, he shall prolong his days;' and yet, this word refers to something antecedent in ver. 9, 'he had done no violence, neither was any deceit in his mouth.' Though he had an unspotted holiness in his nature, an unblameable purity in his life, yet it pleased the Lord to bruise him, as he stood in our stead, and represented our persons.

It pleased the Lord, "chafatz". The word signifies not only a bare will, but a will with delight. The word is used to signify God's pleasure in his church, Isa. lxii. 4, where the word is Hephzibah, my delight is in her, the same word, and it is used to express Christ's delight in his saints, Ps. xvi. 3, 'in whom is all my delight.' Not only his resolve, but his pleasure, his heart was as much in it as his hands;

the word speaks more than a bare permission. He delighted not simply in the strokes he gave, but in his own essential perfections manifested by those strokes; he delighted not simply in the rod, but in that balsam which was to drop from the end of the rod upon mankind; he was pleased with every wound, as it was a necessary medium to redemption; the text intimates it, he was pleased to bruise him, but it was in order to another pleasure that was to prosper in the hands of the bruised person.

To bruise him, "racha'", he has put him to grief. The word signifies to pound as in a mortar, whereby the greatness of Christ's sufferings is expressed. God came armed with his vindictive justice, the sentence of the law in his mouth, and the penalty of the law in his hand; he appeared as a just governor of the world, with a readiness to exercise his authority for the vindication of his law, he glittered in his holiness to right the wronged holiness of his law, and in his justice to revenge the insolences committed against it. His delight in this might very well consist with his love to his Son. As a Father he loved him, as a judge he punished him; as a Father he loved his person, as a God he loved his own honour. A son enters into suretyship with his father for an insolvent debtor; the father loves his son as he is a father, but demands the debt of him as he is a creditor, and has the law passed against him as he is a governor: he did affect him as he stood in relation to himself, and punished him as he stood in relation to us; he loved him for his own holiness, and punished him for our sins.

Again, it is no wonder that it is expressed that the Lord was pleased or delighted to bruise him, since the bruising Christ was a part of the acceptation of the sacrifice: as fire descending from heaven to consume any sacrifice presented to God was a sign of the acceptableness of it to God. This is supposed to be the sign of the acceptation of Abel's sacrifice. Fire from heaven consumed Abel's sacrifice, and not Cain's. Theodotian therefore renders accepted e n e p u r i s e n (enepurisen), and the Scripture gives us frequent examples of this way of acceptation. So it was with Gideon's offering, Judges vi. 21; and so it was with Aaron's, Lev. ix, 24, and with Elijah's, 1 Kings xviii. 38, and with David's, 1 Chron. xxi. 26. God had never kindled the sacrifice, had he not been pleased with it.

When thou shalt make his soul an offering for sin. When God was to deal with him in a way of vindictive justice, as he was a sacrifice for us, he would not spare him, nor abate one stroke due to him for our sins; he would deal with him in the same manner as he would deal with us, in whose place he stood as a sacrifice; he did not bruise him as he was his Son, but as he was a sacrifice, and so would not abate anything of that weight of suffering which was due by the law and by the demand of justice for our iniquities.

The promissory part follows. 'He shall see his seed,' there shall be a succession of generations for the glory of Christ, according to that Ps. lxxii. 17, 'His name shall be continued as long as the sun;' he shall be childed, he shall have a generation of children to keep up his name.

In the verse you see,

1. The greatness of Christ's sufferings, expressed by bruising.
2. The inflicter of them, the Lord.
3. The reason of them, as he was an offering, a sacrifice for sin.
4. The subject, the Redeemer.
6. The fruit of it, a spiritual seed, with duration.

Doct. The greatest punishment inflicted upon Christ, when he stood as a sacrifice for sin, was not the act of men, but the act of God. There were sufferings in the body of Christ, as buffetings, spitting, scourging, crucifying; in these, men were the instruments, but the determinate counsel of God preceded. But there were sufferings in his soul which was beyond the reach of men. God himself made the impressions on this; the fire that as it were scalded his spirit, that made him sweat clods of blood in a cold season, came down from heaven, as the fire did upon the legal altar. He never expressed so great a sorrow under all the calamities he felt in the course of his life as in the garden; he was sore amazed and very heavy: Mark xiv. 38, 34, 'he began to be sore amazed,' as if he had tasted nothing but joy in the time past of his life, and never understood the invasions of any sorrow before. He then began to feel the first impressions of that wrath due to sin, a sudden consternation seized upon his faculties. Both words, e k q a m b e s q a i (ekthambesthai) and a d h m o n e i n (ademonein), signify that his pangs were highly strained; a mere bodily death could not amaze him thus. He had a divine nature to support his human, against a mere separation of his soul from his body, since the divine nature would be separated from neither, and he knew a few days would reunite them for ever in a glorious state. Christ did as well foreknow by the promise, the glory that was to follow upon his sufferings, as he did by the precept the passion he was to undergo. It was the wrath of God, a greater bitterness than any other gall in the cup of death, that the human nature, though supported by the divine, stood looking upon with apprehensions of grief and amazement; he knew the greatness of the punishment due to sin, and the greatness of the passion he was to undergo for sin. He is called 'the Lamb of God,' a lamb of his own appointing, a lamb of his own sacrificing, distinguished from the paschal lamb by the author and giver, called the Lamb of God, whereas those were the lambs of men. In the constitution of Christ in the office of mediator, which was God's immediate act, he acted the part of a wise governor; in punishing sin in the person of our surety, thereby satisfying his justice, he acts the part of a just judge. May not the punishment of Christ be immediate by God's own hand, as well as the constitution of Christ was immediate by his own mouth? Isaac was to be the sacrifice, and Abraham the sacrificer; Isaac a child of promise, in whom the seed should be called, ordered to fall by the hand of Abraham the father of many nations: Christ's suffering represented in the one, and God's striking prefigured in the other, God seeming to intimate, that as Abraham was willing to offer up his son at his command with his own hand, so he would offer up his Son as a sacrifice for him, in whom all the nations of the earth should be blessed. It is true the devils were let loose upon him, with all the powers of darkness, Luke xxii. 53, John xv. 13, and upon the cross he combated with principalities and powers, because there he spoiled them, Col. ii. 15, they bruised his heel by their instruments, and his Father his soul by his wrath. The church of old expected and desired this: Ps. lxxx. 17, 'Let thy hand be upon the man of thy right hand, upon the Son of man,' &c. The psalmist complains of the miserable desolation of the church, for which there was no remedy but in Christ, the man of God's right hand, the man of his love. By the hand being upon a man, is meant punishing, many times in Scripture: as Ps. xxxviii. 3, 'Thy hand came upon me,' i. e. thou did strike me with a plague. Indeed, his Father mixed the cup, would not suffer it to depart from him, though he offered up supplications with strong cries; and God, who, as a righteous judge, will not clear the guilty, did sentence him to the drinking the dregs of it; and it is as righteous an act to inflict the punishment as to pronounce the sentence. He constituted him mediator by an act of sovereign mercy, he inflicted the punishment upon him by an act of sovereign justice, he sent him into the world, as the Father who had the power of mission, and bruised him upon the cross, as a judge who had the power of punishing.

1. The imputation of our iniquities to him was the act of God: Isa. liii. 6, 'The Lord has laid upon him the iniquity of us all;' "panenu", accurrere fecit incursu hostili. He gathered together the debts of men, put them into one sum, and transferred them upon Christ, as to guilt and punishment. He bound our transgression upon the back of his only Son, as Abraham did the wood upon the shoulders of his Isaac. Our sins were laid upon Christ, as the transgressions of the people were laid upon the head of the scape-goat, Lev. xvi. 20, 21, 22, which was but a type of this imputation to Christ; for their sins were not truly laid upon the goat, it had then been the antitype, not the type. Sins were confessed, fathered together by confession, laid upon the beast, which is said to bear them, he, and all that touched him, were accounted unclean. All our sins were laid upon the head of Christ by God. He it was 'made him sin for us who knew no sin, that we might become the righteousness of God in him,' 2 Cor. v. 21; not by inhesion, but imputation; not only a sacrifice for sin, but sin itself. The double antithesis in the text intimates, he was made that sin that he knew not; he knew the punishment by suffering, but he knew not the guilt by commission and practice; he was made that sin which is opposed to righteousness, and that sin was sin itself, which must be understood only as to the imputed guilt; for punishment could not have been indicted on him, unless guilt had first been imputed to him. Had he not first borne our sins, he could not have been driven into the wilderness of desertion and death. Upon this is laid the difference of his first and second appearance: Heb. ix. 28, 'So Christ was once offered to bear the sins of many, and unto them that look for him shall he appear the second time without sin unto salvation.' At his first he bore our sins, not personally inherent, but legally, after the substitution of him in our stead; counted to him as his proper debt; upon which account he 'restored what he took not away.' At the second, he shall 'appear without sin.' His nature was free from sin in his first coming, but not his condition; he had sin as our surety, though none in his person; it was impossible he could be our surety without this imputation. Upon the account of this suretyship, God reckoned him a debtor, as 'made under the law, to redeem them that were under the law,' Gal. iv. 4. That what God in justice might charge upon the bankrupt, he might, after this constitution of him under the law, by the same right charge upon the surety, for this guilt, by the Father's act of imputation, upon his own voluntary submission to take our offending nature, became his; and, therefore, what penalty was by the law due from us was to be paid by him. All punishment supposes a guilt one way or other; but the Redeemer had no personal guilt, for 'he had done no violence,' Isa. liii. 10, 'yet it pleased the Lord to bruise him, when his soul made itself an offering for sin,' imputed to him. This imputation was God's immediate act, and could not be the act of any other, because he was the sole creditor, without any partner; and therefore it is no more rejection upon God immediately to punish him, than it was to transfer our sins upon him, which was an act of God, not possible to be done by any creature. God imputed a world of sins to him, because he undertook for that world God had created by him; therefore God alone indicted upon his soul that punishment which was principally due for our sins. Since he died for our sins, he died under that hand which was to strike us for them; for God made him sin for us, i. e. he handled him as he would have done those sinners in whose stead he suffered, had he not undertaken for them.

2. His greatest sufferings appear to be above the power of any creature to indict. Was it a contest with any creature that made him desirous to waive that death, which was the main end of his coming?

(1.) How was his soul begirt with the wrath of God, before his agony in the garden! What an excess of sorrow do those words signify, Mat. xxvi. 37, Mark xiv. 33, ekqambeisqai, adhmonein, sore amazed, sorrowful, very heavy; an inward quaking, an inexpressible amazement. What a deluge fell from heaven upon our ark, of which that of Noah was a type! How was his soul ground to powder in his agony! How did his soul boil under the fire of wrath, and his blood leak through every pore of the vessel by the extremity of the flame! Must it not be more than a finite breath that thus melted his soul in the garden? Must it not be a stronger than a finite stroke, that wrung out those bitter cries? Was there any visible person to afflict him? Yet his agonies there are thought to have more of hell-fire in them, than his sufferings on the cross; clods of blood dropped from him when there was no visible hand to strike him. Inconceivable must be the afflictions of his soul, that could make such dismal commotions in his body, and put the whole instrument out of tune; that should make a dissolution of the parts, and make his heart like melted wax 'in the midst of his bowels,' Ps. xxii. 14. His spotless conscience could not flash such lightnings, as to melt the sword, when nothing touched the scabbard; his Father was then charging him with our sins, actuating his knowledge and sense of them; he had all his lifetime a knowledge of the ingratitude and rebellion of sin; he knew how it had offended and injured God, how it had deformed and ruined the creature; now was his knowledge actuated, and the charging upon him the punishment of them made his knowledge sensible and experimental. This cup discovers more bitter ingredients than any creature could wring out into it.

(2.) Could it be only the sense of an approaching bodily death, that could so deeply afflict his innocent soul? If so, he had discovered a greater weakness than many of the martyrs; nay, had been outstripped in courage by many moral heathens. His nature sure was as strong as theirs to bear it, had not his sufferings been attended with a more sensible sting than theirs were. Martyrs have suffered as great outward torments with joy, laughing in the faces of their persecutors, and edging their fury to more sharpness. But, alas, he suffered more deaths than one: Isa. liii. 9, 'He made his grave with the wicked, and with the rich in his death,' "bemuto"; the death of the soul in regard of the bitterness, though not in regard of duration. His Father inflicted what was evil, and withdrew that which was good. Were not the clouds of his Father's countenance, and a subtraction of good looks from him, a bruising him? All the outward torments of the world could not have drawn one doleful cry from any man under the full and sensible beams of God's favour, much less from Christ. Could all the instruments in hell, earth, or heaven, draw a veil between his soul and his Father's countenance? This must only be his Father's act, and was a signal stroke. It is clear there was a negative act of God, denying that comfortable presence which was due to him as a holy person by the covenant of works; and could not be denied his humanity, as united to the second person in the Trinity, had he not been in another capacity upon the cross, and not only precisely as the Son of God. The inflicting of the evil of inward punishment was sure as much the act of his Father, as the withdrawing from him an inward good, the light of his countenance. Might there not be more than a bare cloud, might there not be some bitter frowns darted upon him, since he appeared at that time in the condition of the greatest sinner? If the wrath and justice of his Father did not immediately drop upon him, how could he satisfy it; what satisfaction could arise to it, if he were not at all touched by it? The fire upon the typical altar came down from heaven, and so did this wrath which consumed our sacrifice.

3. God had a choice delight in the bruising him. With what ardency does he rouse up the sleepy sword, to sheath it in the bowels of the man that is his fellow! Zech. xiii. 7, 'Awake, O sword, against my shepherd, and against the man that is my fellow; strike the shepherd,' &c. The latter part of the verse is applied to Christ, Mat. xxvi. 31. He commands it to pursue his design with a strength like a man newly refreshed and risen from sleep, and make the deeper gashes. Never was God so pleased in drawing his sword against his creatures, as in drawing it against the man his fellow, against the Shepherd, one of Christ's titles in Scripture. It pleased the Lord to bruise him, Isa. liii. 10. God delighted in his bruising. The word "chafatz" answers to eudokian (eudokian) in the New Testament, when he says that he is well pleased in Christ as his beloved Son. In the formal condition of this action, as it was conversant about punishment, it was not delightful to God, for he does not punish with his heart: Lam. iii. 33, 'He does not afflict willingly, or grieve the children of men'; 'He delights not in the death of a sinner,' much less in the death of his Son, Ezek. xviii. 33. But as finally considered, it is highly pleasant to him in regard of his glory and man's redemption. The reason why God bruised him was not any delight simply in the death of Christ, but because in that act he broke in pieces our sins (which were the cause of the enmity) which were borne by Christ in his body upon the tree: 1 Peter ii. 14, 'Who his own self bore our sins in his own body upon the tree, that we, being dead to sin, should live unto righteousness, by whose stripes we were healed,' which is a comment on Isa. liii. 4, 5. He has home our griefs, he was smitten of God, he was bruised for our iniquities, and with his stripes we are healed. Christ appeared in that state, as bearing the whole body of sin, as well as the body of flesh. The Jews aimed at killing his body, and God aimed at killing our sin. Every stroke he fetched was not ultimately to put his Son to death, but the enmity to death; to destroy the dominion and power which sin by its guilt had derived from the law; for so being dead to sin must be understood, which is clear by observing the like phrase, Rom. vi. 11, 14, where by being dead to sin, he means sin not having dominion, or condemning power over him, which is evidenced by a suitable expression of being 'dead to the law,' Rom. vii. 4, which is no more than the law not having dominion over us in regard of the curse, as appears, ver. 1-3. It was sin which had made the breach, that God principally struck at in the bruising his

Son. He had a pleasure to bruise him as our surety, a trouble to bruise him as his Son. He was afflicted in his afflictions as his Son, and would have the sun in the heavens bear witness to it by hiding its head. But he was delighted with his sufferings as our Redeemer, because they were for the satisfaction of his justice, the condemnation of sin, and the restoration of his creature. In this respect, the death of Christ was the sweetest sacrifice that ever was offered, and consequently the smiting of him the pleasantest work that ever God engaged in.

4. The graces of Christ were most eminent in enduring the inward impressions of wrath from his Father. The odours of his graces brake out more strongly by his Father's bruising him.

(1.) His kindness and tenderness to man. Christ was now upon the highest manifestation of his compassions to mankind. His death was the emphasis of his love; his love was stronger and purer than the love of any creature, not only in regard of the excellency of his person, but the greatness of his sufferings. Had he endured only a death of the body, and not such a death that could have been inflicted only by an infinite hand, his love had lost much of its lustre. His love is principally laid upon the score of his death: Gal. ii. 20, 'Who loved me, and gave himself for me.' If his passion had been only in his body, without impressions from an higher hand upon his soul, he had been in some measure paralleled in this (except in the dignity of his person) by several, who have freely resigned their lives to the enemies' swords, and some to unexpressible torments, for the public good of their country, as the Roman Regulus to the Carthaginians, because his country should not agree to disadvantageous conditions of peace. Besides, by this inward conflict he was fitted for further tenderness, having hereby an experience of the worst men were exposed unto by sin, that he might be more tender of their welfare, and with more melting bowels solicit his Father for relief; hence did arise his strongest sympathising with the condition of men.

(2.) His obedience to his Father. It is a signal testimony given him, that he was 'obedient even to the death of the cross,' Philip. ii. 8. The sharper then his circumstances were upon the cross, the more illustrious his obedience was. The lustre of obedience is seen in engaging upon command with the most affrighting difficulties. It was a more full acknowledgement of his Father's sovereignty, and a stronger asserting his own obedience, in 'making his soul an offering for sin,' Isa. 53. 10, than if he had only made his body so by a temporal death (though I confess by soul, many times in Scripture, is only meant life), and also to have his eye fixed upon the mediatory law, and his own duty arising from thence. When his Father seems to have forgotten all the promises he had bound himself in, and shot frowns into his heart, and denied him both the light of sun and stars, comfort both from heaven and earth, he adds yet holy inflammations to obedience, which under those circumstances was most ravishing to the Father, and most meritorious for us. It was then an offering and 'a sacrifice of a sweet-smelling savour unto God,' 3:ph. v. 2.

(3.) His fiduciary trust in God, and the promises made to him, was more signal and noble. To trust a God smiling, when he does east about us nothing but cords of love, is not a case of difficulty; every man has a strong impulse to this, when God drops sweetness into him. But then is faith at the highest elevation, when a man can trust God though he kills him, and wait upon him when he hides his face and drops hell from his hand. Thus was our Saviour's faith put to the trial by this proceeding; yet he went forth conquering and to conquer, and would not let go his hold. Though his Father's beams were withdrawn, and his bowels seem contracted, the heaven overcast with darkness, and all the curses of the law let fly at him, he would still depend upon God for his help in his greatest passion: Isa. 1. 7, 9, 'The Lord God will help me;' ver. 10, 'Who is among You that fears the Lord, that obeys the voice of his servant, that walks in darkness and sees no light? let him trust in the name of the lord, and stay himself upon his God.' He would not let the storm blow these concerns of the world out of his hands, which then were managed by him; which trust of his, in this dismal time, he seems to set as a pattern for our imitation, in the words immediately following intimating we should have his faith under those dreadful circumstances always in our eyes to encourage ours.

These graces of Christ, tenderness, obedience, and trust, had not been set forth in such orient colours to us, bad not his soul drunk a cup of wrath of his Father's tempering, as well as his body felt the strokes of human fury.

5. I must add a caution or two for the better understanding this, and preventing any mistake.

(1.) Though Christ suffered from his Father an infinite wrath due to us, yet it was not necessary it should be eternally endured by him, because eternal wrath is due to us, for the eternity of punishment arises from the condition the subject suffering, not from the nature of the punishment itself. A creature being a limited nature, cannot give an infinite satisfaction commensurate to an infinite justice, without suffering eternally. Therefore though infinite punishment be due, yet eternal punishment is not in itself due, but falls in for want of the creature's ability to satisfy the demands of legal justice; since it cannot satisfy the law by one or many acts of suffering, it is always suffering, but never fully satisfies. But the infinite dignity of the person of Christ transcending all creatures, made the satisfaction he offered valuable without an eternal duration of those torments, which the insufficiency of the creature could never have made by suffering to eternity. He satisfies the debt, that pays at once the millions he owes;

but he can never satisfy, but must remain in bondage, that pays a farthing in a year when his debts amounts to millions, besides his running farther into debt while he is paying. The eternity of punishment proceeds not only from old debts, but new ones contracted by blasphemies and hatred of God; for though some say that in termino the damned do not sin, I cannot think but loving and glorifying God is the essential duty of a creature; and while he is a creature, let him be in what state he will, he is under the obligation of it. It is impossible a creature can by any conditions be freed from the obligations of loving and adoring his Creator. Christ might suffer the pains of hell, but not with all the accidental circumstances, nor in the place of hell; time and place are but accidental things, and not of the essence of punishment. It is not the place of hell makes hell, but the wrath of God, in what place soever it is poured out. A surety goes not to prison if he pays the debt; the prison is not a place of payment, but a place to enforce the payment where there is unwillingness to pay.

(2.) This act of his Father in bruising him by his wrath was no approbation of the guilt of the instruments in the death of his body. The sufferings in his soul in the garden were before the Jews had laid hands on him to apprehend him. God dropped wrath upon his soul, yet had no hand in the crime of the Jews, in the covetousness of Judas, envy of the pharisees, cowardice of Pilate, and the fury of the people: these did spring from their natural corruption; they had one end, God another; they aimed at the satisfaction of those lusts, God aimed to content his justice, declare his wisdom, manifest his mercy, clear his holiness, remove the enmity, and relieve our souls. Though God approved of the death of Christ, and 'delivered him up,' Acts ii. 23, yet he did not approve of those ends which managed them in that action. It was the highest guilt that ever was manifest upon the stage of the world in them, as it was the highest love that ever God showed in the ordering things to the redemption of man. God determined redemption by the death of his Son, but did not positively determine the evil of the instruments. God laid no inward restraints upon them, left them to act as voluntary agents; he knew what their fury would do, and resolved to govern it for his own glory and the good of the world. God had given them a free power to act otherwise; he did not necessitate them to this rage; their own corruptions met together to commit this horrid crime. They were not impelled by a command, threatening, or promise; his law was a rock against it; the destruction of their city and the dissolution of their state were assured them by our Saviour if they went on in that way; they had no motives from God, but from their own lusts, which were not of God's infusion, but engendered by themselves and inflamed by the devil. God only as a wise governor used them, and ordered them to his own glorious ends, as a man uses the ravenous disposition of his hound to catch the hare, which the hound would of itself do, and governs it to his own ends, different from that of the animal. In short, they acted utterly against the law in shedding innocent blood; God acted according to the mediatory law, in bruising him who had voluntarily substituted himself in our room; they aimed not at any one end which God aimed at in it; their intentions were wholly different. Though God approved of the death of Christ precisely considered, because he delivered him up, yet his death as managed by them was the greatest wickedness that ever the sun saw, so that the Father's bruising Christ does not in the least excuse the Jews, nor had they been excusable had their intentions concurred fully with God's in the act, unless they had received a command from him to crucify him, as Abraham had for the offering his son.

The Father then has been in Christ reconciling the world unto himself: in bruising him by his wrath, glorifying his attributes in that act, which were necessary to be manifested in our redemption, laying all our sins upon him, delighting in it as it was for his glory and our happiness, thereby winding up the graces of Christ, necessary for the exercise of his office and our redemption and imitation, to the greatest height, and thereby relieving us from that curse of the law which we must always have borne and could never have satisfied. So deep a hand had the Father in this work of redemption! The Trinity were signal in it: the Father bruising, Christ receiving the stroke, and the Spirit supporting him under it.

Use 1. How may our meditations swim in this unlimited ocean of love! Oh the depth of the riches of grace, that we should have the cursed pleasure of sinning, and Christ the bitterness of suffering; that the punishment due to us should be charged upon the Son of God by the lathers Priest the Father bruise the Son for us, who had deserved as well as devils to be kept bound in chains of darkness to the judgment of the great day? Might he not snore easily have condemned us, than condemned his beloved Son for us to a bitter death? But here he would have infinite love and infinite justice kiss each other. What could we do to deserve it? If we could merit any good, could we merit so great a gift as this? If we could have deserved that he should open his arm to embrace us, noted we merit that he should wound his Son's heart to redeem us? If we could deserve to be filled with his grace, could all the world deserve that his Son should be emptied of his glory? Could they deserve that God should be wounded by God for their transgressions? God gave Christ to die for us while we were yet sinners, Rom. v. 13, when we wanted motives of love as well as merits of grace, and had no incentive of his grace, unless the want of grace could pass for one. Were God as man, his thunder had crushed the world; the disciples, the best of man Spin earth at that time, would have been prodigal of God's thunderbolts, if they had had them in possession, when they desired fire from heaven upon the poor Samaritans. And had man a storehouse of punishment, he would empty it upon persons that notoriously wrong him; but God poured out those vials upon his own Son, which of right belonged to us. Consider, it was his Son whom he bruised, not a servant, not an unspotted angel; his only begotten Son, the brightness of his glory, the express image of his person, not an adopted Son, having only a dark representation of the divine nature; a begotten Son of his nature, not begotten of his will; a beloved Son, not a disaffected Son; an only Son, not one picked out of many children. God had no more in all the world, and yet he bruised him; he bruised him not only by a temporal death of the body, but by a weight of wrath on his soul, not to purchase some small favour, but an everlasting inheritance. How great is this love, that valued our salvation above the life of an only Son, and shed a blood more valuable than the whole creation to preserve ours, which could not be equivalent to the price of it, and put him into the posture of an enemy to his Son, to make us his friends! If the thunders of the law had been shot upon us, what strength had we to bear them? What merit to remove them? How great is the love of the Redeemer, to be willing not to be spared for a time, rather than millions of men and women should fail of being spared for ever! It was 'for our transgressions he was wounded, for our iniquities he was bruised, and the chastisement of our peace was upon him,' Isa. liii. 5. In every wound God gave him, he minded the full punishment of our sin, in the person of our Saviour, that those whom he represented might go free. He spared him not, abated not a mite of what justice might demand, that so his people might have a full redemption: Rom. viii. 82, 'He spared not his own Son, but delivered him up for us all.' He did not spare him in regard of the strength of justice, wherewith he punished him. What could more enhance the love of God than the terrors inflicted on Christ! And what could more enhance the love of Christ, than that he endured not only a bodily death, but a wrathful death in his soul for us!

2. Let then this love engage every man to come to God through Christ. how should it ravish us into an humble compliance with him, and subjection to him! If he has bruised him for us, he will not bruise us if we come to him. The blood shed by the order of God, is able to expiate a world of sins. God has spent his wrath upon him, and has none for those that accept of him. God has discovered a propensity to be reconciled, though we lie open to the stroke of his justice, and have no strength to withstand him; a higher evidence he cannot give.

3. Spare nothing for God. He spared not the best thing he had in possession, and shall we spare our lust from being mortified by him? The sin of man grieved him more than the death of his Son; shall we preserve that which grieves him, and slight that which was his greatest pleasure? How comes it to pass we are so indulgent to our lusts, and murmur to be parted from that which is the grief of God and the ruin of our souls? Are those destroyers of our souls so extremely dear to us, that we are loath to bring them out of our bosoms, and deliver them to a crucifixion; no, not in love to that God who melted that Son in the fire of his wrath out of love to us, whom he had cherished by the warmth of his bosom from eternity? Sure if our souls were all flint, being smitten by such a love, they should yield some fire to consume our corruptions. Bow hateful should sin be to us, since it is evidenced to be so hateful to God, as that he would not spare his only begotten Son, when he lay under the imputation of our iniquities, and caused the curses of the law to meet on him with all their stings, upon whom our sins had met in all their guilt! Why should we spare that, for which God did not spare his Son who never offended him, but highly pleased him, and in this very act, too, of bowing down under his strokes by reason of our transgressions? Why should we indulge that in our hearts, which God has discovered by this act to be so abominable and odious to him, and so deserving an object of his just indignation? Let not that find rest in our bosoms, under which, while our Saviour was in the form of a servant, he found no rest from the curses of the law and the wrath of his Father, till it had bruised him, and offered him up as a sacrifice of atonement for it.

6. The Father was in Christ reconciling the world, in accepting him, and his expiatory reconciling sacrifice. The steam of his precious blood went directly up to heaven, as the smoke of the sacrifices ascended right up to heaven (as they say), not blown aside by any wind. This gave God a rest, of which sin after the creation had endeavoured to despoil him, for if God had a complacency in the work of creation,ówhich is signified by the word refreshed, Exod. xxxi. 17, "yinafesh", 'In six days the Cord made heaven and earth, and on the seventh day he rested, and was refreshed;'ómuch more must God be refreshed by the work of redemption by Christ, it being a restoring God's rest to him by a new creation, and a greater glory to God than the work of creation was, or, simply considered, could be. God did perform what was incumbent on his part, according to the covenant of redemption, in regard of acceptation, after Christ had trod the wine-press alone; and his grace was of the same tenor in the entertainment of Christ. after his work, as it was in the first designation and call of him to it, the foundation and the topstone being all the fruit of a condescending grace. The grace of God accepted it, and justice could plead nothing against it; grace and justice took him by each arm and led him to the throne of glory. It was God that justified him, Isa. 1. 8. His entrance into heaven, with the same clothes of flesh he wore upon the earth, only changed in the fashion suitable to that glorious country to which he was returning, was an evidence of his full acceptance.

(1.) It is evident that the Father did accept him.

[1.] The types and representations of this reconciling sacrifice were grateful to God upon this account. That first sacrifice after the deluge was a sweet savour, or a savour of rest: Gen. viii. 21, 'And the Lord smelt a sweet savour'; and the Lord said in his heart, I will not any more curse the ground for man's sake,' "hanikhakh". He smelt in that sacrifice a savour of that wherein he should have a rest, and which should fully quiet his mind; and such a rest, that he said in his heart, or swore, Isa. liv. 9. The oath there mentioned can refer to no other place but this. For the sake of the antitype, which was respected in that offering, God swore that he would not any more curse the ground for man's sake. What influence could the steam of the blood of a beast, and the stench of the burning fat, have upon a spiritual substance, an angel, much less upon God? Could the blood and burnt caresses of a few silly animals appease God, so much as to engage him to make so magnificent a promise, not to curse the ground any more for man's sake, when the doleful cries, and vehement supplications of multitudes of dying men in the deluge, could not persuade him to stop his hand, and shut up the flood-gates of heaven? Could this make him order the constant course of nature, and succession of times, when in the very moment he promised it he considered the perpetual fountain of evil in the heart of man, that 'the imagination of his heart was evil from his youth?' No; but God was pleased with a resemblance of Christ, presented to him in the faith of the offerer; as a man is with the picture of his friend whom he dearly esteems, and loves the person that presents such a medal to him, because of the estimation he has of his friend. If the picture be so acceptable, because of the relation it has to a delightful object, how much more dear is the object itself! In the day of the general expiation of the Jews, the sins of the people were atoned by the sacrifice of the beast, and sprinkling of the blood; what force had the blood of a brute to wash off the sins of a rational creature, and those of a nation? But this typified the mighty acceptableness of the blood of Christ, satisfactory to justice, and pleasing to the mercy of God, whence all sacrifices received what efficacy they had. God's being pleased with this sacrifice of Noah, and others of his own appointing, was but to testify how highly pleasing the death of his Son would be to him, as it was an atoning sacrifice, and sweeter than the iniquities of men were loathsome, both being under his consideration at one and the same time.

[2.] The time of Christ's coming, and being in the world, is called by way of eminency an acceptable time, much more was his suffering so, which was the complement of his humiliation work. It was an acceptable time, because it was a day of salvation for man: Isa. xlix. 8, 'In an acceptable time have I heard thee, and in the day of salvation have I helped thee.' They are the words of the Father to Christ, wherein he assures him of the acceptance of his sacrifice extensively for the Gentiles: 'I will give thee for a covenant to the people;' which place the apostle uses as an argument to press the Corinthians to the sincere embracing of the gospel, 2 Cor. vi. 2, because it was an acceptable time, a time wherein Christ was accepted, and all believers accepted upon his account; a time acceptable to God in the prophet; a time which therefore ought to be acceptable to man, as the apostle infers. It is therefore called the acceptable year of the Lord: Isa. lxi. 2, 'To proclaim the acceptable year of the Lord.' The clearest, and serenest time that ever God saw since the creation of the world. Why was it so acceptable? Because it was the day of vengeance of our God, a day of vengeance upon sin, a day of the taking away and removal of that which had caused all the enmity. Upon the knowledge of God's approbation of it, Christ prays for his assistance in the time of his suffering, Ps. lxix. 13. A psalm of Christ, as appears, ver. 9, 21, applied to him in the Gospel, 'As for me, my prayer is unto thee in an acceptable time: O God, in the multitude of thy mercy hear me, in the truth of thy salvation,' when the whole world was set against him, and he was made the song of the drunkards; the time wherein he put it up, and the circumstances he was in, were pleasing to God, as being for his greatest service and glory. Let the mercy which engaged me first in this attempt, and the promise thou hast made me of the salvation of man, move thee to hear me now, and to manifest the truth of thy salvation which thou Last committed to me, and I am now upon the effecting of. When was this acceptable time? this tl81 By? When he was in the mire and deep waters, ver. 14; when he was reproached, and full of heaviness, ver. 20; when they gave him gall for his meat, and in his thirst vinegar to drink; then was the time of this highest acceptation with God for the redemption of man.

[3.] All the fruits of his death manifest God's high acceptation of it.

First, The mission of the Spirit. The great end why the Spirit was sent, was to manifest this acceptance; to evidence to the world that Christ was no impostor, because he was gone to the Father, John xvi. 7-10, and had a welcome in heaven. The coming of the Spirit, and the working miracles in the name of Christ, kept up the credit of his mission and authority from the Father in the world. lie was sent by the Father, in the name of Christ: John xiv. 26, 'The Holy Ghost, whom the Father will send in my name,' i. e. upon the account of his mediation, as a fruit of it. His name would have been of no authority for so great a gift, had not his death been of a grateful efficacy. And by the virtue of his intercession, John xiv. 16, 'I will pray the Father, and he will give you another Comforter,'óGod unlocks to him all his treasures, as a testimony of the pleasure he took in his death, and the completeness of it to appease his anger, and satisfy the most extensive demands of his justice. So high a favour could not be dispensed, if justice had not first been fully contented. This Spirit was also to abide for ever with his people: John xvi. 16, 'That he may abide with you for ever;' which sheds the everlasting acceptance of this sacrifice by God; for since the first coming of the Spirit was upon the first acceptance of his offering, the abiding of the Spirit evidences the perpetual prevalence of it with God; for he could not abide any longer than the ground of his mission did endure, for they must both run parallel. Now, had he not gone away, the Comforter would not have come, John xvi. 7, which refers not only to his ascension, but to his passion. And had he gone, and his death been unapproved by God, the Spirit had stayed in heaven. His work also testifies this approbation. He was to 'bring things to remembrance, whatsoever Christ had said to them,' John xiv. 26, which would never have been, had not Christ in every little been faithful to his Father's instructions. He was not to speak of himself, John xvi. 13; he was not to be the author of a new doctrine in the church, but to impress upon men what Christ had taught, and what he had wrought by his passion; he is therefore called the Spirit of truth, teaching and clearing up to the minds of men that truth which Christ had taught, and confirmed by his blood. There was no error or mistake in any part of the management of this work on Christ's part; for the Spirit is not sent to rectify anything, but to raise the superstructure upon that foundation Christ had already laid. He was to declare only what he heard, John xvi. 13, 14; to act the part of a minister to Christ, as Christ had acted the part of a minister to his Father; to glorify Christ, to manifest the fullness of his merit, and the benefits of his purchase; for he was to receive of Christ, i.e. the things of Christ, his truth and his grace, and manifest it to their souls, and imprint upon them the comfort of both. There had been no foundation to glorify Christ, had not Christ in this work been glorious in the eyes of God, and been acknowledged by the Father to have glorified him to the utmost. Now since all this is come to pass, according as Christ did predict it, it is an undeniable evidence that the Father has fully approved of Christ's faithfulness in his office, and rests highly contented by his death.

Secondly, The answer of prayers in his name. As his acceptance by the Father was the ground of all the miracles which were wrought in the name of the Son after his ascension, 60 it is the ground of all the answers of prayer that any believer receives from God, for our Saviour joins them both together: John xiv. 12, 13, 'He that believes in me shall do greater works than these, because I go to the Father; and whatsoever you shall ask in my name, that will I do, that the Father may be glorified in the Son.' 'Whatsoever you ask in my name,' i. e. says Cajetan, for my glory, not only in the intention of the petitioner, but the direct tendency of the thing petitioned for, I will do. His poker to do it, is an argument of the strength of his oblation, and validity of the price. 'That the Father may be glorified in the Son,' which is the end for which our prayers are answered, and is the event of those mercies we receive as answers from the hands of Christ. The Father is glorified in the success of Christ's mediation, and the 'finishing the work he gave him to do,' John xvii. Every return of prayer, upon the account of the merit of Christ, is a testimony of this success; and glory redounds by it to the wisdom of the Father, for contriving; to the kindness of the Father, for appointing so able a Saviour, who could fully satisfy all the concerns of God, and provide for the necessities of the creature, and lay a foundation for the full communication of all mercies needful for him. His receiving from his Father the keys of all his stores, to dispense to believers, manifests how welcome he was to the Father upon his return, after his conflict in the world, and how successful he was in his execution of his office, and how fully he contented the justice of his Father, which could not by any right keep those stores from him after his meritorious passion, so that in every answer of prayer, the wisdom, love, righteousness of the Father are glorified, in the obedience, merit, and purchase of his Son; the love of the Father is manifested in sending so sufficient a mediator; and the justice and grace of the Father is glorified in accepting him, and performing the conditions requisite on his part by the covenant of redemption. There is a most intimate conjunction of the glory of the Father and the glory of the Son in this mediation of Christ, which is the foundation of the acceptation of him, and his acceptation upon the same foundation will be perpetual; because, as whatsoever he did here was for the glory of his Father, whatsoever he does above also, in distributing his gifts, communicating his grace, is for the same end, and therefore can never be unacceptable; for, by this acceptation of him, the Father has a current and standing revenue of glory established; his exchequer is daily filled with it, by virtue of this approbation. This acceptance is writ upon every return of our supplications, put up in his name, and tending to his glory; the wonderful effects whereof have been known in all ages, and in the private experience of every sincere Christian. Would God ever listen to those pleas in his name, were he not well pleased with the sacrifice of his person? Would God ever expend his gifts to man, to keep up the credit of a person he had disowned? This is the ground of that near communion believers have with God, nearer than Adam was admitted to in paradise, wherein God condescends to the familiar expressions of his grace, and converses with men in and through a mediator, who before were alienated from him, and made the marks of his wrath. The 'golden altar with incense,' Rev. viii. 3. is the pleasant perfume of his merits.

[4.] The content God has in men's believing on Christ manifests it. God has made faith, the acceptance of him by men, the only condition of enjoying the fruits of his purchase; and it is not all the amiable virtues in the world, nor the riches of the whole creation, can procure us any right or title to him without it. So much does the Father stand upon the honour of his Son, that he will not grant an eternal happiness to any but those that join with him in a sincere and hearty acceptation and approbation of him, his meritorious death, and the righteousness evidenced thereby. Without this, no beams of glory can sparkle upon us, but an eternal wrath will swallow us up. As the Father has approved him, so as to give all power into his hands, so he wills us to approve him, so as to bring all our own righteousness to the footstool of Christ, and embrace him only by a naked faith, that nothing of the glory of his work and merit may be clouded by any thing of our own. A true, willing, cordial, lively acceptance is required, a resting on him for salvation, as God rests on him upon his satisfaction. An estimation of him approaching as near as a creature can to that of God's; the knowledge and embracing of him is the best savour to God, next to that of his own oblation; and man only in a believing embracing, stands in his true posture of acceptation with God.

[5.] The naked declarations of Christ to the world are acceptable to God. The very discourses, and the discoursers of it, are a sweet savour to God: 2 Cor. ii. 15, 'We are unto God a sweet savour of Christ, in them that are saved, and in them that perish.' Yea, though men cast away the thoughts of him, and perish in their unbelief; yet the proposal of it to them for their acceptance is very sweet to the thoughts of God. As he will express how high his acceptation of them was, in the gifts of eternal happiness to them that entertain him, so the rejecters shall learn the same in the severity of the punishment inflicted on them. But whatever men do, the sound of it in the world is a sweet savour to him; and all men shall be at last convinced, that his righteousness was acceptable to God, because he is gone to the Father.

(2.) God accepted him with a mighty pleasure. As soon as he was made perfect by his sufferings, he was saluted an high priest, 'called an high priest,' Heb. v. 10, ProsagoreuqeiV saluted; prosagoreuei, aspazetai (Hesych.) When, by the accomplishment of his passion, he became the author of eternal salvation, God congratulates him for his attainment of a new honour by his consecration, as men congratulate one another upon new acquisitions. It was a 'sweet smelling savour to God,' Eph. v. 2; there was eudokia in his mission, and euwdia in his passion. God smelled a greater fragrance in his death than stench from our sins; the sweetness of the one did drown the noisomeness of the other: his death was more satisfying to God than our sins were displeasing. As he was a vine, he sent forth a delicious fruit of his blood to cheer both the heart of God and man; of God, by the fragrance of his satisfaction; of man, by the fullness of his merit. God's soul delighted in him, Isa. xiii. 1. He had an overflowing joy. All the attributes of God, which are the soul and perfections of the Deity, had an undisturbed acquiescence in him. There was an unblemished exactness in his work, because there was a fullness of delight in his Father. The delight he took in his designation was rather heightened than diminished by his faithfulness in the execution. He was, after his death, brought near before God: Dan. vii. 13, 'One like the Son of man came with the clouds of heaven, and came to the ancient of days, and they brought him near before him,' two words to express the height of pleasure, near and before him. As if God would express his pleasure in the strait and intimate embraces of his Son, after his great engagement and return from the battle; and so welcome he was, that God presented him with the dominion of the whole world. For the order of the vision expresses first his incarnation, and then his exaltation; so that this being 'brought near before the ancient of days,' must be upon his ascension just after his death, and before his full investiture in the dominion of the world.

[1.] He pleased him more than all the sacrifices under the Jewish economy; far more than all the devoted creatures, than oxen and bullocks which have horns and hoofs; it is the expression concerning Christ, Ps. lxix. 31. A mark of eminency, a how much more is put upon this offering, above the virtue of the blood of bulls and goats, Heb. ix. 13, 14. Though they were instituted by God, yet they were not acceptable to God for the removal of sin, 'neither could make the offerer perfect before him,' Heb. x. 1. Nor could the heaps of sacrificed animals, the streams of brutish blood, persuade him to the justification of any one offerer: 'In burnt offerings or sacrifices he had no pleasure,' or rest, Heb. x. 6. He had a pleasure in them, not as they were the sacrifices of beasts, but representations of his Son's passion, and appointed as remembrances before him, of what was to be suffered by the true object of his rest in time. Christ is the person, and his death the sacrifice, wherein God only can find a rest: Isa. lxvi. 1, 2, 'Thus says the Lord, The heaven is my throne, and the earth is my footstool: where is the house that you build unto me? and where is the place of my rest? For all those things has my hand made, and all these things have been, says the Lord: but to this will I look, to the poor and a contrite spirit, and that trembles at my word.' The temple and temple-worship was not the place of his rest; God speaks with contempt of them, and seems to cast in the whole created compares of heaven and earth, as no firm object of his pleasure. But to this will I look, i. e. this poor and contrite spirit, "nkheh", stricken; of the same root as "makhah", smitten of God and afflicted: Isa. liii. 4, 'That trembled at my word;' he speaks as of one that trembled under the curses of the law, and felt the weight and bitterness of them; to him will I look, or intently or fixedly look, as the word signifies. The word tremble, "kharad", signifies to be careful or solicitous, as, 2 Kings iv. 13, it is so translated, Thou hast been careful for us with all this care,' though it signifies also to tremble. Who was more stricken than Christ? Who more careful of the honour of God's law than Christ? Or who tasted more of the gall of the curse than Christ? Who can that signal mark this point to, but Christ? Who can be set in the balance with the whole frame of the creation, angels and men, but Christ? 'All those things has my hand made,' which seems to refer not only to the temple, but to the heavens, his throne, and the earth, his footstool; all those have been, and yet no rest found in them. Now after the coming and striking of this person, upon whom the eye of God is intent, an end is put to all the ceremonial sacrifices: ver. 3, 'He that kills an ox, is as if he slew a man; he that sacrificeth a lamb, as if he cut off a dog's neck,' &c. It was a disgrace to him for men to think he could be pleased with such sacrifices, when he had appointed and accepted another; if they then kept them up, they should be an abomination to him, as the blood of swine, and yet they kept them up after this poor stricken spirit, after the offering of his Son: he calls them 'their own ways, their abominations in which he delighted not.' And ver. 4, he would 'bring their fears upon them;' perhaps it may be meant of their fear of the Romans, which you know they pretended, for the putting Christ to death, thereby to prevent any occasion of an invasion; and ver. 6, he prophesies of their destruction. But before this destruction she should be 'delivered of a man child,' ver. 7. You know how he armed the Romans against them, discharged his wrath upon them, gave up the city and temple, which they (and even their enemies) studied to preserve, for the death of his Son, as a prey to the fury and avarice of the enemies. I have been the longer upon it, to show there is some ground to understand this place principally of Christ, though not to exclude the common interpretation; perhaps we might have had more ground for the understanding it so from Stephen's discourse, Acts vii., where he ends his citations with this place of Scripture, ver. 48, 49, and descending to the application of what he had before cited, and charging upon them the blood of Christ, was interrupted by the fury of the Jews from any further light which his discourse might have given us. To consider it again, God demands where the place of his rest was? They might answer, the heavens. No; all these has mine hand made, yet no rest in them; but to this I will look; this is my rest, as the antithesis carries it; this stricken in spirit, as if he had pointed to Christ on the cross and in the garden, trembling under a sense of wrath. An intent look is a look of expectation, or a look of pleasure.

[2.] He shows his mighty pleasure in the acceptance of him by a public proclamation as it were: Heb. i. 6, 'Again, when he brings his first begotten into the world, he says, And let all the angels of God worship him.' Or as some read it, 'And when he brings his first begotten into the world again,' understanding it of his resurrection, he then proclaims him to the angels as an object of worship, He is the heir appointed, as well as the heir eternally begotten, proclaimed to the angels as their head, and the root of their standing. He was 'seen of angels,' manifested to them in such a manner as their head, after he was justified by the Spirit, 1 Tim. iii 16. Methinks being 'seen of angels' should signify something more than the simple vision. he was 'justified by the Spirit,' when he was quickened and raised by the Spirit, 1 Peter iii. 18. His being 'preached among the Gentiles, believed on in the world, and received up into glory,' were evidences of this acceptance of him by the Father. He brings him after his resurrection, as he did Adam after his creation, into the possession of the world, and gave him dominion over the creatures. He brings in his Son, and gives him an empire over the angels as he was mediator, which he had before as he was God blessed for ever; and the angels praise him, and acknowledge him 'worthy,' as the lamb slain, 'to receive power, and riches, and wisdom, and strength, and honour, and glory, and blessing,' Rev. v. 11, 12.

[3.] He declares the pleasure he had in his acceptation of him, by fixing his love for ever upon him. He was settled in his Father's love, because he had performed the mediatory command: John xv. 10, 'If you keep my commandments, you shall abide in my love; even as I have kept my Father's commandments, and abide in his love.' A commandment was given him, and a commandment was kept by him, which obedience has been hitherto the foundation of his Father's love to him as mediator; and when he had fully finished it, would make a fixation of his Father's love. If he had not performed the mediatory command, he had had no interest in his Father's affections; as poor creatures if they observe the commands of Christ, shall for ever be rooted in his love, never to be cast out. So is Christ, upon the observation of the command his Father gave, for ever settled in his affection and acceptation, whereby be has given us assurance, that he was in Christ reconciling the world.

(3.) As the Father accepted Christ, and accepted him with a mighty pleasure, so this acceptation of him and his death redounds to every believer. Grace and glory depend upon this; take away God's approbation, and the whole chain of privileges, linked together by it, falls in pieces.

[1.] It is the stability of the covenant. His approach to God as a surety, having engaged his heart for us, is that which God speaks of with a pleasing astonishment, and is so transcendently taken with it, that he settles the covenant of being their God, and making them his people upon it; that is the issue, Jer. xxx. 21, 22. And the everlastingness of the covenant is founded in his being a witness to the people: Isa. lv. 3, 4, 'I will make an everlasting covenant with you; behold, I have given him for a witness to the people.' All the promises of God are yea and amen, in him the faithful and true witness, Rev. iii. 14.

[2.] Justification is founded upon this acceptance. God was in Christ reconciling the world, i. e. not imputing their trespasses to them, but discharging them. For the pleasure he took in Christ's sufferings upon mount Calvary, he graciously forgets our sins, and of rebels entitles us heirs. There is a fundamental justification of future believers in the discharge of Christ, though not formal and actual till they believe. As there was a fundamental condemnation of all in the loins of Adam upon his fall, not actual till they were in being, and did actually partake of his nature; so Christ having his discharge as a common person, all those whose sins he bore have a fundamental discharge in that of his person from any more suffering. As he bore the sins of many as a common person in the offering of himself and satisfied for their guilt, so he has an absolution as the head from al; that guilt he bore; no more to lie under the burden of our sins, or endure any penalties of the law for them: Heb. ix. 27, 'As it is appointed unto men once to die, and after that the judgment, so Christ was once offered for the sins of many; and unto them that look for him shall he appear without sin unto salvation.' As judgment is appointed for all men, as well as death, and they receive their judgment after death, so Christ after his death was judged by God, and judged perfect, fully answering the will and ends of God, and shall not appear any more as a sacrifice, but as a perfect Saviour. He is no more to appear in a corruptible body prepared to bear sin try imputation, but in a glorious body, as a manifestation of his justification, fitted for the comfort of those that look for him. Unto them does this judgment extend, for upon the score of this judgment passed by God in his behalf, he is to appear at length to them for salvation. For if Christ satisfied for believers, he is accepted by God on their behalf; therefore his sufferings are imputed to them; for it would be strange that Christ should endure a punishment for them, be approved of God as standing in their stead, and his acceptance not be counted to them. If there be an approbation of his sufferings for us, there is an imputation of his sufferings to us, or else no satisfaction is mice to justice upon our account. As he suffered, so he was acquitted as our surety and representative.

[3.] The acceptation of our persons and services redounds to us from the Father's acceptance of Christ. His love to Christ as mediator, is the ground of our acceptation: Eph. i. 6, 'To the praise of the glory of his grace, wherein he has made us accepted in the beloved.' He chose him first as the head, and his members in him; he accepts him as the first beloved, and believers in him. Had not Christ been accepted first, none could have pretended an holiness worthy of the notice of God. The grace of God is the cause, his love to Christ the ground, acceptation of us in him the effect of both. In ourselves, we are the objects of his anger; in Christ, the marks of his choice affection. It is the pleasure God took in the obedience of his Son, which makes believers as his members, and their services, though weak imitations of him, delightful to God.

[4.] The constant wooings of men by God flow from hence. He entreats and beseeches men to embrace him, to be reconciled to him, because he has been thus reconciling the world in Christ: 2 Cor. v. 20, 'As though God did beseech you by us, be ye reconciled to God.' The entreaty and arguments used to persuade men to the acceptance of it, could have no validity without this foundation, that a reconciliation is wrought, and the expiatory sufferings of Christ accepted by God. So much is God in love with Christ's performance, that he condescends to the lowest step, to beseech and solicit the creatures' affections for him, and presses them with that sweet importunity, as loath to take any denial at their hands.

Use 1. See the inexpressible value of Christ's mediation with God. God truth given the highest evidence of the grandeur of it, of Christ's faithfulness in the discharge of the trust committed to him, glorifying the Father in all that he undertook and taught. It is from his being a 'righteous branch,' that he is become the Lord our righteousness, Jer. xiii. 5, 6. He was by his voluntary submission, and his Father's designation, made sin for us, which performance is so grateful, that all that believe in him are made not bare righteousness, but 'the righteousness of God in him.' He seems to become sin itself, wholly guilt, and believers thereby righteousness itself in the presence of God. His death is so valuable as to procure the casting our sins into the depths of the sea, and the advancing our persons to the heights of glory, to stand before God in his kingdom. Our persons, odious in Adam, are made beautiful in Christ; and our duties, that smell rank by nature, smell sweet by his merits, Rev. v. 8. The odours of his merits are so strong as to overcome the stench of our nature. There is no need of any masses, human satisfactions, and additions of any merits of our own.

2. Comfort to believers. Since this acceptance, how does justice itself smile! The rod of God's fury falls out of his hand upon the sweetness of his Son's offering, and gives way to a sceptre of grace; nothing was omitted which was Necessary for the pleasure of God's piercing eye. This may well calm the fears in our hearts, because it smooths the frowns in God's face. If no charge can be brought against Christ since the acknowledgement of the sufficiency of his offering, no charge can be brought against believers. For whom was it performed, but for them? For whom was it accepted, but for them? The acceptation must be for the same ends for which his sufferings were endured, shall not then the influence of it upon them answer the intention of it for them? If it should not, the first acceptation would be in vain, Christ must then return to offer another sacrifice, which shall never be. In the acceptation of Christ for you, he has accepted you in him. He stood in no need of it, but in relation to you, he was the eternal Son of God, acceptable to the Father, but by this he is established an eternal Saviour. An obedient faith on our part will entitle us to salvation on his part: Heb. v. 9, 'And being made perfect, he became the author of eternal salvation unto all them that obey him.' Since God has accepted him for you, God will appear full of omniscience to understand your wants, full of compassion to pity you, full of power to relieve you, full of wisdom to guide you, full of grace to pardon you, full of glory to bless you for ever. Every believer will be accepted by God, because by his faith he owns that which gives

God a rest; and as the grace of God assists him, so he contributes to God's contentment. Oh, then, remember your offences against God, to be humbled; and God's acceptation of the blessed offering, to be comforted. The odour of this sacrifice was so agreeable to God, that, not content to discharge us from the condemnation we had merited, he would also that we should partake of the life, and enjoy the kingdom of his Son, judging it not equity to make any separation between the head and the members, the redeemer and the redeemed, and a disparagement to the greatness of the offer, and offering, to shut heaven against them. Hereby is not only condemnation removed, but eternal glory assured. It is not only a not perishing, but an eternal life upon faith, John iii. 16.

3. This is the main foundation of faith. How invaluable had all Christ's sufferings been and how vain our faith, had God disapproved him; justice had been armed against us if a blemish had been in the oblation. Faith first reads Christ's commission, then casts its eye upon the streams of blood flowing from his heart, listens to his doleful cries, considers them for itself, but ultimately rests itself in God's acknowledgement of the full discharge of the debt, and his cancelling the obligation wherein Christ was bound. After this, none have any excuse for Unbelief, unless they will accuse God of weakness, or falsity, and imposture in bearing witness to the faithfulness of one who had not discharged his office.

4. Glorify God. It is the use Christ in the prophetic psalm makes of it: Ps. xxii. 23, 24, 'Praise ye the Lord, all ye the seed of Jacob; glorify him, all ye the seed of Israel: for he has not despised nor abhorred the affliction of the afflicted; neither has he hid his face from him:' a meiosis. His face indeed was hid for a time, but to return with fresher and brighter beams; and the warmth at the return made a recompense for the clouds upon the cross. How should our beasts swell with praise, as heaven did with joy, and the thankful gladness of our hearts keep time with the joyful acceptance of his Father!

5. Accept Christ. What is worthy of God's acceptation cannot be unworthy of ours. If this be agreeable to the fountain of goodness, why should it not be grateful to the derived streams? That which gratifies an infinite ocean of purity would surely gratify us, were we not abominable sinks of corruption. It is the highest contrariety to God not to seek and acknowledge rest in that wherein God finds a full content. If the pure eye of God behold not the least spot to disturb, but a commensurate goodness to settle his rest, what can we see in Christ which should make us nauseate him? Christ is the object of God's rest, and well may be of ours. As God rested not in anything after the degeneracy of the world but in Christ, so neither should we rest in anything since the degeneracy of our hearts but in the same object. God will love us highly for our acceptance of him. God is highly pleased with his creatures' converse with him in and by a mediator: Deut. xviii. 16, 17, 'They have well spoken that which they have spoken,' when they desired that God would not speak to them but by Moses, a type of the Mediator. God never gave them so great a commendation as in this case, nor ever approved so highly of any action or words that came from the body of this people. God dwells above in the clouds, we cannot come to him but by Christ. He is a God of vengeance; and we the meritors of it; we cannot he screened from his wrath but by Christ; accept him, and God will accept TIS in him; refuse him, and all the other righteousness in the world cannot secure us. Let God's. approbation be the director of ours. Acceptance of Christ is a noble imitation of God.

7. God raised him. There was a necessity of his resurrection in regard of the predictions; for since the Messiah was to die, and not see corruption,ó Ps. xvi. 10, 'Thou wilt not suffer thy holy fine to see corruption,'óit is clear he was to rise again, else his body in a natural course would have seen corruption. This resurrection is a clear evidence of his acceptation; himself uses this as an argument both of the authority of his commission and fidelity in execution: John ii. 18, 19, 21, 'Destroy this temple, and in three days I will raise it up,' speaking of the temple of his body. Rev. i. 5, he is the 'faithful witness,' manifested to be so by being the 'first begotten from the dead.' Without his resurrection, his acceptation had not been manifest; neither could he have appeared in the quality of a Redeemer and High Priest, had he, like one of us, lain rotting in his grave; he had not, without it, been powerfully declared to be the true Son of God, nor consequently evidenced to be our Redeemer, nor been in a capacity, according to the decree, to reign to the ends of the earth. All men would have concluded him an impostor' but by rising up from the power of an ignominious death, he was manifested to angels and men to be not only God's beloved Son, but his obedient servant, faithful in all his will, the exact revealer of his counsels, and grateful to him in his sufferings, whereby not only the valuableness and sufficiency of his passion for a foundation of everlasting reconcilement, but the actual acceptance of it, was evidenced. It was a testimony to Christ of his faithfulness, a testimony to us of the approbation of his sacrifice for those purposes for which it was offered As his resurrection by the Father was, as it were, a new generation of him as the Son of God,óRom. i. 4, 'Declared to be the Son of God with power by his resurrection from the dead,'óso it was as a new constitution of him as the mediator of men. Himself calls his resurrection a regeneration, Mat xix. 28, and he is therefore called not the first risen, but the first-born from the dead: Col. i. 18, 'Who is the beginning, the first-born from the dead,' this being a new birth of him from the womb of the earth. It is a rule in the language of the Scripture, aliquid factum dicitur, cum factum esse demonstratur. Hereby his person was owned to be the Son of God, and his works and suffering, as our Redeemer, were declared highly pleasing; the suit was depending till his resurrection, but then the

controversy between God and sinners upon the account of the law was at an end, and the bond was cancelled in token of full satisfaction. The public decree of God determined it; the decree is extant, Ps. ii. 7; the interpretation of it, Acts xiii. 33, 'God has fulfilled the same unto us, in that he has raised up Jesus again; as it is also written in the second psalm, Thou art my Son, this day have I begotten thee.' Thus was he justified and declared righteous, and his obedience, which run through all his acts, exceeding acceptable. He was indeed approved of God by miracles, which God did by him in the time of tie life, Acts ii. 22; and by such miracles that could not fall under any jealousy, but by those he was testified to be a prophet, a man approved of God, a teacher come from God, as Nicodemus argues, John iii. 2. But by his resurrection he was testified to be more than a man, the Son of God in his majesty. Notwithstanding the miracles of his life, he appeared in the form of a servant, and scarce assumed any other title than that of the Son of man; but after he had by his conquest made death his captive, he illustriously appears to be the Son of God, the glory of which is increased by his ascension, exaltation, and the plentiful effusion of the Spirit: by all which his righteousness and obedience was declared to be pure without any mixture, perfect without any defect, clear gold without any dross, and a full payment of the utmost farthing to divine justice for believing sinners.

(1.) It was the act of the Father. The body of Christ was raised, and resurrection is not the work of either soul or body, but of God only. God raised him from the dead in such a manner as to declare him to be his Son. It being the declaration of the Father, his resurrection was the act of the Father: 'God raised him from the dead,' Acts xiii. 30, 33. Upon which account God is set forth in this raising Christ as the object of faith: Rom. iv. 24, 'If you believe on him, who raised up Jesus our Lord from the dead.' This being, as it were, a new begetting him, was the act of the Father, whose Son he was by eternal generation. It is particularly ascribed to the Father: Rom. vi. 4, 'As Christ was raised up from the dead by the glory of the Father;' by the glorious power of the Father, which was made illustrious in it. Some take glory of the Father for the formal cause, as though the meaning were, Christ in his resurrection was adorned with the glory of the Father; others for the final cause, he rose to the glory of the Father; but to take it for the efficient cause is more natural; as the love of the Father was most magnificent in giving him to die, so the power of the Father is most glorious in unloosing the bands of death, and delivering him from the grave with triumph; because the reuniting the soul to the body, and restoring it to all the functions of life, in an act of creative power. And this resurrection was more glorious than a single creation, in regard of the mighty load of guilt Christ lay by imputation under when upon the cross. It is true this resurrection was the work of the Trinity, it was the work of the Spirit; he is therefore said to be 'quickened by the Spirit,' 1 Pet. iii. 18, and 'justified in the Spirit,' 1 Tim. iii. 16. His resurrection was the justification of his person in all that he performed for the satisfaction of God. Christ also is said to raise himself: John ii. 19, 'I will raise it up,' and had an authority to 'take up his life again,' John x. 18. As he is said to conquer his enemies, 1 Cor. xv. 25, 'he must reign, till he has put all enemies under his feet;' yet the Father is said to do it, Ps. cx. 1; for acts of power are more peculiarly ascribed to the Father, and resurrection is an act of omnipotence, as wisdom is ascribed to the Son, and love to the Holy Ghost. The conquest of his enemies is the act of his Father, and therefore the beginning of his triumph, and the overpowering the great enemy death. And as he waits at God's right hand till his enemies be subdued, so he waited in the grave till his discharge was ordered by the Father.

(2.) It was most congruous and regular for the Father to be principal in the raising Christ. The Father had the power of mission, and therefore of acceptation; and therefore the act whereby it was declared did principally pertain to the Father, as it was a fall manifestation of the faithfulness of Christ in his office. As he received his commission from his Father, so it was most regular he should receive his discharge from the same hand, because he had been faithful to him that appointed him. The Father was the creditor, he had covenanted with his Father to suffer and give him satisfaction; the Father then was the most proper judge whether the articles were performed or no, whether the satisfaction was valid and the debt paid. As the Father was the lawgiver and judge, the delivering Christ to death belonged to him; upon the same account the delivering him from prison and judgment belonged to the Father. None have power to remit or discharge after the sentence but the supreme authority. So that the raising Christ belonged as properly by right to the Father as the power of delivering him to death. When the account was made up in heaven, and not a farthing of what was due was found wanting, but the demands of justice fully balanced by the satisfaction of Christ, 'he was taken from prison and judgment,' Isa. liii. 8, and God sends an angel to roll away the stone, Mat. xxviii. 2; not indeed to make way for the resurrection of Christ, as though there was a necessity of rolling away the stone to give his body passage out of the grace, but to evidence to the women that intended to come into the sepulchre that his discharge came from heaven, and that they might see the grave empty of his body. As he that is in prison for debt ought not to go out without the judge's authority, so Christ was held in the fetters of death till his Father's absolution, and then was delivered from the grave as a debtor from prison. 'God loosed the chains of death,' Acts ii. 24, 'it being not possible that he should be held' in those chains, for it was not equitable that after he had satisfied he should be held longer in his fetters. The judge only can free from prison; and when the law, where any is imprisoned, is satisfied, he is in justice boned to order the discharge, and pronounce in open court the acquittal of the prisoner.

(3.) This act of the Father in raising him was with respect to this work of reconciliation, and the accomplishment of all the fruits of it.

[1.] For the justification of every believer. As the same authority which had delivered him to death raised him from the grave, so in pursuance of the same ends for which he was delivered, he was 'delivered for our offences, and was raised again for our justification,' Rom. iv. 24, 25. It is declared as an encouragement to believe on him that raised up Jesus our Lord from the dead; which argument would have no validity in it to incite the soul to faith in God, if those ends there spoken of were not actually aimed at in those acts of his. The Father, who was the author of both, had the same ends in both those acts; they were the acts of the Father, and therefore the ends of the Father. Though his death was the foundation of his merit, yet his resurrection is the foundation of the application of that merit to all his seed. At this door comes in our justification. As God, in delivering him up to undergo the curse of the law, delivered us in him, and looked upon believers as suffering in him the punishment due to sin, so in raising him he virtually raised them in him, and fundamentally comprehended them in that discharge. His resurrection was not meritorious of our justification, that was the fruit of his death; he paid by his death what was due for our sins, and began to receive at his resurrection what was due for his sufferings; by compact he suffered for us, and by compact he was raised for us. As the expiation of our offences depended upon the death of our surety, so the justification of our persons depended upon the discharge of our surety; and to that end he was raised up by God to be a standing foundation of and encouragement to our faith, to believe the promises of God, and grow up into hope of the enjoyment of them: 1 Peter i. 21, 'God raised him up from the dead, that your faith and hope might be in God.'

[2.] For the regeneration of the seed promised him. This depends upon his resurrection, and was the aim of God in it: 1 Pet. i. 3, 'Blessed be the God and Father of our Lord Jesus Christ, which, according to his abundant mercy, has begotten us again unto a lively hope, by the resurrection of Jesus Christ from the dead.' As the resurrection of Christ was as the Father's new begetting of him to be the Son of God, so in regard that he rose as a common person, his resurrection was a new begetting all his elect to be the sons of God. Herein was the foundation of their regeneration, as well as of their justification, settled. He was 'taken from prison and from judgment,' and then it follows, 'who shall declare his generation?' Isa. liii. 8. For by the resurrection of Christ, God having declared himself pacified, has opened all the treasures of his grace to Christ for the framing a new generation in the world to serve him, without which merit of the suffering, and discharge thereupon, there could not have been a unite of grace given out of God's treasury for the renewal of the image of God in any one person. The spiritual resurrection of any one soul is as much the effect of this resurrection of Christ, as the resurrection of bodies shall be at the last day. That power which does raise any soul from a death in sin, would never have wrought in any heart without this antecedent to it, it would have wanted the foundation of satisfaction, for God only sanctifies as n God of peace. And therefore the power which was exerted for the raising of Christ from the grave was put forth as a power to work in the hearts of all his seed. As the subject of this resurrection was not a private person, but a public representative, as God acted in it in a public manner as the governor and creditor, so the poser whereby he raised him was, as I may call it, a public power, a pattern of what was to be spiritually wrought in the hearts of all those whose debts he paid and for whom the payment was accepted by God. His working in all believers is but 'according to the working of that mighty power which he wrought in Christ, when he raised him from the dead,' Eph. i. 20. It was also a pattern of that power which should be employed for doing all works necessary in the hearts of those that believe. It is the fountain from whence all spiritual life streams don n to us; by this God put into him the spring of the Spirit of life to flow out upon all his seed.

[3.] For to give us the highest security for all new covenant mercies. This security was intended by God in the very act of raising him. 'For as concerning that he raised him up from the dead, now no more to return to corruption, he said on this wise, I will give you the sure mercies of David,' Acts xiii. 34. This was in the thoughts of God when he put forth his hand to the raising of him. There can be no greater security than the fulfilling of the promises made, which the apostle there places in the resurrection of Christ, 'For,' says he, 'we declare unto you glad tidings, how that the promised made unto the fathers, God has fulfilled the same unto us their children, in that he has raised up Jesus again,' Acts xiii. 32, 33. What promise was that which was thus fulfilled? It was the promise of 'an everlasting covenant,' Isa. lv. 3. Whence this is cited, that grand promise that God made to Adam, and in him to all his posterity, was fulfilled in this act of raising Christ; it being a declaration of the bruising the serpent's head, the author of all the enmity between God and man, by the seed of the woman. The promises also of blessing all nations in the seed of Abraham, and the bringing in an everlasting righteousness, were fulfilled. These were but initially performed by the sending Christ and bruising him. But the wisdom of God, the righteousness of God, and the truth of God, did all shine forth in their fullest beams, in the raising him from the dead, which was the top-stone of our reconciliation, as his death had been the corner-stone and foundation. The certain enjoyment of all the blessings of the new covenant is insured to us by this act of God, and so intended by him in the act itself; this giving and dispensing of the sure mercies of David, i. e. the making all the mercies which this our David had purchased by his sacrifice, and had been promised to him in the first agreement, sure and settled for ever.

Use. How strong a ground is here for our faith and comfort! When our Saviour was upon the cross, there was a black cloud of wrath between God and him, the heavens were dusky, the face of God veiled; but in his resurrection the heaven looked clear, the wrath of God was pacified. It left its sting in our Saviour's side. Christ therefore after his resurrection salutes his apostles with peace: John xx. 21, 'And Jesus said to them again, Peace be unto you; as my Father has sent me, so send I you;' which seems to be more than an ordinary salutation, since it is attended with a special commission, the fruit of his reconciling death. Peace dawned at his birth, but was not in its meridian till his resurrection. Thereby he was cleared to all the world, and eased of the burden of men's sins, which bowed down his head upon the cross. Had not God been a God of peace, i. e. fully reconciled by his death, he had not brought him again from the dead, but suffered him to have lain there: Heb. xiii. 20, 'Now the God of peace, that brought again from the dead our Lord Jesus Christ.' Would we be perfect in every good work? Would we do the will of God? Would we have everything well-pleasing in his sight wrought in us? Then we should go to him as a God of peace, as a God lifting up Christ from the grave, that he might with honour to all his attributes work such excellent things in the hearts of all that believe in him, and act faith upon this act of God's power, righteousness, and truth, in the raising the great Shepherd of our souls. He delights now to be called the God of peace, and by this act has laid aside what was terrible to us in the consideration of a judge for the breach of his law. Why may we not hope to attain whatsoever is needful at his hands, since he has clothed himself with a new title? And it is to be observed that the apostle says, God 'brought him again from the dead, through the blood of the everlasting covenant.' He entered into prison as our surety, and paying the price, was delivered by that payment; and freeing himself by that payment from any more satisfaction, he frees all those that are his members; so that the blood of Christ will have the same virtue for those that it has for himself. God manifested it to be the blood of the everlasting covenant, a blood sufficient to establish the everlasting covenant upon, by this deliverance of him. God has no more to lay to his charge, all bonds are cancelled, all actions against him fully answered; he rose not only by his own power and right, but by his Father's warrant, whereby God owned himself his Father, and in him our Father, upon which account he tells Mary, John xx. 17, 'I ascend to my Father and your Father, my God and your God.' This resurrection is the testimony, God is become your Father as well as mine, the enmity is abolished, you stand in a relation to God, and I ascend to him as your Father as well as mine, to take possession from his hands of the inheritance I have purchased for you.

8. God glorified Christ, and so was in Christ reconciling the world unto himself, fully establishing this reconciliation wrought by him. All power was promised to him: Ps. ii. 8, 'I will give thee the heathen for shine inheritance.' It was performed: Mat. xxviii. 18, 'All power is given me.' His resurrection had not attained its full end and perfection, had he not been exalted to a glorious government; it was for this end, dia touto, that he died, that 'he rose again and revived, that he might be Lord both of dead and living.' He died to purchase it, he rose to possess it, and lives for ever to manage it. He was exalted for the honour of God and the happiness of believers, as Joseph the type was advanced to manage things for the interest of the crown and the good of the people.

First, We must premise these two things: there is a double glory and dominion of Christ.

(1.) Essential, as God, which was communicated to him in the communication of his essence; for being God from eternity, he had all the prerogatives of God.

(2.) Mediatory, which was by an agreement between them to be bestowed upon him upon the accomplishment of his work in the world. He had a right to this by the donation of his Father at his conception, for he was made Lord when he was made Christ: Acts ii. 36, 'Know assuredly, that God has made that same Jesus whom you have crucified, both Lord and Christ.' But he had not his actual investiture and full settlement in it till after his resurrection, because his reconciling death was to precede his entrance into glory, where he was to reside for the management of this power. In this respect he is called the heir of all things: Heb. i. 2, 'Whom he has appointed heir of all things;' which inheritance is not meant of his essential dominion, for so he is not appointed but begotten heir. He might then be said to be constituted God as well as heir, which would be an improper speech, like the Socinian's Deus factus. What is natural, cannot be said to be by constitution; the one is voluntary, the other necessary. He is appointed heir, as he was appointed mediator, Heb. iii. 2. He was mediator by a voluntary designation, he was heir by a voluntary donation, and all judgment was committed to him by a voluntary deputation, but he was a Son by a natural generation. Again, an heir succeeds in the place of another; so Christ as mediator succeeds in the place of his Father, in regard of government, as his delegate and deputy; but what the Son has from the Father as God, he has not as his deputy, but by an essential, natural, and eternal communication. So that these two differ.

(1.) The one belongs to his essence as God, the other to his office as mediator.

(2.) The essential is by nature, the mediatory is conferred as a reward of his humiliation and expiation of sin: Philip. ii. 8, 9, 'Wherefore God has highly exalted him,' viz. because of his obedience to death. The one belonged to him without suffering, but his suffering death for us was the moral cause of his exaltation. Since the heavenly sanctuary was shut against us, the expiation of our crimes must precede his entrance into it, and possession of it.

(3.) The essential is an absolute sovereignty, the mediatory is delegated. For it is a judgment committed to him by the Father, John v. 22. In the first he is one with the Father, in the other he is the Father's substitute and deputy; his Father's lord-lieutenant in the world according to a derived authority.

(4.) The essential is wholly free, it has no obligation upon it; the mediatory has a charge annexed to it. It is a dominion with rules, and given him as a means to bring believers to salvation, which is part of the work belonging to the charge of mediator, John xvii. 42. He has this power given him by the Father, 'that he should give eternal life to all that God has given him.'

(5.) The essential is necessary: he cannot possibly be God without an infinite glory and dominion. The other, though due by the covenant, yet is a free gift: Philip. ii. 9, 'God has given him a name which it above every name,' icarisato. Not that God, who is infinite goodness and holiness, would ever let such an exquisite holiness and affection to his glory, which Christ discovered in the whole course of his obedience, pass without a rewarding and crowning it with the greatest glory in his treasury (it being an obedience superior to that of all the angels, it required a recompense superior to all their glory), yet that high exaltation is a free gift.

[1.] In regard that the whole economy, the mission of Christ and his incarnation, is a free gift of God to us; and in his exaltation he is considered as appearing for us, and receiving from the Father those treasures which were to be dispensed to us, and that power and dominion which was to be employed for us.

[2.] Because as it was the free gift of God to unite our flesh to the deity of the second person, it was also an act of free grace to continue the manifestation of the glory of the divinity in the same flesh.

[3.] Because the death he suffered, and the conquest he gained thereby, being by the powerful assistance of the Father, according to those promises of assistance made to him, his glory may be well said to be a free gift from the Father.

[4.] Because given without constraint, with a free pleasure, though upon a valuable consideration.

(6.) The essential is eternal, without beginning and end; the mediatory has a beginning after his death and resurrection, and shall have an end. When all the seed are brought in and perfected, all enemies subdued and conquered, (Christ shall resign his commission and his people, for whose sake he was commissioned and deputed to this government, unto his Father, 1 Cor. xv. 24, when he shall still reign with his Father in the glory of the Deity. The Father lays aside his immediate government, that Christ may- be all in all; at last Christ shall resign the government to the Father, that God may be all in all, and delight immediately in his people, when they shall be fully perfected, and free from sin. The power, in regard of the particular ends for which it was conferred on Christ, ceases when those ends cease; but what belongs of right to him AS God, or what was given him by covenant as a reward for his obedience, will endure as long as the humanity remains united to the divinity.

Secondly, This is to be considered, that it was the person of Christ which was exalted by the Father. The subject of this power is the person of Christ, and the execution of this power is by the person of Christ.

1. His divine nature was exalted and glorified in regard of its manifestation. The Father would manifest that the Redeemer of the world was God blessed for ever, above angels or men. His deity in the time of his humiliation was incapable of any change, and therefore neither did nor could receive any detriment in its nature and essential perfections. It could not be subject to infirmities, or fall under the strokes of death; yet the Son of God emptied himself in taking upon him the form of a servant, and veiled that deity which dwelt bodily in him by the flesh he took, and suffered reproaches and indignities from men, and masked the glory of it by human infirmities; but in his resurrection and ascension, the deity did gloriously spring out of that obscurity, and brake out from under the cloud of his humanity in a glorious lustre, which before had discovered itself in some few sparklings; he was now 'clothed with a gesture dipped in blood, and his name is called the Word of God,' Rev. xix. 13; i.e. he was manifested to be the Word of God after and upon the account of his death.

2. His human nature was exalted and glorified by a new acquisition and addition of perfections of glory, which had been never conferred upon any man or angel. That was really delivered from all that suffering and debasement it had been subject to before in the days of his flesh, and was drawn up into a great and glorious condition, and endowed with gifts above all creatures in heaven and earth, and received a new royalty and power of ruling; and as the Mediator had performed a new work in dying, so he received a new glory in his exaltation. Thus the person of Christ, and each nature, may be said to be glorified in a distinct sense: the divine, in the manifestation of it, from that obscurity wherein it had been disguised; the human, in the reception of that which it had not before possessed. This was fully conferred on him at his ascension, and sitting down at the right hand of God; whereas before the name of a servant was written upon him, the fashion of his vesture being changed, there was a new name writ upon him, King of kings, and Lord of lords, Rev. xix. 16.

These things premised.

1. The exaltation and power of Christ is everywhere ascribed to the Father. It was his promise: Ps. lxxxix. 27, 'I will make him higher than the kings of the earth.' Several monarchies overtopped the Jewish kingdoms throughout the whole duration of that state. He bruised him as he was the rector and judge of the world, to whom belonged the right of punishment; he advanced him as the supreme governor and fountain of all honour; and thus he was in Christ ordering the application, and insuring reconciliation to us upon the conditions in his word.

(l.) In regard of donation. It is a gift from the Ancient of days, Dan. vii. 14. God anointed him to this office as well as to the rest. He sets him in the highest place next to himself, at his right hand:óPs. cx. 1, 'The Lord said unto my Lord;'ógives him all the ensigns of authority, a crown in the day of his espousals, an everlasting throne, a sceptre of righteousness: Heb. i. 8, 'But unto the Son he says, Thy throne, O God, is for ever and ever;' a sword in his mouth, the keys of life and death, all royal prerogatives; subjects all the angels to him, to receive commissions from him, and be at his service; they are now the eyes and horns of the Lamb, ministers and instruments of his jurisdiction. He 'committed all judgment to his Son,' John v. 22; not only a power of judging or sentencing, but a power of governing and conducting all things. In regard of the power he received, he is said to sit down, Luke rxii. 69, 'at the right hand of the power of God.' In regard of the authority invested in him, he is said to sit down at 'the right hand of the throne of God;' in regard of the glory conferred upon him, he is said to sit down 'at the right hand of the throne of the Majesty in the heavens,' Heb. viii. 1. His royal power to manage it, and the glory attending it, being all the gifts of God to him, and that not in a way of common providence, whereby other kings reign, but by a peculiar deputation and special decree, in a mighty affection, whereby he does as it were take him by the hand and set him upon his throne,óPs. cx. 1, 'Sit thou at my right hand,'óand peculiarly calls him his King, Ps. ii. 6; makes him higher than the heavens, gives him by inheritance a more excellent name than all the angels; all which are peculiarly the acts of God towards him, Heb. i. 8, 18, the special orders of God concerning him.

(2.) In regard of fitness for this government. 'The Spirit of counsel and might' did rest upon him for the exercise of this government, as well as for his other transactions in the world; that he might 'reprove with equity,' 'smite the earth with the rod of his mouth, and with the breath of his lips slay the wicked,' Isa. xi. 4; righteousness was to be the 'girdle of his loins,' and 'faithfulness the girdle of his reins.' This was his excellency, conferred upon him as King of the church; he had seven horns, a full power, and seven eyes, a perfect wisdom, for the management of the government, Rev. v. 6. He had need of the highest fitness, because this government upon his shoulders was a charge incumbent upon him above what all the angels in heaven were entrusted with. He has a spirit of wisdom to guide the church, a spirit of power to defend it, a spirit of faithfulness to take care of it, a spirit of compassion to pity it, and inexhaustible fullness to impart unto his people in all their necessities, able to fill the cistern, the church, and every private bucket He was not without power to rescue those out of the hands of the devil by conquest, whom he had redeemed from the wrath of God by his death. He had full power given him to force the jailer, after he had contented the creditor; God fitted him with wisdom against the wiles of Satan, and might against this power.

(3.) In regard of defence and protection in it. He has the whole power of the Godhead to defend him in it, he sits at his right hand. The right hand is a place of honour, and the right hand of a great king is a place of security Though Christ has a power to subdue his enemies, yet the Father is said to make his enemies his footstool. Putting forth his power, to show in the punishment of his enemies the high acceptance of his person and passion, that he will with his own hands bring down all that concur not with him in giving honour to his Son. The power which is essential to the Deity, is promised to be employed for the subduing his enemies under his sceptre and under his feet: Ps. cx. 1, 'Till I make thy enemies thy footstool.' As he did bring him to his throne in spite of all opposition, so he will establish it against the storms and powers of hell. He set him Upon the throne with a mighty zeal for his honour, and indignation against his opposers: 'Then shall he speak to them in his wrath, yet have I set my king upon my holy hill of Sion,' Ps. ii. 5, 6, notwithstanding all their counsels against him and resolutions to cast his cords frown them. So the increase of his government and peace, the ordering of it, the stability of it with judgment and justice, and the perpetuity of it, are Settled, protected, and assured by the same zeal that placed him in it: Isa. ix. 7, 'The zeal of the Lord of hosts shall perform this,' i. e. that vehement love which he has both to the honour of Christ and the eternal peace and security of his seed. The power of God first lifted him to his throne, and the same omnipotence will keep it from being shaken by the powers of darkness. And the Redeemer was still to exercise faith in God as his Father, as his God, the rock of his salvation, even when he had 'set his hand in the sea, and his right hand in the rivers', Ps. lxxxix. 25, 26. Then God does promise to 'beat down his foes before his lace, and plague them that hate him,' and 'his seed' he would make to 'endure for ever, and his throne as the days of heaven,' verse 23, 29.

2. The Father did this upon the account of his death, and to show his high valuation of it, and that reconciliation he wrought by it.

(1.) This exaltation and dominion was upon the account of his reconciling death. His sufferings were the way to his crown; he first surrendered himself as our surety to the justice of God, before God surrendered his power to the management of Christ for the good of man: 'He died and rose again and revived, that he might be Lord of the living and the dead,' Rom. xiv. 9; he obtained a new state of life, not to die again, as Lazarus; and he was not raised barely to a life, but to a royal and princely life, to have an extensive dominion over all, the foundation whereof was laid in his death. God 'lifted up his head,' because he did 'drink of the brook in the way,' Ps. cx. 7, and it was as he was a lamb that had been slain as a sacrifice, that he had both his power and his wisdom, Rev. v. 6.

[1.] The exercise of his dominion before his incarnation, did in order of nature presuppose his death. Though he exercised a power in the world before his incarnation, yet it was exercised by him as a constituted mediator; and his assumption of a mortal body, and offering it up to death, was the condition required at the first constitution of him as mediator, as a reparation of the honour of God, which had been violated in the disorder of his first form of government by the entrance of sin. As soon as ever man fell the government of the world devolved into the hands of Christ by virtue of the covenant between the Father and himself. When sin had undermined the pillars of the world, they would have fallen had he not given a new consistency to them, Col. i. 17, and 'upheld all things by the word of his power,' Heb. i. 3, and 'established the earth,' Isa. xlix. 8, which else would have been overthrown by justice as well as the angels. Had not the government of the world been put into the hands of Christ, and a covenant of grace been erected, the world had been destroyed; the holiness of God would not have endured the sinfulness of it, and the justice of God could not have endured the standing of it according to the covenant of works. And this government was not put into the hands of the mediator, but upon a supposition of his death. What reason have we to think God should constitute a new mode of government without a reparation of his honour in the first? 'The government was upon his shoulders' when he was first given to us as a Son, Isa. ix. 6. He was given to us in promise before he was given to us in the flesh; and in that first promise' wherein his power is ensured to him for us, viz. the bruising the serpent's head, his death is supposed by the serpent's bruising his heel, Gen. iii. 15. He was a Lamb slain from the foundation of the world, and it was upon this presupposed oblation that the world had its standing, that any had grace bestowed upon them, and found acceptance with God. If the great end of the government he is since his death invested with, was performed by him before his incarnation, viz. the salvation of souls, yet with respect to his future death, then the government also, which was but a means in order to this, was conditionally conferred upon him. As believers were saved before his coming, so the world was governed by him, because he was to die. Hence he was the angel of the Lord in delivering his church; the captain of the Lord's hosts in fighting their battles, Joshua v. 14; the guardian of the church, and an advocate for them in their distresses, Zech. i. 8, 12, and attended upon his throne with all the angels as messengers to perform his will, Isa. vi. 1, 2, which, in the evangelist's interpretation, was the Lord Jesus, whose glory Isaiah saw, John xii. 41, when the seraphims celebrated his glory in the earth: it was he, the foundation of whose glory was laid in the earth, in the redemption of the sons of men. They are silent of that glory God has in the vast heavens, and speak only of his glory in the small point of earth, which relates to that of his mediation, wherein the establishing the earth and reducing it to a due order was the maim concern.

[2.] He was absolutely confirmed in it upon his death. There was a confirmation of it in the first instant of his conception, for he eras made Lord when he v. as made Christ; at his birth he was proclaimed by the angels a Lord as well as a Saviour, Luke ii. 11, but his fall investiture was after his death, upon his ascension, when seated at the right hand of the Majesty on high. David had an authority conferred upon him at his anointing, but was not fully inaugurated till his coronation at Hebron. So after the Redeemer had finished his ministerial work, God did fix him in his royal dignity to exercise his power, not only in the divine nature, as he had done before, but also in his human nature assumed by it. There was an 'anointing' of him after his 'bringing in everlasting righteousness' by his death, and 'making reconciliation for iniquity, making an end of sin, and sealing up the vision and prophecy' which centred in him; then was the most holy to be anointed and have his solemn investiture, Dan. ix. 24. Because of that illustrious holiness he had manifested in the whole course of his humiliation, and that signal obedience upon the cross, he then was settled an high priest for ever, which he exercises by himself; a prophet of his church, which he exercises by his Spirit; an everlasting king, which he manages partly by his Spirit, partly by himself. Thus our Noah was brought out of the ark after the suffering, the terror of a deluge, to be the father of a second world, and as Isaac was raised up, after he had appeared as a victim under his father's sword, to be the father of many nations, he was to be Shiloh, a peacemaker, before the gathering of the nations under his sceptre, Gen. xlix. 10; and the Son of man, before he was to have a 'dominion that should not pass away,' Dan. vii. 13, 14. As God brought him again from the dead, 'through the blood of the everlasting covenant,' he raised him because his blood was a covenant blood, Heb. xiii. 20, so by his own blood he entered once into the holy place, Heb. ix. 12. But it was not only after his death, but because it was a death for man voluntarily submitted unto. The conquests made by him in the world, his having a 'portion divided with the great, and the spoil with the strong,' was 'because he poured out his soul to death, made intercession for the transgressors, and bare the sins of many, Isa. liii. 12. It was upon this score of purging and expiating our sins by himself that he 'sat down on the right hand of the Majesty on high,' Heb. i. 3. He expiated sin by the oblation of himself, not as other high priests, by the blood of animals. If any creature had been offered by him, though held in the highest rank in the creation, the priest had been infinite, but the sacrifice had been finite. But it was himself which he offered, a finite, human nature, in conjunction with an infinite person, and that for the atonement of our iniquity; for which infinite obedience, and infinite charity, God rewarded him with an infinite exaltation. It was his own blood which procured his admission into the holy place, and he was crowned because he had combated with the curses of the law and enemies of our peace, and conquered them for us.

There are two things requisite to the exercise of this power and dominion: the knowledge of God's decrees, and authority over the chief ministers in the execution of them; both which Christ has upon the account of his redeeming death.

First, The knowledge of God's decrees. God gave to him the knowledge of his decrees concerning his people, Rev. i. 1. No man on the earth or angel in heaven was found worthy to open the book, i.e. to be acquainted with the contents thereof, nor to unloose the seals, to dive into the depth and mysteries of his counsels and providence, but only the lion of the tribe of Judah. But it was by virtue of his death ins he was the lamb slain, the antitype of the legal lambs sacrificed) that he took the book and opened it, Rev. v. 6, 7. The prevalence of his death with his Father was the cause of the knowledge of all the secrets of his will. As he was the lion of the tribe of Judah' and the root of David, as he had taken human nature according to the will of his Father, and suffered in it, he prevailed to open the book and unloose the seals thereof, Rev. v. 5, that they should not be concealed from him who was the head of the reconciled world. When the justice of God was appeased by the prevailing death of Christ, he gives forth willingly whatsoever may conduce to the salvation of his people; and in order to this, there was a necessity Christ should understand his secrets. How else could he be an executor of all the counsels of God? This revelation is to him as mediator in his human nature, as appointed king by God, which is distinct from that knowledge he had as God, as his mediatory kingdom was distinct from that essential kingdom he had as God. As that was a delegated power, so this is a revealed knowledge; and both one and the other he had, as he was the lamb of God taking away the sins of the world.

Secondly, Authority over the chief ministers employed in the execution of his will. 'Things in heaven' must bow down to him, Philip ii. 10; 'all power in heaven, as well as earth, was given him,' Mat. xxviii. 18, and nothing was exempt from his jurisdiction but only the Father, who did put all things under him, 1 Cor. xv. 27. The innumerable company of angels, which are citizens of the heavenly Jerusalem and mount Zion, the seat of his royalty, Heb. xii. 22, are under his sceptre. His sitting on the right hand of God (as was said) was because he purged our sins by himself, and whatsoever did accrue to him by virtue of this session was upon the same foundation with the session itself. Part of that dominion accruing to him, as sitting at the right hand of God, was the power over angels (1 Peter iii. 22, 'Who is on the right hand of God, angels, and authorities, and powers being made subject to him', who had authority and power from God in the administration of his providence either among other angels or among men; they were subjected to him, i. e. by his Father. He was passive in it, and had it conferred upon him as part of his mediatory glory. As God, he did himself subject the angels to him. Thus, as an honour for the oblation of himself, were they all marshalled under the power of Christ by the Father, who had power to dispose of his creatures under the reins of what government he pleased. And the most excellent orders of them were not exempt from this subjection, but every person to whom God had granted a principality, power, might, and dominion, either in this world or that which is to come, was brought under his sceptre, to be serviceable to him in the execution of those designs he had for the church, which he had reconciled to God by his blood: Eph. i. 21, 'Far above all principality and power;' not only anw, but uperanw, exceedingly above in excellency of dignity and largeness of authority; whence they are called his angels, Rev. i. 1, and fellow-servants of 'those that have the testimony of Jesus,' Rev. xix. 20, and therefore servants to Christ as mediator. And as a testimony of this subjection of them, God sent all his angels to wait upon him at his triumphant reception, as his chariots to convey the human nature of Christ to heaven, and to welcome him after his victory, Ps. lxviii. 17. He was 'among them as in Sinai,' when he came down to give the law; he was commander of them, and gave them directions in that affair. This is spoken with respect to his ascension, as it follows, ver. 18, 'Thou hast ascended on high;' they attended him to his throne and waited upon him, to be employed in the execution of his royal edicts. Now, this adoration which the angels are commanded to render him was because he had expiated sin, Heb. i. 3, 6. Their waiting round about his throne to attend his pleasure, and the joyful acclamations they shout forth in his praise, is because he was the lamb slain, the reconciling sacrifice, whereby God and man were brought together, Rev. v. 11, 12.

[3.] It was very fit and congruous that he should have this glory. This was the agreement between the Father and the Son before he set foot out of heaven. He had glorified God, had given him a foundation by his submission to the sharpness of his mediatory work, to display his wisdom in the highest glory, his justice in the deepest severity, his mercy with the clearest lustre, his veracity in the firmest stability. Without his undertaking this, none of those attributes could have appeared in such glory upon any other foundation; they could never have been thus manifested by any creature, or the undertaking of the whole creation. As he therefore glorified the Father more than all creatures could glorify him, so it was fit he should have a glory transcendently above them. As he had improved his talents above them, so he should be possessed with a rule above them. Without this power he could not have conducted those whom he had purchased to a blessed eternity. It was very reasonable, that as the Father had by him done the hardest work, viz., the expiating sin, he should also by him work the full accomplishment of it. It was congruous that things should be given into the hands of the Redeemer to manage, who had purchased them all by a price so valuable as that of his death. If he died to purchase them, it was fit he should have authority to perfect them. He, being a divine sacrifice, was of infinite price, and as his sufferings surpassed the punishments of all creatures, so the value of his sacrifice exceeded the riches of the whole creation, both of heaven and earth, angels or men. He had not had a reward commensurate to the value of his death, had not a dominion been added to him as mediator, beside that of his deity, which was his by nature, and could not fall within the compass of a purchase, since he never was nor could be dispossessed of it. It was but reason the angels should be subjected to him, who had been preserved and confirmed bv him; for God hall in him 'gathered together things in heaven as well as things in earth, Eph. i. 10' which collection would have signified little, unless by it they had been wrapped up into a permanent state, and a full assurance from any danger of apostasy from God and a fall into misery, as some of their fellows had done. It was very convenient that they who had received so great a benefit by him should be subject to him, that they who had been gathered under his wing should be as well under his sceptre. Besides, as he had discovered himself faithful to death against some reluctance of human nature, he should have an opportunity to discover himself faithful in the other parts which concerned the honour of God; he that was faithful to him under the curse of the law would not be unfaithful to him under the blessing of deliverance. And very fit at last that he that was the innocent sufferer should be the judge of his guilty enemies, and condemn the great head of that enmity which was the occasion of his conflict with his Father's wrath, to remove it out of the way. As he, being rich in the deity and in the form of God, became poor in his humanity and in the form of a servant, eclipsing thereby the glory of his Godhead, it was fit he should reassume his former state as the heir of all things, and exercise that power in his humanity which he had a right unto in his deity.

[4.] This power was conferred upon him for the application nod perfection of the fruits of reconciliation. This power and dominion is given to him for the advantage and full growth of his seed. When his people shall be perfected and his enemies subdued, the government devolves wholly to his Father, there being no longer any occasion for the exercise of his mediatory dominion. If it were conferred upon him only for himself, the power would not cease as long as his person endures; but the cessation of it upon the accomplishment of such effects evidences that those effects were the end for which it was first conferred. It is upon this score the Scripture places the extent of his dominion, Eph. i. 22. He, i. e. the Father, has put all things under his feet, and gave him to be the head over all things to the church, for the church's welfare, for the good of the subjects as well as the glory of his empire. He is the King of saints, to rule them by his grace; and the King of nations, to rule them by his providence. He is set to reign in Zion, the hill of holiness, Ps. ii. 6, as the centre of all the power and wisdom of his government, as the chief city of a prince partakes most of the fruits of his valour in conquering, and his wisdom in ruling. As his prophetical office is not to cease till instruction be swallowed up in vision, nor his priestly till his intercession be succeeded by immediate communion, so neither his kingly till there be a total cessation from all danger, and not an enemy left to disturb their peace.

First, For the bestowing gifts on men for the publishing this reconciliation. He received gifts at his triumph, that he might, as a royal steward of his Father, distribute them for the good of those that had been rebels to the government of God, to fit them for the great fruit of this peace, viz., a communion between God and them, 'that the Lord God might dwell among them,' Ps. lxviii. 18; Eph. iv. 8, 11-13. These gifts come from God as a God of salvation, as the doxology infers, Ps. lxviii. 10, 'Blessed be the Lord, who daily loads us with his benefits, even the God of our salvation.' The intent whereof was to wound the head of the enemy Satan, who had been the first makebait: Ps. lxviii. 21, 'God shall wound the head of his enemy.' The Spirit was not therefore given in that eminency and fullness of gifts and graces till the glorification of Christ, wherein he absolutely received the keys of all the treasures of his Father, as well as the keys of hell and death: John vii. 39, 'The Spirit was not yet given, because that Jesus was not yet glorified.' The giving the Spirit depended on the glorification of him as Jesus, a Saviour. God would receive those gifts for the triumphal coronation of his Son as an evidence of the peace which was made by him, by the effusion of the richest treasures of God. The Spirit was in the world before, as light was upon the face of the creation the three first days, but not SO glorious, sparkling, and darting out full beams till the fourth day, the day of the creation of the sun, and fixing it in the heavens; so was the rich beaming forth of light, when after four thousand years, the fourth divine day, the Sun of righteousness was seated in the heavens to disperse his beams. The first edict he gave out after the receipt of his power, was the commission for preaching the gospel: Matt. xxviii 18, 19, 'All power is given unto me in heaven and in earth; Go therefore and teach all nations.' It was the intention of his Father that he should dispose of his power for this end; for he who did all things according to his Father's will would not use his power in the least, but for those ends for which it was conferred upon him.

Secondly, For the inviting of men to an acceptance of him. As the most beneficial commands that ever he gave, so the most condescending affections he ever discovered, the most gracious invitations that ever he made, were at those times where he had a sense of this power in a more peculiar manner, to show the proper intendment of it, and to what ends he was to manage it. The grant of this power is the foundation of that invitation he makes to weary souls, Mat. xi. 27, 'All things are delivered to me of my Father;' the inference is, 'Come unto me, all ye that labour;' and his governing them as a leader and commander to the people is the encouragement God uses to men to accept of that rich and liberal invitation of coming to the waters and buying wine and milk without money and without price, Isa. lv. 1, 4. God exalted him to all his power, to enable him to make the most gracious offers to men, and encourage their acceptance of him, as himself intimates in that fore-mentioned Mat. xi. 27, that the delivery of all his treasures to him was to make a revelation of his Father to the sons of men.

Thirdly, For the preserving the reconciliation for ever firm. As there is an increase of his government, so there is an increase of his peace: Isa. ix. 7, 'Of the increase of his government and peace there is no end.' His government, and the peace he purchased, go hand in hand; as his glory rises to the meridian, so does the reconciliation. He therefore went to heaven to purify the heavenly things themselves with his sacrifice, Heb. ix. 23, i. e. (say some) heaven itself, which in some sense was polluted by the stench of our sins coming up into the presence of God, into which Christ as the high priest entered with his blood, to settle the sweet savour of that before God, instead of the loathsome savour of our sins which had offended his majesty. But howsoever, this exaltation was that he might 'appear in the presence of God for us,' Heb. ix. 24, and preserve by his intercession what he had wrought by his passion. He has therefore his head encircled with a rainbow, Rev. x. 1, to evidence the perfection of the peace he had made, and the establishment of the security in heaven, against the opening any more the flood-gates of wrath for an overflowing deluge.

Fourthly, For the subduing his and our enemies. He is to continue in the exercise of this power, 'till all the enemies be put under his feet,' 1 Cor. xv. 25. All the enemies, all the enemies to him as God, all the enemies to him as mediator, all the enemies to the great design of his mediation, all the enemies to him in that state and condition wherein he sits at the right hand of God, which is as mediator, and therefore whatsoever is contrary to his mediation and the intendment of it, all those enemies to his members which would hinder their arrival at happiness, and their blessed conjunction with their head, are to be destroyed. And those are,

First, Sin, which has 'reigned unto death,' Rom. v. 21.

Secondly, Satan, who as a prince has reigned in the world, and kept up sin in its vigour, John xii. 31.

Thirdly, Death, the last enemy, which has reigned from Adam to Moses,, Rom. v. 14, and will reign to the end of the world, 1 Cor. xv. 26. Whatsoever sets itself in contrariety to the happiness of believers, is an enemy to the design of Christ, and is to be put under his feet, as one end of the authority granted to him. All the powers of hell must be crushed, all the fortifications of the devil must be demolished, and himself despoiled of 0a arms. This was necessary, that his kingdom should extend over the devils, to repress them, if it did extend over his subjects to secure them; these could not be advanced by his mercy, if the others did not sink under his power.

Fifthly, For the perfect salvation of his seed. His exaltation was tor the perfection and perpetuity of salvation; the apostle's inference else would have no validity: Rom. viii. 34, 'It is Christ that died, yea rather, that is risen again, who is even at the right hand of God, who also makes intercession for us. Who shall separate us from the love of Christ?' But the apostle sets forth the eternal knot between him and believers, upon his session at the right hand of God, with a rather. God 'exalted him to be a prince and a Saviour,' Acts v. 31. A princely Saviour, to bestow the royal gifts of repentance and forgiveness of sins. As he appointed Christ to give it, so he has appointed men to attain it by him, and from him, 1 Thes. v. 9. As he merited salvation by his death, he might perfect it by his life, Rom. v. 10. That as his death was by the ordination of God to purchase a seed, so his exaltation was, by the like designation, for a full sanctification of this seed, that he might at last behold them in their perfect glory; and therefore that he thought his proper work, upon a sense of it in his soul, when he considered his divine original, and his approaching glory, when yet it was not absolutely conferred upon him, John xiii. 3, 4, he will think his work when he is in full possession of it, viz., the full sanctification of his people, the washing their souls, which was symbolically signified by the washing their feet. What seems to be the end of that present sense, will much more be the end and issue of his enjoyment. As he was humbled to save them, so he was exalted to perfect them; and since he was made sin for us in his death, he is in his advancement mode wisdom, righteousness, sanctification, and redemption, a full treasury to supply all our necessities, that as he was the author, so he might be the finisher of our faith. If God delivered to him the full contents of his will because he was a lamb slain, it must be in order to carry on that work for which he was slain, to perfect an eternal amity between God and them, that there might be an eternal rejoicing in one another, The mediator being to reign till the whole church be brought to heaven, the intendment therefore of his heavenly royalty is the perfection of them in a heavenly glory; that as in his humiliation he Divas the way of our access, as by his spirit he was the discoverer of the truth, so by his life he might be the perfecter of our happiness: John xiv. 6, 'I am the way, the truth, and the life.' As he glorified his Father on the earth by a full satisfaction of his justice, so his Father glorified him in heaven, to make a full application of his merits, John xvii. 1, 2.

[5.] By this the Father testifies the highest acceptance of his person, and the sufficiency of his death. John iii. 35, 'The Father loves the Son, and has given all things into his hands.' His coronation testifies the acceptance of his person, and it being after his death, testifies the acceptance of his passion; as Pharaoh's elevating Joseph from a prison, to the highest dignity in Egypt, next to that of the sovereign, was a testimony of that king's high admiration of Joseph's wisdom.

This acceptance is testified by two things: the manner of his reception and settlement; the nature of his power.

First, The manner of his reception and settlement. It was with an infinitely pleased countenance, and all the marks of joy in the soul of God, which rejoiced him more than the crown of pure gold set upon his head, or the length of days for ever and ever granted to him. The psalmist places all the joy of Christ upon his ascension in this: Ps. xxi. 3-6, 'Thou hast made him exceeding glad with thy countenance,' "tekhadehu besimkhah", thou hast made him glad with joy. One frown in the face of God would have damped all the joy of Christ. The psalm was anciently understood of the ascension and glory of Christ, and Ainsworth makes a pretty observation of the word rejoice, "yishmakh", by transposition to be "mashiakh", Messiah. If there be joy in heaven at the return of sinners, how great was the joy of God at the return of the Saviour of them, after the performing unto God so eminent a service! How heartily did the Father take him in his arms! How straitly did he embrace him! How magnificently did he fix him in a throne of immortality and advocacy! And when he did thus constitute him his king upon his holy hill, he established his throne and perpetuity of his kingdom by an oath: Ps. lxxxix. 35, 36, 'Once have I sworn by my holiness, that I will not lie unto David: his seed shall endure for ever, and his throne as the sun before me.' What men are mightily pleased with, they confirm under the highest obligations. As when the daughter of Herodias pleased Herod, he confirms by an oath the grant he had made of whatsoever she should ask him, Mark vi. 22, 23. And the solemnity at Christ's entrance into heaven, and sitting upon his throne, lasted ten days before the sending of the Spirit as the first fruits of his purchase.

Secondly, The nature of that glory and power invested in him. It is not in the orbs of the planets, or the starry heaven, where Christ has taken up his residence, but he is mounted above all the visible heavens: Eph. iv. 10, 'Far above all heavens;' uperanw, not anw, exceedingly above the heavens, into the holy of holies, the habitation of the glorious majesty of God; a place of purity for a pure Redeemer, a place of glory for a glorious Mediator. And he is seated in his humanity in the highest place of heaven, next the Father, at the right hand of the Majesty on high, yea, 'in the midst of the throne,' Rev. vii. 17, an honour never allowed to the highest angels, Heb. i. 13, which stand before the throne of God, but sit not in the throne with him. The obedience of angels never did, never could, equal the obedience of the Son of God. His empire is of the same extent with his Father's; so highly did his Father value his expiatory offering, that he would not exempt an angel in heaven, nor a devil in hell, nor any creature upon earth from a subjection to him, but poured the whole rule and government into his hands, ordered the same worship to be performed to the Son as to himself, John v. 23, and that in heaven, Heb. i. 6, Rev. v. 13. And for duration, it is for ever and ever; he is to reign as Mediator till all the ends of it be accomplished, and afterwards for ever with the Father in the glory of the Deity, Heb. i. 3. He is to reign as Mediator in the place of the Father, till the church be perfected, by reducing all enemies to an entire subjection, and then to resign his power to his Father. As the son of a king, sent to reduce rebellious countries to obedience, has a royal commission from his father to act as king, an authority to pardon or punish, till his conquest be finished; so when Christ shall have gained the full victory, he shall cease his mediation, and God shall reign immediately over all, and Christ shall reign with him, not as Mediator, but as God. 'God shall be all in all,' 1 Cor. xv. 28, which is opposed to Christ's interposition or intercession as mediator; there will be no need of God's communicating himself by a mediator but he will immediately shine forth upon then, when the fruits of sin, and sin itself, is abolished in them. But for the Father to resign things to the management of his Son, as the Son had given himself up to the justice of he Father, in a sort to eclipse his own glory for so long a time, as the Son had eclipsed his Deity in his humiliation, and as it were lay by the immediate exercise of his authority of Judging and governing which originally pertains to him, and veil it, to let the beams of it shoot into the world only through this medium, is such a mark of his acceptance, that higher cannot be given. It cannot be conceived how the Father should do more than this, for a testimony of his pleasure in him and his sacrifice. It is impossible the Father should dethrone himself, and therefore anything higher than what he has done cannot be imagined. For though the authority still resides in the Father, and is extant in every act of Christ's government, yet he acts not immediately, receives no addresses immediately to himself, lint all in and by his glorified Son. lied he had the least displeasure with him, or found the least blemish in him, he had not lodged the exercise of his power in him.

Use of this head.

First, This exaltation of Christ by the Father is a mighty encouragement to faith in Christ.

1. Hereby we have assurance, that all that Christ spoke and did was agreeable to the will of the Father. This exaltation of Christ will not suffer us to think that anything was left undone by him which he ought to have done. Otherwise the exact justice of God would never have consented to have put the government of all things into his hand; an exact obedience was to precede before a glory was to be conferred. Since therefore this glory is conferred, it is evident his obedience was unblemished. All the world, and the concerns of it, would never have been laid upon his shoulders, had the piercing eye of the Father discerned any fault in it. The infinite wisdom of God would never have entrusted him with so great an affair, if he had not been faithful in the management of what had been before committed to him; because, if he had been unfaithful in one, there was no ground to think he would be faithful in the others. But it is a strong argument that he will be exact in the glorious part of his charge, since he has been exact in the ignominious part of his work. It is upon the account of his being a faithful witness, that he is the 'Prince of the kings of the earth,' Rev. i. 5. It is this argument the Spirit uses to convince the world of righteousness, i. e. the righteousness of his person, the righteousness of his mediation, that there is a full expiation of sin, because he is entertained and received by the Father, John xvi. 10.

2. Hereby we have assurances that it is the intent of the Father, that all things should be managed by Christ for the good of those that believe in him. Since he has delivered the book to Christ, containing the secrets of his will, because he was a lamb slain, it is evident that it is the pleasure of the Father, that his government shall be for those ends for which he was slain, and that the book contains the will of God pursuant to the ends of that death. Had that book contained anything contrary to those ends, and to the interest of his people, the Father would not have delivered it into his hands. The end of his exaltation can never cross the end of his passion; nor could the unchangeable love of the Father give him rules for his acting in his government, opposite to those he had designed his humiliation for. Since therefore he was in Christ upon the cross, reconciling the world to himself, he is in Christ upon his throne, pursuing the ends of that reconciliation, and bringing the fruits of it to a glorious maturity by the glorification of the reconciler. How soon were the tears of John dried up, when he looked upon Christ opening the book of God's decrees, and found by the praises of the elders that the world was committed to him, to order all things for the good of the church, Rev. v. 4, 5. What encouragement would they else have had to have fallen down, singing the praises of him, and acknowledging him as their Lord and King, and to present to him their golden vials full of odours, which are the prayers of the saints? The first homage he receives, after his opening the book, and that as a pleasant odour, is the prayers of believers: ver. 8, 'And when he had taken the book, the four beasts and twenty-four elders fell down before the Lamb, having every one of them harps, and golden vials full of odours, which are the prayers of the saints;' which does evidence their good to be the intendment of the Father in delivering it to him, and that the rules in it were to that purpose, and his own resolution to observe the rules of it.

3. It is to be considered who this person is that is thus exalted, in order to the encouragement of faith. It is the same person, in whose humiliation the Father was reconciling us; our kinsman, by the assumption of our nature, but more by the relation of oar faith to him into whose hand this power is put. He is made the steward to dispense his Father's gifts, who knew our indigences and wants of them, and whose tenderness cannot be questioned, since he has had an experience of our infirmities. He that shed his blood to sale us, will not spare his power to relieve us. As he had not died but to reconcile us, so he would not halve been exalted as a reconciler, hut to perfect it by bringing us to the Father: by the one he made way for our access, and by the other for our perfect conjunction. His being quickened by the Spirit, and the glory following thereupon, as well as his being put to death in the flesh, was to 'bring us to God,' 1 Peter iii. 18. He had a tenderness as he is the Son of God, partaking of the same nature with his Father; he has a tenderness as our mediator, and clothed with our flesh; he has also an engagement of faithfulness, since all the treasures of heaven are put into his hands, to be expended for those ends for which he died. He is not only administrator of his Father's goods, but guardian of the souls committed to him by his Father, and faithful he is in both.

How may we then east our souls into this bottom, since the directions he receives from the Father are agreeable to all the former economy? Since, as a lamb slain, he is God's steward to distribute; since both his heart, and the heart of his Father, are so full of love, one in the execution, the other in the acceptation, nothing can be cross to the interest of those for whom the one died and the other accepted it. No higher ground can there be of faith, than the love the Father has strewn to our Redeemer for his reconciling passion, by his glorious exaltation. He loved him in the laying down his life, and he loved him in the taking of it again, John x. 17. Get your thoughts then up into heaven. Behold the Father taking him up in his arms, congratulating his victory, adorning his triumph, conferring upon him, and perpetuating a government. See if in all this you can find a frown on God's face, any doubt in his heart of the validity of his sacrifice; see if any letters, but those of grace, be written about his throne. And if God has no doubt of it, who is more concerned in his glory, than you in your salvation, why should any jealousies remain' in any heart that accepts him, discards all affection to sin, and endeavours to imitate him in an holy obedience to God? 'Be followers therefore of God as dear children,' since he has so magnificently entertained his Son, upon the account of what he did, for all that will believe in him; and wait upon God till he shall send his Son in all his royal attire, to bring you to the full enjoyment of all the fruits of this reconciliation, so strongly wrought, and so heartily accepted, and till that be accomplished, let hope every day pierce through the veil, and enter into that which is within it, more inward, Heb. vi. 19, eis to eswteron tou katapetasmatoV, inning our souls by faith and hope every day in the veil. This faith is a firm anchor, to hold the soul safe in storms, and the Father's admission of Christ into heaven is the rock on which it should fasten.

The second use is of comfort.

1. Sin is fully expiated, since it is upon the recount of the expiation of it that he is thus dignified. The purging of our sins by himself has met not only with a bare acceptation, but an high valuation, with the Father. Since he has thus crowned and enthroned him, what assurance have we of the full atonement by the blood of his cross! How can we doubt the full satisfaction, delight, and content of the Father with him, and with us upon the condition of faith, since it was for the purging, not his own, but our sins, that he did 'sit down,' as of right, 'on the right hand of the throne of the majesty on high'? Heb. i. 3. The gratifications the Father made to our Redeemer, manifest the satisfaction of his justice, since not only God's kindness, but his justice, which is a part of his majesty, was employed in the welcome reception of him. End that frowned, there had been no throne for him to sit on; and if it ever frown upon him, his throne will shake under him. But it never shall, for it is a 'throne for ever and ever,' and that because 'his sceptre is a sceptre of righteousness,' Heb. i. 8. A majesty still offended would never have admitted him to this honour. Is there any room for sorrow and dejection, for jealousies of the sufficiency of the ransom, after so illustrious a discharge from the Father?

2. Accusations shall be answered. We have great enemies; the devils that tempt us, our corruptions that haunt us, and both to accuse us. To whom must they accuse us? To that majesty, at whose fight hand Christ has his residence. Whence must the vengeance they call for issue, but from that majesty upon whose throne Christ sits as a lamb slain, who sits ready to answer the accusations, and stop the revenge? He tore Satan's charge upon the cross, will he let it be pieced together in his triumph? As he bowed down his head upon the cross to expiate our sins, so his head is lifted up on the throne to obviate any charge they can bring against us. Satan knows it is fruitless for him to bring his indictment there, where Christ perpetually appears, and is never out of the way. The perpetuity of our justification results from this sitting of Christ at the right hand of God; for he sits there, not as an useless spectator, but an industrious and powerful intercessor, to keep up a perpetual amity, slid prevent sin from making any new breach: 1 John ii. 1, sin we must not, but 'if any man sin' (not a course of sin, but fall by some temptation), 'we have an advocate with the Father, Jesus Christ the righteous.' He sits as an advocate, as a reconciler, and a propitiation for sin, spreading before his Father the odours of his merits and righteousness, to answer the charge and indictments of sin. 'He appears in the presence of God for us,' Heb. ix. 24, before the face of his glory in the highest heavens. It was through the blood of the covenant he arose, it was through and with the blood of the covenant be entered into the holy place, to carry the merit of his death as a standing monument into heaven. God, by his advancement, would have the sight of it always in his eye, and the savour of it in his nostrils; that as the world, after the savour of Noah's sacrifice, should no more sink under the deluge; so the believers in Christ should no more groan under the curse of the law, though they may, in this world, smart under the corrections of a Father. It is a mighty comfort in the midst of all infirmities (where there is the answer of a good conscience towards God), that Christ is gone to heaven, and is on the right hand of God, to save those that are baptised into his death, and that have the 'stipulation, eperwthma, of a good conscience towards God,' which is the apostle's reasoning, 1 Peter iii. 21, 22.

3. Wants shall be relieved. It is that human nature wherein the expiation was made on earth, which is crowned with glory in heaven by the Father; that human nature, with all the compassions inherent in it, with the same affections wherewith he endured the cross and despised the shame, with the same earnestness to relieve them as he had to deliver them, with the same desire to drink of the fruit of the vine with them in the kingdom as he had to eat the Passover with them upon the earth, to supply their wants as he had redeemed their persons. If the free gift of all things be argued from the Father's delivery of the Son to death, Rom. viii. 32, the full distribution of all things may be expected from the Father's setting him upon his throne, and giving him the keys of death and hell to stop their inroads upon a believer, and the command of his treasures to dispense at his pleasure; what can be denied to the merit of his death, since as our surety he is established in an eternal throne? Since he was admitted as a 'forerunner for us,' Heb. vi. 20, prodromos, what can there be necessary for us, in our journey till we

overtake him, that we may not expect at his and the Father's bands? All our needs will be supplied, since there are riches in glory in Jesus Christ, Philip. iv. 19.

4. Spiritual enemies shall be conquered. All enemies are to be made his footstool, Ps. cx. 1. Satan, who was wounded by him upon the cross, shall not rise, since he is upon his throne. He that could not overpower him while he was covered with the infirmities of our flesh, cannot master him, since all power is delivered to him in heaven and earth, and the keys of hell put into his hands. He bruised him while he was known only to be the seed of the woman, and bruised him for us; and shall he be able to repair his broken strength, since his conqueror is now declared to be the Son of God with power? Our inward enemies shall fall under the same might. It was the purpose of the Father to 'conform his elect to the glorious image of his Son,' Rom. viii. 29. What has Christ this power in his hands for, but to destroy the power of that in the heart, the guilt whereof he expiated by his blood? That as he appeased the anger of God, and vindicated the honour of his lava by removing the guilt, so he may fully content the holiness of God by cleansing out the filth. As he had a body prepared him to effect the one, so he has a power given him to perfect the other; that as there is no guilt to provoke his justice, there may be no dirt to offend his holiness; that, as the Father has been reconciled by the death of Christ, he may delight himself in the soul by the operation of the power of Christ. This will be accomplished. The first fruit of his exaltation was the mission of the Spirit, whose proper title is a Spirit of holiness, in regard of his operation, as well as his nature; and whose proper work is, to quicken the soul to a newness of life, and mortify by grace the enemies of our nature. The apostle assures the believing Thessalonians of it, from this argument, of his being a God of peace: 1 Thes. v. 23, 'The very God of peace sanctify you wholly,' autos o QeoV. That God of peace: ver. 24, 'Faithful is he that calls you, who also will do it.' It is not only a petition, but an assurance; as appears by ver. 24, that it will be done by him as the author of reconciliation; and completely done, of, wholly perfect, universally for the subject, in understanding, will, affections, body, 'in spirit, and soul, and body.' The enmity else would not be taken away; as the enmity is removed from God in the satisfaction of his justice, by the blood of his Son; so the enmity shall be removed from a believer, in the renovation of his image by the grace of his Spirit, that there may be at last no disgusts on either side; for 'he is faithful who has called you.' He is not a God of peace for a day or an hour; it is not an imperfect reconciliation he designed; it is a faithfulness to himself, to his own resolves, to his own honour, to his Son's blood, to the call of his people. And this is a good argument to plead in our prayers for sanctification, since God has manifested himself to be a God of peace in the raising Christ, accepting him, exalting him; all which were evidences of a perfect reconciliation, that he would perfect in you every good work, Heb. xiii. 20, 21.

Use 3. As the Father's exaltation of Christ is comfortable to the believer, so it is as terrible to the unbeliever and unregenerate. He that advanced him to the throne, and conferred upon him a power of asking the heathen for his inheritance, confers also upon him a power of destroying his enemies: Ps. ii. 8, 9, 'Ask of me, and I will give thee the heathen for thine inheritance,' &c. 'and thou shalt break them with a rod of iron.' The breaking refers to ask of me; and as thou shalt have blessings for believers, so thou shalt leave wrath and judgment for unbelievers. Unbelievers that break his bands, and cast his cords far from them, are so far from having the benefit of Christ's intercessions for mercy in his glorified state, that they have a dreadful interest in his pleas for wrath. He has a power of dashing them like a potter's vessel conferred upon him. He that gives Christ the whole world upon asking, will not contradict him in his severest acts against his unbelieving enemies. For that love to him that advanced him, as a lamb slain, will spirit his wrath with a greater fury against the undervaluers of his death and sufferings. Will the Father, who upon his death thought him worthy to devolve the government of the world upon him, and to act all by the hand of his Son, take it well that he is not imitated by his creature? Is it not a reflection upon the Father, as if he had acted a weak part, had set too high a value upon the death of his Son, that his eyes were too dim to pierce into the nature of it? Will God, who is pleased with him, bear with such real blasphemies against him? for so all unbelieving rejection of Christ is. Shall his obedience be so pleasant to God, and be unrevenged, if it be unpleasant to us? Shall God subject the whole host of angels to him, and let worms despise him without severe punishment? If there be not an holy estimation of Christ, obedience to his will and laws, it will not consist with the Father's exaltation of him to suffer the affront, or let his authority be an idle name, au authority without hands, an empty title. No; as he has a sceptre of righteousness, so he has an iron rod to bruise his enemies. What a folly is it to despise that Redeemer, wilfully to violate his laws, who has all power given hen in heaven arid earth, and the power of judging committed to him by the Father! This is to dare the curses of the law, break open the store house of his wrath, and be bent upon hell with violence.

Use 4. Let us accept Christ then, as our Reconciler and our King. God is not contented only with the establishment of him in this honour, but he loves to hear the world ring with acknowledgments of it; he will have every tongue to confess to the glory of God the Father, that Jesus is the Lord: Philip. ii. 11, 'That every tongue should confess that Jesus Christ is Lord, to the glory of God the Father.' For the glory of God, who conducted him through this great undertaking, accepted him for it, and dignified him for bringing in an everlasting righteousness. The way to glorify God the Father, is to acknowledge the dignity of Christ, and to accept him for those ends for which the Father has exalted him. All things are for the glory of God, but this more signally; hereby he has discovered the wonders of his wisdom, justice, power, and love, before men and angels; and he that owns Christ as a glorified Mediator, owns God in the glory of all those perfections; without this acceptation of him, we cannot answer the end for which God has exalted him, 'he has given him a name above every name,' that we might confess and acknowledge him as he has declared him, and pay him a service by our faith. If he do not render him a voluntary homage now, we shall be forced to render him an homage hereafter in a deplorable state. Heartily to accept him for our Lord, is to perform a duty in fellowship with the angels which encompass his throne. Faith is a choice of Christ for head and governor; it is therefore expressed, Hos. i. 11, 'They shall appoint themselves one head,' i. e. the Messiah, they shall believe in him. Christ is an head of God's appointing, and of believers' approving. God sets him as an head authoritative, and we should embrace him voluntarie and obedientialiter, freely and obediently. As the magistrate chooses a public officer, and the people consent to him; the magistrate gives him the authority, and the people encourage him in the exercise. God 'set his Son upon the holy hill of Soon,' Ps. ii. 6, and we are commanded to kiss him, which is a token of acknowledgement, consent, and subjection. As he sits at the right hand of God, he ought to sit in the centre of our hearts. Since he is possessed of the highest place, and does not disdain the lowest, it is unworthy to keep him from it. Serve him as a Lord. As he has made himself a sacrifice for us, and rose again and revived, Rom. xiv. 9, i. e. acquired a new state of life, we should serve him as a living Lord, in obedience to the pleasure and authority of God the Father, who has been in him reconciling the world, and for his work has advanced him to the dominion over all creatures. As God exalted him out of a sense of what he had done for the appeasing his wrath, and the salvation of man, so should we exalt him in our hearts, out of a sense of what he has done for our souls: 'He that honours not the Son, honours not the Father who has sent him,' John v. 22, 23, and who has glorified him. For he contradicts the ends for which God has given all judgment to the Son.

Use. 6. Glorify God in Christ, glorify Christ. 'God is gone up with a shout:' Ps. xlvii. 5, 'God is gone up with a shout, the Lord with the sound of a trumpet; sing praises to God, sing praises; sing praises to our king, sing praises;' alluding to the joy in the fetching up the ark, 1 Chron. xiii. 8. There were shouts of angels at his entrance into heaven: 'God reigns over the heathen, God sits upon the throne of his holiness;' a throne which his holy and righteous obedience purchased, or the holiness of God is now gloriously apparent, fully vindicated. Glorify the Father for it, the Father and the Lamb are joined together in their praises: Rev. v. 13, 'Blessing, honour, glory, and power be unto him that sits upon the throne, and unto the Lamb for ever and ever.' As the Father has enlarged his hand to Christ, as our reconciler, we should enlarge our hearts in thankfulness to him. God was not satisfied with giving a little mite to Christ, a small reward; all the treasures of heaven must be open for him. Why should we put off God with a little praise?

General use of the doctrine

1. Information.
(1.) This declares the excellency of the Christian religion above any other that ever was in the world. All the philosophy and learning in the world can never acquaint us with these mysteries. In the gospel we see the face of God unveiled, whereas with natural light we can but feel or grope after him Acts xvii. 27. He is not far front us by the light of nature, but in a cloud not barefaced; but the light of the glory of God shires forth in the face of Christ. How does this way of the gospel shame all other religions, all other notices of God! It resolves the question, which nonplusses the natural learning of the world, and gives light to the impossibilities of reason. No other knowledge presents us with a reconciled God, and a reconciling Jesus; this only salves the honour of God, repairs the ruins of nature, ensures the happiness of the creature, and discovers an eternal inheritance upon a firm foundation; this varnishes all God's attributes, calms the conscience, cures natural jealousies of God, and restores the creature to answer the end of his creation; this declares things worthy of God, honourable to him as well as beneficial to the world; it shows him in the heights of his wisdom, and the depths of his holiness, the length of his love, and the breadth of his justice.

[1.] It declares the glory of God. We know something of God by natural reason, but the full story of his glorious perfections is not printed in the book of the creation, as in that of redemption. Hence, when he speaks of his redeeming design, he often adds, 'that I may be glorified,' Isa. xlix. 8, lx. 21, as though he had no glory lying in the womb of creation, but all was to spring out from that of redemption. The creation of the world was but a preparation to this; the creation was too dim a glass to show the image of God's glory. He seems to intimate, Isa. xiii. 5, 6, that his creating the heavens and stretching them out, the spreading forth the earth, and that which comes out of it, and giving breath to people upon it, was as a stage on which he would call Christ to act the highest part, as a covenant for the people. He laid the foundation of the old world, to build those new things upon The glory of the creation was too low for a great God to rest in. Upon sin the creation was laid waste, and the glory of God had sunk with the ruins of it, bad not this succeeded. This restored to him the glory of his creation, with interest and increase. His stretching out the heaven and spreading the earth had glorified his power; the damning man upon his fall had honoured his justice; where then should the standing angels have had prospect of his tenderest love, immense wisdom, and severest justice? He had never been known in his full beauty by any creature, had not the platform of this counsel been laid and executed; whence he calls his calling Christ in righteousness, to open the eyes of the blind, and committing the work of reconciliation to him, his glory, that he would not give to another, i. e. entrust in any other hands than in the hands of his Son, Isa. xlii. 6-8, peculiarly his glory, which he does not ascribe to himself so eminently in stretching out the heavens. His attributes were glorified, some in one act, some in another; here they kiss each other with mutual congratulations; mercy rejoices that justice is satisfied, justice rejoices that mercy is manifested, wisdom and holiness join the hands of mercy and justice together. In other things they are scattered in various subjects, here they are banded in one knot, and shine forth with united beams. In which respect Christ may be said to be 'the brightness of his glory and the express image of his person,' as well as in that of his deity, Heb. i. 3, carakthr, wherein we may see the perfections of God engraver as visibly as a stamp upon the seal, his wisdom, mercy, justice, holiness, and truth. 'The light of the glory of God' breaks forth 'in the face of Jesus Christ,' 2 Cor. iv. 6. In the actions and sufferings of Christ, God exhibits himself in the glory of his nature, and gives a fuller view of himself, who was but imperfectly known before. Here the world may see him in the beauty of trig holiness, the condescending sweetness of his nature, the severity of his justice, the inexhaustibleness of his bounty, and brightness of his wisdom; thus he shows himself at once clearly legible in all his perfections. What religion in the world gives us such an account of God? What discovery did so fully evidence him in his robes of royalty at once? Never was the earth seen so full of the glory of God, as in the mediation of Christ; then was there glory to God in the highest ascents, a glory reaching as high as the highest heavens, when there was peace on earth, Luke ii. 14.

First, It manifests his wisdom. which shoots forth with clearer beams in his Son than in the creation. In which regard Christ is called 'the wisdom of God,' i. e. the highest discovery of his wisdom. There is a counsel, as well as will, in the more minute passages of his providence; but there is a more glorious workmanship of wisdom in the work of reconciliation, a manifold wisdom in laying the reconciliation frame with advantage to the glory of his name, and the welfare of the creature, which could not be conceived by angels or men before they saw it unfolded, for it was hid in God from the beginning of the world, and was not then made known to the angels, Eph. iii. 9, 10. What is the frame of heaven and earth to this? Just as his power and wisdom is in the making a clod of earth, to that which appears in the fabric of a man. In the creation it is like a sunbeam through the cranny of a wall, this like the sun facing us in its full glory; he is the only wise God, as he is our Saviour, Jude 25. And the apostle fixes the best note to it, when he calls it 'all wisdom and prudence,' wherein God abounded too: Eph. i. 8, 'Wherein he has abounded towards us in all wisdom and prudence.' All wisdom in contriving and determining the way, prudence in ordering and disposing the means consonant thereunto, wisdom in drawing the platform, and prudence in digging through all impediments, and making even the seeming obstacles serve as steps to the execution. How great was that wisdom that restored us by that logoV, that Word, whereby he had created us, and appointed his Son, who had an holiness exactly to obey him, and a power to bear the weight of whatsoever was necessary, to make up the breach! And this mystery he kept secret in his own breast from the beginning of the world, revealed to none distinctly, but by the gospel, after the incarnation of Christ, that it might evidently appear to be the work only of his wisdom, and therefore called 'hidden wisdom,' 1 Cor. ii. 7; whence the apostle, speaking of this as a mystery kept secret, breaks out into the praise of God for it, as 'The only wise God,' Rom. xvi. 25-27. What religion in the world declares the security of God's rights with man's happiness? What doctrine beside this answers all contradictions, and discovers justice possessing all its rights, and mercy fully answered in all its desires?

Secondly, His power. As the Father was in Christ reconciling the world, Christ was the power of God, as well as the wisdom of God: 1 Cor. i. 24, 'Christ the power of God and the wisdom of God.' The power of God in breaking the heart of the enmity by the death of the cross, and overthrowing all the designs of the evil spirit. The power of God is manifest in sustaining all things after the foundation of the world tottered, more than if he had destroyed this world and made a new one. That man has a mighty power over his own passions, that when he is extremely injured without giving the least occasion, yea, and against multiplied benefits, should study ways of reconciliation with that person, though he knew he should receive new slights from him upon the offers of such kindness; a mightier power would be manifest over himself, if he should part with his dearest friend, or a beloved son, to expose him to contempt and ignominy, for renewing the amity between him and his ungrateful adversary: such a man would have a mighty power and royalty. Rex est qui sibi imperat. Other things show the power of Clod over the creatures, this is as it were power over himself. If the pardon of one sin, or the sins of a nation, argue the greatness of God's power,óNum. xiv. 17, the power of God is pleaded by Moses as an argument to pardon the provoking Israelites, 'Let the power of my God be great,'ómuch more does the reconciling a world. Here is a power over his own wrath, deeply provoked by his offending creatures; a power over his own affections and love to his Son; a power over himself after such vast provocations, and a foresight of more, enhanced by ingratitude and slights of his creatures, and studying ways of reconcilement, while the offender was exercising fresher hostilities against God. It is an inconceivable power, and greater than that which is visible in the creation, and will be acknowledged so by those that understand the evil of sin, and the immense provocations offered to the justice of God. What religion in the world gives us any notice of so vast a power in God, as the gospel does in this case?

Thirdly, The wonders of his goodness. How is the gospel an edition of God's heart, as it wrought from eternity! An unfolding, and opening of his bowels which lay secretly yearning! This 'brings life and immortality to light,' 2 Tim. i. 10, which lay locked up in the cabinet of God's purpose, till they were unlocked and brought down to men in the gospel. In this we may see the scheme and model of his thoughts, the method of his counsels, the treaties about man's recovery, all the motions of his goodness, in its descent to earth and ascent to heaven, carrying at last the creature with it, to the wearing an eternal crown upon its head. How did he prepare all things for man's recovery, before man's fall, which was foreseen by him, and decreed to be permitted, providing a medicine before the disease, and a solder before the crack, casting about to reduce rebels to amity, before they had A being wherewith to rebel! Where is that religion, besides, that presents us with such draughts of divine love, that declares its secret resolves and transactions, that tells us of such an immense flood of bounty flowing down upon mankind! The heathens regarded God as severe, though they saw testimonies of his patience, they saw not those springs of kindness bubbling up in his own breast; they imagined them squeezed out by their sacrifices and solicitations, and purchased by their services. Here is the goodness and tender compassions of God making the first motion, laying on one colour after another, till it was brought to perfection. The gospel shows us God contriving redemption by his own wisdom, drawing it with his own hand, working it by his own power.

All this shows the excellency and amiableness of his nature. Honourable to God, a pattern of goodness to men, the highest incentive to a worship, adoration, and service to him, to all those duties which are most fit for a creature toward God, admiration of him, self-humiliation, dependence, ingenuous obedience: such discoveries of God leave men without excuse in all their contradictions to him. He is not represented in the gospel with his standard up, his weapons sharpened, his bow bent, and his arrows prepared, unless against inveterate and wilful unbelievers; but the gospel draws him to our view sheathing his sword, placing his arrows in his quiver, not in his bow, with his arms open, his countenance smiling; means sufficient to make us sink down in self-abomination, and rise up in the choicest affections to God. No religion represents God so admirably, so amiably to man, so worthy of himself, and with greater motives to those duties which become a creature; and therefore this has an excellency above all other religions in the world.

[2.] It has an excellency above all other religions, in showing the true way of attaining peace with God, and thereupon peace in ourselves. 'God was in Christ reconciling the world to himself;' not in any other methods, not in purifications and washings superstitiously practised by the heathens; not in sacrifices of beasts, though commanded to the Jews; but only as types of the great sacrifice God intended. All other ways of appeasing God are fond and foolish, cannot find a foundation in common and ordinary reason; they disparage God rather than honour him, in such mean and sordid thoughts of him, as though an infinite justice could be bribed by the blood of a beast. All other religions widen the breach, but do not in the least close it. But here we gee a God of peace, and a prince of peace embracing each other, and 'the voice of the turtle is heard' in the world. The gospel is the dove bringing an olive-branch of peace, put into its mouth by God. It brings us news of the allay of his wrath, which was due to our sins, and that his sword is blunted by himself in the bowels of his Son, that it might not be sheathed in ours. It shows us a shelter for storms, a light in God's countenance even in the shadow of darkness. Here God draws near to man, that man may have access to him. He makes his Son like to man, that man might be rendered capable of approaching to God. Two natures are joined in one person, that there may be an amiable conjunction of two different parties; he exposes his beloved Son to the strokes of his justice for a time, that he might reassume his life with honour for ever. It is a way that reason cannot disapprove of, since nothing could conduce more to the honour of God, and nothing more establish the peace of the creature. Other religions have framed mediators of their own, deified men, whereby they might have access to God. God in the gospel presents us with n mediator of his own choosing, of his own fitting, of his own ordering; one that he will not refuse, whose intercessions ho is pleased with; that he might keep off the darts of divine justice from us, that we might 'draw near through the veil of his flesh,' Heb. x. 20, that we may look upon God in Christ, without being dazzled by his glory, or scorched by his wrath. Now may devouring fire and combustible stubble meet together; fire without scorching, stubble without consuming. Here misery may approach to glory, because glory condescends to misery. Hereby guilt is removed, which makes us incapable of access to God; and wrath is removed, which hinders our actual access. Here may all that will believe in God through Christ and conform to his laws, walk in the midst of the furnace of God's justice without having an hair of their heads touched, without feeling the smart of that which will ho quick in consuming unregenerate men. Since nothing else discovers any peace with God, no doctrine else can make any peace in the conscience. It is the old way gives rest to the soul, Jer. vi. 16, the way as old as the first promise of a reconciler. All other ways, if rightly considered, rather promote than allay suspicions of God. Conscience has no ground to make any comfortable reflection, without some plain declaration of God's reconcilableness and reconciliation. Conscience can show us our guilt, but nothing in the world evidences the way of our peace but the gospel; no other religion discovers God in treaty about reconciliation.

Herein the Christian religion transcends all others; it glorifies God, and dignifies the creature. Salvation is bestowed upon fallen man, but the honour of all redounds to God, 'that no flesh may glory in his presence.' Here is an admirable temperament of justice and mercy, in the reconciliation of God and the creature: Hosea ii. 19, 'I will betroth thee unto me in righteousness and judgment, in kindness and mercy.' Judgment in the satisfaction by the surety, an efflux of mercy in requiring no portion at our hands.

(2.) Second information. If God be the author of reconciliation and redemption, then the knowledge of this, the declaration of the gospel, is an inestimable blessing to a nation. What better news can God send to men? The very declaration of it is a lifting a nation up to heaven: Mat. xi. 23, 'And thou, Capernaum, that art exalted to heaven.' The Bibles in our hands are inexpressible blessings, since God has made a large comment upon that first promise which he gave to Adam; God has declared to the world in full, what he gave Adam as it were in a scrip of paper, he has unfolded in his word the mystery, brought it to perfection, and proclaimed it openly, and given us a glass wherein we may see his glory. The discovery of Christ in the flesh was a greater glory belonging to the second temple than what was in the first, notwithstanding all its ornaments and riches. The people wept when they saw the beauty of the second temple inferior to that of the first; and indeed there was wanting in it the propitiatory, the holy fire, Urim and Thummim, the spirit of prophecy, and the ark of the testimony, yet, Haggai ii. 9, God tells them, 'the glory of the latter house should be greater than that of the former,' though it wanted all those things. The matter of it was not so precious, the condition of the inhabitants was more grievous. The temple was often pillaged, by Antiochus, Pompey, Crassus. There must be some other gift proportionable to the majesty of that God who had promised, as the words following declare, 'I will give peace.' Not a temporal peace, for they never had such cruel wars as after the building of that temple; but a spiritual peace, a peace between God and man, between God's justice and our sins, by the means of the Messiah. He would not adorn the temple with riches; he could if he would, for the gold was his and the silver his, ver. 8. But the declarations of peace which should be wrought in that city, and published in that temple, was the glory of the place. What though a nation should be brought to poverty and disgrace, have the waves of all kinds of afflictions go over their heads, while God keeps up the declarations of a spiritual peace, while he proclaims still the reconciliation he is the author of! That nation is still glorious, though externally miserable. God never employed his thoughts so much about the riches and honour of a nation, the gold and ornaments of the temple, as about the reconciliation of man. While God declares that to a people which is the subject of his thoughts, the delight of his heart, the glory of a nation is preserved, but when once he shuts his mouth, and will speak no more

when his voice shall not be heard in our streets, when he shall shake off the dust of his feet against us, then we may write Ichabod upon ourselves, the 'glory is departed,' though wealth and outward glory should stay behind. The proclaiming the everlasting gospel is the fall of Babylon. When the auger comes forth with the everlasting gospel, Rev. xiv. 6, he is presently followed by another that brings the tidings of Babylon's fall: ver. 8, Babylon is fallen, is fallen.' The removing the everlasting gospel is the rising of Babylon, and makes way for an army of judgments. Desolation follows upon a nation when God's 'soul departs from them,' Jer. vi. 8 and his soul departs from them when he breaks off any further treaties With men upon the articles of peace in the gospel. The gospel is nothing else but a proclamation of the articles of peace. His thoughts of peace were the cause of his sending Christ, the accomplishment of the reconciliation is the ground of proclaiming it. He sent Christ to effect it, and his Spirit in the gospel to ratify it. It is called by the title of 'the word of reconciliation,' 1 Cor. v. 19, as though nothing else was intended in it, but to make God and man at peace together actually. It is a declaration of his ardent desire to return into amity with us, that he is satisfied by the death of his Son, and can admit us, without any contradiction to his justice, and with a stronger security than at the first creation. What a mercy is it that God should make known his gospel to us, and not to all in the world! If he did not intend to be reconciled to some in a nation, he would never transmit it from one nation to another. He has made known his Godhead and power to all, Rom. i. 20 but not his placability and mercy to all. Men may know by natural light that God is merciful, and yet not know that he has erected a propitiation for the world in Christ, and without this distinct knowledge no man can be saved under the New Testament; and by all the knowledge of God's mercy in the world, they were never able to arrive to this without a special revelation, no more than by the knowledge of the nature of a candle they can arrive to the knowledge of the nature of the sun in the heavens. Is not this a glory, a happiness? What praise does God deserve from us for it!

(a.) Third information. This doctrine acquaints us with the whole concern of faith. It shows,

[1.] What a strong foundation of faith we have. God chose him, called him, counselled him: he is wise, and would not choose a feeble and uncertain reconciler, unable to manage the business committed to him, he is immutable, and in regard of the holiness of his nature, will not and cannot recede from his own choice and approbation, he has done all that he can possibly to show himself placable and pacified. Christ has done all which concerned him, to the high satisfaction and content of God. All the business lies on our side, whether we will join issue with God in it; whether our hearts shall endeavour to run parallel with the counsel of God in it; whether his approbation shall be the joyful measure of ours. What high ground have we to own and accept this pacification; or what pretence can we have to refuse it? If we do not refuse it, God carrot. His act Lath been already passed, for Christ is a reconciler of his election. It is his glory and our security, that he is a God that changes not: Mal. iii. 6, 'For I am the Lord, I change not, therefore you sons of Jacob are not consumed.' Which seems to me to be spoken in relation to the messenger of the covenant, ver. 1, and not to the words immediately foregoing, ver. 5. As if God should say, I will punish, for I am unchangeable in my justice; which would infer rather their destruction than their preservation: but I have decreed the sending the messenger of the covenant, and I am unchangeable in this purpose, and in the accomplishing all the fruits of his coming, therefore you sons of Jacob are not consumed. The assurance is stronger, since the decree has been manifested, and the satisfaction accepted by the injured Father. God has provided such a satisfaction to himself, in the death of his Son, as is answerable to the greatness of the creature's guilt, a remedy for the creature's fears. The God who was offended is pacified; the law which cursed the sinner is satisfied, the honour of God, which stood in the way of happiness, is repaired, He sent him when we did not desire him, he sent him when we did not expect him; when there was scarce any faith in the promise of the Messiah left in all the land of Judea, and sent him not to procure a temporal good, but the favour of God, which is the womb of inconceivable happiness; and was so far from dealing with us as enemies when we were in his hands, that he did the utmost he could to lay a foundation of amity, and put the management of it into the hands of the person dearest to him, whom he could only trust.

Had God spared any cost to reconcile us, our doubts might be excusable; but since he has discovered a combination of gracious acts about Christ, that his thoughts only run upon this, and had no other intention but the glory of his name in the happiness of the offending creature; there is no room for distrust if we embrace his conditions. The very end of raising him and giving him glory, and therefore of all the actions preceding, was 'that your faith and hope might be in God,' 1 Pet. i. 21, that you might believe him to be a God reconciled, and thereupon hope for all blessings from him which he has promised. As crucified, Christ is the object of faith; as exalted, he is the ground of faith. This sufficiency of Christ as a ground of faith, God Lath witnessed in the highest manner possible: 1 John v. 7, 'There are three that bear record in heaven, the Father, the Word, and the Holy Ghost; and those three are one,' i. e. that give an heavenly and divine authority to this truth. The word heaven is not to be taken for the place or local heaven, for many there bear witness to it, innumerable companies of angels, and martyrs, and glorified spirits but we must understand it of an extraordinary testimony. (As Job xx. 27, when it is said, 'The heaven shall reveal his iniquity,' i. e. God, by an extraordinary judgment, shall manifest to man, that he was a wicked creature.) 'And these three are one,' not only in their essence, but in their testimony, which gives a greater strength to this witness; as the testimony of a man is stronger, when it is in conjunction with the testimony of others, who are worthy to be credited; and this record is, that faith has a strong foundation, and will have a blessed success; it was the whole purpose of the blessed Trinity to join together in this extraordinary witness in all their acts, that Christ is a full ground of faith in God, so that now a faithful person may highly plead this, Lord, I present thee with a mediator of thy own choice. Thou did choose him for me, before I did choose him for myself; thou did counsel him to undertake this office, before thou did command me to accept him; thou did call him to be a reconciler, before thou did call me to be reconciled; thou did bruise him for me; this is thy only act, and this I plead, and upon this foundation will I rest the weight of my soul. It is a ground for a brace plea; for God would not busy himself about any thing that should have no effect. God would not deceive his people, and feed them with vain hopes in a business of so great a concern; he will not go back from his own appointment, he cannot go back from his own word, his own deed, his own counsel, which he is pleased with, especially since it was not by permission, as Adam's sin was, but by his grace, which makes, in the apostle's judgment, the efficacy of Christ's death stronger for reconciliation, than Adam's offence was for the breach of amity: Rom. v. 1a, 'If through the offence of one many be dead, much more the grace of God, and the gift by grace, which is by one man, Jesus Christ, has abounded unto many,' i. e. acting all along in it and with it in a way of grace from the first original of his gift, and therefore it abounds, i. e. is more efficacious to the salvation of men, than Adam's was to their condemnation.

[2.] It shows us the nature and necessity of faith. God has appointed Christ a mediator between himself and man. God has testified himself reconciled in this mediator, all his acts about him signify those things. Faith on our parts is nothing else but an act of our souls, answering to those acts on the part of God. As God chose him, commissioned him, accepted him, glorified him, so faith is a full approbation of all the acts of God in this concern. A choice of Christ, an acceptance and glorifying him, putting our concerns into his hands, receiving him as our mediator and king, upholding him, a; far as creature-ability reaches, in his office; resting in him, in his precepts by obedience, in his promises by dependence; and by such terms faith is set out in Scripture. As God looks to him as his rest, Isa. lxvi. 2, so we are to look to him and be saved, Isa. xiv. 22. As God looks unto him faith all the affections of a God, we should look unto him with all the affections of a creature. A mediator must be accepted by both parties that are at variance, and they must stand to what that mediator does. As when two princes are at difference, and a third interposes to make an agreement between them, they must both consent to accept of that prince for mediator, and both put their Concerns into his hand; he can be no mediator for him that does not accept of him in that relation. God has appointed this mediator, and settled him in this office, because God and man did not stand upon equal terms, God being the sovereign and only offended, man being the offending criminal. God has declared himself fully contented, and has complied with all the conditions of the first agreement; it only rests now that man will accept of him for those purposes for which God did constitute him, and comply with those conditions which God has settled. This is necessary; God saves no man against his will, and he that does not join issue with God in consenting to this, declares he has no purpose to be saved by him.

There must be some mediator to make God and man meet in agreement, to answer all the ends of God, and restore the fallen creature; God has appointed no other than his Son; if men could find out any other and propose him, God is not hound to accept of him. But what mediator can man appoint to treat with God? Without consent to this person, man is utterly undone, for all the wit of men and angels cannot find out a person fit for so great a business. If it were possible, it is an increase of the crime, and a high presumption for a criminal to stand upon terms, and refuse the person the prince chooses to mediate for him, when there can be no exceptions against him, which shows the necessity of faith in Christ, in whom God has been reconciling the world, and only in him, and the duty of the creature to acquiesce in God's contrivance and constitution. God has taken a full measure of Christ and all his sufferings, and found him complete, therefore our faith should be complete in him. As God has singled him out from angels and men to be an expiatory sacrifice and a great king, no faith suits itself to this act of God in singling Christ out from all other competitors to be a reconciler and Lord, and the righteousness of God from all other righteousness. This faith must not be a naked assent, as God's act about Christ was not a naked assent, but a full, hearty consent; a joy in him, an acceptation of him with all his affections. So must ours be.

[3.] It shows us the true object of faith. Not God in the simplicity of his own being, not Christ alone in his incarnation and death, but 'God ire Christ.' As God was in Christ reconciling the world, so God in Christ is the object of faith. God is the ultimate object of faith, Christ the immediate object: John xii. 44, 'He that believes on me, believes not on me, but on him that sent me;' not on me ultimately, his faith is directed to God; as he that believes an ambassador does not only give credit to him, but to the prince that sent him. And to God, not as creator, but as the Father of our Lord Jesus Christ; to God as ordering, to Christ as acting; to God as commissioning, to Christ as commissioned: John xiv. 1, 'You believe in God, believe also in me;' in God as the author of all good, in me as the mediator and purchaser of all grace; in God as the first author, in Christ as the faithful executor. God is the sun, Christ is the beam; our eye ascends to the sun by the beam, but terminates not in the beam, but in the sun. Faith ascends ultimately to God, as being the head of Christ, 1 Cor. xi. 3, and the salutation is first, 'Peace from God the Father,' 1 Cor. i. 3, the fountain and spring of all that Christ did. In Christ, we see the smiles of God; in Christ, we hear the joyful sound of his bowels, in Christ, we feel the beatings of his heart. The Father is the reconciled, the Son the reconciler, faith is therefore called faith towards God, Heb. vi. I, and we are said to 'believe in God through Christ,' 1 Peter i. 21, and 'through his name,' Acts x. 43. God is the primary and principal object, Christ the immediate; both must be taken in. He that believes not in the Son, believes not in the Father; he that believes not in the Son as reconciler, believes not in the Father as reconciled. He that believes not in the satisfaction and mediation of Christ, believes not in the Father satisfied, for 'he that honours not the Son, honours not the Father which has sent him, John v. 23, for they are one in the work of redemption, and in all the grace which flows down to us, as wolf as in nature. As Christ is the Son, equal with the Father, we believe in him as God; as he is mediator, we believe in him as God's servant, furnished by him with authority and ability. He is the proper object of faith, as being one with the Father. If he were not God, he could not be the object of trust: Jer xvii. 5, 7, 'Cursed is the man that trusts in man; blessed is the man that trusts in the Lord.' And a blessedness is pronounced to those that trust in the king God has set upon Sion, Ps. ii. 12, and in the chief corner-stone he has laid in Sion, 1 Peter ii. 6. He is the mediums of our faith, as he is God's servant. We believe in God as the author, we believe in Christ as the means. Faith fastens upon Christ as a gift, upon God as the donor. It receives Christ as God's token and gift of transcendent kindness, and from ravishment with this gift, the soul ascends to confidence in the giver. It reads God's heart in Christ, sees the glory of God in the face of Christ, and mounts up to clasp about one who has declared himself in amity. We eye Christ as the expiation, God as the judge; we see Christ upon the cross and in heaven. But we consider by whose authority he. is there, for what ends he is there, and both the authority and the ends lead us naturally to God, to place our confidence in him as the rector, the acceptor, and in Christ as mediator. For faith is a grace that comforts the soul; joy and peace comes in by believing, John xv. `13. What joy can there be in Christ's actions and passion, unless we regard God the Father as concerned in them? God is a God of all comfort, as being u God of all peace. All Christ's sufferings signify nothing but as they refer to God, and have his approbation and concurrence; so our faith is not right, and signifies nothing, which does not make the whole honour redound to God.

[4.] It shows the acceptableness of faith to God, and the high pleasure he takes in it. Faith is an approbation of God's actions herein, and of the whole scheme; it is a sealing the counterpart, as God's act was a sealing the original deed; it is a testimony to the glory of all those attributes he honoured in the mediation of Christ: as Abraham by his faith 'gave glory to God,' Rom. iv. 20. Faith does actively glorify God, and passively too, for every one that trusts in Christ is 'to the praise of the glory of his grace,' Eph. i. 12. To his truth and to his power, which were concerned, one in the intention of making good his promise, the other in his ability to perform it; so in believing in God as reconciled through Christ, and that he has taken off the curses of the law, and will bestow an everlasting righteousness, and relying upon him in a way of obedience, as Abraham did in that case, we acknowledge God's veracity, wisdom, holiness, justice, love; and we acknowledge (Christy love, tenderness, and sufficiency. It is an applauding the wisdom of God in his choice. Certainly, that God gives us so many exhortations to be followers of him, to be like him, is delighted to see men have the same sentiments with himself, to be like him in their judgments of things in regard of knowledge, and like him in the practice of things in regard of holiness; he delights to see that his Son's blood was not shed in vain; to perceive himself and his Son glorified by men in laying down their weapons. Every act of faith is a new glory to God; it is 'to the praise of the glory of his grace.' God justifies us by this way of reconciliation, and our acceptance of it justifies God from all charge and imputations from the creature, as the approving of John's baptism, Luke vii. 29, was a justification of God. Next to the joy God has in Christ, he has a joy in the beginnings of faith: there is 'joy in the presence of the angels,' Luke xv. 10. Christ has a joy in the faith and obedience of his people, John xv. 11; and when their faith is perfect, they shall at last be 'presented before the presence of his glory with exceeding joy:' Jude 24, 'The presence of his glory;' God will appear more glorious when he comes to see all the purchased and redeemed ones of Christ, that have approved of his gracious and wise contrivance, and given him the honour of his attributes by a believing obedience to his will. 'With exceeding joy;' since the subject of this joy is not determined in the text, it may be understood of the joy of God, of the mediator, of the saints. 'Presented'; God shall receive the presents en egalaliasei, with an exulting joy.

(4.) Fourth information. We see here the strength and sufficiency of Christ for all the concerns of his mediation. God would not have called him out for this work, had he not been able to accomplish it; he would never have laid the government of things, in order to a restoration, upon unable shoulders. God would no more have chosen him, or been pleased with any proposition of it, than he was pleased with sacrifice and burnt offerings. God would not fail of his end; his end was reconciliation; Christ therefore was able to pacify the sharpest wrath. It was not agreeable to God's wisdom to choose an unable or unskilful agent. God was certain of the event; he would never have exposed the human nature, united to the second person, to a task wherein it should have utterly sunk under the justice of God. God had more love to his creature, than to venture the eternal concerns of those he was resolved to save, in a weak bottom, that could not have resisted the sturdiest rocks and most blustering storms. God foresaw the vast number of those sins (though numberless to man) that stood in need of pardon, when he singled out Christ to this charge. It was for 'many offences' he intended the merit of Christ, Rom. v. 16, even for as many offences as those for whom he died would be guilty of, and he would not lay them upon the shoulders of one who was not able to bear them. He was every way able, in regard he had the same nature and glory with the Father; he was every way fit, in the affinity he had with both parties, whereby he could reach out his hand to both: the hand of his deity to the Father, that of his humanity to man. As God, he could satisfy for all mankind; as man, he could suffer. Had he not been every way fit and able, the Majesty of heaven, who was desirous of reconciliation, would not have pitched upon him. No creature could satisfy by suffering, because no creature had an infinite dignity in his person to render temporary sufferings of infinite value; nor could any creature present a service as valuable as the offence was provoking No man can be profitable to God, Job xxii. 2. Good services among men take not off the sentence of the law in a court of judicature, without a pardoning act of the supreme power. Where was there any creature who had strength enough to bear our sins, and dignity enough to satisfy for them? Our offences were too great a load for a creatures strength, or a creature's suffering, or expiation. Here was the humanity in conjunction with the divinity, to be the sacrifice; and the divinity in conjunction with the humanity, to be the altar for the sanctification of it. The whole method of God's proceedings assures us of the sufficiency of Christ for the work of mediation; had he not been fit, God would never have laid all his honour at stake in the choice of him to it. And the sequel shows that God is fully satisfied with it, since, on the consideration of it, justice forgets the injuries done to the Deity, and treats believers as heirs of heaven instead of rebels.

(5.) Fifth information. It gives an assurance of all spiritual and eternal blessings, since God was in Christ reconciling the world, and was the author of all the methods of it, and the acceptor of the performance. Christ must cease to be a reconciler, before God can cease to be reconciled. God was in Christ from eternity in the resolve of it; he has been in Christ in time in the acting of it; he will be in Christ for rendering the fruits of it fully ripe. Christ is the knot and baud of the reconciliation, and is gone to heaven in our nature to secure it. God is in Christ approving it, the second person is in the humanity ensuring it; his conducting Christ through the world in human infirmities to eternal glory, is an assurance that he will dignify all those that by faith lay hold on him, and lay down their weapons against him. If he be in Christ reconciling the world, he is in Christ wrapping up all other blessings for us; since it is an everlasting gospel, the womb of it is full of everlasting blessings.

[1.] God's end is not yet perfected. God has not attained his full end; reconciliation was but in order to further blessings. There may be a reconciliation wrought between parties, whereby a party is freed from punishment, without being partaker of a special amity. God did send Christ to make peace, not simply to be at peace with his creature, but to second it with other mercies which the enmity before was a bar unto. It is a reconciliation that teems with many more inexpressible blessings. The riches of his grace, and the glory of his grace, would not be fully displayed by a single peace. The mystery which he proposed in himself, was, that he might gather together all in one, even in cultist, to the full possession of the purchased inheritance, 'to the praise of his glory,' Eph. i. 10, 14; his glory would not attain its full praise without further blessings at the heels of this. He will rejoice in believers for ever. How can he rejoice in them if they never come to rejoice in themselves; if there be always a defect and indigence in them? The remnants of enmity will drop off, the appearances of anger in his face as a Father will one day for ever vanish, and every frown be smoothed. God is perfectly reconciled, but believers are not yet fully fit for all the fruits of it; but since he has been in Christ laying the foundation in grace, he will be in him rearing the superstructure to glory. God would be at peace with us, that he might bestow the highest kindness upon us. Justice stood in the way, and God would have his justice satisfied, that mercy might flow down without any obstacle. Since, therefore, he has been in Christ contenting his justice, he will be in Christ fully pleasing his mercy As infinite justice was not contented without the death of Christ, so mercy will not be contented without an efflux of benefits upon the believer. We should not understand God fully appeased, if things stood always at one stay.

[2.] The glory of God is concerned in it. If he be the author of it, he will no less be the guardian of it; the same motives of honour and love which excited him to contrive it, and brought it to this issue, will have the same influence on him to ripen all the fruits of it. As ho has the title of 'the God of our Lord Jesus Christ,' in regard of the whole interest he has in this affair of redemption, so the apostle gives him another title in relation to the same work: Eph. i. 17, 'The God of our Lord Jesus Christ, the Father of glory.' He is the Father of glory, as he is the fountain of all the glory which accrues from this work; as well as he is the Father of glory subjectively, in the glory of the divine essence infinitely glorious; and objectively, as all glory is due to him from his creatures. He is the Father of glory, as all the actions of Christ did centre in the honour of the Father; or the Father of glory, as being the author of an those gracious and glorious communications designed to be bestowed by him, as the Clod of our Lord Jesus Christ, upon his creatures. It is by him, as the Father of glory in Jesus Christ, that a 'spirit of wisdom and revelation in the knowledge of Christ' is given, a full and complete knowledge of him, and the riches of the glory of his inheritance in the saints. If God designs to chew himself a Father of glory, as the God of the Lord Jesus Christ, and if he shows himself a Father of glory in increasing the knowledge of Christ by a spirit of wisdom in the hearts of his people and acquainting them with the riches intended for them, the crown of his glory would be dim if there were only n knowledge of it, and no possession at last, and full enjoyment of all that which Christ has purchased. How little glory would God get by acquainting them with it, if the knowledge of it should not at last mount up into fruition!

[3.] All that remains to be done in this kind is more feasible, and hat less obstacles than what already has been done. The grand obstacle to the fullness of his mercy, in regard of the demands of justice, is quite removed, the merit of Christ has surmounted the demerit of men; and what is behind is a lighter thing to the poller, wisdom, and mercy of God, than the laying the first stone of our redemption was. Since the delivery of his Son to death, which might have found resistance from the affections of the Father, has been performed, what is there that can be capable of any demur? How is it possible a believer should perish, since Christ has suffered to reconcile infinite justice, by the will of God? How is it possible he should miss of eternal happiness, since for God to give his Son to die for reconcilement, is infinitely more than the justification of him by his blood, and saving him through his life from wrath? Peace is the root of all joy and blessedness, and in the angels' song, good will towards men follows peace on earth. When peace is made, there is no bar to the highest manifestations of good will.

[4.] No enemies can possibly obstruct it. If God were in Christ reconciling the world, who can prevent the execution of his resolution to the full? Since it has been thus far carried on, all the venom of Satan spit out against a Christian, can no more deprive him of what God will do, than it could hinder what God has done. He was baffled in attempting the hindrance of it, though he engaged all the powers of hell in the contest; and was fooled, since the way he took to prevent it did eventually promote it; and in his resolving to be an hinderer, he was, by a reach of infinite wisdom beyond his own wit, made a furthered of it; and if he could not prevent the foundation, he shall be less able to deface the superstructure; and if the greater sins of unregeneracy did not hinder the influence and application of it, the infirmities after regeneration shall not obstruct the full perfection of it.

(6.) Sixth information. It shows us the unworthiness of man's dealing with God. God cannot do anything higher to sweeten our spirits towards him, he has not another or a dearer Son to give; nothing more can be acted upon the world for the security of the creature. There are no wider channels for the love of God to run in, no higher way to secure his honour from contempt, and his creature from vengeance. He was angry with us, and with good cause; we were children of wrath, and deserved it; God is appeased by the blood of Christ, he delights in the laying aside his anger, he has done his utmost to assure men of it.

Then certainly,

[1.] Our rejecting Christ, and the way of his appointment, is a high contempt of God. It is a slight of God in the glory of his grace, an envying him the honour of the restoration. Adam envied his sovereignty and independence, and every unbeliever envies his wisdom and merciful bowels. Since his heart was set upon this work, that all the counsels of eternity centre in it, a deafness to his proposals is a contradiction to all his counsels, and the great desire of his heart. As faith in Christ redounds to the honour of God, as being an approbation of all God's acts in this affair, so unbelief of Christ redounds to the contempt of God, as slighting all those gracious manifestations of his grace and wisdom. As the murder of a man, and every degree of murder, in the contempt of him who is the image of God, is a dishonour to God in regard of the relation man bears to God in that respect, Gen ix. 6, so every unworthy usage of Christ, every act of unbelief, redounds to the dishonour of the Father, whose ambassador Christ is, and the exact image of his person. If men do not heartily think reconciliation by Christ worth their highest thoughts and entertainments, they reproach God, as if he were busy from eternity about just nothing, or a sleeveless matter, and run through so many stages in his acts about Christ to no purpose. It is a 'making light' of a rich feast of God's providing, Mat. xxii. 5, it is a self-destroying fury, worse than that of devils. It is a making all other sins against God more sinful: John xv. 22, 'If I had not come and spoken to them, they had not had sin,' their sin had not appeared with so much malice.

[2.] Our jealousies of God. Men are fond of suspicions of God when they are struck down with a sense of their sin, though this despair is not so ordinary as presumption. This is a measuring God by man, and bringing him down to the creature's model; a contracting God's goodness according to the creature's scantiness. Can there be any just reflections upon God, after the manifestation of his earnestness for the reconciliation of man? If the owning God in those acts be a justifying God, óLuke vii. 29, 'They justified God,' óthe disowning him is a condemnation of God. As Abraham glorified God when he staggered not at the promise, but clasped it in his arms by faith, so we dishonour God inexpressibly, when we stagger not only at one promise, but at his whole scene of amazing, acts in the founding and carrying of his work in Christ. It is unworthy in any truly humbled soul to imagine God an enemy still, after all his mysterious contrivances for the relief of the creature, and his delight in his Son for answering his purposes.

[3.] Our enmity and disobedience to God, though God be in Christ reconciling the world, as therefore we disparage him by our jealousies of him, we also deal unworthily with him by sinful presumptions. There are terms expected to be performed by us; it is not a lazy belief, an assent to this, accompanied with a love of any one sin (which was the cause of God's anger), that gives men a title to it. As God's love in this, and his acceptation was not a lazy love, &c., neither must our faith. The application of it is not but to such a faith that purifies the heart. For us not to leave the love of sin, when God has quenched his wrath in the blood of Christ, is an unworthy usage of God, and cuts a man off from any interest in this reconciliation. Abraham's faith, whereby he glorified God, appeared eminent in this act of obedience, in a willingness to sacrifice his son. Not to endeavour to please God in a course of obedience, is to keep up our enmity under God's offers of amity. To presume upon his goodness, to act the highest unbelief under pretences of the contrary, to think God will be your friend while you persist in your enmity, is a contradiction to the whole tenor of the gospel. Faith in his promises is never accounted of, without faith in his precepts. As he has been a God in Christ reconciling the world, so he has been commanding in Christ the world to a submission, and it is outrage and high ingratitude not to endeavour to please God, since he has been so careful to please us.

[4.] Omissions of prayer. Has God done so much to render us capable of coming to him, and himself capable to receive us with honour to himself? And is it not very disingenuous and slighting to neglect this privilege, founded upon the counsels of wisdom, and the cost of the blood of Christ? Before, we could with no more comfort approach to God, than a guilty malefactor could to the judge; but since God has laid by his fury in Christ, and discovers an altering glory in the face of Christ, what can we plead for our neglects of his allurements, our seldom approaches to him, or our slight and lazy addresses? He uses his friend unkindly that will not make use of his friendship, and upon urgent occasions desire his assistance. All neglects imply either an inability or unwillingness in God, and both cast dirt upon his reconciling work, since there can be no greater evidences of his power and willingness than he has discovered in the whole working of it. We virtually deny the Father to be the fountain of all grace, when we go not to him; we deny Christ to be the purchaser of all peace, when we go not in his name. God sent Christ to 'consecrate a new and living way for us to enter into the holiest by the blood of Jesus,' Heb. x. 19. By neglects we disparage God's mission, and Christ's consecration, and the liberty he has procured. What should we have done if we had been to approach to God as a judge upon a tribunal of justice, when we will not draw near to him as a judge upon a mercy-seat, through the reconciliation wrought in Christ?

Well, then, let us consider the danger of slighting this reconciliation. Well may that man deserve doubly the curses of the law, that will not believe and obey after God's demonstrations of the riches of grace; well may he deserve to be crushed in pieces under the insupportable burden of his own guilt, that will still be fond of his treason against a reconciling God. Shall the great king descend from the throne of his majesty to become a reconciler, and after that a solicitor, and feel nothing but heels lifted up (John xiii. 18) instead of hearts? Such an one is doubly a child of wrath: first, by nature; and after, by a particular refusal to become a friend. The interest of our souls lies at stake; without changing our unworthy courses, wrath will be executed upon us; God has provided no other reconciler, and is resolved not to let his weapons fall by any other motive than the blood of the Redeemer.

(7.) Seventh information. It shows us the way of all religious worship. If God be in Christ reconciling the world, all our recourse to, and dealing with, a reconciling God, must be in and through Christ. As God's motion to us is in Christ, our motions to Clod must be through the same medium. He is 'the way, the truth, and the life,' John xiv. 6. 'No man comes to the Father but by me;' as no man has the Father coming to him but by Christ, the way whereby God communicates truth and life to us, the way whereby we must offer up our true and lively services to him. As God is the ultimate object of faith, Christ the medium, so God is the object of worship, Christ the medium. As Christ is equal with God, he is the object of faith, the object of worship; as Christ is God's servant, he is the way whereby we believe, the way whereby we have access to God. The soul must be carried altogether by the consideration of Christ, in presenting petitions in his name; in expecting answers upon the ground of his merit. Ye must regard him as the meritorious cause of our access to the throne of grace, and our welcome at it. How can we go to God as reconciled, but in the name of the reconciler? We cannot come with any boldness upon any other account. It is by the knowledge of the Son we ascend to the knowledge of the Father, by the merit of the Son we have access to the throne of the Father, by the intercession of the Son we have access to communion with the Father; in the name of the Son, we are to ask what we want, and by the merit of the Son we must only expect what we beg. It is as 'the Father of our Lord Jesus Christ,' that he communicates himself to us, Eph. i. 8; it is as the 'Father of our Lord Jesus Christ' we must 'bow our knees' to him, Eph. iii. 14, remembering still, that Christ is the band that links God and us together. What confidence can we have in God, if we respect him not as the Father of our Lord Jesus Christ; for in him only he is the Father of believers, otherwise he is the Father of the whole world, a provoked Father; in Christ a reconciled Father. As the Father of our Lord Jesus Christ, our praises must be offered to him, 1 Pet. i. 3. All acts of worship are only acceptable to the rather through Christ: Heb. xiii. 15, 'By him let us offer the sacrifice of praise to God;' all must have the stamp of this reconciler upon them. It is by his satisfaction we have the privilege to come to the holiest, before the seat of God, with our prayers and services. It is in his blood, the sword, set to prevent our entrance into paradise, has lost both its edge and flame. It is by the blood of Christ only we have this boldness, Heb. x. 19, 20. His blood is our best plea, his flesh our only screen from the wrath of God in all our services. We must, therefore, in all our services rest in his office, propose him as the mediator of our services.

(8.) Eighth information. There is then no mediator, no reconciler, but Christ. God is in Christ reconciling the world. In him, and none but him; in him, exclusively of all others. He is indeed 'the Christ, the Saviour of the world,' John iv. 42. By way of excellency! in regard of the danger he saves us from; by way of exclusion, in regard of the sole designation of his person, exclusive of all others. We must believe that Christ is he, the only person designed in the prophecies, promises, and types: John viii. 24, 'if you believe not that I am he.' There was none anciently but he; he was set up from eternity, he was the only lamb slain from the foundation of the world. This seed of the woman was only in the promise, only designed by the types; by this band only were the ancient believers united to God; in this Immanuel he was God with them as well as with us. None were courted God's friends before, but by his mediation; none can be since, because God has accepted no other. No ark, but that of God's appointing, could secure Noah and resist the force of the waters. None hereafter, he is 'the same for ever', he is today, as he was before, Heb. xiii. 8. The heart of God is fixed upon him, and his resolution concerning the duration of his office unalterable; he has summed up all the dispensations of former ages in him: Eph. i. 10, 'He has gathered together in one all things in Christ, even in him,' in no others All other things were preparations to him, shadows of him. But the perfection of all was in Christ; and God, who had various ways of communicating himself to men, has summed up his whole will in his Son, and manifested that all his transactions with men did terminate in his Son Christ, Web. ii. 1, 2. These are the last days, God will speak by no other.

[1.] None else was ever appointed by God. No other sacrifice was ever substituted in the room of sinners; none else was the centre of the prophecies, the subject of the promises, the truth of the types, no name erected for a shelter for the nations to trust in but this name: Isa. xlii. 4, 'The isles shall wait for his law;' Mat. xii. 21, 'In his name shall the Gentiles trust.' None else has the title of peacemaker conferred upon him, Eph. ii. 14, which title he has by his dentin on the cross, Col. i. 20. Those, therefore, that reject this way of mediation, must infallibly perish. He that will have any good by a prince, must go to that minister of state he has settled for that end. God has ordained no other mediator. God has thought none else fit to trust with his concerns, to do his work, restore his honour, receive glory from him. We must acquiesce in God's judgment, and not set up the pride of our reason and will, in contradiction to infinite wisdom. None else was ever honoured by the voice of the Father, testifying him to be his beloved Son, in whom he was well pleased. None besides him had this testimony, none in conjunction with him, none in subordination to him in the work of mediation; that he might be the first born among many brethren, enjoying all the rights of primogeniture. As God employed no other in the creation, so he employs no other in the restoration of the world.

[2.] None else was ever fit for this. Satisfaction there must be for the honour of God, that the law might be vindicated, justice glorified, holiness illustrated; none but Christ, an infinite person, was able to do all this. Security there must be to the Creator, that the honour of God might not be a lain at a loss. This could not be insured in the hands of a mutable creature; so that by any other mediator we cannot honour God by a suitable satisfaction, nor promise ourselves an unshaken preservation. Without infinite satisfaction, guilt must remain; without infinite power to preserve it entire, guilt would return. This mediator only had an alliance to both parties: to God, whereby he could call him Father; to us, whereby he could call us brethren. That God and man might be joined in one covenant of grace, the mediator of that covenant is God and man in one person. Had he been only God, he had had no alliance to our nature; bad he been only man, he had had no alliance to the divine nature, and had been an insufficient mediator, Incapable of performing what was requisite for our redemption. In this posture of fitness, there is none else in heaven and earth. Had the mediator been only man, he had been incapable of satisfying; had he been only God, he had been incapable of suffering; but being God and man, he was capable of both. No motive was powerful enough to appease the anger of the Father, but the blood of the cross; and no power strong enough to bear; no person worthy to present sufferings, but only this mediator. It was upon no other person that the Spirit descended like a dove, to furnish his human nature with all ability for the discharge of this trust. He is infinite,' and what can be added to infinite? If infinite be not sufficient to reconcile, finite beings must for ever come short of effecting it for us.

[3.] None else was ever accepted, or designed to be accepted, but this Mediator. No other surety was ever accepted by God for the payment of our debts. All sacrifices 'could not make the comers thereunto perfect,' Heb. x. 1, could not set them right in the esteem of God, and make a reconciliation with him; they were an image, not the life, and God accepted them as shadows, not as the substance; the repetition of them was a certain evidence of their inability to effect the reconciliation of man, Heb. x. 2, as the iteration of a medicine daily sheers its inefficacy to cure. The law was not able after our fall, by reason of our disagreement with the terms of it, to bring us near to God. God's justice and our sins stood in the way of amity, therefore God commanded bounds to be set to the people when the law was given, Exod. xix. 12, that they should not come near the mount. But the covenant of grace, veiled in the ceremonial law, was laid in the blood of Christ, typified by that blood sprinkled by Moses upon the people, Exod. xxiv. 8, to which the apostle alludes, 'the blood of sprinkling speaks better things than the blood of Abel,' Heb. xii. 24, than the blood of the firstlings, which Abel sprinkled, Gen. iv. 4, which was the first eminent type of the death of Christ upon record, which the Spirit of God mentions here as the first sacrifice, though no question Adam did not spend all that time between his fall and the growth of Abel to man's stature, without a sacrifice. Those sacrifices were poor and feeble, unworthy in themselves of the acceptance of God, not able to expiate sin, nor ever intended for propitiation, because they had no intrinsic value in them for such an end. But the blood of Christ, being the blood of the Lamb of God without spot, is a worthy and valuable price for the sins of the world. These, nor our own righteousness, were ever intended to be of worth, or strength, to expiate the sin of the soul and reconcile us to God; Christ is the only peacemaker, the only peace-conveyer; no other righteousness is called the righteousness of God, the righteousness of God's appointment, or the righteousness of God's acceptance. Anything in ourselves is too low and sordid to be joined with him. God has accepted none else, and we must have recourse to none else. Whatsoever we would join with him is unworthy of God's acceptance. None else was set forth to be a propitiation, and no means appointed of enjoyment, but faith in his blood. This blood was sprinkled upon the mercy-seat in heaven, as the blood of sacrifices was in the temple, which stilled justice, refreshed mercy, and revived it towards us.

[4.] None else ever did do that for us which was necessary to our reconciliation with God. None else ever interposed as a shelter between the irresistible wrath of God and our souls. He alone 'bore our griefs, and carried our sorrows,' Isa. liii. 4; he received into his own bowels that sword which was sharpened and pointed for us; 'by his stripes we are healed;' upon him alone did the scorching wrath of his Father fall for our peace. He trod the wine-press alone, none of the people were with him; he endured the bruises of his Father, and the reproaches of his enemies, and would not desist till he had settled the foundation of our peace. He bore the punishment of our sins, all our iniquities there considered by God in his person, and he paid what we owed. 'In one body' he reconciled us, Eph. i. 16; 'his own bode,' says Peter, 1 Peter ii. 24. None drew in the same yoke with him, none were partners with him in his sufferings, none sharers with him in his office. He sealed heaven alone, and alone made the entrance to his Father easy. None ever did, none ever could, answer the demands of the law, silence the voice of justice, by removing the burden of our guilt. He only filled up that gap and gulf which was between God and us; why should anything in our hearts carry away the honour of a Mediator from him, since none else removed the miseries we had deserved, and purchased the mercies we wanted? Till God therefore confers the title of peacemaker, and prince of peace, upon any other, own nothing else as a sharer with him in this honour; that would be to contradict God's order, deny his sufficiency, and contemn his kindness, and turn our backs upon the only tower that can hinder us from being crushed by the wrath of God. But, alas! men delight in their worm-eaten, withered righteousness, which they set up in the room of the Mediator; this, the grand cheat of the world, claims a precedence of Christ.

[5.] None else is appointed, or can secure to us the fruits of reconciliation. As God is in Christ reconciling the world, so he is in Christ giving out the fruits of that reconciliation, not imputing our trespasses to us. He is not only the Mediator of reconciliation, to make our peace, but the Mediator of intercession, to preserve it. He only took away our sins by his death, he only can preserve our reconciliation by his life. As he suffered effectually, by the strength of his deity, to make our peace, so he intercedes, in the strength of his merit, to preserve our peace. He did not only take away, but 'abolish and slay the enmity,' Eph. ii. 10, 16. He slew it, to make it incapable of living again, as a dead man is; and if any sin stands up to provoke justice, he sits as 'an advocate' to answer the process, 1 John ii. 2. All the gifts of grace, not only in their first purchase, but in their full conveyance and abundant communication, are 'by and through him,' Rom. v. 15. By him only we can come to the throne of grace; in this beloved Son only we are accepted for adopted sons, Eph. i. 6. To none else God gave children for a seed; children to beget, and preserve, and offer up to him at the last day. He rent the veil by his death, opened the holy of holies by his passion, and keeps it open by his intercession, that we may have a communion with God and a fellowship with angels by this only Mediator. Immanuel is a name only belonging to him, Isa. vii. 14; not that this was the name by which only he was called, but that this was his work, to make way for God's dwelling among the sons of men, and communicating to them the richest of his gifts. Not an angel in heaven but has his standing upon the account of Christ as their head; and therefore not a man upon earth can be secure under any other wing, or have the conveyance of grace through any other channel. He is the prosagwgeuV, the introducer of us into the inward chambers of the Father's goodness, where our bonds are cancelled, our pardon assured, and our Father, who was angry with us, falls upon our necks and kisses us. Our constant access to the Father is 'by him,' Rom. v. 2, Eph. iii. 12, 'access,' prosagwgh. He sits in heaven to lead us by the hand to the Father for whatsoever we want, as a prince's favourite brings a man into the presence of a gracious prince. The 'grace of Christ' is put in order by Paul before the 'love of God' and the 'communion of the Holy Ghost' in the benedictions, because it is the only band that knits us to God, and the foundation of every expression of love from the Father, and of every act of communion eve have with the Holy Ghost. Whatsoever grace God works in us is 'through Jesus Christ,' Heb. xiii. 21; he is therefore 'made to us wisdom and sanctification, as well as righteousness and redemption,' 1 Cor. i. 30. God transmits his virtues through Christ; as the heavens, which impregnate all things, transmit their virtues hither by the sun.

Well, then, let us have recourse only to this Mediator; the fire of God's wrath will consume us without this screen. It is the blood of the Lamb of God's appointment which can only secure us Irma the scorching heat of the wrath to come, typified by the blood of the paschal lamb sprinkled upon flee posts of the Israelites' doors; not so much to be a mark to the angel, who could have known both the houses and persons of the Israelites from the Egyptians without that sign on the post, as to represent this mediatory blood of the Lamb of God as our only security from destroying fury. Let men make lies their refuse, and hide themselves under falsehood, the false coverings of their own righteousness, and think to shelter themselves from the overflowing scourge, Isa. xxviii. 15-17. It will be a miserable self-deceit, the hail will sweep away such a refuge, and the waters will overflow such a hiding-place. It is the corner-stone which God lays in Sion that is our only security, because he is only elect, 1 Peter ii. 6, chosen by God, and precious in his account, ver. 6; which is inserted (as some observe) between those two verses to show the miserable shifts of men to provide shelters for themselves, other mediations and mediators, not regarding the foundation God has laid, all which will end in self-destruction, as they began in self-deceit. All human satisfactions, intercessions of saints, refuge in any other righteousness, are weak hiding-places to preserve us from the overflowing waters of divine vengeance. No sure foundation but the stone God has laid in Sion.

One would think there were not so much need to press this information.; but whosoever will look into the world, and into his own heart, will find it necessary. What the papists do one way, many protestants do another; one sets up mediators without him, others set up mediators within them. The great business Christ urged in the days of his flesh was this, that he was the Messiah, the only person sent of God to redeem. Though men profess Christ is so, yet it is too common to bring in some sharer with him.

(9.) Ninth information. We may here see the incomprehensible love of God, in that he did not deal with us summo jure, as a severe law-giver. We are not deeply sensible of it; if we had a due sense of this love, we should have little kindness for sin. It was not a low kind of love, but 'exceeding riches of grace in his kindness towards us in Jesus Christ,' Eph. ii. 7. Grace never appeared in all its royalty but in Christ. A sweet combination of grace in the Father and the Son. Had the Son manifested his love in offering himself, nothing could have been done without the acceptation of the Father; had the Father manifested his lore in moving it, nothing could have been done without the Son's undertaking it. The first motion was from the Father, as the fountain of the Trinity; the execution was from the Son, by a free and dutiful acceptance of the offer of the Father. In this work God 'set his heart upon man,' Job vii. 17; the glorifying his name in the redemption of man was that which ran in his mind, and had the chiefest place in his heart from eternity. How great also is the love of Christ, since he was the person that the first sin was particularly against, as well as against the Father; it being an affecting of wisdom to be like God, and Christ was the wisdom of God. Every day's mercy is a miracle, but the mercies of our lives are to this of reconciling us by his Son, as a molehill to a mountain, a grain of sand to the whole frame of nature. When by our offence we were fallen under the sentence of the law, and shut up in the hands of justice, and could not satisfy for the offence, God pays a ransom out of the treasures of his own bowels, opens the heart of his dearest Son, and redeems us by the most precious thing he had: here love does come to the top of its glory, and does perfectly triumph.

[1.] His own love and compassion was the first rise of this reconciliation. This way by Christ was a 'new' as well as a 'living way,' Heb. xi. 20, not known by all the wisdom of man. New to men, new to angels, it could not enter into any of their hearts to conceive of it before it was declared. He purposed in himself, Eph. i. 9. It lay hid in the womb of his own love. There was none beside him from eternity to put up a request. It was the result of his bowels, before the being of any creature was the effect of his power. Though our justification, sanctification, and eternal blessedness be the fruits of the meritorious death of the Redeemer, yet the first source of all, in his mission and commission, was absolutely from the inconceivable love of God; whatsoever is merited by Christ for us, his first mission was not merited by himself; his personal relation to God rendered him fit for the honour and office of a mediator, but as mediator he did not merit his own sending into the world, because he was settled mediator by God, and sent, too, before he could as mediator merit. Christ did not die to render God compassionate to us, but to open the passage for his bowels to flow down upon us, with the honour of his justice. God's bowels wrought within himself, but the sentence pronounced by justice was a bar to the flowing of them upon man. Christ was sent to remove that by his death, that the mercy which sprang up from eternity in the heart of God might freely flow down to the creature. And when the time came, God looked about and 'saw that there was no man,' none to deprecate his wrath, and therefore 'his own arm brought salvation,' Isa. lix. 16, and 'his own righteousness sustained him,' i. e. his own truth and righteousness engaged in the promises made to the fathers. The satisfaction of Christ does not impair the kindness of God; his pity to us did precede the constitution of Christ. Had there been no compassion, there had been no contrivance, no acceptance of a mediator; but since he had threatened eternal death to sinners, there was need of an honourable reconciliation by death to maintain the honour of God's truth engaged in that sentence, and content his justice, which was obliged to execute the sentence for the honour of his truth. It was by the grace of God that Christ tasted death for us, Heb. ii. 9.

[2.] It is the greatest love that God can show. As Abraham could not skew a greater proof of faith and obedience than by offering his Son, the son of his affections, and his only son, so neither can God show a richer testimony of his affections to us than by making his own Son an oblation for us. Hoe mighty tender was God of our salvation! How valuable was man to him, when he prized him at the rate of his only Son i As high as God did esteem Christ, so highly did he value his own glory in man's reconciliation.

First. His love was more illustrious than if he had pardoned us by his absolute prerogative without a satisfaction. It had been a glorious mercy, but had wanted that enriching circumstance, the death of his Son; in this way he honours his mercy more than our sin had abused it. His mercy had not appeared in such sweetness had not Christ drunk the bitter cup; mercy sung sweetest when justice roared loudest against the Redeemer. Every attribute had a signal elevation in this way of reconciliation, but especially his kindness. We should have been happy had he pardoned us without a satisfaction, but neither his love nor his justice had been wound up to so high a strain. God did not aim only at the praise of his grace, but the praise of the glory of his grace, Eph. i. 6; he would have his grace appear in the richest attire, and with all the ornaments heaven could clothe it with.

This is evident,

First, By the condition of the person. He was his Son. Was it not the victorious triumph of mercy to make his Son a sufferer when we were the sinners, to make his own Son a servant to his justice when we were the debtors? He was his 'only begotten Son,' John iii. 16, not merely his own Son, but his only Son; he had but one Son in the world, and that Son he made a sacrifice for the world; he had not another begotten Son in being. He was 'the express image of his person,' one who was equal with God without robbery, or detracting anything from his glory, Philip. ii. 6; an only Son, enjoying the same majesty and perfections in the Deity with the Father; a Son dearer to him than heaven and earth; the Son he solaced himself with from all eternity, Prov. viii. 30, before ever any stone of the world was laid; and if we could suppose numberless worlds created before this, yet all his joy was placed in him. Can there be a greater assurance of the immensity of his love than in sending a Son that lay in his bosom; a Son who never in the least offended him, nor ever could? He always did the things which pleased him; and when he was in the world there was nothing in him that the devil could fasten upon as any resemblance to himself, John xiv. 30. In this Son was God reconciling the world. The nearer and dearer the Son was to the Father, the greater is the Father's love in pitching upon him to undertake this work. His love bore proportion to the greatness of that Son whom he sent.

Secondly, The condition in which he was sent. He was made lower than angels to stoop to the condition of a servant. To send an only Son out of his bosom to the cross, an innocent Son from glory to ignominy, and not upon a sudden resolve (which might be thought a passion), but by a deliberate counsel, never repenting of it, always glorying in it, even to this day, is a discovery of the most rooted affection. The lower the condition of Christ was, the more wonderful is the kindness of God in sending him in it. If we would walk into the garden and see Christ besmeared with clods of blood, step up to mount Calvary and see him hanging upon the cross, look up to heaven and see the bright sword sheathed in the bowels of the Son of God, see him with his scourged back, his nailed hands, his pierced side, ask then your souls this question, whether here be not bottomless love? whether any affection of God can be more miraculous than this, to give his Son to endure all this for our ransom, the Lord of glory to suffer this for rebellious malefactors? whether this is not greater kindness to you than if he had pardoned you without the sufferings of his only Son?

Secondly, It is a love that cannot be wound up to a higher strain. It is the utmost bound, if I may so speak, of an infinite love: 'God so loved the world,' John iii. 16. So, above the conception of any creature; so, that his affection cannot mount an higher pitch. His power could discover itself in laying the foundation of millions of worlds, and his wisdom could shine brighter in the structure of them; but if he should create as many worlds as there are sands and dust upon the face of this, and make every one of them more transcendent in glory than this, than the sun is above a clod of earth or an atom of dust, yet he could not confer a greater love upon it than he has done upon this; than to be, upon their revolt, a God in Christ reconciling those worlds to himself. There is not a choicer mercy than to be in amity with God, nor a more affectionate way of procuring and establishing it, than by giving his only Son to effect it: in giving whom, he contracts to give himself to be our God, and live with us for ever. If God should take the meanest beggar that lives upon common alms, and transform him into an angel, and make him the head of that heavenly host, it would be incomparably a far less love than the gift of his Son for him. A more condescending kindness cannot be conceived, unless the Father himself should become incarnate, and die for man; but that cannot be supposed. If the fountain of the Trinity, the Judge of all, should take flesh, and suffer, to whom should the offering be made? The rector and judge is to be satisfied, and it is not fit for the judge to make satisfaction to himself; but the Father has given that person next to himself to be our propitiation; most fit, as having the Father, the fountain of the Trinity, to offer the sacrifice of himself unto.

Thirdly, It is a greater love than has yet been shown to angels. The angels in heaven never did partake of such a vast ocean of love, for the Son of God never died for them, though they came under his wing, as a head exalted to that dignity, as a reward of his death. The angels came under him as an exalted head, but not as a crucified Saviour: they have their grace by the will of God, without the death of his Son; we by the will of God, through the death of his Son. What confirmation they have, they have it from Christ, by virtue of his headship over them, not by virtue of any death for them; and therefore they are, in the opinion of several, understood by the 'things in heaven,' which are 'reconciled to God,' Col. i. 20. What reconciliation is to us, confirmation is to them; yet there is not such an excess of love in their confirmation, as in our reconciliation by the blood of the cross. As the preservation of a life from death is less than the restoring life to one that is dead, the latter argues more of kindness, as well as more of power.

Fourthly, Take a prospect of this love by a review of the condition we were in.

First, Our vileness and corruption. What are we in our being but dust, slight and empty pieces of clay? Is it not wonderful that God, who has angels to attend him, should busy his thoughts about worms; that he, who has the beauty of angels, the most glorious piece of the works of his hands to look upon, should cast his eye upon such noisome dunghills; that he should not rest in the praises of angels, but repair such broken instruments as men are, to bear a part in the concert? If the sun knew its own excellency, it would think it a condescension to bestow a beam upon so dark and miry a body as the earth, that can return to it no recompense, much more is it in God, to look upon such pieces of clay as we are, much more to give out his grace and love to man, who can give him no requital. We would be loath to take a toad into our bosoms, and bestow our friendship upon it. By corruption we are worse than the most venomous toad that creeps upon the ground; yet God entertains thoughts of amity, and establishes it for us in the blood of his Con. We are unworthy of any one thought of unbounded goodness, much more unworthy of a thought of so high a strain. Would not any man think that king distracted, that should send his son to keep company with grooms and scullions, to wear the same livery, to advance them to a better state by his own blood? Nothing but the end fair which he does it, and the love which moved him to it, could excuse him. How much more condescending is God than the greatest prince in the world would be in this act!

Secondly, Impotence. When we lay wallowing in our blood, and it was the time of our weakness, that was the time of his love; when we had 'no eye to pity' us, nor a heart to pity ourselves, then were we the objects of his compassion, Ezek. xvi. 4-6, &c. When there was not one solicitor for us among all the holy angels, the peace was broken with them as well as with God, and we were justly hated by those holy spirits upon the Creator's account; when not a man in the whole race of mankind had any thoughts of presenting a petition for recovery; when God looked about, and to his astonishment, 'found none' that had any thoughts of interceding and soliciting a restoration, Isa. lix. 16; when there was not a person in heaven or earth besides himself could save us, 'his own arm,' without the least auxiliary force, 'brought salvation.' It is the glory of his love, that he was 'found of us when we asked not for him,' Isa. lxv. 1. What allurements were there in our nature, unless deformities and demerits could pass for attractives? We had not virtue to merit his love, nor ever shall have power to requite it; both are utterly impossible in a creature. God saw our demerits, it was in his thoughts, otherwise a reconciler had not been appointed; one to merit that for us, which we had forfeited, and never could have recovered. Justice might find cause of punishment in the rebellion of the delinquent, but grace could find no reason but in the pity of our Creator; the amazement of a true believer, when he comes to be seriously sensible of it, does manifest the impossibility of ever thinking of it himself.

Thirdly, Rebellion, which is worse than vileness and impotence. He was a God in Christ reconciling the world, when our enmity to him was as great as our misery; when we had not one spark of love for him, who had a boundless ocean of compassion for us. We had entered a league with Satan, the only enemy God had, rendered ourselves his bond-slaves, and that presently after our creation by his powerful hand; and it was far worse if Adam did know the sin and state of the fallen angels; howsoever his pride in his aspiring thought to be like his Maker was less excusable than that of the devil's, in regard that he was an inferior creature (though the devil's was greater, in regard of his greater knowledge of the excellency of God above him). Pride in a mean person is more odious than in one upon a throne. Then it is that he contrives with his Son, and by the blood of his Son, to redeem rebels; and though he disrelished and loathed the crime, yet he had a tenderness and pity for the malefactor, assured by an oath: Heb. vii. 28, 'The word of the oath, which was since the law, makes the Son, who is consecrated for evermore.' As the word of the oath was after the law the declaration of the oath after the declaration of the law, so in the eternal counsel of God, the constitution of the reconciler supposed a law enacted, and a law violated by transgression. After this, the cry of our sins for vengeance could not alter his resolve of sacrificing his Son, and bringing that vengeance upon the sins which they solicited against the sinner. How easy was it for God to have spurned us into hell, when we lay under his foot without all this expense! One touch of his iron rod would have broke us like a potter's vessel; yet he takes occasion to display his grace, where we give occasion to pour out his wrath. He would inflame us by his love, rather than turn us into ashes by his fury; and reconcile us to himself by the blood of his Son, rather than satisfy justice by our own.

Fifthly, It was a love in the freest manner; without cost to us, but expensive to God. We hear of no strugglings in the heart of God, from the first foundation to the topstone; his affections travel through every stage, without the least relenting; he was in Christ reconciling the world, from one end of his counsel to the other, without any repenting reflections. It cost him the blood of his Son, more expensive than the making millions of worlds. There was no need of any combat in his affections, to make as many worlds as he pleased; but we may wonder (since God represents himself to us often in Scripture according to the manner of men) that there were no pull-backs in his affections to the delivering up of his Son. If there be a conflict in his heart when he is to give up a creature,ó Hosea xi. 8, 'How shall I give thee up, O Ephraim? How shad I deliver thee, Israel? My heart is turned within me,'ócould we reasonably suppose less in giving up his Son? (though indeed the one was eternal, the other temporary), yet in this case we read of no such turnings of bowels, no such kindlings of repentings together. His soul was free in it, and let the peace cost what it would, he would procure it, though with the greatest charge.

Sixthly, Consider what it was his love designed in this. Not a petty inconsiderable thing, but a 'propitiation for sin,' 1 John iv. 10, the non-imputation of guilt, the removing all the bars between him and us, the turning the edge of the sword that was pointed against us, reducing us to an eternal amity. He would draw us out of the condition into which we were fallen, and from a wrath we had merited, to elevate us to an eternal life we had rendered ourselves unworthy of, and exposed his Son to the curses of the law, that the edge of them might be turned from us. And that we might have a free converse with him, he makes the mediator of kin to us, that by reason of the communication of our nature we might with more boldness approach to him. All delightful converse is between those of the same species; we could not have conversed freely with a reconciler of a different nature from us.

Seventhly, This love is perpetual. He was in Christ reconciling the world; he will to the end of the world beseech men to be reconciled to him. Love was the motive, the glory of his grace was the end; what was so from eternity, will be so to eternity. His love is as strong as it was, for infinite receives no diminution; his glory is as dear as it was, for to deny his glory is to deny himself. How great will be the joy of those that accept it i how dismal the torment and sorrow of those that refuse it?

Second use; of comfort. flow great may the joy of believing souls be, to be brought by God, and by ways of his own contriving, into actual favour with him, after they had lain in a state of wrath! To have an almighty, infinite, just God at variance with us, cannot but be a matter of sadness; to have a peace struck, and the light of his countenance shine upon us, cannot but beget a transcendent joy; it is in the very notion of it, to the understanding joyful, yea, tidings of great joy, and in the sense and feeling of it triumphant. The publication of it was ushered in with words of comfort in the prophet: Isa. xl. I, 'Comfort ye, comfort ye my people, speak comfortably to Jerusalem; cry unto her that her warfare is accomplished, that her iniquity is pardoned, for she has received of the Lord's hand double for all her sins.' Three words to note the great comfort should be taken in the gospel administration: the matter of it is the ceasing of the war between God and the creature, the pardon of their iniquities upon the satisfaction of Christ, the fruit whereof is received by the believer; the satisfaction of Christ, in regard of the infiniteness of his person, was great, which is expressed by double; and the fruits of it received by the church are great and double, freedom from the wrath of God, from the tyranny of the devil, and the collation of the gifts and graces of the Spirit. Those words, 'for she has received of the Lord's hand double for all her sins,' cannot be meant of the punishment which they lay under, for that could be no cause of the pardon (as the particle for seems to be causal), neither is it a comfort to think of the greatness of punishment after it is past. But if we consider what follows, ver. 3, &c., it will appear to be a gospel promise, and the believer 'receives of the Lord's hand double:' either it is meant of Christ, who made the satisfaction, the fruits whereof the believer receives; or of the Father, who spared not his own Son, but exacted of him the punishment of our sins, and gives out to us the fruits of his reconciling death. This is the comfort, that the enmity is slain, the war ceased, an end of sin made, and God beheld with comfort, taking away the power of the devil, who first raised this war between God and man; as it is, her. 9, 10, 'Behold your God, behold the Lord God will come with a strong hand, and his arm shall rule for him; he shall feed his flock as a shepherd, he shall gather his lambs with his arm, and carry them in his bosom, and gently lead those that are with young.' All this is the fruit of reconciling grace. God is well pleased with those that are sprinkled with the blood of Christ. As after the 'sprinkling of the blood of the covenant,' God appeared to the elders of the people in a clear, not a cloudy and stormy heaven, Exod. xxiv. 8, 10 (a cloudy and stormy heaven is a sign of God's anger), and his feet, the instruments of motion, standing in a clear heaven, show that all the passages of his providence to his people, are mercy, truth, and kindness, upon the account of the blood of the covenant of peace. God cannot hate those who accept of this reconciliation. Though God hates the remainders of sin in them, yet it is not with such a hatred as redounds to their persons, because their persons are reconciled to God; they believe and apply the reconciliation made by God in Christ. If God deny the acceptance of such, he denies his own act and deed, he denies himself and his whole contrivance from one end to the other. This would be to publish, that he was mistaken in his first design, that it was a fruitless thing, that there was a defect in his wisdom laying the scene of it, or a defect in Christ who undertook to accomplish it, and that things issued not according to his will. If any accept it upon the terms God offers it, nothing can be charged upon him. God must deny his whole contrivance, his commission to Christ, or find some flaw in the execution of it, before salvation can be denied to such a person; but God has already testified again and again how highly pleasing the whole negotiation of Christ was to him, and therefore it is not possible that God (who cannot be deceived in his foresight of events, to whom nothing is contingent) should delight in this before it was acted, please himself with it after it was acted, and yet dart out the frowns of an enemy upon the acceptors of it, who are called 'sons of peace,' Luke x. 6. No; the proper effect of this is non-imputation of sin, as it is in the text, 'God was in Christ reconciling the world unto himself, not imputing their trespasses unto them;' and reconciliation and justification are one and the same thing in the apostle's doctrine; Rom. v. 9, what is called 'justification by his blood,' is called, her. 10, 'reconciliation to God by the death of Christ.' Sincere acceptance of it, with a resolution to obey him, gives an interest in this: Luke ii. 14, 'Good will towards linen.' Some read it, 'Peace on earth to men of good will,' actively, that bear a good will to Christ, that are upright in heart towards God in Christ. But the psalmist is clear in it, that where there is no guile in the spirit in accepting this righteousness, God will not impute sin, Ps. xxxii. 2, and though a believing person may not be sensible of his happiness, yet his happiness is ensured upon faith, though not testified to the soul. Reconciliation and the sense of it are two distinct things; a name may be written in the book of life, and the eye not clear enough to discern it. The prince may have a favour for a malefactor, and his pardon sealed too, yet the prisoner know it not, and perhaps have tattle hopes of it, but casts himself at the foot of the prince's mercy. How comfortable is it to have this peace, and a sense of it too, in our consciences, by the sprinkling of the blood of Jesus! Worldly goods are small; corn, wine, and oil are little things, to the light of God's countenance, shining upon the soul, here is the ground of joy and glorying, that God 'exercises loving-kindness:' Jer. ix. 24, 'Let him that glories, glory in this that he knows me, that I am the Lord which exercises loving-kindness.'

There are several particular comforts arise from hence.

1. The angels, the whole host of heaven, are at peace with the believer. The angels, upon the sin of man, by virtue of their obedience, took part with God, and could not, because of their purity, be friends to a defiled creature; nor because of their affection to God, bear any respect to him to whom the Lord was an enemy. They were placed as a guard to bar man from re-entrance into paradise after his fan, and to 'keep the way of the tree of life,' Gen. iii. 24. Our sins broke the alliance between heaven and earth, so that the good angels could have no converse with the enemies of God; had it not been for this disobedience, they could have had no aversion to man. But since their Lord is satisfied, those obedient spirits cannot be discontented, for this reconciliation ties their hands, and makes all ill intelligence cease between them and believers. The death of Christ expiating our sin, established a good correspondence between the two great parties of the world, angels and men. The monarch being reconciled, the two states of men and angels reassume a mutual commerce. By this they are reduced into one corporation, into one family, and combined under one head: Eph. i. 10, 'All things which are in heaven and on earth, are gathered together in Christ.' That place, Col. i. 20, 'It pleased the Father that in him should all fullness dwell, and by him to reconcile all things unto himself; by him, I say, whether they be things in earth or things in heaven,' is understood by some of the reconciliation of things in heaven to (cod, i. e. believers in the promised Messiah, who died before the coming of Christ, showing thereby the extent of the death of Christ which looked backward; by others, of the reconciliation of heavenly spirits unto us, as being a grand state of the world depending upon the universal monarch. Hence the angels rejoice and sing a hymn at the publishing the gospel, Luke ii. 13, and rejoice more in it than men do; for they delight in the glory of God, but men delight naturally in their enmity to God. They rejoice at the repentance of a sinner, and his acceptance of this reconciliation. They cannot rejoice at men's reconciliation to God, and be unreconciled themselves. They are 'ministering spirits to the heirs of salvation,' Heb. i. 14, instruments of God in the deliverance of his church and people, furtherers of the conversion of men as to outward means, as in the example of the eunuch, Acts viii. 26; and at last conduct the heirs to the possession of their inheritance 'reserved in the heavens for them,' Luke xvi. 22. They are ministers of wrath upon the unbelieving world, ministers of good to the believing creature, and guard him with those weapons wherewith they fought against him, from whence we have many invisible assistances. As God did not hate his creatures as creatures (for then he had hated man as made by him, which is inconsistent with the pure goodness of God), but as sinners, so the angels followed their great pattern in the hatred of men; but now they are reconciled to man, because God, to whom they pay an obedience, is reconciled. They are put under the government of Christ as their head, as he is the mediator, and cannot be enemies to us till Christ, as bead, become an enemy to himself as mediator. Their commission for guarding the heavenly paradise against us is cancelled, and should they now obstruct the way, they would be no longer good angels, but impure and disobedient devils. There is one place which some understand of this peace we have with angels: Rev. i. 4, 5, 'Peace from him which was, and which is, and which is to come, and from the seven spirits which are before his throne, and from Jesus Christ, who is the faithful witness,' &c. The seven spirits are said to be before his throne, as waiting for the commands of God, as the seven angels are said to stand before God, Rev. viii. 2. But it is more likely it is meant of the Spirit of God; it is not reasonable to think the salutations of creatures to the church should be mixed with the benedictions of the Deity, with the exclusion of the third person, who is here to be understood, and called seven spirits in regard of the variety of gifts and graces, given out by him to the church, seven being a perfect number; and placed in the midst of this benediction, perhaps because of his procession both from the Father and the Son.

2. Peace with all creatures. If the Lord of the creation be the author of this peace, then no creatures which are under his conduct can be at enmity with a believer. When Adam fell, he did deserve that all

creatures should act in hostility against him, as the rebel against the sovereignty of their common creator. But when God enters into a new amity with man, and ceases to be provoked, he renews the covenant with the beasts, that all creatures shall be serviceable to the reconciled believer: Hos. ii. 18, 'In that day I will make a covenant for him with the beasts of the field,' in the day of the evangelical espousals, as he had before promised if they continued in obedience, Lev. xxvi. 6. Though no formal covenant can be made between God and irrational creatures, yet they shall hurt no more than if they were tied up by a formal covenant, and were honest and valise enough to observe it; as in the first covenant made with Adam, while he stood on terms of peace with God, and owned a subjection to him as his Lord, all creatures were spontaneously to be under his dominion, which right depended upon the observance of the terms of the covenant which was between God and him. This right is renewed by the satisfaction of Christ procuring the restoration of that which Adam forfeited, and disarming nature, which was before armed against man. The corn and the wine shall hear Jezreel, the seed of God, Hos. ii. 22. The right to all things presents things to come, 'life, death,' all intermediate things, is restored by Christ, 1 Cor. iii. 22, 23. The world, universal nature, all is yours for your good, because you are Christ's, who has purchased those things; and Christ is God's, settled by him in this office for the purchase of them, and accepted by God to that end. The right to all creatures is perfect, the possession insured in the head, who has taken livery and seisin of all; and shall be perfect in the members, when there shall be a new heaven and a new earth; all shall be in an harmonious combination for the glory of the believer. They do yet often instrumentally afflict them, but not hurt them. They hurt the man, not the Christian; they hurt a believer no more than death can, which, though it kills him, yet without a sting, they hurt us, yet without a curse; they are in the hand of a reconciled Father, who uses their natural enmity against us for our good, as the shepherd does the currishness of the dog to reduce the wandering sheep to the fold. The hurts we seem to feel from them issue in mercy, and are so intended by that reconciled God who guides them; they wound us, and thereby break our imposthumes. The same instrument may convey kindness to a believer, which is a mark of wrath upon an enemy; the same knife, which in the hand of an executioner may cut off the arm of a malefactor, in the hand of a chirurgeon may cut off the gangrened member of a patient; the same knife performs a friend's office to the one and a Wrathful to the other. Since we are not perfect in our services of God, we cannot expect the creatures should be perfect in their services of us; as our obedience is only inchoative here, so the performance of God's promises are here in their blade, not in their full harvest.

3. Access to God is another comfort arising from hence. As God was in Christ reconciling the world, so he is in Christ giving believers access to him. As he was in Christ reconciling our persons, so he is in Christ receiving our prayers. As Christ made satisfaction for us by his death, so he sweetens our services by his merit. As Christ was the means of our reconciliation, so is he the means of our access: Rom. v. 1, 2, 'By whom also we have access.' The word also intimates this freedom of access to be as great a benefit as justification. Though justification is a transcendent mercy, yet it would not complete the happiness of a creature, without communion with God. Peace was not the thing God ultimately aimed at; it was but the medium. He would be our friend, that there might be sweet interviews between him and a believer. Before, guilt on our side, and justice on God's, stood as bars to our access. Guilty souls cannot converse with a severe judge; a provoking creature and an offended God can have no commerce; but when the guilt is taken away, the distance is removed. Now may an humble believing creature come to a reconciled God, whose own heart put him upon laying the foundation of friendship, without any desires, or so much as expectations of the creature. We could no more before endure the presence of God than the devil; but by this the bar is taken from us, though not from him. This access is consequent upon this reconciliation. As there was a communion between God and man in innocence, which was broken off by the entrance of the enmity, so0 upon the restoration of the friendship there is a renewing of a mutual converse: that as God reveals his gracious will to the soul, the soul puts up holy desires to God; that as God descends to us in Christ, we may ascend through Christ to him in fruitful meditations, and take a delightful view and prospect of God. It was not only peace that Christ came to procure, but also good will; not only to slay the enmity, but to raise an entire and intimate friendship. The message the angels proclaimed was made up of the one as well as the other: Luke ii. 14, 'Peace on earth, goodwill towards men,' eudokia, a good pleasure in men.

(1.) Access with confidence. We go to our Father, who has had the greatest hand in all this affair. Since he is the author of this peace, what ground of dejection? We have God in Christ to receive us, and Christ by God's order to introduce as. It w as the purpose of God, and his eternal purpose, that by the faith of Christ, and in him, we should have boldness and access, with confidence, Eph. i. 12, parrhsian. And what higher ground of confidence than the consideration of God's appointing and giving this mediator to us for that end? How can a faithful, holy, true God deny his own act, in denying us when we come in the way of his own appointment? for since he has settled such an high priest over his house, we may well draw near in full assurance of faith, if we come with sincere and true hearts, Heb. x. 21, 22, flying with a deep humility to his throne of grace, with a plerophory of faith, a full sail filled by this wind of love. It is not meant of a personal assurance, or a certitudo subjecti, but objecti, a full belief of the doctrine of propitiation, and God's setting forth Christ and preparing him to take away sin, which was the cause of the enmity between God and us; for this is but the use the apostle makes of what he had doctrinally in this point delivered in the foregoing part of the chapter. We may go to God with more confidence upon this account than Adam could in innocence. He had access to a God of goodness, we to a God of grace; he could not look upon God as reconcilable if he should sin; God threatening was a bar to that. If he knew anything of God, he knew him to be just and true to his word, from which knowledge did arise those terrors of conscience upon his face, and his endeavouring to run and hide himself from God; but God in this dispensation Lath given us other notions of himself than Adam had, therefore we may go with more confidence than he could, and pour out our souls before him: Lam. iii. 24, 'The Lord is my portion, therefore will I hope in him.' The Lord is my reconciled friend, therefore will I hope in him for the mercy I beg.

(2.) Delight and joy in our access. We could not come to him before, no, nor think of him, without a slavish trembling; but now we may think of him, and approach to him with joy and comfort, for he deals not with us as an enemy by a strict justice, but as a friend in a way of an obliging mercy. If Adam had a sense that he might fall, he could not come to God without some dejection; the very possibility of falling would not be without fear attending it. But since God was in Christ reconciling the world, we go to him upon the account of an immutable righteousness, a righteousness he settled as an act of grace to us, and security to his own glory; whereas Adam could approach to him but upon the account of a mutable righteousness, which might be as the grass, standing this day and withered tomorrow. Our access to God is with 'a joy in the hope of the glory of God,' Rom. v. 2; and when we take hold of his covenant, this covenant of peace, we have his word that he will make us 'joyful in the house of prayer,' Isa. lvi. 6, 7; actively joyful, full of delight in his service, solacing ourselves in a sweet consideration of the infinite grace of a reconciling God, whereby a transcendent delight is raised in the soul, which is a direct delight in God as the object of faith, discovered in Christ and apprehended by spiritual reason and sense; passively joyful, by receiving in his service more of the refreshing waters of life, and being fed with the 'hidden manna' which God communicates in and by Christ to his friends. And beside, though our services are imperfect, God expects not a perfect obedience from us, but from his Son Christ. It is a full assurance of faith he expects from us, and a true heart, not a perfect obedience; his promise gives us joy, though the sense of our imperfections create a sorrow. Though we cannot delight in ourselves, we may in God, in his promise, in his gracious condescension, in the compensation he has from his Son for us, in his acceptation of it, and application of it to our souls. You are, upon believing, God's friends, not only his servants. It is Christ's speech to his disciples: John xv. 15, 'Henceforth I call you not servants.' It must not be understood of a freedom from all kind of service, which cannot be conferred upon a creature; (it were injustice in God to free a creature from so righteous and noble a virtue as gratitude to himself; God cannot command a creature not to love him, for he should then command the creature not to love the chief good); but it is a freedom from a bondage and servile fear in duties, and bringing to a filial and more dutiful manner of service,óa service from principles of grace, and encouraged by the views of God's reconciled face. Service is not excluded by admission to this friendship, but perfected to a more delightful garb. Peace opens the way for a delightful and successful trade, which war and enmity locks up.

4. The conquest of Satan is insured by this. When we are at peace with God, the devils themselves are subject to us. When God was in Christ reconciling the world, he was in Christ 'destroying him that had the power of death,' Heb. ii. 14, and bringing Satan under the feet of the Mediator, and the feet of his members. This was the intent of God in the first promise of a Mediator, to destroy him who had infected mankind, and brought death into the world. The bruising his head was the design of Christ's mission, Gen. iii. 15, that the great incendiary who had broken the league, and set afoot the rebellion, might feel the greater smart of it. And ever since it is by the gospel of peace, and the shield of faith, that we are only able to 'quench the fiery darts of the devil,' and make his attempts fruitless, Eph. vi. 15, 16, by the reconciliation God has wrought and published by the gospel. God, 'as a God of peace,' 'shall tread him under the feet' of believers, Born. xvi. 20. Unless he had been a God of peace, we had never been delivered from that jailer who held us by the right of God's justice. And since we are delivered, God, as a God of peace, will perfect the victory, and make him cease for ever from bruising the heel of the spiritual seed. As God has given peace in Christ, so he will give the victory in Christ. Peace cannot be perfect till it be undisturbed by invading enemies, and subtle adversaries endeavouring to raise a new enmity. Our Saviour spoiled him of his power upon the cross, and took away the right he had to detain any believer prisoner, by satisfying that justice, and reconciling that God who first ordered their commitment. Me answers his accusations as he is an 'advocate' at the right hand of God; and at the last, when death comes to be destroyed, and no more to enter into the world, the whole design of the devil for ever falls to the ground. Since we are at peace with God, while we are here, the devil himself shall serve us; and the messenger of Satan shall be a means to quell the pride of a believing Paul by the sufficiency of the grace of God, while he fills the heart of an unbelieving Judas with poison and treason against his Master.

5. Comfort in all afflictions. It is a cordial to cheer in the hottest services and sharpest difficulties. What can the greatest danger signify, while God remains reconciled to the soul in Christ, and the peace remains unbroken? God thought the promise of it support enough in all the standing punishment Adam was to endure; he therefore made this promise to him before he denounced the punishment after the fall. We may as well digest all crosses with this peace purchased, as Adam could do with this peace promised; God. was then in Christ promising it, God Lath now been in Christ performing it. The peace as designed was offered to the ancient Israelites as a ground of joy and relief under their oppressing calamities, Isa. ix.; Micah v. 5, 'This man shall be the peace, when the Assyrian shall come into our land.' The peace God has effected in Christ is a more firm matter of joy under oppressions, by how much the comfort of the performance exceeds the joy of the promise, as the joy of harvest does the joy of seed-time. Mercy was manifested in the making the promise truth as well as mercy glorified in the performing. If it were a ground of joy before he wrought it, what a rise is there for a triumphant joy since he has laid an unalterable foundation for it. This was the armour Christ furnished his disciples with against the injuries of the world: John xvi. 33, 'In me you shall have peace, in the world you shall have tribulation.' This was thought by our Saviour to be a sufficient defence for his weak disciples against all the furies of men and rage of devils, an universal remedy against all discouragements. In Christ, God smiles when the world frowns: 'Cause thy face to shine upon us' is thrice repeated, Ps. lxxx. 3, 7, 19, as the chief confidence of a gracious soul under smart distresses. Reconciliation with God changes the nature of everything that is terrible, dungeons into palaces and tears into cordials. It is a shield against fears, a treasure against poverty, physic against diseases, security against danger, and life against death. Indeed, under sharp afflictions a believing soul may not have a strength of faith to discern God as a father, from God as a judge, sense and carnal reason may dispute against faith and stagger it. If he be reconciled, why then does he make me his mark to shoot at? There may be a fatherly displeasure when there is not a wrathful anger, the satisfaction of justice excludes not the rod of mercy. Justice has no plea against a believer, because it is satisfied; mercy is the only attribute that orders all for a reconciled person. The visiting the transgression of the seed of Christ with a rod was knit together with the continuance of God's kindness to them in the covenant of redemption God made with Christ, Ps. lxxxix. 30-33. 'God was in Christ reconciling the world;' it is a less thing for him to be in every affliction, ordering it for good.

6. Comfort in the expectation of all other mercies. If God were in Christ reconciling us to himself, he will be in Christ giving forth all other suitable mercies. If he detains any you seem to want, it is a part of his reconciled wisdom when he sees them not good for you. It is inconsistent with his amity to withhold any you have real need of; it would not be then a much store, as Christ argues, but a much less: Mat. vii. 11, 'If you, being evil, know how to give good things to your children, much more your Father which is in heaven.' But consider, they are only good things he has obliged himself to give, and he in the proper judge of what is good, not we ourselves. If, as a God of patience and goodness, he feeds the unclean birds, will he not, as a God of grace and peace in Christ, feed his friends? Will he let them starve while his enemies fatten? He has struck a covenant of amity and friendship, what may not be expected from a sincere and powerful friend, and one who made it his business from eternity to be casting about for the working of this peace? If this, which neither men nor angels could have imagined, be effected by his wisdom and grace, all subsequent blessings are far easier to God than this could be, since in this he has conquered his own affection to his Son. What can remain unconquered by him, which stands in the way of a believer's happiness? It was a greater act to be in Christ reconciling the world, than to be in Christ giving out the mercies he has purchased. If he has overcome the greatest bank that stopped the tide of mercy, shall little ones hinder the current of it? Justice, and the honour of the law, were the great mountains which stood in the way. Since those are removed by a miraculous wisdom and grace, what pebbles can stop the flood to believing souls? If God be the author of the greatest blessings, will he not be of the least? If he has not spared his best treasure, shall the less be denied? It is the apostle's arguing, Rom. viii. 82, 'He that spared not his own Son, but delivered him up for us all, how shall he not with him freely give us all things?' He cannot but be as free in the least as he was in the greatest, there were more arguments to dissuade him from that, than there can be to stop his hands in other things. If anything you desire be refused by God, know it is your Saviour's mind you shall not have it; for God would deny him nothing of his purchase. Oh how little do we live in the sense of those truths; how does our impatience give God the lie, and tell him he is a deadly enemy, notwithstanding his reconciling grace!

7. There will be peace of conscience. If God be reconciled, conscience cannot charge. If God be the author of this peace, conscience, God's deputy, cannot keep up an enmity against us, for that must speak as God speaks. Peace with the viceroys and governors depends upon peace with the prince. The same blood which was sprinkled on the mercy-seat, is sprinkled upon the conscience of the believer. As it procured peace with heaven, it will produce peace in the soul: Heb. x. 22, 'Having our hearts sprinkled from an evil conscience.' An evil conscience is an accusing conscience; when sprinkled by this blood, it is an acquitting conscience, not from the facts, but from the guilt of them. Whatsoever has a power to

satisfy God, cannot be invalid to satisfy conscience. Where infinite knowledge can raise no objection, a purblind conscience is too weak to find out any. If God has been the contriver of this reconciliation, and accepted it as fully finished, conscience must acquiesce. Adam's conscience flew in his face upon his sin, and did not leave quarrelling till its mouth was stopped with the promise of a reconciler. Guilt sets conscience on fire; when the guilt is quenched, conscience must be at ease. Nothing will satisfy conscience but that which satisfies God, and whatsoever satisfies God must satisfy conscience, for that acts by commission and a derived authority. All other things are too weak to take away the conscience of sin: 'the blood of bulls and goats,' of God's institution, could not do it, Heb. x. 2, it is the proper effect of this peace, all the waters in the world cannot quench the flame of conscience, till God be reconciled. The foundation of this peace of conscience is laid in peace with God, though present actual comfort may not be enjoyed; the day may be clouded, though the winds be still; there may be no storms, yet no sunshine.

8. Comfort against death. If God be the author of reconciliation by Christ, then death, which was the fruit of that sin which is now removed, can be no dreadful apparition. God was in Christ, and is still, conquering his enemies; and this is one enemy which must fall under his sword, and be made his footstool As God v, as in Christ reconciling you, he is in death calling for you to enjoy the full-blown felicities of that peace. It is no more than a departure in peace, when God is a God of peace. Old Simeon thought so, Luke ii. 29; he speaks, says one, like a merchant that had got all his goods on shipboard, and now desires the master of the ship to hoist sail and be gone homeward. Death was before a servant of divine justice; since justice is satisfied, it is the messenger of divine mercy. It was a jailer to enclose us in the prison of the grave, it is now a conductor to the glories of heaven. Where this peace is in maturity, where God's face shines clearly without disguises, veils, and cloudy interruptions, the name death is terrible, but the reconciled soul is beyond the fears of it. It has lost its sting, which was God's justice; Christ satisfying the one, has disarmed the other of what is hurtful. There is a knot between justification (which is termed reconciliation) and glorification; death comes between them, but does not dissolve it: Tom. viii. 30, 'Whom he justifies, them also he glorifies,' which knot cannot be untied by death, though that between our soul and body is: it sends the body to the grave to endure the sentence against sin denounced in paradise, and the soul to heaven, to enjoy the benefit of the promise.

9. This reconciliation is effectual. It is upon this all the other comforts depend. If God was the author of it, contriving, counselling Christ to effect it, furnishing him for the accomplishment of it, it cannot be a weak and imperfect peace. Infinite wisdom would not have spent innumerable 'thoughts, which cannot be reckoned up' (as the expression is, Ps. xl. 5), about a fruitless thing, a peace which might be easily blown away; he would never have sent his Son to shed his blood, and endure his wrath to no purpose, and make his own contrivance to end in a mere chimaera, as though he would be so busy only to deceive his creatures. 'The counsel of the Lord shall stand,' every counsel of his, much more his choicest purpose, to which all his other resolves are as small rivers which run into this great sea, and combine together for the perfecting this counsel; all other thoughts are lines drawn to or from this centre. As all things in heaven and earth are gathered in one, even in Christ, so all the counsels of God gather into this one of Christ and peace in him. This was the great source and pattern of all the rest, Eph. i. 10, 11. Besides, God has received this reconciler into heaven, whereby he has removed all ground of suspicion of his remaining yet unreconciled. If justice had any exception against his sacrifice, it would not have opened heaven's gates to Christ, but have barred, with a flaming sword, Christ's entrance into heaven, as well as Adam's return to paradise. The honourable title of our peace, had not been conferred upon Christ, had an imperfect reconciliation been all the fruit of his blood. By this name he is called, Mic. v. 5, Eph. ii. 14, and by that of our righteousness, Jer. xxxiii. 16. God is the author, and Christ the prince of peace; the reconciliation must be full, and righteous, and effectual, that has such a contriver, such a procurer. We are apt in our unbelieving moods to suspect God; because we have been unfaithful to him, we are jealous he will be unfaithful to us; but he asks the question, 'What could I have done more for my vineyard?' He appeals to men in that case, as if he should say, If men can tell me what I can do more, I will do it, do it to engage them, do it to encourage them. He has contrived it with the choicest wisdom, laid the foundation of it in the richest blood, given the fullest assurances of his sincerity in it, and never refused it to any that desired it; but it has been rejected by many whom his Spirit has solicited. Christ, whose honour lay upon it, would never have assured his disciples of it, after his return from paradise: John xx. 21, 'Peace be unto you,' had it been imperfect; a salutation he used, which is not recorded to be used by him in the time of his life.

10. This reconciliation is perpetual, as well as perfect and effectual; it is durable and fixed. It was an eternal redemption obtained: eternal in regard of its efficacy, eternal in regard of application, eternal in regard of the good things procured for us by it. Man nor devils cannot undo it, because of their weakness, nor God because of his faithfulness. It is a 'grace wherein we stand be faith,' Rom. v. 1, 2, not a tottering, but stable grace. Believers are received into the grace of God's good will, and God is not a light and unstable friend. All human friendship is perfidiousness in respect of this. The tie is everlasting, and knows no dissolution. His own grace and good will moved him to it, and the same good will in an

immutable God will preserve it. Good will made the motion, justice acquiesced in it, but since the death of Christ, the righteousness and mercy of God join hand in hand to keep it entire; Righteousness and peace have kissed each other, mercy and truth have met together,' and congratulated one another for their mutual satisfaction. The mercy of God is as prevalent with him to keep the covenant of peace from being removed, as for the first settlement of it: Isa. liv. 10, 'Neither shall my covenant of peace be removed, says the lord, that has mercy on thee.' Such consultations, such expensive accomplishments of it, cannot be mutable; mercy made it, and mercy perpetuates it. He can no more condemn a believing soul when he looks upon Christ, than he can drown the world against his own promise when he looks on the rainbow. His throne is encompassed with a rainbow, an emblem of a perpetual peace. It was so encircled in Ezekiel's time, Ezek. i. 28; with the same garb he appeared to John some ages after, Rev. iv. 3 and the predominant colour was green, that of an emerald, to note that this peace is always green and flourishing, as fresh in after ages as in the first. God was in Christ reconciling the world, God is in Christ as a priest keeping up that reconciliation. The intercession of Christ, which is a part of his priestly office, was as much in the thoughts of God, for his keeping firm this reconciliation, as the death of Christ was upon his heart to effect it. He confirms his eternal priesthood by an oath, Ps. ox 1, and therefore his intercession for it, otherwise there would be no priestly act for Christ now to perform. Christ by his death quenched the flame of the sword which guarded paradise against us; at his resurrection he sheathed the sword itself; and by his intercession keeps it perpetually in its scabbard, keeps the edge from ever being turned against a believer. Reconciliation is wrought by the death of Christ, and preserved by his merit. Christ's affections remain in his heart to solicit, the Father's affections remain in his heart to grant; Christ has an irrepealable liberty to approach to God to present his reconciling merit. Till, therefore, the unchangeable God change his resolution, and repent of all his counsel, cares, furniture, commission and acceptance of Christ; till Christ's merit become invalid, distasteful, and nauseous to the Father, this peace will stand firm. Christ's merit has been paid, it cannot be unpaid; it has been accepted, it cannot now be refused. If the soul he has redeemed be not safe, Christ can have no satisfaction for all his sufferings. Keep therefore your wills from sin, strive against the motions of it, agree not with it, and the peace will not be broken. As princes enter not into war, but where there is a real affront done, and no satisfaction given, so God breaks not the peace he has made upon every failing. When the will is not engaged, the sin is resisted; but where any give up their wills to sin, and delightfully wear its chains, they are so far from having this reconciliation perpetual, that they never had so much as the least interest in it. It is perpetual to them that embrace it, not by a pretended faith, but a real and obedient faith.

11. The state believers have by this reconciliation is far happier than that Adam had in innocence. It is likely had he persisted in it some time, he might have been confirmed in that state; but how long time he might have lived in that mutable condition, and whether, if he had persisted, he would have enjoyed such a degree of glory, is not upon record. God was in Adam making a covenant of works, he is in Christ making a covenant of peace. Christ came not only to give a simple life or a simple peace, but to give it 'more abundantly,' John x. 10, more abundantly than we had it by creation in innocence. After the fall, we were dead, and Christ restored us to life, but to a more abundant life, not that we had after the fall, for we had none at all, we were dead in trespasses and sins; but more abundantly than we had in Adam before the fall, a better life than man could challenge by the covenant of works. The second creation must be greater than the first, because the thoughts of God about the first were but a step to a second. In the first creation, mere man was the head, God in him gave out the precepts and promises to his posterity; in the second creation, God is in Christ giving out his covenant. As the means of conveyance are higher, so the things conveyed are more glorious. God would provide a way of peace that should not fail again, the security should be built upon a stronger bottom. The Lord give every one of us an interest in this reconciliation, and the comforts of it!

Third use; of exhortation. Is God in Christ reconciling the world? Then it is fit we should join issue with God, and be in Christ reconciled to him. We must comply with God in this his great ordinance. The consideration of it should work relenting, should work believing. Let the design of God prevail with us. It is in this we shall find expiation of sin, the grace of God, peace of conscience; in a word, whatsoever God as reconciled can give, whatsoever Christ as reconciling has purchased. Better to be the vilest slave in the galleys, the scoff and reproach of men, spurned by every foot, than be unreconciled. It was tender mercy, bowels of mercy, whereby the day-spring from on high has visited us,' Luke i. 8. When we lay wallowing in a miry sink, ready to be crushed by God's righteous hand, then he pitied us; the more disingenuous to refuse his amity. The dignity of the donor renders a gift more valuable than it is in itself; a present from a prince is more prized than that which is bestowed by an ordinary merchant. The gift of Christ and the offer of peace by him is incomprehensible in itself, and receives a value from that God that prepared and offers it. What pleasure can we taste in any earthly comfort, though we had a confluence of all princely delights, if we have no share in a reconciled God by a reconciling mediator, while we will force that God, who is the author of peace, to stand over us with a drawn sword pointed to our breasts? Corn, wine, and oil are little things to the light of God s countenance

1. Something must be done on our parts. Though God be the author of our reconciliation by Christ, yet something is incumbent upon us. If all men were reconciled without any condition on their parts, the apostle might have held his pen, and not have added the other clause, her. 20, after the text, 'We pray you in Christ's stead, be ye reconciled to God,' there had been no need of that inference. In the text, he speaks of the fundamental reconciliation; in this, of the actual. If all men had been reconciled to God, it had not been sense to say, You are reconciled, therefore be reconciled. It would have been an exhortation to do that which had been already done to their hands. If all men be actually reconciled, how come any to miss of the fruit of it? why is it not applied to all? Because all that are called do not comply with their call, answer not God's command and entreaty. The purchase and application are two distinct things; the purchase was made by Christ alone upon the cross, without any qualification in us; the application is not wrought without something in us concurring with it, though that also is wrought by the grace of God. God has ordained peace for us. But there is a work to be wrought within us for the enjoyment of that peace: Isa. xxvi. 12, 'Lord, thou wilt ordain peace for us, for thou also hast wrought all our works in us.' The one is grace in the spring, the other is grace in the vessel; the one is the act of God in Christ, the other is the act of God by his Spirit. Though the fire burn, if I would have warmth I must not run from it, but approach to it.

2. This qualification is faith. As grace in God qualified God (if I may use the expression) for effecting it, so faith in us qualifies us for applying and enjoying it. Though Christ be the purchaser, yet faith is the means of instating us in it: Rom. v. 1, 'Being justified by faith, we have peace with God through our Lord Jesus Christ.' Not a man has peace with God till justified by faith. This inestimable mercy is not conferred but upon men of good will, men that affect it, value it, consent to it. We must lay our hands upon the head of the sacrifice, and own him for ours. This is the band which unites us to Christ as the purchaser, and by him to God as the author of this reconciliation; it gives us a right to this peace, and at the last the comfort of it.

3. The order is, first an acceptance of Christ, then of God in and through him. We must first comply with the means before we can attain the end. Our nearness to God was purchased by the blood of Christ, and is actually conferred by union with Christ: Eph. ii. 13, ~ But now in Christ Jesus ye who sometimes were afar off are nnade nigh by the blood of Christ.' faith has recourse first to the atoning blood of Christ, and by that blood to God, Rom. iii. 25, 'Whom God has set forth to be a propitiation through faith in his blood.' This blood only quenched the consuming fire of God's wrath. By him we are reconciled, and by him only we can receive the atonement Rom. v. 11, 'We joy in God through our Lord Jesus Christ, by whom we have now received the atonement.' As God was in Christ reconciling, so we must be in Christ accepting this reconciliation with God. 'You are Christ's, and Christ is God's,' 1 Cor. iii. 23. We must first be Christ's by the acceptance of him, as Christ was God's by his calling and mission. As God goes out to us in him, our return must be by him to God. He paid the debts, made an end of sin, removed the wrath which we had merited. God was the judge, Christ the mediator; we must first go to the mediator, to be conducted by him to the judge. We had offended the law-maker, we must first go to him who is the repairer of the honour of the law; we must take the redemption of Christ along with us, the pacifying blood to present it to God, by whose authority we were under wrath. It is that blood only joins us to God, no cement without it. If we are not first by faith in Christ satisfying, we are still but as stubble before God, who is a consuming fire. Christ is the only band of union between us and God. Think not of standing secure by absolute mercy; mercy through Christ only saves us; it breathes in no other air. We must first take hold of the strength of God before we are at peace with him: Isaiah xxvii. 5, 'Let him take hold of my strength, that he may make peace with me, and he shall make peace with me;' of Christ, who is as well 'the power of God as the wisdom of God,' 1 Cor. i. 24, where you have a direction how to gain it by laying hold of his strength, the end to be aimed at in the act, 'that he may make peace with me,' and an assurance to obtain it in that method, 'he shall make peace with me.'

Motives.

1. Here is the highest encouragement and ground of acceptation. There is no room for any hard thoughts of God after so signal a discovery of himself. He is not a God of unquenchable wrath; he is willing his justice should be appeased: he took all the course that was possible for infinite wisdom to invent, for infinite power to effect, for infinite love to propose. What greater security for our blessings, than that he should make his Son a curse, that we might be blessed by him! How should so much love make us change our unworthy opinions of God! Here are the three persons employed in it: the Father contrives it, the Son effects it, the Spirit stands ready to apply it to every believer. A refusal puts a scorn upon all the three persons. As soon as ever Adam sinned, even the same day, Gen. iii. 15, God applies this remedy of a Redeemer. He did not let a day slip, for any thing we know, not an hour, before he made it known to him. His heart was in travail, and longed to be delivered of the gracious promise of a Mediator. He armed our first parents with this cordial, before he subjected them to their standing miseries. What his heart was then, it is the same still. His kindness was desirous to publish the promise, can his truth have less zeal to perform it? His kindness which moved him to assure it, has moved him to

effect it, and will move him to apply it to every one that seeks to him for it in and by his beloved Son. His wrath, which we were subject to, is overcome by his love to the mediation of his Son, who has honoured him more than sin had dishonoured him. By accepting this, we own the glory of God, and honour him as much by faith as we have dishonoured him by sin; for thereby we own that satisfaction which was as grateful to him as our sins were hateful. As he honoured himself by the death of his Son, so he honours himself by giving forth the fruits of his death. He delights to honour Christ, and to see him honoured by us: we contribute to God's delight, when we approach to him by faith in his blood. Did God make this provision? Did he contrive an expiatory offering before the world was? And will he not communicate this? Would he provide him never to bestow him? Did he bruise him for nothing, but to keep him up as a jewel in a cabinet, not to give out? To whom should God give him, but to those that desire him? Would any father lay up treasures for his children, and not dispense them, when they are earnest for them in their necessities? Can there be a greater argument than this doctrine, to overcome our rebellion, extinguish our fears, hasten our approach, and add confidence to our desires?

2. The terms required are as low as can be imagined. Nothing can be objected against the conditions he requires, repentance and faith. Can any malefactor expect peace with his arms in his hand? Is it not fit there should be such conditions to justify God, since we were the guilty offenders? Can there be less than to cast away our weapons, bewail our crimes, receive his Son as our Mediator, serve him with newness of life, all which are desirable privileges? It was in his power to appoint what conditions he pleased, because he was the free and sole benefactor; what could be less than the believing and receiving the reconciliation? It was impossible the benefit could be without it: it is no benefit unless it be esteemed so; no reason any should enjoy a benefit, that does not think it a benefit. All the self-love of men could not have framed more reasonable terms. Men would have thought of 'rivers of oil, and thousands of rams,' mere impossibilities, Micah vi. 6, 7. God requires no more than to lie humbly at his feet, and reach out our hands to receive the assurance he gives. What can be easier? If faith be difficult, it is so, not in regard of itself, but in regard of our natural enmity to God, and the pride of our own wills; it is hard only as 'the law is weak, through the flesh,' Rom. viii. 3; but nothing could be more reasonable, nothing more easy in itself An ingenuous amazement at unexpected kindness should make us run more swiftly to embrace God, than ever we ran from him. We should subscribe to his articles. As he is a God to contrive the peace, let him be your God to impose the methods of enjoying it, since he Lath given this gift to a brutish world, who he knew would grieve and despise him, yet requires no more at your hands than that you should believe and accept him, which is but a just due to the greatness of the blessing.

3. There is an absolute necessity for this compliance for our happiness. If you have not a peace of God's ordaining, you can have none of your own inventing. There can be no fellowship with God without it. We cannot be happy, because we cannot enjoy God, wherein all the felicity of a creature consists. How can guilt and purity converse together? What society can stubble have with fire, but to its destruction? We cannot see God's face without it; and if the sight of God's face be wanting, felicity is at a distance. The greatest part of hell remains, though there be no positive punishment. This cannot be without a reconciled face. 'How can two walk together unless they be agreed?' Amos iii. 3. What intercourse can there be between a guilty rebel and a frowning judge? between a sinful creature and a provoked Deity? 'If he hide his face, who can behold him?' Job xxiv. 29; but when an agreement is made, there may be mutual endearments. We are enemies to God by birth, God an enemy to us by his law; the enmity will remain on God's part, while enmity remains on ours. Strike up then the treaty with God, since there is a necessity for it, and God has provided all things to that end. Shall not God's love melt you, and sour own necessities move you?

4. Wrath is unavoidable without a compliance with God. If we will not enter into these terms of reconciliation, the heart of God, which was before incensed by our sin, cannot but rise with an higher indignation at a resolve to persist in it. Abused love kindles the hottest wrath. What fence can inexcusable guilt have against an equitable justice? When man, after his creation, proved perfidious to God, there commenced u dreadful war, which only can be ended by him who Lath put an end to sin, or else it will endure for ever in hell. All must have endured what Christ suffered, had he not stood in their stead; and those that refuse him, as he is proffered by the grace of God, must endure the same for ever. If we will not receive him as a friend, eve cannot avoid him as an enemy; his eye will behold us, 'and his hand will reach us, in the thickest coverings of darkness,' Ps. cxxxix. 9, 11. Where he is not accepted as the author of reconciliation in his own way, he will be the author of judgment in his own way. If the satisfaction of his justice, which he has provided, be slighted, that Justice will be satisfied upon our own persons. If we deny him his honour by the sufferings of Christ, he will vindicate it by the sufferings of our own persons. The law was in full force against us, whereby God has obliged himself to inflict death upon the sinner, Gen. ii. 17. It is his law upon record, that damnation shall be inflicted upon every one that believes not. There is no discovery out of Christ, but of wrath prepared against the day of wrath: the day wherein God and his unreconciled enemies shall meet together, is called a 'day of wrath,' Rom. ii. 5, 6; a day wherein there shall be an appearance of wrath only to such. The angel that has a rainbow about

his head, has feet as pillars of fire, Rev. x. i, to consume them that refuse the peace. Consider, then, we are sunk under infinite guilt, and cannot rise up without an almighty hand, vie are defiled with an universal filth, and cannot be cleansed Without infinite purity; sin is strong in its accusations, our righteousness imperfect in its defence, and can make no compensation for the wrongs by the other; our duties are bespotted, and are not fit for a pure eve. An eternal weight of wrath is due to all those; there is but one way of escape which God has provided, but one city of refuge whereby we may escape the edge of the revenging sword. The sword of divine justice reaches all that are without this shelter, touches none that are under Christ's wings, but like a consuming fire devours every thing else. We cannot perpetuate the war against him, but to our own sorrow, one spark of wrath will be enough to consume stubble; death will put a period to all treaties.

5. All other ways of reconcilement are insufficient. To pretend to any other ways is an injury to divine wisdom, as though his contrivance were not sufficient for the creature's restoration and support. Divine mercy will clasp no man in its arms with a wrong to any one attribute, nor to the dishonour of Christ. It will therefore never receive any who denies Christ and the efficacy of his priesthood. Men naturally are studious of making God compensation, applauding themselves in their own inventions and satisfactions of their own coining, unwilling to acquiesce in the wisdom and will of God. Two great things God would advance in the world by his grace, is his wisdom and authority; these are the things men oppose, his wisdom by the pride of reason, his authority by the perversity of will. But consider, do we need reconciliation or no? If we need it not, how came we fiends with God, since we were born enemies? If we do need it, is it not safer to enter into the terms God has proposed, wherewith he is satisfied, than to stand to our false, or, at best, hilt uncertain methods? The safest way is always the choice of wise men. Let us not be fools then in refusing the gospel method, unless we can meet with anything that has as fair a plea to divine revelation. Had we all the angels on our side, and all the men on earth to entreat for us, it would be ineffectual.. God never was in them reconciling the world; this one mediator, whom God has appointed, has done and can do that which neither men upon earth nor angels and saints in heaven can do by their joint intercessions. Place no confidence then in your own humiliations, services, duties, God never was in those reconciling any man; all that is done without faith is but enmity, and that in the best part, your minds, Rom. viii. Whatsoever fair colours they are painted with, they cannot please God. The Scripture settles an impossibility on the head of all of them: Heb. xi. 6, 'Without faith it is impossible to please God,' to gain or keep his favour. Were your righteousness of the highest elevation, it is but a creature, and therefore not the object of trust. Though Adam, while he continued in his natural righteousness, might have entered it as a plea, yet because mutable, it was no fit object of trust for him. But since the fall all pleas of a fleshly corrupted righteousness are overruled in the court of heaven. Absolute mercy, without faith in Christ, cannot save you. As God could not, after the sanction of the law, in regard of his truth, pardon the violations of it without a satisfaction, so since he has settled the way of reconciliation by faith in the blood of Christ, he cannot upon the same score of his truth save any in a way of absolute mercy, especially when that way which he has appointed is refused. As it would be against his truth, against his justice, so also against the honour of his obedient Son; for if he be at peace with one man by absolute mercy, why might he not upon the same terms have reconciled others, and then what need of the sufferings of his only Son to make up the breach? If anything else therefore be chosen as the way of this peace, God at the hour of judgment may remit us to our righteousness, services, carnal confidences, saying, Go to the reconcilers that you have chosen, and see whether they can make your peace, as he did to the Israelites: Judges x. 14, 'Go cry to the gods which you have chosen; let them deliver you;' a dreadful, but a just speech.

6. God seeks it at our hands, and is willing to receive us. He is not only a God in Christ reconciling the world, but he is a God in his ambassadors entreating: 'As though God himself did beseech you by us,' ver. 20, after the text. This is the tenor of his proclamation, 'Be you reconciled to God.' If he had not desired it, he would not have spent so many thoughts about it, and been at such expense to effect it. He was not bound to it; for he might have left Adam to sink into the death he had merited, without exposing his Son to a death he had not deserved, and contracted a necessity of, only as our surety; he was no more bound to seek out Adam and make him a promise of redemption than he was bound to make him a creature. He might have raised a new world, and have filled it with new inhabitants. It must be something of a vast concernment to us, that God has been so busy about, and so desirous of our acceptance of. Both God seek to us to receive wealth and worldly honours? No. This therefore must be a thing of higher value. A God seeks to us, who is infinitely more glorious than we are vile; a God who never did us the least wrong, but has borne with many injuries from us; a God who could as easily send us into hell with his breath, as breathe out a; kind invitation to us; a God who needs our friendship no more than he fears our enmity; a God no more benefited by it than the sun by darting a beam upon a grain of sand. Sure that soul never was sensible of the misery his war with God has sunk him into, who refuses to receive the peace he offers, nor can without an Inconceivable shame look God in the face at the last day, after so notorious a rejecting an entreating God. He seeks it this day, perhaps he will not seek it at our hands to-morrow. There is 'a day' wherein we may 'know the things that

concern our peace,' Luke xix. 41. When the day is over, peace will not return. There is a day v herein he will pour out his wrath upon the unbelieving world. While he is yet a great way off, and his thunders at a distance, he sends an 'embassy of peace,' Luke xiv. 33. He yet seeks to his sworn enemies, and those that were in league with Satan: You may be in league with me, I have not yet shut the door. Listen, do you not hear God's voice in the gospel? He shuts out none that do not shut out themselves. What a guilt will the refusal amount to, when we are to answer for not only the first publication, but repeated offers? Besides, he is willing to receive us into favour, more willing to embrace us than we to receive him. The eternal motions in his heart which gave birth to this gracious design, are of the same force and strength still; he can never forget them. As the remembrance of the years of the right hand of the Most High is our comfort in times of trouble, so God's remembrance of the years of his own right hand, the workings of his own heart, has the like force to excite him to a reception of us, as they had to commission Christ for us. He never broke his word; and less will ho do it at the upshot of all, when his people are almost gathered, the world near its period, and the proclamation of the gospel ready to be taken down and folded up for ever; he will not at the end be worse than he has been all along. Let us be as willing to be at peace with him as he is to be at peace with us. God sets us a pattern, he seeks to us, it is an imitation of God to seek to him.

2. Exhortation. Is God in Christ reconciling the world 7 Then we must be at enmity with sin. God was in Christ reconciling sinners, not sin. God and sin are irreconcilable enemies, so that where there is a peace with one, there must be a war with the other. Fire and water may sooner agree than God and Sin, than a peace with God and a peace with sin. The traitor may be reconciled to the prince, and the treason as hateful to him as before. This is the best evidence to any that he is actually reconciled, when he hates that which made the first separation. Christ expiated sin, not encouraged it; he died to make your peace, but he died to make you holy: Titus ii. 14, 'To purify a people to himself.' The design of God in the manifestation of Christ in the flesh, was 'to destroy the works of the devil,' 1 John iii. 8. The chief work of the devil was to enter man in a league with himself and rebellion against God. God aimed at the death of our sins, when he aimed at the life of our souls. The ends of Christ's death cannot be separated; he is no atoner, where he is not a refiner. It is as certain as any word the mouth of God has spoken, that 'there is no peace to the wicked.' A bespotted conscience, and an impure, will keep up the amity with Satan, and enmity with God. He that allows himself in any sin, deprives himself of the benefit of reconciliation. This reconciliation must be mutual; as God lays down his wrath against us, so we must throw down our arms against him. As there was a double enmity, one rooted in nature, another declared by wicked works; or rather, one enmity in its root, and another in its exercise, Col. i. 21; so there must be an alteration of state, and an alteration of acts. The end of Christ's death was to reconcile God to us, and bring us back to God. We are not therefore linked in a peace with him, unless we be transformed into the image of his Son. How can we expect to be taken into the bosom of God, when we every day wilfully defile our souls! Can familiarity with God be kept up, when daily bars are laid in the way? Why was God in Christ reconciling the world? Because he was a holy as well as a gracious God; and to show his detestation of sin, as well as his affection to the creature. Shall this encourage any practice against the holiness of God? God is of as pure eyes, and can as little endure to behold iniquity, since the reconciliation, as before. God was sanctified in Christ when he was reconciling the world in him, and he will be sanctified in us if we have interest in this reconciliation. All God s acts about Christ are the highest obligation to be at enmity with that, for which the Son of God was appointed, and made a sacrifice; to receive encouragement from hence to sin more freely, is to act Judas his part with God's grace, and betray it to serve our lusts. Be afraid therefore to offend God, not so much because of his power to hurt you, as because of his love whereby he has obliged you. The peace was broken by the disobedience of Adam; it was restored by the obedience of Christ. But our obedience is necessary to the joyful fruits of it. 'Great peace have they which love thy law,' Ps. cxix. 165.

3. Be industrious and affectionate in the service of God. Has God been in Christ reconciling the world, manifesting his desire for it and affection to it by such various acts, and shall we put God off with a little service, who has not put us off with a scanty grace? God has done his utmost to engage our affection and encourage us in the choicest services: there could not be an higher way to procure it and deserve it of us. The view of the creatures, and God's goodness in them, raises a common love to God in the more ingenious natural minds. To what heights should our love ascend, who have such steps to mount by? A weak love is less than is due to him who has discovered such an immensity to us. Shall we return not a drop, or but a drop, for an ocean? How much should we think ourselves obliged to a prince who should but stop a torrent of legal penalties deserved by us? God has done this and more. How should we combine all our thoughts and affections together to serve that God acceptably, who has made all his thoughts conspire to reduce us honourably and successfully? 'I am the Lord thy God, which has brought thee out of the land of Egypt, out of the house of bondage,' is the preface to the Decalogue, as an incitement of them to a choice respect to all his precepts.; I am the God reconciling you in Christ,' is the tenor of the gospel, and much more an incitement to service, by how much the deliverance in the antitype exceeds that in the type; this being spiritual and eternal, that temporal. If you are actually

reconciled, serve God as your friend. As God has given you an higher state, give him a greater honour. Do all things out of love to God as reconciled, without any base ends and sordid designs. God had no other end in being the author of peace but his own glory and your good; have then no other end but God's glory in your own welfare, advancing further to him and enjoying his reconciled favour. Serve him with a delight in him; a dull, slavish spirit becomes not any in his approach to so hearty a friend. Every duty should be performed with a triumph and glory in the God of salvation: Hab. iii. 18, 'I will joy in the God of my salvation.' God would then delight in us; next to the delight he has in his reconciling Son, he has the choicest delight in his reconciled servants, and services springing up from a sense of his love to them.

4. Let all our approaches to God be begun and attended with a sense of this. God in all his communications to his people acted as a reconciled God; we should eye him so in all our approaches to him. As there is not one mercy, one act of grace, God shows to us, but springs from this restored affection, so not any duty we offer up to God but should rise from a sense of it. Whatsoever is not by and through Christ, is not accepted as a duty. This consideration before all addresses would animate them with all those graces necessary, to be acted in them. It would make us humble to consider what we were, and how freely God reduced us. It would make us believing with an holy boldness. What despondency can there be, when God has given so many tokens of his heartiness in it? It would make us earnest; it would be a fetching fire from heaven for the inflaming our souls. Earnestness is grounded upon hope; what greater foundation for hope than the consideration that this was God's sole act? Think before every duty of the great love God bears to Christ as mediator, greater than to all men and angels; this will be a ground of confidence. For the love of God to Christ as mediator, was with respect to all that believe in him. Think much of the virtue of Christ's death, wherewith he sprinkled the throne of God, and turned the seat of justice into a throne of grace. It is the best way to receive answers; by pleading this, we mind God of all his engagements. A very act about Christ is an argument fit to be used in prayer. God will never deny his own acts, nor the ends of them, which was to make a way for communicating himself to his creatures. God is only in Christ entertaining us, as well as reconciling us. Let us not lift up an eye to him without faith in him as a God in Christ, and carry this atoning blood in the hands of faith, in every act of communion with him.

5. Look for grace and spiritual strength from God in Christ. The conduct of mercy and grace is unstopped by Christ, to flow freely down to man. This is the foundation of the regeneration of any soul: 2 Cor. v. 17, 18, 'All things are become new, and all things are of God, who has reconciled us to himself by Jesus Christ.' Having spoken of the new creation, ver. 17, he lays down the true cause, God; the foundation, the reconciliation by Christ. AID things are of God, all the powerful effects and operations of the gospel in the hearts of men are from God as a reconciler by Christ, not from God as creator. The deep meditation of and closing with the promise of God in and through Christ, brings grace into the heart, not a consideration of God's precepts, but of God's promises. The application of the reconciling love of God in Christ by faith, is attended with a powerful benediction of the Spirit, pulling up the foundations of the enmity on our parts; the Spirit is received by the preaching of the gospel, the meditations of the gospel, the applications of the gospel; the Spirit is conveyed with those, not with the precepts of the law, Gal. iii. 5. Men begin at the wrong end, they would rise from obedience to faith, and deal with God as if he were to be appeased and satisfied by them. But begin at faith, a firm assent, a full consent to the gospel and the offers of redemption, and go down, by virtue of that, to obedience; it is by casting ourselves upon God in Christ that we receive vigour for all spiritual obedience. The spirit of holiness is the principle whereby we obey, not the effects of our obedience. Christ is first redemption, then sanctification; God a God of peace, and then a God of grace. We should look upon God as a God of peace, and under that title implore him for increase of habitual grace. As a God of peace, he 'works in us that which is well-pleasing in his sight' Heb. xiii. 20, 21. Our sanctification depends upon our justification. God promised to be as a dew to his people under the gospel, Hosea iv. 5. Dew descends from a clear sky, and grace from a reconciled God. As God in Adam had conveyed a natural righteousness to his posterity, had Adam stood, so God in Christ only conveys a spiritual righteousness to Christ's spiritual offspring.

6. When any rising of enmity is in the soul, go to God in Christ. As God was in Christ reconciling the world, so he is in Christ reconciling a veal after the readmission of guilt through temptation; not that the guilt of the whole mass of sins of a believer returns upon his far], tent a particular guilt of that sin he has committed lies upon him, for which he must have a fresh application of reconciling mercy. He must go to God in Christ for this; as the first application was made in and through Christ. so must the second and third, as often as we need it, even in our daily pardons. Christ sits an officer in heaven to this purpose, and God Lath constituted him an officer to this end, and is in him in his intercession accepting it, as well as in his first satisfaction. The Corinthians the apostle writes to, some of them at least, were reconciled, yet he beseeches them to be reconciled to God, i.e. renew their reconciliation upon every new breach, and regain the favour of God which they had forfeited by their sins, for which he had reproved them in the former epistle. This must be sued out every day. What was the foundation of the

first peace is the foundation of the renewals of it; the same course you took at the first, will be successful for the second. God was not out of Christ in the first, and he will not be out of Christ whenever there is any need. As God was willing and desirous to make reconciliation by the blood of Christ, when all your sins lay before him with their crimson aggravations, much more will he renew it upon a particular fall. But he may hide his face till you sue out a pardon upon his own proclamation and contrivance; and if it be a presumptuous sin, he may deny you the comfort of this peace a long times perhaps as long as you live. Let not any presume upon this, for it belongs not to any man that lives in a course of known sin, which is inconsistent with a reconciled state.

7. How contented should those that are reconciled be in every condition! The peace of God should bear rule in our hearts, to compose them upon any emergency: Col. iii. 15, this will keep the heart and mind from solicitousness Philip. iv 6, 7, this will make us despise the promises of the world alluring us, and the threatenings of the world to scare us. This peace should be the guard of our souls, and will render us happy when the world may account us most miserable, and therefore should render us contented. If you would not have the riches and honours of the world without it, you may well bear the scorns and reproaches of the world with it. The world could not secure you, if you had a war with God, nor defend you from the arrows of his wrath. But since you have peace with God, you are mounted above the enmities of the world, and your spirits should be guarded by it from any tumultuous passions. If the wrath of God be ceased towards us, we may well bear the strokes of a Fathers since we are not like to feel his sword as a Judge. How cheerfully may we kiss the afflicting hand of God, when he is at peace with us! Look upon all your mercies too (though they are of a meaner bulk outwardly than others), as flowing from this fountain, which may make you not only contented with them, but highly value them. It gives a sweeter relish to mercy than Adam could have; he had the goodness of God, but not the goodness of a reconciled Father, while he was in innocence. If this makes heaven the sweeter, it should make mercies here more savoury

8. Let us then be reconcilable to others. Not only where we offer, but from whom we receive an injury. God's reconciliation should be our rule in dealing with others. Hard hearts and uncharitable dispositions are unlike to God, who had a heart full of tenderness to them, who will not part with a grain of their right to their brethren, when God parted with his Son to work their peace with him; and had he not been more forward in it than they, they had perished for ever. God sets his own actions to us as a pattern of ours to others: Luke vi. 36, 'Be ye therefore merciful, as your Father also is merciful,' if we are irreconcilable to others, we are not imitators of God, but reject the noblest pattern, and discover no sense of the kindness of God to us. Since God has made Christ a propitiation for sin, the apostle makes this inference, that 'if God so loved us, we ought also to love one another,' 1 John iv. 10, 11. Did God send his Son out of his bosom, and veil his glory, to be at peace with us, and entreat us to accept his favour, and shall we be upon every occasion at sword's point with our brother? Such a disposition is against the whole tenor of the gospel, and a keeping up a wolfish and brutish nature against the design of the gospel administration, Isa. xi. 6. Christ came to slay the enmity between God and us, between Jew and Gentile; it is a crossing the design of God, to preserve enmity between Christian and Christian; it is to keep up the partition wall, and frustrate (what in us lies) the end of Christ's death, which was to demolish it. The peace God wrought was a matter of grace, the peace we owe to our brother is a matter of debt; it is due to the command of God. God first laid the scene of our reconciliation, not assisted by the counsels of others; not sought to by ourselves, but seeking us. Our doing the like to others is an imitation of God, whereas to be implacable in revenge is to partake of the devil's nature.

9. Glorify God for this. Since God sends out such a blessing to us, we should send out loud prayers to him. Heaven smiles upon earth, and earth should bless heaven Glorify God as the Father of our Lord Jesus Christ. Though we have all immediately from Christ, yet Christ has all from the Father. He is the propitiation for our sins, but he was appointed by the Father. He came to redeem, but he was sent by God upon that errand. He paid our debts as a surety, but he was accepted by God. He was a mediator to bring us to God, but he was Commissioned by God to that end. What a love did God retain to his creatures, though he abominated their Sins, and in the midst of his indignation against their iniquities had bowels for their persons! How did God forecast for us, when we were 'prisoners in the pit wherein was no water,' Zech. ix. 11, the captives of the mighty, and the prey of the terrible! Isa. xlix. 25. When the law of God was against us, and his truth taking part with his law, his wisdom and mercy found a way to preserve his truth, and satisfy the curses of the law, that we might enjoy the blessings of the gospel, when we could not in the least deserve it, unless peevishness and perversity, treachery and disloyalty, weakness and wilfulness could pass for allurements; we had then been inconceivable meriters. Such free and full compassion deserves our thank fullness, though we could not merit his grace. It is not a contracted, half-made, or oppressive peace, It is an extensive, tender, and abundant peace, like a river and a flowing stream, a peace whereby we are borne in his bosom, Isa. lxvi. 12. How should we adore the depth of that wisdom which found a refuge for us, when heaven and earth were at war with us; adore this goodness, that when we were no sooner born, but we were He objects of a cursing law, the scorn of a malicious devil, our Jesus should be sent to pacify the law, and shame the

devil our enemy I Angels glorify him for this peace; should we be outstripped by beings less concerned in it? God is only praised in and through Christ; God and Christ are joined together in the saints' praise: Rev. v. 13, 'Blessing, honour, glory, and power be unto him that sits upon the throne, and to the Lamb, for ever and ever;' and so they should be in ours. How beautiful will this whole work appear, when the whole methods of it come to be read in heaven in the original copy, when they shall be seen in the face, in the bosom of God, in fair and plainer characters! To conclude. If all the sparks that ever leapt out of any fire since the creation, and all the drops of rain that have fell upon the world; were so many angelical tongues, their praise would come short of the excess of this love. Let the praise of God for this, be not the business of a day, but the work of our lives, since eternity is too short to admire it.

End.

The Necessity of Regeneration

Jesus answered and said unto him, Verily, verily, I say unto thee, Except a man be born again, he cannot see the kingdom of God. Jesus answered, Verily, verily, I say unto thee, Except a man be born of water, and of the Spirit, he cannot enter into the kingdom of God.--John iii. 3,5

These words contain the foundation of all practical religion here, and happiness hereafter. It is the principal doctrine Christ, as a prophet, came to teach, and as a king to work in the heart. It is an answer to Nicodemus his compliment, who came to him with some veneration of him. His description is in ver. 1: 'There was a man of the pharisees named Nicodemus, a ruler of the Jews.' 1. By his profession or sect, a pharisee. 2. His name, Nicodemus. 3. His quality, a ruler of the Jews; "Argoon", a prince, one of the great Sanhedrin, who had the supreme power in all affairs which concerned religion, even under the Roman government. His coming to Christ is described, ver. 2 'The same came to Jesus by night, and said unto him, Rabbi, we know that thou art a teacher come from God: for no man can do these miracles that thou doest, except God be with him.' Where we have (1.) the time of his coming, by night; (2.) the manner of coming and speaking to him with reverence, Rabbi, a title of honour. He comes to Christ; therefore is to be commended. He comes by night; has some failure in his respect to Christ, afraid publicly to own him. Nicodemus was one of the member which believed Christ for his miracles, John ii. 28. He comes hereupon to discourse with him about divine things. He acknowledges him a prophet sent by God. The reason of his acknowledgement is the consideration of his miracles, which manifested a divine power, both in the greatness and multitude of them. For he knew that God would not set the seal of his power, to one that had not his commission. Miracles are the credential letters, to signify the divine authority of any person sent upon any new dispensation by God.

Observe,

1. God doth not force any man's belief, but gives such undeniable evidences of his will and mind, that not to believe is flat contradiction to him. When he sent Moses to deliver and give a new law to the Israelites, he attended him with a miraculous power, to testify it to be his will, that what Moses delivered should be entertained. So it was with our Saviour, and in the primitive times, at the first promulgation of the gospel in several places. But when a doctrine is settled and a church established, God forbears those extraordinary works, as he did the raining down manna after the Israelites' entrance into Canaan, where they might have provision in an ordinary way of providence; and they had miracles afterward in a more scanty measure, now and then. We have now rational ways to introduce us to a belief of the Christian doctrine; and though there are no sensible miracles as before, yet there has been in all ages, and is still, a miracle kept up in the world, greater than wrought by Christ upon the bodies of men. And that is the conversion of many obstinate sinners, and subduing them on a sudden, which in Christ's account, was the chiefest miracle he wrought when he was upon the earth: Luke vii. 22, 'Go your way, and tell John what things you have seen and heard: how that the blind see, the lame walk, the lepers are cleansed, the deaf hear, the dead are raised, to the poor the gospel is preached.' Christ had cured many in their sight; but he added in the end of the enumeration, 'To the poor the gospel is preached,' "Ptochoi euangelidzontai". The poor are evangelised, brought into a gospel frame, a renewed state for the kingdom of heaven, which is greater than the raising a man from a natural death to a natural life.

Nicodemus comes by night. He is fond of his own honour, loath to impair it by a free and open confession. He was a master in Israel. Had he come by day, his reputation had suffered in the vulgar opinion, who might well wonder that he, a pharisee, of a profound knowledge, should come to receive instruction from the son of a carpenter, a man despised by his fellows of the Sanhedrin. Yet he comes, though by night.

Observe,

1. It is a hard matter for us to perform a duty we are convinced of, without a flaw in it. Nicodemus is convinced by the miracles of Christ's divine authority; but he forbears an open acknowledgement of him. He creeps to him in the night, unwilling to be seen with him in the day. If Christ were not a prophet, why should he be acknowledged at all? If a prophet, why not in the day as well as in the night? Strange not to consult him in the day, whom he confesses to have his commission from God! How weak is the faith of the best at first! How staggering between Christ and self.

2. Our own reputation will be apt to mix itself in our religious services. It is his fear of the loss of

this makes him choose the darkness. This greatest piece of old Adam in us will be rising in various forms, when we are in the most spiritual exercises. What a contest is there between religion and reputation! He was willing to gratify the one, but not displease the other.

3. Ambition is the great hindrance of a thorough conversion. Nicodemus had a mind to speak to Christ, but his reputation bears too much sway in him against a thorough giving up himself to him. He was ashamed to be taken notice of in this little address he made: John v. 44, 'How can ye believe, that receive honour one of another, and seek not the honour which comes from God only?'

4. Men may have a high esteem of Christ, yet not such an esteem as amounts to a saving faith. Nicodemus acknowledges him a teacher, and that sent from God; but not the teacher, the great prophet Moses had spoken of, Deut. xviii. 15. He confesses him a prophet, but not the Messiah. Look to your estimations of Christ; see whether they be supreme, superlative, the Saviour, the mediator, the Lord and King.

5. Convictions may be a long time before any appearance of conversion. If we consider Nicodemus here, only as one convinced of the divine authority of Christ, and not a thorough convert at this time; for he seems by his questions, verse 4 and 9, to be rather a malcontent, than a convert; yet the seed then sown by our Saviour's discourse sprung up at last in fruit. He does upon a signal occasion plead Christ's cause before a council of pharisees, probably the great Sanhedrin, yet but faintly: John vii. 50, 51, 'Doth our law judge any man before it hears him, and knows what he does?' Before, he would have no witness of his coming to Christ. Here he takes his part, as he might have done any man's upon a common principle of justice and equity, that he should not be condemned before he was heard. But there is more generous fruit afterwards, where he joins with Joseph of Arimathea in doing honour openly to our Saviours crucified body: John xix. 39, 'And there came also Nicodemus (which at the first came to Jesus by night), and brought a mixture of myrrh and aloes, about an hundred pound weight.' What grace he had seems to be in a long sleep, but is very vigorous upon its awaking.

6. True grace does one time or other discover itself most contrary to that which was the natural crime before. In both these places, fear had been his sin. It is now overmatched by confidence. The Holy Ghost takes notice of it, 'which at the first came to Jesus by night.' He came by night before, now he comes by day. He and another never named before, Joseph of Arimathea, who being possessed with the same passion of fear, was a disciple in secret,--John xix. 38, 'Being a disciple of Jesus, but secretly, for fear of the Jews,'--own him publicly at his death, when those that had been familiar with him in his life forsook him. Christ will make timorous hares to own his cause, when those that think themselves courageous lions turn their backs upon him.

Paul had the most transcendent affection to the church, who before was guilty of the smartest persecution. And Peter, after the coming of the Spirit, was as courageous as before he was cowardly in his Master's cause.

We have seen the pharisee. Let us consider our Saviour's answer: ver. 3, 'Jesus answered and said unto him, Verily, verily, I say unto thee, Except a man be born again, he cannot see the kingdom of God.'

Some think that Nicodemus asked a question which is not expressed, but may be gathered out of Christ's answer, and seems to be this, What was requisite to a man's entrance into the kingdom of heaven? Whereupon Christ tells him, that there was a necessity of being born again. Others think that Nicodemus asked no question, and that these words are a very proper reply to Nicodemus.

1. Christ answers not his compliment, but uses his authority, acknowledged by Nicodemus, of a teacher to inform him. Since you acknowledge my commission from God to be a teacher, I will teach you what I have to declare. The great design of my coming is to bring men to the kingdom of God; and the great means to this is a new birth, which can only fit you for evangelical truths here, and eternal happiness hereafter. He acknowledges Christ to be a teacher, and Christ in his reply would teach him how to become a Christian.

2. Christ frames his answer according to the pharisee's corruption. Nicodemus came by night, out of love to his credit, that might be impaired by his coming in the daytime. What would the people think? Surely this man, and the rest of his tribe, are not so knowing as they pretend to be, since he comes to Jesus to be taught, and out of fear of the pharisees, who thereby might be offended.

Christ's answer therefore very well suits him. You must become a new man, if you would have acquaintance with evangelical mysteries. Sway with your old notions, and pharisaic pride. Deny your honour, credit, and whatsoever partakes of the name of self. A legal frame, and a pharisaic righteousness, will not advance you to the kingdom of God. The Jews were proud of being Abraham's children, and thought the gates of heaven could not be shut against any of that relation.

John had touched them before for this: Mat. iii. 9, 'And think not to say within yourselves, We have Abraham to our father.' Christ does tacitly here do the same, and puts him in mind of another birth, and the falseness and deceitfulness of his bottom of legal righteousness.

3. Christ frames his answer according to his weakness and ignorance. Nicodemus acknowledged him a teacher, not the Messiah. Christ would bring him to the knowledge of himself as the Messiah.

Christ therefore by his answer would lift up his thoughts higher, and puts him in mind of the kingdom of God, which the Jews in their common discourse signified the kingdom of the Messiah by, and have entitled it in ages since, the kingdom of God, and the kingdom of heaven. So that Christ would bring him to the knowledge of himself as the Messiah, not only as an extraordinary prophet.

These three things evidence what relation this speech of Christ has to that of Nicodemus.

Observe from the relation of this to Nicodemus his speech:

1. We shall gain nothing by our applaudings and praises of Christ, without a renewed nature. Nicodemus comes with much reverence, gives Christ the title of rabbi, confesses him to be sent of God, owns the divinity of his miracles. Christ does not compliment him again, takes no notice of his civility, but falls roundly to his work, acquaints him with the necessity of regeneration, without which he could not see the kingdom of God, for all his fine praises of him. A glavering reverential religion is insignificant with Christ. A new birth, a likeness to Christ in nature, a conformity to him, is accounted by Christ an higher estimation of him, than all external applauses given to him.

2. No natural privilege under heaven can entitle us to the kingdom of grace or glory. It is not our carnal traduction from the best man. It is no natural birth, with the choicest privileges, gives us a right to either of them. Not the honour of having the law from God's own mouth, the glory of an outward covenant, the treasure of the oracles of God, the seal of circumcision borne in the body, that can instate this Nicodemus into this felicity. It is a birth of a higher strain, from an higher principle, a change of nature, and a removal from the old stock.

See how strangely Nicodemus replied upon this discourse of our Saviour. How strangely astonished is this great ruler in Israel at the doctrine which is absolutely necessary to an entrance into the kingdom of heaven! ver. 4, 'Nicodemus says unto him, How can a man be born when he is old? can he enter a second time into his mother's womb, and be born?' What a childish conception has he of this most heavenly doctrine! Can such an ancient man as I return to my first principles, dig a way into my mother's womb? It is strange that Nicodemus, being a pharisee, and so well versed in Scripture, should be so ignorant, or at least guilty of so much inadvertence, as not to think of that place, Ezek. xxxvi., and other places, which speak of 'a new heart,' and 'an heart of flesh.' He might have considered the design of the legal purifications, which were to represent the inward holiness which ought to be in the persons so purified. Yet he hears him discourse, but does not comprehend him. His carnal notion bears sway against spiritual truths.

Observe,

1. A man may have great knowledge in the letter of the Scripture, and yet not understand the necessary and saving doctrines in it. The doctrine of regeneration was laid down in the whole Old Testament, though not in that term. Let us take heed how we read the Scriptures; not to trouble our heads with needless and curious questions, but with the main mysteries of religion. What could all Nicodemus his knowledge profit him, if it had been ten thousand times more, without the knowledge of this doctrine, and the experience of it!

2. Nothing is more an enemy to the saving knowledge of gospel mysteries than a priding ourselves in head knowledge. Nicodemus his coming by night was not only from fear, but pride, that he might not be thought ignorant by the people. Humble men have the soundest knowledge: 'The meek will he teach his way,' Ps. xxv. 9.

3. How low was the interest of God in the world at that time! How had ignorance and error thrust the knowledge of God out of other parts of the world, when it languished so much in the church! How simple must the poor people be when the students in Scripture were no wiser! It is a thing to be bewailed amongst us, that wrangling knowledge has almost thrust out spiritual. And when Christians meet, their discourses are more about unnecessary disputes than these saving mysteries of Christianity, which might produce elevations of heart to heaven.

To this exception of Nicodemus Christ makes his reply; where observe,

1. A fresh assertion of it, with an explanation: ver. 5, 'Jesus answered, Verily, verily, I say unto thee, Except a man be born of water, and of the Spirit, he cannot enter into the kingdom of God.' In the third verse, Christ lays down the necessity of the new birth; in ver. 6, the necessity of the cause, 'Except a man be born of water, and of the Spirit.' In the first speech, he lays down the doctrine; in this, he explains the principle and manner of it, to remove his false apprehensions, wherein he might mean the transmigration of souls, which seems to be an opinion amongst the Jews.

2. A reason to back it: ver. 6, 'That which is born of the flesh is flesh; and that which is born of the Spirit is spirit.' That which is born of the flesh is flesh, and can be no more by that principle, for the effect cannot be better than the cause; but that which is born of the Spirit is spirit, i.e. has a spiritual nature.

Flesh is taken for man corrupted: Gen. vi. 3, 'For he also is flesh,' degenerate into flesh, grown a mere sensual creature by the loss of original righteousness. For upon the parting of original righteousness, the soul of man was as a body without life; a spiritual carcass, as the body is without a soul.

Flesh signifies the whole nature, as in that place, Mat. xvi. 17, 'Flesh and blood has not revealed it unto thee,' &c. The incarnation of the Son of God, which is the foundation of all evangelical administrations, is above the sphere of nature to discover. Man in his natural generation is but mere nature, and cannot apprehend, cannot enjoy that which is only apprehensible and enjoyable by a spiritual nature; but man regenerated by the Spirit is spiritual, and is advanced above mere flesh, for he is made partaker of the divine nature. So that Christ's argument runs thus: No flesh can enter into the kingdom of God; but every man naturally is flesh, unless born again of the Spirit; therefore no man, unless born again of the Spirit, can enter into the kingdom of God. If you could enter into your mother's womb, and be born again, the matter would not be mended with you; you would still be but flesh, and rather worse than better; therefore that is not the birth that I mean, for the impediment would be as strong in you as before.

These two verses are an answer to Nicodemus his objection. Nicodemus understands it of a carnal birth. No, no, says Christ, it is a spiritual birth I intend; one that is wholly divine and heavenly. That which you mean brings a man into the light of the world; that which I mean, brings a man out of the world, into the light of grace. That forms the flesh to an earthly life; this forms the soul to an heavenly. That makes you the son of man; this forms the soul to an heavenly.

All the difficulty lies in ver. 6, in that expression of water, &c. Some, as the papists, understand it of the elementary water of baptism, and from this place exclude all children dying without baptism from salvation. Others understand it of a metaphorical water, whereof Christ speaks, John iv. 14, 'The water that I shall give him, shall be in him a well of water, springing up into everlasting life.'

Let us first see why by water cannot be meant the baptismal water.

Regeneration is the mystery and sense of that sacred ceremony. It is indeed signified, represented, and sealed in baptism; how, and in what sense, is not my present work.

1. It is strange, that when all agree that the birth here spoken of is spiritual and metaphorical, that the water here should be natural.

2. None could be saved, unless baptised, if this were meant of baptism. As if these words, John vi. 53, 'Except you eat the flesh of the Son of man, and drink his blood, ye have no life in you,' were meant of the supper, none could be saved unless they did partake of it. Whereas Christ lays not the stress upon baptism, but upon faith: Mark xvi. 16, 'He that believes, and is baptised, shall be saved; but he that believes not, shall be damned.' He does not say, He that is not baptised shall be damned, but he lays damnation wholly upon the want of faith. Many have been saved without baptism, none without faith. It is true to say, He that does not believe shall be damned; but it is not true to say, He that is not baptised shall be damned. Christ says the first, but not the second, though his discourse had obliged him to say so, had it been true, or had he meant this speech to Nicodemus of baptismal water. The Spirit is not tied to baptism, but he may act out of the sacraments as well as in them. Understand this of the bare want of baptism, not of the contempt or wilful neglect of it. If it were meant of baptism, it was true then, that none could be saved without it. How did the thief upon the cross enter into paradise, which Christ promised him? So that one may enter into heaven without baptism by water, though not without the baptism of the Spirit.

3. Baptism was not then instituted as a standing sacrament in the Christian church. The institution of it we find not till after Christ's resurrection: Mat. xxviii. 19, 'Go ye, therefore, and teach all nations, baptising them.' And it is not likely Christ would discourse to Nicodemus of the necessity of an institution that was not yet expressly appointed by him, and which he did not appoint till after his resurrection; for he discourses of that which was of present necessity. And if this were meant of baptism, and of that absolute necessity the papists would lay upon it from these words, then all that died before the institution of baptism by our Saviour, unbaptised, could not enter into the kingdom of heaven, though believing. Can anything be necessary before the precept for it be given? It could not be necessary before, as a means, because it is not a natural, but an instituted means. It must be therefore necessary by virtue of a command; therefore not absolutely necessary before the command, and at the time Christ spoke these words. Some say that Christ meant it, not of an absolute necessity at that time, but that it should be so after his death. That is to give our Saviour the lie, for he spoke it of the present time, some years before his death. Besides, it wrongs the goodness of our Saviour (if he had meant it of baptism), to defer the institution of it so long after, when it was at present necessary for Nicodemus his salvation. It wrongs his wisdom, too, to speak of that to be at present necessary, which was not in being, nor could be till after his death.

4. It is strange that our Saviour should speak to Nicodemus of the necessity of baptism before he had informed him of the mysteries of the gospel, whereof it is a seal. To speak of the seal before he speaks of that which is to be sealed by it, is not congruous. For the sacraments being founded upon the doctrine on which they depend, to begin by a sacrament the instruction of a man, is to begin a building by the tiles and rafters, before you lay a foundation; and against the order expressed by our Saviour to the apostles, which puts teaching before baptising, and was always practised in the primitive times, and is to this day in all Christian churches, to the adult and grown up. As circumcision was, amongst the

Jews, not administered to any proselyte before his turning proselyte, and instruction in those laws he was to observe, and then, and not till then, his children had a right to circumcision.

5. Those that understand it of the baptismal water, and so make that of absolute necessity, do by another assertion accuse their own exposition of a falsity; for they say that the baptism of blood supplies the want of that of water, and that if either infants or adult persons be hurried away to a stake or gibbet, or killed for the Christian cause, they are certainly saved; which cannot be, if the baptism of water were to be understood in this place, and so absolutely necessary. It is water that is expressed and blood is not water. One of these assertions must be false. A martyr dying unbaptised must be damned, and cannot enter into the kingdom of heaven, if this place be meant of the water of baptism.

6. It may also be observed that Christ, in the progress of his discourse, makes no more mention of water, but of the Spirit: 'That which is born of the Spirit is spirit;' not born of water and the Spirit, which had been very necessary, if water had been of an equal necessity with the Spirit to the new birth. And since Christ mentions it positively, that he that is born of the Spirit is spirit, will it be said, that if any be born of the Spirit, without water, he is still but flesh?

Water then here is to be taken mystically. Some by water understand the whole doctrine of the gospel; as the waters mentioned through the whole 47th of Ezekiel signify the doctrine of the gospel. To drop, in Scripture, signifies to teach, Amos vii. 16; Ezek. xx. 46, 'Drop thy word toward the south.' Others, by water, understand the grace of regeneration as the principle, the Spirit as the cause, as Titus iii. 5, 6, 'He has saved us by the washing of regeneration, and the renewing of the Holy Ghost.' What washing he means is expressed in the renewing of the Holy Ghost; that is, that renewing which is wholly spiritual, as proceeding from the Spirit of God, whence this grace does flow.

By water and the Spirit are signified one and the same thing, the similitude of water showing the cleansing and generating virtue of the Spirit, as fire and the Spirit are put together, Mat. iii. 11, to signify the refining quality the Spirit has (as fire has to separate the dross from the good metal). Fire and the Spirit, i. e. a spirit of fire, of the force and efficacy of fire.

This water is the same which God had promised: Isa. xliv. 8, 'I will pour water upon him that is thirsty;' and Ezek. xxxvi. 25, 'Then will I sprinkle clean water upon you;' and ver. 27, 'I will put my Spirit within you.' He there explains water to be the Spirit: 'I will pour my Spirit upon thy seed.' And in Ezekiel he joins water and the Spirit; i. e. the water of my Spirit, or my spiritual water, my gospel grace. And Isa. xii. 18, 19, God speaks of the admirable fruitfulness of this water. This shall renew you, and make you fructify in the kingdom of my Son, where none shall be received who is not born of this divine principle.

Now our Saviour having to do with a pharisee, who was acquainted with those oracles, to make him understand this truth, uses those words which the prophets had used, and ranks them in the same order; first water, then the Spirit, that the latter might clear the sense and nature of the former, to hinder Nicodemus from imagining that to be a natural water which was spiritual and mystical. Water and the Spirit signifies the water of the Spirit, or a spiritual water, as 1 Thes. i. 5, 'Our gospel came not unto you in word only, but in power, and in the Hold Ghost;' that is, in the power of the Holy Ghost.

The Spirit is compared to water in respect of its generative virtue. No fruitful plant but is produced by moisture. Water contains in it the seeds of all things. It was from water and the earth that all things in the lower world were in the first creation produced. Water is put here as exegetical of the effect of the Spirit; water being the cause of generation by its moisture, uniting the parts together.

Our Saviour in both places uses an asseveration, Verily, verily, which is spoken,

1. To show the infallible necessity of it, the certainty of the proposition.

2. To urge a special attention. Men press those things in discourse which they would have retained.

It is to be believed because of its necessity; it is to be considered because of its excellency.

Born again. "'Anothen" signifies properly from above; but sometimes it is taken for again. Nicodemus understands it so by his reply, of entering again into his mother's womb, and not of a heavenly birth.

Man was born in nature, he must be born in grace. He was born of the first Adam; he must be born of the second Adam. It is expressed in Scripture by various terms: a resurrection to life, a quickening, a new creation, the new man, the inward man, a dying to the world. It is indeed a putting off the old man, the principles and passions, the corrupt notions and affections which we derive from Adam, to devote ourselves to God, to live to Christ, to walk in newness of life.

The kingdom of God, which is sometimes taken, (1) for the kingdom of glory, (2) it is sometimes taken for the gospel state. And the same thing is signified by the kingdom of God, and the kingdom of heaven. What is called by Matthew 'the kingdom of heaven,' Mat. iv. 17, is called by Mark, relating the same story, 'the kingdom of God,' Mark i. 16. And the gospel is called 'the gospel of the kingdom of God,' Mark i. 14. It is called the kingdom of God;--

1. Because it sets up the rule and government of God in the world above the devil's. The devil had been so long the God of the world, that the interest of God seemed to be overmatched by a multitude of

unclean spirits, and abominable idols; and the true God was not known to be the governor of it. The gospel discovers the true governor of the world, and sets up his rule and authority.

2. It sets up the righteousness of God, above a legal and fleshly righteousness, much in vogue among Jews and Gentiles; but they were wholly ignorant of the righteousness of God, Rom. x. 3.

3. This kingdom is framed and set up by the Son of God; the other kingdom, under the law, was settled by God, but by the hand of Moses, a man. This is administered by him through his Spirit, his vicegerent. His royalty did not so eminently appear as in the times of the gospel.

The Father appoints the gospel state in his wisdom, the Son lays the foundation of it in his blood, the Spirit carries it on in the world by his power.

4. In respect of the service, it is high and heavenly; a serving God in spirit. The service under the legal administration was carnal; the service under the gospel administration is more spiritual, and so more suitable to the perfections of God.

5. In the end and issue of it. It is a translating us into the kingdom of Christ, Col. i. 13. The legal ceremonies could not fit men of themselves for glory; they could not make the comers thereunto perfect. But this kingdom of grace prepares us for the kingdom of glory.

Cannot see the kingdom of God. In verse 5. he cannot enter into the kingdom of God. He cannot,

1. By reason of God's appointment.

2. In the nature of the thing itself; he has no fitness for heaven or heavenly mysteries.

See. Seeing is taken sometimes for enjoying; not a bare sight, but fruition: John iii. 36, 'He that believes not the Son shall not see life;' that is, shall not enjoy life. And Heb. xii. 14, 'Without holiness, no man shall see the Lord;' they may see him in his pronouncing the sentence, but shall not see him in a way of glorious enjoyment of him.

To have a communion with Christ in a gospel state, to have an enjoyment of Christ in eternal glory, it is necessary we be stripped of the corruption of our first nature, and be clothed with another by the Spirit of God.

Observe in the verse,

1. The infallibility of the proposition: Verily, verily.

2. The necessity of regeneration: except.

3. The extension of it in regard of the subject.

(1.) Subjectum quod recipit: man, i. e. every man.

(2.) Subjectum in quo recipitur: man, i. e. the whole man, every faculty.

4. The excellency of it implied: they cannot see the kingdom of God. If he be born again, he shall enjoy the kingdom of God.

Doct. Regeneration of the soul is of absolute necessity to a gospel and glorious state.

By regeneration, I mean not a relative, but a real change of the subject, wrought in the complexion and inclinations of the soul, as in the restoring of health there is a change made in the temper and humours of the body.

As mankind was changed in Adam from what they were by a state of creation, so men must be changed in Christ from what they were in a state of corruption. As that change was not only relative but real, and the relative first introduced by the real, so must this. The relation of a child of wrath was founded upon the sin committed Without a real change there can be no relative. Being in Christ, as freed from condemnation, is always attended with a walking in the Spirit; and walking is not before living. For the better understanding this point, I shall lay down,

I. Propositions concerning the necessity of it.

II. I shall show that it is necessary,

1. To a gospel state.

(1.) To the performance of gospel duties.

(2.) To the enjoyment of gospel privileges.

2. To a state of glory.

I. Propositions concerning the necessity of it.

Prop. 1. There are but two states, one saving, the other damning; a state of sin and a state of righteousness; and all men are included in one of them. All men are divided into two ranks. In regard of their principle, some are in the fiery, some in the Spirit, Rom. viii. 8, 9; in regard of their obedience, some walk after the flesh, some after the Spirit, Rom. viii. 1; some are slaves to the flesh, others are led by the Spirit; some live only to self, some live to God. In regard of the exercise of their minds, their nobler faculty, some mind the things of the flesh, others the things of the Spirit, Rom. viii. 5; some swinishly wallow in sin, others place the delights of their spirits upon better and higher objects.

The Scripture mentions no other. A state of enmity, wherein men have their inclinations contrary to God; a state of friendship and fellowship, wherein men walk before God unto all well-pleasing, and would not willingly have an inward motion swerve from his will. One is called light, the other darkness: Eph. v. 8, 'You were sometimes darkness, but now are you light;' one the children of wrath, the other the children of God. There is no medium between them, every man is in one of these states. All believers, from the bruised reed to the tallest cedar, from the smoking flax on earth to the flaming lamp in heaven, from Thomas, that would not believe without seeing, to Abraham, who would believe without staggering, all are in a state of life; and all, from the most beautiful moralist to the most venomous toad in nature's field, from the young man in the gospel, who was not far from the kingdom of heaven, to Judas, who was in the very bottom of hell, all are in a state of death. Mere nature, though never so curiously garnished, can place a man no higher; faith, though with many infirmities, puts us in a state of amity; unbelief, though with many moralities, continues us in a state of enmity. All men are either the object of God's delight or of his abomination. The highest endowments of men remaining in corrupted nature cannot please him. The delight of God then supposes some real change in the object which is the ground of that delight, for God is wise in his delight, and could not be pleased with anything which were not fit for his complacency. Since original nature in a man cannot displease God unless it be changed by some fault, because it was his own work, so our present nature cannot please God unless it be changed by some grace, though it be otherwise never so highly dignified. Whatsoever grows up from the old Adam is the fruit of the flesh, whatsoever grows up by the new Adam in us is the offspring of the Spirit; and upon one of these two stocks all men in the world are set. Since, therefore, one is utterly destructive, and cannot please God (Rom viii. 8, So then they that are in the flesh cannot please God), though never so well garnished (for being utterly contrary to him it cannot be approved by him), the other is absolutely necessary to salvation.

Prop. 2. It is necessary upon the account of the fall of man and the consequents of it. In Adam we died: 1 Cor. xv. 22, 'As in Adam all died,' therefore in Adam he sinned: Rom. v. 19, 'By one man's disobedience many were made sinners.' Man cannot be supposed to sin in Adam unless some covenant had intervened between God and Adam, whence there did arise in the whole human nature a debt of having righteousness transfused from the first parent to all his posterity. The want of this grace wherein his posterity are conceived is a privation, and a crime which was voluntary in the root and head. This privation of righteousness must be removed. The institution of God stands firm, that Adam and his posterity should have a pure righteousness. It is not for the honour of God to enjoin it so strictly at first, and to have no regard to it afterwards. Now this privation of righteousness, and the unrighteousness which has taken place in the sons of Adam, cannot be removed without the infusion of grace; for without this grace he would always want righteousness, and yet he always under an obligation to have it; he would be under desires of happiness, but without it under an impossibility of attaining it.

Were there an indifference in the soul of man, were it an abrasa tabula, the writing of moral precepts upon it by good education would sway it to walk in the paths of virtue, as an ill education does cast it into the ways of [vice]. This is not so; for take two, let them have the same ways of education, the same precepts instilled into them, as Esau and Jacob had by their father, who were equally taught, yet how different were their lives! Esau's bad, Jacob's not without flaws. Education had not the power to root corruption out of both, no, nor out of any man in the world without a higher principle. There is some powerful principle in the soul, which leads it into by-paths contrary to those wholesome rules instilled into it. Hence arises a necessity of some other principle to be put into the heart to over-sway this corrupt bias. Man goes astray from the womb, as it is in Ps. lviii. 3, 'The wicked are estranged from the womb; they go astray as soon as they be born.' There must be something to rectify him, and expel this wandering humour.

By the fall of man there was contracted,

(1.) An unfitness to any thing that is good. Man is so immersed in wrong notions of things, that he cannot judge fully of what is good: Titus i. 16, 'To every good work reprobate.' The state of nature, or the old man, is described, Eph. iv. 22, to be 'corrupt, according to deceitful lusts;' deceitful, seducing us from God, drawing us into perdition, by representing evil under the notion of good, which evidences our understandings to be unfit to judge without a new illumination; inward and spiritual lusts, which are most deceitful, being accounted brave and generous motions; lusts or desires, which show the corruption of the will by ill habits. Lust and sin is the mere composition of corrupted nature; the whole man is stuffed with polluting principles and filthy appetites.

What was preternatural to man in a state of innocence became natural to him after his depraved state. He is 'carnal, sold under sin,' Rom. vii. 14. The spring being already out of order, cannot make the motion otherwise than depraved, as when a clock is out of order, it is natural to that present condition of it to give false intelligence of the hour of the day, and it cannot do otherwise till the wheels and weights be rectified. Our end was actively to glorify God in the service of him and obedience to him; but since man is fallen into this universal decay of his faculties, and made unfit to answer this end, there is a necessity he should be made over again, and created upon a better foundation, that some principle should be in him to oppose this universal depravation, enlighten his understanding, mollify his heart, and reduce his affections to their due order and object.

(2.) Not only an unfitness, but unwillingness to that which is good. We have not those affections to virtue as we have to vice. Are not our lives for the most part voluntarily ridiculous? Had we a full use of reason, we should judge them so. We think little of God; and when we do think of him, it is with reluctance. This cannot be our original state, for surely, God being infinitely good, never let man come out of his hands with this actual unwillingness to acknowledge and serve him; as the apostle says, in the case of the Galatians' errors, Gal. v. 8, 'This persuasion comes not of him which calls you,' this unwillingness comes not from him that created you. How much, therefore, do we need a restoring principle in us! We naturally fulfil the desires, or "thelemata" 'of the flesh,' Eph. ii. 3. There is then a necessity of some other principle in us to make us fulfil the will of God, since we were created for God, not for the flesh. We can no more be voluntarily serviceable to God while that serpentine nature and devilish habit remains in us, than we can suppose the devil can be willing to glorify God, while the nature he contracted by his fall abides powerful in him. It is as much as to say that a man can be willing against his will. Nature and will must be changed, or we for ever remain in this state.

Man is born a wild ass' colt, Job xi. 12. No beast more wild and brutish than man in his natural birth, and like to remain in his wild and wilful nature without grace, a new birth can only put off the wildness of the first.

(3.) Not only unfitness and unwillingness, but inability to good. A strange force there is in a natural man, which hurries him, even against some touches of his will, to evil.

How early do men discover an affection to vice! How greedily do they embrace it, notwithstanding rebukes from superiors, good exhortations from friends, with the concurrence of the vote of conscience, giving its amen to those dissuasions! and yet carried against those arguments, deceived by sin, slain by sin, sold under it, Rom. vii. 11, 14. This is the miserable state of every son of nature.

Do we not find that men sometime wrapped up in retirement, in consideration of the excellency of virtue, are so wrought upon by their solitary meditations, that they think themselves able to withstand the strongest invasion of any temptation! Yet we see oftentimes that when a pleasing temptation offers itself, though there be a conflict between reason and appetite, at length all the considerations and dictates of reason are laid aside, the former ideas laid asleep, and that committed which their own reason told them was base and sordid; so that there is something necessary, beside consideration and resolution, to the full cure of man.

No privation can be removed but by the introduction of another form; as when a man is blind, that blindness, which is a privation of sight, cannot be removed without bringing in a power of seeing again. Original sin is a privation of original righteousness, and an introduction of corrupt principles, which cannot be removed but by some powerful principle contrary to it. Since the inability upon the earth, by reason of the curse, to bring forth its fruits in such a manner as it did when man was in a state of innocence, the nature of it must be changed to reduce it to its original fruitfulness; so must man, since a general defilement from Adam has seized upon him, be altered before he can 'bring forth fruit to God,' Rom. vii. 4. We must be united to Christ, engrafted upon another stock, and partake of the power of his resurrection; without this we may bring forth fruit, but not fruit to God. There is as utter an impossibility in a man to answer the end of his creation, without righteousness, as for a man to act without life, or act strongly without health and strength. It is a contradiction to think a man can act righteously without righteousness, for without it he has not the being of a man; that is, man in such a capacity, for those ends for which his creation intended him.

Well, then, since there is an unfitness, unwillingness, inability in a man to answer his end, there is a necessity of a new life, a new nature, a new righteousness. There is a necessity for his happiness that he should be brought back to God, live to God, be a son of God, and this cannot be without regeneration; for how can he be brought back to God without a principle of spiritual motion? How can he live to God that has no spiritual life? How can he be fit to be a son of God who is of a brutish and diabolical nature?

Prop. 3. Hence it follows, that it is universally necessary. Necessary for all men. Our Saviour knows none without this mark. There must be a change in the soul: 2 Cor. v. 17, 'Therefore if any man be in Christ, he is a new creature.' There must be the habitation of the Spirit: Rom. viii. 9, 'If any man has not the Spirit of Christ, he is none of his.' There must be a crucifixion, not only of the corrupt affections of the flesh, but of the flesh itself: Gal. v. 24, 'They that are Christ's have crucified the flesh, with the affections and lusts.'

The old nature must be killed, with all its attendants. There is no sonship to God without likeness, no relation of a child of God without a childlike nature. Let a man be of whatsoever quality in the world, never so high, never so low, of whatsoever age, of whatsoever moral endowments, 'except a man,' every man, &c.

And simply necessary. Our Saviour does not say he is in danger not to see the kingdom of God, or he may come short of it; but he shall not, he cannot. There is no possible way but this for any man, no other door to creep in at but by that of a new birth; salvation cannot be attained without it, and damnation will certainly be the issue of the want of it. As there is no other name under heaven by which we can be saved but by the name of Jesus Christ, so there is no other way under hearten wherein we can be saved but by the birth of the Spirit.

It is necessary, therefore, in all places, in all professions. It is not necessary only in Europe, and not in Africa. Let a man be what he will, in any place under heaven, he must have a Jesus to save him, and an Holy Ghost to change him; it is one and the same Spirit acts in all, and produces the same qualities in all. Let men's religion and professions be what they will (men are apt to please themselves with this and that profession and opinion, but), there is no salvation in any profession, or any kind of opinion, but by regeneration. It is not necessary our understandings should be all of one size, that our opinions should all meet in uniformity, but it is necessary we should all have one spiritual nature. It is as necessary to the being of a good man that he should be spiritual as to the being of a man that he should be rational, though there is a great latitude and variety in the degrees of men in grace, as well as their reasons. Some are of little faith, some of great faith; some babes in Christ, some strong men. It is not necessary all should be as strong as Abraham, but it is simply necessary all should be new born, as Abraham; no age, no time excludes it.

(1.) Righteousness was necessary before the fall. The new birth is but the beginning of our restoration to that state we had before the fall. Adam could not have been happy without being innocent. The holiness of God could not create an impure creature. Without it God could take no pleasure in his work.

(2.) After the fall it was necessary, continually necessary from the first moment of the fall. This work of regeneration is included in the first promise: Gen. iii. 15, 'I will put enmity between thee and the woman, between thy seed and her seed.' Naturally we have a mighty friendship to Satan, a friendship to his works, though not to his person. But if any man had interest in that promise, he must exchange that friendship for an enmity.

If Jesus Christ, who is principally meant by the seed of the woman, had an enmity to Satan, then all Christ's seed must be possessed with the same spirit. For when the seed of the woman was to break the serpent's head it was necessary that those that would enjoy the fruit of that conquest should be enemies to the nature of the devil, and the works of the devil, otherwise they could not join with that interest which overthrows him. It is unreasonable to think the head should have an enmity, and the members an amity; and we cannot have an enmity to that which is the same with our nature, without a change of disposition. It is not a verbal enmity that is here meant. While we pretend to hate him we may do his pleasure, and Satan is never troubled to be pretendedly hated and really obeyed. As wicked men do the will of God's purpose, while they oppose the will of his precept, so they do the devil's will many times while they think they cross it; there must be a contrary nature to Satan before there can be an enmity. That foolish appetite, affected sensuality, indulgence to the flesh, the cause of our first friendship with Satan, must be changed into divine desires, affection to heavenly things, a mortification of the flesh, before a man can part with this friendship. There must be a change in the conformity of the soul to the nature of the devil before an enmity against him can be raised. We are never enemies to those that encourage us in what we affect. His nature can never be altered, by reason of the curse of God upon him; therefore ours must, if ever the league be broken. In Isa. lxv. 25 it is said, 'The wolf and the lamb shall feed together, and the lion shall eat straw like an ox: and dust shall be the serpent's meat.' The nature of men may be changed by the gospel, but dust shall always be the serpent's meat. The saving some by water in the deluge was a figure of this inward baptism, which is the 'answer of a good conscience towards God,' 1 Peter iii. 20, 21. As the old world was so corrupt that all must be washed away before it could be restored, so is the little world of man. The cloud and sea through which the Israelites passed signified this, as the apostle informs us: 1 Cor. x. 2, 'And were all baptised unto Moses in the cloud and the sea.' Whereupon some think there were some sprinklings of the water upon them, as they stood like two walls, to favour their passage.

(3.) Necessary in the time of the law. By the moral law this renewing was implied in the first command, of not having any other gods before him, Exod. xx. 3. We cannot suppose that command only limited to a not serving an outward image. Is not the setting up self, our own reasons, our own wills, and bowing down to them, and serving them, as much a wrong to God as the bowing down to a senseless image? nay, worse than the adoring of an image, since that is senseless; but our wills corrupt, and are no more fit to be our God than an image is fit to be a representation of him. So that in the spiritual part of the command this must be included, to acknowledge nothing as the rule of perfection, but God; to set ourselves no other patterns of conformity but God, which the apostle phrases a being new created after God, Eph. iv. 24.

If all idolatry were forbidden, then that which is inward as well as that which is outward. If we were to have no other gods before him, then we were to prefer nothing inwardly before him; we were to make him our pattern, and be conformed to him; which we cannot, without another nature than that we had by corruption.

Upon this are those scriptures founded which speak of covetousness to be idolatry, Col. iii. 5, that 'if any man love the world, the love of the Father is not in him,' 1 John ii. 15; he does not love God.

Now the preferring self before God is the essential part of the corrupt nature. Therefore all men, by the law of nature (which is the same with the moral law), and the Jews, to whom this law was given, were bound to have another nature than that which was derived from Adam, which essentially consisted in the making ourselves our god. Self-esteem, self-dependence, self-willedness, is denying affection and subjection to God.

By the ceremonial law more plainly. Their duty was not terminated in an external observance of the types and shadows under the law, but a heart-work God intended to signify to them in all those legal ceremonies. As sacrifices signified a necessity of expiation of sin, so their legal washings represented to them a necessity of regeneration.

Therefore God is said not to require the sacrifices of beasts: Ps. xl. 6, 'Sacrifice and offering thou did not desire' (that is, sacrifices of beasts), 'burnt-offerings and sin-offerings hast thou not required;' viz. as the ultimate object of his pleasure, but as representations of Christ, the great sacrifice. So neither did he command circumcision, and other legal purifications, for anything in themselves, or anything they could work, further than upon the body, but to signify unto them an inward work upon the heart. Hence they are said not to be commanded by God: Jer. vii. 22, 23, 'For I spake not unto your fathers, nor commanded them in the day that I brought them out of the land of Egypt, concerning burnt-offerings or sacrifices; but this thing commanded I them, saying, Obey my voice.' That is, God did not principally require these as the things which did terminate his will and pleasure, but an obedience to him, and walking with him, which cannot be without an agreement of nature: 'For how can two walk together, unless they be agreed?' Amos iii. 3. Hence God speaks so often to them of the circumcision of the heart, Deut. x. 16, and promises this circumcision of the heart: Deut. xxxvi. 6, 'And the Lord thy God will circumcise thy heart, and the heart of thy seed,' &c. And Paul expressly says, Rom. ii. 28, 29, that 'he was not a Jew;' that is, a spiritual Jew, one of the spiritual seed of Abraham, who had the 'circumcision that was outward in the flesh,' but he that had 'that of the heart.'

So among us many confide in baptism, which signifies nothing to men grown up, without an inward renewal and baptism of the heart, no more than outward circumcision did to them.

(4.) The obligation upon us is still the same. The covenant made with Adam was made perpetually with him for all his posterity, therefore all his posterity, by that covenant, were perpetually obliged to a perfect righteousness. If God had made this covenant with Adam, that he should transfuse this original righteousness to his posterity only for such a time, then indeed, after the expiration of the term, the obligation had ceased, and none had been bound to have it as a debt required by God. The fault of wanting it had been removed without any infusion of grace, because the time being expired, and so the obligation ceasing, it had not been a fault to want it; neither could Adam's posterity have been charged with sin, because the want of righteousness, after the expiration of the time fixed, had not been a sin. But because there was no time fixed, but that it was perpetually of force as to righteousness, which was the main intent of it, we still remain under the obligation of having a righteous nature.

Now God, seeing the impossibility of answering this obligation in our own persons, by our own strength, appoints a way whereby we may answer it in a second head, not pulling the former covenant as to the essential part of it, which was a righteous nature, but mitigating it, as the Chancery nulls not the common law, but sweetens the severity of it.

This latter covenant is called 'an everlasting covenant.' Not that the obligation of the other to righteousness is ceased, but transmitted to another head; which head cannot possibly fail, as our former did, who has both a perfect righteousness in himself, and has undertook for a perfect righteousness in his people, which he is able to accomplish, and to that purpose begins it here, and perfects it hereafter. To this purpose the Scripture speaks of the everlastingness of the covenant: Ps. lxxxix. 28, 'My covenant shall stand fast with him;' that is, with Christ. And if his people sin, as he expresses it afterwards, yet 'my loving-kindness will I not utterly take from him.' In this respect Christ is called the covenant of the people: Isa. xiii. 6, 'I will give thee for a covenant of the people.' And the end of placing David his servant over his people, is not to give way to licentiousness and unrighteousness, and maintain men in an hostile nature against God, but that they might 'walk in his judgments, and observe his statutes,' Jer. xxvii. 24; and that everlasting covenant of peace he would make with them is in order to sanctify them, Jer. xxxvii. 26, 28, compared together. When God would make a covenant of peace with them, an everlasting covenant, it was to set his sanctuary among them, and to let the heathen know that the Lord did sanctify Israel. And the end of the covenant is to 'put his law into the inward parts,' Jer. xxxi. 33.

Christ undertook to keep up the honour of God, which was violated by the breach of that covenant, to 'make reconciliation for iniquity, and to bring in everlasting righteousness,' Dan. ix. 24. This obligation our second head entered into for us, and in him we are complete, even as our head, and as the 'head of all principality and power,' Col. ii. 10, who has undertaken for our perfect righteousness; of our persons, by his own righteousness; of our nature, by inherent righteousness, as it follows, ver 11, &c., 'in whom you are circumcised with the circumcision made without hands, in putting off the body of the sins of the flesh,' &c. This obligation still remains upon our head, and upon us in him, and to him we are to have recourse for a full answering of it. And this cannot be answered without a new birth here, which ends in a perfection hereafter. And Christ, by a plain precept, has made it absolutely necessary now to all under the gospel administration.

So that no age, no time, no administration excludes it. It was as necessary to Adam, the first man, as to the last that shall be born. For being by nature spiritually dead, there must be a restoration to a spiritual life, if ever any be happy. 'God is not the God of the dead, but the God of the living.' What was always necessary is absolutely necessary, and admits of no exception; and therefore the removal of the diabolical nature is indispensable to him and to us, since we are all the posterity of Adam, and the inheritors of his corruption. How can any, in any age, enjoy an infinite holy God, without being changed from their impurity?

Prop. 4. Hence it follows, that it is so necessary, that it is not conceivable by any man in his right wits how God can make any man happy without it. It is not for us, poor shallow creatures, to dispute what God can, and what God cannot do; what God may do by his absolute power. But yet it seems a contradiction, and it is not intelligible by us how God can make a man happy without regeneration.

What semblance of reason can be given that any one who is a slave of Satan, a child of wrath by nature, can be made the son and friend of God, without an expulsion of that nature which rendered him criminal, and restoring that in some degree which renders him innocent?

Without habitual grace, sin is not taken away; and as long as a man remains under sin, how he can be capable of and communion with God I understand not; for he cannot be at one and the same time under God's greatest wrath and his highest love. How is it possible that one can have an enjoyment of eternal life, who has nothing in him but a relation to eternal death?

God made man's nature fit for his communion; man made himself unfit by guilt and filth. This unfitness must be removed by regeneration before this privilege man had by creation can be restored. Not that this restored righteousness is the cause of our communion with God in happiness, but a necessary requisite to it. No doubt but God might have restored this righteousness without admitting man to a converse with him, if there had been no covenant made to that purpose. That God may give grace without glory, is intelligible; but to admit a man to communion with him in glory, without grace, is not intelligible.

(1.) It is not agreeable to God's holiness to make any an inhabitant of heaven, and converse freely with him in a way of intimate love, without such a qualification of grace: Ps. xi. 7, 'The righteous Lord loves righteousness; his countenance does behold the upright.' He must, therefore, hate iniquity, and cannot love an unrighteous nature because of his love to righteousness; 'his countenance beholds the upright,' he looks upon him with a smiling eye, and therefore he cannot favourably look upon an unrighteous person, so that this necessity is not founded only in the command of God that we should be renewed, but in the very nature of the thing, because God, in regard of his holiness, cannot converse with an impure creature. God must change his nature, or the sinner's nature must be changed. There can be no friendly communion between two of different natures without the change of one of them into the likeness of the other. Wolves and sheep, darkness and light, can never agree. God cannot love a sinner as a sinner, because he hates impurity by a necessity of nature as well as a choice of will. It is as impossible for him to love it as to cease to be holy.

This change cannot be then on God's part; it must therefore be on man's part. It must therefore be by grace, whereby the sinner may be made fit for converse with God, since God cannot embrace a sinner in his dearest affections without a quality in the sinner suitable to himself. All converse is founded upon a likeness in nature and disposition; it is by grace only that the sinner is made capable of converse with God.

(2.) It is not agreeable to God's wisdom. Is it congruous to the wisdom of God to let a man be his child and the child of the devil at the same time? Is it fit to admit him to the relation of a son of God, who retains the enmity of his nature against God, to make any man happy with the dishonour of his laws, since he is not subject to the law of God, neither will be: one that cannot bear him, but abhors his honour and the apprehensions of his holiness?

Man naturally has risings of heart against God, looks upon him under some dreadful notion, has an utter aversion from him; alienation and enmity are inseparable: Col. i. 21, 'You who were sometimes alienated, and enemies in your minds.' It does not consist with the wisdom of God to make any man happy against his will; God therefore first changes the temper of the will by his powerful grace, thereby making him willing, and by degrees fitting him for happiness with him.

It is not fit corruption should inherit incorruption, or impurity be admitted to an undefiled inheritance, and therefore God brings none thither which are not first begotten by him to a lively hope, by the resurrection of Jesus Christ from the dead: 1 Peter i. 3, 4, 'Which according to his mercy has begotten us again to a lively hope, by the resurrection of Jesus Christ from the dead, to an inheritance incorruptible, undefiled, and that fades not away, reserved in heaven for you.' It cannot be honourable for the wisdom of God to give a right to eternal life to one that continues a child of the devil, and bestow his love upon one that resolves to give his own heart to sin and Satan.

This which I have now discoursed is founded upon men's natural notions in their right reason. But if we look into the Scripture it is certain there is no other way but this: a man without a new birth can have no right to happiness by any covenant of God, by any truth of God, by any purchase of Christ. God never promised happiness without it. Christ never purchased it for any one without a new nature. No example is there extant of any person God has made happy without this alteration, nor in the strictest inquiries can we conceive any other way possible; therefore if there be any one present that has hopes to enjoy everlasting happiness without regeneration, he expects that which God never yet bestowed upon any, and which, according to our understanding, God cannot, without wrong to his holiness and wisdom, confer upon any person. I beseech you, therefore, let none of you build your hopes upon such vain foundations; you must be holy, or you shall never see God to your comfort.

Prop. 5. It is so necessary, that the coming and sufferings of our Lord and Saviour would seem insignificant without it. That this regeneration was a main end of his coming, is evident by his making this one of the main doctrines he was, as a prophet and teacher, sent from God to make known to the world, it being the first he taught Nicodemus. Jesus Christ came to glorify God, and to glorify himself in redeeming a people. And what glory can we conceive God has, what glory can Christ have, if there be no characteristical difference between his people and the world? And what difference can there be but in a change of nature and temper, as the foundation whence all other differences do result? Sheep and goats differ in nature.

The righteousness which is given through our Mediator is the same, in the essentials and respects it bears to God, as we had at first. And his threefold office of king, priest, and prophet, is in order to it: his priestly, to reconcile and bring us to God; his prophetical, to teach us the way; and his kingly, to work in us those qualifications, and bestow that comely garb upon us that was necessary to fit us for our former converse. Our second Adam would not be like the first, if he failed in this great work of conveying his righteous nature to us, as Adam was to convey his original righteousness to his posterity. As that was to be conveyed by carnal generation, so the righteous nature of the second Adam in to be transmitted to us by spiritual regeneration. In this respect renewed men are called his seed, and counted to him for a generation, as Ps. xxii. 30, 'A seed shall serve him; it shall be accounted to the Lord ("la'adonai") for a generation,' to Christ, it shall be accounted as much the generation of Christ as the rest are the generation of Adam, as if they had proceeded out of his loins, as mankind did out of Adam's. As God looks upon believers as righteous through the righteousness of Christ as if it were their own, so he accounts them as if they were the generation of Jesus Christ himself.

(1.) Christ came to save from sin. Salvation from sin was more his work than barely salvation from hell: Mat. i. 21, 'He shall save his people from their sins.' From sin as the cause, from hell as the consequent. If from sin, was it only from the guilt of sin, and to leave the sinful nature unchanged? Was it only to take off punishment, and not to prepare for glory? It would have been then but the moiety of redemption, and not honourable for so great a Saviour. Can you imagine that the death of Jesus Christ, being necessary for the recovery of a sinner, was appointed for an incomplete work, to remit man's sin and continue the insolence of his nature against God? It was not his end only to save us from wrath to come, but to save us from the procuring cause of that wrath; not forcibly and violently to save us, but in methods congruous to the honour of God's wisdom and holiness, and therefore to purify us: Tit. ii. 14, 'To redeem us from all iniquity,' all parts of it, 'by purifying unto himself a peculiar people, zealous of good works,' that we might have a holy nature, whereby we might perform holy actions, and be as zealous of good works and the honour of God, as we had been of bad works and to bring dishonour to him.

It was also the end of his resurrection to 'quicken us to a newness of life,' Col. ii. 12, 18, Eph. ii. 5, 6. If any man without a new nature could set foot into heaven, a great intendment of the death and resurrection of Christ would be insignificant.

Christ came to take away sin, the guilt by his death, the filth by his Spirit, given us as the purchase of that death. In taking away sin he takes away also the sinful nature.

(2.) Christ came to destroy the works of the devil: 1 John iii. 8, 'For this purpose the Son of God was manifested, that he might destroy the works of the devil.' These works are two, sin, and the misery consequent upon it. Upon the destruction of sin necessarily follows the dissolution of the other which was knit with it. If the sinful nature were not taken away, the devil's works would not wholly be destroyed; or if the sinful nature were taken away, and a righteous nature not planted in the stead of it, he would still have his ends against God in depriving God of the glory he ought to have from the creature. And the creature could not give God the glory he was designed by his creation to return, unless some nature were implanted in him whereby he might be enabled to do it.

Would it, then, be for the honour of this great Redeemer to come short of his end against Satan, to let all the trophies of Satan remain, in the errors of the understanding, perversity of the will, disorder of the affections, and confusion of the whole soul? Or if our Saviour had only removed these, how had the works of the devil been destroyed if we had lain open to his assaults, and been liable the next moment to be brought into the same condition, which surely would have been, were not a righteous and divine nature bestowed upon the creature.

(3.) Christ came to bring us to God: 1 Peter iii. 18, 'For Christ also has once suffered for sins, the just for the unjust, that he might bring us to God.' Was it to bring us to God with all our pollutions, which were the cause God cast us off? No; but to bring us in such a garb as that we might be fit to converse with him. Can we be so without a new nature and a spiritual likeness to God? Would that man who would bring another to a prince to introduce him into favour, bring him into his presence in a slovenly and sordid habit, such a garb which he knew was hateful to the prince? Neither will our Saviour, nor can he bring sinners in such a plight to God, because it is more contrary to the nature of God's holiness to have communion with such, than it is contrary to the nature of light to have communion with darkness, 1 John i. 5-7. Can it be thought that Christ should come to set human nature right with God, without a change of that principle which caused the first revolt from God? Besides, since the coming of Christ was to please God, and to glorify him in all his attributes, as well as to save us, how can God be pleased with the effects of Christ's death, if he brought the creature to him without any change of nature, but with its former enmity and pollution? Will you say his mercy would be glorified? How can that be without a wrong to his purity, and a provocation to his justice? Suppose such a dispute were in God, would not holiness, wisdom, justice, joined together, over-vote mercy?

But since there can be no such dispute, how can we conceive that mercy, an infinite perfection in God, can desire anything to the prejudice of the honour of his holiness, justice, and wisdom?

Well, then, if we expect happiness without a renewed nature, we would make Christ a minister of sin as well as of righteousness, Gal. ii. 17, &c. As there is a justification by him, so his intent was to plant a living principle in us, whereby we might be enabled to live to him. It is in vain, then, to think to find any benefit by the death of Christ without a new nature, any more than from God without it.

Prop. 6. The end of the Spirit's coming manifests it to be necessary. We are said therefore to be 'saved by the washing of regeneration, and renewing of the Holy Ghost,' Titus iii. 5, 2 Thess. ii. 13. As God by his Spirit, moving upon the face of the waters, created the world, so God by his Spirit, moving upon the face of the soul, new creates all the faculties of it. Can the coming of Christ, and the coming of the Spirit, the most signal favours of God to mankind, be intended for no other end than to convey to us the mercy of God, with the dishonour of his holiness, to change our misery without changing our nature, and putting us in a capacity both to glorify God and enjoy him? To what purpose does the Spirit come, if not to renew? Whatsoever was the office of the Spirit, cannot be supposed to be exercised without this foundation. Can there be any seal of the Spirit without some impression made upon the soul like to the Spirit, which is the seal whereby we are sealed? Can he witness to us that we are the children of God, if there be no principle in us suitable to God as a father, no childlike frame? Is the Spirit only to bring things to remembrance for a bare speculation, without any operative effect? Is he to help us in prayer? How can that be, without giving us first a sense of what we need, and a praying heart? And how can we have a praying heart till our natures, so averse from God and his worship, be changed? He is a 'quickening Spirit,' 2 Cor. iii. 6, 'the Spirit gives life.' How can that be while we lie rotting in our former death? It is a 'Spirit of holiness.' Can he dwell in a soul that has an unholy nature? Though he find men so at his first coming, would he not quickly be weary of his house if it continued so? He comes to change our old nature, not to encourage it. What fruits of the Spirit could appear without the change of the nature of the soil?

Prop. 7. From all this it follows that this new birth is necessary in every part of the soul. There is not a faculty but is corrupted, and therefore not a faculty but must be restored. Not a wheel, not a pin in all this clock of the heart but is out of frame, not one part wherein sin and Satan have not left the marks of their feet: Titus i. 15, 'Their mind and conscience is defiled.' It is clearer to a regenerate soul that it is so, since by the light of grace he discerns a filth in every faculty. The more knowledge of God he has, the more he discovers his ignorance; the more love to God, the more he finds and is ashamed of his enmity. And though in our imperfect regeneration here, grace and sin are in every part of the soul, as wine and water mingled together are in every part of the vessel, yet every faculty is in part renewed; and grace and sin lie not so huddled together but that the soul can distinguish them, and be able to say, this is grace, this is part of the new Adam, and this is sin, and part of the old Adam in me.

Because there was an universal depravation by the fall, regeneration must answer it in its extensiveness in every faculty. Otherwise it is not the birth of the man, but of one part only. It is but a new piece, not a new creature. This or that faculty may be said to be new, not the soul, not the man. We are all over bemired by the puddle of sin, and we must be all over washed by the water of grace. A whole sanctification is the proper fruit of reconciliation: 2 Thess. v. 23, 'The God of peace sanctify you wholly.' Reconciliation was of the whole man, so must regeneration. Sin has rooted itself in every part; ignorance and error in our understandings; pride, and self-love, and enmity in our wills; all must be uprooted by a new grace, and the triumphs of sin spoiled by a new birth.

Prop. 8. It is so necessary, that even the dim eye of natural reason has been apprehensive of some need of it. And, therefore, it is a wonder that there should be a need of pressing it upon men under the light of the gospel. Those doctrines that are purely intellectual and supernatural, are not so easily apprehended by men, as having no footing in reason, whereby reason is rendered unpliable to consent to them. But those doctrines that tend to the reformation of man carry a greater conviction, as having some notion of a depravation, which gives them some countenance in the minds of men, though not in their affection. Men cannot conceive any notion of God's greatness, majesty, and holiness, but they must also conceive something necessary to an enjoyment of him (wherein their felicity consists), besides those natural principles which they find in themselves. Natural reason must needs assent to this, that there must be some other complexion of the soul to fit us for a converse with so pure a majesty. The wiser sort of heathens did see themselves out of frame; the tumult and disorder in their faculties could not but be sensible to them. They found the flights of their souls too weak for their vast desires. They acknowledged the wings of it to be clipped, and that they never came so out of the hands of God. That therefore there was a necessity of some restorative above the art of man to complete the work. And I think I have read of one of them that should say, That there could not be a reformation unless God would take flesh. They had 'the work of the law written in their hearts,' Rom. ii. 15. They knew such works were to be done; they found themselves unable to do them. Whence would follow that there must be some other principle to enable them than what they had by nature. To this purpose they invented their purgative virtues; and by those and other means hoped to arrive to an "homoiosis toi theoi", which they much talked of as necessary to a converse with God. As they were sensible of their guilt, and therefore had sacrifices for the expiation of that, so they were sensible of their filth, and had their purifications and washings for the cleansing of that. Hence it was that they admired those men that acted in a higher sphere of moral virtue and moderation than others. Some of them have acknowledged the malady, but despaired of a remedy, judging it above the power of nature to cure. Certainly that which the wisest heathens, in the darkness of nature, without knowledge either of law or gospel, have counted necessary; and since it is seconded by so plain a declaration of our Saviour, must be indisputably necessary. Plato in several places says, That there was a certain divine principle in our minds at first, but that it was abolished, and God would again renew and form the soul with a kind of divinity.

How vain then are men, how inexcusably foolish, to neglect both the light of the gospel and that of reason too; that spend not one hour, one minute, in a serious consideration of it and enquiry after it; in slighting their own reason as well as the express declaration of Jesus Christ. Oh that men were sensible of this, which is of so great concernment to them.

II. I come to show that regeneration is necessary.

1. It is necessary to a gospel state.

(1.) Nothing can exist in any state of being without a proper form. That which has not the form of a thing is not a thing of the same species. He cannot be a man that wants a rational form of a man, a soul. And how can any man be a Christian without that which does essentially constitute a Christian? We can no more be Christians without a Christian nature, than a man can be a man without human nature. Grace only gives being to a Christian, and constitutes him so: 1 Cor. xv. 10, 'By the grace of God I am what I am: and his grace which was bestowed on me was not in vain, but I laboured more abundantly than they all.' Grace there is meant of habitual grace, because he speaks of his labour as the fruit of it. In bodily life brutes go beyond us, in the vigour of senses, greatness of strength, temperance, natural affection. In reason and moral virtues many heathens have excelled us. There is something else, then, necessary for the constitution of a Christian, and that is, Christ's living in him by a new forming of his soul by his Spirit. As the body lives by the soul, which distributes natural, vital, and animal spirits to every part of the body, for the performance of its several functions; so the soul lives by grace, which diffuses its vigour to every part, the understanding, will, and affections.

(2.) There is no suitableness to a gospel state and government without it. In all changes of government in the world there is a change in the whole state of affairs, in those that are the instruments of government, in the principles of those that submit to the government. After the fall of man God set up a new mode of government. All judgment was committed to the Son: John v. 22, 'For the Father judges no man, but has committed all judgment to the Son.' Ver. 27, 'And has given him authority to execute judgment.' The whole administration of affairs is put into his hand; not excluding the Father, who still gave out his orders in the government, wherefore he says, ver. 30, 'I can of myself do nothing; as I hear, I judge.' There must be, therefore, some agreement between the frame of this government and the subjects of it. As there is a new Adam, a new covenant, a new priesthood, a new spirit; so there must be a new heart, new compacts, new offerings, new resolutions. New administrations and old services can no more be pieced together than new does and old garments. The gospel state of the church is called a new heaven and a new earth. Man is by the inclinations of his corrupt nature obedient to the law of sin. There must be a cure and change of those inclinations, to make them tend to an observance of the orders of this new government, and an hearty observation of it, 2 Cor. v. 17, 'Old things are passed away, behold all things are become new, and all things are of God' (so they were before), but now in a new manner and frame; and this is the reason rendered why every man in Christ must be a new creature.

(3.) All the subjects of this government have been brought in this way, not one excepted. Though God has chosen some that he would bless for ever under this evangelical government, yet notwithstanding the purpose of God they are in as great unfitness for this state as the worst of men, till God exerting his power fashions them to be vessels of honour to himself. It is not God's choice of any man which puts any man into a gospel state, without the operation of the Spirit, renewing the mind and fitting him for it. All that were designed by God's eternal purpose were to be brought in by this way of the new birth, as 2 Thess. ii. 13, 'God has from the beginning chosen you to salvation, through sanctification of the Spirit and belief of the truth.' And by this they were fortified against all those workings of the mystery of iniquity, against the government of Christ and the state of the gospel, which would be damnable and destructive to many; for he had spoken of that before, upon which occasion he brings this in. 'A chosen generation, a holy nation, a peculiar people,' are joined together, 1 Peter ii. 9. Peculiar they could not be, unless they had something of an intrinsic value in them above others, and a peculiar fitness for special service, and to offer spiritual sacrifices, therefore called also a royal priesthood.

(4.) The end of the particular institutions, of initiation or admission, under the two different administrations of this government, was to signify this--of circumcision under the law, and baptism under the gospel. Both signified the corruption and filthiness of nature, and the necessity of the circumcision of the heart and the purification of nature. Hence baptism is called 'the laver of regeneration,' Titus iii. 5, many understanding it of baptism. Not that these did confer this new nature in a physical way, or that it was always conferred in the administration of them, but the necessity of having this was always signified by them. Therefore one of the Jews, against the opinion of his countrymen, says absolutely, it is a madness to think that those ceremonies, under their administration, were appointed only for the purification of the body without that of the soul. And Rom. ii. 29, says the apostle, 'He is a Jew which is one inwardly, and circumcision is that of the heart in the spirit.' So that partaking of baptism, and being entrusted with the oracles of God, make a man no more a Christian than circumcision, &c., did make a man a Jew. He is only a Christian that has a Christian nature. The necessity of this nature was evidenced and signified both by the one and by the other.

In every state there are duties to be performed and privileges to be enjoyed. So likewise in the gospel state. Without a new birth we cannot perform the one or be capable of the other.

2. It is necessary to the performance of gospel duties.

(1.) There can be no preparation to any service without it. Man's soul at first could make a spiritual music to God, till the flesh disordered the strings, and no music can be made till the Spirit puts the instrument in tune again. In Jesus Christ we are 'created to good works,' Eph. ii. 10. Therefore no preparation can be before the new creation, no more than there was a preparation in the matter without form and void to become a world. What evangelical duties can be performed without an evangelical impression, without the forming of Christ and the doctrine of Christ in the heart, not only in the notion, but the operative and penetrating power of it? The heart must be first moulded, and cast into the frame of the doctrine of the gospel, before it can obey it, as Rom. vi. 17, 'But ye have obeyed from the heart that form of doctrine which was delivered unto you,' or, 'unto which you were delivered.' The mould wherein a thing is cast makes it fit for the operation for which it is intended. The ship that wants any material thing in its make cannot sail well, will not obey the directions of the pilot; and he that wants grace will be carried away with the breath of every sin and temptation. All the motions and railings naturally in ways of duty by other principles, cannot make an aptitude to divine services, no more than a thousand times flinging up a stone into the air can produce any natural fitness in it for such an elevation any more than it had at first, which was none at all. Where should we have any preparation? It cannot be from Adam; he died a spiritual death by his sin, and had no natural fitness for any spiritual service, and therefore cannot convey by nature more to his posterity than what he had by nature; what grace he had afterwards was bestowed upon his person, not upon the nature which was to be transmitted to his posterity.

(2.) Therefore we cannot act any evangelical service without a new nature. If we have no natural preparation, we can have no natural action. The law must be written in our hearts before it be formed into the life, Jer. xxxi. 33, 34, 'I will put my law in their inward parts, and write it in their hearts.' It is then, and then only, that we have a practical and affectionate knowledge of God, 'And they shall know me from the least unto the greatest.' Restoration to a supernatural life must be before there can be supernatural actions, a just nature before a just walk, as Hosea xiv. 9, 'The just shall walk in them,' that is, in the ways of God. The motion of the creature is not the cause but the effect of life. The evangelical service is not the cause of righteousness but the effect. We cannot walk in one commandment of God till the law be written in our inward parts, Ezek. xxxvi. 14. Those that have not a new heart cannot walk in God's statutes. We can never answer the terms of the covenant without a new nature. For,

[1.] No act can transcend the principle of it. There is a certainty in this rule; that the elevation of an inferior nature to the acts of a superior nature cannot be without some inward participation of that superior nature. The operation of everything follows the nature of the thing. A beast cannot act like a man without partaking of the nature of a man, nor a man act like an angel without partaking of the angelical nature. How then can a man act divinely without a participation of the divine nature? Duties of a supernatural strain, as evangelic duties are, require a supernatural frame of spirit. Nothing can exceed the bounds of its nature, for then it should exceed itself in acting. Whatsoever service, therefore, does proceed from mere nature, cannot amount to a gospel-service, because it comes not from a gospel-principle. We cannot believe without a habit of faith, nor love without a habit of love; for this only renders us able to perform such acts. Justification is necessary to our state as well as regeneration; but regeneration seems to be more necessary to our duties than the former; this principally to the performance of them, the other to the acceptance of them.

[2.] The nature does always tincture the fruit of it. Our Saviour, by his interrogation, implies an impossibility that those that are evil should speak good things: Mat. xii. 84, 'O generation of vipers, how can you, being evil, speak good things? for out of the abundance of the heart the mouth speaks.' The very hissings of a viper proceed from the malice of its nature. As the root is, so is all the fruit. From one seed many grains arise, yet all partake of the nature of that seed. Streams partake of the quality of the fountain. If the seed, root, and fountain be good, so is what-soever springs from them. There is not one righteous man by nature, neither Jew nor Gentile, all are concluded under sin: Rom. iii. 10, 'There is none righteous, no, not one;' none that 'understands and seeks God,' &c. He adds not one twice; he exempts none, not one righteous by nature, not one righteous action by nature: 'none that does good, no, not one.' He applies it to all mankind. A poisonous nature can produce nothing but poisonous fruit. Our actions smell as rank as nature itself. Whatsoever rises from thence, though never so spacious and well-coloured, is evil and unprofitable. If, therefore, we would produce good fruit, we must have a new root, seed, and spring. Our sour nature must be changed into a sweetness and purity. If the vine be empty, the fruit will be so too: Hosea x. 1, 'Ephraim is an empty vine, he brings forth fruit to himself,' or, 'equal to himself,' "yeshaweh". Unless the tree be good, the fruit can never be generous: Mat. vii. 17, 18, 'Neither can a corrupt tree bring forth good fruit.' We must have the Spirit before we can bring forth the fruits of the Spirit. All good services are related to this, as effects to their cause; so that what a man does by an act of reason, and natural conscience, and good education, if his understanding and conscience remain wholly under their natural pollution, the service is not good, because the soul is corrupt; much less are those services good which are the fruit only of humour. How the soul can be habitually sinful, and yet the acts flowing from it be good, is not easily conceivable; it is against the stream of natural observation. It is true, indeed, that a man that is habituated to one kind of sin may do an action that receives no tincture from that particular habit, because it does not proceed from it; as a drunkard gives an alms, his giving alms has no infection inherent from that particular habit of drunkenness, but from the nature, which is wholly corrupt, it has. 'Who can bring a clean thing out of an unclean? not one,' Job xiv. 4. Who can bring a clean service out of a miry heart? Not one man in the world. We cannot, therefore, perform any evangelical service if those foundations be considered.

Not spiritually, because we are flesh. God must be 'worshipped in spirit,' John iv. 44; in a spiritual manner, with spiritual frames. The apostle speaks of 'walking in the spirit,' Phil. iii. 3, and 'praying in the Holy Ghost,' Jude 20. None can act spiritually but those that are 'born of the Spirit;' and no action is spiritual but what proceeds from a renewed principle. The most glittering and refined flesh is but flesh in a higher sphere of flesh, therefore whatsoever springs up from that principle is fleshly, upon the former foundation, that nothing can rise higher than its nature. You may as well expect to gather grapes of thorns as spiritual duties from carnal hearts: Mat. vii. 16, 'Do men gather grapes of thorns, or figs of thistles?' If a natural man 'cannot receive,' and 'cannot know the things of God, because they are spiritually discerned,' 1 Cor. ii. 14, how should he perform the duties belonging to God, since they are spiritually to be performed? We are naturally more averse to motions upon our wills than to the illuminations of our minds. An appetite for knowledge, and a flight from God being both the fruits of Adam's fall, who was both curious to know, as God, and fearing to approach to God after his fall. There may be some services in natural men which may look like spiritual, but in the principle they are not so. Many acts are done by irrational creatures which look like rational acts. As the order among bees, like the acts of statesmen regulating a commonwealth; their carrying gravel in their fangs to poise them in a storm, and hinder them from being carried away by the violence of the wind; yet these are not rational acts, because they proceed not from reason, but from a natural instinct put into them by Gods the supreme governor. So that as no action of an ape, though like the action of a man, can be said to be a human act, so no action of an unregenerate man, though like a spiritual action, can be called spiritual, because it proceeds not from a spiritual principle, but from a contrary one paramount in him. And all actions have their true denomination from the principle whence they flow. They may be fruits of morality, and fruits of conscience, but not spiritual fruits, which God requires.

Well, then, we must be first built up 'a spiritual house,' we must be a 'priesthood' before we can 'offer spiritual sacrifice,' 1 Peter ii. 5. We must have the powerful operation of the Holy Ghost in us before we can have a tincture of the Holy Ghost upon our services. In all human acts, we should act as rational creatures; in all religious acts, as spiritual creatures. Now, as a man cannot act rationally without reason, so neither can we act spiritually without a divine spirit in us. We are indeed to serve God, and worship him as men: therefore rational acts are due to God in worship, and we are constituted in the rank of rational beings to that purpose. But since our minds are defiled, they must be purified; since our understandings are darkened, they must be enlightened. There must be a grace infused, a lamp set up, a spiritual awakening, and invigorating our reasons and wills, before we can worship God as God in a spiritual manner.

We cannot perform any evangelical service, vitally, because we are dead. Our services must be living services, if in any wise they be suitable to a living God. The apostle wishes us, Rom. xii. 1, to 'present our bodies a living sacrifice.' He does not mean only our bodies, consisting of flesh and bones, or a natural life; but he names the body as being the instrument of motion and service, or it may be synecdoche partis pro toto, a part for the whole. Present yourselves as a sacrifice consecrated to God, and living to him, and as living by him.

Upon the loss of original righteousness, another form or principle was introduced, called in Scripture flesh, and a body of death. Hence by nature we are said to be dead, Eph. ii. 1, and all our works before repentance are dead works, Heb. vi. 1. And these works have no true beauty in them, with whatsoever gloss they may appear to a natural eye. A dead body may have something of the features and beauty of a living, but it is but the beauty of a carcass, not of a man. A statue, by the stonecutter's art, and the painter's skill, may be made very comely, yet it is but a statue still; where is the life? Such services are but the works of art, as flowers painted on the wall with curious colours, but where is the vegetative principle? Since man, therefore, is spiritually dead, he cannot perform a living service. As a natural death does incapacitate for natural actions, so a spiritual death must incapacitate for spiritual actions. Otherwise, in what sense can it be called a death, if a man in a state of nature were as capable of performing spiritual actions as one in a state of grace? No vital act can be exercised without a vital principle. As Adam could not stir to perform any action, though his body was framed and perfected, till God breathed into him a living soul, so neither can we stir spiritually till God breathe into us a living grace. Spiritual motions can no more be without a spiritual life than bodily motions can be without an enlivening soul. 'The living, the living, they shall praise thee,' and Ps. lxxx. 18, 'Quicken us, and we will call upon thy name.' There can be no living praise, nor no living prayer, without a renewed heart. If it be one effect of the blood of Christ to 'purge our consciences from dead works, to serve the living God,' as Heb. ix. 14, then it is clear that till our consciences are purged from dead works we cannot serve the living God, for what suitableness can there be between a living God and dead services? Is a putrefied rank carcass a fit present for a king? or a man full of running sores and boils over his whole body fit to serve in a prince's chamber? Our best services, without a new nature, though they may appear varnished and glittering to man, yet in the sight of God they have no life, no substance, but stinking rotten dust, because coming from a dead and rotten heart.

Well, then, we must be born again; it is not a dead nature, nor a dead faith, can produce living fruit for God. We may as well read without eyes, walk without legs, act without life, as perform any service to God without a new nature; no, we cannot perform the least: a dead man can no more move his finger than his whole body.

Not graciously, because we are corrupt. By the same reason that we are to speak with grace, Col. iv. 6, and to sing with grace in our hearts to the Lord, Col. iii. 16, we are to do every other duty with an exercise of grace to God: and without grace, our praises are but hollowings, our prayers but howlings, as the Scripture terms them: Hosea vii. 14, 'They have not cried to me with their hearts, when they howled upon their beds.' How can there be an exercise of that which is not? The skill of the musician cannot discover itself till the instrument be made tuneable. The heart must be strung with grace by the Spirit, before that Spirit can touch the strings to make harmony to God in a gospel service. Our tempers must be changed, our hearts fitted, before he can make melody to God. The principal beauty and glory of a duty lies in the internal workings of the heart; and how can that heart work graciously, that has nothing of God and his grace in it? It is said, 'Folly is bound up in the heart of a child,' Prov. xxii. 15. So is corruption in the heart of a man, like poison in a bundle of stuff; it is entered into the very composition of us. A law of sin is predominant in a natural man, Rom. vii. 93, which does influence all his actions. Strong habits will interest themselves in all we go about, and all a man's services are regulated by it, for he has no other law in his mind to check the motions of it, and to scent his duties, whereby they may carry a pleasing savour to God. The gift of prophecy, the understanding of mysteries, the depth of knowledge, the removing mountains, bestowing alms, dying for religion, are brave and noble acts, but without charity, love to God, without which, no other grace can work, all these profit nothing, 1 Cor. xiii. 2, 3. There is a moral goodness in feeding the poor, but no gracious goodness without charity. A little of this would make those, as a diamond does gold wherein it is set, more valuable. If all those profit nothing without this grace of charity, they would profit much with it. How does grace alter the very nature of services? Those acts which are sensitive in a brute, were he transformed into a man, and endued with reason, would become rational. Those actions which are but moral in a mere man, when changed into Christian, become evangelical; they would be of another nature and another value.

Well, then, look after the new birth, since it is so necessary. There cannot be gracious practices without gracious principles. Can anything fly to heaven without wings? We are to walk as Christ walked; how can we do it without a principle of kin to that which Christ had? We are bound to act from a principle of righteousness; Adam was, and his posterity are; and should we not look after that which is so necessary a perfection, requisite for our services? No doubt but the devil could find matter enough for prayer, and from the excellency of his knowledge, frame some rare strains, as some word it; but would it be a service which came from such a nature? As long as we are allied to him in our nature, our services will be of as little value. He transforms himself into an angel of light, but is still a devil; and many men do so in their religious acts, yet still remain unregenerate.

Not freely and voluntarily, because we are at enmity. A natural man's services are forced, not free. The aversion of our natures from God is as strong as their inclination to evil. We have no fervent desires to love God, and therefore no desires to do anything out of affection to him. When sensual habits are planted in the soul, there is an enmity to God in the mind: it will not be 'subject to the law of God,' Rom. viii., and whilst that habit sways, it cannot. This inclination to sin, and consequently aversion to good, is incorporated in nature, like blackness in a black person, or spots in a leopard; they are accustomed to sin, and cannot do good, Jer. xiii. 23. There is no agreeableness between God and man's soul, whilst there is a friendship between the heart and sin; he affects the one, and is disgusted with the other: one is his pleasure, the other his trouble; he has no will, no heart to come to God in any service, and when he does, he is rather dragged, than sweetly drawn. The things of God are against the bent of a natural heart; there is nothing so irksome as the most spiritual service; when men engage in them, they row against the stream of nature itself. There must, therefore, be something of a contrary efficacy to overpower this violent tide, a law of grace to renew the mind and turn the motions of the will, to another channel. Restraining grace may for a while stop the current, but not turn and change the natural course. A carnal mind conceits the things of God and his spiritual service to be foolishness, and therefore contemns them, 1 Cor. i. 23, 24. The eye of the mind must be opened to discern the wisdom of God in them, before he can affect them. The heart should be lifted up in the evangelical ways of God. Can mere flesh be thus? Force can never change nature. You may hurl lead up into the air, but it will never ascend of itself while it is lead, unless it be ratified into air or fire. Keep up iron many years in the air by the force of a loadstone, it will retain its tendency to fall to the earth if the obstacle be removed; the natural gravity is suspended, not altered. Till the nature of the will be altered, it can never move freely to any duty; there must be a power to will, before there is a will to do, as Philip. ii. 13, 'It is God which works in you both to will and to do.' A supernatural renewing grace must expel corrupt habits from the will, and reduce it to its true object. When faith is planted, it brings love to work by; when the soul is renewed, there is an harmony between God and the heart, between the mind and the word, between the will and the duty; when the appetite and true taste of the soul is restored in regeneration, then spring up strong desires to apply itself to every holy service: 1 Peter ii. 2, 3, 'The sincere milk of the word' is fervently desired, after it is spiritually tasted.

Well, then, there must be a change in us, or in the law. The law is spiritual, man is carnal, Rom. vii. 14. The law can have no friendship for man, nor man no friendship for the law in this state, since their natures are so contrary. What the law commands is disgustful to the flesh, what the flesh desires is displeasing to the law. There must then be a change; the law must become carnal, or man become spiritual, before any agreement can be between them. Where do you think this change must light? It can never be in the law, therefore it must be in man. The wound, in our wills must be cured; the tide of nature, that never carries us to God, must be turned, and altered by a stream of grace, to move us to him and his service. Man has been a slave to his lust by the loss of grace, and is never like to be restored to his liberty in the service of God, till he be repossessed of that grace, the loss of which brought him into slavery. The gospel is a 'law of liberty,' James i. 25; a servile spirit does not suit a free law, neither is it a fit frame for an evangelical service.

Nor delightfully. We can never perform spiritual services with delight, because we are alienated. This we are to do. Paul 'delighted in the law of God,' Rom. vii. 22; and the law was the 'delights' of David, Ps. cxix. 92; his whole pleasure run in this channel. Now, because of that aversion to God, there is no will and freedom in his service, much less can there be a delight. A corrupt nature can have no divine strains; a diseased man has no delight in his own acts, his distemper makes his very motion unpleasant to him. Things that are not natural can never be delightful. There is a mighty distance between spiritual duties and a carnal heart. Things out of their place can never be at rest. Sin is as much a natural man's element as water to a fish or air to a bird; if he be stopped in the ways of the flesh, he is restless till he return. He may indeed have some delight sometimes in a service—not as it respects God as the object, or God as the end, there is no such friendship in a natural man's heart to him—but there is an agreement between a service and some carnal end he performs it for. His delight is not terminated in the service, but in self-love, self-interest, or some external reward, anchored in it by some hopes of carnal advantage, not springing from a living love or a gracious affection to God. He has no knowledge of God, and therefore can have no delight in God or in his service. It is impossible we can come before him without pleasure and delight, if we know how amiable he is in his person, and how gracious in his nature; but we naturally think God a hard master, and man having no delight in God, he can have none in those means which lead him to God, and as they are appointed to bring God and his soul together. He has wrong notions of duties, looks upon them as drudgeries, not as advantages: Mal. i. 13, 'Ye said, Behold, what a weariness it is,' &c. Without a change of nature, we cannot desire communion with God, and therefore cannot delight in the means of it. We can no more do any service cheerfully than the saints without it could 'receive joyfully the spoiling of their goods,' Heb. x. 34. We can never be in a holy ecstasy without this inward principle, to make the gospel services connatural to us. This only makes high impressions upon the soul. It is the law within our hearts, which only makes us delight to do his will: Ps. xl. 8, 'Thy law is within my heart,' in my bowels. He had a natural affection to it, and then a high delight in it. It made our Saviour delight to do his work; and it was the inward man of the heart, wherein the apostle's delight in the law was placed. Unless we have a divine impression of God upon us, we cannot hear his word with any joy in it; as our Saviour says, John viii. 47, 'Ye therefore hear them not,' that is, the words of God, ' because you are not of God.' Unless we have God's light and his truth sent forth into us, we can never make God our exceeding joy, or go to his altar with such a frame, Ps. xliii. 3, 4.

Well, then, there is a necessity of the new nature, to have a warm frame of heart in evangelical duties. What is connatural to us is only delightful. So much of weariness and bondage we have in any holy service, so much of a legal frame; so much of love and delight, so much we have of a new covenant grace. A spirit of adoption and regeneration only can make us delight to come to our father, and to cry Abba to him.

Without regeneration we cannot perform evangelical duties sincerely, because we are a lie, and in our best estate vanity. We must worship God 'in truth' as well as 'spirit,' John iv. 24. God is a Spirit, and therefore must be worshipped in spirit. God is truth, and therefore must be worshipped in truth. Without a new nature we cannot worship God in truth. The old nature is in itself a lie, a mere falsity, something contrary to that nature God created. It was first introduced by a lie of the devil 'ye shall be as gods, knowing good and evil,' Gen. iii. 5), and thereupon a fancy that God lied in his command. How can we serve God with this nature, which had nothing but a lie for its foundation,--a lie of the devil, a lie in our fancy? Therefore our old nature is no better than a lie. How can we serve God with that nature which is quite another thing to that of his framing? Man in his fall is a liar: Rom. iii. 4, 'Let God be true, and every man a liar,' a covenant-breaker, that kept not his faith with God. God, in respect of truth, and man, in respect of lying, are set in opposition by the apostle there. No man but would slight and scorn that service from another, which he knew to be a lying service in the very frame of it. There is no truth can be in any service which is founded only upon an old nature, and performed by one that is acted by the father of lies; and so is every unregenerate man, every 'child of disobedience,' Eph. ii. 2.

Now, sincerity cannot be without a new nature,

(1.) Because there are no divine motives which should sway the soul. Most services of natural men have such dirty springs, so unsuitable to that raised temper men should have in dealing with God, that they produce sacrifices not fit to be offered to an earthly governor: Mal. i. 8, 'If you offer the blind for sacrifice, is it not evil?' &c., 'offer it now unto thy governor will he be pleased with thee?' Had they had divine motives, they had never brought such sickly services. What was not fit for themselves, they thought fit for God. Did but princes know what motives many had in their services they would with as much scorn reject them as they do ignorantly receive them with affection. But it is otherwise with God, who knows all the springs and wards in that lock of the heart of his own framing. Do not most services take their rise from custom, or from an outward religious education barely, or at best from natural conscience, which though it be all in a man, which takes God's part, yet it is flesh, and defiled? And what pure vapours can be expected from a lake of Sodom? Titus i. 15, 'To them that are defiled and unbelieving nothing is pure; but even their mind and conscience is defiled.' The mind, which is the repository of natural light, and the conscience, which is the advocate of natural light, and applies it upon particular occasion, are defiled, and that in every unbelieving person. Can the motives which conscience takes from a dark and defiled principle, as the mind is, be divine? It is fear of death, wrath, and judgment which it mostly applies. These are the motives of defilement. Fear is the natural consequence of pollution; without sin and corruption we never had any fear of hell. That cannot be gracious which springs naturally from the commission of sin, and can this be divine? Were there no punishment feared, there should be no duty performed. Conscience has naturally no basis to stand upon but this. What is the principle of his fear? Self. It is not therefore obedience to God, but self-preservation, says a man. Fear is but a servile disposition, and therefore cannot make a service good. All such extrinsic motives which arise not from a new life, are no more divine than the weights of a clock may be said to have life because they set the wheels on running. The same action may be done by several persons upon different principles and motives, for which one may be rewarded, the other not, as Mat. x. 41, 42, 'He that receives a righteous man, in the name of a righteous man, shall receive a righteous man's reward. And whosoever shall give unto one of these little ones a cup of cold water only in the name of a disciple, he shall in no wise lose his reward.' One may receive a member of Christ out of respect to Christ and the relation the person has to him, another man receive the same person out of a common principle of humanity, the action is the same, the good redounding to the object is the same; nay, it may be greater in him that acts from a commiseration of him, as a man, than a cup of cold water from the other, because his ability is greater; but the inward respect to the object is different. One respects him as a man of the same nature with himself in misery, the other respects him as a member of Christ in misery; one respects him as a man, the other as a righteous man. The principle is different: one relieves him out of a natural compassion, common to a heathen with him, the other out of a Christian affection to his Head. The actions are therefore different, because of their motives: one is rewardable, and promised to be rewarded, the other not; one may be from grace-- I do not say it always is, unless there be a constant tenor of such motives in our actions, for a natural man, under the preaching of the gospel, may do such a thing out of a present and transient respect to Christ, whom he hears so often of, and has some presumption to be saved by, but it is not his constant frame--I say, one may be from grace, the other from nature.

Therefore from hence results a necessity of the alteration of the frame of our souls, to furnish us with divine and heavenly motives for our actions. A man may do a thing by nature from a good principle, a principle of common honesty, good in its kind (brass is good in its kind, but not so good as silver), but not evangelically good, without a renewed affection to God: John xiv. 15, 'If you love me, keep my commandments;' keep what I command you, out of affection to me. Where 'the imagination of the heart is evil, and only evil, and that continually,' Gen. vi. 5, all the service a man in that state performs rises from this spring, and has some infectious imagination in it, highly abominable to God; either wrong notions of God in it, or wrong notions of the duty, or corrupt motives, something or other of the evil imagination of the heart, mixes itself with it.

(2.) Without a renewed nature, as there are no divine motives, so there can be no divine ends. We are bound to refer our natural actions, much more our religious services, to the glory of God. The end is the moral principle of every action. It is that which confers a goodness or badness upon the service: Luke xi. 34, 'If the eye be evil, the whole body is full of darkness' (this is commonly understood of a man's aim). It the intention be evil, there is nothing but darkness in the whole service. The perfection of everything consists in answering the end for which it was framed. That which Jonas the first end of our framing, ought to be the end of our acting, viz. the glory of God. But man has taken himself oil from this end, and has been fond of making himself his chief good and ultimate end. Men naturally have corrupt ends in good duties. Pride is the cause of some men's virtue. And they are spiritually vicious in avoiding crimes, because they intrench too much upon their reputation. The pharisees made their devotion contribute to their ambition: Mat. vi. 5, 'They pray to be seen of men,' and Mat. xxiii. 5, 'But all their works they do to be seen of men.' Not one work wherein they had not respect to this. Their works might well be called the works of the devil, whose main business it was to set up pride and self. All their pretences of devotion to God, were but the adoration of some golden image. Have not many in their more splendid actions, the same end with brutes: the satisfaction of the sensitive part, covetousness, pride, emulation, sense of honour, qualities perceivable in the very brutes, as the end of some of their actions? The acting for a sensitive end is not suitable to a rational, much less can it be the end of a gracious creature. Have not men sinful ends in their religious services? in their prayers to God, , in their acknowledgements of God? The devil could entreat our Saviour's leave to go into the herd of swine. Was this a prayer, though directed to Christ, when his end was to destroy and satisfy his malice in it? At best, a man without grace is like a picture in a room which eyes all, and has no more respect to a prince than his attendants. A natural man's respect to God is but equal to a respect to all his other worldly concerns. Indeed it were well if it were so. He parcels out one part for God, one part for himself, and one part for the world, but God has the least share, or at best, no more than the rest. And truly, as a picture cannot give a greater respect, to fix its eyes more upon a prince than a peasant, because it has no life; so neither can a natural man pay a supreme respect to God in his service, without a spiritual life. There is a necessity then of removing those depraved ends, that man may answer the true end of his creation. The principles then upon which such ends do grow, contrary to the will of God, must be rooted out, that the soul may move purely to God in every service. We are come short of the glory of God: Rom. iii. 23, 'All have sinned and come short of the glory of God;' short of aiming at it, short of his approbation of our acts. Being thus come short, our ends cannot rise higher than the frame of our soul. Grace, grace only can advance our wills to those supernatural ends for which they were first framed. We can never aim at the glory of God till we have an affection to him. We can never honour him supremely, whom we do not supremely love. An affection to God can never be had, till the nature, wherein the aversion is placed, be changed into another frame. We are to glorify God, as God. How can we do this without the knowledge of him? How can we know him but by the gospel, wherein he discovers himself? How can we have right conceptions of the gospel, till gospel impressions be made upon us? How can we act for the glory of God, to whom naturally we are enemies? There is none of us born with a spiritual love to God. There must be an alteration of the end and aim in us; our actions cannot else be good, though ordered by God himself. God employs Satan in some things, as in afflicting Job; but is his performance good? No, because his end is not the same with God's. He acts out of malice what God commands out of sovereignty, and for gracious designs. Our end without it, is not the same with the end of the action; for moral acts tend to God's glory, though the agent has no such intention. So the action may be good in itself, but not good in the actor, because he wants a due end.

Well then, those actions only can be said to be evangelical, when the great end of God's glory, which was his end both in creation and redemption, has a moral influence upon every service; when we have the same end in our redeemed services, as God had in his redeeming love.

Not humbly. We cannot without regeneration perform gospel duties humbly, because of natural stoutness and hardness. Evangelical duties must be performed with humility. Self-denial is the chief gospel lesson, and is to run through the veins of every service. Therefore God speaks of giving 'a heart of flesh,' in gospel times: Ezek. xi. 19, 'I will take the stony heart out of their flesh, and give them a heart of flesh, that they may walk in my statutes, and keep my ordinances, and do them.' Gospel duties require a pliableness and tenderness of heart. Adam's overvaluing himself, and swelling with designs of being like God, brought an incapacity upon himself of serving his creator. And man ever since, is too much aspiring and too well opinioned of himself, to perform duties in an evangelical strain, with that meltingness, that nothingness in himself, which the gospel requires. Our swelling and admiring thoughts of our own natural righteousness, hinders Christ from saving us, and ourselves from serving him. There must then be an humble, and melting, and self denying frame. The angels are said to cover their faces before God, Isa. vi. 2, as having nothing to glory in of their own. And the chief design of the gospel is to beat down all glorying in ourselves: 1 Cor. i. 29, 31, 'That no flesh should glory in his presence; let him that glories, glory in the Lord.' And indeed it humbles us no more than what, upon due consideration, will appear very necessary. Nature then must be changed before this pride be rooted out. Old things must pass away, that God may be all in all in the creature. We cannot without a new nature make a true estimate of ourselves, and lie as vile and base in the presence of God. A stone, with all the hammering, cannot be made soft. Beat it into several pieces, you may sever the continuity of its parts, but not master its hardness; every little piece of it will retain the hardness of its nature. So it is with a heart of stone. The nature must be changed before it be fit for those services which require melting, humble, and admiring frames. There is a necessity of a residing grace, like fire, to keep the soul in a melting temper.

Not constantly. Without a new nature, we cannot perform gospel services constantly, because of our natural levity. Where the nature is flesh, the heart 'minds the things of the flesh,' Rom. viii. 5. The mind thus habituated, will not be long employed about the things of the Spirit. There is a natural levity in man's nature. Do not many seem to begin in the Spirit and end in the flesh? seem to arise to heaven, and quickly fall down to earth? Do not our very promises vanish with the next wind of temptation, and like sparks, expire as soon as they be born, unless grace be in the heart to keep them alive. The Israelites are accused of not having a heart steadfast with God: Ps. lxxviii. 37, 'Their heart was not right with him, neither were they steadfast in his covenant.' Are our natures better than theirs? Do we not all lie under the same charge; so uncertain naturally, about divine things, as if there were nothing but wind in our composition? Nothing can be kept up in motion against its nature, but by force. A top has no inward principle of motion, but is moved by some outward force. When that is removed, the motion languishes. Any motion that depends only upon outward wires, expires upon the breaking of them. When external motives, which spurred men on to this or that service, cease, the service dies of course, because the spring of the motion falls. If fear of hell, terrors of death, some pressing calamity, be the spring of any duty; when these are removed, there will be no more regard to the duty they engendered. But what is natural, is constant, because the spring always remains. Interest changes, conscience is various; and therefore the operations arising from thence, will partake of the uncertainty of thorn. Stony ground may bring forth blades; but for want of root, they will quickly wither: Mat. xiii. 5, 20. A man may mount high in religion, by the mixture of some religious passion, as meteors in the air; but by reason of the gross and earthy parts in them, will not continue their station. There is no being without, stable, but God; and no principle stable within, but grace: Heb. xiii. 9, 'It is a good thing that the heart be established with grace.' Whatsoever service is undertaken upon changeable motives, is as changeable as the bottom upon which it stands. If credit, slavish fear of God, worldly interest, inspire us with some seeming holy resolutions, they will all fly away upon the first removal of those props. There is therefore a necessity of a change of nature and disposition. Where there is no approbation of things that are excellent, there can be no constant operation about them. All action about an object, continues according to the affection to it, and delight in it. We shall then be filled with the fruits of righteousness, to the glory of God, when we have a sincere approbation of the excellency of them: Philip i. 10, 11, first, 'approve things that are excellent;' and then follows, 'without offence, till the day of Christ.' A stately profession can no more hold out against the floods of temptation, than a beautiful building can stand against the winds without a good foundation under ground. It is the Spirit of the Lord within, as well as without, can only maintain the standard against temptation, Isa. lix. 19.

Well then, upon the whole, there is a necessity of regeneration for the performance of gospel duties. We cannot else perform them spiritually, because we are flesh; nor vitally, because we are dead; nor graciously, because we are corrupt; nor voluntarily, because we are enmity; nor delightfully, because we are alienated; nor sincerely, because we are falsity; nor humbly, because of our stoutness; nor constantly, because of our levity. Our natures must be changed in all these respects, before we can be fit for any gospel service.

(2) Regeneration is necessary for the enjoyment of gospel privileges.

[1.] For the favour of God, and his complacency with us. We are not fit for God's delight, without it. That person who has his love, must have his image. If ever God could love an old nature, which he once hated, and delight in that which he once loathed, he must divest himself of his immutability. He never hated the person of any of his creatures, but for unrighteousness. And upon the removal of this cloud of separation between him and them, the beams of his love break out in their former vigour. God's love is not straitened, nor his kindness exhausted, no more than his hand is shortened, or his ear grown heavy, that he cannot hear: Isa. lix. 1, 2, 'But your iniquities have separated between you and your God, and your sins have hid his face from you, that he will not hear.'

For, first, what did make the first separation, was it not sin? God told Adam before, what the issue would be, upon his eating the forbidden fruit: Gen. ii. 17, 'In the day that thou eatest thereof, thou shalt surely die.' It is not a temporal death there only meant; for he should then have died that day wherein he fell, the word surely importing so much. And the punishment of a temporal death was pronounced afterwards: Gen. iii. 19, 'Dust thou art, and unto dust shalt thou return.' Thou shalt surely die; thy integrity and righteousness will expire that very moment, and thou shalt die in my just displeasure. It is a spiritual death that is most properly meant. The punishment of sin is death; the chief part of this death is an 'alienation from the life of God,' Eph. iv. 18; that is, not to have God, and the righteousness of God's image living in him; but to be impure, corrupt, a hater of God, and servant of sin. Now from this punishment no man can be freed, but by a contrary regeneration, the proper effect whereof is to love God, to know his name, to partake of his holiness, to imitate his

virtues. Man forfeited all God's favour upon his fall, and can challenge nothing of it.

Secondly, What then can restore man to God's favour? Can that which first deprived us of it? The cause of our destruction can never be the means of our restoration. Did the loss of Adam's integrity make him unfit for paradise, the garden of God, from whence he was expelled, as a token of God's disfavour? And can the continuance of that loss be a means to regain that love which cashiered us? It was a spiritual death; and is the carcass of a soul fit for God's complacency? There must be not only a satisfaction to his justice for the reinstating man into his favour (this is done by Jesus Christ); but a restoring of his image, this is done by the Holy Ghost. It is as impossible the soul can be beautiful without life, and without holiness, as for a body to be beautiful without a good colour and proportion of parts. Take away this, beauty must cease, and deformity succeed in the place. It is impossible, therefore, that where sin remains in its full vigor, where there is nothing of an original integrity residing, but that the soul must be monstrous, vile, and deformed in the eyes of God. To make it therefore a fit object for God's favour, it is necessary it be beautified with a holy nature, and adorned with its due proportions and vigour. The righteousness of Israel must go forth as brightness; he must be called by a new name, that is, a new nature, for what is a name without a nature? And then it should be Hephzibah, 'the Lord delights in thee.' Isa. lxii. 14, 'The righteousness thereof shall go forth as brightness, and the glory thereof as a lamp that burns.' Righteousness is the glory of a soul, as well as of a church: 'Gentiles shall see thy righteousness, and all kings thy glory: thou shalt be called by a new name,' a new nature wrought by the word of God; 'which the mouth of the Lord shall name.' Then she should be in favour with God, 'a crown of glory in the hand of the Lord, and a total diadem in the hand of her God.' Righteousness is the glory of a soul, and God's delight and complacency is the consequent of a righteous nature.

Thirdly, The elect themselves have no interest in God's favour of delight without it. This follows upon the former, God cannot love the very top of mankind, his own choice, with a love of complacency, without regeneration, without a righteous nature. There is a favour of intention and purpose before it; there is also an executive love in the very infusing the habits of grace, which is a supernatural favour, because there is both a purpose and then an actual conferring a supernatural good. God is free, and may will to give his gifts how, and to whom he pleases. But an elect person, whilst he continues in a state of nature, is not simply beloved, though there be a purpose of love, because there is no gracious quality in him, which is the object of God's special favour. It is regeneration only which is the object of God's delight in us.

Fourthly, Hence will follow, that no privilege under heaven, without it, can bring us into God's favour; no, not if any man were related to Christ according to the flesh. The apostle Paul would not think the better of himself for a fleshly relation to Christ, for being of the same country, descended of the Jewish nation: 2 Cor. v. 16, 'Though we have known Christ after the flesh, yet henceforth know we him no more. Therefore if any man be in Christ, he is a new creature.' Though it be an honour to be of the same descent with Christ, according to the flesh, to be of the same nation and country, yet this does not make a man any more beloved of God. Nothing avails in Christ, but a new creature; and our Saviour himself pronounces it so. It was the highest privilege to he the mother of our Saviour, according to the flesh; yet this had been nothing, without her being born again of the Spirit: 'Who is my mother? and who are my brethren? Behold my mother and my brethren,' pointing to his disciples, Mat. xii. 48, 49. 'My mother and my brethren are those which hear the word of God, and do it,' Luke viii. 21. Those that hear the word, that have the gracious effect of the word wrought in them by the Spirit, are equal to my mother, and my brethren, and superior to any of my fleshly relations, if they be without it. There is a necessity of regeneration upon this account.

[2.] As there is no favour, so there is no union with God and Christ without it. Man has some kind of natural union with all things in the world; he has being with all creatures, rational faculties with angels, sense with animals, vegetation with plants; be wants only that with God which could beautify all the rest. And this can only be by partaking of the image of God's holiness by a new birth. There must be a capability for this union on man's part. A superior and inferior nature man be united together, but never contrary natures. There must be some proportion between the subjects to be united, which proportion consists in a commensuration of one thing to another. What proportion is there between God and our souls? There can be none without a supernatural grace infusing a pure nature. As we come out of the quarry of nature, rough and unpolished, we are not fit to be cemented with the cornerstone in the heavenly building; we must be first smoothed and altered by grace.

First, How can things be united to one another which are already united to their contraries? Separation from one body must make way for union to another. Naturally we are united to the devil as the head of the wicked world. We are by nature his members. Our understandings and wills were united with his in Adam, when Adam gave up his understanding and will to him; and ever since he 'works in the children of disobedience', Eph. ii. 2, 'Who now works in the children of disobedience,' "enegountos en huiois". Working and working in, as a united nature to him, and principle in him. It is necessary this union should be broken before we can partake of the influence of another head. The diabolical nature and principle, therefore, which we have got by sin must be removed, and another nature, which is divine, put in the place first (in order of nature), before we can be united to Christ, and enjoy the benefits of union with him.

Secondly, How can things of a contrary nature be united together? Can fire and water be united, a good angel, and an impure devil? can heaven and hell ever meet friendly and compose one body? We are united to the first Adam by a likeness of nature; how can we be united to the second, without a likeness to him from a new principle? We were united to the first by a living soul; we must be united to the other by a quickening Spirit. We have nothing to do with the heavenly Adam, without bearing an heavenly image, 1 Cor. xv. 48, 49. We are earthly as in the first Adam; we must be heavenly to be in the second, because his nature is so. If we are his members, we must have the same nature which was communicated to him by the Spirit of God, which is holiness. This nature must flow from the same principle, otherwise it is not the same nature; an old nature cannot be joined to a new Adam. There must be one spirit in both; as 1 Cor. vi. 17, 'He that is joined to the Lord is one spirit;' and if it were an union barely of affections, as some would only make it, it is not conceivable how it can be without a change of disposition. But since it is an union by indwelling of the same Spirit in both (Rom. viii. 9, 'If any man has not the Spirit of Christ, he is none of his'), it is less intelligible, how it can be without an assimilation of our nature to the nature of Christ. It can never be supposed the Spirit should unite a pure head, and impure members. Such an union would make our blessed Saviour like Nebuchadnezzar's image; an head of gold, arms of silver, and feet of clay. Shall we loathe to have nasty things about us, and will the holy Jesus endure a loathsome putrefying soul to be joined to him?

Thirdly, How can anything be vitally united to another without life? It is a vital union, by virtue of which believers are called Christ (1 Cor. xi. 12, 'As all the members of that one body, being many, are one body; so also is Christ'); and it is compared to the union of the members of a natural body, Rom. xii. 4, 5. Members have not only life in their head, but in themselves, because the soul, which is the life of the body, is not only in the head, but in all the parts of the body, and exercises in every part its vital operations. The Spirit therefore, which is the band of this union, communicates life to every member wherein he resides, as well as in the head. What man would endure a dead body to be joined to him, though it were the carcass of one he never so dearly loved? It a man were united to Christ, without regeneration, Christ's body would be partly alive, partly dead, if any one member of it had not a spiritual life. A dead body and a living head, a member of Christ with a nature contrary to him, is an inconceivable paradox. Did God ever design such a monstrous union for his Son?

Upon these accounts does result the necessity of regeneration; without it, no union with Christ.

(3.) There can be no justification without it. We are not justified by an inherent righteousness; yet we are not justified without it. We cannot be justified by it, because it is not commensurate to the law by reason of its imperfection; we cannot be justified without it, for it is not congruous to the wisdom and holiness of God, to count a person righteous, who has nothing of righteousness in him, and whose nature is as corrupt as the worst of men. With what respect to God's honour, can it be expected that God should pardon that man's sins, whose will is not changed who still has the same habitualness in his will to commit sin, though he does not at present act it. It is very congruous in a moral way, that the person offending should retract his sin, and return to his former affection. There is a distinction between justification and regeneration, though they never are asunder. Justification is relative; regeneration internally real. Union with Christ is the ground of both; Christ is the meritorious cause of both. The

Father pronounces the one, the Spirit works the other; it is the Father's sentence, and the Spirit's work. The relative and the real change are both at the same time: 1 Cor. vi. 7, 'But you are sanctified, but you are justified;' both go together. We are not justified before faith, because we are justified by it, Rom. v. 1; and faith is the vital principle whereby we live: Gal. ii. 20, 'The life which I now live, I live by the faith of the Son of God.' It is the root-grace, and contains the seeds of all other graces in it; it is habitually and seminally all other grace; so that unless we be new born, no justification can be expected; no justification can be evidenced. God never pardons sin, but he subdues iniquity: Micah vii. 18, 19, 'Who is a God like unto thee, that pardons iniquity?' He will subdue our iniquities. The conquest cannot be made, while the nature, the root of the rebellion, remains. When he turns his compassion to us, he will turn away our hearts from iniquity. If a man were justified before he were regenerate, then he was righteous before he was alive; being 'in Christ,' as free from condemnation, is always attended with a 'walking after the Spirit;' and walking is not before living, Rom. viii. 1. Pardon would be unprofitable, unless he that were pardoned were made righteous inchoately here, and had a right to, and hope of, a perfect righteousness hereafter. If righteousness hereafter were not imparted in this manner, it would be an argument a man were still under the law, which says, 'he that does them shall live in them' (which is impossible in a man that has once sinned, (though his sins are remitted). But it is clear that righteousness is imparted, since there is no man in the world whose sins are pardoned, but finds some principle in him whereby he is enabled to contest with sin more than before he was. Therefore do not deceive yourselves; there is no pardon without a righteous nature, though pardon be not given for it.

(4.) There is no adoption without regeneration. We can no more be God's sons, without spiritual regeneration, than we can be the sons and daughters of men, without natural generation. Adoption is not a mere relation without an inward form. The privilege, and the image of the sons of God, go both together. A state of adoption is never without a separation from defilement: 2 Cor. vi. 17, 18, 'Come you out from among them, be you separate, and I will be a father unto you, and you shall be my sons and daughters.' The new name in adoption is never given till the new creature be framed. 'As many as are led by the Spirit, they are the sons of God,' Rom. viii. 14, "houtoi", those very persons; that is the signal mark, that they are led by the Spirit; therefore first enlivened by the Spirit. A childlike relation is never without a childlike nature. The same method God observes in declaring the members his sons, as he did in declaring the head his Son, which was 'according to the Spirit of holiness, by the resurrection from the dead,' Rom. i. 4. So he declares believers to be his sons, by giving them a spirit of holiness, and by a resurrection from sin, and spiritual death. The devils may as well be adopted sons of God, as we, without a change of nature. To be the sons of the living God, was the great promise of the gospel prophesied of: Hos. i. to, 'Ye are the sons of the living God.' How well will it suit, a living God and a dead son? God is not the God of the dead, but of the living. Our Saviour's argument from the immortality of the soul will evidence not only a resurrection, but a necessity of spiritual life. What advantage is there in being sons of the living God, if we had no more life in us than his greatest enemies? Regeneration, as a physical act, gives us a likeness to God in our nature. Adoption, as a legal act, gives us a right to an inheritance; both the great intendments of the gospel, both accompanying one another. No sonship without a new nature.

(5). There is no acceptation of our services without it. We are not fit to perform any duty without it, and God will never accept any duty from us without it. In the first of Ephesians, 1. election, 2. regeneration, expressed by being holy, 3. adoption, 4. acceptation, are linked together: ver. 4-6, 'He has chosen us that we should be holy, and without blame before him in love, having predestinated us to the adoption of children;' after follows grace 'wherein he has made us accepted in the beloved.' Our acceptation is only upon the account of Christ; but the acceptability is upon the account of grace. Faith makes our persons and our duties acceptable, and Christ makes them both accepted. Acceptability arises from grace, as damnability arises from sin. God damns none, unless they be damnable; neither does God accept any in Christ, unless they be acceptable. The papists that plead for merit, acknowledge nothing of it before grace, but after grace, because then the services have a greater proportion to God, from the dignity of the person, they being acts of God's children, and wrought by his Spirit. God can love nothing but himself, and what he finds of himself in the creature. All services, without something of God's image and Spirit in them, are nothing. As the product of a million of ciphers, though you still add to them, signifies nothing; but add one figure, an unit, the Spirit, grace, it will make the product to be many millions, of high account with God. All the significance depends upon the figure, which, if absent, the rest would be nothing All moral perfections, without a new nature, are but ciphers in God's account: Heb. xi. 6, 'Without faith it is impossible to please God.' Grace is only a good work: Philip. i. 6, 'He which has begun a good work in you, will perform it till the day of Christ;' intimating their morality and their natural wisdom, before their regeneration, were not good works in the sight of God. They were good in their kind; as a crab may be said to be a good crab, but not a good pippin. It is not good, unless it be fruit brought forth in Christ; neither is it ordained as good to the day of Christ, to appear glorious at the time of his triumph. God looks into our services, whether he Spirit frames them, and Christ presents them; all that we do must go through their hands before they can reach God's heart. Acceptation can never be without a renewed nature. The services of the flesh cannot please God: Rom. viii. 8. 'They that are in the flesh cannot please God.' Their persons cannot, therefore their actions cannot, because they are the products of a nature at variance with him, a nature that is not, nor cannot be subject to his law; so that God must be displeased with his own spiritual law; yea with his own holy nature, and change his judgment, and change his nature, before he can be pleased with fleshly services, for at the best, they are but refined brutishness. The image of the devil can never be grateful to God. Services flowing from nature, may seem in the outward form of them, to be as acceptable as the duties of a good man; but considering what a dunghill of filthiness the heart is, from whence they proceed, they cannot be so. Good water is sweetest, and bad water most corrupt, nearest the spring or fountain, the streams may lose some of their corruption in their passage. A gracious man's duties are most pleasant to God nearest the heart, a natural man's services are most distasteful nearest the spring. When the heart is a good treasure, what comes from it is regarded as a rich gift, because it comes from a valuable treasure, Luke vi. 40; hence it is that a less work, coming from a pure and holy principle in a renewed man, is more acceptable to God, than a greater work (in respect of the external glorification of him in the good of mankind), coming from an impure principle in a natural man, as a cup of cold water given to a disciple is more valuable than the gift of a prince from another principle. In the one, God sees a conformity of affection with his holiness; in the other, only a conformity with his providence. One intends God's glory, and the other only acts it, proposing some other end to himself; and we use to value gifts, rather by the affection of the friend, than the quantity of the gift. Well then, consider it; without a new nature, all our services, though they should amount to many millions in number, have no intrinsic value in them with God. For where the nature is displeasing, the actions flowing from that nature can never please him: 'He that turns away his ear from hearing the law,' that is, from a spiritual obedience to the law, 'even his prayer is an abomination,' Prov. xxviii. 9; it is formed by a noisome soul.

(6.) There is no communion with God without a renewed soul. God is incapable on his part, with the honour of his law and holiness, to have communion with such a creature. Man is incapable on his part, because of the aversion rooted in his nature. What way can there be to bring God and man together without this change of nature? what communion can there be between a rising God and a dead heart? God loathes sin, man loves it; God loves holiness, man loathes it. How can these contrary affections meet together in an amicable friendship? what communion with so much disagreement in affections? In all friendship there must be similitude of disposition. Justification cannot bring us into communion with God without regeneration; it may free us from punishment, discharge our sins, but not prepare us for a converse, wherein our chief happiness lies. There must be some agreement before there can be a communion. Beasts and men agree not in a life of reason, and therefore cannot converse together. God and man agree not in a life of holiness, and therefore can have no communion together. We are by sin alienated from the life of God, and therefore from his fellowship, Eph. iv. 18; we must have his life restored to us before we can be instated in communion with him.

[1.] God can have no pleasure in it. God took a delight in the creation, and did rejoice in his work. Sin despoiled God of his rest. It can give God no content, no satisfaction; for to be in the flesh, is to be in that nature which was derived from Adam, which brought the displeasure of God upon all mankind. Regeneration by the Spirit restores the creature to such a state wherein God may take pleasure in him, and strips him by decrees of that sin which spoiled his delight in the work of his hands; as it grows, communion is enlarged. God made man at first after his own image, that he might have communion with him. Since the loss of that, what fitness can there be for communion, till the restoration of that which God thought fit for his delight? Suppose that some one work of a natural man may be good and pleasing to God, it will not argue a communion of God with the person: he may be pleased with the work, but not with the man, for all the goodness he has being in the act, and the act being transient, when that is past his goodness is as the morning dew, vanished. He cannot be the object of God's delight, because he has no habitual goodness in him. If a man be abominable and filthy naturally, he cannot have a converse with God without a nature suitable to God, and a nature so animated, as that God may put some trust in it, and not be at uncertainty: Job xv. 14-16, 'What is man, that he should be clean, he which is born of a woman, that he should be righteous? Behold, he puts no trust in his saints,' &c. No man is clean, but those that delight in sin are much more abominable, that 'drink up iniquity like water.' Now God being infinitely holy, can have no communion with that which he does abominate, and he cannot have a fixed and a delightful communion with that which he cannot confide in. It must be therefore such a nature as is produced and preserved by his own Spirit. If the heavens are not clean in his sight, we must have a nature purer and cleaner than the heavens, before God can delightfully behold us, and pleasingly converse with us.

[2.] As God can have no pleasure in it, so man is contrary to it. Man, as he is by corruption, is at variance with God, and cannot but be at variance with him. An uncircumcised heart will not love God, or at least, will not pay him such a proportion of love, and love of such a quality, as is due to him; for if the end of the circumcision of the heart be to love the Lord with all our hearts, as Deut. xxx. 6, 'And the Lord thy God will circumcise thy heart, to love the Lord thy God with all thy heart,' then it will necessarily infer, that he whose heart is not circumcised, does not love God with all his heart. Holiness and iniquity are so contrary, that no agreement can be made between them. God must deny his nature before he can deny his hatred of sin, and man must be stripped of his nature before he can leave his affection to sin. It is equally impossible for wickedness to love holiness, and for purity to love pollution. There can be no fellowship with God, whilst we walk in darkness, and he is light, 1 John i. 6, 7.

[3.] Nay, thirdly, man naturally resists all means for it. It is the Spirit only which is the bond of union, and consequently the cause of communion. The Spirit can only bring God and us together. Walking in the Spirit hinders us from fulfilling the lusts of the flesh, which make us incapable of communion: Gal. v. 16, 'Walk in the Spirit, and you shall not fulfil the lusts of the flesh.' But every man by nature (as well as the Jews) 'resists the Holy Ghost,' Acts vii. 61. And while this resistance of the great medium of it remains, this communion can never be. This resistance, therefore, must be removed, and there must be a divine stamp and impression upon our very nature, to make it pliable. You see more and more the necessity of regeneration.

(7.) As there is no communion with God without it, so no communications of Christ to our souls can be relished and improved without it. All the communications of Christ relish of that fullness of grace which was in his person, and therefore cannot be relished by any principle but that of the same nature. Whenever Jesus Christ comes to bless us with the great blessings of his purchase, he turns away our hearts from iniquity, Acts iii. 26.

[1.] Ordinances cannot be improved. The word has no place in them, John viii. 37. There is no footing naturally for any divine and spiritual truth. The nature of the soil must be changed before this heavenly plant will thrive. Plants grow not upon stones, nor this heavenly plant in a stony heart. The vine and the weed draw the same moisture of the earth, which in the vine is transmuted, by the nature of the plant, into a nobler substance than that in the weed. The new nature of a good man turns the juice of the word into a nobler spirit in him; and according as the nature of a good man is enriched with grace, the more does he concoct the word, and improve it, to the bringing forth fruit, and fruit of a diviner nature than another. The juice it affords to all is the same, but the nature of the creature turns it in the concoction. Nature must be changed then, to make any profitable improvement of the word and other institutions. A stone receives the water upon it, not into it; it falls off, or dries up as soon as ever it falls: but a new heart, a heart of flesh, sucks in the dew of the word, and grows thereby. The new birth and nature makes us suck in the milk, and grow thereby, 1 Peter ii. 2.

[2.] There can be no communication of comfort. The Spirit comforts by exciting grace, and by discovering grace, not by dashes and enthusiasms. What comfort can there be when grace, the foundation, is wanting? Can the Holy Ghost ever speak a lie, and give any man comfort, and tell him he is a child of God, when he has the nature of the devil, so contrary to him? This were to witness not with our spirits, but against the frame and habit of them, which is not the Spirit's work, Rom. viii. 16. Jesus Christ will not trifle away his comforts upon such as have no conformity to him. This were to put a jewel in a swine's snout, a crown upon a beast's head. Those that are not heirs by a new nature to heaven, cannot claim any title to the first fruits and clusters of it, the comforts of the gospel. As there is a necessity of a likeness to Christ, to make us capable of communications from him in a state of glory, so it is as certainly necessary to the lower degrees of it in this world. Vessels of wrath must be changed into vessels of honour before they are capable of being filled with spiritual comforts. Our blessed Saviour keeps his choicest flowers and richest beams for his dressed garden, not for the wild desert.

(8.) We cannot be in covenant without it. This should have been first, as the foundation of all. Had not Adam had an habitual righteousness in his nature, he had not been a fit person for God to have entered into covenant with. There must therefore be a restored righteousness, that we may come into the bond of the new covenant for eternal life. The very terms of it are, a new heart, a heart of flesh, a new spirit, the law written in the heart. Without this new nature, we cannot depend on him by faith, which is the condition of the covenant. For we cannot confide in him to whom we have an enmity, and of whom we have a jealousy. We cannot have God to be our God unless we be his people, have the nature and disposition of his people, turn to him, act towards him as our God; whereas in our first defection we made the devil our God. God requires righteousness still to our being in covenant, but dispenses with the strictness of the first covenant, and gives our Saviour a power to that end, in committing all judgment to the Son. As the covenant is spiritual, so there must be a spiritual life to answer the terms of it. Without it, we cannot walk in the way wherein we engage by covenant to walk, neither can we have any right to the promises and benefits of the covenant. Does God promise to be our God? It is upon the condition we be his people. Does he promise never to leave us nor forsake us? It is upon condition we continue not in our original apostasy. Does he promise to be present with us? It is more than his holiness will endure, while we continue in our filthy nature.

2. The second general. As regeneration is necessary to a gospel state, so it is necessary to a state of glory. It seems to be typified by the strength and freshness of the Israelites when they entered into Canaan. Not a decrepit and infirm person set foot in the promised land: none of those that came out of Egypt with an Egyptian nature, and desires for the garlic and onions thereof, with a suffering their old

bondage, but dropped their carcasses in the wilderness; only the two spies, who had encouraged them against the seeming difficulties. None that retain only the old man, born in the house of bondage, but only a new regenerate creature, shall enter into the heavenly Canaan. Heaven is the inheritance of the sanctified, not of the filthy: Acts xxvi. 18, 'That they may receive an inheritance among them which are sanctified, through faith that is in me.' So our Saviour himself phrases it in his discourse to Paul upon his conversion by faith, the great renewing principle. Upon Adam's expulsion from paradise, a flaming sword was set to stop his re-entry into that place of happiness. As Adam, in his forlorn state, could not possess it, we also, by what we have received front Adam, cannot expect a greater privilege than our root. Had Adam retained the righteousness of his nature, he had been fit for that place, and that place for him; but poor decrepit Adam could have no leave to enter. The priest under the law could not enter into the sanctuary till he were purified, nor the people into the congregation; neither can any man have access into the holy of holies till that be consecrated for him by the blood of Jesus, and he sprinkled by the same blood for it, Heb. x. 19, 22. It is by the blood of Jesus sprinkled upon our hearts that we enter into the holiest by a way which he has consecrated; 'for there shall in nowise enter into it anything that defiles, neither whatsoever works abomination or a lie,' Rev. xxi. 17, as every unclean thing was prohibited entrance into the temple. Whosoever shall enter into the rest of God, must cease from his own works of darkness and corruption, as God did from his works of creation, Heb. iv. 10. If man fell the sixth day, the day of his creation, the rest of God in his lower works was disturbed by the entrance of sin upon them, as well as it had been disturbed by the sin of the angels in heaven. God rested from his works of creation, but not in them, but in Christ, the covenant of redemption, and restoration by him. We must therefore cease from our own works, to enter into his rest. This entrance we cannot have in an unbelieving, unregenerate state, because by unbelief we approve not of that for our rest, wherein God settled his own repose; and by unregeneracy we oppose the great intendment of it, the restoration of the creature to be a fit object for God's rest and complacency. It is necessary to a state of glory.

(1.) Not that there is a natural connection between a regenerate state and glory, that in its own nature gives a right to heaven, but a gracious connection by the will of God. Though it be morally impossible in nature that a man can have communion with God without a renewed state, yet when he has a new nature, it is not absolutely necessary that God should love him so intensely as to give him an eternal reward, but conditionally necessary, upon the account of the covenant wherein God has so promised. Though it be absolutely unavoidable to God to love goodness (for, because he is perfectly good, he cannot hate it), yet it is not absolutely necessary he should instate it in so inconceivable a glory. A new nature, indeed, makes a man capable of eternal glory, without which it is not possible for him to have it; but it gives him not a right to it, nor instates him in it in its own nature, but by the gracious indulgence of God. For, as I have said before, in the general foundation of this doctrine, that God may give grace without glory, is intelligible; but how he can admit a man to glory without grace is inconceivable. The very having of grace is a reward in itself. It is an ennobling of our nature, a setting us in our right station (the purity of the body is a pleasure, though a man has no hopes upon it to be preferred to a better condition), which may appear to us upon the banishment of Adam from paradise. Had there been any natural connection, he had not been dispossessed, supposing him to have faith infused into him at the time of the promulgation of the promise; or if afterwards, he would have had a re-entry, had there been a natural connection between a new nature and a state of glory.

(2.) Nor is there any meritorious connection between a regenerate state and glory, because there is no exact proportion between a new nature and eternal glory. The papists say, that before habitual grace a man cannot merit, but after it is infused by the Spirit of God into the soul, a merit does result from the dignity of the person brought into a state of grace. No such thing. Glory indeed is merited, but the merit results, not from the new nature, but from the new head, our Lord Jesus Christ. That righteousness whereby God is engaged to give us a crown of glory for a garland of grace, is not a commutative justice; as if grace were of equal value to glory, and heaven no more than a due compensation: 2 Tim. iv. 8, 'There is laid up for me a crown of righteousness, which the Lord, the righteous Judge, shall give me at that day.' But it is the veracity and faithfulness of God which is meant by righteousness there, and otherwhere in Scripture. It is a justice due to the promise, not to the nature of the grace, and due to the covenant made with Christ, which was, that he should have a seed to serve him

upon which compact our Saviour so peremptorily demands his people's being with him in glory: John xvii. 24, 'Father, I will that they also whom thou hast given me be with me where I am.' As much as to say, Father, I will not remit a tittle of that article, which is part of the covenant between thee and me; I will have that performed to the full. And it is observable, though he mentions their faith, and their keeping his word, in other parts of the chapter, as arguments for God to take notice of them, and preserve them, yet his desire of the state of glory he founds upon his will, which must be grounded upon some antecedent agreement, whereby he had a right to plead for it. So that it is from the faithfulness of God to his promise, and the full merit of Christ, and thereupon his fined resolution to have it performed, not from any meritorious dignity in the new nature itself. Grace only fits for glory, but does not merit it.

(3.) It is necessary by a fixed determination of God. Supposing that God could in his own nature, congruously admit of an unregenerate dead creature to a fruition of him in heaven, yet since he has decreed otherwise, and appointed other methods, God is now by his own free resolution under an immutable necessity not to admit him. As God having by a determinate counsel ordained the death of Christ as the medium to redemption, could not in our apprehensions afterwards appoint another way, because his counsel had pitched, not only upon the redemption of man, as the end, but the death of Christ as the means; and had there been a change, it must either be in the end or in the means. If in the end, and he would not have man redeemed, there had been an alteration in his love and kindness; if in the means, it must be either a worse or a better means; if a worse, and not so fit to effect redemption, it had still implied a change in his kindness; if a better means, it would argue a defect of wisdom in his first choice, that he did not foresee the best. By the like counsel and wisdom he has settled this of regeneration as the way to glory: 'Without holiness no man shall see the Lord,' Heb. xii. 14. Without a fixed and permanent holiness, which must be an holiness of nature, not only of action. Supposing any holiness in an action, without a new nature, it is yet but a transient holiness, and though it may make the action acceptable to God, yet it can never make the person that did it acceptable to him.

(4.) Regeneration is necessary in a way of aptitude and fitness for this state. A fitness in both subjects is necessary to the enjoyment of one another. Since therefore our happiness consists in an eternal fruition of God, and that naturally we are a mass and dunghill of putrefied corruption, there must be such a change as to make an agreement with that God whom to enjoy is our happiness; for all aptitude is a certain connection of the two terms whereby they may touch and receive each other. We cannot enjoy God in his ordinances without an holy nature, much less in heaven. As we are under the condemnation of the law by reason of our guilt, so we are under an unfitness for heaven by reason of our filth. We have a remote natural capacity for it, as we are creatures endued with rational faculties. But we have a moral unfitness, while we want a divine impression to make us suitable to it. Justification and adoption give us a right to the inheritance, but regeneration gives us a 'meetness to be partakers of the inheritance of the saints in light,' Col. i. 12. We are not meet for it while we are unholy, and while we are darkness, because it is an inheritance of saints, and an inheritance in light. As the body cannot be made glorious without a resurrection from a natural death, so neither can the soul, which is immortal, be made glorious without a resurrection from a spiritual death. Our corruptible bodies? 1 Cor. xv. 50, cannot possess an incorruptible kingdom unless made like to the glorious body of Christ, much less our souls, which are the chief subjects of communion with him in heaven. A depraved soul is as much unfit for a purified heaven as a corruptible body is for an incorruptible glory. Our Saviour ascended not into heaven to take possession of his glory till after his resurrection from death, neither can we enter into heaven till a resurrection from sin. As Jesus Christ became like unto us, that he might be a merciful and faithful high priest for us, Heb. ii. 17, 'It behoved him to be made like unto his brethren;' so it behoves us to be made like unto him, that we may be fit offerings in the hand of our high priest, to present to God, for him to take pleasure in. The father of the prodigal forgave him at the first meeting after his return, but before he admitted him into the pleasure of his house he took away his garments that smelt of draff, and put other robes upon him. God is said therefore 'to work us to this thing,' "katechradzesthai", polish, that we may be fit to be clothed upon with our heavenly house, 2 Cor. v. 5. If God be happy in his nature, man cannot be happy in a nature contrary to him; for we can never expect to enjoy a felicity in such a nature, which if God himself had, he could never be happy in himself. It is holiness in God which fits him to fill heaven and earth with the beams of his glory, and it is an holy nature in us, which makes us fit to receive him. As without holiness God could not be glorious in himself: Isa. vi. 8, 'Holy, holy, is the Lord of hosts: the whole earth is full of his glory;' so without holiness in our natures we could not be glorious with God. We are no more fit for heaven in a state of nature than a piece of putrefied flesh is fit to become a star. In heaven there are duties to be done, and privileges to be enjoyed. The work cannot be done, the reward cannot be received, without a new nature. The glorifying God, and enjoying him, is the glory of heaven. How can we do the one or receive the other without the change of our affections? Can God have a voluntary glory from his enemy, or can his enemy delight in the enjoyment of him?

[1.] Regeneration and the new nature is necessary to the duty of heaven. Eternity cannot free us from duty. Some duties are essential to the relation of a creature, some result only from this or that state of the creature. The alteration in the state changes the duty proper to that state; but no place, no state, can exempt a creature from those duties which are essential to him as a creature. It is impossible to conceive any relation, without some new debt or service. From every change in relations in the world there does arise some new duty which was not incumbent upon a man before. The relation which a regenerate man has to God here is the same which it is in heaven, but it is manifest there in an higher degree, and a choicer fruition. Thence therefore will arise, though not any new duty that we can conceive, yet fresher obligations to those services which are proper for that place. Without a change of nature it is not possible for any man (were he admitted thither) to perform the duties of heaven. Holy work is troublesome to a natural man here, and the more heavenly it was in itself, the more disgustful to corrupt nature. What was in a little measure holy was a drudgery upon earth; and what is in a greater measure holy cannot be a satisfaction in heaven to an old frame. There are some natural motives to some duties here, and our indigence takes part with them (as in that of prayer); but those of a more elevated strain, as love, and praise, and admirations of God, our natures are more averse to. What duty can be performed without a will? It is concluded by most, that the happiness of heaven consists as much, if not more, in the frame of the will, than in that of the understanding. If the will be not new framed, what capacity is there to perform the service requisite to that happy state? We must first be made just here before we can he made perfect above: Heb. xii. 23, 'Spirits of just men made perfect.' Just by an imputed righteousness, holy by an inherent righteousness, before they were transplanted to a state of perfection. Without a perfect frame none can perform the choice duties of heaven, and without righteousness here, we cannot be made perfect there.

Quest. What are the duties of heaven, that cannot be performed without a new nature?

Ans. First. Attendance on God. Some kind of service which we cannot understand in the state here below. The angels stand before God, and wait his commands; there is a pleasure of God which they do: Ps. ciii. 21, 'Ye ministers of his that do his pleasure.' There is a will of God done in heaven, as well as upon earth. There are acts of adoration performed by them; they cover their faces, Isa. vi.; they are commanded to worship the Lord Christ, Heb. i. 6. Their holiness fits them for their attendance, therefore called 'the holy angels.' It is against the nature of devils to perform such acts as those which the holiness of angels fits them for. Glorified souls shall be as the angels of God in heaven: Mat. xxii. 30, 'But are as the angels of God in heaven.' Equal to angels in their state, as they are angels in heaven; equal to angels in their work, as they are angels of God, attending on God, and ministering unto him, Dan. vii. 10; though what that ministry shall be is not easily known in the extent of it. Is it usual in this world to take up a person from under an hedge, and bring him to an immediate attendance on a prince, without cleansing him, and begetting other dispositions and behaviour in him by some choice education? God picks some out for an immediate attendance on him in heaven; but he sends his Spirit to be their tutor, to breed them up, and grace their deformed souls with beautiful features, and their ulcerous and cancerous spirits, with a sound complexion, that they may be meet to stand before him. When God calls any to do him service in a particular station in the word, he gives them another heart; so he did to Saul for the kingdom, 1 Sam. x. 9. Is there not much more necessity of it for an immediate service of God in heaven? A malefactor, by pardon, is in a capacity to come into the presence of a prince, and serve him at his table; but he is not in a fitness till his noisome garments, full of his prison vermin, be taken off. Can one that is neither pardoned nor purified, one with the guilt of rebellion upon him, and a nature of rebellion in him, be fit to stand before God?

Secondly, Contemplation of God is a work in heaven. There shall be a perfect knowledge; therefore a delightful speculation. The angels behold his face, Mat. xviii. 10, and that always. The saints shall see him as he is, 1 John iii. 2. It is not a stupid sight, but a gazing upon the face of this sun, with a refined and ravishing delight. For this work there must be,

First, A change of judgment. The eye must be restored. It is as possible for a blind eye to behold the sun, or a blear eye to stare in the face of it, without watering, as for a blind understanding to behold God; for it is not a being in the place of heaven, but having a faculty disposed, which does elevate us to the knowledge of him. Things that are corporal cannot know things that are spiritual. We cannot in this sensitive body view the face of an angel, and understand his nature; much less with a body of a total death, see the face of God, which is above all created beings, more than any spiritual creature is above sense. 'In heaven the saints shall know him, as they are known of him,' 1 Cor. xiii. 12, perfectly, as far as the capacity of a creature can extend. Has God any scales upon his eyes? Does he not know perfectly what he knows? So shall the glorified saints. But if a natural man were admitted into heaven, what prospect could he have with a blind understanding? As men under the gospel administrations cannot see the kingdom of God, even in the midst of it, without a new birth, so neither could they see the kingdom of God in the midst of heaven itself without a new frame, if not see it, much less enjoy it.

Secondly, There must be a change of will. Men like not to retain God in their knowledge, when he is represented to them in the dark, yet pleasant glass of nature, Rom. i. 28. The apostle there speaks it of the heathens, and the wisest of them, their philosophers, who, though pleased with the contemplation of nature, yet were not pleased with the contemplation of God in nature; much less will they like him, when he discovers himself clothed with the light of holiness as a garment. That vicious eye, which is too weak to behold with any delight the image of the sun in a glass, or a pail of water, will be much more too weak to gaze upon it in its brightness in the firmament. If there be no delight to know God here, what pleasure, what fitness can there be in the same frame to contemplate him above? Let me ask you, Have you any pleasure in the study of God? What is the reason, then, that in your retirements, when you have nothing to do, your thoughts are no more upon him? What is the reason that if any motion does offer to advise you to fix your thoughts upon him, you so soon shift it off as a troublesome companion, and some slight jolly thought is admitted with gladness into those embraces which the other courted? Can such a temper be fit for heaven, where nothing but thoughts of God run through the veins of glorified souls? If the discovery of God's glory in the gospel is accounted no better than folly by natural men, and therefore not received, 1 Cor. ii. 14, the manifestation of it above would meet with no better valuation of it, unless the temper both of judgment and will were changed. They are spiritually to be discerned here, and no less spiritually to be discerned above. The weak and waterish eye must be cured by some powerful medicine before it can stare upon the light of the sun, or delight itself in its glory.

Thirdly, Love is a duty in heaven. Love is a grace that shoots the gulf with us, and attends us not only to the suburbs, but into the very heart of heaven, when other graces conduct us only to the gates, and then take their leave of us, as having no business there. 'Charity never fails,' 1 Cor. xiii. 8. And, indeed, it is so essentially our duty in every place, that it is concluded that God cannot free us from the obligation of it, whilst we remain his creatures; because God being infinitely good, and therefore infinitely amiable and infinitely gracious to them, it would seem unrighteous, and inconsistent with supreme goodness, to forbid the creature an affection to that which is infinitely excellent, and a gratitude to its benefactor which can be paid only in love. Now, though we are bound to love God in the highest degree, yet every new mercy adds a fresh obligation to return our affection to him. So when we shall have the clearest beams of God's love darting upon us from heaven, we shall also have higher obligations to love him, both for his excellency, which shall be more visible, and his love, which shall be more sensible. Now, can the heart of a natural man cling about God? Can it forget its father's house, and be wholly taken up with the Creator's excellency? Can he that loved pleasures more than God in the world, 2 Tim. iii. 4, love God more than pleasures in heaven, without an alteration of his soul? No. The heart must be first circumcised by God, before we can love God with all our heart, Dent. xxx. 6. If we will not be subject to the law of God here, how can we be subject to the love of God, which is the law of heaven? How can we cleave to God without love, or relish him without delight? No man in a natural estate could stay in heaven, because he does not love the person whose presence only makes it heaven. How can there be a conformity to God in affection, without a conformity to his holiness? A choiceness of love, with a perverseness of will; a supremacy of delight, without a rectitude of heart; a love of God, without a loathing of sin; a fervency of love, with a violence of lust: all these are contradictions. He that has a hatred of God, cannot perform the main duty of heaven; and therefore what should he do there?

Fourthly, Praise is a service in heaven. If a pure angel be not sufficient for so elevated a duty, how unfit then is a drossy soul? What is the angels' note, Holy, holy, holy, Lord God,' Isa. vi. 3, can never be a natural man's; for how can he possibly praise that which he hates? What is the note of glorified saints? It is Hallelujah, Rev. xix. 1, 'Salvation, and glory, and honour, and power unto the Lord our God.' And again they said, Hallelujah, ver. 3. 'Hallelujah, for the Lord God Omnipotent reigns,' ver. 6. Nothing but hallelujah four times, ver. 1, 3, 4, 6. How can that heart frame an hallelujah, that is stuffed with jealousies of him? How can he exalt the honour of God, who was always pleased with the violations of it? How can he rejoice at the Lord's reigning, that would not have one lust subdued by his power? How can a natural man, as natural, ever be wound up to a height fit for such strains, since 'out of the abundance of the heart, the mouth speaks'? The tongue can never be framed to praise while the heart is evil. Our blessed Saviour must be glorified in us, before he can be glorified by us, 2 Thes. i. 10, 12. If a man in a mere natural state be unfit for this heavenly work, how unfit are then their tongues to sound his praise, which are always filled with reproaches of God? And how can their ears endure to hear it from others, which were never offended with the blasphemies of him? They could never rejoice in this heavenly concert were they admitted. Nay, their enmity to the work would not permit their stay. The smoke of pure incense is fitter rather to drive a swine out of the room than to invite his continuance.

[2.] The new birth is necessary, as to the duty, so to the reward of heaven. As the reward is exceeding glorious, the preparation thereto must be exceeding gracious. The rewards of heaven are something incorporated with us, inlaid in the very frame of our souls, and cannot be conceived enjoyable without a change in the nature of the subject. Man was first formed before he was brought into the garden of Eden, or pleasure: Gen. ii. 8, There he 'put the man whom he had formed.' Man must be new-formed before he be brought into that place, which is the anti-type of Eden, the place of eternal and spiritual pleasure. A natural man can no more relish the rewards of heaven, than a dead carcass can esteem a crown and a purple robe, or be delighted with the true pleasure of heaven, than a swine, that loves to wallow in the mire, can be delighted with a bed of roses. A disorder in nature is a prohibition to all happiness belonging to that nature; a distempered body, under the fury of a disease, can find no delight in the pleasures of the healthful; a wicked man, with a troubled and foaming sea of sin and lust in his mind, Isa. lvii. 20, would find no more rest in heaven than a man with his disjointed members upon a rack can in the beauty of a picture. We must be spiritually minded before we can have either life or peace, Rom. viii. 6. Righteousness in the soul is the necessary qualification for the peace and joy in the kingdom of God: Rom. xiv. 17, 'The kingdom of God is not meat and drink; but righteousness, and peace, and joy in the Holy Ghost.' While malice remains in the devil's nature, were he admitted into heaven he would receive a torment instead of a content. A wicked man would meet with hell in the midst of heaven as long as he carries his own rack within him, boiling and raging lusts in his heart, which can receive no contentment without objects suitable to them, let the place be what it will. Heaven, indeed, is not only a place, but a nature; and it is a contradiction to think that any can be happy with a nature contrary to the very essence of happiness.

The pleasure and reward of heaven is,

First, A perfect likeness to God and Christ. This is the great privilege of heaven, which the apostle, in the midst of his ignorance of other particulars, resolves upon as certain as that which results from regeneration, and being the sons of God, and is the full preparation for the beatific vision: 1 John iii. 2, 'Now we are the sons of God; and it does not yet appear, what we shall be: but we know that, when he shall appear, we shall be like him; for we shall see him as he is.' He seems to intimate this, that we can never be like him when he does appear, unless we be now, while we are here, the sons of God, nor ever be admitted to a sight of him. As Christ presented himself without spot to God, when he laid the foundation of our redemption, so he presents his people 'without blemish to God' when he lays the top-stone of it in our glorification, Eph. v. 27. Now as we cannot be like to Christ in our walk here without a new birth, neither can we without it be like to Christ in glory hereafter. It is not the place makes us like to God, but there must be a likeness to God to make the place pleasant to us. When once the angels had corrupted their nature, the short stay they made in heaven did neither please them nor reform them. And when Satan appeared before God, among the angels, Job i. 6, neither God's presence nor his speaking to him did anywise better him; he came a devil, and he went away so, without any pleasure in the place or presence, but by the permission of God, to wreak his malice on holy Job. An unlikeness to God is the misery of the creature. It is therefore impossible, whilst the soul remains in that state, that it can arrive at blessedness, because it is a contradiction to think a felicity can be enjoyed in a contrariety to and separation from the fountain of it: Ps. lxxiii. 27, 'Lo, they that are far from thee shall perish.' It is by faith, beholding the glory of the Lord in the glass of the gospel here, that we must be 'transformed into his image,' before we can be 'changed into his glory,' 2 Cor. iv. 18. And we cannot be like God by holy actions only, though we had performed as many of them as all the holy men in the world ever did as to the matter of them, abstracted from the principle and end; and the reason is, because God is not only holy in his actions, but holy in his nature; and, therefore, we must not only have actions materially good, but a holy nature suitable to the holiness of God, otherwise we neither are, nor never can, be like him.

Secondly, The fruition of God is a privilege of heaven, which necessarily follows this likeness. God is the eternal portion of glorified souls, upon which they live. He is the strength of their hearts, Ps. lxxiii. 25, 26. There is none but God in heaven is the chief object of their love and delight. The presence of God makes 'the fullness of joy,' Ps. xvi. 11. His favour and the light of his glorious countenance constitutes heaven and happiness; not the place, but the countenance. God's frown kindles hell, and his smile renders any place an heaven. Now an old nature cannot have a good look from God; for since he is infinitely holy, he must hate unholiness; infinitely true, he must hate falsity. As it is impossible a man can love truth and falsity, righteousness and unrighteousness, as such, at one and the same time, in an intense degree, therefore an impure nature cannot be happy unless God be mutable. God cannot smile on the old Adam unless he hate himself. What satisfaction can such an one possibly have in God's presence? How can he savour the society of God that never loved it? Do we naturally love any warm mention of God? Have we not a stony deadness to any heavenly motion that falls upon us? A mighty quickness to receive sinful motions in that which we love? Do not our countenances fall, and our delight take wings to itself and fly away at any lively appearance of God? If we have such an enmity to his law, which is but a transcript of his holiness, much greater must our enmity be to the original copy. Hence in Scripture men are said to 'refuse his law,' Ps. lxxviii. 10; to 'forsake his law,' Ps. cxix. 53; to be 'far from his law,' Ps. cxix. 150. Darkness does not more naturally vanish at the appearance of the sun, than an old nature will fly away from the glory and brightness of God. A mass of black darkness and an immense sphere of light may as soon be espoused together, as a friendly amity be struck up between God and an unrenewed man. God is light without darkness, 1 John i. 5; man is darkness itself, as if nothing else entered into the composition of his corrupt nature, Eph. v. 8. If there be therefore a disagreement, contrariety, and unwillingness on both sides, how can any pleasing correspondence be effected? If God should bring a man with his corrupt nature into local heaven, God could not please himself in it, nor such an one delight himself in God, no more than a swine can be pleased with the presence of an angel, or a mole sport itself with the beauty of flowers, or a vitiated eye rejoice at the brightness of light. We must really make God such an one as we shape him in our natural fancy, and like to us, before we can take any pleasure in converse with him. Our nature, therefore, must be changed before we can please him, or be satisfied in him. His presence else will cause fear, while our sinful state remains, an affection inconsistent with happiness.

Thirdly, The company of the saints is an adjunct of that happiness in heaven. A sitting down with Abraham, Isaac, and Jacob in the kingdom of heaven, Mat. viii. 11, in a festival converse, is a part of that felicity. The coming to be with an 'innumerable company of angels, with the general assembly, and church of the firstborn,' is not the least thing in the composition of this happiness, Heb. xii. 22, 23. What joy is that man capable of which should be surrounded with company he has the greatest disaffection to, where he could not meet with any one person without the holy quality he has an antipathy against? A natural man never loved holiness, as holiness, here. The more beautiful the image of God was in any, the more burdensome was their company; the more degrees any good man wanted of perfection in righteousness, the more tolerable was a familiarity with him. If holiness in others, in a lower degree, were disaffected by you, how can you bear the perfection of it? If the mixed and dark goodness in renewed men, which was but a weak flash of the glory of heaven, were unwelcome, how will you be able to endure the lustre of it? Again, glorified saints could not have the least converse with such an one? If carnal nature were a trouble to them here, when they had many relics of corruption, much more must it be above, if they were admitted into that place of glory, because the more holy any creature is, the more it hates that which is contrary to that holiness; the more settled we are in anything, the more we loathe that which is opposite to it; all the folly in their hearts here done away, and the disagreeing principle perfected in the blessed. There must, therefore, be a change in them, to take pleasure in you, or a change in you, to take pleasure in them. They must return to the frame of old Adam, and put off the renewed image of God, before they can delight in you; or you must come up to the frame of the new Adam, and be new created after the same image, before you can delight in them. The truth is, supposing a man admitted into the heavenly place with an old nature, he could not continue there; for the saints must either leave heaven, or he must. Light and darkness cannot agree; what makes the one happy, cannot beatify the other. Saints shall not leave it, because it is their inheritance, it was prepared for them, and they for it; a natural man must, because it was never prepared for him, nor he fitted for it.

Fourthly, Spiritual delights inconceivable are in that state, which, without a new and heavenly nature, it is impossible to relish. 'In the light of God they see light,' and they 'drink of the rivers of God's pleasures,' and are 'satisfied with the fatness of his house,' Ps. xxxvi. 8, 9. Now, is it a fleshly fatness? Are the pleasures of God carnal or spiritual? What is God's pleasure shall be the pleasure of glorified souls. How can the sordid old temper be fit for spiritual delights? Flesh can never savour but the things of the flesh; another palate is necessary to relish the things of the spirit: Rom. viii. 5, 'They that are after the flesh do mind the things of the flesh, but they that are after the spirit the things of the spirit;' "fronousin" signifies to savour or relish. There must be a transformation by the renewing of the mind, Rom. xii. 2, which is the palate of the soul, before we can know what the will of God is, or taste what the pleasures of God are; without it we can no more relish the pleasures of God than we can know his will. All satisfaction does not result from the intrinsic excellency of the object, or the beauty of a place, or a power in anything to affect us, but from a faculty rightly disposed to the object, and a congruity and agreement between that and the understanding, and between that and the will. Brutes cannot be delighted with intellectual pleasures, because they want a faculty, nor fools, because they want a right disposition of that faculty. Purity of heart only gives us a relish of the purity of pleasure: Tit. i. 15, 'To the pure all things are pure; but unto them that are defiled and unbelieving, is nothing pure.' An ill humour on the palate tinctures the meat, and embitters that which was sweet in itself. It must be freed from that vicious juice before it can relish the sweetness of food. Natural men, because of the impurity of their natures, savour not those spiritual delights which the word, and prayer, and other holy duties afford in themselves. What fitness, then, is there in this state for the delights of heaven, which are as much superior to those delights in duties as the sun does surmount a star in brightness? The best unregenerate man is sunk in sense, swallowed up in sense; and what suitableness can there be between a spiritual delight and a sensual frame? True pleasures and contrary desires can never abide together. A carnal man has no apprehensions of spiritual delights but by the measures of animal pleasures. And if there be no conception of them in the understanding, what motion to them can there be in the will, or what fitness for them in the affection? Without a new nature, a new frame, we are no more able to understand or enjoy the pleasures of heaven, than a bat is to take pleasure in a mathematician's lines or a philosopher's books. It is not conceivable how God can make any man happy against his will, because all pleasure consists in the agreeableness of the will to the object. The whole scheme of heaven must be changed to make such men happy that have not tempers suited to its present state. The bright hangings of heaven must be taken down and others put in their place to please a vicious nature.

Use. If regeneration be absolutely necessary to a gospel state, and the enjoyment of eternal glory in heaven, then it informs us,

1. How much the nature of man is depraved; for otherwise there were no need of his being born again, and no reason could be imagined why our blessed Saviour should so pressingly urge the necessity of it, If man's nature were according to his original frame, it would please God, because it was of his own creation. But we are flesh by our natural birth, and therefore to be happy we must be spiritual by a second birth. It is not a new mending, a new repairing and patching, but a new birth. We are by sin as distant from God and grace, as death from life, as nothing from being. It is not a death in appearance, but a certain death. God foretold it to Adam: Gen. ii. 17, 'But of the tree of the knowledge of good and evil, thou shalt not eat of it; for in the day thou eatest thereof, thou shalt surely die,' "mot tamut". I suppose there is nothing here of a corporal death meant (as I have said before), but a death of his integrity and righteous nature, upon this act of disobedience; and the reason is because a temporal death did not ensue presently. And God uses to be punctual when he fixed a time to any threatening, as here he did, in the day, at that very time thou shalt die. Had it been meant of a temporal death, he had died at

that instant. When God threatened Pharaoh, tomorrow such and such a plague shall come, it was certainly so. The destruction of Nineveh in forty days had been too, had they not repented. When he promised and mercy or deliverance at such a time, it was certainly performed: the very day, at the end of the time appointed, the Israelites came out of Egypt, Exod. xii. 41. And though God threatened Hezekiah with death, and bids him set his house in order, yet he fixed no time, Isa. xxxviii. 1. Besides, a temporal death was not necessary to his punishment; God might have flung both body and soul away together into hell. Besides, a temporal death, or death of the body, was fixed after the promise of the seed, Gen. iii. 12, as a punishment superadded upon his sin, as well as the rest, of his eating his bread in the sweat of his brows, and the pain of women's conception and travail, which were to put him in mind of his sin in his redeemed state; therefore I question whether a temporal death, or an obnoxiousness to it, were at all meant there, but a spiritual death, the death of his righteous nature. It is a certain death, a mighty deprivation, a loss of a noble frame, a beautiful rectitude. How may we cry, as the prophet in another case: Isa. xiv. 12, 'How art thou fallen from heaven, O Lucifer, son of the morning! how art thou cut down to the ground!' How is our beauty not only defaced, but changed into deformity? How dreadfully are we fallen, not only to lame ourselves, but dead ourselves, that we cannot rise again, as a man fallen may! We are so inconceivably changed from what we were, that we cannot be recovered without a new make, without a new birth. Oh that we had a true and sensible prospect of this! Give me leave to say that though the fell be the cause of all our misery, yet the true consideration and sense of it is the first step to all our happiness. And we cannot take so full a view of it in the extent of the nature of it, as in the consideration of this doctrine, viz. The necessity of regeneration.

2. If regeneration be so necessary, then how much to be lamented is the ignorance of this doctrine in the world? And strange and sad it is that it should be so little considered. The common talk is observing God and reforming the life, but who of a thousand speaks of the necessity of a new nature? It is a sad case that, when a doctrine is so clear, men should be so stupid and deludingly damn themselves; that they should be so sottishly ignorant of this who have Bibles in their hands and houses, yet not understand this, which is the great purpose for which God even sent the Scripture among the sons of men. It is a shame not to have the knowledge of this great and necessary truth. As the apostle in another case: 1 Cor. xv. 24, 'Some have not the knowledge of God, I speak it to your shame.' How strange and uncouth does this doctrine sound in the ears of the carnal world, which wonder at it, as Nicodemus did at our Saviour's proposal, and think all our discourses of it an heap of enthusiastic nonsense! It is as if we should speak parables, as if you should talk of astronomy to the natural fool, or read divinity in Arabic to a man who understands only his native language. How little sensible is the world of the necessity of this work! They expect Christ should change their misery into glory, without changing their hearts and fitting their spirits for it, which will never be. They think it enough for them that Christ was conceived in the womb of the virgin, without being formed again in their souls, as the poor Jews at this day expect a Messiah, not to alter the frame of their souls, but the frame of the world; not to subdue their spirits, but to conquer the nations to be their vassals. How should this stupidity of men be a matter of lamentation to us!

3. If regeneration be so absolutely necessary, how should Christian parents endeavour all they can to have their children regenerate? There is no necessity they should have great estates, and live bravely in the world; but there is a necessity, a great necessity, they should be new creatures, and live spiritually. In leaving the one to your children, you leave them but earth; in leaving the other, you convey heaven to them. There is an obligation upon you, their old polluted nature was derived from you by carnal generation; make them amends by endeavouring to derive grace to them by spiritual instruction; you made them children of wrath, why will you not endeavour to make them children of God and heirs of heaven? Education of itself will not produce this noble work, nor the bare hearing of the word, or any outward means whatsoever, by their own strength; yet the Spirit does often bless them, and very much, and I doubt not but a great number that are regenerate had the first seeds sown in them by a religions education. And I have made this observation in many. Timothy had a religious education both by his mother and grandmother, though this did not renew him, for Paul, by the preaching of the gospel, was the instrument of that he calls him 'his own son in the faith,' 1 Tim. i. 2, yet no question his religious instructions from his parents did much facilitate this work. Use all endeavour therefore, to convince them of the necessity of a new birth, be earnest with them till you see it produced, that they may not curse you for being the instruments of their beings, but bless you for being the instruments of their spiritual life.

4. This doctrine acquaints us with the insufficiency of everything else without this to enable us to enter into the kingdom of God.

(1.) Great knowledge is not sufficient. Natural knowledge is not. All the wisdom of Solomon in a man, though it may enable him to take an exact measure of nature from the highest star to the meanest insect, does no more fit him for heaven than the stone in the head of a toad expels his venomous nature. We have more relics of Adam's nature in knowledge than we have in righteousness. To be a philosopher, physician, or statesman, is not essential to happiness in this world, much less can it prepare a man for the happiness of another. But grace is as essential to it as natural heat and radical moisture are to the life of a man. Jesus Christ came not to make us scholars in naturals, but to endue us with such a knowledge as is in order to eternal happiness, and with such a renewing principle as might make us capable of heaven. Knowledge and wisdom are some of the choicest flowers in nature's garden; but it will be a small advantage to descend to hell with our brains full of wit and sophistry. One saving cry, from a new born infant soul is of more value than the knowledge of all philosophers. Spiritual knowledge is not, that is, the knowledge of spiritual doctrines, the knowledge of Scripture itself. Nicodemus had a good stock of this; he understood the letter of the Scripture, was well read in all the parts of the law; he was thought fit to be one of the great Sanhedrin. Something else was requisite besides this; a new birth was still wasting. What if we understood the mind of the Spirit of God in every verse in the Bible; were able to discourse profoundly of the great mysteries of the gospel; had the gift of prophecy, and knowledge of things to come, had the interpretation of the whole book of the Revelation writ in our minds; what will all this avail us? An evangelical head will be but drier fuel for eternal burning, without an evangelical impression upon the heart and the badge of a new nature. Men may prophesy in Christ's name, in his name cast devils out of bodies, and devils of errors out of men's brains, yet not be regarded by Christ; but he says to them, 'I never knew you, depart from me ye that work iniquity,' Mat. vii. 22, 23. If they had had this mark and gospel impression, our Lord would have known them. Christ in heaven would have owned himself formed in the heart; he could not have been ignorant of his own nature and offspring.

Well then, a man may have all the learning of Christians and heathens stored up in his head, and not the least stamp of it in his heart; he may be wise in knowledge, and a fool in improvement. A heap and pack of knowledge is not wisdom among men, without an application of that knowledge to particular exigencies and usefulness.

(2.) Outward reformation is not sufficient. Regeneration is never without reformation of life; but this may be without that. We may be outward Christians without an inward principle, though we can never be inward Christians without an outward holiness. The new birth is properly an internal work, and shows itself externally; as the heat of the heart and vital parts will evidence itself in outward motions. 'The king's daughter is all glorious within' as well as without, Ps. xlv. 13. What a vanity would it be to boast of freedom from other diseases, if you have the plague upon thee? What a poor comfort is it to brag of thy being without gross immoralities, whilst the plague of thy nature remains uncured? Outward reformation only (though of excellent use) is but a new appearance, not a new creature, a change of life, not of the heart; whereas this work we discourse of is a new birth in the understanding and will; it begins at the spirit and descends from thence to the body, 1 Thess. v. 23; it is a sanctification in spirit, soul, and then body. Can that which can be no evidence to us in self-examination, be of itself sufficient to waft us to heaven? If you retire to take a view of yourselves whether you belong to God, will you judge by your outward actions or inward frame? There is no characteristical difference in any external action between a true Christian and an hypocrite. That, therefore, which is not a sufficient evidence to us of a right to happiness, cannot be a sufficient preparation of ourselves for it.

This reformation may proceed either,

[1.] From force and fear. Such a reformation is from impediments, not from inclination. The cutting a bird's wings takes not away its propensity to fly, but its ability; the cutting the claws of a lion, or pulling out his teeth, changes not his lionish nature. Fear restrained Herod from putting John to death, when his will was inclined to the act, Matt. xiv. 5. Fear may pare the nails of sin, grace only can hinder the growth and take away its life. This does but only stop the streams, not choke the fountain.

Or, [2.] from sense of outward interest. It may be a rational abstinence from those sordid pleasures which debase a man's esteem and prey upon his reputation; and in the mean time his inward lusts may triumph, while outward appearances are stopped. Such a splendid life may consist with those inward vermin, more contrary to the pure nature of God, and as inconsistent with a man's happiness. The river which ran in open view, may sink and run as fiercely through subterranean caverns. Men may cast out one gross devil to make way for seven more spiritual ones. The interest which restrains outward acts will not restrain inward lusts.

Well then, an outward reformation without an inward grace, can no more rectify nature, than an abstinence from luxury can cure a disease a man has contracted through intemperance, without some other physic to pluck up the root of the distemper. Outward applications of salves and ointments will do little good in a fever, unless the spring of the disease be altered, and a new crasis wrought in the blood. All outward acts are but 'bodily exercise, which profit little,' 1 Tim. it. 3. Outward reformation does but sweeten the conversation, but does not purge the man. He only is a vessel unto honour who has purged himself from these things: 2 Tim. ii. 21, 'If a man therefore purge himself from those, he shall be a vessel unto honour.' Outward reformation only, it is a cleansing of our life, but not ourselves. Self-nature must be purged.

(3.) Morality is not sufficient. By morality, I mean not only an outward reformation, but some love to moral virtue, as the heathens had, raised upon the thoughts of the excellency of it. Nicodemus was a moral man; he had some affection to Christ upon the consideration of his miracles; he had never else ventured to come to him so much as by night. He had no blot upon his conversation, he had desires to be instructed. This was more than a bare abstinence from sin, yet notwithstanding, besides those moral qualifications, he must have a new birth before he can see the kingdom of God. Men may do much good, be very useful to others in their generation, yet be in the very bottom of unregeneracy. A healing witch, as well as a hurting one, is the devil's client, and in covenant with him. There is not so great a difference between the highest degree of glory in heaven and the lowest degree of grace on earth, as there is between the lowest degree of saving grace and the highest degree of natural excellency, because the difference between these is specific, as between a rational and irrational creature; the difference between the other is only in degree, as between an infant and a man. It is one thing to have a love to moral virtue, another thing to have a love to God in it, one thing to move for self, and another thing to move for the glory of the Creator; one thing to be animated by reason, and another thing to be inspired by the Holy Ghost. What can a moral honesty profit that man who values the world's dung above the Creator's glory? What though he be honest and useful to his neighbours, must his affection to God be measured by his honesty among men? The great business is from what principle it flows. What if he does good to others whilst he does his Creator wrong by fostering any one thing in his heart above him? Can his goodness to others make a compensation for his disesteem of God? The bravest man in the whole world, who has no other descent than from Adam, must have a new quality put into his heart before he can be happy; for if a new birth be necessary, all endowments below it are to no purpose for the attainment of that state for which it is intended. Whatsoever is of the old Adam in us, though it be a beautiful flower, must wither and die: 1 Peter i. 28, 24, 'For all flesh is as grass, and the glory of man as the flower of grass, the grass withers, and the flower thereof fades away.' The apostle sets in opposition the incorruptible seed whereby they were born, and the fairer flowers in nature's garden. The best thing which a man glories in is a flower, but withering; it is a glory, but the glory of the flesh; it has no lustre in the sight of God; it is not a flower to be set in heaven. It is only the word of God, and the impressions made on us by that word, which endure for ever. As herbs can not grow without partaking of the natural influence and beams of the sun, so nothing stands and flourishes but what partakes of the nature and spirit of Christ. Nay, it is so far from being sufficient, that it is a great hindrance of regeneration, without the overpowering grace of God, because it is the glory of a man; that is, that wherein a man glories. Men are apt to rest upon their morals without reflecting upon their naturals. They see no spots in their lives, and therefore will not believe there are any in their hearts. They are so taken up, with the pharisee, their proud thoughts of their being above others, that they never think how much they have inwardly of the publican in coming short of the glory of God. Unregenerate morality, therefore, is not sufficient. The heart must be changed before moral virtues can commence graces. When this is once done, what were moral before become divine, as having a new principle to quicken them, and a new end to direct them.

(4.) Religious professions are not sufficient. Can you, upon a serious consideration, conclude that this only is the import of all those scriptures which speak of being born of God, raised from a death in sin, quickened and led by the Spirit, created in righteousness and true holiness? Are not these things, in the very manner of speaking them, elevated above any mere profession, which may be declared to the world without any such work, which is the evident intendment of those scriptures? It is not the naming the name of Christ, but the departing from iniquity; a departing from it in our nature as well as in our actions, that is the badge whereby the Lord knows who are his: 2 Tim. ii. 19, 'The Lord knows who are his: and let every one that names the name of Christ depart from iniquity.' Religious profession only is but a form, a figure, a shape of godliness: a picture made by art, without life and power, and an enlivened faculty, and a divine principle whence it should proceed; it is but a name of life at best under a state of death: Rev. iii. 1, 'Thou hast a name that thou livest, and art dead.' Professions without a new nature, are no more the things God requires of us, than sacrifices under the law without a broken heart. It is not a following our Saviour in profession, but in regeneration, which gives the apostles a title to that promise of sitting upon his throne in glory: Mat. xix. 28, 'Ye that have followed me in regeneration, ye shall sit upon twelve thrones, judging the twelve tribes of Israel.' Judas had followed Christ till that time, and after, in a profession, but not in the regeneration, not from a regenerated principle.

(5.) Multitudes of external religious duties and privileges are not sufficient. Men are very apt to place their security here. It was the great labour of the prophet Isaiah to bring the Jews, in his time, off from them. God does not require attendance on ordinances as the ultimate end, but as means to the beginning and promoting a new birth: Isa. xi. 16, 'To what purpose is the multitude of your sacrifices to me? Wash ye, make ye clean.' The resting in these is the manifest destruction of men's souls, when thousands of sacrifices to God cannot be acceptable without a new nature. We naturally affect an easy religion; and outward acts of worship, especially under the gospel, have no great difficulty in them. Men would rather be at great expense of sacrificing, than crucify one beloved sin, and cringe a thousand times before the cross of Christ, than nail one corruption to it. How easy a work were it to get to heaven, if nothing else were required but to be a member of the Christian visible church? Circumcision was a privilege, but it availed nothing without a new creature, Gal. v. 6. There was another circumcision made without hands, the work of God, that was required, Col. ii. 11; a new creature, without which outward circumcision signified nothing. The practice of some duties may stand with an inward hatred of them, as the abstinence from some sins may stand with an inward love to them. Outward worship is but a carcass, when the soul is not conformed to God, the object of worship, and does not attain an union to, and communion with God, which is the end of worship. What are all acts of worship without a nature suitable to the God we approach unto in them? Judge not, therefore, of your state by any external actions; no outward act, but unregenerated persons may do, yea, they may express much zeal in them. They may have their bodies as martyrs consumed by flames, without having their corruption consumed by grace; a stinking breath may make as good music to the ear in a pipe as a sound one. There is something more necessary than a bare performance of duties.

(6.) Nay, more, convictions are not sufficient. Nicodemus was startled by our Saviour's miracles, believes him to be a prophet sent by God, acknowledges that God was with him, John iii. 2, yet still the necessary qualification of a new birth was wanting. Your spirits may be torn in pieces by terror, the heart of stone may be rent asunder, and yet no heart of flesh appear; the ground may be ploughed, yet not sown. Sensuality and lust may be kept under by a spirit of bondage, when it is not cast out by a spirit of adoption; the sun may scorch you, and not enliven you; the knowledge of the foulness of sin, and the fierceness of wrath, is the work of the Spirit in the law; the new birth is the work of the Spirit in the gospel, the stone may be cut and hewed by the law, and yet never polished by the gospel, never brought into covenant: Hosea vi. 5, 7, 'I have hewed them by my prophets, but they like men have transgressed the covenant.' It is not then great knowledge, fair-coloured fruit, oil in the lamp of life, loud professions, glittering services, or tearing convictions, which are this badge whereby Christ knows his own from all the world besides: all these will be answered, 'I know you not.' Is it not, then, a worthy stork, and high time to get that new nature, whereby God will know thee to belong to him? Professions may be false, outward reformation may be but as a painted sepulchre: knowledge only elevates the understanding, but as our communion lies in the acts of the will, there must be some work upon that to fit us for our great happiness. If these things are not sufficient, then profane men cannot expect heaven by the way of hell.

Use 2. If regeneration be so absolutely necessary to salvation, how miserable is the condition of every unregenerate man! What a miserable case is it, that sinners should dream on in their delusions till everlasting burnings confute their fancies, and turn their hopes into dreadful despair. Oh, how do most men live as if this doctrine were a mere falsity, and act as if they would take heaven by the violence of their lusts, not by the industry of grace? Know you not that an unrighteous nature shall not inherit the kingdom of God? 1 Cor. vi. 9, 'Know you not that the unrighteous shall not inherit the kingdom of God? be not deceived,' &c. Is it possible you should be ignorant of that which stares you in the face in every page in the Bible? If you know not this you know nothing. Be not deceived. Nothing is no natural as heart-deceit and presumptuous confidence. The apostle else would not have spoken of it with such an emphasis, but that he knew how apt men are to delude themselves with hopes of mercy in a state of sin. Self-flattery is one of the strongest branches which grows upon the pride of nature. How vain is it to fancy to yourselves a fitness for heaven, while there are only preparations for hell? Whence should such imaginations arise? Not from God; it is contrary to all his professed declarations. Is it from yourselves? What reason have you to believe your fancies in spiritual things, who are so often mistaken in temporal? Is it from the devil? What reason have you to believe your greatest enemy? If this work be brought, he has for ever lost you. It is he that cherishes such notions, for he has no pleasure to undo his kingdom, and lose his subjects. Never did any man use so much diligence to get a new nature as the devil does to hinder him.

Will you seriously consider,

1. It is highly irrational to expect security and glory in an unregenerate state. Is it for us to separate those things which God has joined, flesh and destruction, a new birth and a kingdom? That which does naturally tend to hell can never conduct us to heaven. Can the old nature, which frames a fit subject for eternal vengeance, ever fashion it to be a vessel of eternal glory? There is as great a tendency in the old nature to hell as there is of a stone or lead to the earth. If men may be saved in their unregeneracy,

(1.) God must be false to himself. False he must be to his truth, false to holiness, false to his Son, false to the whole tenor of the gospel. God must change the covenant of grace, blot out all his threatenings in Scripture, give the lie to all his declarations in the word, proclaim himself unwise in all his administrations, if ever such a man be happy; and is it not a damnable conceit, and a provoking wish, to desire that God should belie himself to befriend us? There must be a new gospel before any can be saved without a new nature. This cannot be. Must God change his law, or we our lusts? God has settled and declared a decree, that none that are not born again shall enter into the kingdom of God. His decree stands irreversible, the change must necessarily therefore be on our side.

(2.) As far as I can understand, God must put himself out of heaven before that such a man can come thither. There can be no pleasure on either side with unsuitableness. If God be absent from heaven, as to his glorious presence, how can there be happiness? He loves his own righteousness better than to endure such men's presence, and they love their unrighteousness so much as not to bear his. No man cares for coming into a place which is possessed by one that he hates; they can have no pleasure to be in a heaven with God, who were delighted to be in a world without him, Eph. ii. 12.

(3.) Jesus Christ must be a liar, and the gospel false, if ever there be a heaven enjoyed by an old nature. He has asserted it, that is truth itself; and is it not a madness to imagine a possibility of coming thither in spite of him? You may upon better grounds hope to be crowned monarch of the whole world tomorrow, than to enter into heaven without being born again. Christ values his truth, though he did not his life, above our souls, and his word will stand firm against all presumptuous confidence whatsoever.

(4.) Suppose God should reverse his gospel (which cannot be), and declare another, I cannot see how the ease would be mended, for what gospel can God frame, with a salvo to his own honour, without the creatures being righteous to enjoy the benefit of it? Must God conform himself to the will of our lusts? Must he cast his holiness into the depths of the sea? Must he paint himself black to agree with our hue? as the Negroes picture him of their own colour. In a word, must God cease to be God that you may cease to be miserable? To desire happiness without a new nature shows a contempt of God, since it is to desire it on terms on which it is dishonourable for God to give it.

Well then, this doctrine is so certainly true, that if an angel from heaven should declare the contrary he ought not to be believed: Gal. i. 8, 'Let him be accursed;' that is, he would be more a devil than an angel, and it could be an accursed doctrine. He must found his doctrine upon another gospel, and a gospel printed in hell, but impossible to hare an imprimatur from heaven. Is it possible, then, for any man, after such an assertion of our Saviour, to live under the hearing of the Christian doctrine, and fancy a heavenly glory belonging to him without a heavenly nature?

2. As it is highly irrational, so it is highly sinful to lie in an unrenewed state. To continue in it after the declaration of God's holiness, in so eminent a manner, in the death of his Son, is a high approbation of unrighteousness, and a contempt of his infinite purity; for since he has shown himself a hater of sin, and the old nature of Adam in the death of the Redeemer, more than he could any other; the fostering the old nature in us is a valuing that which God has manifested his hatred of, and a slighting all the expressions of his love. It draws a greater guilt upon our persons than Adam did by his fall upon our natures: John xv. 22, 'If I had not come and spoken to them, then had not had sin.' If I had not told them those things, and preach heavenly doctrine to them, their sin had been as it were a petty larceny, in comparison of what it is now, a treason against my Father's crown and dignity; 'but now they have hated me and my Father'.

3. Hence it follows that such a man's condition must be exceeding miserable. Those that 'have a part in the first resurrection,' on them it is said 'the second death shall have no power,' Rev. xx. 6; whether he means the resurrection of Christ, or the spiritual resurrection of the soul. The second death then shall have power over them that have no part in the first resurrection.

(1.) Such are peculiarly miserable. Such a man had better have been any other creature,--a toad, a serpent, a beetle, liable to be trod to death by the next comer,--than have been a man, and live and die with a serpentine nature, and without renewing grace, would be glad one day to chance states with them; and it had been better to have been born in the darkest part of America than in England, and better to have lived in the blindest corner in England than in London, where he has heard so much and so often of the necessity of the new birth, and yet cherished an old nature. It is an astonishing madness that. Better never to have been born a man than not be a real Christian, which he cannot be without this new birth, this necessary regeneration; better never to have entered by the door of baptism into the Christian society, than not have a nature answerable to the baptismal intendment. There is not the meanest beggar that creeps in the street, the most ulcerous Lazarus that lies at the door, but if renewed is infinitely happier than any one unrenewed can be with all worldly felicity.

(2.) Such are unavoidably miserable. The mercy of God can never make you happy against his truth, the righteousness of God can never do it without the necessary qualification. Is it just with God to give his worst enemies the same reward of glory with his choicest friends; to those that never endeavoured to reform their lives according to the methods of the gospel, as to those who have had the holy image of his Son drawn and wrought in their hearts? In 2 Tim. iv. 8 he is said to be a 'righteous judge,' which could not be if he gave the same rewards to both the contrary qualifications. The devil may as soon be eased, as any man without a new birth. Though there be enough written against the salvation of devils, yet there is more written in the book of God against the salvation of men living and dying in an unregenerate state than against the salvation of devils. Do any expect to see the kingdom of God without it? Why, that form on which you sit, that dust under your feet, far cleaner than ourselves by nature, are fitter to be brought into that place of glory. The holiness of God can better endure them than an unrenewed man. He pronounced their kind good at the creation, but never was an unrenewed nature pronounced good by God. You can no more shun an eternal misery without it, than you can a temporal death with it, you can no more fly from hell than from yourselves. Our blessed Saviour, the redeemer of the world, will know none for admission into happiness without his badge upon them: Mat. vii. 23, 'I never knew you:' you had nothing in you worthy my knowledge and affection. Where is the evangelical impression upon your soul? will be the only question then asked.

Well, then, I wish every unregenerate man would put the question to his soul, Can I dwell with everlasting burnings? Can I, with a cheerful security, meet the wrath of God in its march against me? Is eternal darkness a delightful state? Is an eternal separation from the blessed God to be desired? Is a present sensual life to be preferred before a joyful eternity? Is there any one Scripture in the whole book of God can give me comfort in this state? What, then, dost thou, O my soul, spend thy thoughts about, since there is nothing to procure thy felicity, but this new birth?

Use 8. Is of comfort. Is it so, that without regeneration there is no salvation? Then how great is the comfort of that person, who has attained this necessary thing! What a foundation is here for the composition of never songs for spiritual exultings! What a diffusion may there be of pleasure through the whole soul! That little regenerating principle within you is more necessary than the wisdom of Solomon, the power of Nebuchadnezzar, the glory of Ahasuerus, the reaching heads of the most knowing men in the world, and shall make you happy, when others in their unrenewed wisdom and unsanctified wealth shall descend to destruction.

1. The least true grace has comfort from hence. 'Except a man be born again, he cannot see the kingdom of God;' therefore if he be born again, he shall see it. Our Saviour does not say, except a man has been born so long, arrived to such a stature, but simply born again; it lies upon the essence, not upon the degree. A child that cries the first minute it is born, is in a state of life, as well as the man in the prime of his strength. A child has the nature of a man, though attended with some strong disease and great infirmities; though every true Christian has not the same growth yet he has the same birth, the same renewing Spirit. 'If a man be in Christ he is a new creature;' the apostle does not say, he is a strong creature, or a tall creature. St John reckons three different states of Christians, 1 John ii. 13, 14, children, young men, and fathers, and all in a state of the knowledge of God.

2. Here is comfort in the ignorance of the time of the new birth. 'Except a man be born again,' not except he know the time of his being born again; the want of the knowledge of the time has troubled some, but it is no matter for the time, if we find the essential properties; our happiness is secured by the essence, not by the circumstance. It is the glory of those that were born in Sion, that they 'were born there,' Ps. lxxxvii. 5, though the time of their birth were not exactly known by them. Many may tell the first preparations to it, the first strong conviction, the first time they found their hearts affected; this is more easy than to tell the very time when spiritual life was infused, any more than to tell the punctual time when the child was quickened in the womb; this is no more known, than that particular minute when this or that addition was made to our stature and growth, though the growth itself be discernible.

3. Such are new born to the enjoyment of God in glory. If none shall see God without it, then those shall certainly see God who have it; it is for the undefiled inheritance that God did first beget you: 1 Peter i. 3, 'He has begotten us to a lively hope, to an inheritance undefiled, incorruptible that fades not away, reserved in heaven for you.' Had not God intended you for an everlasting converse with himself, he would not have taken such pains, but have let you lie in your blood, and run down the stream of nature into the ocean of a miserable eternity with the common mass of the world. What comfort will this be, when you see the old house of your bodies full of gaps, ready to fall, that your reborn souls are ready to take possession of their eternal inheritance! Paul was one of the highest rank in Christianity, both in grace and office, yet the 'crown of righteousness' was not only laid up for him, and to be given to him, but to 'all that love the appearing of Christ, 2 Tim. iv. 8, that is, to all those that, from the principles of the new nature, aspire to that perfection, which shall be at the appearance of Christ. There is as certain a tendency, by the ordination of God, of a renewed soul to heaven, as of flame into the air. Grace and glory are in nature the same thing as a seed and a plant.

4. It is comfort upon this account, If new-born to heaven, then to all things which may further your passage thither and assist you in it. To God, as your God and king to protect you, as your Father to cherish you; to the promises as your promises, as assurances and deeds for heaven; to a sanctification of all states for a furtherance of you in your travel to and fitness for this kingdom; to a sight of God in his ordinances, and in his providences; he will not deny a beam here in his institutions to those for whom he reserves his full face hereafter; to a fellowship with God in duties of worship, as a foretaste of a perpetual communion with him; to an improvement of all graces, to the most perfect dress at last of all beautiful grace, which may completely fit you for an everlasting sight of God in heaven.

Use. 4. If without the new birth there is no entering into heaven, then it stands upon you to clear up your evidences for the new birth. If the existence of it be necessary for our felicity, the knowledge of it is necessary for our comfort. This is the great distinguishing evangelical sign; without an inward principle of life, we have not reached the intendment of the gospel: John vi. 63, 'The words of Christ are spirit and life.' John x. 10, 'I am come that you might have life.' He has no interest in the gospel that has not this in his heart. Every man in Christ must be a new creature.

To encourage you in this work, consider,

1. It is by this you must know your justification. Justification is our blessedness: Rom. iv. 8, 'Blessed is the man to whom the Lord will not impute sin.' And this is the way to know our blessedness:

forgiveness of sin precedes the inheritance, and both this and that are received only by the sanctified through faith in Christ: Acts xxvi. 18, 'That they may receive forgiveness of sin, and inheritance among them which are sanctified by faith which is in me.' The alteration of our frame is motifs, more discernible to us, than that of our relative states; the new dispositions discover what relation we stand in to God. This is a certain truth, he that does not find the draught of God's image in him, has no reason to conclude he has any saving interest in the propitiatory sacrifice of the Redeemer. As the blood and water were not separated in the effusion upon the cross, neither are they in their application to the soul; water to renew us, and blood to justify us. The 'washing of regeneration' evidences our being justified by grace, Titus iii. 57; the apostle infers the one from the other.

2. Therefore, by the knowledge of this only you can gain comfort. The great desire is, Oh that I were assured! Let it be your great business to clear up the new birth. It is the office of the Spirit not only to comfort but renew, and to comfort by renewing. The hope of eternal life is founded upon the renewing of the Holy Ghost, as well as on justification by grace, Titus i. 5-7; the Spirit as a comforter is to guide into all truth, John xvi. 13, into that truth which is sanctifying, John xvii. 17. The property of the Spirit is to guide us into sanctifying truth, and sanctify us by that truth; the Spirit does witness with our spirits that we are the children of God; its witness is by something within us, not without us. There must be something in our hearts as a foundation of this testimony; what witness can there be in an old nature? Look after, therefore, those essential properties of the new nature. Christ preached duty and comfort together; his first sermon, Mat. v., is made up of both. The clear evidence of a new life seated in the centre of the soul, will be a surer testimony of our right to, and fitness for glory, than if an angel from heaven should assure us in the name of God, that we are some of his heirs, the testimony of an angel is but that of a creature, lower then the verbal testimony of the Son of God. The evidences of the beginnings of glory, by the operations of grace and a Godlike nature, are more uncontrollable than the highest assurances all the angels in heaven can give us. Clear up this, therefore. There are many counterfeits; men may take morality, outward reformation, heaps of religious duties, to be this work, but these are all insufficient, and men without good examination may cheat themselves, and take copper for gold, and tin for silver. There is a natural or moral integrity, and an evangelical integrity; the natural integrity God owns in Abimelech: Gen. xx. 6, 'Yea, I know that thou did this in the integrity of thy heart.' He was king of the place where Abraham thought there was no fear of God, ver. 12. And it is likely there was not. God puts none of them upon prayer for themselves, but Abraham upon praying for them.

Then ask yourselves these two or three questions.

1. How stand your hearts to God and sin? Is there a bias in the will, which does naturally carry it to God? What light is there in your minds? what flexibleness and tenderness in the will and conscience? what sprightliness in your affections to the things of God? what readiness to meet him in his motions to you? what closing with Christ? Are there strong cries, struggling, wrestling, Jacob-like prayers? A new-born babe not to cry; a child not to call to his father, and follow him, and press to him: it is inconsistent with such a nature, since it is the first fruit of the 'spirit of adoption' received by us, to cause us to cry, Abba, Father, Rom. viii. 15. How stand your hearts to sin? Are there deep humiliations for it, utter detestation of it? Are your affections dead to the flesh and the world, and alive and quick to the things of God? Rom. viii. 10, 'The body is dead because of sin, and the spirit is life because of righteousness.' What humbling of inward pride, what striving against inward sins, what loathing of inward corruptions?

2. What delight have you in spiritual duties? Do your souls spring up in a service? Are your hearts in heaven before the words are out of your mouth? What is agreeable to nature is not burdensome. Spiritual services are as pleasant to a new nature, as sin is to an old, as sweet wines and delicious food is to a gluttonous disposition: Ps. cxix. 103, 'How sweet are thy words unto my taste! yea, sweeter than honey to my mouth!' Honey, one of the staple excellencies of Canaan, which is described to be a land flowing with milk and honey. Does your delight in the law of God spring up from the inner man? There is a delight in doing some things of the law (the Gentiles did by nature the things contained in the law, Rom. ii. 14), by a moral nature, not a new nature; if by nature, they had then a delight in them, and it was as all delight is, inward in the soul and heart, no doubt but many of them had pleasure in their morality. That is not the meaning of the apostle; but he does distinguish his delights from theirs by the object of it, and by the subject or spring of it. It was the law of God, as it was the law of God, that he did delight in; and it was not only an inward delight, but a delight arising from an inner nature, a man distinct from that man composed of soul and body; it did arise from a spirit possessed with nobler principles and higher ends.

Well, then, is it your meat and drink to do his will? Has the glory of God been dearer to you than the dearest worldly concerns you have? Are your converses with him very delightful to you? Do the thoughts of God, and delights in him, frequently return upon you? What bears the most grateful relish in your souls? holy thoughts and duties, or sinful and foolish vanities?

3. How do you live? Have you another life 'by the faith of the Son of God?' Gal. ii. 20; another faith beside the common faith, not resting in assent, but 'working by love,' Gal. v. 6. Do you live to

yourselves? That is proper to a state of nature. Or do you live to God? 2 Cor. v. 18. That is proper to a state of grace: Gal. ii. 19, 'I am dead to the law, that I might live unto God.' Is there a closing with Christ, not only as your Saviour, but as the principle and end of your lives? Is there a living the life of God, the life of Christ? Can Christ be formed in the heart, and there be nothing of the qualities of Christ, nothing of the spirit of Christ? Is Christ formed in the heart, a hard, low, dead, cold, dark, lifeless Christ? This frame is a quite contrary thing to Christ. If we are born of the will of God, we are born to answer the will of God. Is it the will of God that we should be loose in our hearts, and vain in our lives? That is the will of the flesh, not the will of God. According as our hearts are, so is our birth; sin or grace must have dominion in the soul; they cannot live amicably together; a man cannot be a sinner and a saint with the same will, cannot equally love holiness and iniquity. We may as well say that a man may be in heaven and hell at the same time; not but that a renewed man may in a sudden fit do a thing against his nature, as Moses, one of a mild disposition, was transported with a strain of passion against his nature. If sin reigns in the heart, though it does not in outward acts; if we yield ourselves servants, to obey it in the lusts thereof, though not in the outward fruit of those lusts, this new-creature principle was never settled in the heart: Rom. vi. 12, 'Let not sin reign therefore in your mortal body, that you should obey it in the lusts thereof: neither yield ye your members as instruments of unrighteousness unto sin.' He makes a manifest difference between the inward lust obeyed, and the outward commission of it in the members, and places the reign of sin in one as well as the other; and, ver. 16, concludes them in a state of nature or a state of grace, according as they yield themselves servants to this or that. A regenerate practical atheist is just as true as to say a regenerate devil.

(1.) Be diligent observers, therefore, of what solid alterations you find in your spirits; what motions, starts, principles, ends you can perceive there; and if you find you have this excellent and necessary new birth, admire God's grace in you, that he should pass by so many thousands in the world and renew you; that he should leave many soaking in their sins, and swimming to destruction in their old nature, and bestow this heavenly plant upon your souls. And prize it too. Aquinas has an excellent saying, The good of one grace is greater than the good of all nature; which words Cajetan commends as fit to be writ upon our minds, and constantly reviewed by us, to raise our admirations of God and his grace.

I speak now but little of these things, because the next discourse will lead me to speak more of them.

(2.) Seek it. If it be necessary to be had, it is necessary to be sought. We are all at this present before God in an old or new nature; and if we die in the nature we have received from old Adam, without another from the new, it is as certain that every one of us shall be excluded out of the kingdom of God, as it is certain we live and breathe in the places where we stand or sit. We are born of the earth, we must be born from heaven; we must have a spiritual as well as an animal life. Oh that every man and woman had the same thoughts of the necessity of it as they have who are past hope in hell of ever attaining it! Riches are not necessary, honours are not necessary; this is of absolute necessity. Were you like Solomon in all his glory, you could not have the privilege of entering into God's kingdom without a new nature; but a new nature without the glory of Solomon, nay, without a rag to your backs, will admit you. If those that are already renewed must be every day putting off the old and putting on the new man, Eph. iv. 22, 24, how much more need have you who have not dropped one scale, or sweat out one spirit of the old man, nor have a grain of the new man in you? As original corruption stood up in the place of original righteousness, so a gracious regenerate frame must rise up in the place of original corruption, for God will never befriend corrupt nature so much as to give a happiness to that which he hates. Men do not choose weeds but flowers to plant in their delightful gardens. God indeed does choose weeds, but they are turned into the nature of flowers before he transplants them to glory. We must have a wedding garment to fit us for his feast, and oil in our vessels to prepare us for his nuptials.

Seek it, for,

(1.) It is an indispensable duty. God has resolved that only 'the pure in heart shall see God,' Mat. v. 8. It is a duty incumbent on us to love God. Since we are bound to love God, we are bound to love whatsoever has any relation to him. Therefore we must love ourselves, not with a sordid, carnal love, but as we are the image of God. Hence we are bound to do what we can to brighten and clear this image, and restore it to its primitive perfection in our souls. We are answerable to God for the presenting this image of God in the same state wherein it was when he conferred it upon Adam, and upon us in his loins. Since the Redeemer has undertaken to restore it, it is our duty to seek to this Redeemer for the restoration of it, for he came 'that we might have life,' John x. 16; a vital principle in us to fit us for eternal life, and to 'have it more abundantly,' in a more glorious and fixed manner than Adam had.

(2.) Seek it, for something of this nature, or equivalent to it, seems necessary to all rational and intellectual creatures. The first nature of man was sown in mutability, and there was a necessity of something equivalent to this regeneration to fix and establish his nature; as the confirmation of angels under the head Christ is in some sort a regeneration of them, for it is an alteration of their state, from mutable to immutable, not by nature, for so God only is immutable, but by grace: Eph. i. 10, 'He has gathered together in one all things in Christ.' There is need now of it to change our nature, and afterwards to fix us in it. Most think that Adam, had he stood some time, had been confirmed in the state of innocence, and advanced to a more excellent state than that of paradise, which would have been an alteration of his state. If, then, an alteration of state was necessary for the fixing his happiness, an alteration of state is much more necessary for us for regaining the happiness we fell from.

(3.) Seek it, because in not seeking it you act against your own reason and natural experience. You have by the fight of nature, improved by the light of the gospel, so much knowledge as to perceive that you are not as God first made you. You cannot but acknowledge it impossible that so filthy and disorderly a piece can come out of his hands; that there is something wanting to you. And are those relics of nature left only to show us our indigence, and not also to spur us on to seek a remedy? Melanchthon says, I have seen many epicures who, being in some grief for their sins, have argued, How can I expect to be received by God, when I find not a new light and new virtues infused into me? When you are stilled after the rage of carnal affections or glut of pleasures, and you do in silence turn in upon yourselves, and make inquiry after your future state, if your conscience do not lie and flatter, will they not tell you to your faces that you are men of death, prepared against the day of slaughter? Besides, will not every man confess in his most raised retirements that he cannot find any real satisfaction in things below? And are there not sometimes some natural aspirings to something above these? Do not all men one time or other inquire, Ps. iv. 6, 'Who will show us any good?' Have you ever a more delightful pleasure than when you find yourselves inflamed with some desires for it? But, alas! do you not feel yourselves in a depraved state, and that these motions are but weak flutterings, and that the soul is quickly wearied in them? Is not this an evidence that there must be a more vigorous nature infused both to attain and enjoy them? Is it not then an acting against your own sentiments not to seek it? Do you not offer violence to that little reason in you to cut the wings of such motions? Let me add this too, you act in a way contrary to the nature of every thing, not to seek that state which was designed for the perfection of human nature. Is it not natural for everything to endeavour its recovery to its primitive purity, and struggle under that which is preternatural to it? A fountain will not rest till it has wrought out the filth which has been cast into it; so neither should man be quiet till he recover himself from the dominion of sin in his nature, and his pollution by it. Are you contented with a nasty, impure, and diseased body? are you not restless till it be cleansed and cured? and is it no trouble to you to have your souls in a dirty and foul condition? Do you not hereby act against your own nature in other things?

(4.) Not to seek it is to despise the general mercy of God, and the general kindness of the Mediator to human nature. There are in man desires for and inclinations to happiness, and some knowledge that this happiness lies in God. These desires were left in man by the mercy of God upon the interposition of the Mediator; therefore some call them not relics of nature, but restored principles, as a foundation to work upon; for upon the fall man did forfeit all, and sin despoiled himself of all de jure, but by the mediation of Christ, those were left (Col. i. 17, 'By him all things consist'), otherwise there had been no stock to work upon. These are left as foundations upon which God grafts this grace of regeneration, as they that spin do not spin out the whole thread, but leave some end) that they may add to it another thread; so God, having a purpose to do good on man in renewing him, did not suffer the stock of nature to be wholly rooted out, but left that as a root to graft upon, to make him the better capable of happiness. Had not man had a natural desire to happiness, there were no ground to work upon him to induce him to such a thing; therefore in not seeking it you reproach God for leaving this stump in you, and seem to be so well pleased with corrupt nature as if you would not have any remainder of the former. It is a striving against the relic of original nature left in us.

(5.) Seek it, for it is as necessary as justification. You should therefore seek it with as high an esteem of it as you have of pardon, none but would desire pardon of sin. You must be as desirous of the regeneration of your nature; they are equally necessary. Those who will not have an inherent righteousness can never expect an imputed righteousness from Christ; he never came to that end. Two things happened to us by the fall: another state and another nature; the regaining of the former must be equally sought with the latter, a being in another covenant by justification (for naturally we are in the covenant with Adam), and a being beautified with another image, because naturally we are deformed by the image of Adam. As long as we are only in a state of descent from, and union with, the first Adam, we are under the strictness of his covenant and the deformity of his image; when we are united to the second Adam, and spiritually descend from him, we are in his covenant of grace, and are adorned with his image. Both, therefore, must be looked after as equally necessary: Rom. v. 21, 'That as sin has reigned unto death, so might grace reign through righteousness unto eternal life by Jesus Christ our Lord.' Let us, then, look after this reign of grace; let not that be the last which should be first in our thoughts. Since our natural descent from Adam, we are born God's enemies: we must be spiritually new-born before our enmity can expire.

(6.) The advantages that accrue by regeneration are high. When we are received, we part with impurity for purity, with dross for gold, with corruption for holiness, with flesh for spirit, with nature for grace, with sin for God, and the enjoyment of him for ever. Our present nature is a nature of death and bondage; a new nature is like the new law, a law of life and liberty, James i. 25. It will put our souls in order, and set the Israelite free from the Egyptian taskmaster; it will quell the rage of sin, and diffuse a serenity in our souls. Grace and peace are not unfitly joined together by the apostle, in respect of peace in ourselves, which cannot be without habitual grace, as well as peace with God, which cannot be without his favour. It will enable us to perform spiritual services. As all natural actions flow from a natural form in the creature, so all spiritual actions flow from a spiritual nature in the soul, and without it a carnal heart can no more do any spiritual work than a rock can perform the work of a balsam-tree. It is but highly reasonable and just we should endeavour to regain that state wherein we were created, as the best for us, since the estate wherein God created us was certainly the best. It is inconceivably better to be a righteous man than to be a man.

(7.) Seek it; you will never repent your labour, because it is necessary. Necessity makes us contend with the greatest difficulties; men will do more at a pinch than they can do at other times, when no necessity is upon them. Never did any repent of it, never any will; it has been a comfort upon a deathbed to all that had it: it never was any man's sorrow. The universal consent of all who have found it wrought should quicken our desires and endeavours for it. Ask a renewed man whether ever it troubled him that he was regenerate? whether he would be without that state rather than undergo the same pains again? Would not his answer be, No, not for all the world? When the blessed apostle Paul considered his late regeneration, he expresses it with some regret, 1 Cor. xv. 8, 'as one born out of due time.' It implies a sorrow that he was not born sooner; and Austin cries out, Sero te amavi, Domine, I have loved thee too late, Lord. So does every renewed man repent that he was not regenerate sooner. A regenerate man come under the yoke of Christ finds such a pleasure in it, such a suitableness, such an advantage to his interest, that he would not be free from those delightful engagements, and the sweetness of that yoke, for all the delights and commodities of the world.

Exhortation. 3. Seek it presently; let not a minute pass without some ejaculation to God for the new birth; and when you come home, fall upon your knees, end rise not till you find a change of resolutions and dispositions. If you did well understand the necessity of it, you would not be one hour without begging it. You have heard the necessity of it now, are you sure you shall ever hear the doctrine preached on again? Are you sure you may not be past the hope as well as the happiness of the new birth before mans days be run, if the present opportunity be neglected? When God commanded Abraham to circumcise himself and his family, it is said he did it that very day wherein God commanded him, Gen. xvii. 23. Why should you not imitate Abraham in the ready and speedy circumcision of the heart? Though God does wait long, it cannot be thought he should always be courting dead souls. It must be now; there is no hope of such a change after death: 'The redemption of their soul ceases for ever,' Ps. xlix. 8; no more under the offers of a redeeming Saviour, no more under the motions of a renewing Spirit. Christ breaks the nations like a potter's vessel, Ps. ii. 9. A vessel before it be burned may be macerated in water, and formed anew; but when it has been burned in the furnace, it cannot be changed. Well, if thou wilt be new born this day, God will bless the memory of this day, for he will gain a son; Jesus Christ will by his blood put this day in red letters in his calendar, for he will gain a brother; the Spirit will rejoice, for he will gain a temple; angels will rejoice, for they will gain a fellow-servant; you will gain a fitness for an everlasting inheritance. Let me, therefore, press young men and women to this necessary and important concern; I know not when I may have so fit an opportunity or subject for it. It is not said, except an old man be born again, but except a man; therefore be not careless, as if you were not concerned in it, nor put it off to a longer day from the probability of the length of your life in a course of nature. Consider,

1. An early regeneration makes for God's honour.

(1.) In preventing much sin. How ripe are young ones, yea, even children when they are scarce green in age, as though iniquity had been their tutor in the womb! Youthful blood is the devil's tinder. Job knew it; therefore when his sons feasted he sacrificed, chap. i. 5. He was jealous of their inbred corruption, from the sense of the sins of his own youth, which we find him complaining of, Job xiii. 26; therefore he feared his children, having the same temptations, might fall into the same transgressions. Sow, by an early regeneration, many diseases of the soul are prevented, as well as the great crack of nature cured, as the distempers of the body are prevented by altering the habit of it in the spring. Though by a late regeneration, that of an old man, the soul is fitted for heaven, yet it will be grievous to him to think that his former dishonouring of God in his natural state was not prevented. It is otherwise with the early regenerate; they cannot complain, as Paul did, Oh, how have I persecuted the church of God! how have I breathed out threatenings against Christ and his people! how have I wallowed in all kind of sin! They have indeed as much reason to complain of the stock of the old nature within them, but not of so many bitter fruits of the flesh as others. How does the devil hang the wing when he is deprived of an active servant! As nothing makes heaven so glad, so nothing makes hell so sad, as to be frustrated of the full crop of sin it expected from such an instrument.

(2.) In doing much service for God. Young men are usually of active spirits and vigorous affections, whereas age does freeze all youthful warmth. Such, like Peter, can 'gird themselves, and go whither they please,' John xxi. 18, and travel about for God; but age damps the spirits. We are not so fit for service when the vigour of our youth is spent. And would you be saved, and God have no more glory from you? Now what parts, or strength, or mettle, a young man have, grace will bias, put into a right channel, and direct to an useful end. The early regenerate will be eminent in piety; for in a course of nature, they have a longer time to grow in. Their faith and love, by a larger exercise, will be the stronger; and the stronger the grace the more glory will be brought to God, Rom. iv. 20. Abraham, it is said, was 'strong in faith, giving glory to God.' He that rises betimes in the morning, will do more work than he that lies in bed till noon, or loiters till the sun declines.

(3.) In manifesting the power of the grace of God. An early regeneration is the great ornament of the gospel. It evidences the dignity and strength of habitual grace, in quenching youthful heats and powerful temptations, in making such to deny themselves, and prefer God's precepts before their own pleasures. It magnifies grace, when the devil is beat upon his own dunghill, where he had so great an interest, by reason of the corruptions such are subject to. What an eulogy is it to the beauty and power of grace, to see a young flourishing plant in God's garden! It shows the power of his grace upon such to salvation, that they are strong in the power of the might of God, to wrestle against principalities and powers, as well as against flesh and blood. It manifests the power of God's grace in the work of faith, and that there is a spirit of power residing in them.

2. As an early regeneration makes for God's honour, so it makes for your own interest.

(1.) Your new birth will be the gentler. The work of conscience will be more kindly, without the horrors they have, who have lain many years soaking in the old nature. More of hell must be flashed in an old sinner's face, to awaken him from his dead sleep. Paul, who had sinned some years with an high hand, was struck to the earth. Christ, as it were, took him by the throat, and shook him: Acts ix. 6, 'He trembling, and astonished, said,' &c. There will be more amazing aggravations of sin to rack the conscience, and consequently more anguish. Putrefied wounds require more lancing; and therefore are more painful in the cure than those which are but newly made. The more we are alienated from the life of God, the harder it will be to return to live that life again. The further a man is gone out of his road, the longer he must travel to come in again, and the more pains he must take in running or riding, than he that wandered but a little from it.

(2.) Your new birth will be the more grateful to God. God loves the first fruits. He would not have the gleanings, but the first crop of everything under the law, which was laid upon the altar as God's portion. The kindness of the youth is most respected by God. He cherished Israel because they were 'the first fruits of his increase,' Jer. ii. 2, 3. 'I remember the kindness of thy youth, the love of thy espousals, when thou went after me in the wilderness,' under many discouragements. God writes down the time of the new birth, and it runs in his mind a long time after. 'Epenetus, the first fruits of Achaia,' is saluted by Paul, just after the salutation of the whole church, with the title of well-beloved: Rom. xvi. 5, 'Greet the church that is in their house, salute my well-beloved Epenetus, who is the [first] fruits of Achaia unto Christ.' And surely more beloved by the Lord than by the servant. God has most affection for such as come in at the first sound of the gospel. Daniel was a young man, yet the holiest man of his age; and God has so great an affection to him that he joins him with Noah, that famous preacher of righteousness, and Job, that mirror of patience,--Ezek. xiv. 14, 'Though these three men, Noah, Daniel, and Job, were in it, they should but deliver their own souls by their righteousness,'--as those that had the greatest power with him, to keep off judgments from the place where they were.

(3.) Comfort will be the greater by an early new birth. What a long time will such an one have to enjoy the comforts of the Spirit! whereas those that are renewed later, have fewer comforts, because their grieving the Spirit has been the longer. You will be always ready, and fit for the kingdom of God, let God call when he will. Your foretastes of heaven greater, and much acquaintance with the life of it, before you arrive at the place of full enjoyment. John, the youngest disciple, lay in Christ's bosom; he had afterwards the most spiritual illuminations, and the discoveries of the state of the church in after days revealed to him. When our sluggishness makes God wait for our return, his justice will make us wait long for his comforts. The earlier your new birth, the sweeter will be your death, as being more stored with experiences of God's grace, and goodness, and truth, wherewith to answer all the devil's affrighting charges in your departing hence. No doubt can arise, but there will be a treasure of experience whence to draw an answer. The longer acquaintance you have with God, and the longer likeness to him in your natures, the more joyful will be your passage to him, and the more confidence against the fear of death.

(4.) The earlier your new birth, the sincerer and stronger will be your grace. To row against the strong stream and tide of nature, temptations of a youthful age, the inconstancy and lightness of your humour, and the inconsiderateness of your temper, are arguments of sincerity. To seek God, when a man has fair and frequent invitations to sin, is not so liable to suspicion, as when a man can live no longer. The latter proceeds rather from a fear of wrath than love to their Creator, or affection to his glory. Grace will be the stronger, the more full of juice. He that is new-born betimes, when he is young, will grow to a greater stature and a mighty strength in his age; for it is not with grace as it is with our bodies, the older the weaker; but as the outward man decays, the inward man grows, and is renewed day by day, 2 Cor. iv. 16. A young plant in the house of God will be fat and flourishing, and full of fruit in old age, Ps. xcii. 18, 14. The weakness of the body in such is the youthfulness of grace.

(5.) The earlier the new birth, the weightier will be your glory in the kingdom of God. God rewards according to our works: Rev. ii. 23, 'I will give to every one of you according to your works.' Not only to the wicked, the children of the woman Jezebel, according to their works, but to them whose charity, service, faith, patience, he knew, ver. 19. The longer you are without a new life, a vital principle, the fewer will your works be, and the shorter your wages. Though God in regeneration works as a sovereign, and has mercy on whom he will have mercy, yet, in rewarding, he acts as a righteous judge, according to the rules of justice: 2 Tim. iv. 8, 'The crown which the Lord, the righteous Judge, shall give me;' and so does proportion the glory to every man's service. Young ones regenerate, that bear head against the temptations of their violent nature, shall have crowns get with more jewels. They shall not only have an entrance, but 'an abundant entrance into the everlasting kingdom of our Lord and Saviour Jesus Christ,' 2 Peter i. 11. They shall enter into the port with a full gale. The more violent storms they bear up against, the brighter will be their glory. For if he that endures temptation, but one temptation, shall have a crown, by proportion, he that endures many shall have a greater: James i. 12, 'Blessed is the man that endures temptation; for when he is tried, he shall have a crown of life.' How comfortable will it be to feel the weight of your crown and the richness of your robes, according to your years of service. If there be any sorrow in heaven, it is because they were not sooner new-born, that they might more have glorified God on earth, who bestows so much honour upon them in heaven. If any of you were sure to be regenerate after you had spent so many years after the course of the world and fulfilling the lusts of the flesh, yet how great would your loss be, both of the comforts of the Spirit in this life, and of degrees of glory in the other!

3. Deferring the seeking after this new birth till more years grow upon you is a mighty folly. It is a matter of the highest concern, the greatest necessity, in comparison of which all other things are but toys and superfluities. Is it not folly to prefer superfluous things before necessary? Is it not a madness for a man to be mending the mud-wall about his garden, and neglect to quench the fire which has got hold of his house? You are poisoned in your nature, you have plague-spots upon your hearts. Would it not be ridiculous for a man that has drunk poison, and spilt some upon his clothes, to be more careful to have the stains fetched out of his garments than the poison out of his stomach? You are careful about the concerns of the body and flesh, oh be not such fools as to let the poison within get the greater head, and the plague continue in the heart.

Folly it is,

(1.) Because of the uncertainty of life. You are not lords and keepers of your own times, they are in God's hands: Ps. xxxi. 15 'My times are in thy hands.' What if he should fling that time out of his hand tomorrow, what would your condition be? Those that are in a dead state now, as they are here, if judgment find them so, are irrecoverable. Because thou art a child of wrath, if he take thee thus away with his stroke, as Job speaks, chap. xxxvi. 18, then a 'great ransom cannot deliver thee.' Hell followed death close at the back, Rev. vi. 8. Shall sin reign in a body? That is base. But in a mortal body, a body that may drop into the grave every hour? That is folly in the highest degree. It is the apostle's exhortation: Rom. vi. 12, 'Let not sin therefore reign in your mortal bodies.' Many a candle has been put out before half burnt, how often has a clear sun in the morning been overcast before noon! Were none of you the last week at the funeral of some strong and vigorous person? Perhaps there is no more time left you than just what will serve for to seek this new birth. God seizes upon some suddenly, that they have not time so much as to cry out what ails them: Job xxxvi. 13,14, 'They cry not when he binds them. They die in youth, and their life is among the unclean.' It is better to be new-born many years too soon (if it can be supposed to be too soon), than to defer it one minute too late. He that defers the new birth today, may not have a morrow to be new born in. And to be surprised by death before you are new born, better for you, you had never been born at all.

(2.) It is folly, because if you neglect the present time, though you may live, yet your return to God by a new birth may be very uncertain. There is such a thing as a day of grace, shorter than the days of a man's life: Luke xix. 42, 'The things of their peace' were then 'hid from their eyes,' though their destruction was deferred forty years. There is such a resolve in heaven sometimes, that 'the Spirit shall strive no longer' with this or that man: Gen. vi. 3, 'My Spirit shall not always strive with man,' or 'in man,' with this or that man; 'for that he also is flesh.' It is a threatening to those in the church, in opposition to the profane world, ver. 2. The church began then to be corrupted. My Spirit shall not strive with them; though they make a profession of me, and attend upon me in worship, yet they are flesh, degenerated into mere flesh, and flesh they shall be. And sometimes it is confirmed by a solemn oath. Rev. x. 5, 6, The angel swears in a most solemn manner, 'by him that lives for ever, who created heaven and earth' &c., 'that there should be time no longer;' that is, no time of repentance, as appears if you refer it to Rev. ix. 20, 21. It is not therefore without great reason that the apostle does double both the notes of attention, behold, and the time too, now, now, when he exhorts them not to receive the grace of

God in vain; that is, sit under the gospel administration to no purpose, without having a gospel impression and signature upon their hearts: 'Behold, now is the accepted time; behold, now is the day of salvation,' 2 Cor. vi. 2.

4. As it is a folly to neglect it; so if it be not presently sought, and endeavoured for, the more difficult it will be every day to attain it.

(1.) In regard of the increase of moral indisposition and unfitness. It is true indeed there is in every man a moral indisposition to a spiritual renovation, but the indisposition is greater when the habits of sin are more than ordinarily strengthened. The more the soul is frozen, the harder it will be to melt. A body dead some few hours is a subject more capable of having life breathed into it than when it is putrefied and partly mouldered to dust. A young tree may more easily be taken up and transplanted than a strong old oak, which has spread its roots deep into the earth. The more rooted the habit of sin, the harder the alteration of the soul. Every sin in an unregenerate man is an adding a new stone to the former heap upon the grave to hinder his resurrection. It is a fetter and bond--Acts viii. 23, 'bond of iniquity'--and the more new chains are put upon thee, the more unable wilt thou be to stir. The habits of sin will become more connatural to the soul, and fortify themselves with new recruits.

(2.) In regard of the industry of the devil. If you remain in a state of nature till you are old, that devil which blinds you now will have increased your blindness by that time; he will bestir himself in your age, that he may not lose that which he has possessed so long. It is a shame for Satan, as well as for a man, deficere in ultimo actu. He that struck the first fatal blow to us, and occasioned this degenerate nature, will not want watchfulness and care to strengthen it in you. He will be diligent to keep up his own work; the longer his possession, the more difficult his departure. Judas was a devil in our Saviour's judgment all his time--John vi. 70, 'One of you is a devil,' --but when he had withstood the force of our Saviour's discourses, and nourished his covetousness against his Master's frequent conviction, the devil 'entered into his heart,' John xiii. 27. Perhaps there had been before some strugglings of natural conscience in Judas, as there may be in some of you; but when he had, against the sight of our Saviour's miracles, the hearing of his sermons, the checks of his own conscience, continued in a natural state, Satan enters into him in a more peculiar manner, in a way of more special efficacy; and, by an uncontrollable power, breaks the bridle of conscience, which had held him in so long, and runs furiously with him to what wickedness he pleased. Satan reigned in him before; but as the regenerate, being by degrees filled with spiritual gifts, and having additions of grace, are said to be 'filled with the Spirit,' so natural men, as they increase in sin by degrees, are said to have a new entrance of Satan into them, because there is an increase of his efficacy in them, and power over them, binding them in stronger chains and fetters of iron.

(3.) In regard of spiritual judgments, which will make it impossible. Such judgments upon men that sit under the gospel, and admit not the influence of it, are more frequent than is usually imagined, though they are not so visible. Open sins God punishes many times by visible judgments, but wilful unregeneracy by spiritual. Though a man may sit under the same means of grace which God does bless to regenerate others, they may be an accidental means to harden him: 'The miry places shall not he healed, but be given to salt,' as it is Ezek. xlvii. 47, when others shall grow like trees on both sides the river, and bear a never-fading leaf. If once your neglects and provocations put God to his oath, and make him swear, as he once did, that you shall not enter into his rest, Heb. iii. 11, his oath will be irreversible; he will blow up heaven and earth before he will break it. And that it may not be evaded that this was an oath against the Israelites, it is intimated by the apostle that even in the times of the gospel this oath is of force, ver. 12. He from thence exhorts them at that time to take heed of 'an evil heart of unbelief.' What need of this exhortation to them, if this oath did only concern the Israelites murmuring in the wilderness, and were not valid against unbelievers and unregenerate men in the time of the gospel? It is a terrible place that in Isa. vi. 9, 'Make the heart of this people fat, and make their ears heavy, and shut their eyes, lest they see with their eyes, and understand with their heart, and convert, and be healed;' which dreadful place is no less than six times quoted in the New Testament, as though it belonged only to them that sit under evangelical light with a wilful unregeneracy. Certainly as the mercies of the gospel are most spiritual, so the judgments inflicted upon the neglecters of it are the most spiritual judgments. Then a man is made the centre of divine fury, and his heart sealed up from any seizure by sanctifying grace: Ezek. xxiv. 13, 'Because I have purged thee,' that is, offered thee purging grace, 'and thou was not purged, thou shalt not be purged from thy filthiness any more, till I have caused my fury to rest upon thee.' When God passes such a secret sentence, if all the men in the world, and all the angels in heaven, should, with their most affectionate strains of reason, attempt the persuading of you, they were not able to open an heart which God has judicially locked up and sealed. It is observed by some, that the work of the gospel, for conversion, is usually dose in those places where it comes, in the space of seven years, as to those who have sat under it so long; and they ground it upon Dan. ix. 27, 'And he shall confirm the covenant with many for one week,' that is, one week of years. And that our Saviour preached three years and an half among the Jews, and the apostles three years and an half or thereabouts before the Jews were discovenanted. I will not affirm it positively, but offer it as worthy consideration to those that have sat under the gospel more than seven years without any renewing work on their souls.

Well then, let me beseech you, resolve upon this work presently. We are not to bid a poor man 'go away, and come again tomorrow,' Prov. iii. 27, 28; and shall we bid the Spirit, knocking at our hearts in the gospel, go away, and come again another time? Our blessed Saviour did not defer his death for us till he was old, and shall not we live to him till we are old? As his death is an argument used by the apostle, to move us to live to him, 2 Cor. v. 14, 15, so the time of his death should be an argument to us to live to him betimes. How many has this foolish tomorrow deceived! and many have perished today before the dawning of tomorrow. Defer it not therefore a night longer; reflect upon yourselves, and say, Have I lived so long, pleased with my old nature? O Lord, what had become of me without thy wonderful patience? Let your motion be as the lightning, as the prophet Ezekiel speaks of the motion of four beasts, chap. i. 14. God may make up the match between himself and you before midnight: there was less time in God's working upon the jailer.

Quest. What shall we do to get this new birth?

Answer 1. Begin with prayer; seek it from that Saviour that first made so plain a declaration of it. 'A man cannot receive anything, unless it be given him from heaven,' John iii. 27. Then from heaven beg it; let God hear of you as soon as ever you come home. God usually lets in renewing grace at the same gate at which honest prayer goes out. Prayer is a compliance with God's grace; he never refuses it to them that heartily desire it. Go therefore to God, give him no rest; if you do so, it may not be long before you will hear that joyful word drop from his gracious lips: 'My grace will be sufficient for you,' sufficient to renew you, sufficient to cure you. Let the fervency of your prayers be proportioned according to the necessity of the thing, and the greatness of your misery without it. Plead, therefore, with God for it; Lord, is it not better to make me thy friend than to let me continue thy enemy? Is it not more thy glory to raise a soul from sin than a Lazarus from the grave? Thy power and mercy are more illustrious in turning a dry stock into a fruitful and flourishing tree. Overcome, therefore, my base nature by thy merciful power; change me from a venomous to a dove-like nature. Oh how fain would I glorify thee, by answering the end of my creation! Glorify thyself by new creating my heart, that I may glorify thee in a newness of life. I cannot get a new heart by my own strength; but it is a work not too hard for thy power, and suitable to thy promise. Plead the promise: Ezek. xi. 19, 'I will take the stony heart out of their flesh, and I will give them an heart of flesh;' and Ezek. xxxvi. 26, 'a new heart will I give you, and a new spirit will I put within you;' but he 'will be inquired of, to do it for them,' ver. 37. Breathe and aspire after it; beg for it as earnestly as you would in extreme hunger for food for the satisfaction of your natural appetite; God will not deny it for such as breathe after it, Mat. v. 6, Hunger and thirst after righteousness, and you shall be filled; beg the operation of the Spirit. Our Saviour provided the plaster, but left the Spirit to apply it; he provided the colours, his blood, to draw his image, but none but the Spirit can lay them on. Ask therefore the Spirit of the Father in the name of Christ; the Father sends him into the world, and sends him into the heart, but in the name of Christ. It is called a holy Spirit, because without it there can be no holy nature.

2. Be deeply sensible of the corruption of nature. The more we are sensible of our inherent depravation, the more we shall breathe after a real change. Can he ever imagine the necessity of a cure, who understands not the greatness of his disease? Be fully convinced, as Paul was, that in you, that is, 'in your flesh, dwells no good thing,' Rom. vii. 18. I know; I am experimentally sensible of it. Did we but truly see the defilement of our nature, and the monstrous alteration of it from that of our creation, as we can the deformity of some monster in the world, we should loathe ourselves, we should fly, if we could, from our own nature, and send forth nothing but groans for a deliverance from the body of death, and have no rest till we were stripped of so abominable a frame. Let us, therefore, turn in upon ourselves, take a view of our condition, see if there be any suitableness between our depraved natures, and the glory of another world. There is not, unless we conceit heaven a place filled only with carnal pleasures. But reason will tell us the contrary, and a carnal soul can never, in that state, be fit for a spiritual glory.

3. View often the perfection of the law of God. This will make us sensible of the contrariety of our nature to God's holiness, and consequently make us look about for a remedy. See whether your nature answers the exactness of the law; for although you were alive without the law, yet, when the commandment and your hearts come to look upon one another, you will see sin in its life and power, and all the conceits of your own excellency will die: Rom. vii. 9, 'For I was alive without the law once, but when the commandment came, sin revived, and I died.' Paul thought himself a righteous person, till he came to measure himself by the exact and spiritual image of the law. He had been instructed in the literal knowledge of the law, for he was brought up a Pharisee; his head and the law were acquainted, and then he thought himself a living person; but when his heart and the law came to be acquainted, then he found himself dead, and his high opinion of himself fell to the ground. Consider, then, how the law requires a perfect righteousness, an inward principle. All duties it commands are not only to be done materially, but formally; for they are so commanded in such a manner, from such a principle, to such an

end. Then reflect, have I such a righteousness? can I answer the law? do I come up to the measures of it in any one action? Surely I do not. Then consider further, Does not this law stand? will God lay it in the dust? has he thrown it out of doors? Surely it is holy, just, and good, and therefore a standing rule. I must have a principle suitable to that which Jesus Christ came not to destroy, but establish. How shall I do it with this corrupt nature, wherein I do not one action that does sincerely respect it, as the law of God, that is, accompanied with a delight in it? Certainly this temper, so contrary to the law, must be changed. I must have an inner man to delight in this law, a principle that must in some measure, though imperfectly, suit it. This orderly consideration would put you upon the seeking out for such a righteousness as may in part answer it.

4. Observe the motions of the Spirit. There is an assisting work of the Spirit, and an informing work. There is not a man but has, or once had, the strivings of this Spirit with him. There are the knockings of Christ by his Spirit at the door; there are calls, 'Zacchaeus, come down; this day is salvation come to thy house.' Did you never hear a voice from heaven, saying, 'Come to me that you may have life'? Did you never hear a groan from heaven, 'When shall it once be?' Did you never see a tear trickling down the cheek of Christ, as when he wept over Jerusalem? Did you never hear a sigh of a grieved Spirit waiting upon you? Can you see, and hear, and hear again, yet no compliance, when that is of absolute necessity you are exhorted to? Smother not these motions; answer them with suitable affections. If Christ looks upon you, as he did upon Peter, think of what you are, and weep, Mark xiv. 72. If the Spirit calls, answer presently, 'Thy face, Lord, will I seek.' The neglect of the time of the Spirit's breathing is the cause of a continuance in unregeneracy Repel not those sweet motions that strike upon your hearts.

5. Attend diligently upon all means of grace. They are the pipes through which the Spirit breathes, the lungs of the Spirit, the instruments whereby our natures are altered: 'Faith comes by hearing.' It is by the hearing of faith that the Spirit is ministered: Gal. iii. 5, 'He therefore that ministers to you the Spirit, does he it by the works of the law, or the hearing of faith?' None can expect it who will not use the means to have it, no more than men can expect to live without eating and drinking. Would we be warm? we must approach to the fire. Would we be clean? we must wash in the water. Would we be renewed? we must attend upon the breathings of the Spirit in the institutions of God. This we may do, though we cannot renew ourselves; we may read the word as well as a piece of news; we may hear the word, and attend to it, as well as to any worldly concern; we may meditate upon it, and consider it, as well as a story. This we have power to do, and it is by the word that this great work is done. By a powerful word Christ called Lazarus out of the grace, and by his word spoken by his Spirit, his great deputy he sent after him, he calls us out of our state of death. Beg of the Spirit to breathe upon you before you come to attend upon his institutions. We profit little by the Word, and our old nature attends us, because we take no notice of the Spirit of God, who is appointed the principal officer in this business. It is he that is to guide us into truth, John xvi. 13. Though men may speak truth to us, yet the Spirit can only guide the truth into our hearts, and guide us into the heart, and bowels, and inwards of truth, to taste the marrow of it.

6. I might add, Study the gospel. Look upon Jesus Christ in that glass; this transforms us into his image; as the beholding the light of the sun in a glass, paints an image of that light in our faces; so does the beholding Christ in the gospel: 2 Cor. iii. 18, 'But ye all, with open face, beholding as in a glass the glory of the Lord, are changed into the same image.' The gospel is the cause of our first change, and of our growth in it, 'from glory to glory,' but by the Spirit of God in the gospel, 'as by the Spirit of the Lord.' Study the promises of the gospel, and the end of the blood of Christ, which was to purge our conscience from dead works. It is by believing the promises of pardon in the blood of Christ that 'the conscience is purged from dead works,' Heb. ix. 14.

Discourse of the Nature of Regeneration

Therefore if any man be in Christ, he is a new creature: old things are passed away; behold, all things are become new.--2 Cor. v. 17.

The apostle in those words, ver. 13, 'For whether we be besides ourselves, it is to God; or whether we be sober, it is for your cause,' defends his speaking so much of his integrity; though some men would count him out of his wits for it, yet he regards not their judgment; for if he were in an ecstasy, or 'beside himself,' his purpose was to serve God and his church, and therefore he did not regard the opinion of men, whether he were accounted mad or sober, so he might perform the end of his apostleship. The sense therefore of it, as Calvin renders it, is this: Let men take it as they will, that I speak so much of my integrity, I do it not upon my own account, but have respect to God and the church in speaking of it, for I am as ready to be silent as to speak, when my silence may glorify God and advantage the church as much as my speech; 'for the love of Christ constrains me,' ver. 14, for whom I am bound to live; and so he passes on to inculcate the duty of every man that bath an interest in the death of Christ. The love of Christ constrains us actively; the love wherewith Christ has loved us is a powerful attractive to make us live to him. It is the highest equity and justice that we should live to him who died for us. Whence observe,

The true consideration and sense of the love of Christ in his death, has a pleasing force, and is a delightful bond and obligation upon us to devote ourselves wholly to his service and glory. There is a moral constraint upon the soul to this end: 'if one died for all, then were all dead,' then all were obnoxious to eternal death. Others (Vorstius, Calvin, editor) dislike this interpretation, and understand it not of the death to God brought in by the first Adam, but a death to sin and the flesh, procured by the second Adam, which death is spoken of Rom. vi. 2, 'How shall we, being dead to sin,' &c., and called 'a suffering in the flesh, and a ceasing from sin,' 1 Peter iv. 1. If one died for all, then all for whom he lied are dead, jure et obligatione, dead to themselves, that they might not be under their own power, but the power of him that died for them, and rose again. Since, therefore, we are dead to sin, we should take no care to maintain the life of it. And this seems, by the following verse, to be the true meaning of it: ver 15, 'And that he died for all, that they which live should not henceforth live unto themselves, but unto him which died for them, and rose again.' He has redeemed us by the price of his blood, that he might have us in his own power, as his own property, so that we are no longer our own masters, and have no longer right to ourselves. They ought to die to themselves, that they may live to Christ; it being fit they should live not to their own wills, or own honour, but to the glory and will of their Redeemer. It was to this end that Christ died, that he might have a seed to serve him, and live to him. It is ingratitude and injustice to deny him our service, since thereby we endeavour to frustrate the design of his coming. and the end of his death. Observe,

1. Self is the chief end of every natural man. 'That they which live, should not henceforth live unto themselves.' Implying that all men living, who are not under the actual benefit and efficacy of our Saviour's death, do live to themselves. The greatest distinction between a regenerate and a natural man is this, self is the end of one, and Christ the end of the other. The life of a natural man, and all the dependencies of it, is to gratify corrupt self, with the greatest detriment to his natural and moral self, the happiness and flood of his soul, but the life of a new creature, with all the dependencies of it, is for the glory of God and the Redeemer. This self-dependence, and a desire of independence on God, which was the great sin of Adam, whereby he would malice himself his own chief end, has run in the veins of all his posterity, and is the bitter root upon which all the fruits of gall and wormwood grow.

2. The end of our Saviour's dying and rising again was to change the corrupt end of the creature. The end of redemption, and consequently the end of the Redeemer, must be contrary to the end of corruption and the end of the first Adam. As Adam dispossessed God of his dominion to set up self, so does Christ pull down self to advance God to his right of being our chief end. It is called, therefore, a redemption of us to God: Rev. v. 9, 'For thou was slain, and hast redeemed us to God by thy blood;' redeemed us from a slavery under sordid lusts, to God as our end.

3. Therefore we must be taken off from ourselves, as our end, and be fixed upon another, even upon Christ, else we answer not the end of Christ's death and resurrection: 'He bore our sins in his own body on the tree, that we being dead to sin, should live unto righteousness,' I Peter ii. 21. And if the ends

of our Saviour's death and resurrection be not accomplished upon us, the fruits of it shall not be enjoyed by us. The whole work of regeneration, and conversion, and sanctification, and the efficacy of the death of Christ in the soul, consists in these two things: a taking us off from self, and pitching us upon God and Christ as our end. The terminus a quo is self, the terminus ad quem is Christ. We are 'redeemed by the precious blood of christ from our vain conversation received by tradition from our fathers,' I Peter i. 18, even from our first father Adam. This is properly to set up no other gods before him, and to abhor the grossest idolatry.

4. It is highly equitable, that if Christ died for us, and was raised for us as our happiness, we should live to his glory, and make him our end in all our actions, and the whole course of our lives. The apostle uses this consideration as an argument, and as a copy and exemplar. As Christ died not for himself, nor rose again for himself, but he died for God's glory and our redemption, to vindicate God's righteousness, and justify us in his sight, and rose again to make it appear that he had done our business in redeeming us, and went to heaven to manage our cause for us, so we are to rise to keep up the honour of God's righteousness and holiness, and to justify Christ in our professions of him, and conformity to him in the design of his death and resurrection. It is a high disesteem of ourselves not to live to Christ, which is both a more rightful and a more satisfying object of our affections, who returns our living to him with a happiness to ourselves. By his dying he purchased a dominion over us; by his resurrection his dominion over us was confirmed, and thereby our obligation of love and service increased. He died as our surety to satisfy our debts, and rose as our Saviour to justify our persons; so the apostle, Rom. iv. 26, 'He was delivered for our offences, and rose again for our justification.' Therefore, as he rose to justify us, we must rise to glorify him. And indeed it is a great sign of a spiritual growth when we grow in our ends and aims for God.

5. The resurrection of Christ, as well as his death, was for us. He rose again, it must be understood, for them for whom he died; he died as a public person, bearing our sins, and rose again as a public person, and head of the believing world, acquitted from our sins: Heb. ix. 24, 'He is entered into heaven, to appear in the presence of God for us.' And in a conformity to these two public acts of Christ does our regeneration and communion with Christ consist; in a mortification of the body of sin in conformity to his death; in newness of life, by quickening grace, in conformity to his resurrection, Col. ii. 12.

The apostle proceeds on, and makes his inference in the 16th verse, 'Henceforth know we no man after the flesh; yea, though we have known Christ after the flesh, yet now henceforth know we him no more.' To know is used in Scripture for love and delight, both on God's part,--Ps. i. 6. 'The Lord knows the way of the righteous, that is, loves and delights in the way of the righteous,--and on man's part: Hosea iv. 1, 'No knowledge of God in the land,' that is, no love of God. Not to know men after the flesh then, is either not to judge of men according to the endowments, though never so glittering, which arise only from fleshy principles; to esteem no man according to his greatness, his knowledge, and worth, in the account of the world, or, not to love men for our secular interest; or, not to regard men according to those fleshly privileges of circumcision and carnal ceremonies. Not ourselves, which is included in no man; not to esteem of ourselves by our knowledge, wealth, credit, honour, or any other excellency which falls under the praise of men, but by inward grace, living to God, fruitfulness to him, which falls under the praise of God. Men esteem not their fields for the gay wild flowers in them, but for the corn and fruit; 'yea, though we have known Christ after the flesh, yet now henceforth know we him no more.' We do not glory in him because he was of kin to us, and our countryman according to the flesh; we look upon him no more only as a miraculous man, but we have more noble thoughts of him; we know him as the great Redeemer of the world; we consider him in those excellent things he has done, those excellent graces which he has communicated, those excellent offices he does exercise, we know him after a spiritual manner, as the author of all grace, appointed by God for such ends, accepted by God upon such works, glorified by God for such purposes; we regard him as transacting our great affairs in heaven, where he is entered as a forerunner for us, Heb. vi. 20, and as such we serve and honour him; we desire not his company in the flesh, but in the spirit, in his heavenly appearance and glory. Observe,

1. Natural men have no delight in anything but secular concerns; love nothing, but for their own advantage; admire not any true spiritual worth; they know and love men, yea, what love they pretend to Christ is only a fleshly love, a love from education, a customary love.

2. An evidence of being taken from ourselves and living to Christ, is our valuation either of ourselves or others, according to holiness. Though a civil respect be due to men according to their station in the world,--such a respect the writer of this epistle gave to Agrippa;--yet our inward valuations of men ought to be upon the account of the image of God in them. God, who loves righteousness, knows no man after the flesh, but as he finds the image of his own righteousness in him; and as a new creature is framed after the image of God, so his affections and valuations of men or things are according to God's affections to them, or esteem of them.

3. Our professions of Christ, serving him and loving him barely for ourselves and for fleshly ends, does not consist with regeneration. Such a love is a love to ourselves, not to Christ, a making him only subservient to us, not ourselves subservient to Christ.

4. We should eye Christ, and arise to the knowledge of him, as he is advanced and exulted by God. Look upon him as our head, delight to come under his wing, and have our whole dependence on him, know him in his righteousness to justify us, know him not only as a Saviour risen, but in the power of his resurrection in our souls, and the fellowship of his sufferings, and to be made conformable to his death; such a knowledge the apostle aims at, Philip. iii. 8-10; the other knowledge is a knowledge of him in the head, this a knowledge of him in the heart; the other is a knowledge of him after the flesh, this a knowledge of him after the spirit, in the draught of Christ in our hearts by the Spirit, an inward conception of him in the womb of our hearts.

The text is another inference made from that position, ver. 15. If there be such an obligation upon us to live to Christ, because he has died and rose again for us; then certainly whosoever has an interest in the death and resurrection of Christ, as to the fruits of it, must be a new creature, a changed person; old things have passed away, all things are become new in him. Whosoever is in the kingdom of Christ, engrafted into him, under the participation of his death and resurrection, is a new creature; all other excellencies are defective, though they may be useful to the world; it is a 'new creation' only makes a man excellent and worthy of the kingdom. 'Old things are passed away,' old affections, old dispositions of Adam; those things, the "archaia", things that are very near of as old a standing us the world. Adam would be his own rule and ruler; he would be the rule of good and evil to himself; he would be his own end. These things must pass away; we must come to a fiduciary reliance upon God, under the new head of his appointment, and make him our highest good, our chief end, our exact rule, and therefore what is called the 'new creature, Gal. vi. 15, is called 'faith working by love,' Gal. v. 6. Adam's great failures were unbelief and self-love; he would not believe God's precept and threatening; he would not depend upon God. To this is opposed faith, which is a grace that empties us of ourselves, and fixes us in our dependence on another. He would also advance himself, and be his own rule and end, to know as God; to this is opposed love, which is an acting for God and his glory. And these two are the essential parts of the new creature. Some of late would understand, by the new creature, only a conversion from idolatry to the profession of Christianity. But there must be a greater import in the words than so. The apostle makes it a qualification necessary both to Jew and Gentile, that neither the circumcision of the one did avail without it, nor the uncircumcision of the other prejudice them that possess it. Besides, men may turn from one profession to another without living to God, and directing all their actions to the glory of Christ. Some translate it, 'Let him be a new creature;' others, 'He is a new creature.' One notes his state, the other his obligation. 'Old things are passed away.' It is a reason rendered; there is a change in the whole frame of things. If you understand it of the old economy, the old legal state, then it is an argument showing the necessity of the new creature. Old things are withered; there is a new frame in the church, in the kingdom, therefore there ought to be so in the subjects of it; for the prophets use to speak of the state of the gospel under the names of a 'new heaven and new earth,' Isa. lxv. 17. As old rites in the church are removed, so the old principles and the old frames of Adam should pass away. The old rubbish must be thrown out when the house is new built. And they are passed away in a regenerate man, jure, obligatione, potestate, though not wholly in actu. 'All things are become new', but not of ourselves, but by the grace of God, ver. 18, 'and all things are of God.' It is likely the apostle expresses himself thus, to pull down the swelling thoughts of the Corinthians which they had of themselves. They were proud of their gifts, wherein, by the apostle's own confession, they came behind no church in the world, 1 Cor. i. 7; and he discourses to them much of the excellence of charity above knowledge, and advises them to 'covet the best gifts,' 2 Cor. xiii. He depresses their confidence in knowledge without grace, which does but puff up, not edify to eternal life. He wishes them, therefore, to look more to the new creature in them, to try themselves whether they be in Christ or no, by the change they found in their hearts. 'If any man be in Christ,' that is, be a member of Christ, engrafted into him.

In the words observe,

1. The character of a true Christian by his state, a new creature.

2. The necessity of this new creation, if any man; if he be not a new creature, he is not in Christ; he has nothing at present to do with him, he is no true member of his body.

3. The universality, any man; not a man can be in Christ by any other way, without this new creation pass upon him.

4. The advantage of it: if he be a new creature, he is certainly in Christ, it is an infallible token that the Redeemer did die and rise again for him.

5. The nature of it.

(1.) Removal of the old form: old things are passed away.

(2.) Introduction of a new: all things are become new, as without in the church, so within in the soul.

6. The note of attention: behold, more particularly set to this passage, of all things becoming new, to remote the deceit that men are liable to. Old things in some measure may pass away, but look to that, whether new things come in the place contrary to those old, whether there be new affections, new dispositions; old things may pass away, when old sins are left, and no new frames be set up in the stead

of them. The doctrine I shall insist upon is this:

Doct. Every man in Christ has a real and mighty change wrought in him, and becomes a new creature.

I pitch upon these words to show the nature of regeneration, the necessity of which I have already discoursed of.

It is difficult to describe exactly the nature of regeneration.

1. Because of the disputes about the nature of it; whether it be quality, or a spiritual substance; whether, if a quality, it be a habit or a power, or whether it be the Holy Ghost personally. Many controversies the wits of men have obscured it with. The Scripture discovers it to us under the terms of the new creature, a new heart, a law put into us, the image of God, a divine nature; these, though Scripture terms, are difficult to explain.

2. It is difficult, because it is visible, not in itself, but in its edicts. We know seed does propagate itself, and produce its like, but the generative part in the seed lies covered with husks and skin, so that it is hard to tell in what atom or point the generative particle does lie. We know we have a soul, yet it is hard to tell what the soul is, and in what part it does principally reside. We know there are angels, yet what mortal can give a description of that glorious nature? It is much like the wind, as our Saviour describes it: John iii. 8, 'The wind blows where it lists, and thou hears the sound thereof, but can not tell whence it comes, nor whither it goes: so is every one that is born of the Spirit.' The wind, we feel it, we see the effects of it, yet cannot tell how it arises, where it does repose itself, and how it is allayed; and all the notions of philosophy about it will not satisfy a curious inquirer. So likewise it is in this business of regeneration; the effects of it are known, there are certain characters whereby to discern it; but to give a description of the nature of it is not so easy.

3. It is difficult, because of the natural ignorance which is still in the minds of the best. A man cannot understand all iniquity, for there is a 'mystery of iniquity;' neither can he fully understand this work, for there is a 'mystery of godliness,' 1 Tim. iii. 16; not only in the whole scheme of it without, but in the whole frame of it in the heart. It is called the 'hidden man of the heart', 1 Peter iii. 4; hidden from the world, hidden from reason, hidden from the sight sometimes of them that have it; a man can hardly sometimes see it in his own heart, by reason of the steams of corruption; as a beautiful picture is not visible in a cloud of smoke. The blindness the god of this world has wrapped us in, that we might not know God, or the things of God, is not wholly taken off: And even what we know of the truths of God, suffers an eclipse by our carnal conceptions of them; for all the notions we frame of them have a tincture of sense and fancy.

4. It is hard for those to conceive it who have no experience of it. If we speak of the motions of natural corruption, as wrath, passion, distrust of God, and enormous sins, men can easily understand this, because we have all sad experiments of an inward corruption; but the methods and motions of the Spirit of God in this work are not comprehended, but by those who have felt the power of it. The motions of sin are more sensible, the motions of the Spirit more secret and inward, and men want as much the experience of the one, as they have too much of the other. Hence it is that many carnal men love to have the nature of sin ripped up and discovered; partly, perhaps, for this reason among others, that they can better understand that by the daily evidence of it in their own practices; whereas other things, out of the reach of their experience, are out of the grasp of their understanding; and therefore seem to them paradoxes and incredible things: the spiritual man is not judged or discerned by any but them that are spiritual, 1 Cor. ii. 15. It is certainly true, that as a painter can better decipher a stormy and cloudy air than the serenity of a clear day, and the spectator conceive it with more pleasure: so it is more easy to represent the agitations and affections of natural corruption, than the inward frame of a soul wrought by the Spirit of God. I shall therefore describe it consonantly to the Scripture thus:
Regeneration is a mighty and powerful change, wrought in the soul by the efficacious working of the Holy Spirit, wherein a vital principle, a new habit, the law of God, and a divine nature, are put into, and framed in the heart, enabling it to act holily and pleasingly to God, and to grow up therein to eternal glory. This it included in the term of a new creature in the text. There is a change, a creation, that which was not is brought into a state of being. If a new creature, and in Christ, then surely not a dead but a living creature, having a principle of life; and if a living creature, then possessed of some power to act, and habits to make those actions easy; and if a power to act, and a habit to facilitate that act, then a law in their nature as the rule of their acting; every creature has so. In this respect the heavens are said to have ordinances: 'knows thou the ordinances of heaven?' Job xxxviii. 33; and they seem to act in the way of a covenant, Jer. xxxiii. 25, according to such articles as God has pitched upon. And, lastly, as in all creatures thus endued, there is a likeness to some other things in the rank of beings; so in this new creature there is a likeness to God, whence it is called 'the image of God in holiness and righteousness,' and a 'divine nature.' So that you see the divers expressions whereby the Scripture declares this work of regeneration are included in this term of the new creature, or the flew creation, as the word is, "kaine ktisis". It is a certain spiritual and supernatural principle, or permanent form, per modem actus primi, infused by God, whereby it is made partaker of the divine nature, and enabled to act for God.

Let us therefore see,

1. How it is differenced from other states of a Christian.
2. What it is not.
B. What it is.
1. First, How it is differenced from the other states of a Christian.

(1.) It differs from conversion. Regeneration is a spiritual change, conversion is a spiritual motion. In regeneration there is a power conferred; conversion is the exercise of this power. In regeneration there is given us a principle to turn; conversion is our actual turning; that is the principle whereby we are brought out of a state of nature into a state of grace; and conversion the actual fixing on God, as the terminus ad quem. One gives posse agere, the other actu agere.

[1.] Conversion is related to regeneration, as the effect to the cause. Life precedes motion, and is the cause of motion. In the covenant, the new heart, the new spirit, and God's putting his Spirit into them, is distinguished from their walking in his statutes, Ezek. xxxvi. 27, from the first step we take in the way of God, and is set down as the cause of our motion: 'I will cause you to walk in my statutes.' In renewing us, God gives us a power; in converting us, he excites that power. Men are naturally dead, and have a stone upon them; regeneration is a rolling away the stone from the heart, and a raising to newness of life; and then conversion is as natural to a regenerate man as motion is to a living body. A principle of activity will produce action.

[2.] In regeneration, man is wholly passive; in conversion, he is active: as a child in its first formation in the womb, contributes nothing to the first infusion of life; but after it has life, it is active, and its motions natural. The first reviving of us is wholly the act of God, without any concurrence of the creature; but after we are revived, we do actively and voluntarily live in his sight: Hosea vi. 2, 'He will revive us, he will raise us up, and then 'we shall live in his sight;' then we shall walk before him, then shall we 'follow on to know the Lord.' Regeneration is the motion of God in the creature; conversion is the motion of the creature to God, by virtue of that first principle; from this principle all the acts of believing, repenting, mortifying, quickening, do spring. In all these a man is active; in the other merely passive; all these are the acts of the will, by the assisting grace of God, after the infusion of the first grace. Conversion is a giving ourselves to the Lord, 2 Cor. viii. 5; giving our own selves to the Lord is a voluntary act, but the power whereby we are enabled thus to give ourselves, is wholly and purely, in every part of it, from the Lord himself. A renewed man is said to be led by the Spirit, Rom. viii. 14, not dragged, not forced; the putting a bias and aptitude in the will, is the work of the Spirit quickening it; but the moving the will to God by the strength of this bias, is voluntary, and the act of the creature. The Spirit leads, as a father does a child by the hand; the father gave him that principle of life, and conducts him and hands him in his motion; but the child has a principle of motion in himself, and a will to move. The day of regeneration is solely the day of God's power, wherein he makes men cavilling to turn to him, Ps. cx. 3; so that, though in actual conversion the creature be active, it is not from the power of man, though it be from a power in man, not growing up from the impotent root in nature, but settled there by the Spirit of God.

(2.) It differs from justification. They agree in the term to which, that is God: by justification we are reconciled to God; by regeneration we are assimilated, made like to God. They always go together. As our Saviour's resurrection, which was the justification of him from that guilt which he had taken upon himself, and a public pronouncing him to be his righteous servant, is called a new begetting him: Acts xiii. 33, 'God has raised up Jesus again, as it is also written in the second Psalm: Thou art my Son, this day have I begotten thee;' because it was a manifestation of him to be the Son of God, who before, being covered with our infirmities, did not appear so to the world: so our justification from guilt, and new begetting us, and manifesting us to the angels to be the sons of God, are at one and the same time, and both are by grace; 'by grace you are justified,' Rom. v. 1, the quickening and raising us together with Christ is by grace, Eph. ii. 5, 6. The blessing of Abraham, which is the application of redemption from the curse of the law, and the receiving the promise of the Spirit by faith, are both together, Gal. iii. 14.

But [1.] it differs from justification in the nature of the change.

Justification is a relative change, whereby a man is brought from a state of guilt to a state of righteousness; from a state of slavery to a state of liberty; from the obligation of the covenant of works to the privilege of the covenant of grace; from being a child of wrath to be an heir of promise. Regeneration is a physical change, and real, as when a dead man is raised from death to life; it is a filling the soul with another nature, Eph. ii. 1, 'And you has he quickened, who were dead in trespasses and sins.' The translators have inserted those words, 'has he quickened,' because those words are put in the 5th verse; but methinks the words refer better to the 23rd verse of the first chapter, speaking of Christ, 'who fills all in all,' and fills you too with a spiritual life; or he passes from the power of God in raising Christ, to his power in raising us. It is a change of nature, and of that nature whereby we are children of wrath, not only by the first sin, but by a conversation according to the course of the world. And this quickening respects the change of that nature which was prone to a worldly conversation, and a fulfilling the desires of the flesh. The first is a change of a man's condition, this a change in a man's disposition. When a man is made a magistrate there is a change in his relation; when a servant or slave is made a freeman there is an alteration of his condition; but neither the one's magistracy nor the other's liberty, fills their hearts with new principles, or plants a new frame in their nature. Relation and nature are two distinct things. In creation there is a relation of a creature to God, which results from the mere being of the creature; but there is also the nature of the creature in such a rank of being, which is added over and above to its mere being. The apostle in the verses following the text, speaks of reconciliation, or non-imputation of our trespasses, as distinct from that change wrought in us in the new creation. In justification we are freed from the guilt of sin, and so have a title to life; in regeneration we are freed from the filth of sin, and have the purity of God's image in part restored to us.

[2.] They differ in the cause, and other ways. Justification is the immediate fruit of the blood of Christ: 'Being justified by his blood,' Rom. v. 9. Regeneration is by the immediate operation of the Spirit, therefore called 'the sanctification of the Spirit,' the matter of that is without us, the righteousness of Christ; the matter of the other within us, a gracious habit. The form of the one is imputing, the form of the other is infusing or putting into us; they differ in the end, one is from condemnation to absolution, the other from pollution to communion. In the immediate effect, one gives us a right, the other a aptness. In their qualities, the righteousness of one is perfect in our head, and imputed to us. The righteousness by regeneration is actively in us, and aspires to perfection.

(3.) It differs from adoption. Adoption follows upon justification as a dignity flowing from union to Christ, and does suppose reconciliation. Adoption gives us the privilege of sons, regeneration the nature of sons. Adoption relates us to God as a father, regeneration entrances upon us the lineaments of a father. That makes us relatively his sons by conferring a potter, John i. 12. This makes us formally his sons by conveying a principle, I Peter i. 23. By that we are instated in the divine affection; by this we are partakers of the divine nature. Adoption does not constitute us the children of God by an intrinsic form, but by an extrinsic acceptation; but this gives us an intrinsic right; or adoption gives us a title, and the Spirit gives us an earnest; grace is the pledge of glory. Redemption being applied in justification, makes way for adoption. Adoption makes way for regeneration, and is the foundation of it: Gal. iv. 5, 6, 'God sent forth his Son to redeem them that were under the law, that we might receive the adoption of sons. And because you are sons, God has sent forth the Spirit of his Son into your hearts, crying, Abba, Father.' Because you are thus adopted, God will make you like his Son, by sending forth the Spirit of his Son, to intimate the likeness it shall produce in the hearts of men to Christ, that you may cry, Abba, Father, behave yourselves like sons, and have recourse to God with a childlike nature. The relation to Christ as brethren is founded upon this new creature: Heb. ii. 11, For both he that sanctifies and they who are sanctified, are all of one.' they are all of one nature, not the divine nature which Christ had by eternal generation, but that divine nature Christ had by the Spirit's unction. And being of one nature, he is not ashamed, though glorious in heaven, to call them brethren; and being Christ's brethren by a divine nature, thence result also the relation of the sons of God.

(I.) It differs from sanctification. Habitual sanctification, indeed, is the same thing with this new creature, as habitual rectitude was the spiritual life of Adam; but actual sanctification, and the gradual progress of it, grows from this principle as from a root. Faith purifies the heart, Acts xv. 9, 'purifying their hearts by faith,' and is the cause of this gradual sanctification, but faith is part of this new creature, and that which is a part cannot be the cause of the whole, for then it would be the cause of itself. We are not regenerated by faith, though we are sanctified by faith; but we are new created by the Spirit of God, infusing faith into us. Faith produces the acts of grace, but not the habit of grace, because it is of itself a part of this habit, for all graces are but one in the habit or new creature, charity, and likewise every other grace is but the bubbling up of a pure heart and good conscience, 1 Tim. i. 5. Regeneration seems to be the life of this gradual sanctification, the health and liveliness of the soul.

2. The second thing proposed is, what it is not.

(1.) It is not a removal or taking away of the old substance or faculties of the soul. Some thought that the substance of Adam's soul was corrupted when he sinned, therefore suppose the substance of his soul to be altered when he is renewed. Sin took not away the essence, but the rectitude; the new creation therefore gives not a new faculty, but a new quality. The cure of the leprosy is not a destroying of the fabric of the body, but the disease; yet in regard of the greatness of man's corruption, the soul is so much changed by these new habits, that it is as it were a new soul, a new understanding, a new will. It is not the destroying the metal, but the old stamp upon it, to imprint a new. Human nature is preserved, but the corruption in it expelled. The substance of gold is not destroyed in the fire, though the metal and the flame mix together, and fire seems to be incorporated with every part of it; but it is made more pliable to what shape the artist will cast it into, but remains gold still. It is not the breaking the candlestick, but setting up a new light in it; not a destroying the will, but putting a new bias into it. It is a new stringing the instrument to make a new harmony. It is an humbling the loftiness, and bowing down the haughtiness of the spirit, to exalt the Lord alone in the soul, Isa. ii. 11, speaking of the times of the gospel. The essential nature of man, his reason and understanding, are not taken away, but rectified. As a carver takes not away the knobs and grain in the wood, but planes and smoothes it, and carves the image of a man upon it, the substance of the wood remains still; so God pares away the rugged pieces in man's understanding and will, and engraves his own image upon it, but the change is so great that the soul seems to be of another species and kind, because it is acted by that grace, which is another species to from that principle which acted it before. New creation is called a resurrection. Our Saviour in his resurrection had the same body, but endued with a new quality. As in Christ's transfiguration, Mat. xvii. 2, neither his deity nor humanity were altered, both natures remained the same. But there was a metamorphosis ("metamorfosen"), and a glorious brightness conferred by the deity upon the humanity which it did not partake of before. So though the essence of the soul and faculties remain the same, yet another kind of light is darted in, and other qualities implanted. It was the same Paul when he complied with the body of death, and when he complained of it, but he had not the same disposition. As Adam in a state of corruption had the same faculties for substance which he had in the state of innocence; but the power, virtue, and form in those faculties, whereby he was acceptable to God, and in a capacity to please him, was wholly abolished. We lose not nor substantial form, as Moses his rod did, when it was turned into a serpent; or the water at Cana was turned into wine. Our nature is ennobled, not destroyed; enriched, not ruined; reformed, not annihilated.

(2.) It is not a change of the essential acts of the soul, as acts. The passions and affections are the same, as to the substance and nature of the acts, but the difference lies in the object. And acts, though for substance the same, yet are specifically distinguished by the diversity of objects about which they are conversant. Whatsoever is a commendable quality in nature, and left in man by the interposition of the mediator, is not taken away; but the principle, end, and objects of those acts, arising from those restored qualities, are altered. The acts of a renewed man, and the acts of a natural man, are the same in the nature of acts, as when a man loves God and fears God, or loves man or fears man; it is the same act of love, and the same act of fear; there are the same motions of the soul, the same substantial acts simply considered; the soul stands in the same posture in the one as in the other, but the difference lies in the objects; the object of the one is supernatural, the object of the other natural. As when a man walks to the east or west, it is the same motion in body and joints, the game manner of going; yet they are contrary motions, because the terms to which they tend are contrary one to the other: or, as when we bless God and bless man, it is with one and the same tongue that we do both, yet these are acts specifically different, in regard of the difference of their objects. The nature of the affections still remain, though not the corruption of them, and the objects to which they are directed are different. If a man be given to thoughtfulness, grace removes not this temper, but turns his meditations to God. The solitariness of his temper is not altered, but something new offered him as the object of his meditation. If a man be hot and earnest in his temper, grace takes not away his heat, but turns it into zeal to serve the interest of God. Paul was a man of active disposition; this natural activity of his disposition and temper was not dammed up by grace, but reduced to a right channel, and pitched upon a right object; as he laboured more than any in persecuting, so afterwards he 'laboured more than any' in edifying, 1 Cor. xv. 9, 10. His labour was the same, and proceeded from the same temper, but another principle in that temper, and directed to another term. As it is the same horse, and the same mettle in the beast, which carries a man to his proper stage that carried him before in a wrong way, but it is turned in respect of the term. David's poetical fancy is not abolished by this new principle in him, but employed in descanting upon the praises of God, which otherwise might have been lavished out in vanity, and foolish love-songs, and descriptions of new mistresses. So that the substance and nature of the affections and acts of a man remain; but anger is turned into zeal by virtue of a new principle, grief into repentance, fear into the fear of God, carnal love into the love of the creator, by another principle which does bias those acts.

(3.) It is not an excitation, or awakening of some gracious principle which lay hid before in nature, under the oppression of ill habits, as corn lay hid under the chaff, but was corn still. Not a beating up something that lay sculking in nature, not an awakening as of a man from sleep; but a resurrection as of a man from death; a new creation, as of a man from nothing. It is not a stirring up old principles and new kindling of them; as a candle put out lately may be blown in again by the fire remaining in the snuff, and burn upon the old stock; or as the life which retired into the more secret parts of the body in those creatures that seem dead in winter, which is excited and called out to the extreme parts by the spring sun. Indeed, there are some sparks of moral virtues in nature, which want blowing up by a good education; the foundation of these is in nature, the exciting of them from instruction, the perfection of them from use and exercise. But there is not in man the seed of one grace, but the seeds of all sin: Rom. vii. 18, 'I know that in me, that is, in my flesh, dwells no good thing.' Some good thing may be in me, but it arises not from my flesh; it is not from any seed sown by nature, but it is another principle put into me, which does seminally contain in it all grace; it is a putting a new seed into the soil, and exciting it to grow, 'an incorruptible seed,' 1 Peter i. 23. Therefore the Scripture does not represent men in a trance, or sleep, but dead; and so it is not only an awakening, but a quickening, a resurrection, Eph. ii. 6; Col. ii. 12; Eph. i. 19, 20. We are just in this work as our Saviour was when the devil came against hem: John xiv. 30, 'The prince of this world comes, and has nothing in me.' He had nothing to work upon in Christ;

but he rakes in the ashes of our nature, and finds sparks enough to blow upon; but the Spirit finds nothing in us but a stump, some confused desires for happiness; he brings all the fire from heaven, wherewith our hearts are kindled. This work, therefore, is not an awakening of good habits which lay before oppressed, but a taking off those ill habits which were so far from oppressing nature that they were non-natural to it, and by incorporation with it, had quite altered it from that original rectitude and simplicity wherein God at first created it.

(4.) Nor is it an addition to nature. Christ was not an addition to Adam, but a new head by himself, called Adam, in regard of the agreement with him in the notion of an head and common person: so neither is the new creature, or Christ formed in the soul, an addition to nature. Grace grows not upon the old stock. It is not a piece of cloth sewed to an old garment, but the one is cast aside, the other wholly taken on; not one garment put upon another: but a taking off one, and a putting on another, Col. iii. 9, 10, 'putting off the old man, putting on the new man.' It is a taking away what was before, 'old things are passed away,' and bestowing something that had no footing before. It is not a new varnish, nor do old things remain under a new paint, nor new plaster laid upon old; a new creature, not a mended creature. It is called light, which is not a quality added to darkness, but a quality that expels it; it is a taking away the stony heart and putting an heart of flesh in the room, Ezek. xxxvi. 26. The old nature remains, not in its strength with this addition, but is crucified, and taken away in part with its attendants: Gal. v. 24, 'They that are Christ's have crucified the flesh with the affections and lusts.' As in the cure of a man, health is not added to the disease; or in resurrection, life added to death; but the disease is expelled, death removed, and another form and habit set in the place. Add what you will without introducing another form, it will be of no more efficacy, than flowers and perfumes strewed upon a dead carcass, can restore it to life, and remove the rottenness. Nothing is the terminus a quo, in creation; it supposes nothing before as a subject capable; nothing in a natural man is a subject morally capable to have grace, without the expulsion of the old corrupt nature. It is called a new creature, a new man; not an improved creature, or a new-dressed man.

(5.) It is not external baptism. Many men take their baptism for regeneration. The ancients usually give it this term. One calls our Saviour's baptism his regeneration. This confers not grace, but engages to it: outward water cannot convey inward life. How can water, a material thing work upon the soul in a physical manner? Neither can it be proved that ever the Spirit of God is tied by any promise, to apply himself to the soul in a gracious operation, when water is applied to the bow. If it were so that all that were baptised were regenerate, then all that were baptised would be saved, or else the doctrine of perseverance falls to the ground. Baptism is a means of conveying this grace, when the Spirit is pleased to operate with it. But it does not work as a physical cause upon the soul, as a purge does upon the humours of the body; for it is the sacrament of regeneration, as the Lord's Supper is of nourishment. As a man cannot be said to be nourished without faith, so he cannot be said to be a new creature without faith. Put the most delicious meat into the mouth of a dead man, you do not nourish him, because he wants a principle of life to concoct and digest it. Faith only is the principle of spiritual life, and the principle which draws nourishment from the means of God's appointment. Some indeed say that regeneration is conferred in baptism upon the elect, and exerts itself afterwards in conversion. But how so active a principle as a spiritual life should lie dead, and asleep so long, even many years which intervene between baptism and conversion, is not easily conceivable.

3. Let us see what it is positively.

(1.) It is a change; and, as to the kind of it is,

[1.] A real change, real from nature to grace, as well as by grace. The term of creation is real; the form introduced in the new creature is as real as the form introduced by creation into any being. Scripture terms manifest it so. A 'divine nature,' the 'image of God,' a 'law put into the heart,' they are not nominal and notional; it is a reality the soul partakes of; it gives a real denomination, 'a new man,' a new heart', 'a new spirit', 'a new creature,' something of a real existence; it is called a resurrection: John v. 25, 'The hour is coming, and now is, when the dead shall hear the voice of the Son of God, and they that hear shall live.' If Christ had said only that the hour shall come, it had been meant of the last resurrection, but saying that it was already come, it must be meant of a resurrection in this life. There is as real a resurrection of the soul by the trumpet of the gospel, accompanied with the vigorous efficacy of the Holy Ghost, as there shall be of bodies by the voice of the Son of God at the sound of the trumpet of the archangel. All real operations suppose some real form whence they flow, as vision supposes a power whereby a man sees, and also a nature wherein that power is rooted. The operations of a new creature are real, and therefore suppose a real power to act, and a real habit as the spring of them. It is such a being that enables them to produce real spiritual actions, for the 'spirit of power' is conveyed to them, 2 Tim. i. 7, whereby as when they were out of Christ they were able to do nothing, so now being in him they are able to do all things, Philip. iv. 13.

[2.] It is a common change to all the children of God. 'If any man be in Christ, he is a new creature;' every man in Christ is so. It is peculiar to them, and common to all of them. The new creation gives being to all Christians. It is a new being settled in them, a new impress and signature set upon them, whereby they are distinguished from all men barely considered in their naturals. As all of the same species have the same nature, as all men have the nature of men, all lions the nature of lions, so all saints agree in one nature. The life of God is communicated to all whose names are written in the book of life. All believers, those in Africa, as well as those in Europe, those in heaven as well as those on earth, have the same essential nature and change. As they are all of one family, all acted by one spirit, the heart of one answers to the heart of another, as face to face in a glass. What is a spirit of adoption in them below is a spirit of glory in them above; what in the renewed man below is a spirit crying Abba Father, that is in them above, a spirit rejoicing in Abba Father. The impress and change is essentially the same, though not the same in degree.

[3.] It is a change quite contrary to the former frame. What more contrary to light than darkness? Such a change it is, Eph. v. 8; instead of a black darkness there is a bright light. As contrary as flesh and spirit, John iii. 6, 'that which is born of the flesh is flesh; that which is born of the Spirit is spirit.' Where both are put in the abstract, one is the composition of flesh, the other of spirit: as contrary as east to west, as the seed of the woman to the seed of the serpent, as the spirit of the world and the Spirit of God. The frame of the heart before the new creation, and the frame of the heart after, bear as great a distance from one another as heaven from earth. As God and sin are the most contrary to one another, so an affection to God and an affection to sin are the most contrary affections. It is quite another bent of heart, as if a man turn from north to south. It is a position quite contrary to what it was. The heart touched by grace stands full to God, as before to sin; it is stripped of its perverse inclinations to sin, clothed with holy affections to God. He abhors what before he loved, and loves what before he abhorred. He was alienated from the life of God but now alienated from the life of his lusts; nothing would before serve him but God's departure from him; nothing will now please him but God's rays upon him. He was before tired with God's service, now tired with his own sin. Before, crucifying the motions of the Spirit, now crucifying the affections and lusts. That which was before his life and happiness is now his death and misery; he disaffects his foolish pastimes and sinful pleasures as much as a man does the follies of his childhood, and is as cheerful in loathing them as before he was jolly in committing them. It is a translation from one kingdom to another: Col. i. 13, a translation 'from the power of darkness into the kingdom of his dear Son.' "Metestese", a word taken from the transplanting of colonies: they are in a contrary soil and climate, they have other works, other laws, other privileges, other natures. As Christ's resurrection was a state quite contrary to the former, at the time of his death he was in a state of guilt by reason of our sin; at his resurrection he is freed from it. He was before made under the law; he is then freed from the curse of it. He was before in a state of death, after his resurrection in a state of life, and lives for ever. God pulls out the heart of stone, that inflexibleness to him and his service, and plants a heart of flesh in the room

a pliableness to him and his will, Ezek. xxxvi. 26. It is as great a change as when a wolf is made a lamb; that wolfish nature is lost, and the lamb-like nature introduced by corruption man was carnal, and brutish; by the new creation he is spiritual and divine. By corruption he has the image of the devil; by this he is restored to the image of God. By that he had the seeds of all villainies; by this the roots of all graces. That made us fly from God; this makes us return to him. That made us enemies to his authority; this subjects us to his government. That made us contemn his law; this makes us prize and obey it: 'Instead of the thorn there shall come up the fir-tree; instead of the briar shall come up the myrtle-tree,' and God will preserve it from being cut off, Isa. lv. 13, speaking of the time of redemption.

[4.] It is a universal change of the whole man. It is a new creature, not only a new power or new faculty. This, as well as creation, extends to every part; understanding, will, conscience, affections, all were corrupted by sin, all are renewed by grace. Grace sets up its ensigns in all parts of the soul, surveys every corner, and triumphs over every lurking enemy; it is as large in renewing as sin was in defacing. The whole soul shall be glorified in heaven; therefore the whole soul shall be beautified by grace. The beauty of the church is described in every part, Cant. 1-4, &c.

First, This new creation bears resemblance to creation and generation. God in creation creates all parts of the creature entire. When nature forms a child in the womb, it does not only fashion one part, leaving the other imperfect, but labours about all, to form an entire man. The Spirit is busy about every part in the formation of the new creature. Generation gives the whole shape to the child, unless it be monstrous. God does not produce monsters in grace; there is the whole shape of the new man. You mistake much if you rest in a reformation of one part only; God will say, Such a work was none of my creation. He does not do things by halves.

Secondly, It bears proportion to corruption. As sin expelled the whole frame of original righteousness, so regenerating grace expels the whole frame of original corruption. It was not only the head or only the heart, only the understanding or only the will, that was overcast with the blackness of sin, but every part of man did lose its original rectitude. Not a faculty could boast itself like the Pharisee, and say, It was not like this or that publican; the waves of sin had gone over the heads of every one of them. Sin, like leaven, had infected the whole mass; grace overspreads every faculty to drive out the contagion. Grace is compared to light, and light is more or less in every part of the air above the horizon, for the expulsion of darkness when the sun arises. The Spirit is compared to fire, and therefore pierces every part with its warmth, as heat diffuses itself from the fire to every part of water. The natural man is denominated from corruption, not an old understanding or an old will, but the 'old man,' Eph. iv. 22. So a regenerate man is not called a new understanding, or a near will, but 'a new man,' ver. 24.

Thirdly, The proper seat of grace is the substance of the soul, and therefore it influences every faculty. It is the form whence the perfection both of understanding and will do flow; it is not therefore placed in either of them, but in the essence of the soul. It is by this the union is made between God and the soul; but the union is not of one particular faculty, but of the whole soul. 'He that is joined to the Lord is one spirit;' it is not one particular faculty that is perfected by grace, but the substance of the soul. Besides, that is the seat of grace which is the seat of the Spirit, but this or that particular faculty is not the seat of the Holy Ghost, but the soul itself, whence the Spirit rules every particular faculty by assisting grace, like a monarch in the metropolis sending orders to all parts of his dominions. The Spirit is said to dwell in a man, Gal. iv. 4, Rom. viii. 9; in the whole man, as the soul does in the body, in forming every part of it, if it dwelt only in one faculty there could be no spiritual motion of the other. The principles in the will would contradict those in the understanding; the will would act blindly if there were no spiritual light in the understanding to guide it. The light of the understanding would be useless if there were no inclination in the will to follow it, and grace in both those faculties would signify little if there remained an opposing perversity in the affections. The Spirit, therefore, is in the whole soul, like fire in the whole piece of iron, quickening, warming, mollifying, making flexible, and consuming what is contrary, like Aaron's ointment, poured upon the heart, and thence runs down to the skirts of the soul.

Fourthly, Therefore there is a gracious harmony in the whole man. As in generation two forms cannot remain in the same subject; for in the same instant wherein the new form is introduced the old is cast out; so at the first moment of infusing grace, the body of death has its deadly wound in every faculty, understanding, will, conscience, affection. The rectitude reaches every part; and all the powers of the soul, by a strong combination, by one common principle of grace acting them, conspire together to be subject to the law of God, and advance in the ways of holiness: Ps. cxix. 10, it is with 'the whole heart' that God is sought. In the understanding there is light instead of darkness, whereby it yields to the wisdom of God, and searches into the will of God: the spirit of the mind is renewed, Eph. iv. 23. In the will there is softness instead of hardness, humility instead of pride, whereby it yields to the will of God, and closes with the law of God. In the heart and conscience there is purity instead of filth (whereby it is purged from dead works, Heb. ix. 14, settled against the approbation of sin), and a resolution to be void of offence, Acts xxiv. 16. In the affections there is love instead of enmity, delight instead of weariness, whereby they yield to the pleasure of God, have flights into the bosom of God: 'Oh how love I thy law! it is my delight day and night.' The memory is a repository for the precepts and promises of God as the choicest treasure. It is a likeness to Christ; the whole human nature of Christ was holy, every faculty of his soul, every member of his body, his nature holy, his heart holy. If we are not formed, Christ is not formed in us; look therefore whether your reformation you rest in be in the whole, and in every part of the soul.

Fifthly, It is principally an inward change. It is as inward as the soul itself. Not only a cleansing the outside of the cup and platter, a painting over the sepulchre, but a casting out the dead bones and putrefied flesh; of a nature different from a pharisaical and hypocritical change, Matt. xxiii. 25-27. It is a clean heart David desires, not only clean hands, Ps. li. 10. If it were not so, there could be no outward rectified change. The spring and wheels of the clock must be mended before the hand of the dial will stand right. It may stand right two hours in the day, when the time of the day comes to it, but not from any motion or rectitude in itself. So a man may seem by one or two actions to be a changed man, but the inward spring being amiss, it is but a deceit. Sometimes there may be a change, not in the heart, but in the things which the heart was set upon, when they are not what they were. As a man whose heart was set upon uncleanness, change of beauty may change his affection; the change is not in the man, but in the object. But this change I speak of is a chance in the mind, when there is none in the object; as the affection of a child to his trifles changes with the growth of his reason, though the things his heart was set upon remain in the same condition as before.

First, It is a change of principle.

Secondly, A change of end.

First, A change of principle. The principle of a natural man in his religious actions is artificial; he is wound up to such a peg, like the spring of an engine, by some outward respects which please him; but as the motion of the engine ceases, when the spring is down, so a natural man's motion holds no longer than the delight those motions gave him, which first engaged him in it. But the principle in a good man is spirit, an internal principle, and the first motion of this principle is towards God, to act from God, and to act for God. He fetches his fire from heaven to kindle his service; an heat and fervency of spirit precedes his serving the Lord, Rom. xii. 11. There may be a serving God from an outward heat, conveying a vigour and activity to a man, but the new creature serves God from inward and heated affections. Examine therefore by what principles do I hear, and pray, and live, and walk? For all acts are good or evil, as they savour of a good or bad root, or principle in the heart. The two principles of the new creature are faith and love. What is called the new creature, Gal. vi. 15, is called 'faith working by love,' Gal. v. 6.

Faith. This is the first discovery of all spiritual life within us, and therefore the immediate principle of all spiritual motion. A splendid action without faith is but moral, whereas one of a less glittering is spiritual with it. The new creature being begotten by the seed of the word, and having thereby an evangelical frame, has therefore that which is the prime evangelical grace, upon which all other graces grow; and consequently all the acts of the new creature spring from this principle immediately, viz., faith in the precept, as a rule; faith in the promise, as an encouragement; faith in the Mediator, as a ground of acceptation. Therefore if we have not faith in the precept, though we may do a service not point-blank against the precept, yet it is not a service according to a divine rule; if we have not faith in the promise, we do it not upon divine motives; if we act not faith in the Redeemer, we despise the way of God's ordaining the presentation of our service to him. All those that you find, Heb. xi., acting from faith, had sometimes a faith in the power of God, sometimes in the faithfulness of God; but they had not only a faith in the particular promise or precept, but it was ultimately resolved into the promise of the Messiah to come: ver. 14, 'Those all died in faith, not having received the promises, but having seen them afar off,' &c. The performance of particular promises they had received, but not the performance of this grand promise; but that their faith respected. They, as new creatures, did all in observance of God promising the Mediator; and we are to do all in observance of God sending the Mediator, being persuaded of the agreeableness of our services to him, upon the account of the command, and of the acceptation of our services by him upon the account of the Mediator. This put a difference between Paul's prayer, after the infusion of grace into him, and before; so that our Saviour sets a particular emphasis upon it: Acts ix. 11, 'Behold he prays.' Paul, no doubt, had prayed many times before his believing, but nothing of that kind was put upon the file as a prayer; before, they were prayers of a self-righteous pharisee, but these of an evangelical convert; these were prayers springing from a flexibleness to Christ, a faith in him; from a Lord, what wilt thou have me to do?

Love. There are many principles of action, hope of heaven, fear of hell, reputation, interest, force of natural conscience; some of those are inward, some outward, which are the bellows that blow up a man to some fervency in action; but the true fire, that contributes an heavenly frame to a service, is the love of God. The desire of the heart is carried out to God; his heart draws near to God, because his sole delight is in God, and his whole desire for him: Ps. lxxiii. 25, 'Whom have I in heaven but thee?' Then, ver. 28, 'But it is good for me to draw near to God.' This choice affection in the new creature spirits his services, makes his soul spring up with a wonderful liveliness. The new creation is the restoration of the soul to God from its apostasy; a casting down those rebellious principles which contended with him, and reducing his affections to the right centre; and when all the lines meet here in one centre, in God, all the returns to him flow from this affection. It is but one thing settled in the soul as the object of its earnest desire, and that should be the spring of all its inquiries and actions, the beholding the beauty of the Lord. Ps. xxvii. 4. Things may be done out of a common affection; as when a man will raise a child fallen into the dirt, out of a common tenderness, but a father would raise him with more natural affection, which is a sphere above that common compassion. Every attraction therefore is not the renewed principle, but a choice affection to God. This is a mighty ingredient in this change, and does difference the new creature from all others. One acts out of affection to God, the other out of affection to itself. Men may be offended with sin, because it disturbs their ease, health, estate, &c. He may pray, and hear, merely out of a respect to natural conscience; but how can these be the acts of the new creature, when there is no respect to God in all this? But a new creature would quench the fire of corrupt self-love, to burn only with a spiritual and divine flame; he depresses the one to exalt the other, and would be disengaged from the burdensome chains of self-love that he might be moved only by the spiritual charms of the other purer affection; it is a death to him to have any steams of self-love rise up to smoke and black a service.

Secondly, A change of end as well as principle, The glory of God is the end of the new creature, self the end of the old man. Before this new creation, a man's end was to please self; now his end is to please God. A man that delights in knowledge, to pleasure his understanding, and for self improvement, when he becomes a new creature, though his desire for knowledge is not removed, yet his end is changed, and he thirsts after knowledge, not merely to please his inquisitive disposition, but to admire and praise God, and direct himself in ways agreeable to him. As the end of the sensualist is to taste the sweetness in pleasure, so the end of a renewed man is to know more of God, to taste a sweetness in him, and in every religious duty. This is the distinguishing character of the new creature. This design for the glory of God was not to be found among any of the heathens, who were so great admirers of virtue. Most of them intended only an acquiring a reputation among their countrymen; and though some of them might esteem virtue for its native dignity, yet this was to esteem it by the moiety of it, when they referred it not to the honour of God, from whence it flowed to the world. Man was not created for himself, and to be his own end; he therefore that does chiefly aim at his own satisfaction in anything, is not a new creature: he has his old deformed end into which he sunk by the fall. But grace carries a man higher, and reduces all to God, and to his well-pleasing. Col. i. 9, 10, the apostle desires they may be 'filled with the knowledge of the will' of God, that they may 'walk worthy of the Lord, unto all well-pleasing'. The very first motion of this new principle is towards God, to act for God; as the first appearance of a living seed in the ground is towards heaven; thither it casts its look, from whence its life came. What the new creature receives, is from God: 1 Thes. ii. 13, 'They received it as the word of God,' and therefore what he does is for God.

(First.) The principal intent of God in the new creation is for himself: Hosea ii. 23, 'I will sow her to me,' speaking of the church in the time of the gospel; not to sin, not to the world, not for herself, but I will sow her to me. Husbandmen sow the ground for themselves, for their own use, to reap the harvest, and the corn grows up to the husbandman that sowed it. What the seed does naturally, the new creature does intentionally, grow up for God. Since the new creature is a divine infusion, it must needs carry the soul to please God, and aim at his glory. God would never put a principle into the creature, to drive it from himself, and conduct it to his own dishonour; this consists not with God's righteousness, this would be a deceit of the creature. It is impossible, but that which is from God in so peculiar a manner, and with gracious intentions to restore the creature to his happiness, must tend to the advancement of God. Where there are no aims fit the divine glory, there is no divine nature, nothing in the soul that can claim kindred with God. Regeneration is a forming the soul for God's self, and to show forth his praise, Isa. xliii. 21, hence they are said to be 'a peculiar people,' in respect of their end, as well as their state. Certainly that man, who makes not God his pattern and his end, that does not advance the praise and glory of God, was never new formed by him. What comes from God, must naturally tend to him. Is it possible that the living image of God should disgrace the original? that a divine impression should be unconcerned in the divine author?

(Secondly.) The new creation is an evangelical impression, and therefore corresponds in its intention with the gospel. This is the instrument whereby the new creature was wrought; and this was appointed and published for the glory of God: 'Glory to God in the highest,' Luke ii. 14. It is to promote holiness in the creature, which is the only way whereby we can honour God. This is the prime lesson the grace or gospel of God teaches, to live godly, Titus ii. 12, to live to God. What, therefore, is produced by the efficacy of such an instrument, cannot but aim at the glory of God, which was intended in it; otherwise the gospel would work an effect contrary to itself, which no instrument does produce when managed by a wise agent; and contrary to the end of the agent too, viz., the Spirit of God, whose end is to glorify Christ: John xvi. 14, 'He shall glorify me.' The frame and acts of a renewed man are like the grain or seed of the word sown in the heart. Nothing the gospel designs more than the laying self low, even as low as dust and death. The first lesson is self-denial. It is in self that the strength and heart of the body of sin and lust lies; and it is the principal end of the gospel to bring the creature to sacrifice self-love to righteousness, self-interest, self-contentment, wholly to God, and his law, and his love, that God may be all in all in the creature. Before the heart was touched with the gospel, it had not the least impulse to bring forth the virtues and excellencies of God into the world; but when it is changed, it is filled to the brim with zealous desires to have his name exalted upon a high throne among men.

(Thirdly.) A new creation is the bringing forth the soul in a likeness to God. The end, therefore, of the new creature, is the glory of God. As God is the cause, so he is the pattern of the new creature, according to which he does frame the soul; it is 'after God created in righteousness,' &c., Eph. iv. 24. There can be no likeness to God where the creature dissents from him in the chief end. Without such an agreement, there can be nothing but variance between God and the creature. All the commotions and quarrels upon earth are founded upon the difference of ends. God aims at his own glory, so does the new creature, otherwise it were impossible he should walk with God, or follow him as a dear child. It consists also in likeness to Christ: his resurrection is the pattern and cause of our regeneration: 'Ye are risen with Christ,' Col. iii. 1. What, to contrary ends? Did Christ rise only to live to himself? No; but to live to God, as the great end for which he was appointed Mediator. Did he design to glorify God on earth, and does he live to dishonour God in heaven? No; he lives to the same end there for which he lived and died here. Our spiritual resurrection, is not only a restoring us to a spiritual life, but to the ends of this life; a living to God and Christ, and to the ends of his mediation. Surely the new creature cannot be so brutish, as not to mind the honour of that nature to which it is so near allied, the glory of that God unto whom it has the honour to bear a resemblance. A new creature has a mighty sprightliness, and a height of spirit in some measure, when anything in his hands concerns God, more than when it concerns himself; for his will being framed according to the will of God, is filled with an ambition for the promoting the excellency of his name.

(Fourthly.) The end of the new creation is to advance the soul. It can never be advanced by an end lower than itself, or equal to itself. Any interest lower than God would be a degrading of it, a disparagement to its state, and too sordid for the soul to drive at; for it is the excellency or sordidness of the end which does elevate or debase a man's spirit, and his actions also: the one enlarges, the other shrivels up the soul in its operation. All things below God are unworthy of the boundless nature of the soul of man, much more unworthy of a soul rectified by a new creation. The soul is only perfected in a tendency to this end, and disgraced and lost in the mud and dirt of lower aims. That grace that is most durable, and does most ennoble the spirit of a man, has this property, that it 'seeks not her own,' nor 'vaunts itself,' 1 Cor. xiii. 4, 5.

(Fifthly.) It is impossible the soul can have this new creation without a change of end. It is not conceivable how anything can return to that, which it does not eye as its end. The soul, as deriving its original from God, has an obligation in all its motions to return to him as its chief end. The new creature has an higher obligation by grace. Does that, therefore, deserve the name of the new creature, that is so far from answering a gracious tie, that it does not so much as answer a natural one? That is yet below the sphere of inanimate creatures, who all run back to their fountain, and one way or other declare the glory of God. He is no new creature, therefore, who is devotedly fawning upon himself, caressing himself; he is one that is yet bemired in his old nature, and has not yet partaken of the fruit of Christ's purchase, redeeming and renewing grace. Those that are under the efficacious influence of it, and are the temple of the Holy Spirit, 'do glorify God in their body and spirit' too, inwardly as well as outwardly, because they are God's, 1 Cor. vi. 19, 20. The understanding and will are both elevated by grace. The more intelligent any creature is, the more noble is his end, or ought to be, and the more he does intend his end. The aim of a man is higher than that of a child; the aims of men in this or that station, are still more noble than the ends of men in a lower rank. Since the new creation, therefore, endues man with the most excellent nature he is capable of, it must fix a man upon the most excellent end, which is God and his glory; it were not else a new creature, or worthy of such a title.

(Sixthly.) This change of end does only fit the soul for its proper service. From this end does arise a quickness and an heartiness in every service. When God and his glory is not our end, our hearts flag, and we feel our spirits tired at our entrance into any service for him. When the apostle had made the glory of God his end in testifying the gospel of the grace of God, then his life was not counted dear to him, that he might finish his course with joy, Acts xx. 24. Where this end sits uppermost in the heart, all allurements to the contrary are mightily despised. What a scornful eye does the apostle cast upon all other things! and sets no higher value upon them than he would upon dross and dung, when they were not conducing to his main end, which was the knowledge of Christ, Philip. iii. 8, 10.

Well, then, this is one of the most essential properties of the new creature, and that which is the clearest discovery of this state. A new creature is as earnest in secret for the glory of God, and as industrious for God, as if the eyes of all the world were upon him; the bent of his heart always stands this way; he glorifies God in his spirit as well as body, 1 Cor. vi. 20. When men will be zealous in things that concern God before men, and negligent in their spirits and inward part of the soul, then the glory of God as not their end, but themselves. For what is a man's end, sets an edge upon his spirit in private as well as public. But a new creature is of another frame. When he finds that he has missed of his full aim, and has not had that single respect as he ought, he is unsatisfied and troubled that God has been no more glorified by him. But he that is not renewed is well pleased if any concerns of self have been advanced, though God be not glorified; and his soul is at rest in that act, as it has lived to himself, and brought in something to increase the treasure of his self-ends.

Thirdly, As it is an inward change in respect of principle and end, so, thirdly, it is a change of thoughts. Being new, he is new in the choicest faculty. As when he was after the flesh he minded the things of the flesh, so now being after the spirit he minds the things of the spirit, Rom. viii. 5. As a child has not the thoughts of a man, so neither has a natural man the thoughts of a new creature. A principle is placed in his understanding which does emit other beams different from that smoky light which was in it before. Though a new creature cannot hinder the first motions, yet he endeavours to suppress their proceeding any farther, and excites others in his heart to make head against them; and would, as far as he could, hinder the rising of any wave, the least bubbling against right reason and the interest of God. When David had an inclination in his heart to God's statutes, the immediate effect of it is to 'hate vain thoughts', Ps. cxix. 112, 113, 'I have inclined my heart to perform thy statutes;' and it follows, 'I hate vain thoughts.' The vanity of his heart was a burden to him, and he loathed all the inward excrescences, any buds from that bitter stump he still bore within him. A new creature is as careful against wickedness in the head or heart, as in the life. He would be purer in the sight of God than in the view of men. He knows none but God can see the workings of his heart or the thoughts of his head, yet he is as careful that they should not rise up as that they should not break out. The soul is so changed that it is no longer a stranger and ill-willer to the motions of the Spirit; it will welcome them upon their entrance, conduct them into the innermost room, converse familiarly with them, and delight in their company, it invites their stay, pursues them when they seem to depart, holds them fast, and will not let them go, as the church does to Christ. He turns much in upon himself, sets his eye upon his own heart, keeps that with all diligence, to observe what issues of a spiritual life are there; as it is directed in Prov. iv. 23, 'Keep thy heart with all diligence, for out of it are the issues of life'. If he perceives any weeds to spring up there, or mushrooms (as they will in a night), he cuts them up and throws them out. The understanding is more quick and sensible to discern them in the first risings, to receive good ones or check bad ones, than it was before; the new creature is sensible of any touch contrary to its interest. A corrupt mind draws to it the vilest things, and unproportionable to the true nature of the soul, as a corrupt stomach does unwholesome food, till by a new creation it be set higher, and by a sanctified reason becomes more choice about its objects; and then, like David, the heart is filled as with marrow and fatness, when he meditates on God in the night watches, Ps. lxiii. 5, 6. The thoughts of God are an inward spring of pleasure to him, more than the thoughts of sin can be to a deformed and depraved soul.

Fourthly, Change of comforts follows upon this. Since there is a change of nature, there is a change of his complacency. The former nature is his trouble, therefore all his delights which arise from it are its discontents and burden. Every nature has a peculiar pleasure belonging to it: the nature of a dove will not acquiesce in that which pleases a swine, nor the new nature in that which pleases the old. The comforts of manhood are of another make than those of a child, and the comforts of a prince more elevated than those of a peasant, because he has another spirit. That Spirit who is appointed to renew him is appointed an officer to comfort him; as therefore he gives him new principles, so ho gives him new consolations. He is, as a comforter, to glorify Christ, to receive of his, and show it unto the new creature. They are Christ's own words--'He shall glorify me: for he shall receive of mine, and shall show it unto you'--being described before under the title of a Comforter, John xvi. 14. He shall receive of mine; grace from me, suitable to the grace in me, wherewith to beautify; and comforts from me, suitable to those comforts in me, wherewith to refresh you. As they are brought to live the life of God in holiness, so they are brought to live the life of God in joy and comfort. Righteousness, peace, joy are the trinity which make up the kingdom of God in the heart: Rom. xiv. 17, 'The kingdom of God is not meat and drink; but righteousness, and peace, and joy in the Holy Ghost.' As the grace of God is their life, so the joy of the Lord is their strength; strangers to God intermeddle not with it, and have no share in it. There is a joy put into the heart together with this new creature: 'Thou hast put gladness into my heart,' Ps. iv. 7--a gladness not founded upon any worldly consideration as the joy of men, not a joy of their own putting in; but the new creature's joy is a joy of God's putting in. Other men's comforts are in the creature, the new creature's comforts in the Creator. Others cannot joy if worldly things be removed, because the foundation of their joy is without them; but these, by the loss of worldly things, have their comforts rather increased than impaired, because the foundation of their joy is within them. The comforts of a natural man are sucked from the dry breasts of creatures, the comforts of a new creature are derived from the full fountain of life, which makes their very sufferings gloriously comfortable to them, 1 Peter iv. 13, 14. The prodigal by his change of mind had a change of refreshment: robes for rags, and a fatted calf for husks. It is as much his comfort to loathe himself as derived from Adam, and to love the self implanted by God, as it was before the contrary. He can never look upon the new creature in him but with delightful views, and a pleasure mingles itself with every cast of his eye upon it. For certainly from making God our end, and doing all things for his glory, endows the highest delight; since God is the only happiness of that soul that is in conjunction with him as his main end, he must needs have a share in the happiness of God as well as his nature. Felicity and consolation follow it, as the shadow does the body; and every act of the new creature towards God is edged with comfort in the very acting.

Fifthly, As it is an inward change, so it is also an outward change. I call it outward in regard of objects, in regard of operations; though it is principally inward in regard of the prime seat of it, in regard of the form, which causes the outward. The power of seeing is in the soul, though the vision itself be in the eye. The change our Saviour made in those he cured was in the organ, when he made the blind to see, the deaf to hear, and the lame to walk, which did necessarily infer a change of objects and a change of actions. So a man by this new creation sees the things of God, hears the voice of God, walks in the ways of God. All outward changes argue not an inward, but an inward is always attended with an outward.

First, In regard to objects. The world and sin was before the object of his inquiries and endeavours. Now he seeks the face of God; his soul follows hard after him. The world and God are so contrary, that the love of the one is the enmity to the other. >From multitudes of objects which distracted him, he is come to unity, which quiets and settles him: Ps. xxvii. 4, 'One thing have I desired of the Lord, that will I seek after; that I may dwell in the house of the Lord all the days of my life, to behold the beauty of the Lord, and to inquire in his temple.' It is no lower an object than this, that the soul is conversant about, about God himself, to embrace him; about what has most of God in it, to value and cherish it; about the word of God, to direct him in his ways, and to do his work. The understanding is conversant about the things of God, in the apprehension of them; the will in the election, the affections in complacency in them. Spiritual objects are set up by every faculty, as the delightful things which it heartily embraces. Before, a man had no affection to God, you might as well have persuaded a swine to love the music of a lute, as a natural man supremely to love God. All his desires were set upon the dross of the world, the customs, coarse corruptions, pleasures of the world, but a truly regenerate man can as little make the world his chief object of desire and affection, as a man used to choice viands can feed upon chaff and husks. The intendment of the gospel is to set forth God in Christ as an amiable object, as infinitely glorious. It declaims against the world, to draw men from the affectionate considerations of it. The renewed work then does consist in fixing upon God in Christ, as the main object of desire and affection. When the heart, therefore, complies with the gospel, there must be a compliance with the chief subject of the gospel, and in such a manner as may answer the intendment of the gospel. While Paul was in his natural and pharisaical state, Christ and his truth was accounted as dung, trampled upon as dross, fit to be thrown out of the converse of mankind; but when his heart is changed, there is a change in the object of his valuation: Christ is then his treasure, his all, and other things but dross in comparison of him, Philip. iii. 8.

Secondly, In regard of operations. 'Old things are passed away,' old actions as well as old affections. Operations are never constantly against nature, *operari sequitur esse*. The heart and the actions do not always contradict one another. 'According to the abundance of the heart, the mouth speaks,' Mat. xii. 24. According to the spring of grace in the heart will the hand of the life stand. It will vent itself more or less, according to the quantity of it. It is an inward baptism with fire, which will quickly break out and show itself in the members: Mat. vii. 20, 'By their fruits you shall know them.' New apprehensions infer new operations. An alteration of judgment cannot be without an alteration of acting. As he has received Christ Jesus the Lord, so he walks in him,' Col. ii. 6. The very intendment of God in the new creation was this: Eph. ii. 10, 'Created in Christ to good works, which God has before ordained, that we should walk in them.' If there be not then new works, there is no new creation, for the chief intention and aim of God cannot be frustrated. Christ formed in a man is not a sleepy and inactive being: actions will scent of him. Fruits bear the image of the root whence they spring, and upon which they flourish. A new root cannot bring forth old fruits. If the nature of a crab-tree be changed into that of a vine, it will bear no longer crabs but grapes. Where holiness is implanted in the nature, holiness will be imprinted in the fire. A man that has reason superior to sense does use his sense rationally; a renewed man that has grace superior to reason uses his reason graciously. The operations were rational when bare reason held the sceptre, but they are spiritual when grace ascends the throne; for it cannot be that that person who is acted by the Spirit, 'lives in the Spirit, walks in the Spirit' (Gal. v. 18, 25), should do anything without a spiritual tincture, in that wherein he is acted by it. For it is impossible but every action must be dyed of the same colour with the principle whence it flows, and by which it is directed. Actions of sensitive nature are be reason of grace ordered be a new rule, directed to a new end. He ate and drank to the flesh before, now to God, 1 Cor. x. 31. He degraded his soul to invent ways to pamper his body. Now he puts his body in its due posture to serve the soul, and both to exalt God. Yea, his religious duties are changed, not as to the matter, but the manner. He knew them before, as he did Christ, after the flesh; he now knows them and performs them after the Spirit. There is zeal instead of coldness, liveliness instead of deadness, brokenness instead of presumption, a spirit of liberty instead of the whip of conscience, confidence in God instead of confidence in duty, melting pleading of promises instead of a pharisaical pleading of works. In a word, grace instead of nature, spirit instead of flesh. Paul, of a pharisaical boaster, becomes a Christian suppliant; 'behold he prays.' This change is outward as well as inward. In a man of an exact morality it is chiefly inward; he walks in his old outward ways with a new heart. In a loose man renewed it is apparently outward; he has left both his old ways and his old nature; but a man only outwardly reformed, without any inward change, walks in new ways with an old spirit. 'He that lacks these things,' says the apostle, after an enumeration of several graces, 'has forgotten that he was purged from his old sins;' for indeed he never was.

Thus have I considered this new creation in the nature of a change.

2. Let us consider it in the nature of a vital principle. This new creation is a translation from death to life: 1 John iii. 14, 'We know that we have passed from death to life.' And we have not a spiritual life till we are in Christ. 'He that has not the Son has not life,' 1 John v. 12. When our Saviour called Lazarus out of the grave, he gave him a principle of life and motion. The same he does when he calls men from a spiritual death in sin. Whatsoever we had from the first Adam is mortal, whatsoever we have from the second Adam is vital; the one communicates a spiritual life, as the other propagated a spiritual death. The new creature is a vital powerful principle, naturally moving the soul to the service and obedience of God, and does animate the faculties in their several motions, as the soul does quicken the members of the body. It is called the hidden man, the inward man, implying that it has life and motion. As the life of the body is from the soul, as the effect from the cause, so the life of the soul is from grace. Christ is the meritorious cause of this life in his person, the efficient cause of it by his Spirit; but grace is the formal cause of this life, as God is the cause of our bodily life efficiently, and the soul the cause of it formally. It is not, then, a gilding, but a quickening; not a carving, but an enlivening. Whatsoever does proceed from an external cause is not life or a living motion. A piece of wood may be carved in the shape of a man, but remains wood still in such a form and figure. But a Christian has a spiritual life breathed into him, as Adam had a natural. When Adam's body was formed of the earth, it was no more than earth, till a heavenly spark was breathed into him by God, to set him upon his feet, and enable that piece of earth to move. It is distinguished therefore from hypocrisy, which is but the shadow of Christianity. This is a living principle; that a form, this a power; that a piece of art, this a

nature. A picture may have the lineaments of a man, but not the life, understanding, and affections of a man.

3. Let us consider it as a habit, and then see what light the consideration of it, as a vital principle and a habit, give us into the nature of this new creation. By habit we must not understand, as we do in common speech, a clothing, as when we say, Such a one was in such a habit; but by habit we mean an inward frame, enabling a man to act readily and easily, as when an artifices has the habit of a trade. Since this new creation is not a destruction of the substance of the soul, but that there is the same physical being and the same faculties in all men, and nothing is changed in its substance as far as respects the nature of man, it is necessary, therefore, that this new creation consist in gracious qualities and habits, which beautify and dispose the soul to act righteously and holily. Corruption of nature is the poison, the sickness, and deformity of our nature; grace is the beauty, health, ornament of it, and that which gives it worth and value. When a debauched man is become virtuous, we say he is another man, a new man, though he has the same soul and body which he had before, but he has quitted those evil habits wherewith he was possessed. It is impossible to conceive a new creature without new habits. Nothing can be changed from a state of corruption to a state of purity without them. The making darkness to become light, in the very nature of it, implies the introducing a new quality, Eph. v. 8. This is meant by the seed: 1 John iii. 9, 'His seed remains in him.' As seed makes the earth capable to bring forth good fruit, which had a nature before to bring forth, not corn, but weeds, till the grain was put info it; and it is expressed by 'a fountain of living water springing up into eternal life,' John iv. 14 ("pege").

(1.) There is such a habit. God does provide as much for those that he loves, in order to a supernatural good, as for those creatures that he loves in order to a natural good; but God has put into all creatures such forms and qualities, whereby they may be inclined of themselves to motions agreeable to their nature, in an easy and natural way. Much more does God infuse into those that he moves to the obtaining a supernatural good, some spiritual qualities, whereby they may be moved rationally, sweetly, and readily to attain that good; he puts into the soul a spirit of love, a spirit of grace, whereby, as their understandings are possessed with a knowledge of the excellency of his ways, so their wills are so seasoned by the power and sweetness of this habit, that they cannot, because they will not, act contrary thereunto. And this habit of grace has the same spiritual force in a gracious way, as those principles in other creatures in a natural way. As the habit of sin is called flesh in regard of its nature, and death in regard of its consequent, so the habit of grace is called the new creature and spirit, Gal. v. 17, in regard of its term and consequent, life. This habitual grace is the principle of all supernatural acts, as the soul concurs as an immanent principle to all works by this or that faculty. As Christ had a body prepared him to do the work of a mediator, so the soul has a habit prepared it to do the work of a new creature. To this purpose, there is a habit of truth or sincerity in the will, and a 'hidden wisdom' in the understanding, Ps. li. 6. As the corrupt nature is a habit of sin, so the new nature is a habit of grace; God does not only call us to believe, love, and obey, but brings in the grace of faith, and love, and obedience, bound up together, and plants it in the soil of the heart, to grow up there unto eternal life; he gives a willingness and readiness to believe, love, and obey.

(2.) This habit is necessary. The acts of a Christian are supernatural, which cannot be done without a supernatural principle; we can no more do a gracious action without it, than the apostles could do the works of their office unless endued with power from above, which our Saviour bids them tarry at Jerusalem for, Luke xxiv. 49. If there were not a gracious habit in the soul, no act could be gracious; or supposing it could, it could not be natural, it would be only a force. New creation is not from the Spirit compelling, but inclining; not like the throwing a stone contrary to its nature, but changing the nature, and planting other habits, whereby the actions become natural. As sin was habitual in a man by nature, so grace must be habitual in a new creature, otherwise a man is not brought into a contrary state (though the acts should be contrary) if there be not a contrary habit; for it is necessary the soul should be inclined in the same manner towards God as before it was towards sin; but the inclination to sin was habitual.

(3.) This habit is but one. For it is an entire rectitude in all the faculties, and an universal principle of working righteously. As the corrupt nature is called the 'old Adam', and a 'body of death', the gracious nature is called the 'new man,' Col. iii. 9, 10. As a man is but one man, a body one body, though consisting of divers members, and several parts, all formed by one spirit, and making up but one habit, so that as all sins are parts of that body of death, so all graces are but strings of this one root. As from that primogeneal light, kindled at the first creation by God, were framed the stars and lights of heaven, which have their several appearances and motions, and are distinct from one another, though all arising from the womb of that first light, so all particular graces, though they have their stated seasons of action, and are distinct in themselves, yet all flow from, and are contained in, this habit as in a root. They are so many grapes growing upon one stalk, clusters proceeding from one root of the new nature. It is from the participation of the divine nature that all those graces arise, the exercise of which the apostle exhorts them to, 2 Peter i. 4, &c; and indeed it being a divine nature, must needs include all the perfections due to it. As the divine essence of God is one, yet contains all perfections eminently; and if there were a deficiency of any, it could not be the divine essence; so the grace infused into the heart contains in it virtually all the perfections wherein it may agree with the nature of God's holiness, otherwise it were not a divine nature, if there were any defect in the nature of the habit, I say, in the nature of the habit. And it cannot be otherwise; for though the Spirit may give one gift to one man, another gift to another, 1 Cor. xii. 8, 9, yet when he would make a new creature, there must be a nature or habit containing all graces. It could not else be a divine nature; for if the Spirit does purpose to make a new creature, he cannot but give all grace, which belongs to the essence and constitution of that new creature, otherwise he would either wilfully or weakly cross his intention.

(4.) This habit receives various denominations, either,

[1.] From the subject. It is subjectively in the essence of the soul, but as it shows itself in the understanding, it is called the knowledge of God; as it is the will, it is a choice of God; as it is in the affections, it is a motion to God. As the body of death is in the understanding, ignorance; in the will, enmity; in the conscience, deadness; in the affections, disorder and frowardness. As diseases receive several names, as they are centred in several parts, yet are but the dyscrasy or distemper of the humours.

[2.] From the object it is diversified. As it closes with Christ dying, it is faith; as it rejoices in Christ living, it is love; as it lies at the feet of Christ, it is humility; as it observes the will of Christ, it is obedience; as it submits to Christ's afflicting, it is patience; as it regards Christ offended, it is grief; yet all arising from one habit, and animated by faith, so that it is the love of faith, the joy of faith, the humility of faith, the patience of faith, they all spring from one habit, seated in one soul, conversant about one object, God in Christ: such a unity there is in all these diversifications. As the holy oil wherewith the vessels of the tabernacle were anointed was but one ointment, though composed of many ingredients, Exod. xxx. 25, 26; as all the perfections of creatures are eminently in one God all the evil dispositions of the creatures seminally in man by nature: so all the beauties of grace are eminently included in this habit.

Hence we may take a prospect of the nature of the new creature. It being thus a vital principle, and a habit, therefore the motion to God, and for God, must be,

1. Ready in respect of disposition. He stands ready and disposed to every good work upon God's call. As the habit of sin disposes the soul to every evil work, so the habit of grace prepares it for every good work, and makes it meet for its master's use: 2 Tim. ii. 21, 'If a man therefore purge himself from these, he shall be a vessel unto honour, sanctified, and meet for his Master's use, and prepared unto every good work.' It is just as it was with Isaiah, chap vi. 6, at the first sight of the vision he complains, 'Woe is me, a man of unclean lips,' taken up with self-reflection, no offers to act for God; but when a live coal was taken from the altar and laid upon his mouth, there is a ready answer to God's question, ver. 7, 8, 'Whom shall I send? Here am I, send me.' No demurs; it was a live coal from the altar had quickened him into a new frame for God. David does not say he had performed the statutes of God, but he had 'inclined his heart' to perform them, Ps. cxix.

That I may not grate upon any troubled spirit, consider,

(1.) This readiness is seminally in every renewed person, yet it does not always actually appear. As the old nature contains in it seminally all sins, yet every men is more prone to one than another, according to education, temper of body, or a set of temptations; so the heart of a renewed man has an habitual disposition to the exercise of all grace, because it has the seeds of all graces in it, yet it does not act all alike for want of vigorous occasions. As the attributes of God, though in the highest perfection, yet in their exercise in the world, sometimes one appears more triumphant than another, sometimes more of patience, sometimes mercy, sometimes justice, sometimes wisdom, one is more eminently apparent than another; so the divine nature has seminally in this habit all grace, and an agreeableness to every duty enjoined, a principle to send forth the fruits of all when an object is offered, and the grace excited by the Spirit of God; yet sometimes one is more visible than another, according to the call it has to stand forth and show itself. This habitual disposition may be when there is not a present actual fitness for some service of a higher strain, by reason of some particular commission of sin, which has sullied the soul, as a vessel of honour in respect of its formation may be fit for use, but in respect of some foulness contracted may not be immediately fit for some noble service, till a new scouring had passed upon it. A grown Christian, who has his senses exercised in the ways of God, does not always actually exercise this habit, yet he is ready upon the least motion actually to do it; as a new creature having a change of end does habitually mind the glory of God, yet he does not in every action actually think of it, or will it as his end; but he is ready to bring this habitual aim into exercise upon the least motion, and reaches out his arm to embrace and stand right to that point. David had an habitual repentance in him while he lay asleep in his sin, and by virtue of this habit, he does without any resistance comply with the first touch God gave him by Nathan. His repentance flowed, and never ceased till it had done its perfect work. It was a sign of a heart of flesh; a heart of stone could not have been so flexible. Job was eminent for patience, but being a new creature, he had a disposition to all the rest, and had acted them with as high a strain, had he had the same occasions.

(2.) This readiness to every service does not actually appear in persons newly regenerate. I think the lowest degree of this habit in one newly regenerate, is a purpose of heart to cleave unto the Lord: Acts xi. 23, 'When he came, and had seen the grace of God, he was glad, and exhorted them, that with purpose of heart they would cleave unto the Lord.' Certainly when there is such a fixed and constant purpose, it is a token of the grace of God; yet to this purpose there may not always be connected an actual readiness to every service. For at the first beginning of the new creature there is a strong resistance, it is in a strange soil, the armies of hell are in array against it, it is like a Daniel in a lion's den, or a Lot in Sodom, only God restrains the force of these enemies. As it is in a child derived from Adam, there is a principle in the natural corruption to exert all kind of wickedness; yet it does not presently rise to the utmost of its force, till ripened by time and other intervening causes. So though the new creature has in it a readiness virtually to the most raised action, to be as believing and laborious as Paul, as zealous as Elijah, as patient as Job, yet it mounts not presently to this state; a time must be allowed for growth. There is an infancy in grace, as well as in manhood. And as a child, though his soul be of the same nature with that of a man, yet he cannot exercise those acts of understanding and reason, because of the predominance of sense, and the indisposition of the organs; so neither can a young Christian: he may have a disposition equal to the best Christians, but not an equal strength; the reluctance of the corrupt habits is more vigorous, not being much mortified; he wants also that additional strength gained by exercise. There may be a greater resistance to one grace more than to another, from the strength of some corruption particularly opposite to that grace; yet 'to will is present with him,' though he 'cannot perform that which is good,' Rom. vii. 18. The posture of the soul to God was as natural to him as the posture of the heart was before to sin; as a young boy first come to school may have as strong a purpose to get learning as a man that has taken all his degrees in the university. The first graces which appear in a renewed soul are repentance and faith; because regeneration being a rooting up from the odd stock and setting up a new, as it relates to the old stock, it does necessarily produce repentance upon the sight of his misery, and for being upon the old stock so long; and faith, as a necessary grace for closing with the Redeemer upon a sight of him, and for engrafting him upon a new stock, and then love, admiration, and thankfulness, walk the stage, from a reflection upon the greatness of the misery escaped, and the great deliverance attained. Sprouts from a root grow up, some faster, some slower, yet all arising from the same root. So some graces appear at the very first setting this habit in the soul, other graces lie hid till new occasions draw them out. This disposition, inclination, will, readiness, purpose, is the first language of a habit.

2. A second thing wherein you have a prospect of the new creature is this; as it is ready in respect of disposition, so it is in activity of motion. Since it is a life infused by infinite activity, since it is a habit bearing the impression of God, and maintained by a union with him, it is impossible it can be sleepy and dull in a constant way. All life has motion proper to the principle of it: rational life is attended with rational actions; sensitive life, with acts proper to sense. It is as impossible then that a spiritual life should be without acts consonant to it, as that the sun should appear in the firmament without darting forth its beams. All life is accompanied with natural heat, which is the band of it, whereby the body is enabled to a vigorous motion. The new creature is not a marble statue or a transparent piece of crystal, which has purity, but not life. It is a living spirit, and therefore active; a pure spirit, and therefore purely active, according to the degree of it. It is the same habit in part renewed, winch Adam had by creation, which was not a sluggish and unwieldy principle; it must therefore have an activity, it could not else be a proper principle to contest with the contrary principle, which is active like the sea, casting out mire and dirt. Since the old Adam conveyed such a vigorous principle of corruption, the new Adam is not venting to endue the principle of his conveyance with a suitable activity. Grace abounds in its vigour, as well as sin has abounded in its kind, Rom. v. 20. Upon Christ's call, Matthew left his receipt of custom; the other apostles their nets; motion presently follows an enlivening call of God. It is first a habit, then an act; first a 'spirit of grace and supplication,' then a 'looking upon him whom they have pierced,' by an act of their understanding, and a 'mourning' by an act oft he will, Zech. xii. 10, 11. First a 'sanctification of the spirit,' then a 'belief of the truth,' to the obtaining of glory, 2 Thes. ii. 13. When anything ceases to act, there is either an oppression, or a death of nature.

(1.) This principle of the new creature is naturally active. All vital motions are natural; sometimes in men there are natural actions without any actual exercise of reason, as when the spirits flow out to any part for the defence of it upon the motion of any passion, as blood starts to the face upon shame, &c, which all the reason of a man cannot hinder. It is as natural to this new habit to produce new actions, as for anything to engender according to its own likeness and species, as for a living tree to spring out in leaves and fruits. A renewed man, whose seed is within himself, brings forth fruit after its kind, as well as the herbs and the trees, Gen. i. 12. All living creatures move agreeably to their natures, with a spontaneity and freedom of nature. The bramble does not more naturally bring forth thorns, than a habit of sin does steam out sinful actions; nor a fountain more freely bubble up its water, than a habit of grace springs up in holy actions. For shall the workmanship of God be more unapt to the proper end of it, than the workmanship of the devil, since good works are the end of God's new creating us, that we should walk in them? Walking is a natural motion: Eph. ii. 10, 'We are his workmanship, created in

Christ Jesus to good works.' A well dressed vine does not more naturally bring forth grapes, than a soul rooted in Christ does the fruits of the spirit; neither does the sun more naturally enlighten the world with its beams, than the new creature shoots forth its desires and affections to God; for it is impossible but this habit should tend to him, since it is planted by him. The new creature's services are his meat and drink, not his work; it is as natural to him to do it, as for a creature to desire and take its proper food; you need not hire a child to suck, by the promises of fine things, it will naturally, without imitation, take the breast. The new creature having a righteous and just nature cannot but do righteous things; nothing can act against its nature, while nature is orderly, and not disturbed by some disease or frenzy. As God, whose image a regenerate man bears, cannot but do good, because his nature is goodness: Rom. vi. 2, 'How can you that are dead to sin, live any longer therein?' He can no more naturally do it than a dead man can walk. Not but that there are some mistakes sometimes, which proceed not from nature, but from some obstructing humour. Nature does not err in its right course unless hindered by some adversary; the errors renewed men are subject to proceed not from the regenerate principle in them, but from that remainder of corruption which by degrees is weakened by the other, and at last wholly put off.

(2.) It is voluntarily active. There is a kind of natural necessity of motion from life and habit, yet also a voluntary choice, it is a power which constrains and inclines the will: Ps. cx. 8. The apostle tells us there was a 'necessity laid upon him to preach the gospel,' 1 Cor. ix. 16, yet it was not a compulsion, but a voluntary act, after his will was changed. The new creature is not constrained from without, but flows freely, is not forced; the chief work is upon the will, the proper effect of any work upon the will is voluntariness. The Spirit works to make it willing; its motion then is not by compulsion: there is a sweet necessity of the new nature, and a gracious choice of will, which meet together and kiss each other; a natural, not a coactive necessity. How freely does the soul, winged with grace, move to and for God, as a bird in the air! With what a free and ready spirit does the new creature go to prayer, reading, and hearing! How freely does it breathe in the air of heaven! Not spurred by outward interest, or dragged by the threatenings of the law, nor chased to it by the clamours of conscience; but gently moved to it, and upheld by it, by a soft, and dove-like, and 'free spirit,' Ps. li. 12. How great is the difference between the flowing of a fountain and the dropping of a sponge; one is free, the other squeezed: between a statue drawn upon wheels, and a living motion; one moves, the other is moved. Our Saviour, by washing us from our sins in his own blood, 'has made us kings and priests unto God,' Rev. i. 6. First kings, putting into the new creature a royal and magnanimous frame, as he did into Saul when he advanced him to the kingdom; and then priests, to offer sacrifices to God with this royal and generous spirit. So that it is as troublesome to a soul, having this royal spirit, to omit things proper to this frame, as it is for a legalist to do them. Therefore where there are frequent omissions of duty, or a constant dullness in it, it shows the want of this kingly frame, and consequently that we are not washed from our sins in the blood of Christ. There is both such a nature and such a choice, that as the apostle says, 2 Cor. xiii. 8, 'We can do nothing against the truth, but for the truth.' So the new creature cannot but do the things which are holy, just, and good, so far as he is regenerate, were there no rule without to guide him, because he has a habit of holiness with him, a will set to the right point. His former state made him have an aversion from holy services this makes all spiritual duties connatural to him. So that it is as irksome for him to live without God in the world, as before it was to live with him; he can as soon strip himself of his own soul, as act, from a renewed principle, contrary to God and righteousness.

(3.) It is fervently active. The nobler the being of anything is, the greater degree of activity it is attended with; the more spiritual the quality, the more vigorous the effect. Both the spirituality of the principle, excellency of the object, and affection to the end, conspire together to increase this activity. The principle is spiritually vital; the operation therefore is vigorous: the object is God as amiable; the warmer therefore the zeal; the acts are, loving God, trusting in God, depending on God, promoting his kingdom in the heart, acts delightful in themselves, delightful in their issue, the motion in them more quick; the end is the glory of God, the happiness of the creature; the higher the end, the more elevated the soul. There is an innate principle in everything to preserve its happiness; it is as natural as life itself. Inanimate creatures are endued with this nature. The flame aspires to heaven, and waves on this and that side greedily, to catch what man supply a fuel; much more will other creatures act vehemently for that which preserves their being: the toad to its plantain, the swallow to its celandine, the babe to the breast. and the Christian to the word. There is in the new creature an impetus and force settled in the soul to do good. It is a baptism of fire following that with water. The Spirit is first as water, washing us from our filth; then as fire, quickening us with grace: Mat. iii. 11, 'I baptise you with water, he shall baptise you with the Holy Ghost and with fire.' In this respect it is likened to creatures of the greatest activity, fire, wind, a spring of living water; what more active in the rank of corporeal beings than fire and wind, either above or in the bowels of the earth? Witness the many stately buildings speedily consumed by the one or overthrown by the other. The new principle in the creature fills every part, dissolves the hard, melts the lumpish leaden heart, and makes it moveable in the ways of God with a glowing heat. But above this there is a higher denomination; the new creature is called spirit: John iii. 6, 'That which is born of the Spirit is spirit;' that is, a spiritual creature. The activity of a spirit does inconceivably

174

surmount that of a body; what vast strides can a spirit take in a moment, from heaven to earth! The habit of sin in respect of its vehemence to evil is called a spirit, 'a spirit of whoredom,' Hosea iv. 12; as well as the habit of grace, in respect of its vehemence to good, 'a spirit of love,' 2 Tim. i. 7. How active is the new creature in its motion to God! It can fly in a thought from earth to heaven, enter the bosom of God, clasp about him, hold him fast, even till almightyness bids him let him alone. Where there are rivers of living water in the belly, they will flow, John vii. 38; where there is a divine habit, the soul will have a paroxysm of divine heat for the glory of God, Acts xvii. 16. Paul's spirit was stirred in him upon the sight of the Athenians' idolatry. If created to good works, then not to a dull and sluggish motion in them, this was not the intendment of the Creator, and therefore not the disposition of the creature.

(4.) It is unboundedly active. This new creature's desires are as large as his nature, he cannot be bound up in the narrow and contracted motions of his former disposition. The natural activity of the soul overflows, like a swelled river, all natural bounds, since it is possessed by a spiritual habit. A man without a habit in an art, does but bungle at his work, is quickly tired, desponds of attaining what he would; but he that has a habit, suppose of mathematical knowledge, finds one proposition following upon another, one deduction rising up from another, that he has a largeness, he knows not where to end; so the new creature finds one affection coming upon the neck of another many times in transports and out-goings to God, which knows no limits. It is unfoundedly active;--

[1.] In affections to God. The new creature would be as unlimited in its affections to God, as God is in his affection to him. It will not fix lower than the object it has pitched upon in heaven; all its operations tend thither; nothing below can give them a cessation, though they may suffer an interruption; it flies up, and is pulled back; it mounts again and again, follows hard on after the Lord. His affections are larger than his ability. 'Whom have I in heaven but thee? and there is none in earth that I desire besides thee,' Ps. lxxiii. 25. H seems to scorn everything else in comparison of God, though it were an angel, like a man that makes haste to some mark, turns the impediments on this side and that side. The new creature puts by the temptations of the flesh and the world, to make its way into the bosom of God, the centre of its rest, and the boundless limit of its soul. The sun, so many thousand miles distant from us, sends its rays as far as the lowest valley of the earth; and the new creature, the darlings of his soul to the highest heavens. 'Where the Spirit of the Lord is, there is liberty,' 2 Cor. iii. 16,17, the veil is taken away, it 'beholds, as in a glass, the glory of the Lord;' like an eagle, mounts up as near as it can to the sun, peers upon it till its eyes be dazzled with its brightness; he is never glutted with the views of him; his desires for him are never bounded but by him; one breathing after another, that he may fill God, as it were, with his affections. as he is filled by him with his Spirit. In his obedience, too, he would have his 'heart enlarged,' that he may 'run,' not creep, in the ways of God's commandments, Ps. cxix. 32; it is his grief that he cannot keep pace with God's commandments; it is his joy that God flies upon the wings of the wind to him, and his sorrow that he cannot fly upon the wings of the wind to God. He groans under his dullness, and his pleasure consists much in a liberty in God's service.

[2.] In disaffection to sin. He hates that body of death which hinders the accomplishment of the desires of his soul, and regards it at no other rate than his fetter, disease, and torture. He is discomposed when he meets with any cheek in his religious course; it is a violence to his new nature, and he cannot bear it without regret. His anger and impatience rises with as much force against any obstacle to a free converse with God, as it did before against any impediment in the way of his lust. Nature is restless till it has got the conquest of the disease and corrupt humours of the body. Neither can a new creature be at quiet, till all that is against the interest of the new nature be purged out; and to that purpose he daily knocks at heaven gates for new strength and recruits of power against sin in the spiritual conflict. It is a trouble to him that he has not as full a sense of his own corruptions as he would, and therefore he goes frequently to God to beg new discoveries of sin, that he may fetch his enemy out of his holds and skulks, and beat it to death; for by this habit the understanding is more quick in discerning the first rising of any sinful motion, and sensible of the least touch contrary to the new interest of it.

(5.) The new nature is powerfully active. There is not only an unbounded affection, but there is a power inherent in this habit to enable the soul to act; all habits add strength to the faculty. It is therefore called 'might in the inner man,' Eph. iii. 16; and a 'spirit of power,' 2 Tim. i. 7. It is put as a stock into the heart, to maintain the acts of holiness; as there is a stock of sap in the root to produce branches and fruit. A power of acting is always united with a form, and rooted in it. In regard the new nature is implanted by a higher cause than any moral habits, even by the Spirit of God, it must be able to do more than any moral nature can; and being more excellent than moral nature, must produce more excellent operations, otherwise it were not of a more excellent kind, if it had not a more excellent power. Jesus Christ was appointed to be a quickening Spirit, to convey a powerful life, to enable us to live to God. 'The kingdom of God' in the heart, as well as that in the world, 'is not in word, but in power,' 2 Cor. iv. 20. Move steel as often as you will, you can never make it of itself move towards the north; but by the impression made on it by the loadstone, there is a power derived to turn and stand that way of its own accord. By nature we are 'without strength,' Rom. v. 6, because without life, Eph. ii. 1. But in the renewing there is strength conveyed together with life, an ability to walk in God's statutes, convoyed with the new heart; out of weakness the soul is made strong; and the grace within, in concurrence with the supplies of the Spirit, is sufficient for it. It is not only an outward strength, as is from a staff in a sick man's hand, but an inward might. But besides this inherent strength there is an adherent ability; for Christ, who is his life, Col. iii. 4, is also his strength: Philip. iv. 13, 'I can do all things through Christ which strengthens me.' So that whatsoever active power is wanting in itself can be supplied by the head. And therefore the new creature has a kind of almighty power of activity, by the communication of another, which is called a greatness of power, and a mighty power which works towards them, or, "eis hemas", in them that believe, Eph. i. 19. This power does reside in the heart, and this adherent power is ready for it, but neither of them is always perceptible, but upon some emergency, as a sound man has a greater power to act than he puts forth upon all occasions.

(6.) It is easily active. Since that motion to God, and for God, is connatural and voluntary, and a power and ability also in the new creature, it must follow, that the motion is very easy. Habits are to strengthen the faculty, and facilitate the acting of it. Bubbling is no pain to a fountain; rivers of water flow out of the belly easily, because naturally. The motion of this habit is as easy as the motion of the lungs, or the pulse of the artery; though constant, yet not troublesome or painful in itself, but by reason of some imparted humour settled in them. This stock of grace is called the unction: 1 John ii. 20, 'But you have an unction from the Holy One;' the inward oiling the soul, as oil communicates agility to the body. This unction some understand of habitual grace conveyed from the Holy One by the Spirit. As this unction upon our Saviour was the cause of his activity for God in doing good,--Acts x. 38, 'God anointed Jesus of Nazareth with the Holy Ghost and with power; who went about doing good,'--so it being the same in the new creature, will have the like effect upon him. Supernatural motions are as easy, by the strength of a supernatural habit, as natural motions are by the strength of natural habits. A bird does with as much ease fly upward as a beast walks upon the ground, and the seed does with as much ease spring up, and put its ear out of the ground, as a bitter root does its unwholesome fruits and flowers. So when the soul is filled with this new habit, the walks in the ways of God are as easy by virtue of it as a course of sin and folly was before. The yoke of itself is easy, Mat. xi. 30, and the motion under a light yoke cannot be grievous. The very yoke is not a shackle and burden, but a privilege. There is indeed some reluctance sometimes, which arises not from the will as renewed, but from some evil habits resident in the soul, not yet fully conquered by renewing grace. You know how the apostle Paul does distinguish between the posture of his will, and the interruptions by that sin which dwelt in him, Rom. vii. 18-20.

(7.) It is pleasantly active. "Hedu men to kata fusin", says the philosopher. As all actions which flow from life are pleasant, so those which flow from a divine life in the soul. It is a joy to a just man to do judgment, Prov. xxi. 16. That is, the entire inclination of the soul stands right to such actions; and as much a joy to him to do judgment, when enabled thereunto by a gracious habit, as it is to a sinful man under the bonds of iniquity to commit it. His soul leaps as much at an opportunity of pleasing God, as John Baptist did in his mother's womb at the appearance of Christ, as much as his heart sprang up before at the proposal of a sinful object. Never did the sun naturally rejoice so much 'like a strong man to run its race' in the heavens, Ps. xix. 5, as the new man does spiritually rejoice to run his race to heaven. It is a mighty pleasure to have our spiritual enemies under our feet, to be estranged from them. It is the purest delight to comply with God, and be embosomed in him. He is shallowed up in these choicer pleasures, as a man that has had his full draughts of learning is in his studies, whence his diseases cannot draw him, though in his childish time he counted them his task and burden. The delights of an heart seasoned with habitual grace are more ravishing than all the pleasures of sense, because they arise from an habit planted in the soul by that Spirit which is a Spirit of joy as well as of grace. The fatness of God's house, the sacrifices presented by him, are his delight, and he drinks of a river of pleasure in his very acts of worship: Ps. xxxvi. 8, 'They shall be abundantly satisfied with the fatness of thy house, and thou shalt make them drink of the rivers of thy pleasures.' 'In keeping thy commandments there is great reward,' Ps. xix. He finds much sweetness in the very acts of worship. Ah, how can the motions of the habits of sin, under the quarrels of conscience, yield as much delight as the habits of grace under the breathings of the Spirit! The very marks of Christ in his body are his delight and triumph. He takes pleasure in distresses for Christ's sake: 2 Cor. xii. 10. says the apostle. 'I take pleasure in infirmities, in reproaches, in necessities, in persecutions, in distresses for Christ's sake.' The motions of his soul to Christ are his life and joy. He chides his soul that her flights to Christ are not so strong as Christ's flights to him. He would have a delight in doing the will of God's precept, as Christ had in doing the will of the mediatory command. He rejoices in his breathings after God, though he wants him, and is glad his soul can have any flights towards him though he cannot find him. The tabernacles of God are amiable, when his 'heart and his flesh cries out for the living God': Ps. lxxxiv. 1, 2, 'How amiable are thy tabernacles, O Lord! my soul longs, yea, even faints for the courts of the Lord.' And when, by reason of some distemper, he cannot move so readily, some disease fetters him, some corruption has cast a clog upon him, yet he delights in the thoughts of what he had, as a man in the former converses with his friend, though now at a distance, and cheers up his soul with the thoughts that he will again return: Ps. xiii. 6,

11, 'Why art thou cast down, O my soul? hope thou in God, for I shall yet praise him,' He grieves because he at present cannot do what he would, and hopes for another frame, and rejoices in the faith that he shall repossess it: 'He will turn again,' &c., Micah vii. 19. A natural man without an habit of grace may move in some ways outwardly good, but with some reluctance, and without any pleasure in the goodness of the thing enjoined, or the goodness of that God who enjoins it. He may have a sudden inclination to do a good action, but he is not pleased with that inclination itself. Ahab's humiliation was good in itself, no doubt, but Ahab was pleased with it, but not as it was a humiliation, or had a likeness to a gracious action, or a tendency to the pleasing God, but as it was a means of removing the judgment threatened, so that his pleasure was only in the issue of it; but a gracious soul is pleased with the habit itself, for he considers it as the perfection of his nature, regards it as an ancient inmate, though separated from his nature by Adam's degeneracy, as friends long absent rejoice in one another. When this rectitude is in part restored, and understood to be of kin to it by creation, but lost and now returned, there must needs be an high complacency in the soul, and a joyful compliance with it. And the stronger and more vigorous this inward rectitude is in habit, the more pleasure a man has in the exercise of it. As God, who is infinitely righteous in all his ways and in all his works, has an infinite pleasure in the exercise of this righteousness, and an infinite loathing of what is contrary to it, because it is his infinite nature, so the stronger the habit in a man, the more contentment there is in the exercise of it, because his nature is more elevated. And what is natural is delightful, and the more natural, the more delightful. Mercy is natural to God, therefore he delights in it; and because infinitely natural, therefore he does infinitely delight in it.

Well then, since all the motions of nature are pleasant, the new nature is not inferior in the pleasure of acting to any other nature whatsoever. It being the most perfect nature, must beget the most delightful operations. What a pleasure is it to draw near to God, to melt before him, to pour out a prayer to him, and dissolve itself into love and affection in any address to him!

(8.) It is a permanent activity. There is a spring of perpetual motion. The fountain does constantly bubble. The sun does constantly move, because naturally. Whatsoever is natural is constant in its posture; a fire perpetually burns, and water perpetually cools. What is the essential property of a thing does competere semper. A man is always rational, and ready to act reason; if there be any indisposition, it is not in the soul, but in the organ or ill habit of the body, which does obstruct the motions of the soul, and is an unfit instrument for it to act by. This habit is not a passion, but a principle; not a motion, but a spring of uniform motion; it is wrought in the nature, and like the heart is continually beating. The principle is permanent, it is an abiding anointing, 1 John ii. 27, it is settled by God, given to us in Christ, backed and assured by the earnest of the Spirit in the heart, where this habit is seated. All is expressed, 1 Cor. i. 21, 22, 'Now ho which establishes us with you in Christ, and has anointed us, is God, who has also (that is, beside this) sealed us, and given the earnest of the Spirit in our hearts.' It is a life and habit more fixed than that in Adam: his life depended upon the rectitude of his soul, but this depends principally upon the power of the Spirit, and the everlasting life of Christ. It is a water which quenches all thirst, and never leaves springing till it mount up to eternal life, John iv. 14; it is perpetually active and springing, till it be swallowed up in glory, as rivers in the sea. Others may move by some wires, and have some strains of a natural religion, by some sudden impulses which touch the strings and faculties of the soul but the wires break, the touch ceases, and the motion with it, it has no living spring. Nay, sometimes those motions in natural men under the gospel may be more quick, and warm, and violent for a time than the natural motion of this habit; as the motion of a stone out of a sling is quicker than that of life, but faints by degrees, because it is from a force impressed, not implanted and inherent in the nature. They are just like water heated by the fire, which has a fit of warmth, and may heat other things; but though you should heat it a thousand times, the quality, not being natural, will vanish, and the water return to its former coldness. But the new heart being in the new creature, causes him to walk in the statutes of God, not by fits and starts, but with an uniform and harmonical motion, Ezek. xxsvi. 27, 'Ye shall keep my judgments and do them;' you shall treasure them in your minds and act them in your lives. Not but that there are in the new creature some faintings; it is sometimes more vigorous, sometimes more weak in its motion; it has its sicknesses; it meets with wounds, but none of them to death. Every one that is born of the Spirit is like the wind, John iii. 8, it moves and blusters, and when you think it is passed away, it returns, resumes its force, and you feel as stiff a motion as you did before. A man is never weary of that which is habitual to him. There may be a weariness in duty and service, but not a weariness of it, so as to throw it off; but after he has refreshed and recruited himself, his habit will put him upon a delightful return to it. Where the ways of God are in the heart habitually, such shall go from strength to strength, till they appear in Sion, though there may be some rests and intermissions by the way: Ps. lxxxiv. 5, 6, 'In whose heart are the ways of them;' some read, 'the high way of God in their hearts,' more consonant to the Hebrew.

(9.) It is an orderly motion and activity/. Natural motions are orderly. As affirmative precepts bind semper, but not ad semper, so this habit enables the soul semper, but not ad semper; I mean, not to this or that service at all times. Natural things have their stated times, places, and measures. As trees bring forth fruit in their season, so does the new creature bring forth fruit 'in his season,' Ps. i. 3, in a season proper for that fruit. It is always producing some fruit or other, according to the particular seasons, sometimes love, sometimes humility, sometimes patience. This habit is ready at hand, whence he draws out fruits new and old. As God does all things in weight, and number, and measure, so does this habit of his own implanting. As God gives every creature meat in due season, so the new creature renders God his fruit in due season. As a wicked man is always acting sin, sometimes one, sometimes another, according to the seasons of them, so does this habit in the new creature act grace, sometimes one, sometimes another.

From all these things put together there follows,

1. A predominance of grace in the new creature. As a state of nature consists in the prevalence of the corrupt habit which leavens the whole man, so the state of grace in a predominance of the gracious habit, which spreads itself over the whole soul, striving with the powerful opposite, which in part resides there still. It is a habit put in to mate and destroy that habit of sin which was there before; the soul by it is made alive from the dead: Rom. vi. 13, 'Yield yourselves to God, as those that are alive from the dead.' Life triumphs over death, grace over nature, whereby the members become instruments of righteousness unto God, instead of being instruments of unrighteousness unto sin. It is put in to guide reason and will, and therefore is invested with the sovereign power. As sense was first in man, but that veiled when reason stepped into the throne, as being a more excellent principle than sense, so must reason descend and give place to grace when that comes in, as being a more excellent principle than reason. It is reason, it should have the sovereignty, for it does but regain its own right, and take possession, which by the law of creation it ought to have kept till violently ejected by man. He that has this habit has a spirit of might as well as of the fear of the Lord; the same spirit which was in Christ, which is a 'spirit of might,' Isa. xi. 2. 'They that are Christ's have crucified the flesh, with the affections and lusts,' Gal. v. 24: have, not shall. As soon as ever they are Christ's, which they are by this principle, a deadly wound is given to sin; such a one scorns to have anything more to do with idols, Hosea xiv. 8. He overcomes the world: 1 John v. 4, 'Whatsoever is born of God overcomes the world.' He can do all things: enter the lists with the strongest Goliath, repel the sharpest temptations, through Christ which strengthens him, Philip. iv. 13, so that grace is predominant.

2. There follows from hence a difficulty to sin. No creature can easily act against a rooted habit; how hard is it to make a beast do that which is different from and contrary to his nature, To act contrary to nature is burdensome and intolerable. What creature would willingly change its element? Will a bird sink of its own accord into the water, or a fish delight to leap upon the land, whose only element is the water? What creature would court the destruction of its life? What man would willingly deform and gash his own body? Men never do so by nature, but when frenzy has dispossessed them of their reason. Sin must dispossess a Christian of his grace before it can be easy for him to run into ways destructive to his nature and blessedness. That principle which is in all natures must be more eminently in the highest nature, and proportionately in every nature that is of nearest approach to it. Righteousness and holiness is the very constitution of the new creature: Eph. iv. 24, 'That new man, which after God is created in righteousness and true holiness.' It is as impossible for the new creature to sin by the influence of habit, as for fire to moisten by the quality of heat, or water to burn by the quality of cold. It is as impossible for that habit to bring forth the fruits of sin, as for the sun to be the cause of darkness, or a sweet fig-tree to bring forth sour fruit. Yet as there is darkness in the air, though the sun be up, by the interposition of thick clouds so is there darkness in the new creature from the habit of sin in the soul, which is not only a lodger, but an unwelcome inhabitant: Rom. vii. 20 'Sin that dwells in me' still, and acts according to its nature, though much over-powered and weakened by degrees by that habit of grace. Therefore it is a hard thing for him to sin: 1 John iii. 9, 'He cannot sin.' It in as hard for him to contradict the new nature as before to cross the old: 'I cannot do this wickedness,' says Joseph; it is against the frame and disposition of my soul.

(1.) It must be difficult to sin against 'purpose of heart,' which is the lowest step of the new nature, Acts xi. 23, though it be not hard to sin against a flashy resolve.

(2.) It is hard for a man to sin who has cordially chosen God for his portion, which every new nature does, with a fixed revelation to keep his word: Ps. cxix. 67, 'Thou art my portion, O Lord: I have said that I would keep thy word.' When it is carried out with a free motion to God, it cannot easily be diverted from that charming object; he cannot but value any diversion at no better a rate than that of punishment.

(a.) It is difficult for him to contradict the new habit, wherewith he is so highly pleased, and which he is assured has nothing but happiness in the womb of it.

(4.) It must be difficult for him to act that which, by virtue of this habit, he is daily in the mortification of.

(5.) It is difficult for the habit of sin in him to do the same acts after it has received a deadly wound, as for a wounded man to do that which he could when he was sound.

(6.) This nature cannot be in a man without an universal enmity to sin, though it may without an universal victory, this belongs to the perfection of it, but enmity to the very constitution of it: Gen. iii. 16, 'I will put enmity between the seed of the woman and the seed of the serpent.' He can at the best but half sin, and scarce that; he could not commit sin very freely before, because of the reluctance of natural conscience; he can less freely do it now, since there is a habit of grace in him, which does more powerfully fly in the face of sin when it appears; therefore there can be but a partial will to it or delight in it. The new man in the heart can never do it; the old man remaining cannot fully do it, because of the contradiction it receives from the new habit. If he does at any time sin, this new nature can no more be pleased with it than the nature of a man is with the poison which he has wilfully taken, which will contest with it, and endeavour to expel it, whether a man will or no. So that if a new creature be caught at a disadvantage, and be bemired by the remaining habit of sin in the heart, his spirit is wounded, his soul bleeds, his conscience upbraids him, he is displeased with himself and with his sin, runs to God, searches into himself, calls heaven and earth to his assistance, sharpens his spiritual weapons, and by virtue of this habit in him is dissatisfied, and in little ease, till he has overcome this rebellion of lust, dispossessed it, removed the guilt, and cast out the filth.

4. As we have considered this work as a change, a vital principle, a habit, so we will consider it as a law put into the heart. Every creature has a law belonging to its nature, so has the new creature. Man has a law of reason, beasts a law of sense and instinct, plants a law of vegetation, inanimate creatures a law of motion. A new creature has a law pot into his heart: Jer. xxxi. 23, 'I will put my law in their inward parts, and write it in their hearts,' cited by the apostle, Heb. viii. 10. It is called the 'law of the mind,' Rom. vii. 23, it beginning first in the illumination of that faculty. As sin begun first in a false judgment made of the precept of God, 'You shall be as gods, knowing good and evil.'

Now, as to this law put into the heart, you may know what is meant by it in some propositions.

(1.) This law of the mind, or law written in the heart, is not wholly the same with the law of nature. Some indeed tell us that it is nothing but the law of right reason. But certainly they are mistaken,--it is a law of grace. The law of nature was the law of a covenant of works, this law of the mind is the law of the covenant of grace. The law of nature is in all men, this law of grace only in some; the law of nature was in Paul before his conversion, this law of the mind was in him upon his conversion. The law of nature consists not of faith in a mediator, but faith is a main part of the law of grace. The law of nature acquaints not a man with the knowledge of all sins, not with unbelief; this law of grace does, for the conviction of this is a work of the Spirit: John xvi. 8, 9, 'Of sin, because they believe not in me.' The law of nature is the general work of the mediator in all men, 'who enlightens every man that comes into the world,' John. i. 9. This is the peculiar work of the Mediator, by his Spirit, in the hearts of those that believe; the law of nature does not oppose sin as sin, this law of grace does; the law of nature is no part of sanctification, for this is in men that are born of the flesh, are flesh still; but the law of the mind is a part of sanctification, and wars against the law of the members; there is indeed a war and a contest from the law of nature against some gross sins, but not against the law of sin in the members. As sin wars against the law of the mind, as a law of direction, so the law of the mind, or the law of grace, wars against sin, as it is a law which pretends to guide and order the ways of a man.

(2.) Yet it is the restoring of that law which was the law of nature originally. It is a renewing in the heart that law which was written in the heart of Adam: Eph. iv. 24, 'That new man, which after God is created in righteousness and true holiness;' or after God was created "ktisthenta", alluding to that righteousness wherein Adam was created, lost by him, and restored by Christ. This righteousness which Adam had was the righteousness of the law: holiness towards God, which includes the duties of the first table; righteousness, including the duties of the second table; and truth being added (as it may be referred both to holiness and righteousness), shows the sincerity of it in the manner and the end of being holy to God and righteous to man. This was the law written in the heart originally, which was defaced by the fall, and whatsoever relics there were of this law in man, were only upon the account of the mediation of Christ, it is this law which is new engraved in the soul by regeneration. God does not say, I will write another law in their hearts, but 'my law' Jer. xxxi. 33,--that which was my standing law, my law to Adam, and to your fathers. The law written in the heart is not substantially distinct from that in the nature of Adam. Man by his fall did blot this law, lost his righteousness, had an enmity in his heart to it, and to the very relics of it. He is not naturally subject to the law, nor can be, as it is the law of God, because of his enmity to God, Rom. viii. 7; the law of sin had taken place instead of it. Regeneration is a taking down the law of sin, and fixing the law of God in its due place and posture.

(3.) This law is written in the heart wholly. The whole law, every command which has the print of God upon it, is written there. As God wrote his whole law in tables of stone, so he writes the whole law in the 'fleshly tables of the heart,' 2 Cor. iii. 3. It is true holiness and righteousness; true, as to its essential and integral parts. God does not write one part of the law upon the heart, and leave out another; it is not a moiety of it, the impression of one command, and the defect of another. If it were not the whole law, something belonging to the essence of a new creature would be wanting. It would not be a new creature, because it would be a monster, wanting something necessarily requisite to the constitution of it, and would not be a new creature according to the original copy. Where there is an agreeableness in one nature to another, it is to the whole nature, the nature of the soul to the nature of the law.

(4.) This law written in the heart does not make the outward law useless, for that is still a rule. This inward law written in the heart is a conformity to the outward rule, and therefore is not a rule itself. The law in the heart is imprinted by the external word in the hand of the Spirit; and therefore to try the truth of the law within, we must have recourse to the law written. If a man has any notions of any human law, he must consult the law written, to know whether his notions of it be right, and whether his actions be according to the letter and reason of the law or no. As the law of sin within a man is not the rule of judging of sin, but the law of God, so neither is the law of grace within the rule of judging good, but the word of God. The law within, though it be commensurate to the law in its essential parts, yet it is imperfect as yet; but a rule ought to be perfect, Ps. xix. 7, and so the written law is. It is this law written in the word that we are to take heed to, for the cleansing of our ways: Ps. cxix. 9, 'Thy word have I hid in my heart, that I might not sin against thee.' When this writing of the law in the heart was promised, ver. 11, there was also an inward teaching promised: Jer. xxxi. 32, 'And they shall teach no more every man his neighbour, saying, Know the Lord;' which is spoken in regard of the abundance of the knowledge which should be in the time of gospel light, above what was in the twilight of Jewish ceremonies; so that the weakest Christian under the gospel knows more of God and his attributes in Christ, than the greatest Jewish doctor did before the coming of Christ. This was not so understood by Christ, as if teaching others were utterly useless; for then why should he institute apostles, pastors, teachers, &c., and promise to be with them to the end of the world, if this promise of inward teaching made outward teaching useless? In like manner, neither does the limiting the law in the heart make the outward written law useless, but rather it does establish and advance it, and the esteem of it. The outward law is the rule, as the model of a house is the rule by which a carpenter is to make a building, and to which he is to conform that idea he has in his mind of it; but that idea or figure of it which he has in his mind, is to be suited to that role which is prescribed to him in the outward pattern; and therefore that pastern is to be consulted with. The law of God is of eternal duration; and as it is a law of holiness and love of God, does oblige every reasonable creature, in what condition soever he be, whether of nature, grace, or glory.

Quest. Wherein does this writing of the law in the heart consist?

Ans. (1.) In an inward knowledge of the law, and approbation of it in the understanding. The knowledge of righteousness and the being of the law in the heart, are put together as the proper character of the people of God: Isa. li. 5, 'Hearken to me, ye that know righteousness, the people in whose heart is my law.' Lest they should think a knowledge were enough, he adds, 'In whose heart is my law;' not in the head, but in the heart. There is in a renewed understanding, a principle teaching how to make use of the law. It is like the inward skill of a pilot, who guides the ship by the compass and rudder. The outward law is the compass by which we must steer; the inward law is the practical knowledge of this; an inward skill to make application of it to particular occasions. The word of God being a seed, does, as every seed, produce a being like itself, and like that plant whose seed it is: from the seed of corn arises a grain of the same nature. This seed being sown first in the understanding, is there cherished, and grows up in principles and thoughts agreeable to itself, whereby the mind becomes the epistle of Christ, 2 Cor. iii. 3, and an ark to preserve the tables of the law; whence David speaks of his soul keeping God's testimonies, Ps. cxix. 167, and not forgetting them, ver. 16. The new creature by its new light sees an amiableness in the law, a holiness in the precepts, and a filthiness in himself thereby.

(2.) It consists in an inward conformity of the heart to the law. The soul has a likeness to the word and doctrine of the gospel within it; it is delivered into that mould: Rom. vi. 17, 'You have obeyed from the heart that form of doctrine, into which you were delivered.' He considers the gospel as a mould, and the Romans as a metal poured into it, and putting on the form of it. As melted metal poured into a mould loses its former form, and puts on a new shape, the same figure with the mould into which it is poured; the soul, which before was a servant of sin, and had the image of the law of sin, being melted by the Spirit, is cast into the figure and form of the law. As when a seal has made its impression upon wax, the stamp in the one answers exactly to the stamp on the other, put the seal on again, and they both will meet as close as if they were one body, the wax will fill every cavity in the seal; but put this seal to any impression made by another seal, there will be an inequality, the stamp on the seal and that on the wax will not close. The law of sin and the law of God, being contrary impressions, cannot close together; but the law of grace in the heart and the law of God close, they being but one and the same stamp. So that when any command of God appears, a new creature finds something within it of kin to it; as a natural man finds something ready to close with sin upon the appearance of it. The heart answers to the law as a lock to a key, ward for ward; sometimes it may not answer but resist, as a lock does, because of some rust or some filth got up into it; but then it needs not a new making but a new cleansing, to answer exactly to the key of the law. So that as the 'Gentiles, having not the law, are a law to themselves.' Rom. ii. 14, having it written upon their minds in those notions common to mankind, so the new creature, if he had not the written law, would be a law to himself. So natural is this conformity, that were there no law without, the renewed soul would naturally be carried out in the ways of holiness. 'The law,' says the apostle, 'is not made for a righteous man,' 1 Tim. i. 9, it is not chiefly intended for the righteous, but for the unrighteous, who would not stir one step in any good action without it, and will hardly stir with it. There would be no need of any written law in a commonwealth, if all men had an exact justice and righteousness in their own minds, and did conspire to the good of the community. But when disturbers of the peace and common welfare start up, there is need then of public laws to restrain them. But there is no need of a public enacting of a law for them that are good, because what the law enjoins they do by their one judgements and inclination. So that what a new creature does in observance of the law, is from natural freedom, choice, and judgment, and not by the force of any threatenings annexed to it.

(3.) It consists in a strong propension to the obedience of it. As there was a strong impetus in the old nature, inclining it to sin, so there is a strong impulse in the new nature, biasing it to observe the commands of the law. In this respect it is chiefly called a law written in the heart, in regard of the efficacious virtue of this new nature, sweetly constraining and directly conducting to the performance of it. The law without us commands us, the law within constrains us. That enjoins a thing to be done, this inclines us to the doing of it. The first law is written in the Scripture or in the conscience, whereby we judge those commands to be kept; the other consists in the propension of love, or faith working by love. As the impulse of concupiscence is called 'the law of sin,' Rom. vii. 25, so the impulse of grace is called the law in the heart; not as a thing distinct from the law without, but only a counterpart of it, an indenture answering to the other. They are but two parts united between themselves, and compose one perfect law; one as the direction, the other as the practice. That lays the injunction, this embraces it; and as naturally from the disposition of the new nature as he did embrace the law of sin from the disposition of the old. It is a powerful operative law of the Spirit of life, which 'sets us free from the law of sin and death,' Rom. viii. 2; not a dead letter, but an active principle, quickening the heart to close with the law, and delivering it from that which was the great hindrance to it. As the devil does act in men's hearts, Eph. ii. 2, not personally, but by a principle in the heart, the law of sin, so does the Spirit of life by the law of grace; for being written by a living Spirit, it is a living law. This is the chief intent or the whole new creation, to cause us to walk in God's statutes, Ezek. xxxvi. 26, 27. Ps. xxxvii. 31, 'The law of God is in his heart, none of his steps shall slide.' The soul being thus evangelised and spiritualised, may be said to do by nature the things contained in the gospel, as the Gentiles are said to do by nature the things contained in the law, Rom. ii. 14, because there was a law of nature engraved in them.

(4.) It consists in a mighty affection to the law. What is in the word a law of precept, is in the heart a law of love; what is in the one a law of command, is in the other a law of liberty. 'Love is the fulfilling of the law,' Gal. v. 14. The law of love in the heart, is the fulfilling the law of God in the Spirit. It may well be said to be written in the heart, when a man does love it. As we say, a beloved thing is in our hearts, not physically, but morally, as Calais was said to be in Queen Mary's heart. They might have looked long enough before they could have found there the map of the town, but grief for the loss of it killed her. It is a love that is inexpressible. David delights to mention it in two verses together: Ps. cxix. 47, 48, 'I will delight myself in thy commandments, which I have loved: my hands will I lift up to thy commandments, which I have loved;' and often in that psalm resumes the assertion. Before the new creation, there was no affection to the law; it was not only a dead letter, but a devilish letter in the esteem of a man: he wished it razed out of the world, and another more pleasing to the flesh enacted. He would be a law to himself, but when this is written within him, he is so pleased with the inscription, that he would not for all the world be without that law, and the love of it: whereas what obedience he paid to it before, was out of fear, now out of affection; not only because of the authority of the lawgiver, but of the purity of the law itself. He would maintain it with all his might against the power of sin within, and the powers of darkness without him. He loves to view this law; regards every lineament of it, and dwells upon every feature with delightful ravishments. If his eye be off, or his foot go away, how does he dissolve in tears, mourn and groan, till his former affection has recovered breath, and stands upon its feet! If he finds not his heart answering the law, he longs after the precepts, as the prophet says: Ps. cxix. 40, 'I have longed after thy precepts, quicken me in thy righteousness.' He longs to join hands again with the holiness of them. As his heart is inclined to obey it, so it is wounded upon any neglect of it, and never at ease, till he be reduced to his former delight in it. He has no mind ever to part with it, because of its intrinsic goodness, as well as convenience for him. It is his pleasure, not his confinement; his ornament, not his fetter; he hates every thing that is contrary to it. How does Paul grieve and groan under 'the body of death,' when he considered what opposition 'the law in his members made against the law of his mind'? Rom. vii. 23, 21. The law in his members 'brought him into captivity to the law of sin.' Then, 'Oh wretched man that I am! though he knew he was in part delivered from it. How does he long for a perfect redemption from his shackles, which hindered him from following the law of his delight! And he that never murmured at his sufferings, but could glory in persecutions and death for Christ, seems to be impatient till he could hear the last expiring groan of this enemy: all which says the effect of his 'delight in the law of God after the inward man,' ver. 22. And that this writing the law does principally consist in this affection, those two expressions, 'putting the law into the inward parts,' and 'writing it in the heart,' intimate. The nature of man being enmity against the law of God, the writing it argues, not a change of the law, but a change of the frame of the heart to the law, that should be so fashioned, that the law should reign there, and all his affections subscribe to it. As the writing the law in the heart of Christ was nothing else but the agreeableness of the mediatory law to him, and his delight in it, Ps. xl. 8, so it is with a new creature.

(5.) It consists in an actual ability to obey. Writing the law in the heart implies a putting a power and strength into the soul, enabling it to run the ways of God's commandments, as well as to incline the heart and affections to them; the promise is made to the latter times: not but that the ancient patriarchs were regenerate, but not by the law, not by any covenant of works: this ability did not reside in the law, but was transferred to them from the gospel. In this respect it is called 'a letter,' 2 Cor. iii. 6, because it did only instruct the eye or ear, when read or heard: this teaches the heart; that a killing letter, this a quickening Spirit; that exacted the observance of its precepts, but wrote nothing in the heart to answer it, but condemned upon neglect, this commands the observance of the law, and gives an ability evangelically to perform it. That was a ministration of condemnation, this of righteousness, 2 Cor. iii. 9; that could do no other but condemn, because it gave no intrinsic power to observe it. It is through Jesus Christ that we are enabled, by virtue of this inward writing, to serve with our minds the law of God, though in our flesh we be captivated by the law of sin. As an unregenerate man is dragged to any good, but willingly obedient to the motions of sin, so a regenerate man is sometimes under the rape of sin, but is willingly obedient to the motions of grace. So that the law is written in the heart, in respect of the assent of the understanding, consent of the will, pleasure of the affections: in the understanding, by the clearness of the light of faith, in the will, by the heat of the fire of love. In the understanding there is a judicious approbation of it; in the will, a motion to it, closing with it, and an affection to keep it; and, according to its ability, an endeavour to keep pace with it.

5. The fifth thing. As there is a vital principle, an habit, a law written in the heart, so there is a likeness to God in the new creature. Every creature has a likeness to something or other in the rank of beings: the new creature is framed according to the most exact pattern, even God himself. In this the form of regeneration does consist. The new creature is begotten; begotten, then, in the likeness of the begetter, which is God. As sin is the impression of Satan's image, which was drawn over all by the fall, so renewing grace is the impression of the image of God; for it is a quite contrary thing to corruption. This likeness to God was man's original happiness in creation, and is his restored happiness in redemption: Col. ii. 10, 'renewed in knowledge after the image of him that created him.' His misery consisted in losing it; our felicity, therefore, does consist in recovering it. Hence it is called a 'divine nature,' 2 Peter i. 4. Every thing receives its denomination from the better part. A man is denominated rational, though he has both a sensitive principle common with beasts, and a vegetative, or growing principle, common with plants; so a new creature is denominated divine, because grace, a divine principle, is superior in the soul. Every perfection in the creature is supposed to be essentially somewhere. Every impression supposes a seal that stamped it, every stream a fountain from whence it sprang, every beam a sun from whence it is shot. Grace being the highest perfection of the creature, must be somewhere essentially. Where can that be but in God? His womb and power is the womb that bare it, and the breasts which gave it suck. It must then have a resemblance to him, as a child to the father, the copy to the original. We are said to be 'born of God,' 1 John iii. 9. Now to be born of any thing is to receive a form like that, which the generating person has. But,

(1.) It is not a likeness to God in essence: it is no participation of the essence of God. It is a nature, not the essence, a likeness in an inward disposition, not in the infinite substance, which is communicated by generation only to the Son, and by procession to the Holy Ghost. The divine essence is incommunicable to any creature. Infiniteness cannot be represented, much less communicated. Man is no more renewed according to God's image, than he was at first created according to it, Gen. i. 27; which was not a communication of the divine essence, but of a righteousness resembling the righteousness of God, according to the capacity of Adam's nature; which image of God in Adam is by the apostle restrained to that of 'righteousness and true holiness,' Eph. iv. 24. The likeness in a state of glory is founded upon a sight of God as he is, 1 John iii. 2; which may more properly be meant of the seeing of Christ as he is in glory; for the apostle goes on in the discourse without naming of Christ, but without question means him, ver. 5, when he says, that 'he was manifested to take away our sins.' We shall be like him, as we shall see him; therefore not in essence. His essence is concluded by most to be invisible, even in glory. How can finite creatures behold an infinite being? He must be God that knows God's essence. We shall understand him in his bowels, as a father; in his wise acts, as a governor; in his judicial acts, as a justifier; in his merciful acts, as a reconciler. We shall see him in all his relations to us. Such a vision we shall have, whatsoever it is which shall transform us into as high a likeness to him as a finite creature is capable of. There can be no participation of the substantial perfections of God, which are incommunicable; for then it would not be a participation but an identity, oneness, or equality. God put in one letter, and the chiefest of his name, Jehovah, "he", which is twice repeated in it, into the names of Abraham and Sarai, reckoned Nehem. ix. 7, as one of his favours to Abraham, but not the whole name, that is incommunicable; and Jacob's name is changed to that of Israel, putting in "el", a

---

communicable name of God.

(2.) Yet it is a real participation. It is not a picture, but a nature: it is divine. God does not busy himself about apparitions. It is a likeness, not only in actions, but in nature. God communicates to the creature a singular participation of the divine vision and divine love, why may he not also give some excellent participation of his nature? There is a nature; for there is something whereby we are constituted the children of God. A bare affection to God does not seem to do this. Love constitutes a man a friend, not a son and heir by generation. The apostle argues, 'if children, then heirs,' Rom. viii. 17. He could not argue in a natural way, if friends, then heirs. And the Scripture speaks of believers being the children of God, by a spiritual generation as well as by adoption. So that grace, which does constitute one a child of God, is another form whereby a divine nature is communicated. Generation is the production of one living thing by another, in the likeness of its nature, not only in the likeness of love; so is regeneration. Were not a real likeness attainable, why should those exhortations be of being 'holy as God is holy, pure as he is pure'? 1 Pet. i. 15, 1 John iii. 3. The new creature receives the image of God; not as a glass receives the image of a man, which is only an appearance, no real existence; and though it be like the person, yet has no communion with its nature; but as wax receives the image of the seal, which though it receives nothing of the substance, yet receives exactly the stamp, and answers it in every part. So the Scriptures represents it: Eph. i. 13, 'You were sealed with that holy Spirit of promise.' Something of God's perfections are in the new creature by way of quality, which are in God by way of essence. In a word, it is as real a likeness to God as the creature is capable of, laid in the first draughts of it in regeneration, and completed in the highest measures in glory.

(3.) It is the whole image of God which is drawn in the new creature. It is 'the image of God,' Col. iii. 10, not a part: a foot or a finger is but the image of those parts, not of a man. The members in a child answer to those in a parent, that is but a chip from the body of his father, though not in so great a proportion. The image of a man has not only the face, or eyes, but the other members. Though a Christian may have one or too parts of this image more beautiful than the rest, as a man may have a sparkling eye that has not a proportionable lip, yet he has all the members of a man. The painter's skill appears in some lineaments more than in others. So the Spirit's wisdom appears in making some eminent in one grace, some in another, according to his good pleasure; yet the whole image of God is imprinted there. It would be else not a likeness, but a monstrous birth in defect. 'The fruit of the Spirit is in all goodness, righteousness, and truth,' Eph. v. 9; and therefore the immediate effect of the Spirit in the soul is the engraving all goodness, righteousness, and truth in the essential parts of it. As God's nature is holy, his perfections holy, his actions holy, so holiness beautifies the nature, spirits the actions, and is written upon all the endowments of a renewed man. There is an impression of the wisdom of God in the understanding, and of the holiness of God in the will.

(4.) It is more peculiarly a likeness to Christ, wherein we partake of his nature: 'He that does righteousness is righteous, as Christ is righteous,' 1 John iii. 7. There is a real likeness to Christ in righteousness, though not an equal perfection. The new nature is a draught of Christ, something of Christ put into the soul, such a likeness to Christ, that it seems to be (as it were) another Christ, as the image of the sun seems to be another sun in a pail of water, therefore called a 'forming of Christ in us,' Gal. iv. 19. Not by any communication of his substance, either of the divine or human nature, but by conveying such affections into us, which bear a likeness to the affections of Christ. Hence we are exhorted to have 'the same mind which Christ had,' Philip. ii. 5, and to 'arm ourselves with the same mind,' 1 Peter iv. 1, which supposes such a mind put into the new creature which he is to excite, and put into actual exercise. And the apostle speaks of a conformity to Christ in his death and resurrection, Philip. iii. 10. And God did 'predestinate' all his own 'to be conformed to the image of his Son,' Rom. viii. 29, "summorfous", of the same form and shape. Jesus Christ conformed himself to us, by assuming the human nature; and God conforms us to Christ, by bestowing upon us a divine. Hence we are said to be the seed of Christ, Isa. liii. 10; not a carnal seed as the Jews say, and therefore deny Christ to be the Messiah, because he left no posterity. Whereas seed is spiritually understood, as in the first promise, the seed of the serpent or the devil. Devils do not beget, but metaphorically, as they instil their cursed principles into men; so Christ sows his principles in us, whereby we become his seed. Hence also renewed men are called 'his fellows,' Heb. i. 9. If fellows with him in the covenant, and fellows with him in glory, fellows also with him in his disposition of loving righteousness, and hating iniquity. This disposition was the inward motive of his death, and the foundation of his advancement. Without this disposition we cannot be conformable to him in his death, and consequently not his fellows in his advancement. The new creature is a likeness to Christ, therefore called the new man; as the natural man is like to Adam, therefore called the old man. The new man and old man are titles of Christ and Adam, and transferred upon others by a figure, metonymia causae pro effectu. These are the heads and roots of the two distinct bodies of men in the world. All are in the old Adam by nature, and so partake of the old man; all believers are in the new Adam by faith, and so partake of the nature of the new man. As we did partake of Adam's nature by our natural birth, so we partake of the nature of Christ by our spiritual: by the one we have the 'image of the earthly,' by the other the new creature has the 'image of the heavenly,'

1 Cor. xv. 48, 49; the one derives sin, the other righteousness; they both imprint their image according to the quality of their extraction. Christ is full of purity, righteousness, charity, patience, humility, truth, and in a word, all the parts of holiness; then the form and image of Christ in the new creature can be no other than a lively representation of those divine qualities, a soul glittering with goodness, humility, &c., which the apostle comprehends in two words, 'righteousness and true holiness.' Therefore, if there be not a likeness to Christ in the frame and qualities of our souls, we are not born of him. No man will say an ox, or a sheep, or a dog descends from Adam, because they have not the likeness, shape, and qualities of Adam, neither can any man without such a likeness to Christ in faith, humility, patience love, obedience, and minding the glory of God, number himself in the spiritual seed of Christ. He retains the nature poisoned by the serpent, creeping upon the earth, feeding upon the dust, not the nature formed by the eternal Spirit.

(5.) It is a likeness to the Spirit, which is the immediate cause of it. Therefore the new creature is called spirit in the abstract, as a natural man is called flesh in the abstract: John iii. 6, 'That which is born of the flesh is flesh; and that which is born of the Spirit is spirit.' As that which is born of the flesh is like to flesh in its nature, so that which is born of the Spirit is like to the Spirit in its nature, as light in the air, being the natural effect flowing from the sun, is like to that light which is in the sun, its relishes, delights, breathings, are according to its spiritual original; its motions, purposes, dispositions, are like those of the Holy Ghost, of whom it is born. The principles and impressions in the nature must be agreeable to those the Spirit has. The Spirit is a Spirit of holiness, grace, love and zeal to the glory of God; his office is to exalt and glorify Christ. If we are renewed, then we shall have the same draught in our hearts, the same design; the fleshly principle will be changed into spiritual. They will be habitual too, as the frame of the Holy Spirit is. A natural man may do some acts that look like spiritual by fits and starts, but there is no settled principle; whereas the spirit in a new creature is a spirit of meekness, and curbs the passions; a spirit of humility, and overthrows pride; a spirit of zeal, and fires the heart; a spirit of power, and arms the soul against sin; a holy spirit, and therefore cleanses it, an heavenly spirit, and therefore elevates it.

Quest. Wherein does this likeness to God chiefly consist?

Ans. 1. In a likeness of affections. God is no bodily shape; we cannot be like him in our bodies, but in our souls, as they are spirits; but if there be a dissimilitude of affection and disposition, the unlikeness to God is greater than a likeness to him in point of the natural being. There is no draught of this image in us, unless we have a conformity of affections to God; it is then chiefly evidenced by a delighting in him, by faith and love, wherein we bear a resemblance to him in his affection to himself, by delighting in his image in others, wherein we imitate his affection to his creatures. He that loses not that image of God which is visible, cannot love the invisible original, 1 John iv. 12, 20, and so, having no likeness to God in his affection, can have no likeness to God in his nature. And the apostle positively affirms, that 'he that loves, is born of God,' 1 John iv. 7. The new creature extends its arms to every thing which has a resemblance of that whose image it bears. The divine nature is chiefly seen in the objects of the affections, when they are set upon the same objects, and in a like manner as God's and Christ's are. When we grieve most for sin, for this grieves the Spirit, when we desire most an inward holiness, this God most longs for: 'Oh that there were such an heart in them!' When we hate sin as God hates it, because of the inward filthiness; when we love grace as God loves it, because of its native beauty; when we can love God and Christ above all the world, and other things in order to him and his glory, when we can trust Christ with all our concerns, and God does trust him with his glory; then, and not till then, there is an image of God in us, which God values above all the world. When the soul is thus touched and quickened by grace, she can no more strip herself of the object and manner of her affections, than she can of the affections themselves. And when she does reach out herself to all that is good, and has a complacency in it, it is her happiness, because it is the great likeness to the spring of happiness. When we have the like affections with God, we have in our measure a like happiness and blessedness with God.

2. In a likeness of actions. Men by sin are 'alienated from the life of God,' Eph. it. 17, by restoring grace then they are brought to have communion with God in his life, to live as God lives. By nature men live the life of beasts and devils; by grace they come to live the life of Christ. If he lives then the life of God, be must be conformable in his actions to the acts of God. No nature is stripped of affections and actions proper to it; it would be else a picture without breath, a body without motion, a lifeless colour. The divine image is not a painted statue, but an active being. The nearer any thing approaches in its nature to the fountain of life, the more of liveliness and activity it must needs partake of. The communicable perfections of God are stamped upon the soul as a pattern to imitate, and as a principle to quicken. A new creature acts like God, as melted and inflamed gold will act after the nature of fire, by the assistance of that quality communicated by the fire to it, so does the soul by that divine quality it partakes of. It is as impossible that this image of God can produce anything but divine acts, as that the image of the sun in a burning glass should produce a darkness and coldness in the air. There will be the manifestation of the life of Christ in the motions of our soul, as the apostle speaks in case of sufferings

for him there will be in our bodies, 2 Cor. iv. 10. Natural men are called the devil's children, because they resemble him in nature and works, egging on to sin, and delighting themselves in their own and others' iniquities, John viii. 44; so renewed men are God's children, because they live the life of God, and abound in the works of God, 1 Cor. xv. 58. As there is the same nature and the same spirit which Christ had, there will be a following of him in his works; all creatures of the same species have the same instinct, the same nature, the same acts that the first creature of that kind had originally in its creation. Grace being a new excellency advancing the soul to a higher state, endues it with a more noble kind of operation. Nothing is lifted up to a more perfect state of being, but in order to a more perfect manner of acting, if a beast should be elevated to the nature of man, would you then expect from him the actions of a beast still? And can any have the implantation of the divine nature, who has only the actions of a man which bear no resemblance to God?

3. This likeness to God consists principally in a likeness to him in holiness. It is only 'he that does righteousness is born of him:' 1 John ii. 29, 'If you know that he is righteous, you know that every one that does righteousness is born of him'. It is by this the children of God are manifest from the children of the devil, 1 John iii. 10 in doing righteousness. If we are unlike to God in this, we are like him in nothing; God has not a pretence of holiness, but a real purity. He that has not 'escaped the corruption that is in the world through lust,' is no 'partaker of the divine nature'; the apostle puts that as a necessary qualification, 2 Peter i. 4. If by afflictions good men are partakers of God's holiness, much more by regeneration: Heb. xii. 10, 'He chastened us for our profit, that we might be partakers of his holiness.' If God aim in his corrections at the bringing his people to partake with him in holiness, as a father does at the reformation of his child, that he may be a follower of his virtues, much more does God aim at it in regeneration, when a spirit of holiness is infused into the soul. The near creation is a drawing this excellency of God in the soul; if any attribute lift up his head above another, it is this, in this we chiefly are to imitate him; this is the greatest evidence of the divine nature. By sin we 'come short of that which is the glory of God', Rom. iii. 23; by the renewing of the soul we attain the glory of God; that is, attain a state of holiness and at last a perfection of it, a communion with him in holiness here, and a full enjoyment of it hereafter. Whatsoever our fancies, our hopes, our presumptions are, if this be not drawn in our soul, if we have not an internal holiness, we are not new creatures, and therefore not in Christ.

Use 1. It serves for information. If regeneration be such an inward change, a vital principle, a law put into the heart, the image of God and Christ in the soul; then,

1. How few in the world are truly new creatures! Is the law transcribed in many men's lives? nay, can we all read it copied in our own hearts? Cannot many see the image of the devil sooner than the image of God in their own souls? Is not the law of sin written in text letters, and with many flourishes, when the law of God is written in characters hardly legible, and crowded into a narrow room? How many are changed from childhood to youth, from youth to manhood, from manhood to age, and the old nature still remaining in its full strength, and the body of death more vigorous than twenty or thirty years ago! Changed years, and unchanged hearts, are a very sad spectacle.

(1.) Profane men are numerous. None will offer to rank these in the number of new creatures. Such nasty souls are no branches of Christ, nor habitations for him, we read of the devil in swine, but never of our Saviour in swinish souls. Are such regenerate? Can brambles be ever accounted vines, or thistles fig-trees? These rather look like hellish than divine creatures; diabolical, not God-like natures. A devotedness to the sins of the flesh is inconsistent with the circumcision made by Christ: Col. ii. 11, 'Putting off the body of the sins of the flesh, by the circumcision of Christ;' that is, the body of sins which exert themselves in the flesh or natural body; whereas such have the body of sin, with an activity in every member of it. Is the image of Christ in such men? Is not he meek as a lamb? Are not they fierce as lions? Is not he holy, and they defiled with intemperance? Did not he labour for nothing but the glory of his Father, and the salvation of souls; and they mind nothing but the dishonour of God, and the destruction of themselves and others? Did not he do good to his enemies, and they scarcely spare their friends? Alas, with this contrariety, how can they pretend the image of Christ, when they have nothing but what looks like the image of his enemy the devil? Is not the gospel counted as great a foolishness by such, as at the first times of its publishing? Are not the great mysteries of God, and the contrivances of eternity, entertained with coldness, and sometimes with scoffs, and the word, the great instrument of this change, unregarded? Are such new creatures, that contemn the very means to attain it? Surely they are so far from being near the kingdom of God, that they are in the very suburbs of hell. Is a hugging base lusts against the light of nature, a contempt of God's law and authority, the nature of Christ? Were any such spots upon our Saviour's garment? Is this to be like him who was holy, harmless, separate from sin and sinners?

(2.) Among professors, is there much evidence of a new creation? When men shall say, All that the Lord speaks to us we will do, has not God as great occasion to say as he did of old, Deut. v. 24, 'Oh that there were such a heart in them, that they would fear me, and keep my commandments!' We may find a change of language in some, a change of outward actions in others, but how few are there among many who stand up before God with the breath of life! Here and there a man or woman, wherein God may see the image of his own nature. How few are they with whom Christ can shake hands, and justly call them his fellows! Christ may be in the mouth, and the devil formed in the heart; the name of Christ may lie upon them, and the nature of Christ not in them. They may he born of the will of man in a religious education, but not born of the will of God in a spiritual regeneration. Is it not a graceless Christianity in many men, a faith without holiness, a Christianity without Christ? Regeneration is never without faith, love, and righteousness. They depend upon grace, as the property upon the form. Wherever the new creation is, these are, for they are the qualities created; wherever they are not, there is nothing of a new creature, let the pretences be never so splendid. There may be a nearness to the kingdom of God by profession, when there is no right to it for want of regeneration. Instead of humility, according to our Saviour's pattern, does not 'pride compass men as a chain,' Ps. lxxiii. 6, counting that their ornament, which is the strength of their old nature. Instead of patience, roaring passions; instead of meekness, boiling anger; instead of love a glowing hatred. How few then are renewed! But few shall be saved and therefore few regenerate. How little is the report of a likeness to God believed by the incredulous world! How few are the strivings of any towards heaven! Most lie quiet without any such motions, like the dust on the ground, unless some stormy affliction raise them a little towards heaven, whence they quickly fall back to their old place.

2. It informs us that a dogmatical change, or change of opinion, is not this new creature. It is not, if any man change his opinion from Gentilism to Christianity he is a new creature, but 'if any man be in Christ,' by a vital participation from union with him. As men generally place saving faith in dogmatical assents, so they place the new creation in a change of opinion, as well from truth to error as from error to truth, though there be no spiritual knowledge of God, nor internal cordial closing with the gospel, nor practice of it. Such a change may endue the head with a knowledge which never gently slides down to the affections. It may indeed have some influence upon the life, as this or that principle comes nearest to, or is divine truth, and is settled as an opinion in the soul; yet this great change may not be wrought. That is but a change in the head, this in the heart; that of opinion, this of affection; that perfects the understanding, this both the understanding and will, and the whole soul. There is a natural desire of knowledge, but a natural aversion from grace; whence this change becomes easy, the new-creature change difficult. A hot contriving head may have a cold and sapless heart. A head informed by the knowledge of truth may be without a heart enlivened by the Spirit of truth. A head changed in opinion only will descend into the bottomless pit, when the least grain of renewing grace shall not receive so much as a singe from those flames. A change from error to truth, without a heart framed to the truth, does but more settle a man upon his lees, and makes him not only more regardless, but opposite to a true change to God. It stores up wrath for him, and his very judgment will be a witness for the condemnation of his practice. The knowledge of God will not justify, but condemn a practical denial of him; but for all that, they are abominable, Titus i. 1b. This new-creature change is not from one doctrine to another, barely considered as doctrine, but a change to the gospel in the main intendment of it, as it is 'a doctrine according to godliness,' 1 Tim. vi. 8, as it may affect, purify, and direct the soul in its motion. And by the way observe this: whenever you are solicited to a change of opinion, consider the truth of it by this rule, whether it have a tendency to encourage and promote internal godliness, since this doctrine of regeneration was the first gospel lesson taught, to which all succeeding truths refer as to their end and centre. The apostle tells us what the issue of all such doctrines are that refer not to this, 'pride, doting about questions, envy, strife, railings, and evil surmisings,' verse 4. A heap of motions may consist with a body of death in its full strength, but a spirit of grace cannot; a nationalist may speak great things, but a new creature acts them. Great speculations only are but leaves without fruit, like cedars, that by their shadows may give a refreshment, but have no fruit to fill the soul hungering after righteousness.

3. Morality is not this new-creature change; that is, moral honesty, freedom from gross vices, &c. I have before spoken something about it, showing it insufficient, when I handled the necessity of regeneration, we cannot speak too much against it, it being a soft pillow, from whence many slide insensibly into destruction. How many, upon this account, think themselves new creatures, who are yet deeply under the image of Satan; and though they have blown off some dust from the law of nature, yet never had a syllable of the law of grace written in their hearts! Nay, the image of the devil may be more deeply engraved in a soul whose life is free from an outward taint. Profane men express more of the beast; a civil and moral conversation may have more of the devil and serpent within, in spiritualised wickedness.

(1.) Yet morality is to be valued. It is a comely thing among men, a beauty to human societies, satisfaction to natural conscience, security to the body, example to others: men are to be applauded for it, and encouraged in it. It is a fruit of Christ's mediation, left for the preservation of human societies, without which the world would be a mere Bedlam and shambles. The works of kindness, justice, mercy, love, pity, &c., are useful and commendable. It is a thing which our Saviour loved, yet not with such a love as eternally to reward it. He looked upon the young man with some affection, Mark x. 21, but scarce upon the Pharisees without anger and disdain.

(2.) Yet we must not set the crown belonging to grace upon the head of it, and place it in a throne equal to that of the new creation. It is too amiable for men to be beaten off from it, yet with just reason we may persuade them to arise to a higher elevation. It is a curious paint, a delightful picture, an useful artifice, but not a vital principle. A glow-worm is a lovely light, yet it is not a star. We press not men to throw off morality, but to advance it, to exchange it for Christ, that their moral virtues may commence Christian graces. It is an elevation near the kingdom of God, not a translation into the kingdom of God; it is nature improved, not nature renewed; it is a well-coloured picture without a principle of life; an outward resemblance, not an inward power, 2 Tim. iii. 5; a form of godliness; as a change that is made upon does in the draught of a picture, but no change in it by the conveyance of life. For,

[1.] It removes not the body of death. It is a cutting away the outward luxuriances, not the inward root. It removes the stench and putrefaction, not the death, an embalmed carcass is as much dead as a putrefied one, though not so loathsome. It removes not that wherein the strength of sin lies, though it does somewhat of the stench of sin. It may check those degenerate lusts inconsistent with the peace of natural conscience, but not heal the corrupt nature. It may be a change from scandalous to spiritual sins; from vanity in the outward life, to vanity in the mind from debauched practices, to a vainglorious and envious spirit: Eph. iv. 17, 18, 'Henceforth walk not as other Gentiles walk, in the vanity of their minds; having the understanding darkened, being alienated from the life of God.' By the Gentiles, from whom the apostle would have the Ephesians differences, he means not the lower sort, but the whole rank, ver. 21, there was a 'truth in Jesus' which they had been 'taught;' he makes no distinction between the looser rabble, and the professors of wisdom, whom he calls fools, Rom. i. 22, the followers of the divine (as they called them) philosophers, were alienated from the life of God, and walked in the vanity of their minds. The new man he exhorts them to put on was another kind of thing than what the greatest moralists among the heathen were acquainted with. It was at best human, not divine; an old nature purified, not a new implanted; or as the apostle phrases it, a walking in the vanity of their mind, in the darkness of their understandings, though not in a vanity of gross actions. It can never remove that body of death, which was introduced into the world while this outward morality stood. What immorality against the light of nature do you find in Adam? He did break a positive command in eating the forbidden fruit; you find nothing of drunkenness, lying, swearing; his great sin was inward pride and unbelief, nothing of those sins, the freedom from which you boast of, and rest on. Some would make Adam guilty of the breach of every command in the moral law; virtually I confess they may; expressly I do not see how they can; and also virtually the highest mere moralist is guilty of the breach of the whole; yet all his morality, after the breach of this one command, could not preserve him in paradise, nor all the morality without a new nature restore you to it. You may have Adam's morality with Adam's corruption; a freedom from gross vices, with a heap of spiritual sins in your hearts, as Adam had, but not a true righteousness without the new Adam, the quickening Spirit.

[2.] Therefore the highest morality without a new creation is but flesh; all men out of Christ agree in a fleshly nature. It is the highest thing in the rank of flesh, but it is not yet mounted to spirit. Water heated to the highest pitch is but water still, and morality in the greatest elevation of it is but refined flesh; an old nature in an higher form. A profane man reduced to a philosophical morality is putrefied flesh reduced to some sweetness, endued with a fresh colour, but wanting life as much as before; it is an old nature new mended. But a new creature is Christ formed in the soul. Moral virtue colours the skin, renewing grace enlivens the heart; that changes the outward actions, this the inward affections; that paints the man, this quickens him; that is a change indeed in the flesh; not of the flesh into spirit; it is a new action, not a new creation. There is a difference indeed among men in this respect, as there is of cleanly lambs from a filthy swine, or a ravenous wolf; yet both are in the rank of beasts. There seems to be a difference in the wickedness and malice of devils. Our Saviour tells us of a kind that are 'not cast out but by fasting and prayer,' Mat. xvii. 21, intimating that there are other kinds of them, not altogether so bad or so strong, yet all agreeing in one common diabolical nature; as there is a difference in gracious men, one shining like a star, another of a lesser light, yet all agree in the nature of light, and light in the Lord. So though there be a difference among men, in point of moral virtue, yet all agree in the nature of flesh: 'That which is born of the flesh is flesh,' John iii. 6. Let it be what it will, a Nicodemus as well as Judas, it is flesh, a more refined sensuality, an animal life.

[3.] It must needs be differenced from the new creature, because its birth is different. Moral virtue is gained by human industry, natural strength, frequent exercises; it is made up of habits, engendered by frequent acts. But regeneration is an habit infused, which grows not upon the stock of nature, nor is it brought forth be the strength of nature; for man being flesh, cannot prepare himself to it. That may be the fruit of education, example, philosophy; this is of the Spirit; that is a fruit of God's common grace, this of his special grace; that grows upon the stock of self-love, not from the root of faith, and a divine affection; that is like a wild flower in the field, brought forth by the strength of nature; this like a flower in the garden, transplanted from heaven, derived from Christ, set and watered by the Spirit. And therefore the other being but the work of nature, cannot bear the characters of that excellency, which the affections planted by the Spirit do. That is the product of reason, this of the Spirit; that is the awakening of natural light, this the breaking out of spiritual light and love upon it; that is the excitation of an old principle, this the infusion of a new; that a rising from sleep by the jog of conscience, this a rising from death by the breath of the Spirit, working a deep contrition, and making all new.

[4.] It differs from the new creature, in regard of the contractedness of the one, and the extensiveness of the other. That is in part a purifying of the flesh, this a purging both of flesh and spirit, 2 Cor. vii. 1; that binds the hands, this clears the heart; that purges the body, this every part of the soul; that, at the best, is but oil in the lamp of life, this oil both in lamp and vessel, that is a change of outward postures, modes, and fashion of walking, this of nature, heart, and spirit; that seems to be a dislike of some sins, this of all. If anything in moral honesty be given to God, it is but a certain part, the greatest and best is kept back from him. That may be a casting away some iniquity, but not making a new heart, when both are commanded together: Ezek. xviii. 31, 'Cast away from you all your transgressions, and make you a new heart and a new spirit.' That is a casting away the loathsome works of the flesh, this a new root to bring forth the fruits of the Spirit.

[5.] It differs from the new creature in the immediate principle of it, and its tendency. That is a cleansing the outward flesh in the fear of man, out of reverence to superiors (as it is said of Jehoash, he did that which was right, while he was under the awful instructions of Jehoiada, 2 Kings xii. 2). This is a 'perfecting holiness in the fear of God,' 2 Cor. vii. 1. That is an outward reformation from the hearing of the word, some acts materially performed from the newness of the thing, John v. 35, this from a judicious and hearty approbation of the law and will of God; that arises from a natural love to reason, justice, equity, this consists of love to God; that avoids some sins, because they are loathsome, this because they are sinful; that tends not to God for himself, but for something extraneous to him, it is an acting for self, not for the praise of God. The actions of unregenerate morality, as well as loathsome profaneness, are to gratify the flesh in some part of it; they all meet in that point, as the clearest brooks, as well as the most rapid and muddy streams, run to feed the sea.

Well, then, deceive not yourselves, conclude not yourselves new creatures by your moral honesty; it will not follow, that because you have some virtues you have therefore true grace, but it will follow that if you are new creatures, and have faith and love, you have all graces in the root; and they will appear in time, though they may lie hid a while in that seminal principle; the greater virtues contain the less, but the less do not infer the greater.

4. It will certainly follow from hence, that restraints are not this new creature. Restraining grace and renewing grace are two different things; the one is a withholding: Gen. xx. 6, 'I withheld thee from sinning against me;' the other an enlivening with a free spirit against it. Restraint may be from a chastisement, attended also with something of natural conscience. Abimelech had some natural integrity in his conscience not to meddle with another man's wife, which God acknowledges: 'I know that thou did this in the integrity of thy heart; for I also withheld thee.' Yet without this restraint by a punishment, this natural integrity might have been baffled by the temptation. Restraints may spring from the law in the hand of the magistrate, when it does not spring from the law of God in the heart. Men may love that which they do not act, at least they may love it in others, though not in themselves, for some extrinsic considerations, and wish they had as fair a way to commit it as others have; they may hate what they practise. Do all that hear the word, love the word, hide it in their hearts, and let it sink down into the bottom of their souls? Do all that abstain from sin, loathe what they abstain from? The restraints of many being barely outward restraints, are no more arguments of regeneration, than God's withholding the devils by the chain of his powerful providence is a sign of the new creation of them. The damned are hindered from committing many of those sins which were their pleasure upon the earth; it is not a change of their disposition, but of their condition. Neither punishments in hell, nor punishments upon the earth, alter the nature; though after lying a thousand years in hell, they should have leave to dwell upon the earth again, they would have the same inclinations without an inward change. Do we not see it daily in men's afflictions, though the sense of the smart nips a little those inclinations, yet when that sense is extinguished, those inclinations bud forth afresh? The bare pruning a tree makes it bear more fruit of the same kind as long as the root remains, rather than diminishes it: Isa. i. 5, 'Why should you be stricken any more? you will revolt more and more: the whole head is sick, and the whole heart is faint.' While the head is sick and the heart faint, though there may be a weakness to act some sins under the stroke, yet afterwards the revoltings are more violent many times than they were before. The best that restraints work of themselves, is but a cautiousness to sin more warily. The act may be repressed, while the habit remains.

5. A serious fit of melancholy, or a sudden start of affections, is not this work of the new creature. It is an habit, a law written in the heart; not a transient pang, or a sudden affection; not a skipping of fancy, or a quick sparkling of passion, but a new nature, a divine frame, spreading itself over every faculty; knowing God in our understandings, complying with him by our wills, aspiring to him by a settled and perpetual flame of our affections, rising heavenward, like the fire upon the altar, conforming ourselves to him in the whole man, a denial of whole self for God. It is not a working of the imagination, or a melancholy vapour, which may quickly be removed, or a flash of joy and love; but a serious humility, a constant grief under the remainder of corruption yet unextirpated; a perpetual

recourse to God, and delight in him through Jesus Christ. Are your affections raised sometimes to God? and are they not oftentimes raised higher to objects extrinsic to God? Such affections may arise rather from the constitution of the body than alteration of the soul. They are but a taste of the heavenly gift and the good word of God, Heb. vi. 4, 5; a taste, and no more, and is but a transient work. The object about which our affections are stirred may be divine, yet the operation but merely natural. May not sometimes affections be stirred much at the hearing the sufferings of our Saviour pathetically expressed, yet only out of a natural compassion, from an agreeable impression upon the fancy? The story of Joseph in the pit, and Christ upon the cross, may be heard with the same workings of passion. And may not the same be done at a well-humoured play, or at the hearing a report of the lamentable death of a Turk or heathen, pathetically expressed? These are but the workings of natural spirits. Some affections are as moveable as quicksilver, upon the least touch; they sweat like marble in moist weather, but resemble it also in hardness. You do not find the affections to be the chief seat of the law; this would be as to write letters upon melted wax or running water, but the tenor of the covenant runs upon the mind: 'I will put my law into their minds,' Heb. viii. 8, 10. And when God works upon the mind, the affections will attend the dictates of that, and the motions of the will. But a work upon the affections only, is like water in a sponge, easily sucked up, and upon the least compression squeezed out. These may be where there is no root of grace; they suddenly rise, and suddenly vanish. When unrooted notions are received only into the fancy, without any illumination of the understanding, or determination of the will, the affections to them will be as volatile as the fancy which entertained them. Those in Mat. xiii. 20, 21, that received the word with a sudden joy, were as suddenly offended for want of a root: 'anon with joy receives it, by and by he is offended.' The word translated anon, and by and by, euthus", is the same, a lightning of affection, and a sudden vanishing; therefore this is not the new creature, sudden affections, or a melancholy fit. The law of God seated in the heart, mind, and will, though a constant course of affection is a very good character to judge of the new creature.

6. It informs us of the excellency of the new creature. How excellent is this new creature? It is a change, a divine nature, a likeness to God, an excellency above that of the greatest moralist under heaven. The apostle calls it a change from 'glory to glory,' 2 Cor. iii. 18, implying that the first change wrought upon the soul is glorious, and a new creature excellent in its first make, more glorious in its progress, inconceivably glorious when God shall put his last hand to the completing of it. Regeneration is more excellent than creation. It is more noble to be formed a son of God by grace, than made a man by nature; nature deforms, grace beautifies. By nature we are the sons of Adam, by the new nature the members of Christ. As grace excels nature, and Christ surmounts Adam, so much more excellent is the state of a Christian, a real Christian, above that of a man. Can there be a greater excellency than to have a divine beauty, a formation of Christ, a proportion of all graces, suited to the imitable perfections of God? Man is an higher creature than others, because he has an higher principle. A life of reason is more noble than that of sense. To live by sense, is to play the part and live the life of brutes; to live by reason, is to live the life of a man: but he that lives by the Spirit, lives the life of God, answers the end of his creation, uses his reason, understanding, will, affection for God, by whom they were first bestowed; acts more nobly, lives more pleasantly, than the greatest angel could do without such a principle. A new creature does exceed a rational creature, considered only as rational, more than a rational does a brute. The apostle makes a manifest distinction between the natural or the "psuchikos", the rational and the spiritual man, 1 Cor. ii. 14, 15. A man with the richest endowments, is no more to be compared in excellency with a regenerate man, than the top of a craggy mountain is with a well-dressed garden. That must needs be excellent, the forming of which is the end of all God's ordinances in the world, the end of the Spirit's being among the sons of men, the end of keeping up mankind, the end of his patience in forbearing his punishment upon contempt of the gospel. The end of his preserving the world, is to form Christ in the heart; and when the last new creature is formed, God has no more to do in the world: when all that are given to him shall come to believe, Christ shall then 'come, to be admired in them,' 2 Thess. i. 10. He does not come, therefore, till all his chosen ones are brought in to believe in him, for then he would not be admired by all those that are saints in his purpose. This, therefore, must needs be excellent. One new creature is more excellent than the whole unrenewed world with their choicest ornaments. It was never pronounced of them, that they were 'partakers of the divine nature.'

7. How much therefore should new creatures be esteemed and valued? Is anything, next to God, more worthy our esteem than that which bears his image? Is anything, next to a crucified Christ, glorified in heaven, more worthy our valuation, than Christ formed in the heart of a believer? What esteem have men had for those who have had tempers like to some heroes, some generous and useful men in the world? How much more respect should be given to them that bear the characters of God upon them, and have communion with God, and Christ, and the Spirit, in their nature! If the dead image of God in a natural man ought to be respected, much more the living image of God in a renewed man. If a picture is to have respect, much more the life. To slight them, therefore, redounds to the slighting that infinite perfection, whose image it is. They are his living images, sent into the world to represent him. He then that disesteems them for that work, disesteems him that wrought and engraved them, by the

same rule that he that despised the disciples despised Christ, and the Father that sent him, Luke x. 16: 1 Thess. iv. 8, 'He therefore that despises you, despises not man but God, who has also given us his Holy Spirit.' Yet no better must be expected here; for the contracted spirit of the world can love no other birth but its own, no other similitude but what draws near unto it: 'If you were of the world, the world would love his own; but because you are not of the world, therefore the world hates you,' John xv. 19. The copy can expect no better usage than the original. The nearer any approach in likeness to Christ, the more they will be exposed to contempt and scorn in the world.

8. It the new creature be such a thing as you have heard, then the sin of a regenerate man has a greater aggravation than the sins of any in the world. If you slip into sin, the sins of the whole unregenerate world have not so great a blackness. It is true a new creature may, and does sin, for though a new man is created in him with all his members, and essential and integral parts, yet the body of death does remain still with all its members, and a seed-plot still, though not in the same strength and fruitfulness as before. For the apostle Paul does not complain of a member of death, or a piece of sin, but the whole 'body of it,' and 'the law of sin in his members,' Rom. vii. It seems it did reside there still, and so it does in all the renewed, though but faint and feeble, an old man indeed, growing older every day, losing its teeth and strength, less able to bite, less able to assault. Yet sometimes a new creature may fall into sin, but not without great aggravation. For other men sin against natural, you against spiritual principles; others sin against an habit of common notion, you against an habit of divine grace. A natural man sins against the light of God in his conscience, a renewed man against the life of God in his heart. Others sin against a Christ crucified and risen from the grave; he sins against a Christ new-formed and risen in his heart. Others sin against the law of God in the word, he against the law written in his mind and word too. Such cast dirt upon the Spirit's work, cross the end of so noble a piece, bring a thief into the Spirit's temple, and grieve the Holy Spirit, who instructed him better. Whenever you sin, it must cost you more grief, because your sins are more grievous; and you must grieve the more for them, because the Spirit is grieved by them. Grief for sin is a standing grace in the new creature, and part of a likeness to the Spirit of God, whatsoever some men dream to the contrary.

Use 2. Is of comfort. There is ground of joy unspeakable and full of glory that results from this. Are you of this new creation that I have been discoursing of? Then take your portion of comfort. The jewel of comfort belongs only to the cabinet of grace. It is fit you should have the comforts of heaven in your hearts, who have a fitness for heaven in your nature. The day of the new birth was a happy day, to be brought from under the rule of sin and death in it, to the rule of the Spirit of God and life in it; from bearing fruit to death, to bringing forth fruit to God and everlasting life. If sin be a torment to the womb that bare it, no joy can reside in an unregenerate spirit, if sin be the soul's rack in its own nature, grace must be its pleasure; for it carries as much contentment and satisfaction in its bowels, as sin does disquietness and sorrow.

1. You have, by the new creation, a relation to the blessed Trinity. Such are the sons of God, the seed of Christ, the temple of the Spirit; what a connection is there between you and the three persons! God in Christ, and Christ in you, that you may be 'made perfect in one,' John xvii. 23. God in Christ reconciling the world, you in Christ reconciled to God; God in Christ as a father in a son, you in Christ as members in the body; Christ in you as a head in the body, the Spirit in you as an informing and enlivening principle. It makes you related to the Father as his friends, by the ceasing of your enmity; to the Son as his propriety, for then you are his; to the Spirit as the tutor of you and inhabitant in you, all implied, Rom. viii. 8-10. By your former birth you were children of wrath; by this, children of God: by that, partakers of the serpentine nature of the destroyer; by this, partakers of the divine nature of your Creator and Redeemer: by nature you descended from the loins of Adam, and thereby were related to all the corruption of the world; by the new birth you are descended from the Son of God, and 'counted to the Lord for a generation,' Ps. radii. 30, and thereby related to all the perfection of heaven; as really descended from Christ by a spiritual, as from Adam by a natural generation. What an overflowing comfort is this! To be a king's son is a higher privilege than merely to be his subject; subjects have protection, sons affection; subjects partake of the kindness of the prince, sons of his nature. As a son, he has a right to the inheritance of the lather; as a subject, not. Men are subjects by covenant, though born of others, sons by generation. By being a new creature, the regenerate man acquires a more noble relation, than by being a creature. That relation that he lost by a prodigal corruption, is restored to him in a more excellent way by his spiritual regeneration.

2. If you be new creatures, you are the delight of God. It is impossible but God should have the most tender respect to his own likeness; he must needs take a pleasure in a resemblance to his own nature, in a habit of his Spirit's infusing. Can God despise the work of his own hand? Can he then despise the work of his heart, a likeness to himself, to his Son, to his Spirit? His delight is strengthened by a threefold cord, 'he delights not in the strength of a horse, nor takes pleasure in the legs of a man,' but 'in them that fear him, in them that hope in his mercy,' Ps. cxlvii. 10, 11. You are the first fruits of his creatures, peculiarly dedicated to him as his portion by the new birth: James i. 18, 'Of his own will begot he us, with the word of truth, that we should be a kind of first fruits of his creatures,' taken out of

the mass of the world for a holy offering to himself; the more refined part of his creation, not barely creatures, but first fruits peculiarly belonging to him, upon whom he looks with a delightful eye, and under another relation. God cannot but love himself, and therefore that which approaches most near to himself, for nothing in the creature is a fit object for God's love, but his own living image in him. As he loves himself in himself, so he loves himself in his creature. To deny his truth, is to deny himself; to deny his love to his image, would be to deny his love to himself. He can as soon hate his Christ glorified at his hand, as hate Christ formed in the soul. If sin makes men the objects of his hatred, as being contrary to his nature, grace then makes them the objects of his love, as being agreeable to his nature. He cannot but delight in his own birth, and delight in the seals of his own Spirit. You could not but displease him by being in the flesh; 'those that are in the flesh cannot please God,' Rom. viii. 8; you then please him by being in the Spirit. Shall the pleasure of the Father of spirits, in his own image, be of a lower degree than that of a natural father in his son, which bears the lineaments of his body? He has no pleasure in anything in the world, if not in you. Sin soon deformed all after he had pronounced them good, and stopped the joy God had in his works; it is by your redemption by his Son, and regeneration by his Spirit, that the joy in his works is restored to him; if he should not delight in you, what has he in the world to please himself with? Your services please him; a new spirit, a new beauty is added to all your addresses. A new creature prays not as before, hears not as before, he refers all to God; there is a brokenness instead of pride, every sacrifice is washed in contrition, a zeal of spirit, a heavenly warmth, a sweet and delightful savour ascends up to him. It is you only that with grace 'serve him acceptably,' Heb. xii. 28, with such a godly fear and frame wherein he takes a pleasure.

Well then, the new creature is the delight of God, though the scoff of men; the pleasure of him that commands the world, though reproached by them that shall fill hell with their souls.

3. How great a foundation then is laid in this for your happiness! New creatures, divine nature, a relation to God, the delight of heaven: 'If any man be in Christ, he is a new creature; old things are passed away, behold, all things are become new.' New for them, as well as in them. Distance and dissimilitude from God is the foundation of all misery; a likeness then to him is the basis of all blessedness. Divine happiness is non-natural to the divine nature, and due to it, as it were jure intrinseco; as new creatures you are heirs, as sanctified creatures you are made meet for the inheritance; you have a hereditary right, and an aptitudinary right. Can any comfort be greater, than to have right to an inheritance, and a fitness to enjoy it? 'Now are we the sons of God,' 1 John iii. 2, we have this real relation; not only named so, but are so, which is a certain foundation of a happiness which does not yet fully appear to us. But such a knowledge we have, that when the original of this new nature shall appear, our imperfect likeness shall arise to a full perfection, 'we shall be like him, for we shall see him as he is;' upon the account of this relation we know there will be an exact likeness between him and us. I suppose it is properly meant of a likeness to Christ, we shall see him as he is; for the apostle, verse 5, refers it to Christ, without altering the person he had spoke of before; so that it is not meant of a seeing the essence of God, but the sight of Christ. Where lust reigns, the natural consequence is storms and dissatisfaction; he that has the image of the devil, has a model of hell; the new creature having the image of God, has a model of heaven. A drop of grace is a drop of glory; so much as there is of the new creation, so much of heaven is put into the soul. It is 'a lively hope' of heaven here, and a full enjoyment of heaven hereafter, that the soul is 'begotten unto,' 1 Peter i. 8, 4. The greater the progress in this state, the more lively are the hopes of it, and the nearer approaches of heaven to the soul; such a foundation of happiness, with the hopes and foresight of it, cannot but be attended with inconceivable pleasure.

4. How highly comfortable is it to view yourselves, and consider the draught of this image, and the progress of the new creation in your souls? How comfortable is the work of self-examination to such a soul! With what pleasure may you look upon your present estate, and be filled with ravishments at every view? When you look back upon your former condition, and think of your state of death, the noisomeness of your hearts to God, the stiffness of your souls against him, when you consider how spiritual death reigned over every part; and now see your nature changed, your souls upon a lively and quick motion to God, your relishes of the sweetness of spiritual pleasures to be greater than those of sensual; how comfortable is it to behold those diffusions of God in your souls, and to feel them full of love to him, and full of love from him! How comfortable to view the original, and copy from it, and to see how near the one does resemble the other; to cast your eye upon the state of wrath you were in by your first birth, and upon the state of grace you are in by the latter; to consider your former drudgery under sin, and your present freedom in the service of righteousness! It would make you perform those commands so often repeated of rejoicing in the Lord always, and shouting for joy, since mercy does so compass you about, Ps. xxxii. 11, Philip. iv. 4. As upon the awakenings of conscience, and the exercise of its reflective office, there must needs arise an anguish and torment in an unrenewed soul, so upon the reflections of the same faculty in a new creature, there must spring a sparkling delight. As God by the reviews of himself and contemplation of his own excellency has an infinite joy, so the new creature by the views of itself has a joy in its measure proportionable to that of God himself. As it is in itself the image of God, so it is a lower fruition of him. I enjoy my friend somewhat in his picture when the

original is absent; and this joy is greater when a beam from heaven does shine upon this image, and both illustrate and discover the beauty of it, which in the darkness of ignorance and mistakes cannot be seen. But take heed that in these reviews you impair not your comfort by any proud and God-neglecting reflections, but with humble and debasing thoughts of yourselves, and thankful admirations of the grace of God, and praises of him for so excellent a draught in your hearts. It is wonderful to perceive how by such a carriage the comforts of heaven flow in upon the soul, when thus humbly and thankfully it opens itself before God in this review. And let this add to your comfort, that if the reviews of so imperfect an image in you, and the dark sight of God, whose image it is, be so delightful, how much more pleasant will it be when your souls shall be elevated to the highest perfection and the most satisfying fruition!

5. And how great a comfort it is to consider that this imperfect image, which is the foundation of happiness, will in time be perfect, and as fully resemble him whose image it is as the creature is capable of! There is a day of perfect and glorious regeneration coming, wherein you will appear in all your royalty as heirs of God. The divine nature shall glitter without any filth of sin to sully it; holiness shall hold the sceptre without any lust to shake it. There is a day wherein Christ shall make all things new in the church, and in the; he sits upon his throne and says it: Rev. xxi. 5, 'Behold, I make all things new.' It will be so new and admirable, that when you look back upon that mean draught of it while you were in the world, you would think you never had a grain of the divine nature before in you. As the vision of God will be perfect, so will your likeness to him, 1 John iii. 2; as it will be a vision without any clouds, so it will be a likeness without any dissimilitude, according to the creature's capacity. The vision of Christ here transforms us into a likeness to him in his death and resurrection, the vision hereafter transforms us into a likeness to him in glory; the close look of the soul upon God shall divest it of all carnal conceptions; the understanding shall perfectly behold the original, the will closely embrace it, the affections centre in it without distraction; the whole soul shall be changed from a less degree of glory to an inconceivable perfection in it, changed 'from glory to glory,' 2 Cor. iii. 18, when the well of living water springing up in thee to eternal life shall spring into it. This fire-baptism will not leave till it has fully consumed your dross, and refined your souls. That Spirit that begun the work will fill the heart with the knowledge and love of God, as his promise is to fill the earth, Isa. hi. 9. He will not leave despoiling you of the oldness of the flesh till there be not a mite left, and clothing you with a newness of the spirit till there be not a grain of the soul free from this new enlivening. As he began, so he will finish, in abolishing that which remains of vanity, and in filling this holy temple with the glory of the Lord. There is certainly as much power in the second Adam to perfect, as well as to begin this new creation, as there was in the first to convey his soul and defiled image to his posterity. The honour of Christ and the good of the new creature are concerned in it; the honour of Christ in point of power and affection, the good of the new creature in point of happiness; his honour would suffer if he did not perfect what he had begun. As Moses pleads with God for the perfecting the Israelites' deliverance in bringing them into Canaan, that the nations might not say, God was not able to deliver them, Num. xiv. 16. In point of affection he loves his Father, therefore the image of his Father; he loves himself, therefore the picture of himself; he loves his Spirit which glorifies him, therefore will perfect the draught he has made. It will, then, in time be perfect, not a lineament of God but will be illustriously drawn; there shall be no more complaints of a body of death, nor any snarlings of sin and lust.

Upon these considerations you may apply the comfort this new creation affords you,

(1.) Against troubles in the world. Old things are passed away, even the old events and issues of your afflictions, they are no longer used merely to trouble you or punish you, but to perfect this new creation, to engrave more deeply or exercise this divine image. All things are but fellow-labourers to throw out the rubbish, and blow up this divine spark: Rom. viii. 28, they 'all work together for good, to them who are called according to his purpose.' As regenerating grace gives us a relation to God, so it should expel fear: Isa. vliii. 1, 'Fear not: for I have redeemed thee, I have called thee by name; thou art mine.' What reason is there to fear when he has called you by name, in a special manner, not in a general way? What reason to fear when thou hast the badge of God upon thee, who has new created thee? The grace wherein you stand, or the state of grace, should make you not only to 'rejoice in the hope of the glory of God,' but to 'glory in tribulations also,' as well as the apostle, Rom. v. 2, 3, because it 'works patience,' &c. It dresses up the new creature; and draws the several parts of the gracious habit into exercise. Though it seem strange, yet the 'glorying in tribulation' is as proper an effect of this new creation as 'rejoicing in hope of the glory of God.' Grace, being the foundation of your glory in heaven, cannot but be the foundation of glorying in everything else which heightens it, and pushes it nearer to its centre. Let not affliction, crosses, reproaches, molest your new nature; be new creatures as to four respects to them as well as relation to God. Our Saviour's sonship, and the meat the world knew not of, supported him under greater injuries than we can ever be subject to. What clouds of trouble should ever sadden that heart which has the living image of God in his soul? This alone should turn the wormwood of affliction into honey, and bitterness into sweetness.

(2.) You may apply the comfort of your new creation against temptations. Will not the power of God be employed in the defence of that which is his only image in the world, since he knows that Satan is most active against it, because it is his image? And upon the same account will not God be active for it? Surely that Spirit which begot it broods upon its own birth, and watches for the defence of it against its mighty adversaries. Satan watches to cast dirt upon the divine nature; the Spirit watches to hinder it, and if cast on, to wipe it off, and restore it to its beauty. Can it enter into the heart of an infinite affection nakedly to expose his own work, his affectionate new creature, made up of faith in him and love to him, that which maintains his honour in the world, designs all for his glory, values his honour above his own credit, yea, his life; opposes everything that opposes him, hates everything that is loathsome to him, would endure any misery rather than displease him; I say, shall a God of infinite tenderness expose this creature to the violences and furies of hell without any defence? What should we make of God, by entertaining such thoughts of him, but a hard master, a cruel tyrant, one that would make his own work the sport of devils, to stand by carelessly and see his image trampled upon, and leave the best subjects he has in the world to the mercy of his mortal enemy? Let not such a thought enter into any new creature, nor let us believe that the love in the heart of the new Creator is less than the power in his hand. It was the sonship and resurrection of our Saviour secured him against the counsels of enemies: Ps. ii. 2 and 7 compared, 'Thou art my Son, this day have I begotten thee.' So our communion with him in his resurrection secures us against the malicious designs of Satan. Thou art my son, this day have I regenerated thee, is the voice of God to a new creature; and by this relation his happiness is secured under the greatest assaults, if he keep up faith, which will fetch vigour from the Head. The devil by his whole legions of temptations cannot more prevail against the seed of God, than Haman could against Mordecai, because he was of the seed of the Jews, as his wife prudently advised him, Esther vi. 13.

(3) This comfort of the new creation is applicable against fears of falling away. Were grace like a moral habit, acquired by moral acts, it might sink under a force, it might be lost; but it is a divine work, a new creation in Christ, not anything gained by moral philosophy, and a road of virtuous actions. Men may seem to begin in the Spirit and end in the flesh; but does the Spirit begin this regeneration work, to suffer it to end in the flesh? When the apostle speaks of men's works, he fears the consequence; but when he speaks of God's working in a man, he is confident of a good issue, Philip. i. 6. God never begins but he resolves to perform and finish. As it is impossible for one united to Adam in a natural way not to partake of his sinful life, so it is impossible for one united to Christ in a gracious way not to partake of his spiritual life. And as every man is really in the loins of Adam, so every believer is, in a sort, spiritually in the loins of Christ, and is as truly denominated his seed, and as no man can be cut off from the stock of Adam but be the grace of God, so no man can be taken off from the stock of Christ, when once implanted, but by the retraction of that grace, against which there is sufficient security in the covenant of grace, and several promises in Scripture, like stars in the heavens, set to give light to this truth. The new creature under the gospel shall grow in beauty as the lily, in strength like a cedar, his beauty shall be as fresh as that of the rose or lily, his root as firm as that of a cedar; and this from God, who will be as the dew unto it: Hosea xiv. 5, 'I will be as the dew to Israel: he shall grow up as the lily, and cast forth his roots as Lebanon.' As dew quickens the plant, so will God enliven Israel; what withering can there be under such an influence? If you have been made new creatures in Christ, you are made stable creatures, his charge is as great to preserve you as it was to renew you. Besides, the divine nature is so delightful a thing, that he that once is a possessor, has no mind to be a loser of it. He that has once put off the old man, and put on the hew, will have little heart to make another exchange, and divest himself of his beautiful robe, to be clothed again with the old tattered rags which he has dung upon the dunghill. The new creation is a 'fellowship with Christ in his resurrection,' Philip. iii. 10, and therefore in the consequents of it. As Christ did not rise to die again, so the soul is not made new to become old again. Christ formed in the soul is like Christ incarnate in the world: the divine nature may be obscured, it may and will have its humiliations; it cannot indeed die, but though it seem to die, it will have its resurrection, and afterwards its ascension into glory.

(4.) It is comfort against weakness of grace, and strength of corruptions. The whole frame of the new creature is wrought at once: the soul is infused at once, but not as Adam was, created in his full stature, and perfect strength, and exercise of all his faculties. But as Adam's posterity were generated, first infants, then men, others may be more honourable creatures, but the weakest grace is a new creature; others may be more noble members, but every new creature is a member of the body; others may have more grace, but not a better title; the weakest is a heaven-born heir, and has the same title by the purchase of the Redeemer, the reality of the new creation, and the spirit of adoption. I do not mean by the weakest grace a superficial desire, or a velleity not to sin, and yet a daily running into it; but a grace mating and mastering corruption, though residing with it, a grace that is daily eating into the bowels of lust, and growing up to a sharper animosity and strength against what is contrary to it; for the least degree of grace is prevalent against sin, and is not overpowered by it, though it be mightily opposed. The essence of grace is the same in every new creature, though the degrees be different: it is one thing to have the nature of fire, another thing to have the strength of it; a spark is essentially fire, and will burn, though not so much as a flame. If the frame be new, though the draughts be not so clear, nor the lineaments drawn with such lively colours, yet there is a representation; the first draught of a picture bears a likeness to the person, but it will be more lively after the second or third sitting, when the limner has laid on his fresher colours.

[1.] If your complaints of the weakness of grace and strength of corruption be sincere, it is a comfortable sign you will hold out. Hasty pretenders and proud boasters are not durable. The seed sown in the stony ground 'presently sprung up,' Mat. xiii. 5; grew faster, as if it would outstrip the common harvest, but as soon withered, whereas that which was sown in the good ground sprung up leisurely to perfection, and endured the storm.

[2.] You cannot reasonably think you should presently be rid of your corruptions. Some spice of a cured disease will remain in the soul as well as the body, and a certain spiritual weakness after the raising of the new creature. The law in the mind does not presently raze out the law of sin in the members. There is a diabolical nature as well as divine. The Platonist could say, The virtuous man who does something, "aproaireton", is both a god and a demon. Christ formed in the heart does not presently dispossess the serpentine nature, but master it. A man restored to health from a sharp disease may do the actions of a sound man, yet not in that manner and soundness, for all his motions are infected with the relics of that disease which lately mastered his body. Original corruption is not as a cistern (then it may be emptied), but a spring; pump out all you can at one duty, it will rise again, you will see it, before the next service. It is true that 'he that is born of God commits not sin,' he sins not with such a frame as he did before; but it is as true that 'if we say we have no sin, we deceive ourselves, and there is no truth' of grace 'in us,' 1 John i. 8. There will be a running issue, that you may frequently touch the hem of Christ's garment for a cure. The soul of the best is never like to be 'without spot or wrinkle' till it be glorious, Eph. v. 26.

[3.] All God's communications of grace are gradual. Doth the mustard seed spring up in an instant to the tallness of a tree? Grace is sown in an instant, but grows not up so suddenly. Christ formed in the heart is like Christ in the flesh; first in his cradle, before he be upon his legs. The new creation is not a sudden leap from corruption to perfect purity; the day dawns in the heart, but the light takes a time to expel the darkness: Prov. iv. 18, 'The path of the just is as the shining light, that shines more and more unto the perfect day.' The first appearance at the dawning is an earnest that the victory will be complete at last. God did not make a full discovery of Christ to Adam, his revelations of him grew brighter with every age; the nearer his coming, the clearer was the foresight of him. The divine nature has its time of discovery in the creature, as it had in Christ the original; there were forty days between his resurrection and ascension, wherein he was but in the first degree of his exaltation. Christ risen in the heart will take some time before he ascends and carries up the soul to spiritual heights with him.

[4.] Consider well how it is with thy will. It is not the having of lusts, but the fulfilling of them, wherein our danger lies: Rom. xiii. 14, 'We have then put on the Lord Jesus Christ, when we make no provision for the flesh, to fulfil it in the lusts thereof,' but endeavour to walk holily. The author of the Epistle to the Hebrews could pretend to little more than will: chap. xiii. 18, 'willing to live honestly,' "kalos", comely, beautifully. And herein Paul 'exercised' himself, Acts xxiv. 16. He manifested this will by compliance with all seasonable occasions to that purpose. Is there grace in thy whole soul? Is there an enlightened judgment to see the foulness of sin and the loveliness of Christ? Is there a renewed will to incline to God and to close with the Redeemer? Is there a rectified affection, consisting of love, desire, delight, though yet but weak in all the faculties? Are there dissatisfactions in you upon internal reviews? Have you not strong bewailings and laments for the strength of sin and weakness of grace, and breathings after a more vigorous and active grace? Let not then your complaints of the body of death stifle your praises of God for what he has wrought in Christ in order to your full deliverance. They did not so in Paul, Rom. vii. 24, 25; let them not do so in you. Take comfort in what God has wrought, bless him for it, and solicit him to confirm that which he has wrought in you, Ps. lxviii. 24. He that provides food for the ravens that cry, will not stop his ears at the voice of his own image.

(6.) It is comfort against the fear of death. If you were born only of the old Adam, you were spiritually dead, and you must eternally die; it were unavoidable, if not changed; but if born of an incorruptible seed, the dissolution of your body shall be the consummation of your glory. Death strikes the outward man, and the new creature elevates the soul. The new nature will as naturally ascend to heaven, when it is unclothed of flesh, and has left all the relics of corruption behind it, as the pure flame aspires into the air, and seems to long to embody itself with the son, the first fountain of light. How joyfully will the original and copy meet: Philip. i. 23, 'to depart from hence,' is 'to be with Christ.' The truth of grace in the creature, and the infinite righteousness in the Creator, kiss each other. How affectionately will God entertain that image of himself! How delightfully will Christ view himself in the soul, and the soul view itself in the heart of Christ! The soul shall see Christ in glory, and Christ shall behold the soul in perfection, where there will be nothing but life and love, love and life for ever. Is death then to be feared, that brings the new creature to this happiness?

Use 3. Is for examination. Of all things, this deserves the strictest inquiry, in regard of its absolute necessity, and in regard of its superlative excellency.

1. It is possible to know it, and not very difficult to know it. You may know the acts of your own

heart. Can you not view your own thoughts? Can you desire, or love, or hate, or grieve, but you must know that you do so? Can you not tell what is the object of your inclinations, what your affections run most greedily after? No man can be such a stranger to his own soul, if he look into it. Can you not tell whether you are the same men as before; whether you love what before you hated, and hate that which before you loved? A soul may know whether it loves God supremely or no, so as to appeal to God for the truth of it, as Peter to our Saviour: John xxi. 17, 'Lord, thou knows that I love thee.' It is in this reflexive power that a man excels a brute.

2. You must inquire into the effects and operations of it. Where there is this spiritual change, there is life; where there is a spiritual life, there will be spiritual operations. You must inquire, then, what sense and motion you have, that is superior to a life of nature. This new creation is not only the taking down the old frame, but setting up a new. The old creature frame will grow more inactive, the new creature form more sprightly. Regeneration is never without some effect; if we have not the properties, we have not the nature. If the air be dark and pitchy, that a man cannot see his way, it is a sign the sun is not up to enlighten that hemisphere. A thick darkness cannot remain with the sun's rising. The works of darkness, with their power, cannot remain with a new creature state. The old rubbish cannot wholly remain with a new building. Look well, therefore, whether old principles, aims, customs, company, affections, are passed away, and whether new affections, principles, ends, be settled in the room. Be sure to distinguish well between the form and the power, between a paint and life, and regard well your inward acts. The acts of the new creature are principally in the proper seats of it, the mind, the heart, the will, the conscience, the affections. Outward acts are no sign at all; no man can perfectly judge of another by them, nor any man judge of himself. As the strength of sin, so the strength of grace, the new creature, lies in the heart. Those waters which are bitter, are bitterest, and those which are sweet, are sweetest, at the fountain; they lose somewhat of their qualities in the streams, by the mixture of other things with them.

3. In general observe, what contrariety there is to what you were before, and the very point wherein this contrariety does consist. It is a spiritual habit, a divine nature, the law of God in the heart. It must principally be discerned in its motion to God, in its respect to God, whose law, nature, habit it is, directly contrary to the sinful habit, the law of sin in the heart, the old serpentine nature which moved to sin. Let us see in general how it was with Paul, who speaks so much of the new creature. He was quite another man after his being in Christ than he was before. He was before an admirer of his own righteousness, a contemner of grace, a persecutor of Christ and his members. After the new creation, his pharisaical plumes fall, his own righteousness is as dross, he lays it down at the feet of Christ; grace is highly admired by him, and his whole labour is spent in glorifying Christ, and edifying his church. He abhors that which before he delighted in: he did before his own will, and the will of his sect; now, 'Lord, what wilt thou have me to do?' He is now an admirer, where he was a despiser; his industry, passions, heart, are for Christ, as before they were against him. The doctrine of the cross is no longer folly, but wisdom: he glories as much in being persecuted for Christ, as in being a persecutor of him and his people. His ravaging wolfish nature is gone, and a lamb-like nature in the place of it; he has as much sweetness toward the people of Christ, as he had sourness against them. Of an executioner, he becomes a martyr; and would not only lose his life, but be an Anathema, to do them good whom before he hated. Christ was his life, Christ was his joy, Christ was his all, and nothing but Christ dear to him. A quite contrary strain. And this is a new creature; and therefore examine yourselves. Is there faith instead of unbelief, the knowledge of God instead of ignorance, a constant glowing affection to him instead of enmity, or a coldness of love, the love of the Creator instead of that of the creature? This is to have the image of God instead of that of the devil.

But, in particular,

1. What fervent longings have you after a likeness to God? The first draught of this image begets strong desires for a farther perfection. The sighs and groans for a likeness to God are the first lineaments of God in the soul, and arise from some degree of affection to him, and delight in him. The breathings of the soul are 'for the living God,' as David, Ps. xiii. 2; Ps. lxxxiv. 2, for God, as a principle of life and spirit in him. This hungering and thirsting after righteousness is a sign of righteousness already in the soul, and an earnest of a further fullness, Mat. v. None can fervently and unweariedly long for a divine nature but such as have had some taste of it. The divine nature in the soul will be returning to that nature whence it derives its essential purity. The principle coming from God will be aspiring to that nature which it is a part of, as rivers to the sea, and swell if they be hindered. He must needs long after a full draught, and can no more satisfy himself with imperfect lineaments, than a sick man can with an imperfect cure. It is to this end he breathes after heaven, because it is a state of perfection, not from any carnal notion of it. He knows he is not already perfect, and therefore presses forward with eager desire and endeavour, 'if by any means he may attain the resurrection from the dead,' Philip. iii. 11-13, &c. He does not only desire a freedom from sin, but to be as pure and elevated in affection to God as an angel. God is not only free from unrighteousness, but full of righteousness; and therefore those desires of a divine nature are not limited to, and centred in, a negative holiness. He would set himself no other

pattern but God. It is an excellent speech of a heathen, exhorting not only to live the life of a good man, which civil virtue and the vogue of men approved of, but to look above that to the choicest desire of a divine life; for, says he, our endeavours should be for a likeness to God, not to good men. To endeavour to be like to man, is to make one image like another; but a new creature aims at the highest exemplar; it aspires after no lower a pattern than God himself, his will, his rule, his glory, his pleasure. Do the breathings of your spirits rise as much for it, as the steams of your lusts did before against it?

2. Put this question to yourselves, What inward authority has God over your hearts? Is the government of God set up in your souls? Can you with joy say, The Lord reigns, and none but he shall reign over me? The new creature coming under another government, has frames suitable to it, and delightfully owns that supreme authority, and pleases himself more in a subjection to God, than the wicked can in their slavery to sin. Do you 'yield yourselves to God, and your members as instruments of righteousness unto God'? Are the motions of your souls guided by him? You are then 'alive from the dead;' it is the apostle's assertion, Rom. vi. 4. Sin does reside; but which reigns, God or lust? An usurpation may be on sin's part, when no voluntary subjection on ours. Is it an absolute, or only a partial resignation of yourselves to him? Do you give him a moiety, or do you give him the whole? Has he the sole sovereignty? or would you give him an associate? Are any evil ways hated, out of a respect to his word, to his authority, wisdom, goodness, or a respect to yourselves? Ps. cxix. 128, 'I esteem thy precepts concerning all things to be right, and I hate every false way.' Ver. 133, 'Order my steps in thy word, and let not any iniquity have dominion over me.' Are God's dictates readily obeyed? Does a free submission to his authority govern and act thee in his ways? Do you count his yoke easy, and his burden light? Do you glory in the chain of grace, and count the service of sin as iron fetters? Is the will of God above your own wills? Do you defy the one to observe the other? Is God's will sacred with you, when it thwarts your own, or only when it suits your interest? It is not then the authority of God which prevails with you, but the authority of some extraneous thing which has the chief moving force. If so, there is no sign of the new creature in such a frame.

3. How are your affections to God? It is a new creature we are speaking of, and that is inward chiefly. Sin may be left in the practice, and not hated: goodness may be practised, when it is not affected. Where, then, is the new creature? It is not only a change of professions. Simon Magus had changed that before his baptism, but not his heart, either before or after, Acts viii. 21. The strength of sin, lies in the understanding, will, and affections, and it is there that the strength of grace must appear, and set up its banners. Are your affections and lusts of your flesh crucified? They must be so, if you are Christ's new creatures, Gal. v. 24. The strong stirring of natural conscience may weaken a present resolution to an act of sin, but not an affection to it, and to the habit of sin. It may restrain from outward exercises, not from inward dispositions. Natural conscience informs of the evil, but does not confer upon us a disaffection to that evil. What are the inclinations of your affections? Are they pitched upon God? What are they for duration? Are they constantly in motion to him? Is it your pleasure to think of him, to live to him? Are the remainders of unlikeness to him your grief, your yet imperfect image your delight, not because it is imperfect, but because it is his image? Every sigh, or a slight affection, is not a new creature. It is a deep engravement, a constant inclination, contrary to what it was before, as white to black. Do your affections correspond with the affections of God? Do you hate everything that he hates? Or is there any one lust thou should caress and hide among the stuff? Such a frame is not the new-creature frame. God loves not one sin, neither must we, if we be like him. Is the love to God and Christ more settled than love to father or mother, which is an inbred affection, born with our natures? Mat. x. 37. It must be so supreme. What desires have you to magnify his name? Do you love him so intensely, as to part with your lives to glorify and enjoy him? If you be new creatures, God and his glory will be dearer to you than friends, credit, life. He said not amiss, that no man is a true Christian who is not an habitual martyr; that is, that has not a disposition to lay down his life for the honour of God. And that apostle who has spoken so much of the new creature had such a raised affection, Acts xx. 24, he would 'not count his life dear, so he might finish his course with joy;' which was 'to testify the gospel of the grace of God.' He could lay down his head more willingly upon a block than upon a pillow, if he might finish his course to his Master's honour, and publish his grace. Where there is no concern for the honour of God, there is little sign of a likeness to him; for this is an essential part of true Christianity. If we have a new nature, we cannot but love that nature, wherever we find it. And where we find it in a greater degree, and infinitely perfect, as in God, we cannot but love it there above all; else we offer violence to the divine nature; and in not loving it in God, we love it not in ourselves. It is impossible there can be this divine nature without spiritual affections, and that the image of God can be in us without having an intense love to him whose image it is. If anything, then, lie nearer the heart of any man than God, the image of God is not in him. Therefore look into your hearts. How does your hatred break out against sin? How is your sorrow poured out for sin?

4. How stand your souls to inward and spiritual duties? How vile are you in your own eyes because of sin? What grief is there even for your least imperfections? Are you every day defacing your pride, and strengthening your humility? Pride is the great fort of the old man, humility the great security

of the new. How are you in prayer? Are you constant, are you fervent, have you daily converses with God? I mean secret prayer and meditation: there are the most intimate converses with God. I appeal to you that neglect those duties; can you pretend to this new creation? Do you think that the image of God in the heart would not often move to its original? Can a likeness to God consist with an estrangedness from him? Can any man live the life of God that does not care for the presence of God, either speaking to him, or thinking of him? Can that law in the heart, which is put in that we may not depart from him, consist with this which is the prime departure, never to seek him, or to seek him coldly? All the affections of the new creature bend to him, and centre in him. Can this be without a drawing near to him? The 'spirit of grace' is followed with a 'spirit of supplication:' Zech. xii. 10, 'the spirit of grace and of supplication.' The Spirit is not a dumb spirit in the new creature. The first work in the heart is to cry, 'Abba, Father': Gal. iv. 6, 'God has sent forth the spirit of his Son into your hearts, crying, Abba, Father.' The first impression made by the Spirit is upon the eye of the soul to look to God, and the voice of the soul to cry to him. It is the first work of a regenerate man as regenerate. It is the argument our Saviour uses to Ananias, to have confidence that Paul was not the same man as before: Acts ix. 11, 'Behold, he prays.' Our old nature being made up of aversion from God, the proper language of that is, 'Depart from us.' The new nature being made up of an inclination to God, the proper language of that is, 'It is good for me to draw near to God;' for upon this renewing grace God is the proper centre of the soul, and the same principle which moves other things to the centre will move the soul to God. It is made the effect of a pure heart: 2 Tim. ii. 22, 'Peace with them that call on the Lord out of a pure heart,' and the characteristical note of a saint: 1 Cor. i. 2, 'Saints, with all that in every place call upon the name of Jesus Christ our Lord.'

5. What valuations and relishes have you of the word and institutions of Christ? As the life is, so is the food; a spiritual appetite for spiritual food is a comfortable sign of a renewed nature. In every nature there is an aversion to what is destructive, an inclination to what is preservative. Every creature does as much desire its proper food, as it abhors that poison that would blast it. The new nature has a new taste, his palate is embittered to his former pleasure, and refined and prepared for his new delight: he relishes what before he loathed, esteems that sweetest that before was most unpleasant. The law in the heart, being an impression of the word, will answer it with a choice affection. The first cleansing of the heart, and the progressive sanctification of it, is wrought by the word: Eph. v. 26, 'That he might sanctify and cleanse it with the washing of water by the word.' The image of God in the heart cannot but value the image of God in his law; since the soul is brought to a love of God, it will love his operations, and all the methods of them, and therefore his word. A rectified judgment will have a rectified affection; there will be a spiritual palate, whereby it proves and 'approves what is the good, acceptable, and perfect will of God,' Rom. xii. 2. What is pleasing to God is good and pleasing to him. And the same apostle sets it as a sign of a perfect man, or a sincere new creature, to esteem that the wisdom of God which the world counts foolishness: 1 Cor. ii. 6, 'We speak wisdom among them that are perfect.' The Spirit of truth in the new creature will fill it with a strong affection to those truths in the word. Truth in the heart, and truth in the word, being so near of kin, cannot be strangers or unwelcome to one another. What sympathy, then, is there between the word and your hearts? What exercise of grace in it? What improvement of grace by it? Do you desire it to satisfy your curiosity, or to further your growth? 1 Pet. ii. 2, 'As new-born babes, desire the sincere milk of the word, that you may grow thereby.' Are you like the plants, both cleansed and quickened by the showers, and discovering themselves in a fresh verdure? How do you dilate your souls for it? How do you work it upon your hearts? Do you desire it should be stamped upon you? Do you long for a more perfect intimacy with it? Do you prize it above the satisfactions of wealth and the pleasures of sense? Is it 'more excellent than gold,' Ps. xix. 10, 'and sweeter than honey?' Ps. cxix. 103. Do you spiritually concoct it, and turn spiritual meat into a spiritual juice, as the stomach does meat into chyle, and other parts of the body into blood? Life can only do this. Do you love to have it dwell richly in you, and bring down the highest imaginations to the foot of it? Do you cut the throat of your dearest Isaacs when the word commands you? Is it a pleasure to you to see the face of God in his ordinances? Is your pleasure raised most by the spirituality of truth? The more spiritual any truth is, the more satisfactory it is to a spiritual taste. Do your hearts burn within you at the warm breath of Christ? Are they not only warmed, but raised into a flame, and that lasting? Not like the straw, which does blaze and vanish.

6. What holiness is there in your hearts and lives? God cannot be otherwise than holy, therefore holiness is the perpetual concomitant of the divine nature; and so the apostle makes it to consist in 'escaping the pollutions that are in the world through lust,' 2 Pet. i. 4. There is a principle which springs up in holy motions and thoughts. It is in the soul the image of God is stamped, and it is there that the new creature does chiefly exercise and preserve it. Holiness must be the proper effect of that which is planted by the Spirit of holiness. He that pretends to a likeness to God without it, fathers an irregularity upon him, and makes him a monstrous begetter. It is not born of the will of the flesh, to follow sensual pleasures, nor of the will of man, to follow only rational delights; but of the will of God, and therefore follows that will it was born of, John i. 13. 'Let thy kingdom come, thy will be done,' is the natural

language of the new creature, and glad he is to have the Spirit point him to those ways that are most conformable to the divine will, for it is not a strained holiness, but natural, such a one as arises from the 'fear of God in the heart,' Jer. xxxii. 40, and a care to please God in his walk: 2 Cor. vii. 11, 'Yea, what care!' It is holy as God is holy, in some measure, and therefore like him whose infinite purity cannot endure pollution. And it can no more divest itself of its inclinations to righteousness than the soul can strip itself of its natural activity. There is a certain connection between a 'heart of flesh' and 'walking in God's statutes,' Ezek. xxxvi. 26, 27. To what purpose does God give it? either for his own work or for the devil's? There is no need of it for the latter; the heart of stone would have done his work effectually: therefore for the service of the former, and that constantly, for the new creature is 'created to good works,' not to do them by fits and turns, but 'to walk in them,' Eph. ii. 10; and he is described by the apostle to be one that 'walks after the Spirit,' Rom. viii. 1, the ordinary course of his heart is spiritual. How is it with you, then? Is holiness your proper element? Is it a death to you when any thing contrary to it buds up in your hearts? Is there a purity of heart joined with a zeal for goodness, Titus ii. 14? They go hand in hand, as being both the ends of our Saviour's death, and both the works of the Spirit. Is there an angry detestation of the loathsomeness of sin, and a kindly affection to the purity of grace? It will be thus if the new creation be wrought, for as in original sin there was the root of all evil, therefore all holiness may be opposed, and all sin practised; so in the habit of grace there is the root of all grace, therefore all sin will be loathed, and every part of holiness will be loved. But on the contrary, if your old lusts be rather improved than impaired; if you are more charmed by swinish pleasures, and enamoured of them; if the enmity in your hearts or the loathsomeness in your lives remain, is there anything of a new creature in you? Judge for yourselves. Do you make as rich a provision for the flesh as before? Is your heart and life set upon it with as much affection? Are you joyful when employed in its drudgery? Is this to be a new creature? Can there be such darkness, if the sun of grace were risen upon you? Such fruits evidence the standing of the old root. He that has the black mark of the devil in his life has no reason to think he has the spiritual badge of Christ in his heart; and if he do, he does deceive himself.

7. How is your disposition against those things which are contrary to a divine nature? No creature has a greater antipathy to that which is contrary to its nature, than a regenerate man has against that which is contrary to the divine. It is as impossible there can be a friendly neighbourhood between the new man and the old, as between the ark and Dagon, between heat and cold, which are always quarrelling, yea, between Christ and Belial, 2 Cor. v. 16.

(1.) Against the motions of Sin. An irreconcilable war is commenced between grace and corruption. At the first inlet flesh is in arms to hinder; the spirit in arms to maintain its standing, Gal. v. 17. The contest is in the whole man; grace being seated in the heart, sends out its commands, and despatches forces to every part to meet with its enemy, as motion beginning at the centre diffuses itself through the whole sphere, shaking every part to the circumference. Light will oppose darkness in every part of the air; they cannot shake hands together; the increase of one is the decrease of the other. Sensibility is a sign of life; a dead man complains not of wounds and cutting; you may take out his bowels, cut limb from limb, but a living man will complain of the least prick of a pin or a pinch. Natural men cannot complain of that which they do not feel. There is a mighty friendship between a dead carcass and rottenness, nothing is noisome to it. Loads of sin may lie upon him, like mountains upon a dead body, and no complaint: 'The motions of sin work in his members' without resistance, and 'bring forth their fruit unto death,' Rom. vii. 5. But the new creature counts the least sin that has stolen in upon him his torture, like the stone in the bladder, a worm in the root, and can find no rest till he routs the beginnings of the disease. If there be no antipathy then to that which is contrary to the life and being of a Christian, it is a sure sign that there is nothing of a divine life, for as a renewed man 'esteems all the precepts of God to be right,' and 'hates every false way,' Ps. cxix. 128, so he must abhor every motion which would divert him from what he values, and entice him to what he hates. How are your understandings sensible of the first risings contrary to the interest of the new creature? Are they more ready to dissent from them, your wills more ready to check them than before? What counterworkings against the flesh, with its affections and lusts? Are you ready with weapons in your hand to stay the first stirrings of corruption? Are you ready to pluck those buds, and fling them away with disdain? Does both your courage and strength increase? Can you more readily be in arms against the rising of a lust than formerly you were, and cannot without horror bear the approaches of them? Does a little dust of sin got into your eye set you a-weeping before God?

(2.) How stand you affected to spiritual sins? Here you should lay the great stress in your examination of the new creation, for your lives may be the lives of saints, while your hearts are the hearts of devils; we may have no spots of the flesh upon our garments, and a world of them upon our souls; spiritual sins may revel where the more fleshly and sensual iniquities are excluded. There is a war in the heart of the new creature against spiritual wickedness: Eph. vi. 12, 'For we wrestle not against flesh and blood, but against the rulers of the darkness of this world, against spiritual wickedness in high places;' or wickedness spiritualised in the high places, "Pros ta pneumatika tes ponerias en tois epouraniois", the choicest faculties of the soul. Satan does most excite those sins in the heart, and natural conscience makes no resistance against them. It is only an enlightened conscience that understands and abhors this darkness, and loathes those steams which others cherish. Do you wrestle against these which partake most of the devil's nature? Do you dandle them in your minds, or do you groan at the appearance of them? Do you fly from them as you would do from a visible apparition of the devil? These are most contrary to the divine nature and life of God. And a renewed man can no more avoid contesting with them than the nature of a living creature can with poison. But if you can without any reluctance play the wantons with these in your hearts; if you think pride, vain-glory, ambition, speculative wickedness, &c., no evils, if your hearts never start at the appearance of them; if you entertain them as welcome guests, though you be never so free from the filthiness of the flesh, you have yet the strength of Satan's image in you, nothing of a Christian formed. A natural man may quarrel with some sins, not with all; renewed men with all, because all are enemies to God, and to the life of grace in the heart. He is always with arms in his hand to extirpate sin, and drive the Canaanite from his forts as well as the open field.

(3.) Are you in the like manner affected against temptations and occasions of sin? The state of regeneration makes the soul more subject to the assaults of temptations than before, from the envy of Satan, who stomachs the happiness of the new creature. Do your souls start at the appearance of a temptation? Do you regard any enticement to a departure from God as your torment? Do you discountenance it at the first approach, and give it more civil entertainment, than 'Get you behind me, Satan'? Christ in the flesh did so, and Christ formed in the heart will do no less; if he happen to come near the way of evil men, he will observe the wise man's counsel, Prov. iv. 14, 15, he will 'avoid it, pass not by it, turn from it, and pass away.' His spirit will rise against anything that would intrude upon him, which looks unfriendly towards God. The nobleness of the new nature will make him disdain a sordid temptation, and inspire him with a holy generosity; and the stronger the nature, the more vigorously will it oppose that which would deform it. And if any temptation break in upon it at any time, and master it, how restless is it to be delivered from it, applies itself with all its force to heaven, complains against it, engages God's power on its side, makes up the gap where sin has broken in, and fortifies the place to prevent a future assault! In short, a natural man nourishes inward lusts, meets motions to sin half way, smiles upon an approaching temptation A new creature starts at the first appearance for the most part, frowns upon satanic suggestions, turns away his eyes from beholding vanity. One makes provision to maintain them, the other to destroy them; one submits to the tempter, the other arms himself against him.

8. Put this question to yourselves, What delight do you find in God and his ways? This indeed is an evident sign of the new nature; by this men may judge of themselves, if they will not deceive and flatter themselves in their search. This is the greatest evidence of sincerity in all the ways of God. For the law cannot be in any man's heart, unless he delight to do the will of God: Ps. xl. 8, 'Thy law is within my heart, I delight to do thy will, O my God.' He will be carried out with a spiritual joy and triumph to the acting what is spiritually good, with a mighty pleasure, as great as the body takes in eating when it is hungry, or drinking when it is thirsty. It was thus with our Saviour in the flesh, it is thus with Christ formed in the heart, it is his meat and drink to do the will of God; not so much in the new creature as it was in Christ, because in that there is a remaining principle of resistance, in Christ none. It is then he can 'delight himself in the Lord,' Isa. lviii. 14, and count him his 'exceeding joy,' Ps. xliii. 4. As it is an argument that Seneca gives of the divine original of the soul, that it is most pleased with divine speculations, it is no less an argument of the new creation, when it is delighted, not only with the speculative, but with the practical contemplation of God, when the soul that triumphed before in the pleasures of sin can burn with an ardent love to God, and solace itself in communion with him; and unless holy services be our delightful element, we have not a likeness to that God, who is not only righteous, but delights in 'righteousness, loving-kindness, and judgment,' Jer. ix. 24. Every being owes so much respect to its own welfare, as not to act sluggishly and drowsily in its main concern; for the same love which excites it to perform those things which are essential to its preservation will oblige it to act with the highest complacency; and the more conducing they are to the well-being of the creature, the more powerful is the joy which spreads itself through the whole essence of the creature; therefore holy services being as intrinsical to a holy principle as the most inward operations of any creature can be to its nature, will be done with a vigorous frame, and an edged intenseness of spirit. Without this, in some degree, nothing requisite to the operations of a new creature can be performed; without it we have no aversion to that which is contrary to the law, nor an inclination to what is conformable to it. It is a consent of the will to the whole law, Rom. vii. 16, a delight of the affections in it; a consent to it in respect of the goodness; a delight in it (ver. 22), in respect of the authority enjoining it, as it is the law of God; not principally as it is in some parts conformable to human reason, but as it is the divine will, whereby both the sovereignty, holiness, and righteousness of God is owned by the whole inward man; the understanding, will, and affections, conspiring together with a strong delight in God and his law. Hence you find David so often expressing his delight in it, Ps. cxix. 14, 35, 47, 70, 77, &c. And indeed so much of weariness as we have in any service, so much of an old nature and a legal frame; so much as

we have of love and delight, so much we have of a new creature, and new covenant grace. A natural man cannot have any of this choice joy in any spiritual service, because it is against his nature; no more than a fish can delight to be upon the land out of its proper element; but a new creature has little delight in anything, but as it regards God, and tends to him; other men's delights are terminated in the flesh, but the elevations of a renewed soul are highly spiritual. How then is it with you? Are the duties of religion, communion with God in them, your delightful element? Is a flight of your love to him, the acting for his glory, as pleasant as flattery to a proud nature, or gain to a covetous disposition? Have you little satisfaction in what you do, but still breathe and strive after a higher frame, and cannot rest, till with your choice embraces of your souls you clasp about God himself? O happy man! None but a divine nature could fill thee with such pleasing transports.

Use 4. Is of exhortation.

1. To those who are new creatures, that have some comfortable evidence in their souls, that there is the image of God renewed in them.

(1.) How should you admire and glorify God? Is it possible that so noble a work can be unattended with a spirit of gratitude? How should you be filled with a sense of divine goodness, and formed to set forth his praise? Surely this of thankfulness is not one of the least good works you are created unto. Before, when you were alienated from the life of God, you were estranged from his love and his praise, you would never glorify him whom you did not affect; but since a heavenly nature is introduced, a heavenly work should become the very life of your souls; tongues and hearts should be set on fire by grace.

[1.] Has not God made you differ from the whole mass of the corrupted world? There is as great a difference between a new and an old creature as between the clearest day and the darkest night; as between Christ, who is glorified in heaven, the head of his own flock, and the devil, who is damned in hell, the head of the unbelieving world; so they are opposed by the apostle, 2 Cor. vi. 14, 15. Might you not have run down the stream with others, lived only a natural life with others, and at last died an eternal death, and descended, with all your intellectual and moral endowments, to the place only due to corrupt nature? But God, the God that is blessed for ever, has breathed into you a breath of life, caused you to stand up before him with a resemblance of his nature, set you apart for himself, wrought you for glory, and made you live another life, a life by the faith of the Son of God. And is it not reason you should differ from all the world in your praises of him, who has made you differ so vastly in your state and condition?

[2.] Has not God in this bestowed upon you a higher perfection than all natural perfection in the world? The lowest degree of sense is more excellent than the highest inanimate perfection; therefore a fly, in regard of life, is more excellent than a diamond, or the sun itself. The lowest degree of reason is above the highest degree of sense, and the lowest decree of renewing grace transcends the highest degree of reason, because this in the highest degree is but human and natural, that in the lowest degree spiritual and divine. Therefore you owe more to God for your regeneration than all creatures of the world do for their natural existence. He has done more for you, in communicating to you his own nature, than if he had made you viceroys over men and angels and put the whole created world under your feet, without investing you with this new creation.

[3.] And this God has done for you, when you were in the common lump, and had no more worth in yourselves to move him to it than the rest of the world. No other motive on your part but misery. All the world had the same; for it lay in the like condition. All that you had, all that you were, was proper to move him to a contempt of you, and a loathing you forever. It was the invention of his own overflowing love, not any persuasion of your worth. What were you, and what was your father's house, that he should thus translate you from the drudgery of sin to the liberty of grace, from a spiritual death to a divine life? Had God called you out of the womb of nothing, unshaped as the great chaos, and asked you what degree of creatures you were willing to be raised unto, would you have presumed to desire God to make you like himself? Yet God in regeneration raised you to a state you dared not ask, above a rational creature, even to a divine, when he had no motive to anything, but to turn you, with Nebuchadnezzar, to graze among the beasts, and partake with devils in the eternal misery of that image you had contracted.

[4.] It is therefore a wonderful and miraculous change. If the framing the body of man be so 'wonderful' a work, Ps. cxxxix. 14, and a curious piece of embroidery, how much more admirable is this new formation of the soul into the likeness of God. If we should see a silly fly or a poisonous spider, a clod of earth, or a glow-worm, transformed into a glittering star, it would not be so great a miracle; it would be a change from one natural image to another. But this is a change from hell to heaven, from being a limb of the devil to become a member of Christ, from a worse than Egyptian darkness into a marvellous light. That is but a change of one innocent nature into another; this a change of a nature hateful to God into a nature delightful to him, a corrupt creature into an holy one, a change of something worse than a bare creature into something like the great Creator and Redeemer. This is your change, therefore the highest obligation in the world lies upon you, to praise and glorify God. It is in the day of your regeneration that God has rolled away the reproach of your corruption and death, as he said of the Israelites when they were circumcised in Canaan, Joshua v. 9.

To quicken you to praise,

First, Often reflect upon your former state. Cast your eyes back upon what you were, that you may be thankful for what you are. Ah, what was I once? A hater of God, and hated by him; one bearing the image of Satan, and delighting in it; a noisome heap of lusts, estranged from God, sold under sin, dead to goodness, an enemy to the law. What a condition was I in then! Good Lord, how astonishing was thy mercy, how wonderful thy love, how great was thy power, to draw me out of this state!

Secondly, Review what you are. What am I now? Here is a new light in my understanding, new inclinations in my will; I can now look upon God with pleasure and run his ways with delight. Christ is my only joy, and Christ is my only gain. My old nature is wearing away, my new nature is rising higher and clearer; now am I freed by the blood of Christ from my guilt, and by the Spirit of Christ from my filth. What shall I render to the Lord for these inestimable benefits towards me? O blessed God! O dear Redeemer! O infinite condescending Spirit, to work these things for me, in me; to clear such a nasty soul, imprint such a heavenly image, conform me to so excellent a pattern, and by grace to fit me for a glorious eternity! Let then the love of the author, the excellency of the work, the misery of your former state, the happiness of your new, be joined together in your considerations to enhance your praise; and since you live the life of God, be sure to live the life of thankfulness.

(2.) As it is your duty to admire and glorify God for making you new creatures, so it is your duty and advantage too to preserve in its vigour this new nature in you. When Adam's life was infused, he was to preserve it by feeding upon the fruits of paradise, Gen. ii. 29. And you must preserve your spiritual lives by the fruits of divine institutions placed in the church. The inner man is to be strengthened; Paul prays to this purpose for the Ephesians, Eph. iii. 16, 'that he would grant you to be strengthened with might by his Spirit in the inner man,' which is not, as some understand it, a strengthening of reason, mind, and understanding, The Scripture by heart understands the mind, will, and judgment, but the apostle joins this inner man so with the heart (ver. 17, 'That Christ may dwell in your hearts by faith'), that he does manifestly put a difference between this inner man and the heart, making one the seat, the other the root in it. The apostle wishes them not a strength of the soul, but a strength of the new man and image of Christ in the soul. The devil is a mighty enemy to it; he has lost a servant: he will leave no stone unturned to recover him; his servant will be his judge; he will therefore endeavour to overthrow him. Go to God, therefore, for new supplies in the case of Satan's assaults; desire him to put a vigour into your grace, water the seeds, and blow up the divine spark. Our Saviour desired assisting and strengthening grace for Peter, when he foresaw the devil's preparations to worry him, Luke xxii. 31, 32. So should we for ourselves, and Christ will not be backward to second us in it; yea, he will prevent us, and send in an auxiliary force over and above the standing habit which makes up the new creature. We need the gales of heaven to blow us forward, the concourse of God to his gracious creature, as well as his common concourse to his natural. Is it not the highest reason to engage all in the defence, and strengthening that which is the delight of God, the happiness of the soul, and the envy of the devil? What is worth our care, if this be thought worthy of our neglect? Sloth in preserving and strengthening argues a lesser value of a thing. Would you lose beauty for deformity, health for sickness? Would you lose the pleasures of heaven for the anguish of hell? Preserve this image then from being defaced, and look that Satan draw no more black lines in your hearts. 'Skin for skin, and all a man has will he give for his life;' eat his own flesh to preserve his life as long as he can. Oh then, if I may so say, soul for soul, and all that you have, you should give and employ for maintaining this spiritual life, which is as much above a natural life as the sun above a dunghill. Blow it up every day, dress the lamps as the priests in the temple. It is for want of this strengthening it, that we have so little liveliness in duty. It is for want of this excitation that we walk so often in darkness. What have we else to do but this? Preservation and strengthening of life is the chief design of men in the world. Is not a divine life of more worth? Let not then the cares of our bodies surpass those for our souls, and our fondness to natural life exceed our affection to spiritual life. We know but in part, we see but as in a glass darkly. The inclinations of our hearts to righteousness are not in their full strength.

(3.) Grow up to a taller stature. There must be a daily putting off the old man, and a putting on the new, a renewing the inward man day by day, 2 Cor. iv. 16. And though at the first regeneration there is the forming all the essential parts of grace, yet afterwards there is a daily augmentation (the Galatians were both knowing God, and known of him, Gal. iv. 9, yet of these did the apostle travail, till Christ was formed again, ver. 19), till the design of Christ be fully complied with, and the soul grown up to the measure of the stature of the fullness of Christ, by the participation of his nature. As providence is a continued creation, so growth is a continued regeneration. As a man grows in reason by new improvements, so ought a Christian in grace, by new additions. Things are not ripened at once. The spirits in raw and immature bodies are depressed by gross and earthy mixtures with them, till they are encouraged by the sun and showers, and thereby able to digest the crude parts, and arrive at perfection.

[1.] This must be: Job xvii. 9, 'The righteous shall hold on his way, and he that has clean hands shall be stronger and stronger.' The new nature can no more stand at a stay, than a living tree can, till it come up to the measures of its nature. It is the nature of seed to propagate itself, and spread its virtue into branches and fruit. It will be aspiring to that perfection which nature has allotted to it. If you do not grow, it is a sign there is no life in you. It is but a common gift, or a common grace, at best; the counterfeit, not the reality of the new creature. Living natures do thrive; pieces of art stand at a stay. He is no member of Christ, but as a wooden leg or arm; not knit by any vital band, but some extrinsic ligaments; not fed with the increases of God, because he does not grow. To content ourselves with a low degree of grace, makes us unworthy of the benefit of regeneration, and below those that pretend to a likeness to God.

[2.] It must be uniform. As it is one habit which is infused, so it equally thrives in all the parts of it. An unequal growth is the effect of a disease, not of nature. As nature causes a proportion of parts in the make, so likewise a proportion of parts in the growth. It is not a growth in faith, and a decay in love; or a growth in love, and a decay in faith. To pretend to the one without the other, is to have an head without an heart, a life without blood or spirits. A natural man may grow in some moral ornaments, as a dead man in hair and nails; but a spiritual vitality shows itself in an equal increase of all the members in the new creature. And it is best discerned by the thriving of those graces which are most contrary to your natural disposition which cannot so well be discerned in those which have some foundations in moral natures, as humility has a mild disposition, which by the addition of grace, advances to an eminent humility. But a new creature thrives in those graces which were most contrary to his corrupt nature, now over-mastered. The second draught of a picture defaces not one line or two of the former, but the whole frame, to make it more near the original. And thus a new creature ought to grow as the vine, and revive as the corn, in all the branches and fruits proper to its nature, Hosea xiv. 7.

[3.] By this we please God and pleasure ourselves. The more illustrious any work is, the more glory redounds to the artist. If the beginnings of the new creation be so amiable as to make heaven itself in love with it, how infinitely will God be pleased to see it grow to maturity among the whirlwinds and storms of temptations; every increase, adding new colours and lustre to this beauty, will renew the jubilee in heaven. Thus will God pronounce it good at first, and very good the nearer it comes to perfection, as he did in the creation of the world. By this growth you will have a greater capacity for heaven; for if the first new creation capacitates a man for glory, the higher it springs, the more beautiful the divine nature grows, the nearer it is to glory and the fitter to be planted in an eternal paradise, the more right to heaven will appear to yourselves.

(4.) A fourth exhortation. Behave yourselves in your ordinary walk, as new creatures of another rank from the world. It is the inference the apostle makes from the new state wherein the Ephesians were, 'For you were sometimes darkness, but now light in the Lord: walk as children of the light,' Eph. v. 8. You must bring forth fruits meet for regeneration, meet for him by whom you are renewed, as the ground does herbs, meet for him by whom it is dressed, Heb. vi. 7.

[1.] Adorn the gospel, whereby the divine impression is made upon you. The apostle argues against lying, and by the same reason against all sin, from this head, Col. iii. 9, 10. The gospel adorns the soul by its impression; the soul should adorn the gospel by its conversation: Titus ii. 10, 'Adorn the doctrine of God our Saviour in all things.' Let the writing of the law in the heart appear on the other side of the life, and the divine light in your hearts shine in your outward man, as a candle through a lantern, that God may be glorified, Mat. v. 16. Let not lust and sin, extraneous to the new creature, bear any rule in any action; let no unworthy action reproach your profession. Do nothing unbecoming one who is like him that rules the world, unbecoming that word and gospel which God has magnified above all his name. Defile not your garments; we can never walk with God but in white, Rev. iii. 4, in the whiteness of purity, not in the blackness of sin. Do not any works of Satan with the nature of God upon you. Indeed, we may be ashamed, that when there is so much of the image of Christ in the gospel, there should be so little of the image of Christ in our lives. Walk as those that are enrolled among the spirits of just men made perfect, as those who have the honour to be of the assembly of the first-born; live to God, not to yourselves. The more wicked the generation is you live in, the more it is your duty to shine, as the lights of heaven in the darkness of the earth, Philip. ii. 15, and the more it will be your commendation, as it was the praise of Job, that he was upright in the land of Uz, among the race of profane Esau, not among the offspring of praying Jacob: Job i. 1, That man was perfect, and feared God.'

[2.] Live above affections to a drossy world, if you would honour your new nature. An earthly spirit cannot be the effect of a heavenly birth. Let not the rattles of your childhood be your present pleasure, or the bewitching world have any influence upon you. The world is no fit boundary for the soul in its natural capacity, much less in its spiritual; it is too empty for an immortal soul, much more for a divine nature. Let not anything on this side God be your darling, but your footstool, to mount you nearer heaven. Value them only as they enable you to do the higher duties of religion without distracting cares, and are subservient to the honouring God in the world. As the new creature was not redeemed with a vile price, so it is not endued with so sordid a nature, as to be much in love with these things. The conquest of this is one of the first fruits of the new birth. 1 John v. 4, 'Whatsoever is born of God, overcomes the world;' there is a mighty antipathy between the world, and anything that is the offspring of God. There cannot be so much ignorance of the things of another world, as to prize so vile a piece, as a house with walls and furniture, infected with a sinful leprosy. Let the inward contempt of the blandishments of it grow up in you; distract not yourselves with cares for it, but trust in God's promise, and leave things to the conduct of his wise providence. It is inconsistent with a new nature to lie at the bottom of this great sea, sucking up weeds and sand, and never peep its head above water, towards heaven.

[3.] Be much in the thoughts and views of the divine original of your nature. Shall the new nature seldom look up to that place whence it descended, or cast its eye upon that beautiful hand that framed it? Surely the new creature cannot be so unnatural. Employ your souls in exercises of an unbounded love to God, a settled delight in him, a high esteem of the righteousness of his nature, and an habitual walking with him; let the esteem of him, and vilifying yourselves, be your daily employment. The looking upon him will transform you more into his image; by this spiritual converse you will partake of a new brightness, and clearer lineaments. Every view will leave a greater perfection upon his image in you, by a reflection of a glory, 2 Cor. iii. 18: By this your hearts will be more suitable to those regions of blessedness to which the divine image is hastening. It will make you sweat out some corruption every day, and advance you some steps toward the state of bliss.

[4.] Fix your aims on a state of perfection. You are to walk, not to stand still. Never rest till all that righteousness which of right belongs to that divine nature in you, be conferred upon you: breathe after a more close conjunction with the original. Keep up in a due sprightliness your detestations of sin, which you had when you were first enlivened, with what a holy indignation you flung away your lusts, with a Get you hence, and, What have I to do any more with idols? Set an edge upon this hatred every day, sharpen your indignation more and more. Preserve in your souls those affections which did rise up in you, when the irresistible charms of divine love did first allure you, when you first cast your eyes upon this new likeness and image of God; quicken them daily, and 'press forward towards the mark for the prize of the high calling of God in Christ.'

[5.] Let your affection be carried to everything which partakes of the same image. There is in all creatures a kindness to those of their own nature; the most ravenous do not prey upon their own species; all men, descending from Adam, having the same nature, have some kindness to those of their own kind and all descending from Christ have the same nature, the same affections and instincts. It is in love and holiness wherein God does decipher himself in the soul, he would not be drawn in any other attributes in the heart of man; and thus in the Scripture he publishes himself in the abstract as holiness and love, delighting to be imitated by his creature in those two perfections, 'God is love, and he that dwells in God dwells in love,' 1 John iv. 16. Love is, therefore, the nature of the new creature, and love to the same objects whereon God's love is pitched, first himself, then his image in his creature. So the love of God and that of a new creature go hand in hand together; first, the affections of the new nature stream out to God as the prime and original beauty, then to all new creatures, as they partake more or less of this divine image. This universal charity to God, grace, and good men, is the inseparable property of the new creature, the highest perfection of it, and the beginning of a state of glory. Love all those that partake of this divine nature.

[6.] Endeavour to propagate your new nature to others. It is the property of goodness to be diffusive of itself; and God, the highest goodness, is the most communicative. The divine nature should imitate him in this. No nature but delights to propagate itself. The new nature ought not to be sluggish in it; since the great change lies in the end, since the glory of God is set up as its main intendment, it will oblige it to propagate holiness and righteousness, whereby God is most glorified; for thereby the number is increased to represent him on earth and praise him in heaven. No sooner was Paul renewed, but he endeavours to bring all the world into the same frame. The apostate angels, being revolted from God, labour to sink all the world into the same disposition. Fire communicates by a touch its own nature to all matter that comes near it, and turns the hardest metals into its own likeness. So ought that holy fire in a new creature to labour to convert everything into its own flames. This is a peculiar mark set upon the evangelical times, and the special fruit of a gospel impression: Isa. ii. 3, 'Many people shall say, Come se, and let us go up to the mountain of the Lord, to the house of the God of Jacob.' It should be your endeavour that all about you may be the better for you. Strive to affect your children and servants with a sense of the corruption of nature derived from Adam, and the necessity of being implanted in the new head of the world, and partaking of another nature from him. Thus to be a fellow-worker with God is the most absolute work of grace, as to beget in its own likeness is the most perfect work of nature.

And to persuade you to walk and act as new creatures, consider,

First, The excellency of your birth. It is a birth of heaven, a resemblance to God, do nothing below it or unworthy of it. Is it fit for you to lie among the pots and smut yourselves? The consideration of the relation you bear to God should inspire you with heroic resolutions for his glory. You are the only persons that keep up God's honour in the world, and his final anger from it. Whenever you are tempted, reflect upon yourselves, as Nehemiah: 'Should such a man as I' do this? Neh. vi. 11. Or as Joseph to his mistress, 'Behold, my master has committed all that he has to my hand;' behold, God has put his divine nature in my heart, and 'shall I do this wickedness?' Consider in every action what that God you call Father by regenerating grace, that Christ who is the great exemplar and copy of the image in you, would do in such cases and circumstances. How unworthy is it for a living man to do dead works! As your life springs from the highest principle, let it be employed for the highest ends. Was ever any prince ashamed of his honour? And shall any new creature be ashamed of the particular badge of heaven upon it; of that righteousness which is the true nobility of his nature? Holiness is the beauty of an intellectual and rational creature; it must then be your highest honour to live conformably to the dignity of your nature.

Secondly, It was the intendment of God you should walk in a nobler manner than the rest of the world. Did God infuse into Adam a soul of a higher nature than that of beasts, to enable him to live only the life of beasts? God intended by the infusion of this new principle, that you should live above the sphere of humanity and the rate of man. How does the apostle chide the Christians because they did not advance above the life of mere man; and therefore gives them a title chiefly belonging to the unregenerate world: 1 Cor. iii. 3, 'Are you not carnal. and walk as men?' Our Saviour expects a more worthy carriage from his children than what barely nature can teach them. He would have them as God, and imitators of him, Mat. v. 44-47,

and do something peculiar to this new state, which cannot be done by any unregenerate man in the world. Your holiness is not to be of the common level with the morality of the world, but such as may set forth the 'praise of God,' I Peter ii. 9; they are a 'chosen generation,' therefore should have choice conversations; a 'royal priesthood,' therefore princes' deportments; a 'holy nation and peculiar people,' therefore should have holy and peculiar behaviours. They should thus be public evangelists, to set forth "edzangeilete", the graciousness and righteousness of God. There is also the highest obligation, because he has called them out of darkness into his marvellous light. God intended that their conversations should be such as should amaze the world into a love of holiness, and admiration of that light which gives them such excellent directions, and that nature which enables them to so exact a walk. God's temples were not intended to be made dunghills.

Thirdly, Not to walk as new creatures is a dishonour to God. You that do not walk answerable to your high calling do more highly dishonour him than all other persons. You are quite contrary to his image, and represent God to the world as they would have him, not what he is in his own nature; for by a careless walk the world will judge God to be like you, or you very unlike to God. Is God holy, and you impure; God merciful, and you revengeful; God a God of peace, and you fomenters of malice and contention? To pretend to his image with such qualities is to disparage his nature, and rather degrade God to a likeness to the flesh than to mount up to a true resemblance of him: Ps. l. 21, 'Thou thought I was altogether such a one as thyself' It is a disgrace to a noble father to have a swinish, clownish, ill-bred person pretend to be his son. But how much is the contrary a glory to Christ, as delicious fruit and choice flowers credit the beams of the sun! What a mighty pleasure is it to God to behold a suitable walk of his new creatures! He loves them, and 'his countenance does behold the upright,' Ps. xi. 7. How much must he, who is holiness itself, take complacency in the holiness of it. If he loves it while in a low degree, no question but he loves it more in a higher exaltation. How does the Holy Ghost repeat Enoch's walking with God twice in Gen. v. 22, 24, to witness his pleasure in it?

Fourthly, Not to walk suitable to your new creation is a mighty disadvantage to yourselves. Though a new creature does not totally lose his grace if a temptation deflower his purity, yet his grace suffers an impair, and perhaps he may never recover the same degree of grace and comfort he had before. It is a question whether David ever had his sails filled with such strong gales of the Spirit after his fall as he had before. The marks of a disease will hang about us after the disease is cured, and the same stock of health may never be restored again. If you do let your hearts run out at any time to any sinful pleasure, though it may not raze out the image, yet it will make you more unfit for those views of God which can only maintain it. When you come before him, after such a departure, how will your hearts recoil upon you? With what pleasure can you look upon him whom you have so abused in his image in your souls, and in his image in his law? Besides, every unworthy walk detracts somewhat from the weight of that crown you might otherwise expect to be reserved in heaven for you, and makes it of a greater alloy. But if you keep close to the law in the word, and the law in your hearts, what communications will you have from God? What inward torches and feelings of him? How hastily will he run to meet you half way, and kiss you with the kisses of his mouth? 'Thou meets him that rejoices and works righteousness,' Isa. lxiv 5. How intimately will he wind himself into the secret corners of your hearts, as John xiv. 23, 'and make his abode with you;' and like fire in every part of iron, fill every part of the new man with a glowing and divine heat?

Fifthly, Such an exact walk will mightily stop the current of sin. It may justly be feared, the sins of many have taken too much heart from the unsuitable carriages of professors. But a walk according to the rule of the new creation might inflame others to godliness, at least stifle some corrupt motions, suspend some inclinations to sin, and for a time bind up the devil in them. This is the greatest charity to the world; by other benefits we advantage particular persons, by a holy example all that behold us. It strikes an awful reverence into the hearts of men, as being a ray of God; what the gospel enjoins are things comely, and of good report, many of them lovely and illustrious, even in a carnal eye, therefore such expressions of a gospel impression would engender admirations of it, cast a lustre upon the truth of God; men will look upon such works with reverence, and 'glorify God in the day of their visitation' or conversion, as Calvin understands it. To be a holy people is to be 'sought out,' they are both joined, Isa. lxii. 12. Many by seeing the holiness of the church in gospel times shall be induced to give up their names to the Lord; it will tend more to the regeneration of others than a thousand sermons; it will raise the reputation of Christianity, and cause them to believe it to be of a divine extract; it would stir men up to a holy emulation to be like them. And beholding the law of God transcribed in the life, it would convincingly answer the cavils of the world, and demonstrate the commands they count grievous to be in themselves practicable. But whither is this gospel ornament we have been speaking of fled? Where is it to be found? How few walk as new creatures, 'as becomes the gospel,' however they profess it, and pretend a zeal for it!

Exhortation 2. To those who lie still buried in the ruins of the old Adam, who carry the image of beasts in their lives, or of devils in their hearts, or both, such I would advise earnestly to seek this new creature state. Let not your hearts be besotted to a neglect of it, and stupefied into endless torments, which will, as surely as you live, be the dreadful issue, if this be not attained. To be so long under the gospel, and retain the obstinacy of an old nature to God, is a high aggravation. Talk not of sparing the old man; it is your enemy, wound it to death, use the utmost severity towards it; put it off, leave not a rag, if possible, behind; send it away, as Abraham did Hagar, and without so much as a bottle of water, to despoil it of any hopes of return. But, alas, how do you cherish and hug this enemy! How do you value it, as if it were a part of yourselves; as if you could not live without poison, or be happy without misery! How do you bid the new man stand far from you, as if it were a real torment to be in the arms of Christ, and the new creation your disease, not your felicity! Though you were the most unblameable in your lives, free from any pretence of an accusation there, what were you without this change, but devils in the garb of angels of light, poison in fair cabinets, and the natures of serpents in the bodies of men? What is become of your souls? Are they so immersed in flesh, that nothing of spirit can make impressions upon them? Have men quite forsworn the attaining any other excellency than what mere nature bestowed upon them? What deformity do you find in God, that you slight his image, which should be imprinted on you? What frightful thoughts have you of the Spirit that solicits you? How come your souls so senseless of their real happiness? Oh what a happy thing were it, if this day Christ were formed in all our hearts; that though we are nasty dunghills, worse than the stable wherein our Saviour was born in the flesh, we might become the sanctuary of our Lord and his Spirit; it is then the angels would renew their song at the birth of Christ in the heart as well as that in the world, 'Glory to God in the highest,' peace and eternal good will to such a soul. If you have any strugglings in your hearts, any convictions upon your consciences, and make not a further progress, these will be so far from being your advantage, that they will add an emphasis to your damnation.

Let me use some motives to press you.

(1.) Shall not the loathsomeness and misery of your present state startle you? It is a nature that makes you 'the children of wrath,' Eph. ii. 3. Were your old natures acceptable to God, what need any change? But the requiring this change demonstrates the old nature to be abhorred by God. This nature is the devil's filth, the serpent's poison, a deformed leprosy; it is the pain, anguish, torment, rack of every man that dies in it; it smells rank of hell. Is not another nature then desirable? When you commit some grievous sin, to which you are not accustomed, are you not dejected? If you not think worse of yourselves for it? And are you not pleased when you can escape it? If the reformation of one sin be a desirable thing, how much more the reformation of the whole nature! For if a drop of that filth bubbling up in the life be so loathsome, what loathsomeness is there in the heart, where the fountain springs! What gall of bitterness must be in the root, when a little of the fruit is so bitter to your taste! Corruption is the dishonour of your natures, the poison of your souls, the cause of all your unhappiness. It is this that banished you from paradise, ravishing away your pleasures, subjected you to vanity, the wrath of God, the hatred of angels, and tyranny of devils; it is this that has deformed your souls. Despoil yourselves of this cursed old man, give yourselves no rest till you have conquered it; never say, it is incorporated in your entrails and marrow. Where the question is about your everlasting happiness, let no excuse prevail.

(2.) Shall not the excellency of another state allure you? It is the excellency of any piece of art to come nearest its original; that star is most glorious that does most partake of the sun's light and power. The very light of nature tells us the state wherein we are is not our perfection, something the soul flutters at beyond this, though it naturally understands not what it is. Is it not, then, the happiness of the soul to be reduced to its true centre, to be reinstated in an unspotted nature, to return to a due respect to those ends for which it was made, to have the understanding conversant about the loveliest object, the will inclined to the most amiable goodness, and the affections twining about it, and growing up with it?

Can it be anything else but the highest excellency, to live the life of God; to have the image of God wrought upon you, and your souls conformed to his holiness? Can that be an imperfection, which makes you like an infinite righteousness? It was the highest perfection of man to be made according to the image of God, wherein God, as in a glass, might see a resemblance of himself. Is it not then a desirable thing to have it drawn again with more lively and lasting colours, after sin and Satan have so basely defaced it? All other things are not the perfection of man's nature; for whatsoever else there is, is possessed by beasts or devils; the pleasures of sense, by beasts; the endowments of knowledge, by devils; but the divine nature by neither. This therefore, which neither devils can be blessed with, nor beasts capable of, is only the perfection of the soul, more excellent than the soul itself, since that which perfects is more excellent than that which is perfected by it. Original corruption destroys your health, sullies your purity, enslaves your liberty. Regeneration restores your health, expels your filthiness, and knocks off your fetters. Let the excellency of this better state prevail with you.

(3.) Will the honour of the thing allure you? Where shall you meet with so honourable a relation? It is more honour to be a new creature in rags than a carnal prince in purple, though the greatest in the world, for you will then be settled heirs of all the promises. Is it not, then, more glorious to partake of the nature of that God, who created and commands the world, than by the force of the old nature to be slaves to sordid lusts, which are both a drudgery and a disease? As a spirit is more excellent than the body, so a spiritual being and frame is more honourable than a fleshly. There is a greater relation between God and a new creature than between natural fathers and sons. The sons of men have but a little particle of the vile matter and flesh of their fathers, but a renewed man has the whole divine Spirit in him; and by virtue of this, all things will, one time or other rise up and call you blessed; you will be more allied to Jesus Christ, by the inward formation of him in your hearts, than the blessed virgin by the conception of Christ in her womb, Luke xi. 27. She was more happy by partaking of Christ in her heart, than by conferring a flesh on Christ from her body. What an honourable thing is it to be moulded into the divine likeness! Can you be more glorious, unless you were gods?

(4.) Will pleasure charm you? View it here. Pleasure must necessarily follow this new state, as light the sun; there is no state without a pleasure pertaining to it. Pleasures of sense belong to a life of sense; intellectual pleasures to a life of reason; divine pleasures to a divine nature. 'All the ways of wisdom are ways of pleasantness,' Prov. iii. 17. An infinite perfection is attended with an infinite happiness; the more lineaments, then, you have of the divine perfection, the more tastes you will have of the divine happiness. God has an infinite perfection in his own perfections; it is his felicity to enjoy himself, to view himself. Pleasure then must naturally result from this image drawn in the soul, and as naturally, I conceive, according to the degrees of it, as the pleasure God has in his own holiness and love. The pleasure of heaven is the perfection of holiness; therefore there is a pleasure also attending the draught of it here; an imperfect pleasure from the imperfect form of it, as a perfect pleasure from the completing of it in glory. What want can there be of pleasure, if you come into this state? Will you not be conversant about the highest object, and that with your choicest faculties? Can this be without some communications of the pleasure of God, as well as his nature? You will find a pleasure in the very strugglings to get into this state, much more in it.

(5.) Do you profess yourselves enemies to the devil? Why then will you gratify him by continuing in an old nature? He keeps a jubilee when he can draw men into great sins, and bind them under them, his main industry is to make men like himself, and continue them in that likeness. The whole world, that are not of God, lie wrapped up in the devil's image: I John v. 19, 'The whole world lies in wickedness, or 'in the wicked one,' "En toi poneroi"; more consonant to the former verses. Satan and natural men lie nugging together, though the latter dream not of it. His intent in assaulting man in paradise was to destroy the righteousness of his nature; his design now is to hinder the restoration of it, by keeping men off from the means, making them have false thoughts of the unpleasantness of it, as though it were a state injurious to man's tranquillity, by suppressing convictions, which are the first portals to the courts of blessedness. Oh, gratify not the devil; fly from his image, that you may fly from his misery.

(6.) Why will you cross your own sentiments, when sober reason in you may have leave to speak? What do you think was the end for which you came into the world? Was it to serve the devil or God? Whose image is it most rational for you to bear? Are there not innate desires in man to be as God? Adam desired it unlawfully; the same spirit runs through the veins of his posterity. God has shown you a way in his word whereby you may lawfully desire it, and successfully accomplish it. Do not all creatures, one way or other, instruct you in it? Do they not all run back to their fountain; rivers into the sea, that they may have a new formation in it; beams retracted to the sun; and why not the soul to God? Do they not all declare the glory of God? And shall man stand alone? And what way is there for him to declare God's glory, but by the reformation of his nature? You once had this desirable nature in your first head, and lost it; you may have the re-possession in the second head, and for ever preserve it. You cannot deny your obligation to have it, therefore you cannot deny your duty to seek it. You know your souls received their original from him; you likewise know that there is an obligation to return to him. As the spirit naturally returns to God who gave it, so it cannot be happy in that return, unless it first morally return to God, to be formed like him.

(7.) Nothing else can advantage you if you want this new-creature state. You can no more enjoy happiness by Christ without it, than Adam did in paradise, in the presence of God, with the nakedness of his nature. His being in paradise, the richer part of the whole lower creation, could neither heal him nor content him, after the loss of the purity of his nature. In that happy place his conscience racked him. There he fled from his Creator, which in his innocent nature he never attempted to do; and all the pleasures of that place could not restore him to God's favour or his own peace, without the promise of a seed, and by that seed the restoration in part of his former image.

(8.) Lastly, take this for your encouragement, it is attainable by the meanest person, Col. iii. 11. In the new creation 'there is neither Greek nor Jew, circumcision nor uncircumcision, barbarian, Scythian, bond nor free; but Christ is all and in all;' that is, there is no distinction of any. The eloquence of the Greek, or the rudeness of the barbarian; the uncircumcision of the Gentile, or the circumcision of the Jew; the baseness of the slave, or the liberty of the freeman, does neither advantage nor disadvantage them in this work of the new creation; and he names Scythians, as being the rudest and most unpolished among all the known Gentiles. No natural endowments advantage us; no worldly indigences hinder us. The soul of the meanest is as capable of the new creation as the soul of the highest. There is nothing required to the putting on the new man, which is not attainable by the one as well as the other; yea, sooner by those of the meanest endowments, as wanting that fuel for their pride, which is the chief hindrance to a gospel impression. God values nothing but his own image; neither is he any more taken with the glittering parts and wisdom of men than our Saviour with the glory of the temple, which his ignorant disciples did so much admire.

Quest. But what means must be used to obtain this excellent privilege?

Aim. It is indeed the work of God, yet means may be used. He that observes precepts of morality shall gain moral habits; and by practising acts of temperance become temperate. So he that follows the rules given in the word for attaining the new creation, shall have it produced in him; and the more assuredly, because it is not produced by him but by God, who is more able to create new hearts in us than the unregenerate man is to work a moral reformation.

For means:

1. Be deeply sensible of original corruption. View yourselves in the glass of Adam; reflect upon the fall, and the dreadful consequences of it; take an exact account of the enmity of thy nature, as the word represents it. We must acquaint ourselves with our sin and misery, and have self-emptying thoughts, before we can seek after a new creature. Man is apt to think his nature good enough; and this makes him the more miserable and wretched, and causes him to think there needs no change, Rev. iii. 17.

2. Be deeply humbled before God. Lay yourselves low before him, and abhor yourselves in dust and ashes. Complain of your corrupt nature, melt before God, dissolve into tears. When you are weary and heavy laden, sensible of it by contrition, Christ will give rest by regeneration. The heart must be melted before it be made new. Pride must be humbled; we must be vile in our own eyes, as well as vile in our own nature. 'The Lord is nigh to them that are of a broken heart,' Psalm xxxiv. 18.

3. Often meditate of the excellency of this state, as it is represented in the word. Men hear and forget; they leave behind them what they have heard; they hide it not in their hearts; therefore does not the word profit them. Think often of the honour of being a new creature, as well as the necessity of being a new creature; if you have any thoughts arising of resting upon your knowledge, or morality, or good meaning, say to your soul, as the apostle in another case, O my soul, 'covet earnestly the best gifts, yet show I unto thee a more excellent way.' If any imagination arise which flatters you with hopes of being in Christ without an inward change, regard it as an angel from the bottomless pit, sent from the great impostor to seduce you from your happiness.

4. Fixedly resolve not to be at rest till you procure it at the hands of God. Perhaps you may have had some resolutions before, and some diversion has chilled those purposes; weaver not with uncertain velleities between inclination and aversion. Content not yourselves with sluggish wishes, and yawning desires, but put heart and hand to the work. Set vigorously to it, and those sons of Anak, those seeming terrifying difficulties, will fly before you. Where does the Scripture tell you, that God will neglect his laborious creature, and stand by without assisting him in his serious endeavours? No, no; God will not be wanting in his power, nor the Spirit in his operations, if we firmly purpose and strongly pursue. 'God is near to all that call upon him in truth,' Psalm cxlv. 18; that is, to all that call upon him with a true purpose and desire for his mercy: he is near by his merciful presence, not by his essential presence only. Fool not away your vows in vain mirth, nor drown your resolutions in sensual pleasures. Say as David in another case, 'I have sworn, and will perform it,' that I will in good earnest endeavour that I may become a new creature, Psalm cxix. 106.

5. Pray. Regeneration is against the inclinations of old nature; intermit not therefore to call earnestly for help from heaven; it is best attained upon the knee. God is the foundation of all vitality; the life of grace is no less the effect of his breath than the soul of Adam. Go to Christ, in whom, as in a

steward, is treasured up a fullness of grace, to dispense to him that seeks it. Beg earnestly of the Spirit, who is the officer appointed, the great limner to draw this image in us. Why can you not go to Christ as well as the leper, and lie sobbing before him, 'Lord, if thou wilt, thou canst make me clean,' thou canst change my nature? Do it constantly, do it fervently, and take notice with what inspirations you will be filled. But do you solicit him for this mercy at all? Has God one breath from thee in a whole week to this purpose? Have you, since you heard it, pressed from the necessity of it, made your case known to God? Has there been one groan, one sigh for it? What a stupid creature is man! Time will not always last; God will be solicited for it, and it is fit he should. An old nature is like an old devil, it cannot be cast out without fasting and prayer. The great changes of the soul are chiefly wrought in prayer and the word: our very looking up to God and upon God in humble prayer makes a gradual transformation in our souls: we never are in the mount with him, but our souls (as Moses his face) look quite of another hue and colour. By frequent converse with friends, we grow more into an imitation of the excellent qualities we perceive in them. Converse with God in frequent prayer and meditation, and you will grow more and more into a holy likeness to him.

6. Attend diligently upon the word. To pray to God to renew you, and slight the word which he has appointed as an instrument to effect it, is to dishonour God; for while you pray to him to be a father to beget you, you contemn him as a governor, by neglecting the means he has appointed for such ends. As the devil formed himself in the soul by man's listening to and sucking in his temptation, so Christ forms himself in the soul, by our sucking in the milk of the word, as the disposition of the nurse is by the milk conveyed to the infant. It is wrought by the gospel, 1 Cor. iv. 15, 'for in Christ Jesus I have begotten you through the gospel.' Not by the word of God at large, which consists of law as well as gospel. So the regenerations of old were wrought, not by the law, but by that of gospel mixed in that administration. By this means you may get a spiritual knowledge, and discard that ignorance which is the foundation of an alienation from the life of God, Eph. iv. 18, 'alienated from the life of God through the ignorance that is in them, because of the blindness of their hearts.' Study the promises, and plead them before the Lord, for 'by these you are made partakers of the divine nature,' 2 Peter i. 4. Resist not any divine impressions, by a sluggishness and a listlessness. Be not in love with your spiritual death, nor cherish the bondage to sin in your will, when God makes motions to enliven and enlarge you. Welcome the breathings of the Spirit. Open your souls, as some flowers do for the sun; drink in the drops of heaven, as the earth does the rain; and when the Spirit quickens you by its influences, quicken the Spirit by your earnest supplications, Cant. iv. 16; make much of him, persuade his stay. Breathe, O blessed Spirit, upon this wilderness. Never leave till it be changed into a fruitful garden, both pleasant to, and fruitful for, my blessed Creator and gracious Redeemer.

End of A Discourse of the Nature of Regeneration.

A Discourse of the Efficient of Regeneration

Part 1

Which were born, not of blood, nor of the will of the flesh, nor of the will of man, but of God.-- John 1:13.

This evangelist so plainly describes the deity of Christ, and in so majestic a style, in the beginning of the chapter, that the accidental view of it in a book lying open by neglect, was instrumental for the conversion of Junius, that eminent light in the church, from his atheism.

We shall take our rise only from ver. 9, 'That was the true light, which lightens every man that comes into the world.' John Baptist, who, ver. 6, &c., was to bear witness of this light, was a light by our Saviour's assertion, 'a burning and a shining light,' John v. 35, but not that 'true light' which was promised, Isa. xlix. 6, to be 'a light to the Gentiles, and the salvation of God to the ends of the earth.' The sun is the true light in the heavens and of the world; not but that other stars are lights too, but they all receive their light from the sun. Christ is called the true light, by nature and essence, not by grace and participation: 1 John v. 20, 'We know him that is true; and we are in him that is true, even in his Son Jesus Christ,' the natural light and Son of God.

1. True, as opposed to types, which were shadows of this light.

2. True, as opposed to false. Philosophical lights, though esteemed so, are but darkness, and ignes fatui, in comparison of this.

3. True original light, ratione officii, illustrating the whole world with his light. Whatsoever is light in heaven or earth, borrows it from the sun; whosoever is enlightened in the world, derives from him 'which lights every man that comes into the world.' Some join coming into the world, to lift, and read it thus, 'He is the light coming into the world, which lights every man.' The Greek is something ambiguous, and it may be referred to light, though not so commodiously. But the translation which we have has been followed in all ages of the church; and is contended for (the other is contended for? editor) only by those who deny the deity of our Saviour, or are somewhat affected to them that do.

How does Christ light every man that comes into the world?

1. Naturally. So Calvin; the world was made by him, and therefore that which is the beauty of the world, the reason of man, was made kindled by him. As all the light the world has had since the creation flows from the sun, so all the knowledge which sparkles in any man is communicated by Christ, even since the creation, as he is the wisdom of God, and as mediator, preserving those broken relics of the fall: Prov. xx. 27, 'The spirit of man is the candle of the Lord,' lighted and preserved by him. The light of nature, those common notions of fit and just in men's consciences, those honest and honourable principles in the hearts of any, those beams of wisdom in their understanding, though faint, and like sparkles raked up in ashes, are kept alive by his mediatory influence, as a necessary foundation for that, reparation which was intended in his first interposition.

2. Spiritually. So not only the Socinians, but some very sound, understand it; not that all are actually enlightened, but,

(1.) In regard of power and sufficiency, he has a power to enlighten every man; able to enlighten, not a few, but every man in the world, as the sun does not light every man, though it has a power to do so, and does actually light every man that shuts not his eyes against it.

(2.) Actually, taking it distributive, not collective; that whosoever is enlightened in the world, has it communicated from Christ; as Ps. cxlv. 14, 'The Lord upholds all that fall, and raises up all those that are bowed down;' as many as are upheld and raised, are upheld and raised by God' He does indeed 'shine in darkness,' his light breaks out upon men, but they are not the better for it, because 'the darkness comprehends it not'; as when there is but one schoolmaster in a town, we usually say, he teaches all the boys in the town; not that every individual boy comes to school, but as many as are taught, are taught by him. I embrace the former, because the evangelist seems to begin with his person, as God; his office, as mediator; and then descends to his incarnation; and it is a sense which puts no force upon the words.

And I suppose that every man is added, to beat down the proud conceits of the Jews, who regarded the Gentiles with contempt, as not enjoying the privileges conferred upon themselves; but the evangelist declares, that what the Gentiles had in natural light, and what they were to have in spiritual light, did, and was to come from him, who would disperse his beams in all nations, ver. 10. And therefore 'he was in the world,' before his coming in the flesh, in regard of his virtue and efficacy, by the spreading his beams over the world, enlightening men in all ages and places with that common light of nature; he was near to every man; 'in him they lived, and moved, and had their being;' but the world by their natural wisdom knew him not, and glorified him not. 'The world was made by him, yet the world know him not.' Ingratitude has been the constant portion of the mediator, from the world; they knew him not in past ages, knew him not in the present age of his coming in the flesh; they did not acknowledge him with that affection, reverence, and subjection that was due to him.

He aggravates this contempt of Christ,

1. By the general right be had, 'he came to his own,' "Eis ta idia", ver. 11, meaning the world, it being put in the neuter gender. The whole world was his property and his goods, yet they knew not their owner. In this, worse than the ox or ass.

2. By the special privileges conferred on those to whom he first came, and from whom he should have the most welcome reception; implied in these words, 'and his own,' "hoi idioi", in the masculine gender, his own people, that had been his treasure, to whom he had given his law, entrusted with the covenants and oracles of God, these 'received him not.' His own, some say, as being peculiarly committed to him, the angel of the covenant; whereas other nations were committed to angels to receive laws from them. His own flesh and blood, who expected a Messiah, to whom he was particularly sent, as being the lost sheep of the house of Israel. Christ is most rejected where proffers most kindness. Those of Tyre and Sidon, those of Sodom and Gomorrah, would not have used him so ill as Capernaum and Jerusalem, his own people. He descends to show the loss of them that rejected him, the benefit of those that received him: ver. 12, 'But as many as received him, to them gave he power to become the sons of God, even to them that believe on his name.'

Where is,

1. The subject: these that received him.

2. The benefit: the dignity of sonship.

3. The manner of conferring this benefit: 'gave them power.'

4. The instrumental cause: 'believe on his name.' Though his own rejected him, they lost a dignity which was conferred upon those that received him: he lost not his pains, for he gathered sons to God out of all parts of the world. 'To as many as received him.' It was not now peculiar to the Jews, who boasted of being Abraham's seed, and to have the covenant entailed upon them to be the people of God. It was now conferred upon those who were before Lo-ammi and Lo-ruhamah, Hos. ii. 23. It was nothing but faith on his name that gave men the privilege of being the sons of God, and this was communicated to Gentiles as well as Jews. Power: not a power, but a dignity, as the word properly signifies. Not a power if they would, but a will, for they were born of the will of God. Faith brings men into a special relation to God; which faith is more than an assent and giving credit to God; for to believe on God, to believe on his name, is a phrase peculiar to Scripture. 'To become the sons of God;' some understand this of sonship by adoption, but the following verse gives us light to understand it of a sonship by regeneration. St Paul uses the word adoption, but St John, both in his gospel and epistles, speaks more of the new birth, and sonship by it, than any of the other apostles; 'who were born not of blood,' or 'of bloods.' He removes all other causes of this, which men might imagine, and ascribes it wholly to God. This place is variously interpreted. 'Not of blood.' Not by natural instinct, says one; not by an illustrious stock. The Jews imagined themselves holy by their carnal generation from Abraham in a long train of ancestors. Grace runs not in a blood. It is not often a flower growing upon every ability; 'not many wise, not many mighty.' Not hereditary by a mixture of blood. Natural generation makes men no more regenerate than the rich man in hell was regenerate by Abraham, his natural ancestor, whom he calls 'father Abraham.' Religious parents propagate corruption, not regeneration; carnal generation is by nature, not by grace; by descent from Adam, not by implantation in Christ. Abraham had an Ishmael, and Isaac an Esau: man begets only a mortal body, but grace is the fruit of an incorruptible seed. 'Nor of the will of the flesh.' Not by human election, as Eve judged of Cain that he should be the Messiah, or Isaac of Esau that he should be heir of the promise, as the Jews say. Not by a choice of those things which are necessary, profitable, or delightful to the flesh; not by a will affected to the flesh, or things of the flesh. Not by any sensual appetite, whereby men used to adopt one to bear up their names when they scanted posterity of their own. I would rather conceive it to be meant of the strength of nature, which is called flesh in Scripture; not by legal observances, the ceremonies of the law being called carnal or fleshly ordinances, Heb. ix. 10. It is not a fruit of nature or profession. 'Nor of the will of man.' Calvin takes the will of the flesh and the will of man for one and the same thing, the apostle using two expressions only to fix it more upon the mind. I rather fudge it to be meant thus: not by natural principles, or moral endowments, which are the flower and perfection of man as man. It is not arbitrary, of the will of man, or the result

naturally of the most religious education. All the power of regenerate men in the world joined together cannot renew another; all the industry of man, without the influence of the heavens in the sun and rain, cannot produce fruit in the earth, no, nor the moral industry of men grace in the soul; 'but of God,' or the will of God; his own will: James i. 18, 'Of his own will begot he us,' exclusive of all other wills mentioned before. It is the sole efficiency of God; he has the sole hand in it; therefore we are said to be both begotten and born of him, 1 John v. 18. It is so purely God's work, that as to the principle he is the sole agent; and as to the manifestation of it, he is the principal agent. Not of the will of the flesh, that is only corruption; nor of the will of man, that at best is but moral nature. But whatsoever the meaning of those particular expressions is, the evangelist removes all pretences nature may make to the efficiency of this regeneration, and ascribes it wholly to God.

1. There is a removal of false causes.
2. A position of the true cause.
(1.) The efficient, God.
(2.) The manner, by an act of his will.
Showing thereby,
[1.] To necessity in him to renew us, no motive but from himself.
[2.] No merit on our parts. Man cannot merit, say the papists, before grace, no child can merit his own birth, no man grace.

Doct. 1. Man, in all his capacities, is too weak to produce the work of regeneration in himself.

It is subjectively in the creature, not efficiently by the creature, neither ourselves nor any other creature, angels, men, ordinances.

Doct. 2. God alone is the prime efficient cause of regeneration.

Doct. 1. For the first. Man, in all his capacities, is too weak to produce the work of regeneration in himself. This is not the birth of a darkened wisdom and an enslaved will. We affect a kind of divinity, and would centre ourselves in our own strength; therefore it is good to be sensible of our own impotency, that God may have the glory of his own grace, and we the comfort of it in a higher principle and higher power than our own. It is not the bare proposal of grace, and the leaving the will to an indifferent posture, balanced between good and evil, undetermined to the one or the other, to incline and determine itself which way seems best to it. Not one will, in the whole rank of believers, left to themselves. The evangelist excepts not one man among them; for as many as received Christ, as many as believed, were the sons of God, who were born; which believers, every one that had this faith as the means, and this sonship as the privilege, were born not of the will of the flesh nor the will of man.

For the proof of this in general,

1. God challenges this work as his own, excluding the creature from any share as a cause: Ezek. xxxvi. 25-27, 'I will sprinkle clean water upon you, I will cleanse you, I will give you a new heart, I will put a new spirit into you, I will take away the heart of stone, I will give you a heart of flesh, I will put my Spirit into you.' Here I will no less than seven times. Nothing is allowed to man in the production of this work in the least; all that is done by him is the walking in God's statutes by virtue of this principle. The sanctifying principle, the actual sanctification, the reception of it by the creature, the removal of all the obstructions of it, the principle maintaining it, are not in the least here attributed to the will of man. God appropriates all to himself. He does not say he would be man's assistant, as many men do, who tell us only of the assistance of the gospel, as if God in the gospel expected the first motions of the will of man to give him a rise for the acting of his grace. You see here he gives not an inch to the creature. To ascribe the first work, in any part, to the will of man, is to deprive God of half his due, to make him but a partner with his creature. The least of it cannot be transferred to man but the right of God will be diminished, and the creature go shares with his Creator. Are we not sufficient of ourselves to do any thing? and are we sufficient to part stakes with God in this divine work? What partner was the creature with God in creation? It is the Father's traction alone, without the hand of free-will. 'None can come, except the Father, which has sent me, draw them,' John vi. 44. The mission of the Mediator, and the traction of the creature, are by the same hand. Our Saviour could not have come unless the Father had sent him, nor can man come to Christ unless the Father draw him. What is that which is drawn? The will. The will, then, is not the agent; it does not draw itself.

2. The titles given to regeneration evidence it. It is a creation. What creature can give itself a being? It is a putting in a law and a new heart. What matter can infuse a soul into itself? It is a new birth. What man did ever beget himself? It is an opening the heart. What man can do this, who neither has the key, nor is acquainted with the wards? Not a man knows the heart; it is deceitful above all things, who can know it?

3. The conveyance of original corruption does in part evidence it. We have no more interest of our wills in regeneration, than we had in corruption. This was first received by the will of Adam, our first head, thence transmitted to us without any actual consent of our wills in the first transmission; that is conveyed to us from the second Adam, without any actual consent of our wills in the first infusion. Yet though the wills of Adam's posterity are mere passive in the first conveyance of the corrupt habit from

him by generation, yet afterwards they are active in the approbations of it, and production of the fruits of it. So the will is merely passive in the first conveyance of the grace of regeneration, though afterwards it is pleased with it, and brings forth fruit meet for it.

4. Scripture represents man exceeding weak, and unable to do any thing spiritually good. 'So then, they that are in the flesh cannot please God,' Rom. viii. 8. He concludes it by his so then, as an infallible consequence, from what he had discoursed before. If, as being in the flesh, they cannot please God, therefore not in that which is the highest pleasure to God, a framing themselves to a likeness to him. The very desire and endeavour of the creature after this, is some pleasure to God, to see a creature struggling after holiness; but they that are in the flesh cannot please him. 'Can any good thing come out of Nazareth?' was said of our Saviour. So may we better say, Can any good thing come out of the flesh, the enslaved, possessed will of man? If it be free since it was captivated by sin, who set it free? Nothing can, but 'the law of the Spirit of life,' Rom. viii. 2. To be 'sinners,' and to be 'without strength,' is one and the same thing in the apostle's judgment: Rom. v. 6, 8, 'While we were yet without strength;' afterwards, 'while we were yet sinners;' he does not say, We are without great strength, but without strength, such an impotence as is in a dead man. Not like a man in a swoon, but a man in a grave. God only is almighty, and man all impotency; God only is all-sufficient, and man all-indigent. It is impossible we can have a strength of our own, since our first father was feeble, and conveyed his weakness to us; by the same reason that it is impossible we can have a righteousness of our own, since our first father sinned: Isa. xliii. 26, 27, 'Declare, that thou may be justified. Thy first father has sinned.'

5. This weakness is universal. Sin has made its sickly impressions in every faculty. The mind is dark, Eph. iv. 18, he cannot know, 1 Cor. ii. 14, there is a stoniness in the heart, he cannot bend, Zech. vii. 12; there is enmity in the will, he cannot be subject, Rom. viii. 7. As to faith, he cannot believe, John xii. 89. As to the Spirit, the worker of faith, he cannot receive; that is, of himself, John xiv. 17; acknowledge Christ he cannot, 1 Cor. xii. 3. As to practice, he cannot bring forth fruit, John xv. 4. The unrighteousness introduced by Adam poured a poison into every faculty, and dispossessed it of its strength, as well as of its beauty: what else could be expected from any deadly wound but weakness as well as defilement? The understanding conceives only such thoughts as are pleasing to the law of sin; the memory is employed in preserving the dictates and decrees of it; the imagination full of fancies imprinted by it; the will wholly submitting to its authority; conscience standing with fingers in its mouth, for the most part not to speak against it; the whole man yielding itself and every member to the commands of it, and undertaking nothing but by its motions, Rom. vi. 19.

6. To evince it, there is not one regenerate man but in his first conversion is chiefly sensible of his own insufficiency; and universal consent is a great argument of the truth of a proposition; it is a ground of the belief of a deity, it being the sentiment of all nations. I do not speak of disputes about it from the pride of reason, but of the inward experience of it in any heart. What more frequent in the mouths of those that have some preparations to it by conviction, than I cannot repent, I cannot believe, I find my heart rotten, and base, and unable to any thing that is good! There have been instances of those that would elevate the power of man, and freedom of will in spiritual things, who have been confuted in their reasonings, and acknowledged themselves so, when God has come to work savingly upon them. Indeed, this poverty of spirit, or sense of our own emptiness, insufficiency, and indigence, is the first gospel grace wrought in the soul, and stands in the head of all those noble qualifications in our Saviours sermon, as fitting men for the kingdom of God: 'Blessed are the poor in spirit; for theirs is the kingdom of heaven,' Mat. v. 3. And God in the whole progress of this work keeps believers in a sensibleness of their own weakness, thereby to preserve them in a continual dependence on him; and therefore sometimes withdraws his Spirit from them, and lets them fall, that they may adhere more closely to him, and less confide in themselves.

2. What kind of impotency or insufficiency is there in the soul to be the cause of this work?

Ans. 1. It is not a physical weakness for want of faculties. Understanding we have, but not a spiritual light in it to direct us; will we have, but no freedom to choose that which is spiritually good. Though since the fall we have such a free will left, which pertains to the essential nature of man, yet we have lost that liberty which belongs to the perfection of human nature, which was to exercise acts spiritually good and acceptable to God! Had the faculties been lost, Adam had not been capable of a promise or command, and consequently of ever sinning after. In Adam, by creation we were possessed of it. In Adam, by his corruption, we were stripped of it; we have not lost the physical but the moral nature of these faculties; not the faculties themselves, but the moral goodness of them. As the elementary heat is left in a carcass, which yet is unfit to exercise any animal action for want of a soul to enliven it; so, though the faculties remain after this spiritual death, we are unfit to exert any spiritual action for want of grace to quicken them. If man wanted faculties, this want would excuse him in his most extravagant actions: no creature is bound to that which is simply impossible; nay, without those faculties, he could not act as a rational creature, and so were utterly incapable of sinning. Sin has untuned the strings, but did not unstring the soul; the faculties were still left, but in such a disorder, that the wit and will of man can no more tune them, than the strings of an untuned lute can dispose themselves for harmony without a musician's hand.

2. Neither is it a weakness arising from the greatness of the object above the faculty. As when an object is unmeet for a man, because he has no power in him to comply with it; as to understand the essence of God; this the highest creature in its own nature cannot do, because God dwells in inaccessible light; and it is utterly impossible for any thing but God to comprehend God. If man were required to become an angel, or to rise up and kiss the sun in the firmament; these were impossible things, because man wanted a faculty in his primitive nature for such acts: so if God had commanded Adam to fly without giving him wings, or to speak without giving him a tongue, he had not been guilty of sin in not doing it, because it was not disobedience, for disobedience is only in what a man has a faculty to do; but to love God, praise him, depend upon him, was in the power of man's original nature, for they were not above those faculties God endued him with, but very correspondent and suitable to him. The objects proposed are in themselves intelligible, credible, capable to be comprehended.

3. Neither is it a weakness arising from the insufficiency of external revelation. The means of regeneration are clearly revealed in the gospel, the sound is gone into all the earth, Rom. x. 18, and the word of the Lord is an apprehensible object; it is 'near us, even in our mouths,' Rom. x. 8; 'the commandment of the Lord is pure, enlightening the eyes,' Ps. xix. 8. If the object were hid, the weakness lay not on the part of man, but on the insufficiency of revelation; as if any thing were revealed to man in an unknown tongue, there were an insufficiency in the means of revelation.

But, 4, it is a moral weakness. The disability lies chiefly in the will, John v. 40; what is there, 'You will not come to me,' is, ver. 44, 'How can you believe?' You cannot, because you will not. Carnal lusts prepossess the heart, and make their party in the will against the things of God; so that inward propensities to embrace sin, are as great as the outward temptations to allure to it, whereby the soul is carried down the stream with a wilful violence. In this respect he is called dead, though the death be not of the same nature with a natural death; for such a one has not the natural faculty to raise himself, but this is an impotency arising from a voluntary obstinacy; yet the iniquity of a man binds him no less powerfully under this spiritual captivity, than a natural death and insensibility keeps men in the grave; and those fetters of perversity they can no more knock off, than a dead man can raise himself from the grave. By reason of those bands they are called prisoners, Isa. xiii. 7, and cannot be delivered without the powerful voice of Christ commanding and enabling them to go forth: Isa. xlix. 9, 'That thou must say to the prisoner, Go forth.' The apostle lays the whole fault of men's not receiving the truth upon their wills: 2 Thess. ii. 10, 'They received not the love of the truth;' they heard it, they knew it, but they loved not that which courted them. It is not seated in any defect of the will, as it is a power of the soul; for then God, who created it, would be charged with it, and might as well charge beasts to become men, as men to become gracious. Man, as a creature, had a power to believe and love God; to resist temptations, avoid sin, and live according to nature; but man, as corrupted by a habit derived to him from his first parents, and increased by a custom in sin, cannot believe, cannot love God, cannot bring himself into a good frame; as a musician cannot play a lesson when he has the gout in his fingers. When the eyes are full of adultery, when the heart is full of evil habits, it 'cannot cease to sin,' it cannot be gracious, 2 Pet. ii. 14.

Now, these habits are either innate, or contracted and increased.

(1.) Innate. By nature we have a habit of corruption, fundamental of all other that grow up in us. Man made a covenant with sin, contracted a marriage with it; by virtue of this covenant sin had a full power over him. What the apostle speaks of the marriage between man and the law, Rom. vii. 1-4, is applicable to this case. Sin as a husband, by way of covenant, has a powerful dominion over the will, and binds it as long as sin lives; and the will has no power to free itself, unless a higher power make a divorce, or by the death of the husband. This is the cause of man's obstinacy against any return to God, the will is held in the cords of sin, Prov. v. 22. The habit has obtained an absolute sovereignty over it: Hosea v. 4, 'They will not frame their doings to turn unto their God.' Why? 'For the spirit of whoredoms is in the midst of them,' that is, in their hearts. This adulterous or idolatrous habit holds their wills in chains, and acts them as a man possessed by the devil is acted according to the pleasure of the devil. The devil speaks in them, moves in them, and does what he pleases by them. And which binds the will faster, this habit is not in a natural man by way of a tyranny, but a voluntary sovereignty on the part of the will, the will is pleased and tickled with it. As a woman (to use the similitude of the Holy Ghost in that place) is so overruled by her affections to other lovers that she cannot think of returning to her former husband, but her unlawful love plays all its pranks, and rises with that force against all arguments from honesty and credit, that it keeps her still in the chains of an unlawful lust, so this is not a habit which does oppress nature, or force it against its will, but by its incorporation, and becoming one with our nature, has quite altered it from that original rectitude and simplicity wherein God at first framed it. It is a law of sin, which having razed out the purity of the law of nature, commands in a greater measure in the stead of it. Hence it is as natural to man, in his lapsed state, to have perverse dispositions against God, as it is essential to him to be rational. And the chariot of that weak remaining reason left us, is overturned by our distempered passions; and the nobler part of man is subject to the rule of these, which bear down the authority both of reason and God too. That one sin of the angels, howsoever complicated we know not, taking place as a habit in them, has bound them for ever from rising to do any good, or disentangling themselves from it, and may perhaps be meant by those 'chains of darkness' wherein they are reserved and held to the judgment of the great day, having no will to shake them off, though they have light enough to see the torment appointed for them.

(2.) New contracted and increased habits upon this foundation. Custom turns sin more into another nature, and completes the first natural disorder. An unrenewed man daily contracts a greater impotency, by adding strength to this habit, and putting power into the hands of sin to exercise its tyranny, and increasing our headstrong natures in their unruliness. It is as impossible of ourselves to shake off the fetters of custom, as to suppress the unruliness of nature: Jer. xiii. 23, 'Can an Ethiopian change his skin? or a leopard his spots? then may you also do good that are accustomed to do evil.' The prophet speaks not here of what they were by nature, but what they were by custom; contracting thereby such a habit of evil, that, like a chronic disease could not be cured by any ordinary means. But may he not accustom himself to do good? No, it is as impossible as for an Ethiopian to change his skin. Those habits draw a man to delight, and therefore to a necessity, of sinning. The pleasure of the heart, joined with the sovereignty of sin, are two such strong cords as cannot be untwisted or cut by the soul itself, no, not without an overruling grace. It was a simple wound in Adam, but such as all nature could not care, much less when we have added a world of putrefaction to it. The stronger the habit, the greater the impotency. If we could not raze out the stamp of mere nature upon our wills, how can we raze out the deeper impressions made by the addition of custom? If Adam, who committed but one sin, and that in a moment, did not seek to regain his lost integrity, how can any other man, who by a multitude of sinful acts has made his habit of a giant-like stature, completed many parts of wickedness, and scoffed at the rebukes of conscience?

Let us now see wherein this weakness of our wills to renew ourselves does appear.

1. In a total moral unfitness for this work. Grace being said to make us meet for our Master's use, it implies an utter unfitness for God's use of ourselves before grace. There is a passive capability, a stump left in nature, but no fitness for any activity in nature, no fitness in nature for receiving grace, before grace; there is nothing in us naturally which does suit or correspond with that which is good in the sight of God. That which is natural is found more or less in all men; but the gospel, which is the instrument of regeneration, finds nothing in the nature of man to comply with the main design of it. There is indeed some compliance of moral nature with the moral precepts in the gospel, upon which account it has been commended by some heathens; but nothing to answer the main intendment of it, which is faith, the top grace in regeneration. This has nothing to commend itself to mere nature, nor finds an internal principle in man that is pleased with it, as other graces do, as love, meekness, patience, &c. For faith strips a man of all his own glory, brings himself from himself to live dependently upon another, and makes him act for another, not for himself; and therefore meets not with any one principle in man to show it countenance: 'No good thing dwells in the flesh,' Rom. vii. 18. There may be some motions lighting there, as a fly upon a man's face; but they have no settled abode, and spring not up from nature. If the apostle, who was renewed, found an unfitness in himself to do that which was good, how great is that unfitness in a mere natural will, which is wholly under the power of the flesh, and has no principle in it correspondent to spiritual truth, to renew itself! If this regeneration had any foundation in nature, it would be then in most men that hear the gospel, because there is not a general contradiction in men to those things which are natural; but since there is no good thing dwells in any flesh, how can it be fit of itself to be raised into a conformity to God, which is the highest pitch of the creature's excellency? The Scripture represents us not as earth, which is fit to suck in showers from heaven; but as stones, which are only moistened in the superficies by the rain, but answers not the intendment of it. Adamants are unfit to receive impressions; and the best natural heart is no better, like a stone, cold and hard. The soul with its faculties is like a bird with its wings, but clogged with lime and clay, unfit to fly. A barren wilderness is absolutely unfit to make a pleasant and fruitful garden. There is a contractedness of the heart till God enlarge and open it, and that in the best nature. Acts xvi. 14, Lydia, it is said, worshipped God; there was religion in her, yet the Lord opened her heart for the gospel. Can anything be more indisposed than a fountain that is always bubbling up poison? So is the heart of man, Gen. vi. 5. The least imagination rising up in the heart is evil, and can be no better, since the heart itself is a mass of venom. If the renewed natures find so much indisposition in the progress of sanctification, though their sails be filled with grace, how great must it be where corrupt nature only sits at the stern! As when Satan came to tempt our Saviour he found nothing in him, no touchwood in his nature to take fire by a temptation, so when the Spirit comes, he finds no tinder in man to receive readily any spark of grace. This unfitness is in the best mere nature, that seems to have but a drop of corruption: a drop of water is as unfit to ascend as a greater quantity.

2. There is not only an unfitness, but an unwillingness. A senseless sluggishness and drowsiness of soul, loath to be moved. No man does readily hold out his arms to embrace the tenders of the gospel. What folding of the arms! yet a little more slumber, a little more sin. Man is a mere darkness before his

effectual calling: 'Who has called us out of darkness,' 1 Peter ii. 9. His understanding is darkened; the will cannot embrace a thing offered, unless it have powerful arguments to persuade it of the goodness of that thing which is offered; which arguments are modelled in the understanding, but that being darkened, has wrong notions of divine things, therefore cannot represent them to the will to be pursued and followed. Adam's running away from God to hide himself, after the loss of his original righteousness, discovers how unwilling man is to implore God's favour. How deplored is the condition of man by sin! since we find not one prayer put up by Adam, nor can we suppose any till the promise of recovery was made, though he was sensible of his nakedness, and haunted by his conscience: 'I was afraid, because I was naked: and I hid myself,' Gen. iii. 10. He had no mind, no heart, to turn suppliant unto God; he runs from God, and when God finds him out, instead of begging pardon by humble prayer, he stands upon his justification, accuses God to be the cause by giving him the woman, by whose persuasion he was induced to sin. What glass will better discover the good will of nature to God than the first motions after the fall!

3. There is not only an unfitness and unwillingness, but an affection to something contrary to the gospel. The nature of outward objects is such, that they attract the sensitive appetite, corrupted by sin, to prefer them before that which is more excellent; the heart is forestalled by an inordinate love of the world, and a pleasure in unrighteousness: 2 Thess. ii. 12, they 'believed not the truth, but had pleasure in unrighteousness' ("Eudochesantes"), a singular pleasure. Where the heart and the devil agree so well, what liking can there be to God or his will? Where the amity between sin and the soul is so great, that sin is self, and self is sin, how can so delightful a friend be discarded, to receive one he thinks his enemy! This weakness arises from a love to something different or contrary to what is proposed. When a man is so tied to that object which he loves that he minds not that contrary object which is revealed by a fit light, as a man that has his eyes or his heart fixed upon a fair picture, cannot observe many things that occur about him; or if he does consider it, he is taken so much with the things he loves, that he seems to hate the other; that though he does count it good, yet compared with what he loved before, he apprehends it as evil, and judges it evil, merely by the error of his mind,--a practical, affected, and voluntary ignorance. So though a man may sometimes judge that there is a goodness in the gospel and the things proposed, yet his affection to other pleasures, which he prefers before the gospel, causes him to shake off any thoughts of compliance with it. Now, all natural men in the irons of sin are not weary but in love with their fetters, and prize their slavery as if it were the most glorious liberty.

4. There is not only unfitness, and unwillingness, and a contrary affection to the gospel, but according to the degrees of this affection to other things, there is a strong aversion and enmity to the tenders of the gospel. This enmity is more or less in the heart of every unrenewed man; though in some it is more restrained and kept down by education, yet it will appear more or less upon the approaches of grace, which is contrary to nature. As a spark as well as a flame will burn, though one has less heat than the other, there is the same nature, the same seminal principles in all. The carnal mind, let it be never so well flourished by education, is enmity to God; and therefore 'unable,' because unwilling, 'to be subject to the law,' Rom. viii. 7. By nature he is of the devil's party, and has no mind the castle of his heart should ever come into the hands of the right owner. It is in every faculty. Not one part of the soul will make a mutiny within against sin, or take part with God when he comes to lay siege to it; when he 'stretches out his hands,' he meets with a 'rebellious and gainsaying people,' Rom. x. 21. It can converse with anything but God, look with delight upon anything but that which is the only true object of delight. It can have no desire to have that law written in his heart whose characters he hates. All the expressions in the Scripture denoting the work of grace, import man's distaste of it; it is to deny self, crucify the flesh. What man has not an aversion to deny what is dearest to him, his self; to crucify what is incorporated with him, his Isaac, his flesh? The bent of a natural heart, and the design of the gospel, which is to lay man as low as the dust, can never agree. A corrupt heart, and the propositions of grace, meet together as fire and water, with hissing. The language of man, at the proposals of the gospel, is much like that of the devils, 'What have we to do with thee? Art thou come to destroy us?' Luke iv. 34.

5. This aversion proceeds on to a resistance. No rebels were ever stouter against their prince than an unrenewed soul against the Spirit of God: not a moment without arms in his hand; he acts in defence of sin, and resistance of grace, and combats with the Spirit as his deadly enemy: 'You always resist the Holy Ghost; as your fathers did, so do you,' Acts vii. 51. The animosity runs in the whole blood of nature; neither the breathings of love, nor the thunderings of threatenings, are listened unto. All natural men are hewed out of one quarry of stone. The highest rock and the hardest adamant may be dissolved with less pains than the heart of man; they all, like a stone, resist the force of the hammer, and fly back upon it. All the faculties are full of this resistance: the mind, with stout reasoning, gives a repulse to grace; the imagination harbours foolish conceits of it; in the heart, hardness and refusing to hear; in the affections, disgust and displeasure with God's vans, disaffection to his interest; the heart is locked, and will not of itself shoot one bolt to let the King of glory enter. What party is like to be made for God, by bare nature thus possessed? Nature indeed does what it can, though it cannot do what it would; for though it resist the outward means and inward motions, yet it cannot efficaciously resist the determining

grace of God, any more than the matter of the creation could resist the all-powerful voice of God commanding it to receive this or that form, or Lazarus resist the receiving that life Christ conveyed to him by his mighty word. God finds a contradiction in our wills, and we are not regenerate because our will has consented to the persuasions of grace; for that it does not do of itself; but the grace of God disarms our will of all that is capable to make resistance, and determines it to accept and rejoice in what is offered. Nature of itself is of an unyielding temper, and removes not one scale from the eye, nor any splinter from the stone in the heart; for how can we be the authors of that which we most resist and labour to destroy?

6. Add to all this, the power of Satan in every natural man, whose interest lies in enfeebling the creature. The devil, since his first impression upon Adam, has had the universal possession of nature, unless any natural man free himself from the rank of the children of disobedience: Eph. ii. 2, 'The spirit that now works in the children of disobedience;' where the same word "enengein" is used for the acting of Satan, and likewise for the acting of sin, in Rom. vii. 5. as it is for the acting of the Spirit, Philip. ii. 13. In whom he works as a spirit as powerfully according to his created strength, as the Holy Ghost works in the children of obedience. As the Spirit fills the soul with gracious habits to move freely in God's ways, so Satan fills the soul (as much as in him lies) with sinful habits, as so many chains to keep it under his own dominion. He cannot indeed work immediately upon the will, but he uses all the skill and power that he has to keep men captive for the performance of his own pleasure: 2 Tim. ii. 26, 'Who are taken captive by him at his will,' or for his will, "Eis to ekeinou thelema". It is in that place a dreadful judgment which God gives some men up to for opposing the gospel, taking away his restraints, both from the devil and their own hearts, but more or less he works in every one that opposes the gospel, which every unrenewed man under the preaching of the gospel does, he is the strong man that keeps the palace, Luke xi. 21. Can the will of man make a surrender of it, at God's demand, in spite of his governor? What power have we to throw off these shackles he loads us with? We are as weak in his hand as birds in a fowler's. What will have we, since we are his willing slaves? The darkness of nature is never like by its own free motion to disagree with the prince of darkness, without an overpowering grace, able to contest with the lord as well as the slave; for by the fall he is become prince of the lower creation, and holds it in chains too strong for weakness to break. How great, then, is man's inability! How unreasonable is it to think that the will of man possessed with such unfitness, unwillingness, affection to other things, aversion to the gospel, resistance of it, and in the devil's net, can of itself do anything towards its recovery, from that it counts no disease; or to turn to that which it accounts its burden? If unspotted and sound nature did not preserve Adam in innocence, how can filthy and craze nature recover us from corruption? If it did not keep him alive when he was living, how can it convey life to us when we have not a spark of spiritual life in us? Man was planted a 'noble vine,' but turned himself into 'a degenerate plant;' nothing that has decayed can by its own strength recover itself, because it has lost that strength whereby it could only preserve itself.

1. Man cannot prepare himself for grace.
2. He cannot produce it.
3. He cannot co-operate with God in the first work.
4. He cannot preserve it.
5. He cannot actuate it.
1. Man cannot prepare himself for the new birth.

I shall premise a few things for the better understanding of this,

(1.) Man has a subjective capacity for grace above any other creature in the inferior world; and this is a kind of natural preparation which other creatures have not. A capacity in regard of the powers of the soul, though not in respect of the present disposition of them. A stone or a beast are not capable of habits of grace, no more than of habits of sin, because they want rational natures, which are the proper seats of both. Our Saviour did not raise trees or stones to life, though he had the same power to do that as he had to raise stones to be children to Abraham; but he raised them that had bodies prepared, in part, for a receptacle of a soul. As there is a more immediate subjective capacity in a man newly dead for the reception of life upon a new infusion of the soul, because he has all the members already formed, which is not in one whose body is mouldered into dust, and has not one member organised fit for the acting of a rational soul. These faculties have a spring of natural motion in them, therefore are capable of divine grace to make that motion regular; as the wheels of a clock out of order retain their substance and their motion if their weights be wound up, but a false motion unless the disorder of the spring be mended. Man has an understanding to know, and, when it is enlightened, to know God's law; a will to move and run, and, when enlarged by grace, to run the ways of God's commandments; so that he stands in an immediate capacity to receive the life of grace upon the breath and touch of God, which a stone does not, not the most sparkling jewel any more than the meanest pebble; for in this it is necessary rational faculties should be put as a foundation of spiritual motion. Though the soul be thus capable as a subject to receive the grace of God, yet it is not therefore capable, as an agent, to prepare itself for it or produce it; as a piece of marble is potentially capable of being the king's statue, but not to prepare itself by hewing off its superfluous parts, or to raise itself into such a figure. If there were not a rational nature, there were nothing immediately to be wrought upon. If there be not a wise agent and an omnipotent hand, there were nothing to work upon it.

(2.) Besides this passive capacity, there are more immediate preparations. The soul, as rational, is capable to receive the truths of God; but as the heart is stony, it is incapable to receive the impressions of those truths. A stone, as it is a corporeal substance, is capable to receive the drops of rain in its cavities; but because of its hardness is incapable to suck it in, and be moistened inwardly thereby, unless it be softened. Wax has a capacity to receive the impression of the seal, but it must be made pliable by some external agent to that purpose. The soul must be beaten down by conviction before it be raised up by regeneration; there must be some apprehensions of the necessity of it. Yet sometimes the work of regeneration follows so close upon the heels of these precious preparations, that both must be acknowledged to be the work of one and the same hand. Paul on the sudden was struck down. and in a moment there is both an acknowledgement of the authority of Christ, and a submission to his will, when he said, 'Lord, what wilt thou have me to do?' Acts ix. 6. The preparation of the subject is necessary, but this preparation may be at the same time with the conveyance of the divine nature: as a warm seal may both prepare the hard wax, and convey the image to it, by one and the same touch.

(3.) Though some things which man may do by common grace may be said in some sort to be preparations, yet they are not formally so, as that there is an absolute causal connection between such preparations and regeneration They are not causae dispositivae of grace, not disposing causes of grace. Grace is all in a way of reception by the soul, not of action from the soul. The highest morality in the world is not necessary to the first infusion of the divine nature. Mary Magdalene was far from the one, yet received the other. If there were anything in the subject that was the cause of it, the most tender and softest dispositions would be wrought upon, and the most intelligent men would soonest receive the gospel. Though we see them sometimes renewed, yet many times the roughest tempers are seized upon by grace; and the most unlikely soils for fructifying God plants his grace in, wherein there could be no preparations before. It is not with grace as it is with fire, which gives as much heat to a stone as to a piece of wood; but the wood is sooner heated than the stone, because it is naturally disposed, by the softness and porousness of its parts, to receive the heat. Moral nature seems to be a preparation for grace; if it be so, it is not a cause howsoever of grace, for then the most moral person would be soonest gracious, and more eminently gracious after his renewal, and none of the rubbish and dregs of the world would ever be made fit for the heavenly building. There seems to be a fitness in morality for the receiving special grace, because the violence and tumultuousness of sin is in some measure appeased, the flame and sparks of it allayed, and the body of death lies more quiet in them, and the principles cherished by them bear some testimony to the holiness of the precepts. But though it seems to set men at a greater nearness to the kingdom of God, yet with all its own strength it cannot bring the kingdom of God into the heart, unless the Spirit opens the lock. Yea, sometimes it sets a man further from the kingdom of God, as being a great enemy to the righteousness of the gospel, both imputed and inherent, which is the crown of the gospel: to imputed, as standing upon a righteousness of their own, end conceiving no need of any other; to inherent, as acting their seeming holiness neither upon gospel principles, nor for gospel ends, but in self-reflections and self-applauses. What may seem preparations to us in matters of moral life, may in the root be much distant and vastly asunder from grace; as a divine of our own illustrates it, two mountains whose tops seem near together may in the bottom be many miles asunder. The foundation of that which looks like a preparation may be laid in the very gall of bitterness; as Simon Magus desiring the gift of the Holy Ghost, but from the covetousness of his heart. Other operations upon the soul which seem to be nearer preparations, as convictions, do not infer grace; for the heart, as a field, may be ploughed by terrors, and yet not sown by any good seed. Planting and watering are preparations, but not the cause of fruit; the increase depends upon God.

(4.) There is no meritorious connection between any preparation in the creature and regeneration. The Pelagian opinion was, that by a generous love of virtue we might deserve the grace of God, and the farther assistance of the Spirit, we first (say they) put our hearts into the hands of God, that God may incline them which way he please; and by thus making our wills depend on God, we merit help from God, and make ourselves worthy of him. Whether this be the opinion of any now, I know not. This is to assert, that man gives first to God, and then God to man in way of requital. What son can merit to be born? What desert before being? Nothing can be pre-existent in the son which merits generation by the father. The fair hand of moral nature more induce God to confer on man the state of grace, than the deed of conveyance of a manor, fairly drawn, can dispose the lord to pass it away. In what part of Scripture has God indulged mere nature with any promise of adding grace upon the improvements of natural abilities? Whatsoever conditional promise there is, supposes some grace superior to nature in the subject as the condition of it. We do not find that God has made himself a debtor to any preparation of the creature.

But there is no obligation on God by anything that may look like a preparation in man. For,

[1.] If man can lay any obligation on God, it must be by some act in all parts his own, for which he is not in the least obliged to God. Thinking is the lowest step in the ladder of preparation. It is the first act of the creature in any rational production, yet this the apostle does remove from man, as in every part of it his own act: 2 Cor. iii. 5, 'Not that we are sufficient of ourselves to think anything as of ourselves, but our sufficiency is of God.' The word signifies reasoning. No rational act can be done without reasoning; this is not purely our own. We have no sufficiency of ourselves, as of ourselves, originally and radically of ourselves, as if we were the author of that sufficiency, either naturally or meritoriously. And Calvin observes that the word is not "autarkeia" but "hikanotes", not a self-ability, but an aptitude or fitness to any gracious thought. How can we oblige him by any act, since, in every part of it, it is from him, not from ourselves? For as thinking is the first requisite, so it is perpetually requisite to the progress of any rational act, so that every thought in any act, and the whole progress, wherein there must be a whole flood of thoughts, is from the sufficiency of God. We cannot oblige God after grace, much less before, for when grace is given there must be constant effluxes of grace from God to maintain it; and the acts of grace in us are but a second grace of God. How can we then oblige him by that which is not ours, either in the original or improvement? If when a man has given to another a rich gift he must also give him power to preserve it, and wisdom to improve it, the person cannot be said by his improvement of it to oblige the first donor. What has any man that he has not received? 1 Cor. iv. 7. The apostle excludes everything in us from the name of a donation to God. If there be no one thing but is received from God, then no preparation to grace but is received from him. The obligation then lies upon the receiver, not upon the donor. But may we not oblige God by the improvement of such a gift? The apostle includes everything, challenges him to name any one thing which was not received, which will contain improvements as well as preparations. If we have power to improve it, wisdom to improve it, hearts and opportunities to improve it, all these are by way of reception from God.

[2.] If man can lay any obligation upon God, it must be by some pure, spotless act. This cannot be; no pure act can spring from man. God has taken an exact survey of the whole world in its dark and fallen state, and could not, among those multitudes of acts which spring from the will of man find one piece of beauty, one particle of the divine image, for he has pronounced this sentence upon them, with repetition, too, as his infallible judgment: 'There is none righteous no, not one: they are all gone out of the way, they are together become unprofitable; there is none that does good, no, not one,' Rom. iii. 10-12. The most refined nature derived from Adam was never found without fault, a pure virtue is a terra incognita. The productions of nature are always evil. If not one action be fully good in the nature of man, what meritoriousness can there be in any preparation of nature for the grace of God? Can the clearest virtue that ever was since Adam oblige God to pardon its own defects, that is, the defects of that very act of virtue? Much less can it challenge a higher degree of grace to be transmitted to it.

[3.] If any preparation were our own, and were pure, yet being natural, how could it oblige God to give a supernatural grace? If there be anything of meritoriousness, it is only something of the same kind with the work in a greater degree, but there is no proportion between natural acts and supernatural grace. There is no one scripture, or one example, declaring grace to be given as a reward to mere nature, or any act of nature. God indeed, out of his infinite righteousness, and equity, and goodness, has rewarded some moral acts with some worldly advantages, or the withdrawing some judgments threatened, as Ahab's reprieve from judgment upon his humiliation, 1 Kings xxi. 27, 29; and the temporary pardon to Nineveh, upon their submission to the prophet's threatenings, Jonah iii. 8-10. But what obligation lies upon God to reward men doing thus with super-additions of grace? for there is no proportion between such a moral act and so excellent a reward. Are may as well say that a coal by glowing and sparkling may merit to become a star; or that the orderly laying the wood and sacrifice upon the altar might merit the descent of fire from heaven to kindle it.

[4.] If there was any obligation on God, by any preparations of nature, then such acts would be always followed with renewing grace. There would be an obligation on God's righteousness to bestow it. And if it should be denied, the creature might accuse God of a failure in justice, because he gave not what was due. God sure would observe that rule of justice which he prescribes to man, not to detain the wages of a hireling, no, not for a night. Were grace a debt upon the works of nature, God were then obliged not only to pay it, but pay it speedily, it being exact righteousness so to do. But we see the contrary. Publicans and harlots are raised and beautified, while pharisees lie buried in the ruins of nature. These preparations are many times without perfection. The pangs of conviction resolve sometimes into a return to the old vomit, and make no progress in a state of life and grace. The apostle's rule will hold true in the whole compass of the work, Rom. vi. 11, 'If it be of works, then it is no more grace.' So much as is ascribed to any work or preparation by the creature, so much is taken from the glory of grace, and would make God not the author, but assistant, and that too by obligation, not by grace.

[5.] From this it follows, that man does not prepare himself by any act of his will, without the grace of God. What preparation can he make, who is so powerfully possessed by corrupted habits, which have got so great an empire over him, struck their roots to the very bottom of his soul, entrenched themselves in the works of custom, that if he goes about to pull up one, his arm shakes and his heart faints? How strongly do these rooted habits resist the power of grace! How much more easily do they resist the weakness of nature in confederacy with them! What is said of the remnant of Jacob as a 'dew from the Lord,' as 'the showers upon the grass,' that it 'tarries not for man, nor waits for the sons of men,' Micah v. 7, may be said of the grace of God, it waits not for the preparations and dispositions of the creature, but prevents them. It is a pure gift; though we are active with it, yet we are wholly indisposed for it. We can no more prepare ourselves to shine as stars in the world, than a dunghill can to shine as a sun in heaven. What preparations does God wait for in the heart of an infarct when he sanctifies it? If 'without Christ we can do nothing,' John xv. 5, then no preparations without Christ; for they are something, and very considerable too. There is no foundation to think there should be any preparation in the creature, as of the creature.

First, The first promise of redemption and regeneration intimates no such thing in man to either of them: Gen. iii. 15, 'I will put enmity,' &c. The putting enmity into man against Satan is promised by God as his own work. There was a friendship struck up, a confederacy made, the devil entertained as a counsellor; God would now break this league, he only puts enmity into the heart against Satan: 'It shall bruise thy head,' &c. The bruising the serpent's head is wholly the act of Christ. It, not the man or the woman, but the promised seed. As there were no preparations in the creature to that which Christ acted in the flesh, so there are no preparations in that creature for what Christ is to do in his Spirit. He bruised Satan in his flesh upon the cross without any preparations in the creature; and so he bruises Satan in the heart, by his Spirit, without any preparations on the creature's part. For anything I see, had man in the state of innocence been sensible that his dependency, as to any good, and motion to good, ought to be upon God, and he to have waited upon God for his change and confirmation, he might have stood; but when he would practically assert the liberty of his own will in a way of indifference to good and evil, he fell. And by the way, those that assert the freedom of their own will naturally, without the grace of God, either common or special, seem to me to justify Adam's first affected independence of God.

Secondly, God is as much in the new creation as he was in the old. Not only the creation of the matter, but the preparation of it to receive the form, was from God; neither the matter, nor any part of it, prepared itself. If nothing prepared itself to be a creature, how can anything prepare itself to be a gracious creature, since to be a new creature is more than to be a creature; and every preparation to be a new creature is more than any preparation to be a creature? The new creation differs, I must confess, from the old creation; but it is such a difference which makes it rather harder than easier.

First, The object of the old creation was nothing, the object of the new is something; but a thing that has no more active disposition to receive a new form, than nothing had.

Secondly, The object of the first creation was a simple and pure privation; the object of the second is a contrary form, which resists the work of God: there was only an action of creation in the first, there is an action of destruction in the second, the destruction of the old form and the creation of a new. Is it likely that any nature would voluntarily prepare itself for its own destruction? God in the first creation found no disposition in the subject to entertain a form, here he finds a contrary disposition to resist the form.

Thirdly, What preparation had any of those we read of in Scripture from themselves? What disposition had Paul, when he was struck down with a heart fuller of actual enmity than he had at his birth? Did the apostles expect any call from their nets, or set themselves in a readiness before they heard that call? A voice from Christ was attended with a divine touch or power upon their hearts; both the preparation and the motion itself took birth together. And what preparations are there in Scripture, but are attributed unto God? If a conviction be thorough and full, and consequently a preparation, it must refer to that Spirit which our Saviour asserts to be the principal cause of it, John xvi. 8, 9, 'When he is come,' that is, the Comforter, 'he will reprove the world of sin.' It is laid wholly upon this, as the end of the almighty Spirit's coming, whereby it is not likely men would be convinced without him. Is there any desire or prayer for it? Even this, if true, is from the Holy Ghost; 'no man can call Christ Lord, but by the Holy Ghost,' 1 Cor. xii. 3. Did any of those our Saviour cured of bodily infirmities, prepare themselves for that cure? Neither can any man prepare himself for his spiritual cure.

Fourthly, What thing in all the records of nature ever prepared itself for a change? All preparations in matter for receiving any form arise not from the matter itself, but from some other active principle, or the new form in part introduced, which by degrees expels the old; as in water, when heat comes in the place of cold, the preparation is not from the water, but from the new quality introducing itself. The grace of God is to the soul as form is to matter. The body is formed in the womb, for the reception of the soul, but not by the embryo, but by the formative virtue of the parent, fashioning the parts of the body to make it a fit lodging for the soul; or, as some think, the soul itself, as the bee, fashions its own cell; but howsoever it is not from itself. The preparations of Lazarus to rise were from the voice of Christ, not from the stinking body of Lazarus. The nature of all is alike. That one lute is better prepared for an harmonious touch, is from the musician's skill, not any art of its own. If one man of the same nature with another be endued with rich morals, it is from the common grace of God exciting natural light, and the common notions of fit and just; as the reason one vine of the same kind brings forth more generous fruit than another, is from the stronger influence of the sun. All nature assents to this truth, that nothing does prepare itself for a change.

Fifthly, If man did prepare himself for grace, it would be a disparagement to God, it would violate the sovereignty of God. It would be derogatory to the majesty of God to have his grace depend upon the conditions and previous preparations in the creature; it would lay the foundations of grace in a man's self, and impose a necessity in God to come in with further grace, and make his actions dependent upon the actings of the creature. The beginning of faith would be from us, and the supplement from God; the work of grace would be of him that 'wills and runs,' and not 'of God that shows mercy,' Rom. ix. 16. It would change the whole tenor of the Scripture, and make conversion not God's drawing of us, but our traction of God; for he that does dispose himself to grace, is in some sort the cause of that grace, as he that does dispose the subject for such a form is in a sort the cause of that form. If the preparations were from the will of man, man would begin the noblest work that ever was wrought, and God would be made no more than an attendant upon the creature's motion; whereas the very beginning in the will, as well as the perfection, is ascribed to God: Philip. ii. 13, 'God works in you both to will and to do of his good pleasure.' God's good pleasure is the original cause of this work upon the will, not the will's good pleasure. The work then depending on God's good pleasure, excludes any dependency on the will of man; it is therefore called a creation, to show God's independence upon anything as to this work.

Sixthly, Where should this preparation begin? in what part of the soul? Shall it begin in the understanding? That has lost the reins whereby it governed the lower parts of the soul. Nothing is more discomposed in its acts than that faculty. It is well compared to a charioteer or coachman fallen from his box, and his feet entangled in the reins of the horses, which hurry him about. The sensitive appetite, like a wild horse, has got the bit between his teeth, runs about, and draws the understanding after it. Indeed a charioteer that has lost the government of his horses endeavours to remedy that violence; he cries out, makes all resistance, has a will to help himself; but the understanding is so far from resisting, that it takes pleasure in the disorder of the passions; it prompts the will to follow them, and this is properly to be a servant to sin. Shall it begin in the appetite? How can that incline to range itself to the order of reason? It has no reason itself; it submits not to the laws of reason; it has got the mastery of it, and has prescription for its dominion, of a long standing, ever since the fall. The dominion of sin is in the understanding, will, appetite, whence all of them are called flesh, so that all the motions of the soul depending upon them, the slavery must needs be voluntary. Therefore neither the understanding conceives, nor the will wills, nor the appetite desires, anything against themselves; how, then, should the will, which is captivated by a corrupt understanding and disorderly affections, recover itself, when it must necessarily be under the guidance of one of these jailers? Suppose the understanding were illuminated, are those evil habits in the will corrected barely by the illumination of the understanding? If they are corrected, why does not the will always follow the dictate of the understanding? But, alas! those evil habits determine the will to evil, as good habits determine it to good; for it is the nature of habits to incline the faculties to those things which are suitable to the nature of those habits; therefore as long as it remains under the command of those evil inclinations, it is impossible it should pass from evil to good. But that the will has evil inclinations, appears by the Scripture calling the whole man flesh; else corruption would not be universally seated in the soul, but only accidental in the will, from the darkness of the understanding. But certainly, as Adam in innocence had an habitual holy disposition in his will, so man, in his fall, has a corrupt inclination in his will, an habitual quality, whereby he drinks iniquity like water, Job xv. 16. What power of the will can take those cords off, which hold it prisoner, whereby it must be prepared for a free motion?

To evidence this further, we shall consider,

1. That man does not naturally, neither can, understand the new birth.

2. He cannot desire it. Understanding and desire are necessary preparations to any rational change a creature can make in itself.

1. Man cannot understand it. This is necessary to a change. Whatsoever is done by the will, must be done by the impulse of some other faculty. Sensitive appetite cannot instruct the will to this work. Sense is not capable of reason, much less of religion, though it be the portal to both. The will can never be moved to any good thing, unless the mind propound it as good and amiable. The act of thinking must precede the act of believing, for we cannot believe without thinking of what we believe. It is less to think than understand. If we cannot, then, do that which is less in the preparation, we cannot do that which is greater, especially when it is impossible to will without thinking; and thinking is a necessary means to willing. He that cannot prepare himself for a good thought, how can he prepare himself for a gracious habit? What ability have we to the act of faith, when we have no ability to any thought of faith? We cannot by the strength of nature understand it, if we consider,

(1.) The first blot caused by sin was upon the understanding. Man was first deceived by the sophistical reasonings of the serpent. The first effect of sin was to spread a thick darkness upon Adam's understanding. Though the whole house, and every beam of it, fell together, yet this faculty was first unfastened, and brought all the rest to ruin. As soon as ever he ceased from glorifying God as God, a darkness was brought upon his foolish heart: Rom. i. 21, 'When they knew God, they glorified him not as God, but became vain in their imaginations, and their foolish heart was darkened,' where the apostle describes the state of man in corrupt nature after his fall. Folly first in the heart to desire the forbidden fruit, and then darkness came upon the understanding. Their "dialogismoi", their reasonings, became empty and contradictory; their primitive light departed, and darkness, as a privation, took place. What true motion can there be in the will, when there was so thick an obscurity in the understanding? Where there is but a false knowledge in the mind, there can be no true motion in the will. There must then be a restoration of this light, before there can be any preparation to a good act of the will. Adam recovered not this light by his own strength, no, nor by the outward declaration of the gospel in the promise; for no outward object proposed to the understanding confers any power upon the faculty. How can it then be recovered by our strength, since we have rather added to the scales than diminished them? For,

(2.) There is a darkness transmitted from him to the understanding of every man by nature. The light is darkened in the heaven of the soul, the more spiritual part of the mind, Isa. v. 30, as the prophet speaks in another case. Our understandings are so closed up with the thick slime of sin, that we cannot see the beauty of gospel truths; 'darkness comprehends not the light,' John i. 5. Though the light of the sun did shine a thousand times brighter than it does, and strike upon the face and eyelids of a man with the greatest glory, yet if there be a spot upon the apple of his eye, if he scants a seeing faculty, he can apprehend nothing of it. Hence the apostle prays for the illumination of the understanding of the Ephesians, chap. i. 17, 18, and that they might have 'a spirit of wisdom and revelation in the knowledge of God.' And our Saviour tells them that they 'must be taught of God,' John vi. 45, by an internal teaching of the Spirit, as well as by himself in an oral instruction. What a thick cloud was upon Nicodemus his mind, when he discoursed with him about regeneration, who was the ablest teacher to illustrate it to his fancy and understanding! It is not such a darkness as if he might understand the mysteries of heaven, if he would exert the strength of his own reason. This would be only as a man shutting his eyes who had a visive faculty; but it is such a darkness as cannot be expelled by flesh and blood, or anything arising from it: 'Flesh and blood,' says our Saviour to Peter, 'has not revealed it unto thee, but my, Father which is in heaven,' Mat. xvi. 17. Flesh and blood includes everything in opposition to God. Our Saviour had externally owned himself, in the face of the Jews, to be the Messiah, the Son of God; but besides this, there was an inward illumination granted to Peter, for the apprehending and embracing so great a truth. There is not only a darkness upon the minds of those who have no outward revelation of the will of God in Christ, but upon those who are in the midst of the sunbeams: Deut. xxix., 'Yet the Lord has not given you an heart to perceive, and eyes to see, and ears to hear, unto this day.' They wanted not the beams. No people in the world had the ordinances of God besides them; but they wanted an organ fitted to receive and use them, which was not in their power, but is mentioned as the gift of God. God promises to make his people to know his ways. What needs that, if they could know them without him? We have indeed the light of the gospel, we have also a faculty, but without an eye disposed for the light, Ye enjoy no benefit by it. Now who ever heard that darkness could prepare itself for its own expulsion? It cannot comprehend the light, much less prepare for the reception of it. Now who ever heard of one born blind, in a capacity to prepare himself for sight? We are blind in naturals, much more in spirituals. The most polished reasons among the heathens, both for knowledge in naturals and prudence in civil affairs, coated, and with all their wisdom knew not God.

(3.) There is an unsuitableness and a contrariety in the mind of man to the gospel, which is the instrument of regeneration. There is a mighty distance between the spiritual object and the natural faculty. The understanding, though never so well furnished with natural stuff, is but natural, and flesh; the object is supernatural and spiritual; therefore the richest mere nature can no more attain to the knowledge of spiritual things, than the clearest sense can attain to the knowledge of rational. Though every man 'by nature has the things contained in the law,' Rom. ii. 14, 15, yet no man has by nature the things contained in the gospel. The gospel has not the same advantage in the hearts of men as the law hash, for it finds nothing of kin to it. Though a natural heart has some broken pieces of the law of God deposited in it, yet there is not the least syllable of Christ or regeneration written in the mind by the hand of nature. The understanding therefore naturally cannot prepare itself for the reception of the gospel, because it has not any principle in it which suits the doctrine of it. It seems a ridiculous thing to the wisest carnalist, who receives not the things of God, because, out of the pride of natural wisdom, he counts them foolishness, 1 Cor. ii. 14. Hence not many wise are renewed in their minds. Had the gospel truth been as agreeable to reason as the other common notions imprinted in man, it would have been preserved in the world longer than it was, since, without question, Adam did communicate to his posterity the notion of a redeemer, which did soon die among them, because not consonant to that reason they had derived by nature from Adam. It was a knowledge given to Adam by revelation, not imprinted in his nature by creation. Besides, there is a contrariety in the mind to the truth of the gospel. As we say of liberty, so of enmity. Though it be formally in the will, yet it is radically in the understanding. The mind is the seat of those hostile principles which act the will against God, Rom. viii. 7. The mind of man regards the things of God as unpleasant, and an intolerable yoke and hard bridle.

Let light, the most excellent thing in the world, glare upon a man that has sore eyes, he will turn away from it, or shut his eyes against it; for though he understands the worth of it, yet it has a quality offensive to him. So is the gospel to those notions settled in the distempered mind. Men give not credit to the declarations of the gospel; 'Who has believed our report?' has been the voice of God's messengers in all ages, Isa. liii. 1. No man, unless known by all never to speak truth, but is more believed than the God of infallible and unerring truth! What principles, then, are there in the understanding to prepare it for the reception of that which is so contrary to its ancient inmates?

(4.) Besides this, the natural levity of the understanding does incapacitate it to prepare itself. It is with the understanding as with a line, the farther it is stretched out the weaker and more wavering it is. So is the understanding, being at a distance from God. How do vain thoughts intrude into the mind! No man can keep a door locked against them. We feel them rushing upon us while we endeavour to avoid them. We are confounded and overwhelmed by them, and drawn to things against our own resolutions. Man has not the command of his own heart, so much as to think steadily of a divine object. How can he then prepare his own heart, when he cannot without grace fix in any holy meditation which is necessary for the renewal of it, since nothing is more discomposed in its acts than the mind of man, which is always dancing about, like cork in the water, or feathers in the air? Whence should come any preparation to good orders but by some supernatural ballast, to establish it from fluctuating? This disease every man is sensible of, and whatsoever disease is inherent in nature cannot be cured by any preparations by that nature which is wholly overgrown with it.

(5.) Hence it follows that a natural mind has no right notion of grace. To the right notion of a thing is required suitableness, pleasure, and a fixedness of the mind upon it. A natural mind wants all these. How can it then prepare itself for that which it has no knowledge of? And without knowledge it cannot commend it to the will. The apostle asserts a plain cannot in this business: 1 Cor. ii. 14, 'He cannot know them, because they are spiritually discerned.' Being destitute of the Spirit, they cannot discern the things of the Spirit. Sense can discern things sensibly, not rationally. Reason can discern things rationally, but not spiritually. The light whereby a natural man judges of the things of the gospel is a star-light or a moonlight, which gives not a distinct view of the object. The evil disposition must be removed from the mind, before the object be entertained according to its worth. As if any natural object have such excellent qualities in it, that if it be embraced it will draw the will and affections after it; yet if the mind be ill-disposed, and does not judge of the object according to the merit of it, it will refuse it. Offer a man gold who understands not the worth of gold, it will not allure him. Man with his eyes is spiritually blind, and with his ears is spiritually deaf. So God calls the Gentiles, which were to be brought to Christ for a restitution of their eyes: Isa. xliii. 8, 'Bring forth the blind people that have eyes, and the deaf that have ears.' Such can no more judge of the excellency of spiritual things than a blind man can have regular conceptions of colours, or a deaf man of the excellency of music. If 'no man can call Jesus Lord, but by the Holy Ghost,' 1 Cor. xii. 8; if no man can have a magnificent conception and speech of Christ, but by the Spirit giving him both that conception and utterance, he cannot have a notion of the formation of Christ in the heart without the gift and impression of the same hand. What preparations, then, can arise from nature, when the mind can have no conception of Christ but by the Spirit of God?

Well, then, to conclude this. What preparations can there be in nature, since we cannot understand the things of God, when yet we have more clearness in our understanding to see them than we have force in our wills to love them and embrace them? It is in the understanding that the common notions, which are the grounds of knowledge, are deposited. There is less of ignorance in our understanding than of enmity in our will. The eye can see further than the arm can reach. If therefore we cannot think or understand, by all that help of common notions, without the grace of God, hove can we then prepare our wills for it, to comply with it, and renew that faculty which is chiefly possessed with a contrariety to it?

2. As we cannot understand it, so we cannot naturally desire it. What is not spiritually discerned cannot spiritually be desired. Not but that according to those unformed conceptions which men have of it by common grace, there may be some weak velleities, but they are wishings without a will, not desires according to the value of the thing. Mercy first breathed on our first parents, before they breathed after that. The first motion came from God. So soon were they turned obstinate enemies against their Creator, without any thoughts of turning supplicants, though they had not lost the conceptions of their late integrity. which if they had, they had been wholly insensible, without any trouble of conscience. What desires can we naturally, then, have for it, who have far weaker conceptions of that happiness than they had immediately after they lost it? We cannot desire what we do not apprehend. A beast cannot desire to be a man, because he has no conceptions of the excellency of the human nature above his own. No nature can ever affect that which is contrary to it. Do flesh can ever desire its own crucifixion. If we seek, we shall find; if we ask, we shall receive, but who first touches the heart to seek or to ask? If we cannot think a good thought of ourselves, how can we think so good a thought as a desire of regeneration? To say, then, we can desire the new creation of ourselves, without some kind of grace, is to assert another doctrine than what the apostle Paul asserted to those already

regenerate. The first will, which is the necessary spring of all actions, is wrought by God, Philip. ii. 13. The frame of man's will and desire stands to another point: John viii. 44, 'The lusts of your father you will do.' The best renewed man 'knows not what to pray for as he ought,' without the instruction of the Spirit, Rom. viii. 26. We cannot give our hearts a lift to heaven, or breathe out an unutterable groan, without the help of an infinite Spirit. The root of man's affections groves downward, not upward. What breathings can be expected in a soul choked up with sin? There was no motion of the church till 'the hand of her beloved was put in by the hole of the door,' and made a motion in her bowels, Cant. v. 4. The church owed no obligation to her free will and her own predispositions. There is not a smoke in the heart to heaven without a spark first from heaven; not a step till God enlarges the heart. Velleities are from common grace, under the preaching, of the word, fervent and saving desires are from special grace, by the hand of the Spirit. So that there are no preparations from nature to this, since both our apprehensions of it and desires of it spring not out of that stock.

The second main thing is this, As man cannot prepare himself for it, so he does not produce and work it in himself. This is evident from the former. If he cannot make any preparation, which is the less, he cannot cause any actual production of it, which is the greater.

But to evidence it more, let us spend some time in this.

As it does not depend upon the will of man in the preparation, so neither in the production.

I shall evidence it, first, by arguments drawn from the consideration of God.

If this work depended upon the will of man, as the first cause in the production, it would deprive God,

1. Of his sovereign independence. If man's will were the first cause of regeneration, God would not be the supreme independent cause in the noblest of his works. This work is nobler than creation in respect of the price paid for it. The world was made without the death of anything to purchase the creation of it. But the divine image is not restored without the death of the Son of God, every line in this new image being drawn with his blood. Is there anything happens in the world but by the conduct and efficacy of his providence? Do all the motions of the heavens, the productions of creatures, the universal events of nature, depend upon the will, power, and wisdom of God? And shall the soul, the most excellent of the lover creatures, bearing the characters of God's wisdom and goodness upon it (the acts of the soul in the way of religion, being the noblest acts it can produce), be left wholly to itself in the production and management of these? Shall God, the supreme cause in everything else, be an inferior and secondary cause in this affair? It is 'not he that plants, nor he that waters, but God that gives the increase,' 1 Cor. iii. 7. God is the first cause, upon whom man depends in all kind of actions, much more in supernatural actions, chiefly in the understanding and will, upon which faculties no creature can have any intrinsic influence to cause them to exercise their vital acts. If the will of man were the first cause, God would be an attendant to the creature in the noblest works. God would not then be the first mover, but man. The will willing would then be the cause of God's working, not God's working the cause of the will's willing and choice. God's working would be consequent upon the will, and so the effect of the will's free motion. Man would then be the *dispositiva causa* in relation to God. It would make God the second cause, and represent him expecting the beck, and the preparations of man, before he did exert any act. It would make God to will that which man wills, and make God to will that which man may reject. It would follow that God concurs not to regeneration by way of sovereignty, but by way of concomitance. It would not be a victorious but a precarious grace, which is against the whole tenor of the Scripture, which represents God as holding in his hands the first links of all second causes: Rom. xi. 36, 'For of him, and through him, and to him, are all things.' He is the first governor of all the wills and powers of the creatures, the first cause of all motions. He orders all, without being ordered by any. Now this is below the majesty of God, to be conducted in his motion by the will of the creature, to have the purposes of his goodness brought into act by an uncertain and slippery cause. How can it be conceived that God should put his hand to the more ignoble works of nature, and turn over the noblest work of the new creation to the airy will of the creature.

To conclude; God must either be precedent in his operation to the act of the will, or follow it. If precedent, we have what we would, if subsequent, then God is a mere attendant upon the motions of the creature, and a servant to wait upon man. This is to advance free will to the throne of God and depress God to the footstool of will; this is to deify the creature, by placing the crown of the sovereign independence of God on the head of free will.

2. It puts a blot upon the wisdom of God. If God expects the determination of the will of man, whether he shall act or no, then God is disposed by the will of man to the intention of his end. But it is very inconsistent with that unfathomable and unerring wisdom, to have the attainment of his end depend upon an agent wherein nothing is wrapped up but folly and madness, Eccles. ix. 3. This is to make his power depend upon weakness, and his gracious ends towards his creature hang upon the extravagancies of one distracted, which no wise man would be guilty of. Is God in all things else a God of power and wisdom, working all things in number, weight, and measure, springing up every motion in the lower world, by an unblameable counsel? And shall he leave the forming of the image of his Son, wherein his

wisdom is most seen, to the slight irregular will of man, which has neither weight nor measure in itself? This would make the immutable counsel of God depend upon the mutability of the creature; which would be inconsistent with the wisdom of man, who chooses the firmest means he can for the conduct of his designs; for if man wills this day, then God wills, if man reject it the next day, then he rejects that which God wills. So God's will most be at uncertainty, according to the will of man. How shall his counsel stand upon so tottering a bottom? How shall he do all his pleasure if it were a mere dependent upon the pleasure of the creature, contrary to what he is pleased positively to assert: Isa. xlvi. 10, 'My counsel shall stand, I will do all my pleasure.' The apostle does couch these into arguments together: Eph. i. 11, 'Who works all things according to the counsel of is own will;' he argues (1) from the power of God, 'who works all things', whereby our own works, and power, are excluded, and God asserted to be the supreme cause of everything, in an efficacious and energetical manner, as the word "energein" signifies. (2.) From his wisdom, 'according to the counsel of his own will,' wisely and justly, and therefore not according to ours, wherein there is nothing but folly and evil. This excludes all our own wills in the first work. Now, to assert that this beautiful image were brought forth upon the stage of the heart by the will of man, as the first cause, would destroy God's prerogative, and represent his operations under the conduct of our own counsel and will, not of his own. Certainly if there be a secret and wise Spirit of providence, running through the whole world to preserve his honour in his works, as certainly there is, the most honourable declaration of them in the heart cannot be thought to be left to the conduct of wild and hare-brained nature.

3. If the will of man were the prime cause of regeneration, it would deprive God of his foreknowledge and prescience; it would make that foreknowledge, which is certain and infallible, merely contingent. For if the will of man were wholly left to its own determination, the motions of the will were doubtful and uncertain, till the will does determine itself; and so God's knowledge of them would be uncertain, for it is clear, that from a thing wholly uncertain, there cannot arise a certain knowledge. Therefore, God could not be said certainly to foreknow the conversion of man, if the efficacy of grace depended upon so contingent a cause as the liberty of man's will; for then it might not be, as well as be; the will might not embrace it, and so the knowledge of God be but merely conjectural,--a knowledge unworthy of a deity, which must be supposed to be omniscient; a knowledge depending upon a peradventure, or at best, it is but a very likely it will be so. This would be a debasing the deity to an opinionative knowledge, which could not be certain, because depending upon so undetermined and wavering a cause. God cannot know this or that man's regeneration from eternity but he must see it infallibly in himself willing it, or in the causes of it, irresistibly producing it. But if the efficacy of grace depends upon the will, then God does not certainly determine the regeneration of man. And for God to foreknow that which he himself has not determined, and when nothing in the creature, nor anything in the circumstances, does determine it, is to make God see that (as one says) which neither in the creature nor in himself is to be seen.

Obj. Some may object, How does God come to foreknow sin, for that depends upon the liberty of the will?

Ans. It would be too long to inquire into this, I shall only at present say this, it is certain God does foresee every sin, otherwise the evil acts of men could not be predicted. Our Saviour could not then have foreknown what the scribes and priests would do to him, as he does foretell: Mat. xvi. 21, 'Christ began to tell them how many things he was to suffer of the chief priests and scribes.' And since God cannot fail in his predictions, but they will certainly come to pass, the hearts of the Jews could do no other thing, supposing the prediction, than what Christ does here foretell, for their wicked wills would certainly determine themselves that way. And God, by a concurrence of causes which he had linked together in his hand, orders things so, that meeting with the corruption in their wills, their wills determine themselves to such actions there foretold; yet is not God therefore the author of sin. For sin being no positive thing, cannot have an efficient, but a deficient cause; and God determines the withdrawing of his common grace, and the ordering of such and such circumstances, and so did foresee how a free creature, with that corruption in his heart, would determine himself in such occasions, when involved in such circumstances. But now in the work of regeneration, outward circumstances cannot cause any determination of the will, because those outward circumstances of grace meet with nothing in the heart full of corruption, to take part with them, which outward circumstances of sin do. Therefore since there can be no foresight of God in this case, depending upon the concurrence of outward circumstances, unless there were something in the heart which did suit them, the determination of the will cannot proceed from them, but from God himself, willing and determining the will by a positive influx of his grace. The determination of the will to sin comes from within, from its natural corruption concurring with such occasions, which, joining together, determine the will to it. Therefore God foresees what a free creature will do; but there being no principle in the will by nature to correspond with any gracious external circumstances, it cannot determine itself to grace, because it wants a principle of determination within itself, the corrupt habits determining it quite otherwise. Sin proceeds not so much from the liberty as the captivity of the will; and God knowing the corrupt frame, can foresee what man in such a frame will do upon occasion; as we may easily resolve that an habitual drunkard will be drunk when he has sensual objects placed before him.

4. Another consideration is this: to make the will of man the efficient of his regeneration, is to make the truth of God a great uncertainty.

(1.) First, In the covenant he made with Christ. If his having a seed depended upon the will of man, the promise of God to give him a seed might be null and void; for at least it must be granted possible, that not one man under heaven would have accepted of his terms; and then his coming to save had been in vain, because there was a possibility that not one man would have embraced the salvation offered. Since the number of rejecters of him is greater than the number of receivers, it is likely the less number, if left to their own wills, would have followed the greater, since the prevalence of evil examples above good ones is every day evident. It had not been, then, 'the pleasure of the Lord shall prosper in his hand,' Isa. liii. 10, 11, but the pleasure of man shall prosper in the hand of the will of man. The great resolve of God, the priesthood of Christ, the design of drawing a generation of persons out of the world to praise him, had hung upon a mere haphazard and a maybe, if it had depended only on man's will; and God should have waited the leisure of free will, to see whether the most glorious design that ever was laid should prosper, and whether he should have been a God of truth, or a liar to his Son. Though our Saviour had laid the foundation of our redemption in his own most precious blood, yet he must have depended on our will for the fruits of his purchase; it had been a great uncertainty whether he had seen one grain of fruit for all his expense. He might have been a king without one subject, or the destruction of one potent enemy he came to conquer, not one sin subdued, not one devil cast out of any son. This might have been; for though by God he was made a king, yet according to the other assertion, it depended on the will of man whether he should have one subject to own his authority; and, if so, God had been very unwise to enter into covenant with him, and Christ very unwise to come upon such grand uncertainties at the best, when it was a question whether any one person should have enjoyed the fruits of his death. How can it enter into any man's heart, that so great a contrivance as the sending of Christ to be the means of salvation, with such great promises to see the fruits of his death in a seed to serve him, should depend in the main fruits and effects of it on any thing undetermined by the will of God; that so great a weight should hang upon so thin a thread as the will of man?

(2.) In the promises he makes to men. How could God promise that so absolutely as he does, Ezek. xxxvi. 26, 'A new heart will I give you,' if this work did depend upon the will of man, which might frustrate the truth of God in his promise? And when God knew there was no principle in their hearts that could rise higher than to shame and confusion, not to so excellent a work as regeneration, as is intimated, ver. 32, 'Not for your sakes do I do this: be ashamed and confounded for your own ways, O house of Israel,' what reason was there for God to depress them to confusion, if they had had power to renew themselves? If this promise of God depended not upon any thing in them in the first making, it could not depend upon any thing in them in the full performance of it. We must either make God a liar, or unwise, or remove any efficiency in the will of man as the first cause. What blasphemy would it be to say, that God was so unwise as to promise that which depended upon the power of another, whether it should be wrought or no; that God could not be certainly true to his word, unless freewill assisted him!

5. It despoils God of his worship, in those two great parts of it, prayer and praise.

(1.) Prayer. With what face can any solicit God for that grace, which he conceives to be in his own power to have when he will? It is a mocking of him to desire that strength of him, which he has given us already, inherent in our nature. If it were the work of our wills, it would require only the excitation of them, not any application to God. Who begs for what he has? Who desires an alms that has thousands in his purse? As prayer would be a vain thing in any man that should deny a providence overruling the affairs of the world, so it would be as vain a thing to call upon God for grace, if the whole affair of regeneration were left to the conduct of man's will. The end of God's making promises of a new hearts and a new spirit, is to be inquired after to do it for us, Ezek. xxxvi. 26, 37. The natural consequent, then, of asserting the power of our own wills, is not to call upon God, but direct our desires to another cause, to solicit our own wills, not God. It would not be, then, according to the language of the church, 'Turn thou us, O Lord, and we shall be turned;' 'Draw me, and I will run after thee,' Lam. v. 21, Cant. i. 4, but, I will turn to thee, and then shalt thou be turned to me; I will run after thee, and draw thee to myself. The royal authority, and power of God, and his glory in granting, is the foundation of prayer; therefore the Lord's prayer is concluded with this, as an argument to move God to grant what is asked, 'Thine is the kingdom, the power, and the glory;' that is, thou art rich and powerful, and hast all sorts of blessings to bestow. With what face can any one go to God with these words in his mouth, when he ascribes the kingdom, power, and glory, in so great a work, to his own will? We can never pray in confidence to God for it, for all confidence is wrought by a consideration of the will of him we pray to, to accomplish what we desire, and of his power to effect it. What confidence, then, can we have in his will particularly to work it for us, if we conceive he has left it to our hands, as the proper work of our own wills? This was the ground of our Saviour's supplications, with strong cryings and tears, that 'God was able to save him,' Heb. v. 7: able naturally, in respect of his power, able morally, in respect of his truth to his promise. If God were careless in this concern, and had cast off all from his own hands, on the hand of free will, God might well say to and man, as he did to Moses, 'Why criest thou unto me? Speak to the children of Israel that they go forward,' Exod. xiv. 15. Why cry you to me? You may do it yourselves. Go forward with your own wills. The natural language of man to God would not be, Lord, let thy kingdom come, thy will be done, give me a new heart; but, I will have thy kingdom come, I will have thy will be done, I will procure myself a new heart, I will change my heart of stone into a heart of flesh.

(2.) Praise. It does deprive God of this part of his worship also, praise even for his greatest blessings. If our own wills did produce this work, the greatest cause of glorying would be, not in God, but in ourselves. We have as little ground to praise God, if it be our own work, as we have to pray to him for it. All that can be said is, that we have ground to praise him for the means of regeneration; and this is no more ground than they have that are not regenerate under the enjoyment of the same means. If a man could give himself a natural being without God, he could be his own creator, his own foundation; so if he could give himself a spiritual being without the grace of God, he would be a god to himself; for in this case he would really do more to his conversion than God. If God offer grace equally to all, and the pliableness of one man's will to receive it above another were from himself, he would then owe an obligation to himself, but no more to God than the other that rejected it owes. The apostle, by asking the question, 'Who Has made thee to differ? And what hast thou that thou did not receive?' 1 Cor. iv. 7 (though it be meant of a difference of gifts, yet it is argumentum a minori), clearly implies, that what difference there was between them and others, was not of their own planting, nor grew up from the stock of nature. But if regeneration be wrought by a man's own will, it is not God that makes the difference, therefore the glory does not belong to him. He is the author of a general call, therefore the glory of that pertains to him, it is true; but yet as much from the damned that have lived under the gospel, as from the glorified saints in heaven, because the special entertainment of this call was not from the efficacy of God's grace, but the liberty of man's will; for, according to this assertion, the love of God would be equal both to the damned and saved, and would not shine with a fairer lustre in heaven than it does in hell. The apostle wishes the Philippians to 'work out their salvation with fear and trembling,' and encourages them by this argument, because God is the author of all that good which they do. If the determination of the will, then, is from itself, is it not a brave ground to glory in ourselves? How shall any man give God the glory of his salvation? If it be said, God did enlighten their understandings by the preaching of the gospel, this is an illumination common to all; and the reason some believe and others not, is not from the gift of God, but from themselves; how can we give God a peculiar praise for that wherein there is no difference between the best and the worst of men? But the apostle says, God gives us to will, that is, the operation of our will, and not only the illumination of the understanding; therefore, that our wills do terminate in that which is good, we hold of God; the apostle does not say, God has given us power to will, but produced the will in us, and that of his good pleasure. If, therefore, God work no more in one than in another, there is no place for God's good pleasure, because there is no difference. Let us see with what kind of language the praise of God would be clothed, according to the doctrine of free will. A renewed man may say thus: Lord, I give thee thanks, that thou hast conferred upon me a supernatural grace; but thou did also give as much grace to my neighbour, but I added something to that which thou did supernaturally give me; and though I received no more than he did receive from thee, yet I did more than he, since he remains in his sin, and I am regenerate; therefore I have no more obligation to thee and the grace, than he that believes not; for, Lord, thou did not make me differ from the other, because he had equal gifts with me; but I made myself to differ, because I superadded my own velle to thy divine assistance. How much of the glory of God would be pared off by such a half-witted praise as this! How low would be the acclamations of glorified saints in heaven! What foundation of pride in the creature, contrary to the intendment of the gospel, which is chiefly to humble man, if man were the cause of the most excellent work in himself! It would write vanity in a great measure upon that excellent exhortation of the apostle, 'Let him that glories, glory in the Lord,' 1 Cor. i. 31, since there would be a bottom for flesh to glory in his presence, contrary to the design of God in his works, ver. 29, which is, 'that no flesh should glory in his presence.'

Arg. 2. The second sort of arguments is drawn from the nature and state of man.

1. In creation. Man did not create himself; to be a new creature is more than to be a creature. As man contributed nothing to nature, so neither can he contribute anything to grace, any more than a passive capacity in respect of faculties, which yet are the gift of God to him, nothing of his own acquisition. The soul, though framed with all its faculties, is as little able to engrave the image of God upon itself, as the body of Adam, formed with all its parts and members, was able to infuse a living soul into itself; there is no reason therefore to attribute our creation to God, and regeneration, the glory and excellency of a creature, to ourselves. I know such similitudes ought not to be strained too high; yet when this doctrine agrees with other parts of Scripture, we may form an argument from this metaphor of creation whereby regeneration is expressed in Scripture. It is confessed by most, if not all, that no creature, not an angel, can be an instrument in the very act of creation of another thing, much less the chief efficient of its own creation, for creation is an act of omnipotence, and an incommunicable

property of the Deity, not to be delegated to any creature. The creation of man, in a state of such perfection as to be endued with the image of God, was a greater work than simply the creation of his body or the essential faculties of his soul, yea, greater than the creation of the whole world, because the attributes of God did more lively appear in him, and particularly his holiness. The restoration then of this righteousness to man, after it is lost, is a greater work than the first creation of his body and soul, it being the same thing with the conferring at first his original rectitude upon him. If man therefore could create this in his own soul after it is lost, he would do a greater work than simply the creation of a world. Surely there is as much power and wisdom required to the new creating righteousness in the heart, after it is perished, as there was in the placing it there at first; and then it will follow that none can new create it but an infinite wisdom, power, and holiness. If man therefore can create it in itself, he must have a wisdom, power, and holiness equal to that of God his first creator, for what could not be done by any creature at the first conferring it, but it was necessary that it should be a work of infinite power, cannot be done by a less power non, because the work is every whit as great; and no less power is requisite to a second creation of a thing after it is perished, than was necessary to the first creation of it, since this power of creation cannot be derived to any creature. As when life is gone from a fly, and the body of it dried and shrivelled up, all will grant that the restoring life to this fly must be done by an omnipotent power. The case is the same with us by nature, spiritual life, upon the fall, was wholly fled, no good thing dwells in our flesh, Rom. vii. 18, not one thing spiritually good, that which is born of the flesh is flesh, wholly flesh in every part of it. If the making a living fly or worm is above the power of nature, much more the creating of so glorious a fabric as grace in the soul. Man might as well have implanted the divine image in his soul at first, as restore it after it was lost. To ascribe such a power to man to raise himself is a greater power than Adam had by creation, because to restore a man's self from death to life is greater than to preserve the vital principle he has already, and act naturally from it.

2. In the state of innocence. Let us consider man in that, and it will appear he is unable to renew himself. If man did not keep himself up, with so great a stock of natural rectitude in paradise, how can he recover himself and that stock after it is lost? 'Man in his best estate is vanity; all Adam is all vanity.' In the estate of pure nature, he is vanity in respect of his mutability, much more vanity then in his fallen state, from the experience of which Adam rightly called his second son Abel, vanity, Hebel, the word used here. How soon did the breath of the serpent melt the impression upon him! And if he did not by his innocent will preserve that purity which he had received, how can he by his corrupt will recover that purity which he has lost? If Adam had had a will to preserve, he might have stood, but in losing his will he lost his power; if he did not maintain his will in his rectitude, nor (as some say) could not without the grace of God, how can he, by the mere force of his own will, restore that lost rectitude to himself? If an universal integrity stood in need of grace to preserve it, an universal depravation stands in need of a more vigorous force than that of our will to eject it. If Adam, who had no disorders in nature to rectify, did not stand by his own will, it is not likely that we, who have strong habits to conquer, can be restored by the strength of our own wills. What nature did not do when it was sound, it is not likely to do a greater thing when it is wounded. We cannot now have more power than Adam had in innocence; but he was not then endued with a power to regenerate himself if he should fall, but death was pronounced, both spiritual and eternal. If temptations corrupted him, and if he, being in a good condition, did not maintain himself in it, but pass from a good condition to a bad, how can we, by the only liberty of our will, pass into a good one? Are temptations less powerful now than before? Is the devil less vigilant to take all occasions to subvert us? Suppose our wills were not so evil as they are, would it not be more easy for the enemy to draw the will to himself, when it is unresolved between two parts, when the guide of it is so easy clouded, than it was to draw Adam's will to evil from that good to which he might readily have determined himself? Adam had the greatest advantages human nature, in a natural way, was capable of; he was created with a fullness of reason. But how long do we converse with sense, which fastens upon temptations, before we come to a use of reason! After we are come to some smatterings of reason, and a growth in it, as we think, what whisperings and impulses to sin do we feel! What an easiness to embrace incentives, a deafness to contrary admonitions! What languishing, velleities, and palsy desires at best, for that which is good; a mighty mist and darkness upon our understandings, irresolution in our wills? How can we with all these fetters be able of ourselves to put ourselves into a better state, and act against nature, which is impossible any creature can do but by a superior power!

8. Consider man also in the state of corruption.

(1.) If the will of man by nature were the cause of regeneration, it would follow that corruption were a cause of regeneration. 'The imagination of the heart of man is only evil, and that continually,' Gen. vi. 6. That which is evil, therefore, cannot be the cause of that which is man's greatest happiness. All actions are according to those innate qualities and habits which the agent has; all corrupted things act no otherwise than corruptly, because every act has no more in it than what the principle, which is the spring of the action, conveys to it. If the heart, then, be wicked, it cannot do anything but what is wicked, and a wicked act can never be the foundation of regeneration. If a corrupt man, as corrupt, can be the cause of regeneration, then he can act graciously, not only without a gracious habit, but by and from a corrupt habit. If the acts are corrupt, the product of them must be corrupt, for man, in renewing himself, must act either as corrupt or good. If as good, then he was renewed before he set about the renewing himself. The question will then be the same, How came he by that restoration to goodness? If as corrupt, then corruption is the spring of the noblest happiness of the creature. It would then follow that a man can perform acts of life before he lives; that vital acts may be exerted by dead principles; that sanctification can grow up from an unsanctified root; and that the will, with its old corruption, can be the cause of its elevation to another state, and that the old creature can perform a new creature's act before it be a new creature. Then a carnal mind, while it is carnal, may be subject to the law of God, which the Scriptures say it cannot be, Rom. viii. 7. Then those that are in the flesh may please God in an high manner, by the renewing themselves. This would be more strange than if we should see a crab-tree bring forth pomegranates; a corrupt tree would then bring forth good fruit, and that the highest fruit, contrary to our Saviour's assertion, Mat. vii. 18. It would follow that the stony heart would be the cause of the fleshly, and so an effect would rise from a cause quite contrary to it, and the complying principle in man be wrought by the resisting principle. It is as much as if the fire should cool, and the water burn, by their own innate qualities. If the will of man corrupted be the cause of principles of grace, then the old creature brings forth the new. The image of the devil is the cause of producing the divine nature, and hell the cause of an heavenly principle. It would follow that an act of one kind can be produced by an habit of a contrary nature, and that a man can act graciously before he be gracious. Before grace, no action is essentially good, because there wants a gracious principle, whence it must receive its denomination as good. One act, then, of corrupted man, or a multitude of acts, cannot be the cause of grace, because they all centre in that denomination of evil. How the acts of the will, whereof not one can be called good till the will has a good principle, can produce so noble a work and habit as grace is, is not easily intelligible. Our being engrafted into the good olive tree is contrary to nature, Rom. xi. 24. Nature cannot naturally contribute to that which is opposite to it. We are wild by nature, our new implantation is contrary to nature. A good nature, therefore, cannot be the natural effect of a wild nature.

(2.) Since corruption, the power of man is mighty weak in naturals and morals, much more certainly in spirituals.

[1.] In naturals. No natural body that lies under a grievous disease can repair itself by its own power without some external assistance. A wounded member must be beholding to oils and plants for a cure. No man can cast out a disease when he will. He may be sick when he will, by eating that which is contrary to nature; but the cure does not depend upon his will, but upon physic. Outward medicines must recover that which he lost by his own wilfulness. The will indeed is conditio sine qua non; there must be a will to use the means, or a man must be forced to use them, as we deal with madmen and children which are unwilling to take physic. But who ever heard of a man that could cure himself by his own will without the application of medicines? How can the soul then be restored to its vital integrity, by its own force? How can it change its own temper without some superior power operating upon nature? 'Man is like a wild ass's colt,' Job xi. 12. What wild creature ever tamed itself? If any say that the will of man, by the use of outward ordinances, can cure itself, it is answered, Those ordinances are operative, not in a physical but moral way, and therefore such an efficiency as is in plants and drugs cannot be expected from them. There must be an operation of our own wills to make them efficacious. But what shall cure the will where the disease principally lies, and the love of the disease is seated? Who shall remove the beloved inclination from the will? Can nature cast out nature, or Satan cast out Satan? What can make us willing? When we are made willing, the cure is half wrought, as, when a madman is willing to be cured of his infirmity, you can hardly count him any longer mad. The evil principles in the will will never aim at their own destruction. If this work of regeneration were only the curing of a man that were sick or wounded, it could not be done by the power of man's will, but by the application of some external medicine, though nature did concur with it. But it is not a sickness but a death, therefore cannot come under the influence of the will of man in the first work. Shall a man have more power to cure his soul of mortal sins, than to cure his body of mortal wounds?

[2.] In morals. Whence comes that intemperance, incontinence, luxury, which overflows mankind, who are carried to those things which impair health, even in meats and drinks, against the reluctance of reason, whose will is led not by reason but appetite, and choose not like men but beasts, under the notion of pleasant and lustful? Is not this from the will conducted by appetite? The temperance and continence opposite to this is not in Scripture counted part of the extraction of nature, but the gift of God: 1 Cor. vii. 7, 'But every man has his proper gift of God, one after this manner, another after that,' speaking of continence. That which is God's gift is not merely the fruit of human will; for in the apostle's language they seem to be opposed, viz., to be from God, and from ourselves; to be God's gift, and yet our own. In Eph. ii. 8 there is a plain antithesis, 'Not of yourselves: it is the gift of God.' It is the same expression of that moral virtue of continence as it is of the divine grace of faith; 'it is the gift of God.' We are nothing in morals without God, no more than a beam is when the sun is clouded or withdraws its light. Shall we, then, allow a greater power to man in spiritual things than the Scripture does in morals? Shall the one be the gift of God, and the greater the acquisition of nature? Cannot the clay form itself into a vessel of moral honour? Shall it, then, be able to form itself into a vessel of grace? If we are not intrinsically sufficient of ourselves to exercise a morel act, since our natures are so overgrown with corruption, we are less sufficient of ourselves to exercise a supernatural act without a divine motion. Can anything assume an higher nature than what it originally has? Man has assumed a lower nature than that wherein he was created, which no creature besides him in this lower world has. Since he has brutified himself, and cannot moralise himself without common grace, how can he advance himself into a participation of the divine nature without special grace? How can man, so habitually evil, ascend up to an higher nature?

[3.] In this corrupt state of man, any one sin beloved will hold a man down from coming to God. It is impossible for a man, wedded in his heart to his riches, and bemired in earthly confidences, to enter into a renewed gospel state. 'How hard is it,' says our Saviour, 'for them that trust in riches, to enter into the kingdom of God!' Mark x. 24, 25. This one corruption commanding in the heart, will hinder any resurrection by the power of nature, for on man's part Christ pronounces it impossible for such an one to enter into the kingdom of God, ver. 27, that is, into a gospel-state; and that upon the score of this single sin, which only appeared at this time in that young man. The like he pronounces of another sin, that of ambition: John v. 44, 'How can ye believe, which receive honour one of another?' That one fancy of the Jews, of a temporal conquering Messiah, did so possess their brains, that it barred the door against all the power of our Saviour's miracles; and the bare objective proposal of him, though unanswerable by reason, could not remove this rooted fancy. One sin in the will, has more power than any imagination in the fancy. When Adam disfigured his nature by one sin, he had no strength to recover himself, though his righteousness was but very lately fled from him. We need not question his recovery of it, had it been in the power of his will to will it, and the power of his nature to regain it. If one sin, then, in the will, is a bar against the power of nature, what are all those lusts which swarm in the heart of man, and swell up this lake of natural venom in the soul? If one fetter stakes down a man to an impotency and impossibility, how great is man's weakness under all those fetters which every day he loads himself with! One string about a bird's leg will keep it from flying away, much more many.

Arg. 3. Another sort of considerations, is from the state of man under the gospel.

1. If regeneration depended on the will of man, what is the reason more do not receive the gospel than are seen by us to receive it? If the faculty of believing were given to all, then all would believe upon the promulgation of the gospel, because the gospel is 'the power of God to salvation,' Rom. i. 16. If it be the power of God in the outward preaching of it, then all would believe. If all do not believe, then some other secret power attends it, which makes it efficacious in one, not in another; it is 'to them that are saved' only, 'the power of God,' 1 Cor. i. 18; to others, though of great reason, foolishness. If the strength of arguments be the cause in one, what is the reason those arguments have not force upon another? What is that which makes the difference? All men have reason; and what is common reason does conduct all men more or less. If men could open the eyes of their mind to understand the excellency of gospel proposals, what is the reason that among those great multitudes to whom it is preached, so few in all ages have embraced it, though the things proposed are in themselves desirable, and suit so well, in respect of the blessedness promised, to the natural desire of man for happiness! When it was preached by the apostles! it was edged with miracles, attended with a remarkable holiness, yet they complained that few received their report. When in that age, and succeeding ages, men have been so far from receiving it, that they have scoffed at it, persecuted with all their fury the professors of it. It has been thus despised, not only by the meanest and blindest sort of people, but by men of the most elevated understanding among the heathen philosophers, that could pierce into the depths of nature; and by the Jews too, who had the Messiah promised to them, expected him about that time, had so many prophesies deciphering him, which all met with their accomplishment in his person; who were also amazed at the miracles he wrought in his life, and those which accompanied his death. Does not all this show the natural blindness of man, that there is need of some higher power to open his eyes, besides the objective proposal, that he may acknowledge the excellency of those things which are presented to him? Do we not find men ready to acknowledge reason upon other accounts, to be wrought into warm affections by pathetical speeches? Why are they not as ready in this, if it were in the power of their own understandings and wills? Do we not find the wills of men averse from it, though in their consciences they approve of the doctrines of it? What is the reason a man is renewed at one time, and not before, when he has heard the same arguments inculcated many a time? Many drops would not work it before, and one drop works it not in an instant. Is it from the power of reason in man? What reason is there, then, that he should be mastered by one reason now, who was not mastered by the same reason, and many more as strong, formerly? Whence comes that light into the mind? What is the reason such a man was not regenerate before, when he has in some fits meditated upon former arguments, and afterwards one effects it, by a secret insinuation, without any previous meditation, and a sudden turn of the will is wrought? Can this be supposed to be from the will principally? Rather from some divine spirit spreading itself over the soul, and opening the passages of it which were before shut. That place, Mat. xi. 21, where our Saviour speaks of the Tyrians and Sidonians, if the gospel had been preached to them,

they would have repented in sackcloth and ashes, does not prove the power of man to renew himself, but that they would have testified some outward humiliation, as Ahab did at the threatening of Elijah; or rather, Christ exaggerates the hardness of the Jews' hearts in comparing them with the Tyrians in a hyperbolical manner of expression; as we do when we reproach a man for unmercifulness, we say, Had I entreated a Turk or barbarian as much, I should have bent him; not that we commend the humanity of the Turks, but aggravate the cruelty of those we have to do with. The proposal of an object is not sufficient without the inspiration of a will, whereby that concupiscence which masters that faculty may be overpowered.

2. If regeneration were the fruit of man's will, what is the reason that men convinced by the preaching of the gospel, and under great terrors too, find themselves unable to turn to God? What is the reason they are not presently renewed? Would they be torn with such horrors, and bear about them such racks in their consciences? Would they fill heaven and earth with complaints, were it in their own power to make themselves such as God commands them to be? If this were found in the more ignorant sort of people, the reason then might be charged upon their want of knowledge; but men of great wits and insight are filled with those complaints when God begins to rebuke them. And such as have a great deal of grace, as David, when God charges sin upon him: Ps. li. 10, 'Create in me a clean heart; renew in me a right spirit;' why should they solicit God for renewing grace, were it in the power of their own hand? Would any that fear God, as David did, mock him at such a rate, as to desire that of him which they are able to do without him? Were there a natural power in man to turn himself, why did not Judas, after his conscience lashed him, go to his Master's knees to desire pardon, rather than to the gibbet? He had long experience of the merciful disposition of his Master; had not grace given him to incline his will to such an act; yet Peter was turned after his denial of his Master, was there anything more by nature in him than in Judas? Or did Peter do that by the strength of his own will, which Judas did not do? No, the Scripture assures us, it was from the prevalence of Christ's prayer, a secret influence from Christ's look, stirring up that grace that was already in his heart; he might else have gone out cursing his Master as long as he had lived: 'No man can come to me, except the Father draw him,' says our Saviour; though he be convinced, there must be the Father's traction as well as conviction to complete the work. All drawing implies a resistance, or at least a heaviness and indisposition in the thing so drawn, to come of itself. There is much difference between the proposal of the object, and the cause of our entertaining it. The object is the final cause which puts us upon motion; the object moves the will as an end, but it gives no power to move. If a man hear of an alms to be distributed at such a place, and he knows he stands in need of it, and has a desire to go to receive it, this knowledge of the necessity of it will not give him legs to go, if he be lame and unable to go; and he that does go to receive the alms, the desire to receive the alms puts him upon motion; but the intention of receiving the alms was not the efficient cause of that motion. If he had not had strength in him from some other cause than the alms, he could never have gone. Our motion to God must proceed from some higher cause than barely the proposal of the object, and a conviction by it.

4. Argument is drawn from the condition of the regenerate themselves. They are not able to rid themselves of the remainders of sin, much less can natural men of the body of sin. From the impotency after grace, we may rationally conclude a greater weakness in a natural man that has not one spark of grace within, to be blown up from any breathing of grace from without. The flesh lusts against the spirit in a regenerate man; how peaceably does it enjoy its dominion in a natural man, where there is no spirit to control it, and lust against it? Regenerate men 'cannot do the good they would,' and they 'do the evil which they hate,' Rom. vii. 16, 19, though they have a law of grace in their mind, set up in contradiction to the law of sin in their members. How can a natural man then, do so good a thing as the renewal of himself, and the destruction of his sin, who has no will to the one nor hatred of the other, who has the law of sin flourishing in him, and delights to read the characters of it and perform the wills of the flesh! If there be such an inability in a renewed man, who has a relish of God and the goodness of the law, who has sin in part mortified, and cast out of the mind, to the members and suburbs, how much greater must the inability and resistance be when there is nothing but opposing flesh! What need the apostle issue out such heavy complaints: 'O wretched man that I am, who shall deliver me from the body of this death?' Rom. vii. 24, if he had power in his own hands to free himself from this oppressing sin? If Paul, a living tree in God's garden, having both the root and sap of grace, be so wretched, so weak and unable to free himself from those suckers, how wretched then is a dead rotten stake, which has no spiritual root! How can he free himself from a total spiritual death, when this great apostle could not free himself from a partial spiritual death by all that stock of grace already received? If a good man finds it so laborious a task to engage against the relics of nature, and manage an open hostility against the wounded force of his sensual appetite, much more is it a difficult task for a natural man to row against the stream of unbroken nature, when the natural resistance is in its hill strength, and the bent of nature standing point-blank against God. If a well-built and well-rigged ship, with her sails spread, can only lie floating upon the waves, and make no way till a fresh wind fills the sails, surely the rough timber that lies upon the ground can never fit and frame itself into a stately vessel.

5. It is against the whole order which God has set in the world, for any thing to be the cause of itself, or of a higher rank of being than what it has by nature. No effect is nobler than its cause; grace is more noble than nature. A seal cannot convey and other image than what is stamped upon itself, and no further than its own dimensions; neither can nature stamp anything of grace upon the soul, because it has no such image engraver on it by God. Nature, though never so perfect in its own kind, can never produce a thing of higher perfection than itself; a plant can never produce a beast, nor a beast a man, nor a man an angel. No natural quality can be changed in any subject by itself, but by the introduction of some other quality superior to it. The fire can never freeze while it is fire; water cannot part with its coldness without some superior acting upon it; and can those that are naturally bad ever become spiritually good but by an almighty power? No nature can exceed its own bounds, because nothing can exceed itself in acting. Whatsoever a natural man does is but natural, and can never amount to grace, without a change of nature and addition of a divine virtue. If any thing could rise above its own sphere, it would be stronger than itself. Nothing can never make itself something; the best apostle counts himself no better,--2 Cor. xii. 11, 'I am nothing,'--and entitles grace the sole benefactor of all his spiritual good, 2 Cor. xv. 10. What thing ever gave itself its own shape? Every piece of art is brought into figure by the workman, not by itself. Conformity to Christ is a fruit of the election of God, not first of the choice of our own wills. Rom. viii. 29, 'Whom he did foreknow he also did predestinate to be conformed to the image of his Son.' The first link of the chain in the providential and in the gracious administration is in the hands of God. Hence in Scripture the gracious works in the soul run in the passive for the most part: 'Ye are justified, ye are sanctified;' not you justify or sanctify yourselves; though sanctification and purging and working out salvation is ascribed to them that have received grace and life, as acting afterwards for such ends, and producing such effects by the strength of grace received from God, and grace accompanying that first grace in its acts.

As we have proved that man by his own strength cannot renew himself, let us see whether he can do it by his additional capacities.

1. Man, by the help of instituted privileges, does not produce this work of regeneration in himself, without a supernatural grace attending them. Ordinances cannot renew a man, but the arm of God, which does manage them, edges them into efficacy, as the arm that wields the sword gives the blow. Means are the showers of heaven, but they can no more make the heart fruitful till some gracious principles be put in, than the beams of the sun, the dews of heaven, and the water pots of the clouds, can make a barren ground bring forth flowers, without a change of the nature of the soil, and new roots planted in it. All the spectacles in the world cannot cure a man's eyes, he must have a visible faculty to make use of them. Our faculty must be cured before we can exercise it about objects or use means proper to that faculty. All persuasions will not prevail with a dead man; the fairest discourses, the most undeniable arguments, the most moving rhetoric will not stir or affect him, till God take away the stone from the grave and raise him to life. The report of the prophets will do no good without the revelation of God's arm, Isa. liii. 1, because all those things do not work in a physical way, as drugs and plasters, which attain their end without any active concurrence of the patient, but in a moral way; the will therefore and nature must first be charged before those can do any good. You can never by all your teachings teach a sheep to provide for winter, as an ant does, because it has no such instinct in its nature. If any thing were like to work upon a man, the most stupendous miracles were most likely to produce such an effect upon the reasons of men; yet those supernatural demonstrations without a man only cannot make him believe a truth. Miracles are a demonstration to the eye as well as preaching to the ear; though they be confessed to be above the strength of nature, yet all the spectators of them are not believers: John xii. 37, 'But though he had done so many miracles before them, yet they believed not.' Many of those that saw our Saviour's works did not believe his doctrine; nay, they irrationally ascribed them to the devil, when they could find no reason in the nature of them to charge them upon such a score. The raising Lazarus from the dead was as high a miracle as ever was wrought yet, though many of them believed, yet others did not, but accused him to the pharisees, who thereupon more vigorously took counsel to put him to death, John xi. 45, 46, 47, 53, though they acknowledged that he did many miracles. They had reason as well as others; the miracles were undeniable, as being acted before many witnesses; the natural force of them upon all reasons was equal, the considerations arising from them unanswerable. There were evil habits in the will, not removed by grace, which resisted the unanswerable reason of the miracles. What made the difference between them and those that believed? Why did not the wills of the enemies follow the undeniable reason, as well as the wills of others? Miracles may astonish men, but cannot convert them without a divine touch upon the heart. 1 Kings xviii. 39, the people were astonished by that wonderful miracle of fire falling from heaven and consuming the sacrifice, and licking up the water in the trench; and some reverential resolutions were produced in them: they fell upon their faces and said, 'The Lord he is God;' they showed their zeal in taking Baal's prophets, and helping, or at least suffering, Elijah to slay them; yet those people revolted to idolatry, and continued so till their captivity. The easiness of faith upon the apparition and instruction of one risen from the dead was the opinion of one of the damned: Luke xvi. 80, 'If one went to them

from the dead, they will repent;' but this opinion was contradicted by Abraham, ver. 31, who positively asserts, 'If they did not hear Moses and the prophets, they would not be persuaded though one rose from the dead.' If their wills were obstinate against the means God had appointed for their conversion, the same wills so corrupted would be as obstinate against the highest sort of miracles. If that, then, which is above the hand of nature to act, and bears the character of omnipotence upon the breasts of it, does not work upon men's hearts and wills of themselves, surely nature itself cannot turn the heart to God.

The two great dispensations of God are law and gospel; neither of these can of themselves work this.

(1.) The law. The law will instruct, not heal. It acquaints us with our duty, not our remedy; it irritates sin, not allays it; it exasperates our venom, but does not tame it; though it shows man his miserable condition, yet a man by it does not gain one drop of repentance. It tells us what we should do, but corrects not the enmity of our nature whereby we may do it. The apostle takes notice of the enmity of man to the law: Rom. v. 6, 7, 'Yet enemies', 'yet sinners.' That yet may refer to what he had spoken of the law in the chapter before. Though men had had so much time from the fall to recover themselves, and had so many advantages by the law and the ceremonies of it, yet all those years spent from the foundation of the world had produced no other effect than the weakening of them; as creatures that are wounded, by their strugglings waste their own strength. Yet sinners, till this time sinners, whereby the load of sin which lay upon the world was made more heavy by the continual addition made to those heaps. The offence did rather abound by the law than was diminished: Rom. v. 20, 'The law was given that sin might abound.' Though it made a clear discovery of the will of God, yet it rather aggravated sin; it added no power to perform that will. The motions of sin were exasperated by it, ex accidenti, and brought forth fruit unto death; all the means by the law for the repressing of sin did rather inflame it. Sin could not be overcome by it, because the law was 'weak through the flesh;' that is, had not so much power as sin had; it was like a little water put upon fire, which did rather enrage than quell it: Rom. vii. 8, 9, 'Sin revived' when the law came, it had a new life, and the apostle found himself utterly unable to overpower it. There were, ver. 5, 'motions of sin,' "pathemata", not only a power in sin, but an enraged power, which adds to the strength of a person, 'sin slew him: taking occasion by the commandment,' ver. 10, and a dead man is wholly at the disposing of his conquerors. The law was 'holy,' it had an impression of God's holiness upon it, Rom. vii. 12-14, there was also equity and convenience in it, it was 'just and good,' and though these were considerations enough to spur men on to rid themselves of this tyrant sin, yet they could not, they had not strength enough to do it; though it was holy, just, and good, yet it was not strong enough to rescue them; and the reason of it, the apostle lays upon the difference in the nature of both: ver. 14, 'We know that the law is spiritual, but I am carnal, sold under sin;' there was an enmity in his nature to it, and therefore he must lie under the power of it till a mighty deliverer stepped in to conquer it. Do we find any better effect of the ceremonial law, which was the gospel in a mask, and which was the instrument of all the regenerations among the Jews? How few do we find renewed among them under that means which they enjoyed solely, and no other nation in the world partners with them in it! How frequent were their revolts, and rebellions, and idolatries, inconsistent with regeneration, we may read in Joshua and Judges. The inefficaciousness of means appears evidently in that nation which had greater advantages than any in the world besides; the covenants, sacrifices, oracles of God, warnings by prophets, yet so frequently overgrown with idolatry from the time of their coming out of Egypt to the Babylonish captivity; and ten tribes wholly cashiered for it.

(2.) The gospel. Though the veil of ceremonies be taken off from it, and it appears open faced, yet till the veil be taken off the understandings of men, it will produce little fruit among them, 2 Cor. iii. 14. The gospel is plain, but only to him that understands, Prov. viii. 9, as the sun is clear, but only to him that has an eye to see it. The gospel itself cannot remove the blindness from the mind. The proposal of the object works no alteration in the faculty, without some acting on the faculty itself. The beams of the sun shining upon a blind man make no alteration in him. The Jews, to whom the gospel was preached by our Saviour himself, could not believe, because God blinded their eyes, &c., John xii. 39, 40. There must be a supernatural power, besides the proposal of the object, to take away this blindness and hardness which is the obstruction to the work of the gospel. Though the Son of God is come, and the gospel be preached, yet the understanding whereby we know is given us by him: 1 John v. 20, 'And we know that the Son of God is come, and has given us an understanding, that we may know him that is true;' the light of the gospel shines upon all, but all have not an eye given them to see it, and a will given them to embrace it. The mere doctrine of it does not regenerate any man; some have tasted of the heavenly gift, that is, have had some understanding of Christ, who is the heavenly gift, the Son given to us, Isa. ix. 6, and are partakers of some common illumination of the Holy Ghost, yet are not regenerate. Was not the gospel preached to the Jews, even by the mouth of our Saviour whom they crucified? And was it not preached to the Gentiles by the mouths of those apostles whom they persecuted? Were there not proposals that suited the natural desires of men for happiness, yet did not many that seemed to receive it, receive it not in the love of it? If God himself should appear to us in the likeness of a man, and preach to us as he did to Adam, it he did not overpower our hearts with an inward grace, he would do us no good at all by his declarations. We do not read of any work immediately upon Adam at the promulgation of the gospel by God himself, though it appears that afterwards there was, by his instructing his sons to sacrifice, and his expectations of a Messiah. But we certainly know that our Saviour, God manifested in the flesh, declared the gospel in his own person, and found no success but where he touched the heart inwardly by the grace of his Spirit. All mere outward declarations are but suasions, and mere suasion cannot change and cure a disease or habit in nature. You may exhort an Ethiopian to turn himself white, or a lame man to go; but the most pathetical exhortations cannot procure such an effect without a greater power than that of the tongue to cure nature; you may as well think to raise a dead man by blowing in his mouth with a pair of bellows. Judas had enjoyed the best means that ever were, yet went out of the world unrenewed; and the thief upon the cross, who never perhaps was in any good company in his life till he came to the cross, nor ever heard Christ speak before, was renewed by the grace of God in the last hour.

2. Neither can a man renew himself by all his moral works, before faith. Our calling is not according to our works, but 'according to God's own purpose and grace,' 2 Tim. i. 9. Paul, before his conversion, was 'blameless as to the righteousness of the law,' Philip. iii. 6, yet this was loss; a bar rather to regeneration, than a means to further it. For all this legal comeliness he ranks himself, before his conversion, in the number of the dead: Eph. ii. 5, 'When we were dead in sins;' not you, but we, putting himself into the register of the dead. Whatsoever works a man can morally do before faith, cannot be the cause of spiritual life; they are not vital operations; if they were, they were then the effects of life, not the cause; the Scripture makes them the effects of grace: 'created to good works,' Eph. ii. 10. What is an effect cannot be the cause. The best works before grace are but a refined sensuality, they arise from self-love, centre in self-satisfaction, are therefore works of a different strain from those of grace, which are referred to a higher end, and to God's well-pleasing. In all works before grace there is no resignation of the soul to God in obedience; no self-denial of what stands in opposition to God in the heart; no clear view of the evil of sin; no sound humiliation under the corruption of nature; no inward purification of the heart, but only a diligence in an external polishing. All those acts cannot produce an habit of a different kind from them. Let a man be stilted up with the highest natural excellency; let him be taller by the head and shoulders than all his neighbours in morality, those no more confer life upon him than the setting a statue upon an high pinnacle, near the beams of the sun, inspires it with a principle of motion. The increasing the perfection of one species can never mount the thing so increased to the perfection of another species. If you could vastly increase the heat of fire, you could never make it ascend to the perfection of a star. If you could increase mere moral works to the highest pitch they are capable of, they can never make you gracious, because grace is another species, and the nature of them must be changed to make them of another kind. All the moral actions in the world will never make our hearts, of themselves, of another kind than moral. Works make not the heart good, but a good heart makes the works good. It is not our walking in God's statutes materially, which procures us a new heart, but a new heart is in order before walking in God's statutes, Ezek. xxxvi. 27. Our regeneration is no more wrought by works of our own than our justification. The rule of the apostle will hold good in this, as well as in the other: Rom. xi. 6, 'If it be of grace, it is not of works; otherwise grace is no more grace;' and faith is 'the gift of God, not of works, lest any man should boast,' Eph. ii. 9. And the apostle, Titus iii. 5, opposes the 'renewing of the Holy Ghost' to 'works of righteousness.' He excludes works from being the cause of salvation; and would they not be the cause of salvation, if they were the cause of the necessary condition of salvation?

Prop. 3. As man cannot prepare himself to this work, nor produce it, so he cannot co-operate with God in the first production of it. We are no more co-workers with God in the first regeneration, than we were joint purchasers with Christ in redemption. The conversion of the will to God is a voluntary act; but the regeneration of the will, or the planting new habits in the will, whereby it is enabled to turn to God, is without any concurrence of the will. Therefore, say some, we are active in primo actu, but not in primo actus; or we are active in actu exercito, but not in actu signato. Some say, the habit of faith is never created separate from an act, as the trees at the creation of the world were created with ripe fruit on them; but the tree, with the power of bearing fruit, and the fruit itself, were created at one and the same time by God. Yet though the habit be not separate at first from the act, yet there is no co-operation of the creature to the infusion of that habit, but there is to the act immediately flowing from that habit; for either that act of grace is voluntary or involuntary. If involuntary, it is not a gracious act; if voluntary, it must needs be; since the tone of the will is changed, then the creature concurs in that act; for the act of believing and repenting is the act of the creature. It is not God that repents and believes in us; but we repent and believe by virtue of that power which God has given us. In the first act, therefore, there is a concurrence of the creature; otherwise the creature could not be said to repent and believe, but something in the creature, without or against the will of the creature. But in the first power of believing and repenting, God is the sole agent. Jesus Christ is the sun that heals our natures, Mal. iv. 2; the rain that moistens our hearts: Ps. lxxii. 6, 'He shall come down like rain upon the mown grass.' What co-operation is there in the earth with the sun to the production of flowers, but by the softness it has received from the rain? It would else be parched up, and its fruits wither. The Holy Ghost does by his own power make us good trees; but we afterwards, by virtue of that power, work together with him, in bringing forth good fruit. Yet this is also a subordinate, not a co-ordinate working; rather a sub-operation than a co-operation.

1. The state wherein man is at his first renewal excludes any co-working with God. The description the apostle gives of a state of nature excludes all co-operation of the creature in the first renewal: Titus iii. 3, 'For we ourselves were sometimes foolish, disobedient, deceived, serving divers lusts and pleasures, living in malice and envy, hateful, and hating one another.' And Eph. ii. 2, 3, 'Among whom we all had our conversations in time past, in the lusts of our flesh, fulfilling the desires of the flesh and of the mind.' Every man is naturally taken up in the fulfilling the desires of the flesh; not only the Gentiles, to whom Paul writes, but himself; for he puts himself and the rest of the Jews in the number. In the second verse it was 'ye walked;' in ver. 3, it is 'we all;' and in Titus iii. 3, 'we ourselves.' We who had the oracles of God, that had greater privileges than others, were carried out with as strong an impetus naturally, till grace stopped the tide, and after stopping, turned it against nature. When the mind was thus prepossessed, and the will made the lusts of the flesh its work and trade, there was no likelihood of any co-operation with God in fulfilling his desires, till the bent of the heart was changed from the flesh and its principles. The heart is stone before grace. No stone can co-operate with any that would turn it into flesh, since it has no seed, causes, or principles of any fleshly nature in it. Since we are overwhelmed by the rubbish of our corrupted estate, we can no more co-operate to the removal of it, than a man buried under the ruins of a fallen house can contribute to the removal of that great weight that lies upon him. Neither would a man in that state help such a work, because his lusts are pleasures; he serves his lusts, which are pleasures as well as lusts, and therefore served with delight. There is naturally in man a greater resistance against the work of grace, than there is in the natural coldness of water against the heat of the fire, which yet penetrates into all parts of the water.

2. Regeneration is a new principle. What operation can there be before a principle of action? All co-operation supposes some principle of working; as actus secundus supposes actum primum. But a man, before his first regeneration, is blind in his mind, perverse in his will, rebellious in his affections, unable to know the truth, unable to do good, dead in sin. If he does co-operate with God before the habit be settled, then we can act before we have a power to act. We can please God in taking his part, and joining issue with him, before we have a gracious principle; which is contrary to the Scripture, which tells us we are first begotten of God before we can keep ourselves, or exert one act for the bettering ourselves: 1 John v. 18, 'He that is begotten of God keeps himself.' The preservation of ourselves, and every act tending thereto, follows the infusion of the first principle. And the apostle Paul implies, that God works in us to will before we work: Philip. ii. 12, 13, 'Work out your own salvation with fear and trembling; for God works in you both to will and to do,' &c. The apostle supposes not any operation in them before, because he supposes not their working without God's giving them a will, the act of volition. The working of the creature supposes some divine work first upon the will. Did the dust of the ground, whereof Adam's body was formed, co-work with God in figuring it into a body? or does the body contribute any more than a passive receptivity to the infusion of the rational soul? Lazarus did not concur with Christ till his powerful voice infused life and strength into him. His rising and walking was from a power conveyed, wherein Christ did work; but there was no co-working in him in the conveyance of that power. We do not say that a man co-works with the sun in enlightening a room, because he opens the shuts which barred out the light; the opening whereof is no cause of the sun's shining, but a conditio sine qua non. But do we so much in the first renewal? It is God alone who darts his beams, and opens our hearts too, to admit it: Acts xvi. 14, it is said, 'the Lord opened Lydia's heart.' The will cannot concur in the actual infusion of a gracious principle, because it has no spark in itself by nature, suitable to that principle which is bringing it into the soul itself. The shining of God into the soul is compared to the chasing away that darkness which at the first creation was over the face of the deep: 2 Cor. iv. 6, 'For God, who commanded the light to shine out of darkness, has shined in our hearts, to give the light of the knowledge of the glory of God.' What co-working was there in that darkness to remove itself, but a necessity upon it to obey the command of God who had the sovereign power over his own works? If the creature did co-work with God at first, it could no more be said to be dead than a man asleep may be said to be dead; and grace were only an awakening, not an enlivening.

3. If there were any co-working of the will with God in the first infusion of grace, God would not be so much the author of grace as he is of nature in any other creature. The creature would share with him in the first principle of its action, which no creature in the world can be said to do. It would rather be a concourse of God than a creation; but all the terms whereby God sets forth himself in the work of regeneration import more than a bare concourse or a co-operation with the creature: ' I will take away the heart of stone; I will write my law in their hearts; I will put my Spirit into them,' are loftier expressions than are used to signify a co-working only. He appropriates the whole work to himself, without interesting the creature in any active concurrence, any more than at his creation.

4. If the will of man did co-work with God in regeneration, it would then share part of the glory of God. The whole glory would not belong to God, which he challenges to himself in Scripture. He were then but an half Saviour, an half new creator. We should be in joint commission with him, by the power of our own wills, in the first motion. If creation and resurrection are acts of an almighty power, man co-operating with him in the very act of creation and resurrection would partake with God's almightyness, and in some sort be co-equal with him, and a joint partner with God in a work which required almightyness for the effecting it. Surely since the same power which raised Christ from the dead works first in every believer for his spiritual resurrection, he contributes no more to it than the body of Christ in the grave did to its resurrection, which was a work not of his humanity, but divinity. Plucking out of the power of Satan is an effect of the power of grace, and God's gift, 2 Tim. ii. 25, 20. God first 'gives repentance, that they may recover themselves out of the snare of the devil.' A slave, whose hands and feet are laden with fetters, can contribute nothing to his deliverance but a will and desire to be delivered; nor that, if he be in love with his fetters, which is the case of every one of us by nature, who are as fond to be in the devil's custody as he is to have us. What co-operation can there be in this ease? Whatsoever is an act of mercy, and an act of truth in God, he is to have the sole praise of; it does not in any sort belong to the creature. The psalmist emphatically excludes man from it: Ps. cxv. 1, 'Not unto us, O Lord, not to us, but unto the name give glory, for thy mercy, and for thy truth's sake.' Not unto us, twice repeated, but to thy name give glory. Do believers beg of God the giving glory to himself, and not unto them; and will they contradict their prayers, by sharing the praise with God? This is expressed for deliverances. Much less does any praise and glory belong to the creature for the most excellent deliverance of all, from the power of sin, Satan, and death.

5. How can men co-work with God in the first regeneration, when they must needs acknowledge that in the progress of it they are oftener hinderers than furtherers of it? If God did not work more strongly in us than the best of us do in ourselves, and breathe a willingness into our wills, after regeneration, we should come short of salvation for all the first stock. How often do the best complain of their disability! Is it not frequent in the mouths of Christians in all ages as well as of Paul: Rom. vii. 18, 'To will is present with me, but how to perform that which is good I find not'? How easily are our purposes shaken, and our strength staggers! Can we then co-operate with God, when we have no purpose, no strength? Let every man's experience speak for himself, how apt he is to check the motions of the Spirit; to let our Saviour stand and knock, and not open. What strugglings of the body of death! What indispositions in an holy course! Is there not often a kind of rustiness of soul, cold damps in spiritual duties? What faint hands in any holy work! What ebbs and floods, ups and downs in his heart! What feeble knees in his walk! What hung-down heads in laying hold of Christ in repeated acts of faith! What frequent returns of spiritual lethargies! And all this after habitual grace. If our co-operations with God after grace received, are but a remove from non-acting, next neighbours to no working at all, we must conclude it to be worse with man before grace was settled in the soul, and that there was no active concurrence with it in any manner of acting; otherwise there would be as much co-operation before the implantation of habitual grace as after, which is hard to be imagined, that a man should be no stronger with grace received than under the want of it.

Prop. 4. Man by his own strength cannot actuate grace after it is received. To what purpose did the saints of old pray to quicken them, if they stood not in as much need of exciting grace from God as of renewing grace: Ps lxxx. 18, 'Quicken us, and we will call upon thy name;' Ps. cxix. 25, 27 and many places in that psalm. The new creature is little better than an infant in the best, and cannot go unless God bear it in his arms, as he speaks of Ephraim, Hosea xi. 1, 3. They cannot move unless led by the Spirit. The child has a principle of motion in it, but cannot go without the assistance of the nurse; nor the soul, without the assistance of God, actuate that principle of grace. Habitual grace is the instrument, not the principal agent. A sword, though it has an edge, cuts nothing till it be moved by some strong arm. The first principle of the motion of grace resides in God. Purification in its progress is attributed to faith as an instrument, but to God as a principal agent. It is said, Acts xv. 8, 9, 'God gave them the Holy Ghost, as he did to us, and put no difference between us and them, purifying their hearts by faith.' Yet the will of man concurs in this actuating of faith, as a subordinate cause: 1 John iii. 3, a man is said to 'purify himself by hope.' A well-rigged soul, with its habit of grace spread, as well as a ship with its sails, must wait the leisure of the wind before it move. Paul acknowledges his acting for the service of God to be not from himself principally: 1 Cor. xv. 10, 'Yet not I, but the grace of God which was with me.' It was the grace of God used me as an instrument; the glory must not stick to my fingers; it was the grace of God with me, affording strength and help to that grace which was in me. If this concourse of God be necessary in all natural actions, it is much more in the spiritual frame of the soul to keep it up, and to keep it acting. It is not we that work to will and to do, but God works to will and to do. It is to be considered that the apostle writes to them that are in a state of grace, exhorting them to a progress in salvation depending upon God, who worlds the after will and the alter doing, as well as the first will and compliance with the grace of God. Do we not find renewed men not able, with all the grace they have, to quicken themselves sometimes in duty? What is the reason they lie spiritless before God, often with breathings, sighs, and groans for quickening, and it is far from them? They stir themselves up, meditate, summon up all the powerful considerations they can, yet find themselves empty of a spiritual vigour. Surely there is some principal power wanting to spirit their grace, and make them leap in duty; some invisible strength has withdrawn itself, which did before conduct and breathe upon them, and fill their souls with a divine fire. They find it not in the power of the hand of their own will to actuate and quicken the grace they have, much less is it in the power of any man's hand to renew himself. The work of grace is not only a traction at the first, but a continual traction, as conservation is a continual creation: 'Draw me, and we will run after thee,' Cant. i. 4. The church there speaks it as regenerate, desiring a continual traction from God, as the first ground of her race after Christ. Life she had, for she promises to run; yet this race she could not begin nor continue, without traction from God.

Prop. 5. Man cannot by the power of his own will preserve grace in himself. Our Saviour's prayer to his Father, John xvii. 11, 15, to 'keep them,' imports, that they were too weak to keep themselves: 'Unless the Lord keep the city, in vain does the watchman wake,' Ps. cxxvii. 1. Unless God preserve the soul, all the watchfulness of habitual grace will be to little purpose. All creatures, if God hide his face, are troubled, Ps. civ. 29, much more the new creature, whose strength does more necessarily depend upon God, because of its powerful opposites. Were it not for the assisting grace of God, the unruly lusts in our hearts would soon bear down habitual grace in the best. How many temptations are prevented which we cannot foresee! How many corruptions are restrained, which the best grace cannot fully conquer! How is the tide and torrent of these waters beaten back, which otherwise would go over our heads! The poor will of Adam preserved him not against a temptation, when he had no indwelling corruption to betray him; nor did the will of the angels, who had no temptation, keep them from forsaking their habitation. How can any renewed man, alive with all his grace, merely by the strength of his own will, keep himself from sinking down in the lake of his old corruption? He that would ask the fallen angels in the midst of their torments, what was the reason of their fall, would receive no other answer but that their strength was unsuccessful, because it depended upon their own will. The knowledge of the gospel and evangelical impressions are never like to keep up without the Holy Ghost: 2 Tim. i. 14, 'That good thing which was committed unto thee, keep, by the Holy Ghost,' not by thine own strength. It we cannot keep a form of sound words, which, as it is knowledge, is more agreeable to the natural appetite of man, without the Holy Ghost, much less can we preserve grace in us, which is more stomached by corrupt nature. Neither are good frames like to be preserved in us without God's keeping: 1 Chron. xxix. 18, 'keep this in the imagination of the thoughts of the heart of thy people.' Our hearts will not let any good motion sink into them, unless God give a pondus to his own motion. If, then, regenerate men are unable of themselves to actuate and preserve grace received, much more inability is there in a natural man to gain that which he has not a

spark of in his own nature, but an enmity to.

Quest. But, do you divest man of all power, all freedom of will? Is he able to do nothing in order to regeneration?

Ans. We do not divest man of all power; therefore, before we consider what power belongs to man, we may consider,

(1.) Man simply in his fall. So man lost all his natural ability by his first sin, and was the meritorious cause of his losing supernatural grace, which God by a judicial act removed from him, and in this state man had no ability unto anything morally good. Nothing was due to Adam but the state of the devils, who have no affection to anything morally good, but always do that which is in its own nature evil, and always sin with evil intentions. Adam would have been thus, had the threatening, according to the tenor of it, been executed; there had been no common affections, no more light in his understanding than what might have served for his torment, as wicked men, after death, are deprived in a judicial way of that light in their minds, those velleities and good motions which sometime hovered in them, those affections which were here exercised now and then towards God. The sentence given against Adam is then pronounced against them, and they laid under the final execution of it, which was to die the death: Gen. ii. 17, 'Thou shalt surely die,' a death of all morality, all affections to anything that has the resemblance of goodness. It might be a prediction of what would be in course, as well as what would be inflicted in way of judicial recompense. None of these things can be looked for in Adam, or any of his posterity, as fallen; not a grain of life, or anything tending that way, was due to him, but only death.

(2.) Man is to be considered as respited from the present suffering this sentence by the intervention of Christ; whereby he is put into another way of probation. So those common notions in our understandings, and common motions in our wills and affections, so far as they have anything of moral goodness, are a new gift to our natures by virtue of the mediation of Christ. In which sense he may be said to 'taste death for every man,' Heb. ii. 9, and be 'a propitiation for the sins of the whole world.' By virtue of which promised death, some sparks of moral goodness are preserved in man. Thus his 'life was the light of men;' and he is 'The light that lightens every man that comes into the world,' which sets the candle of the Lord in the spirit of man a-burning and sparkling, John i. 9, and upholds all things by his mediatory as well as divine power, Heb. i. 3, which else would have sunk into the abyss. By virtue of this mediation, some power is given back to man, as a new donation, yet not so much as that he is able by it to regenerate himself; and whatsoever power man has, is originally from this cause, and grows not up from the stock of nature, but from common grace.

Which common grace is either,

[l.] More general, to all men. Whereby those divine sparks in their understandings, and whatsoever is morally praiseworthy in them, is kept up by the grace of God, which was the cause that Christ tasted death for every man: Heb. ii. 9, 'That he by the grace of God should taste death for every man;' whereby the apostle seems to intimate, that by this grace, and this death of Christ, any remainders of that honour and glory wherewith God crowned man at first are kept upon his head; as will appear, if you consider the eighth Psalm, whence the apostle cites the words which are the ground of his discourse of the death of Christ.

[2.] More particular common grace, to men under the preaching of the gospel. Which grace men 'turn into wantonness' or lasciviousness, Jude 4. Grace they had, or the gospel of grace, but the wantonness of their nature prevailed against the intimations of grace to them. Besides this common grace, there is a more special grace to the regenerate, the more peculiar fruit of Christ's mediation and death for them. All this, and whatsoever else you can conceive that has but a face of comeliness in man, is not the birth of fallen nature abstracted from this mediation. Therefore when the Gentiles are said to 'do by nature the things contained in the law,' it is not to be understood of nature merely as fallen, for that could do no such thing; but of nature in this new state of probation, by the interposition of Christ the mediator, whose powerful word upheld all things, and kept up those broken fragments of the two tables of law, though dark and obscure. And considering God's design of setting forth the gospel to the world, there was a necessity of those relics, both in the understanding, and affections, and desire for happiness, to render men capable of receiving the gospel, and those inexcusable that would reject it. So that by this mediation of Christ, the state of mankind is different since the fall from that of the evil angels or devils. For man has, just, a power of doing that which is in its own nature good; secondly, a power of doing good with a good intention; not indeed supremely for the glory of God, but for the good of his country, the good of his neighbours, the good of the world, which was necessary for the soldering together human societies, so that sometimes even in sins man has good intentions. Whereas the devil does always that which in its own nature is evil, and always sins with evil intentions. Without this mediation, every man had been as very a slave to sin as the devil; though he be naturally a slave to sin, yet not in that full measure the devil is, unless left in a judicial manner by God upon high provocations.

There is then a liberty of will in man; and some power there is left in man. And here I shall show,

1. What kind of liberty this is.

2. That there is some liberty in man.

3. How far the power of man by common grace does extend.

Quest. First, what kind of liberty this is.

Ans. 1. The essential liberty of the will remains. Liberty is of the essence of the will, and cannot be taken away without extinction of the nature of man; it is free from compulsion, otherwise it were a not-will, which liberty does not consist in a choice of good or evil. For even under this depravation it cannot choose evil qua malum, as such. It can choose nothing but what appears to it under the notion of good; though it many times embraces that which is materially evil, yet the formal consideration upon which it embraces it is as good, either in reality or in appearance; as the sight in every colour sees light. And when it is carried out to that which is really evil, and only apparently good, it is by force of those habits in the understanding, which make it give a false judgment; or, by the power of the sensitive appetite, which hurries it on to the object proposed, but always it respects in its motion everything as good, either an honest, pleasant, or profitable good.

Ans. 2. Though the essential liberty of the will remains, yet the rectitude whereby it might have been free only to that which was really good is lost. Man by creation had a freedom of will to choose that which was really good, yet had a mutability, and could choose evil; and by choosing evil rather than good, sank his posterity into this depraved liberty which now remains. Though since the fall man is preserved in his natural freedom, and cannot be forced, yet he has not a power to will well, because that righteous principle whereby he did will well is departed from him; yet because the essential freedom due to his nature remains, whatsoever he wills he wills freely, so that though something the will wills may be materially good, yet it wills that good in an ill manner, for being overcome naturally by sin man can do nothing but according to that law which sin, as a master that has conquered him, imposes upon him: 2 Peter ii. 19, 'They themselves are the servants of corruption: for of whom a man is overcome, of the same is he brought in bondage.' And of all men in a state of nature, though under common grace, the apostle pronounces, Rom. iii. 11, that 'there is none that seeks after God;' that is, in any thing they do, though never so good, they seek not God but themselves. 'There is no fear of God,' no respect to God 'before their eyes,' ver. 18, whence it comes to pass, that by reason of this dominion of sin nothing can be done well. Hence man is said to be dead; not that the life which does constitute the nature of the soul is taken away, but that which renders it fit for performing actions pleasing to God; for such a life does consist, not in the nature of the soul or will, but in that habitual integrity which was in man by creation. As the body when it is dead does not cease to be a body, but ceases to be animated, by the separation of the soul from it, so the soul may be truly said to be dead, though the power of the soul be not taken away. If the spiritual rectitude in that power which did constitute it spiritually living be departed, by the removal of this righteousness, the will is not free to spiritual things, though it be to natural. It is 'free among the dead,' as the psalmist speaks of himself; Ps. lxxxviii. 5; free to dead works, not to living; to this or that dead work, to any work within the verge of sinning, as a bird in a large cage may skip this way and that way by its natural spontaneous motion, but still within the cage.

Ans. 3. Therefore, though man has lost this liberty to good, he retains a freedom to the commission of sin, under the necessity of sinning. This freedom is a power of choice and election of a thing, which differs from that spontaneity which is in beasts, who act by instinct, without any reasoning in the case, because they want a reasoning power. Though man be under a necessity of sinning, yet it is not a necessity of constraint, but a necessity of immutability, which is consistent with liberty, though the other be not. A creature may be unchangeably carried to good or evil, and yet be free in both: to good, as the angels and glorified saints cannot will to sin, because their wills are immutably determined to good. They cannot but praise and love God, yet they freely do both, and our Saviour did freely do that good which he could not but do by reason of his hypostatical union, otherwise he could not have merited, for all merit requires the concurrence of the will. To evil; the devils cannot will to do good, because their wills are unchangeably determined to evil, yet they sin as freely as if there were no immutable necessity upon them. So man cannot but naturally sin in all that he does yet he is not constrained to sin, but sins as freely and voluntarily as if there were no necessity upon his nature to corruption,--as freely as if God had not foreseen that he would do so. Man sins with as great a pleasure as if he were wholly independent upon the providence of God, and the more a man is delighted with sin, the greater freedom there is in it. Hence the Scripture lays sin upon the choice of man: Isa. lxvi. 3, 4, 'They have chosen their own ways, and their soul delights in their abominations.' They have their own ways, that is, ways proper to corrupt man; but they chose them and delighted in them. Man is voluntary under his depravation, free in his aversion from God, a free necessity, a delightful immutability. The will cannot be compelled to will that which it would not, or not to will that which it would. Then sin arises from a settled habit, the freer is a man in his sin; and though he cannot act otherwise than according to that habit, yet his actions are most voluntary, because he is the cause of that habit which he acquired by evil acts, and by succeeding acts testifies his approbation of it.

2. That there is some liberty in man, some power in man. Not indeed such a power as the Jews thought man had naturally, of exercising himself about anything that God should reveal, without the infusion of a new power, to enable him to act that which God required by supernatural revelation. Some power and liberty must be allowed,

(1.) To clear the justice of God. No just man will punish another for not doing that which was simply and physically impossible; and 'shall not the Judge of all the earth do right?' It is a good speech of Austin, If there were not the grace of God, how could the world be saved? If there were not free will, how could the world be judged? If man were divested of all kind of liberty, he might have some excuse for himself; but since the Scripture pronounces men without excuse, Rom. i. 20, some power must be granted to clear the equity of God's justice. No man sins in that which he is under an inevitable constraint to do, and so would be unjustly punished. It does not appear that God does condemn any man simply for not being regenerate, but for not using the means appointed to such an end, for not avoiding those sins which hindered his regeneration, and which might have been avoided by him if he would, though indeed every unregenerate man will be condemned. The pouring out the wrath of God upon man is principally for those sins which they might have refrained, and had sufficient reason against: Eph. v. 6, for 'because of these things,' that is, for those gross sins which they might have avoided, mentioned ver. 5, 'comes the wrath of God upon the children of disobedience,' "apeithias"; men that would not be persuaded, which obstinacy was in their will. As these are the causes of God's wrath, so these will be alleged as the principal reasons of the last sentence. And our Saviour in his last judgment does not charge men with their unregeneracy, but with their omissions of what they might have done, and that easily; and commissions which they might have avoided, Mat. xxv. 41-43, with their not feeding his members when they were hungry, &c., which were things as much in their power as anything in the world. And the reason Christ renders of the sentence passed upon men, to depart from him, was their working of iniquity: Mat. vii. 23, 'Depart from me, you that work iniquity,' that work it voluntarily, and work that you might have forborne. Though unregeneracy does exclude a man from heaven, as a condition without which a man cannot come there, yet nothing of this is mentioned in the last sentence. If man had a firm will to turn to God, and had not then a power conferred upon him to turn, I know not what to say; but man has no will to turn, yea, he has no will to do those things which he might do. Supposing man has a power to avoid such and such sins, he is justly punished for not making use of that power. Nay, supposing he had no power to avoid them, yet if his will be set to that sin he is justly condemned, not for want of power, but for the delight his will took in it. From which delight in it, it may be gathered that if he had had a power to have shunned it, he would not have shunned it. If a man be assaulted by murderers that will cut his throat, if he will not use his power against them, but take a pleasure in having his throat cut, is not this man a self-murderer, both in the judgment of God and man? Let me use another illustration, since the end of all our preaching should be to humble man and clear God. If a man be cast out of an high tower, and be pleased with his fall, would he not be justly worthy of it, and to be neglected by men, not because he did not help himself in his fall, for that was not in his own power, but because he was mightily pleased and contented with his fall, and with such a pleasure, that if he had been able to have helped himself he would not? So though man be fallen in Adam, yet when he comes to discern between good and evil, he commits the evil with pleasure. So that supposing he had no power to avoid sins, yet he is worthy of punishment because he does it delightfully. Whence it may be concluded, if he had had power to avoid it, he would not, because his will is so malignant.

(2.) Without some liberty in the will, free from necessity of compulsion, man would not be capable of sin, nor of moral goodness. No human law does impute that for a vice, or a virtue, to which a man is carried by constraint, without any power to avoid. Where anything is done without a will, it is not an human action. Beasts therefore are not capable of sin, because they want reason and will. If man had not liberty of will, he would be as a beast, which has only a spontaneous power of motion without reason. Sin could not be charged upon man, as God does all along: Ps. xcv. 10, 'It is a people that do err in their hearts;' and Ps. cxix. 21, 'Thou hast rebuked the proud that are cursed, which do err from thy commandments.' It had been no error in them, if they had not done it voluntarily. The erring from God's commandments arises from pride of heart, they had not else deserved a rebuke. Who would chide a clock for going wrong, which has no voluntary motion? Man without a liberty of will could not be the author of his own actions, and sin could no more be imputed to him, than the irregular motion of a watch can be imputed to the watch itself, but rather to the workman or governor of it. Without a voluntary power, man would be as all engine, moved only with springs, and human laws, which punish any crime, would be as ridiculous as Xerxes' whipping the sea, because it would not stop its tide. Neither were any praise due to man for any moral virtue, no more than praise is due to a lifeless picture for being so beautiful, or to the limner's pencil for making it so: the praise is due to the artist, not to the instrument.

(3.) Without some liberty and power of motion in the will, all the reason of man, and those notions in the understanding, left by the virtue of Christ's mediatory interposition, would be to no purpose. The reason why men do err is because they do not take right ways of judging according to those means they have: 'Ye err,' says our Saviour, 'not knowing the Scripture, nor the power of God,' Mat. xxii. 29. They have a faculty of judgment, and means whereby to judge, which would prevent errors. There is therefore some suitable power in man to follow the judgment of reason, if he will. He would be in vain endowed with that power of reasoning, if there were not a power of motion in some measure suitable to that reason. The authority of judging in the understanding would be wholly insignificant; all debates about any object proposed would be to no end, if the will had not a liberty to follow that judgment. How can God make appeals to men as he does, if they had not a power of judging that they ought to have done otherwise, and might have done otherwise than they did? Though man has not a sufficient light left in his nature for salvation, yet he has such a light of reason in him to which he might be more faithful than he is, otherwise the apostle could not have argued from that light the heathens had to their conviction, as he does, Rom. i. 19-21, &c., and manifests their unfaithfulness to that truth which God had manifested to them, and manifested in them in their nature. Most sins do arise from the neglect of being guided by that light which is in men.

(4.) The glory of God's wisdom in the government of the world would not have been so conspicuous, if some liberty had not been allowed to the will. It is no great matter to keep in order an inanimate thing, as a clock that must obey a necessity; God would have been but like a good clock-keeper only, as ones says. But how much does it make for the wisdom of God, to make the free motions of his creature, the various humours in the will of man, centre at last in his own glory, contrary to the will and design of the creature, that they have their natural motions, their voluntary motions, and God superintends over them, and moves them according to his own will regularly, according to their nature, without crossing them? 'The determinate counsel of God,' in the death of our Saviour, and the free will of Pilate and the Jews, meet in the same point: God acting wisely, graciously, justly; their wills acting freely and naturally, reduced, without injury to their nature, to the due point of God's will.

Quest. 3. The third question, How far does the power of man by common grace extend?

Ans. As in a body deprived of the soul there is some power of growth left in the hair and nails, so some power is left in the soul, though it be spiritually dead. As a regenerate man by special grace has a power of doing that which is spiritually good, so a natural man by common grace has a power of doing things morally good, if he will. God keeps the key of regenerating grace in his own hands, and unlocks what hearts he pleases, and brings in a vital spirit into whom he pleases; but there is by common grace an ability in men to do more than they do, but that they harbour, cherish, and increase those vicious inclinations in their own souls. But let it be remembered that this power is not to be abstracted from God's common grace, as the power of a renewed man after grace is not to be abstracted from special grace, nor the natural powers of motion to the actual motion, not to be abstracted from God's general providential concourse.

(1.) Man has a power by common grace to avoid many sins: I say, a power by common grace; for sometime, upon the neglecting the conduct of natural light, God pulls up the sluice of his restraining grace, lets out the torrent of their natural corruption upon them, which forcibly hurries them to all kind of wickedness; as it is said, Rom. vii. 24, 26, 'Wherefore God also gave them up to uncleanness, through the lusts of their own hearts; for this cause God gave them up to vile affections.' Therefore, and for this cause, that is, for going contrary to that natural light they had, God let the lusts of their own hearts, which he had restrained, have their full swing against them. In this case sin can no more be avoided, than a man can stop a torrent.

Again; though a man, as he is in a state of nature, cannot but do evil, yet he is not necessitated to this or that kind of sin, but he may avoid this or that pro hic and nunc in particular, though he cannot in general; as a man who has the liberty of walking where he pleases in a prison, he may choose whether he will come into this or that walk within the liberty of the prison; but let him move which way he will, he is a prisoner still.

Quest. If it be said, if a man has power to avoid this or that sin, why may he not avoid all?

Ans. I answer, If he had power to avoid all, he would be restored to the state of Adam. But the reason is this, the power to avoid this or that particular sin arises from a particular cause, the natural subjection of appetite to reason, the lightness of temptation; or if the temptation be more vehement, the stirring up reason and pressing considerations against it; but the power to shun all sin depends upon the subordination of the faculties one to another, in the due order of their creation, and an universal subjection of them to God. Though a man, by a careful watch, may withstand a particular temptation, yet as long as he is alienated from God, and has corrupt habits in him, which are prone to sinful acts, he will one time or other, by some sudden temptation, be carried out according to his natural inclination, before he is able to premeditate, and set reason on work. And sometimes the motions to sin come in such troops, that he cannot stir up his force against all, so that while he is combating against one, another comes behind and surprises him. As another Romanist illustrates it, a vessel has three holes to leak at; a man with two hands may stop two of them, which he will, but the third will remain open of necessity. None will say that the devil can avoid all sin in general, and become holy for the future, because his will is determined to sin, but this or that individual act of sin he may; for he may choose whether he will assault this man or that with such a temptation, or whether at this time or another. As if two commands were given to the good angels, and it be left to their wills whether they will do that or the other, though they cannot but do good, because their wills are so determined, yet they have a liberty to choose which command they will at present follow. And the reason of this is this: there is no physical necessity upon a man to this or that sin, as there is that the fire should burn. Lusts only offer themselves; they have no force upon a man, but be his own will; they have no authority from God to compel him; then God should be the author of sin. Satan can give no commission to them to break open our hearts; and though he be a strong adversary, he cannot break them open. If the door be open, it is our own act. Is there any necessity upon a man to run into this or that infectious company, or drink brimful cups, till he has drowned both his reason and sentiments of morality? Has he not power to quell many incentives to sin? Show me that man in the world that, upon serious consideration, would say, it is utterly impossible for him to avoid this or that particular sin when he is tempted to it. What men do in this case, they do willing, though a strong temptation may be the first motive of it. It is said, Hos. v. 11, 'Ephraim willingly walked after the commandment,' though the first motive to it was the command of their prince Jeroboam.

To evidence this, let me do it by some queries, which may both satisfy that we divest not man of all power, and prevent the ill use men may make of this doctrine, to encourage sluggishness.

1. Cannot you avoid this or that foreseen occasion of sin? Cannot he that knows how prone he is to overthrow his reason when the wine sparkles in the glass, avoid coming within the sight of it? What force is there upon his legs to go, or his hands to take the cup? Can we not starve those affections we have to this or that particular sin, by neglecting the means to feed them? If a man stood by with a drawn sword to stab you if you went into such a place, could you not forbear going in? What is the reason? Fear. And why might not a natural fear of God, heightened by consideration, be of as much force with you as the fear of man, unless atheism has swallowed up all sentiments of a Deity? Do you not rather wish for opportunities, and court a temptation? put you heads out of the window, with Sisera's mother; why is the chariot of the devil so long a coming? It is said, Prov. xxi. 10, 'The soul of the wicked desires evil.'

2. Have you not a power to avoid gross sins? Is there any force upon men, to open, sensual sins? Have they not a power to abstain from fleshly lusts? Has not the will a commanding power over the members? What hinders it from exercising that power? The members are not forced, but they are

'yielded up' by consent of the will to sin, Rom. vi. 19. Had not Achan as much natural power to forbear taking the wedge of gold and the Babylonish garment, as the rest of that vast number of the Israelites? Not one of their hands touched any of the spoil. Had he not as much power as any of them to have restrained his hands, though he could not quench his covetousness? The law of nature tells us, we ought not to do that to another which we would not have done to ourselves. Have we not as much power to observe this as the Gentiles, who did by nature the things contained in the law? Why may not a man's will command his tongue to speak that which is true, as well as that which is false? Is there not power to control it from speaking blasphemy, and belching out cursed oaths? Cannot you command the hand to forbear striking another wrongfully? Has not a murderer power to keep his sword in his scabbard, as well as to sheath it in his neighbour's bowels? Can any man say, that there was one gross sin in the whole coarse of his life, but he had a power to avoid it if he would? Forbearance of gross sin consists in a naked omission and a not acting, which is far more easy than a positive acting, and every man has a power to suspend his own act.

3. Did you never resist a temptation to a particular sin? Why may you not then resist it afterward if you will, since the same common grace attends you? If the will be disengaged one moment from a sin under a great temptation, why not another moment from sin, under a less temptation? No temptation can overpower your strength, unless the will freely shake hands with it: Acts v. 3, 'Why has Satan filled thy heart, to lie to the Holy Ghost?' His meaning is not, why Satan has done it, for Ananias could not render a reason of that; but why did thou suffer Satan to fill thy heart? If you have given a check to Satan before, is it not as easy to say again, 'Get thee behind me, Satan'?

4. Have you not power to shun many inward sins? Man, where he has least power, yet he has some, viz. over his thoughts. We cannot, indeed, hinder the first risings and motions of them, which will steam up from the corrupt fumes and lake whether he will or no; but cannot we hinder the progress of them? Is there not a power to check the delight in them if we will, or divert our thoughts another way, not listen to their suggestions, and hold no inward converse with them? Though you cannot hinder their intrusion, may you not hinder their lodging? 'How long shall vain thoughts lodge within you?' Jer. iv. 14. Sure we have a power by common grace to forbear any conference with the motions of flesh and blood.

5. When you do sin, had you not many assistances against it, which if you had hearkened to, you might have avoided it? Were there not previous dissuasions from that inward monitor, conscience? When sin has been enticing you on one hand, and conscience warning you on the other, have you not more willingly listened unto the pleasant reasoning of sin, than the wholesome admonitions of conscience? Can you not as well listen to what conscience as to what sin does propose? But have you not wilfully scorned its judgment? Have you not raged against it with a confidence in sin (which is the case of the foolish sinner, Prov. xiv. 16, 'The fool rages, and is confident'), and would 'not consider any of the ways of God' it minded you of, Job xxxiv. 27, and gave no more regard to its sober dictates, or its louder pressings, than you have to the barking of little curs in the street? Why could you not, with those assistances, have avoided that particular act of sin? The fault was clearly in your wills. Can you not rather choose a cup of wine, than a cup of poison? clear streams, than muddy waters? Besides those assistances, you might have had more, if under the batteries of temptation you had sought to heaven for them. Might you not, then, have avoided this or that sin, when you had such assistances, and might have had more?

6. Have you not avoided sin upon less accounts and considerations? The heathen philosopher could observe, that men may live better than they do. The wrestlers and champions in the Olympic games lived most temperately and continently during that time, to be more fit for the gaining the prize. May not rational considerations do as much, if excited in your minds, as an ambitious desire of honour and affection to victory did in them? Had not Saul a power to withdraw his hand from the unrighteous persecution of David before, as well as when he was sensible of David's kindness in sparing his life when he might have killed him? A drunkard under the disease and pain caused by his sin, can forbear his cups; does his disease confer any power upon him more than he had before? No; why could he not then have forborne his drunken revellings? Can men be restrained from some sins by the eye of a man, the presence of a child? What power do their eyes confer upon them? They only excite that which they had before. Cannot men forbear a sinful act for a sum of money if it were proffered them or in the presence of a king, who is said to 'scatter away evil with his eyes,' Prov. xx. 8, or in a visible and imminent danger? If a gibbet or a stake were set before men, that they should be immediately executed if they did not forbear such a sinful action, or if they did not go to hear a sermon; can any be so foolish, to think that the glister of gold, the penalty of the law, the sight of a gibbet, should confer a power upon you which you were not before possessed with? It is not then the want of power to avoid sin, but the want of will.

7. Why does conscience check any man after the commission of sin, if it were not in his power to avoid it? All those actions which fall under the cognisance and check of conscience, are actions in our own power, and within the verge of our wills. For the pain of conscience is of another kind than that

pain or grief which is raised by those accidents we could not avoid. It arises from the liberty of the will, and galls the soul when it considers, that that which it has done was in its power to be done otherwise. This is the common language of men upon the regrets of conscience: I might have done otherwise, I was warned by my friends; I slighted their warnings, I had resolutions to the contrary, but I stifled them. All men have laid the fault upon themselves, and what is universal consent has a truth in it; the consciences of all men would not gall them for that which they had no power to decline. Indeed, if men wore necessitated to sin, they could not be tormented in hell, for the torment there is conscience acting rationally, and reflecting upon them for their wilfulness in the world. If man had not a power to refuse sin, conscience would have no ground for any such reflections to rack and torment them. And it is observable, that natural men, somewhat awakened upon a deathbed, are not so racked by their consciences simply for not being regenerate, as for not avoiding those sins which were hindrances, and not using those means which were appointments of God for such an end, because those were in their power; but they wilfully embraced the one, and as wilfully refused the other.

Prop. 2. Man has a power, by common grace, to do many more good actions (actions materially good) than he does. Evangelical works we cannot do without union to Christ, so himself says, 'Without me you can do nothing,' John xv. 5; nothing according to the order of the gospel, nothing spiritually, nothing acceptably, because no such fruits can arise, where faith, the root of such works, is wanting. Though man be much crippled in regard of morals, yet he is not wholly dead to them, as he is to spirituals. A man may 'break off his sins by (moral) righteousness, and his iniquity by showing mercy to the poor;' by taking off the yoke of oppression, and restoring of what he has rifled, which counsel Daniel gives to Nebuchadnezzar, chap. iv. 27. Though a sick man cannot do all the acts of a sound man till he be perfectly cured, yet he has some power of acting some things like a sound man, remaining with his disease. The young man in the Gospel (yet out of Christ) morally kept the law; so may men under the gospel keep the outward and material part of the precept. There are not only some common notions left since the tall, but also some seeds of moral righteousness in the nature of man. The Gentiles did not only, by nature, in part restored, know the things written in the law, but they did by nature do them, Rom. id. 14; upon this stock they bore many excellent fruits. What patience, chastity, contempt of the pleasures of the world! What affections to their country, and bowels of compassion to men in misery! And what devotion in the external worship of their gods, according to their light, were exemplary in them, though only under the conduct of nature! And these works, though they were not according to the exactness of the law, and failed also in the manner of them, and could not please God for want of faith, yet so far as they were agreeable to the law of nature, and in regard of the materiality of them, were not offensive to God. This moral righteousness of theirs was only external, and rather an image of righteousness than a true one. Abimelech had a natural integrity, which God acknowledges to be in him, and did arise from his moral nature, though he also appropriates to himself the restraint of Abimelech, and his concurrence with an approbation of that moral integrity: Gen. xx. 6, 'I know that thou did this in the integrity of thy heart: for I also withheld thee from sinning against me, therefore suffered I thee not to touch her;' "lo netaticha", I gave thee not up to touch her. If men did nourish a moral integrity, which they might do, God would concur with them to preserve them from many crimes. If those which were only under the guidance of natural light had so much power to do many moral acts by a common grace, is man's power less under the gospel, whereby they have an addition of a greater light to this natural? If man was able to do so much by the light of nature, there can be no inability brought upon him under the light of the gospel, unless men, by their sluggishness and obstinacy, provoke God judicially to deprive them of that power, and withdraw his hand from them, and so give them up to all kind of wickedness, as it is the dreadful case of many in these days. Man may keep the law of nature better than he does, and for not keeping that he is condemned.

Prop. 3. Men have a power to attend upon the outward means God has appointed for regeneration. Though man cannot renew himself, yet he has a natural power to attend upon the means God has afforded. Though a man has not power to cure his own disease or heal his wound, yet he has power to advise with others, and use the best medicines for his recovery. There is not an outward duty a renewed man does, but a natural man has power externally to do it; though what is essentially good in all parts, cannot be done without special grace, yet what is externally good may be done by the assistance of common grace. Have you not passions, fear, love, desire, grief? Why cannot you exercise them about other objects than ordinarily they are employed about? Why can you not make hell the object of your fears, and heaven the object of your desire? Why might not Esau have wept for his sins, as well as for the loss of the blessing? Might he not have changed the object if he would? Why may we not exercise our inward affections more in our attendance on God? Is not a little excuse sufficient to put off from duty, a great excuse not sufficient to keep you from committing sin? Great business must be laid aside for sin, not the least laid aside for God. Every little thing is a lion in the way then. Do you not many times rack your minds to invent pleas for neglect of duty? Why can you not set them on work to consider reasons to move you to service? Have we not power to be more serious in the use of means than we are? We can be so when some affliction presses us, or conscience gnaws us. Neither of these furnishes us with a new power. Conscience is like the law, acquaints us with our duty, but gives us no strength. The charge God brines against Ephraim was, that he 'would not frame his doings to turn towards God,' Hosea v. 4; he would entertain no thoughts, not one action that had the least prospect towards repentance, he would use no means for that end, or have a look that way. If a man will not do what is in his power, it is a sign he will not be renewed. Can he pretend to a desire to live, who will not eat, and endeavour to prevent foreseen dangers? Or can he pretend to a desire to build, that will not use materials when he may?

There are two great means: hearing the word, and prayer.

(1.) Hearing the word. Have not men power to go to hear the word, to hear a sermon, as well as to see a play? Have they any shackles upon their feet, that they cannot carry them to a place of worship as well as to a place of vanity and sin? Can you not as well read the Scripture as a romance? Has not the will a despotic power over the members of the body? How came Herod to have more natural power to hear the word, and to hear it 'with pleasure,' Mark vi. 20, than other men have? May you not strive against diversions, resist carnal affection, rouse up your souls from their laziness, and endeavour to close with the word? How smilingly would God look upon such endeavours? If men do not, it is out of a natural sluggishness and enmity of will, not for want of power if they would. Men do not what they might. Certainly he does no more desire regeneration who neglects and despises the great instrument of it, than he can be said to desire his own preservation, who neglects medicines proper for the cure of his disease.

(2.) Prayer. I do not mean a spiritual prayer, which is by the special assistance and indwelling of the Holy Ghost, but of a natural prayer by common instinct; such a one as the apostle puts Simon Magus upon, who he knew was destitute of any air of the Spirit to breathe out, as being 'in the gall of bitterness and bond of iniquity,' Acts viii. 22, 23, yet supposes him to have a power in some manner to express his desires to God; or such a power that was common in heathens, upon any distress to run to their altars, and fill their temples with cries to their gods. You cannot pray in the Holy Ghost, but you may send up natural and rational cries to God. Did not Jonah's mariners cry every man to his god? Have you not as much power to cry to the true God as the heathens to false ones? There is the natural prayer of those mariners, as well as the natural integrity of Abimelech, which was not a new-covenant integrity. Can you not be as devout as the publican, and cry, with more seriousness of affection than generally men do, 'Lord, be merciful to me a sinner'? When men are upon a death-bed, ready to take their leave of the world, they can then cry. It is not their death-bed inspires them with power, more than they had before, but they have more mind, and see a greater necessity of crying to God. They have more power in the time of their health, by how much the habit of sin wanted that strength which has been acquired by a continuance of acts till the time of their sickness; for the fewer sins have been committed, the less is the power impaired. Though God has kept other things in his hand, yet he has given us a power of begging, we will use it as a means to obtain them. Can you not kneel down before God, and implore his assistance? Can you not acknowledge before him that it is impossible for you to change yourself, but that your eyes are upon his grace; that you cannot attain by your own strength a spiritual heart; that you will seek nowhere else for it but from his hand; and that you will not be at rest till he has put in his hand and dropped upon your hearts? Can you not thus cry out, Oh that I were a renewed person! as well as cry out, Oh that I were rich and honourable in the world! Had Paul a new tongue when he cried out, 'Who shall deliver me from the body of this death?' Was it not the same member wherein he had breathed out threatenings against the disciples?

Prop. 4. Man has a power to exercise consideration. He has seminals of jus and aequum, and a power of judging according to them: Luke xii. 57 'Yea, why even of yourselves judge you not what is right?' Our Saviour checks them for not making use of their natural power; in the searching their own consciences, and judging their own acts, as well as they did in discerning the face of the sky, and what weather would follow. There is a power of consideration in a rebellious heart; for God acknowledges it in a rebellious nation: Ezek. xii. 3, 'It may be they will consider, though they be a rebellious house.'

1. Can you not reflect upon yourselves? Every man has a reflexive faculty; otherwise he is not a man. Reflection is the peculiar privilege of a rational creature, without which he is not rational. The Pharisees could reflect upon themselves, and say, 'Are we blind also?' John ix. 40. Can you not then take a survey of your past lives; cast up the accounts of your souls, as well as your books? Can you not view your particular crimes, with the aggravations attending them? Yea, you can, if you would. Can you not look back upon the means you have neglected, the love you have slighted, and the light you have shut your eyes against? As long as a man has reason, he may use his reason in these things as well as in others. Why may he not reflect upon himself in spiritual concerns, as well as civil affairs in the world? Cannot he, by comparing the face of his soul with the glass of the word, understand his own state, and by self-reflection come to an understanding of his own lost condition and weakness?

2. Can you not consider the word? Cannot your reasons be employed about the objects the word offers, as well as the objects the world offers? Though you cannot act spiritually in the duties of religion, can you not act rationally in them, as men? Are you endued with a rational soul, to consider the

proposals of worldly affairs and concerns, and can you not exercise the same power in considering the proposal made to you by the gospel? The gospel is not only spiritual, but rational. As long as you have a thinking faculty, can you not consider what the reasonable meaning of it is? Though you have not a spiritual taste, you have a rational understanding; why may it not be busied about one object as well as another? The natural repentance of the Ninevites at Jonah's preaching, implied the consideration of his threatening sermon. Why is there not a power in you to think of what is proposed to you out of the word, as well as you can think of what you read of a mathematical or philosophical book, or some history? The power is the same in both, the faculty the same. As the object proposed adds no power to the faculty, so it takes away no power the faculty already has. Surely man is not such a block or stone, but he may turn these things over and over, press them upon his own soul, which may make way for the sensibleness of his state, and putting the will out of its sinful indifference. What any natural man has done, that may all under the same means do, if they will. Why may not the veriest wretch among us humble himself at the hearing of the word, as well as wicked Ahab? 1 Kings xxi. 27, 29, 'When Ahab heard these words, he rent his clothes. Seest thou how Ahab humbles himself?' He discovered an external humiliation, after the consideration of the threatening denounced by the prophet.

3. Can you not cherish, by consideration, those motions which are put into you? There is not a man but the Spirit strives with, one time or other, Gen vi. 3. Has not man a power to approve any good counsel given him, if he will? Have you not had some supernatural motions lifting you up towards God, and pressing obligations upon you, to walk more circumspectly? Why might you not have cherished them, as well as smothered them? Why could you not have considered the tendency of them, as well as have considered how to divert and drown them, by engaging in some sensual dust? Was the power of consideration lost? No; you could not then have cast about in your minds, by what means you should be rid of them, or how you should resist them. Have you not wilfully rejected them, even when consideration has been revived at a sermon? And yet you did industriously let that good motion die for want of blowing up the spark, by following on the consideration which was raised upon its feet. When you have 'begun well, who did hinder you' from a further obedience? 'This persuasion comes not of him that calls you,' Gal. v. 7, 8. There was no necessity upon you, to fortify yourselves in your corrupted habits against the attempts of the Spirit. Could you not as well have fallen down before the throne of grace, to have begged grace to second them, as kicked at them, and spurned them away? Was it want of power to do otherwise? or was it not rather your own obstinate wilfulness? Since I appeal to you, whether your own consciences have not tugged at you, and spurred you on at such seasons, why could you not then beg of God, that such a good motion might not have departed out of your coasts? Because a man cannot renew himself, therefore to lie down in sluggishness is not the design of this doctrine.

4. Can you not consider those notions you have be natural light? Man has a conscience which minds him of moral good, and pulls him from evil. No man can deprive himself of these. It will check in those things wherein others commend us, and commend us in those things wherein others accuse us. May we not observe the motions of conscience within us? May we not consider the charge it brings against us for any act committed, so as to avoid the like for the future; and the excusations of conscience, in commending us, so as to do the like acts for the future? As we have a law without us, which we may consider, so we have a conscience within us, which witnesses to the equity of the law, accusing us for what we do contrary to it, and excusing us for what we do in observance of it, Rom. ii. 15; and this in man's corrupt state. Cannot man then observe the dictates of conscience? Can he not find out the sense of this law in his mind, though it be much blurred? Cannot he act like a man, in following the dictates of this rational principle, as well as like a beast follow the allurements of sense? No rational principle in man puts him upon evil, but upon moral good; whatsoever draws him from good, or puts him upon evil, are principles common to him with one brute or other, profit, pleasure, honour, all which are found in some beast or other. Why may not a man then consider the rational reports of his own conscience, as well as the brutish whisperings of sense? But does not man endeavour to shuffle off his conscience, and is mighty jolly when it keeps silence, or when he can stop its mouth with an excuse? Do not men wilfully choke the sentiments of it, and keep the truth deposited in their souls, in unrighteousness, Rom. i. 18; and like the scorner, 'hear not its rebukes,' Prov. xiii. 1? Whatsoever man has by the relics of natural light, he may think of. He knows by nature there is a God; he knows something of his attributes, and of his law; may not those be his morning thoughts? Is he not stirred up sometimes to contemplate on them? May he not do it at other times, since this common grace is always with him, and leaves him not till he leaves valuing and embracing its divine assistances? Let it be remembered, that in all this which man may do, the power is to be ascribed to common grace through a mediator, keeping up by his interposition the pillars of the earth, and preserving some relics of natural light, and the seeds of moral righteousness in man, not in the least to be ascribed to bare nature; and that man's corrupt will, stuffed with sinful habits, is the cause he makes no use of this power.

Quest. 2. If we have not an ability to renew ourselves, why does God command us to do so? And why does God make promises to men if they will turn? Is not this a cruelty? as if a man should command another to run a race, and promise to reward him if he did, and yet bind him with fetters that he cannot run? Both the command would be unjust and the promise ridiculous.

Ans. In general. God may command, and his command does not signify a present ability in man.

(1.) He may command, because we have faculties suited to the command in respect of their substance. For the death of a sinner was not a physical death, but a moral. Man lost not his faculties, but the rectitude of them; he lost the purity of his sight, the integrity of his will, but not the understanding and will itself.

(2.) God's command does not signify a present moral ability to perform it. God's command, which acquaints us with our present duty, is no argument of a present power; for if a command signified more than the duty man owes, it signified more than a command in its own nature could signify. Gods command to us to renew ourselves implies no more an ability inherent in the creature to do so than Christ's voice to putrefying Lazarus, 'Lazarus arise, come forth,' John xi. 43, implied a power in Lazarus to raise himself, or his speech to the palsied cripple, 'Arise, take up thy bed,' implied a power in himself to do it himself before a supernatural conveyance of it. Do not men exhort every day to sobriety those that have contracted a profound habit of drunkenness and lust, that philosophy does acknowledge it is not possible for them to abstain from; yet no man accuses those that exhort them of impertinence, nor those that chastise them of injustice. God's commands are not the measures of our strength, but the rule of our duty, and do not teach us what we are, but what we should be.

But to clear this more particularly:

God may command, though man has not a present moral ability to renew himself. For

[1.] First, Man once had a power to do whatsoever God would command him; he had a power to cleave to God. He had not else, in justice, been capable of any such injunction; there had been ground of a complaint and charge against God, if man had been created defective in any of those abilities necessary for his obedience to this command. The command is just; God would not else have imposed it, because of his righteousness, and every man's conscience testifies that it is highly just he should honour God, love God, and cleave to God. If it were just, then man was capable to perform this command, for man, as a rational creature, is capable of a law, and cannot be governed otherwise; and no law could be given so proper for him as to stand right to his Creator. Since, therefore, the law was just in itself, and since God did justly impose it, man was certainly created by God in a capacity to observe it. No question but God, who furnished other creatures with an ability to attain their several ends, and perform the orders God had set them in at the creation, was no less indulgent to man. He that was not deficient to the lower creatures would not be deficient to the noblest of his sublunary works. He would have been worse in his rank, without a sufficient stock, than other creatures were in theirs. There would not have been a physical goodness and perfection suitable to his station in the world, and his excellency above other creatures. How could God then have pronounced him good, among the rest of his works, if there had been in his creation a natural inability to answer the end of his creation? If God had created man in such a state that he could not do righteously, and yet commanded him to do righteously, and, because he did not, punish him, he would have been unjust; as if a man should command another to reach a thing too high for him, and that when his hands were tied behind him, and because he did not, beat him. This would have been the case had not man had power at first to do righteously. Had man preserved himself in that created state, no just command of God (and it was impossible any unjust command should have proceeded from infinite righteousness) would have been too hard and too high for him.

[2.] God did not deprive man of this ability. Man was not stripped of his original righteousness by God, for man had lost it before ever God spake to him, or passed any sentence upon him after his fall: Gen. iii. 10, 'I was naked.' If God had taken it away without any offence of Adam, he might have expostulated the case. It had been alike unjust, as if God had never given him power at first to observe the command he enjoined him. It would have been unreasonable to require that of man which God himself had made impossible. But God did not take away man's original righteousness. If God had taken it away before man's fall, then man was unrighteous before he fell, and God, taking it away from him while he was perfect, had made him, of an holy and righteous man, unholy and profane; as he that deprives a malefactor of his sight, for his demerit, makes him of seeing blind. If God took it away after he spake to Adam in the garden, it would then follow that Adam was righteous after his fall till God deprived him of it, and so was innocent while he was sinful, and strong while he was weak. God did not take it away from him before, but had told him that the loss of it would be the natural consequent of his eating the forbidden fruit, Gen. ii. 17, nor after for after we find only temporal punishments threatened. God indeed did judicially deny him the restoration of it, which, as a governor and a judge, he might justly do, resolving to govern him in another manner than before. So that it would be an unjust imputation on God to say, God cut off man's legs, and then commanded him to run, and come to him. What if God did foresee that man would fall; was God therefore the cause of his fall? God's prescience, though it is infallible, is not the cause of a thing, no more than our foreknowledge that the sun will rise to-morrow morning is a cause of rising of it.

[3.] Therefore, since God did not deprive man of it, it follows that man lost it himself, and not barely lost it, but cast it away. He did voluntarily by an inordinate intention of will, cast away this original perfection, and fell a-hunting after his own 'inventions', Eccles. vii. 29. He did not stick to that command God had given him, nor implore God s assistance of him, as by

His natural ability he might have done. He consulted not with his command upon the temptation, but was very willing to cast off that righteousness wherewith God had endowed him, for an affected godhead. Man readily swallowed the bait; he did not debate the business with Eve, 'She gave to her husband with her, and he did eat,' Gen. iii. 6. So that the fault

was wholly in himself, and his present state voluntarily contracted, for though the devil tempted him, yet he had no power to force him. He was easily overcome by him, for it was not a repeated temptation, but a surrender at the first parley.

[4.] Therefore God's right of commanding, and man's obligation of returning and cleaving to God, remains firm. God's right still remains. God gave him a portion to manage, though man prodigally spent it. God may challenge his own. Cannot a master justly challenge that commodity he sent his servant with money to buy, though he spent it in drunkenness and gaming? God gave Adam a sufficient stock; he trifled it away. Must God's right suffer for his folly, and man's crime deprive God of his power to command? The obligation to God is natural, therefore indelible; the corruption of the creature cannot render this first obligation void. Righteousness is a debt the creature, as a rational creature, owes to God, and cannot refuse the payment of it without a crime. Who deprived him of the power of paying? Himself. Should this voluntary embezzlement prejudice God's right of exacting that which the creature cannot be excused from? A debtor, who cannot pay, remains under the obligation of paying. The receipt of a sum of money brings him into the relation of a debtor, and not his ability to pay what he has received. Such a doctrine would free all men who were unable to pay from being debtors, though the sums they owed were never so vast. That judge would be unjust that would excuse a prodigal debtor, because he could not pay when sued by his creditor. No doubt but the devils are bound to serve God, and love him, though by their revolt they have lost the will to obey him. If, because we have no present power, our obligation to turn to God and obey him ceased, there would be no sin in the world, and consequently no judgments. Who will say, that if a prince had such rebellious subjects that there were little hopes to reclaim them, he should be therefore bound not to command them to return to their duty and obedience? If it be reasonable in a prince, whose rights are limited, shall it not be reasonable in God to exact it, who has an unbounded right over his creature? Either God must keep up his law or abrogate it, or, which is all one, let it lie in the dust. His holiness obliges him to keep up his law; to abrogate it, therefore, would be against his holiness. To declare a willingness that his creature should not love him, should not obey him, would be to declare that which is unjust, because love is a just debt to an amiable object and the chief good, and obedience to a sovereign Lord. Must God change his holiness because man has changed his estate? The obligation of man remaining perpetual, the right of God to demand remains perpetual too, notwithstanding the creature's casting himself into an insolvent condition. If man still owes this duty to God, why may not God exact his right of man? Much more may God call for a right use of those means and gifts he has, as a benefactor, bestowed upon man since his fall. No man will deny this right to God upon serious thoughts. These new gifts and means were given him not only for himself, but for his Lord, to improve for his glory. God may justly require the right use of those moral principles and evangelical means for the ends for which he appointed them.

[5.] It will appear more reasonable, because God demands no more, nay not so much as he required of Adam in innocence. It is but *obedientia redintegrata*, a return in part to that perfect boldness which was inherent in man, and to that obedience in part which was in a great measure due to God. As when a prince demands the return of rebels, he demands a restoration of that subjection which they paid him before. God required a perfect obedience in the first covenant, he requires not so much in the second, so that for want of it a creature shall be cast off; but a sincere obedience is required, though not in degree perfect. Adam had a fundamental power in him to perform that obedience which is required, in faith and repentance, the two great parts of regeneration. Faith is nothing but an embracing and accepting of Christ the mediator. Adam had a power of believing and accepting Christ for his head, had he been proposed to him in paradise, as the mediator of consistency and confirmation, and the vinculum of holding him for ever close to God. Had not Adam a power to accept him under this notion, as well as the good angels have accepted him for their head, and worship him as mediator; that is, pay him an obedience as mediator when he comes into the world, Heb. i. 6. Had he not a fundamental power to grieve, though since sin was extraneous to a state of innocence, he could not have exercised that grief for himself, repentance being extraneous to obedience, and unmeet for him in a sinless state? Suppose God had commanded him to grieve for the sins of the fallen angels, Adam having this passion in his nature, might have done it. He might have known what sin was in them, and might have grieved for the dishonour of God by them; even as our Saviour did grieve for the sins of others, Mark iii. 5, who knew no sin himself. And in grieving for his own sin, there was only a change of the object.

[6.] It is yet more reasonable if we consider, that every natural man thinks he has a power to renew himself, and turn to God when he will practically, though not all of them notionally. What reason then has man to quarrel with God, and accuse him of demanding that which he thinks he can give to God, and will not at present, but take his own time to do it, when he sees it fit? This practical opinion runs in the reins of every natural man under the gospel, as well as in the heathens, which appears by the general wilful delays of men about their eternal concerns, by their vows and resolutions upon the blows of conscience of reforming their lives, and becoming new men without having recourse to the grace of God, or taking any notice of him in their resolves. This I think is a clear case. 'Yet a little more sleep,' says a man, that thinks he can rise time enough when he will, and despatch his business in a moment, Prov. vi. 10. With what face can man accuse God of not giving him power, when he thinks he has power enough himself? or be angry with God for demanding his debt, when he thinks himself in a solvent condition? No man will blame another for requiring that of his servant, which his servant boasts he has power in himself to do. The Israelites thought so when they said, Exod. xxiv. 3, 'All the words which the Lord has said we will do,' without any applications to the grace of God to enable them. All men are like Israel in this; only the regenerate are most sensible of their own impotence, and scarce any man else.

[7.] From all this it follows, that God is not bound to give grace to any; and where he does bestow it, it is an act of his sovereign pleasure. If God has given man power, and never took it away, but it was cast away by man, therefore God's right is not prejudiced, but he may justly demand of man what once he gave him power to do, especially since it is less than what man at first owed him; and when man thinks he has power to pay him, it will evidently follow, that God is not bound to give any new power. If God were bound to give a new power to accept of the gospel, he were then unjust not to confer it; if he be not bound, it is of mere grace that he bestows it. God proposes pardon to all upon such conditions, but he is not bound to give the condition to any; he commands all to renew their obedience to him, but he is not bound to renew any one person. He gives the command to turn, as a lawgiver and governor; he gives the grace to some to turn, as a benefactor. It is grace therefore, not debt. When God confers it, it is an act of his compassionate mercy; when he denies it, it is an act of his just sovereignty. He may, if he please, 'suffer all nations to walk in their own ways,' Acts xiv. 16. Yet if he please to propose the means of grace to any, the very knowledge of those mysteries of heaven is a peculiar gift, as well as the outward proposal: Matt. xiii. 11, 'To you it is given to know the mysteries of the kingdom of heaven, but to them it is not given.' If we improve reason to the highest, God is not obliged to give us grace, no more than if a beast improved sense to the highest, he were bound to give him reason. Though if there could be a man found in any age of the world, who did improve reason to the utmost of his power, I would not doubt God's giving him the addition of supernatural grace, out of the largeness of his bounty, though still there is no obligation upon God, because man does no more than his duty.

And that God does not give grace to all to whom the means are offered, and yet does command them to turn, and promise to receive them;--

(1.) It does not entrench upon his sincerity in his proposals. His proposals are serious, though he knows man will not receive them without an over-powering grace; and though he be resolved not to give the assistance of his grace to every one under those means, but leave them to the liberty of their own wills. The gospel is to be considered as a command ordering men to believe, or as a promise alluring men to be renewed, by representing to them the happiness of such a state. Consider it as a command, God is serious in it, though he resolve not to give grace to all to whom the precept comes, for under this consideration of a command it is a declaration of man's duty, and a demonstration of God s sovereign authority. Does God's resolution of not giving grace weaken the obligation of man to his duty, or diminish God's authority, or give ground to man to charge him with insincerity? Consider it as a promise, does it hinder God's seriousness in it if he resolves not to give the condition of it to all? It is sufficient to show God's seriousness in it, to declare, that if men will be regenerate, it will be very pleasing to him; that he will make good to them what he has promised, that if they be renewed, he will make good every tittle of the promise to them; and if they will seek, and ask, and knock, he will not be wanting to them to assist them.

(2.) It does not disparage his wisdom to command that to man which he knows man will not do without his grace, and so make promises to man upon the doing it. If man indeed had not a faculty naturally fitted for the object, it might entrench upon God's wisdom to make commands and promises to such a creature as it would be to command a beast to speak. But man has a faculty to understand and will, which makes him a man; and there is a disposition in the understanding and will which consists in an inclination determined to good or evil, which makes us not to be men, but good or bad men, whereby we are distinguished from one another, as by reason and will we are from plants and beasts. Now the commands and exhortations are suitable to our nature, and respect not our reason as good or bad, but simply as reason. These commands presuppose in us a faculty of understanding and will, and a suitableness between the command and the faculty of a reasonable creature. This is the reason why God has given to us his law and gospel, his commands, not because we are good or bad men, but because we are men endued with reason, which other creatures want, and therefore are not capable of government by a command. Our blessed Lord and Saviour did not exhort infants, though he blessed them, because they were not arrived to the use of reason, yet he exhorted the Jews, many of whose wills he knew were not determined to good, and whom he told that they would die in their sins. And though God had told them, Jer. xiii., that they could no more change themselves than an Ethiopian could his skin, yet he expostulates with them why they 'would not be made clean;' verse 27 'O Jerusalem, wilt thou not be made clean? when shall it once be?' Because, though they had an ill disposition in their judgment, yet their judgment remained, whereby to discern of exhortations if they would. To present a concert of music to a deaf man that cannot hear the greatest sound were absurd, because sounds are the object of hearing; but commands and exhortations are the object, not of this or that good constitution of reason, but of reason itself.

(3.) Neither does it disagree with his justice. It is so far from being unjust for God to demand what men are obliged to do, though he knows that they will not do it, that God would be unjust to himself if he did not demand it, if he let men trample upon his rights without demanding restitution of them. If a prince sets forth edicts to rebels to return, and promise them pardon upon their returning, though he knows they are rebelliously bent, that they will not entertain a thought of coming again under his sceptre, but will still be in arms, and draw down his wrath upon them, will not all interpret this to be an act of clemency and goodness in the prince? Neither is God an acceptor of persons, because he does not give grace unto all; for may he not do with his own what he please without injustice? Those to whom we give alms have reason to thank us; those to whom we give not an alms have no reason to complain; we have gratified the one, but we have done no wrong to the other. We are all by nature criminals, deserving death; should God leave us in that deplorable estate wherein he found us, can we accuse him of injustice? Those that by grace are snatched out of the pit, have reason to acknowledge it an admirable favour, as indeed it is; those that are destitute of grace, and by their own wilful rejection left to sink to the bottom, cannot impute their unhappiness to him; for he left them not without witness; he presented them the word, exhorted them to hearken to him; but, instead of paying their duty, they fiercely rejected him, abhorred his exhortations, and gave themselves over to sin and vice. If a man proclaim by a crier that such that can bring such a mark shall receive such an alms, he sends this private mark to some, they come and receive an alms. Had he not power to do what he pleased with his own, to send his distinguishing token to whom he pleased? What injustice is done to the other, to whom he sends not this mark?

We have shown that God may command. Let us see why God does command, when he knows man has no power to renew himself?

1. The first reason is,

To make us sensible of our impotency. The design of God is not to signify our power to perform it, but sensibly to affect us with our inability, that we may be the better prepared for a remedy; as the moral law was given with such terrifying marks, to make men despair in themselves, and the ceremonial law annexed to it, to give some glimpse of a Mediator in whom they might have strength. And therefore when the Israelites were so affected, Deut. xviii. 16-18, as to desire not to hear the voice of the Lord in that manner, nor to see that great fire any more which attended the law, that they might not die, he commends them for it: verse 17, 'They have well spoken that which they have spoken.' God is highly pleased with this sense of their own inability to answer the terms of the first covenant, since it makes them fly for help and supply to the prophet of the second covenant. The cabalists therefore say, that the law was given to take away the venom of the serpent; that is, not that we should fulfil the law, but that we might learn how far we were swerved from the duty we owed to God, and how unable to gain the happiness we had lost. A conceit of self-sufficiency secretly lurks in every one of us; we should think ourselves gods to ourselves if we saw not the picture of our own weakness in the spirituality of the command. Therefore, though we cannot ourselves perform this command of regeneration, it is necessary it should be directed to us, to make us abject in our eyes, and strip us of all confidence in the flesh, which is the first step toward a being endued with the Spirit; to make us hang down our proud plumes, and sink into that despair in ourselves, which is necessary to the superstructure of a saving faith. It is necessary the law should be commanded, to make sin appear exceeding sinful, to give us a true prospect of ourselves in the glass of the command: the rectitude of it shows us our crookedness; the holiness of it, our impurity; the justice of it, our unrighteousness; the goodness of it, our wickedness; and the spirituality of it, our carnality and fleshliness. God does not command us (though we have no power) to upbraid and triumph over us, but to lay us low, and humble us.

2. To make us sensible of the grace of God, and urge us to have recourse to it. It is necessary that man should understand the perfection of divine righteousness, and what the condition of man was before the fall, that thereby he may understand the necessity of the remedy, and be more willing to come under God's wing than Adam has to keep under it; but without a sense of his own weakness man would never come to God. God commands us, not that he expects we should renew ourselves, for he knows we cannot; but that being acquainted with our feeble frame, we should implore his grace to turn us, and have recourse to him, who delights to be sought unto and depended upon by his creature. That this command of renewing ourselves, and returning to our due obedience, is given to this end, is evident by the promise of the gospel, which did accompany the command, both to encourage and direct men where

to find assistance for the performance of what the first covenant exacts, and the second accepts. Therefore, with the commands of the law, there is the promise of a great prophet to teach them, an ordaining typical sacrifices to relieve them, and the gospel, under the mask of the ceremonial law, attended the fiery and impossible commands of the moral. God might have exacted his right without making any promise, it had been summum just; but God exacts not his right now, but with a promise; where there is jus in one, and remissio juris in the other. And very frequently in the Scripture, where the command is given to show us our duty, yet a promise is joined to it, to show that though obedience be our duty, yet sanctification is God's work, as Lev. xx. 8, 'Ye shall keep my statutes and do them;' whereupon it immediately follows, 'I am the Lord which sanctify you.' The precept is to acquaint us with our duty; the promise, to acquaint us with the sight of a gracious ability; the precept minds us of our debt, the promise minds us of the means to pay it: what is required in the precept is encouraged in the promise. Every precept, being a part of the law, is to 'shut us up' to faith, and to 'bring us to Christ,' Gal. iii. 23, 24. God makes us amends; that as he requires of us what we lost by another's fault, he has provided us a remedy by another's righteousness, which we never performed; and by his own Spirit, which we never purchased, if we will but seek it. If God did work it in us without commanding us to work it ourselves, we could not have a foundation to make such sensible acknowledgements of his grace and omnipotent kindness. It is our work as a due debt; it is God's work as a fruit of his grace; Isa. xxvi. 12, 'Thou hast wrought all our works in us.' The promise, therefore, of a new heart and a new spirit, is made indefinitely; none are aimed in it, nor any excluded, that will but seek it. And supposing they are predictions rather than promises, yet they run in the nature of a promise: they are to be pleaded, for God 'will be inquired after concerning them;' and the fulfilling of them to the soul is as pleadable as the fulfilling other prophecies to the church; the grounds of the plea are the same in both, the truth of God: Ezek. xxxvi. 37, 'Thus says the Lord God, I will yet for this be inquired of by the house of Israel, to do it for them;' which may reasonably be concluded to respect the whole antecedent promising discourse of God.

3. These commands and exhortations are of use to clear the justice of God upon obstinate sinners. God is a judge, and judges by law; commands therefore are necessary, because a rational creature is only governable by law. If God were not a lawgiver, he could not be a judge; his judicial proceedings depend upon his legislative power. Men being to be judged by their works, must have some law as the rule of those works; and his law is no more than the first law in innocence, that is, to return to obedience and righteousness. These commands and exhortations are the whips and scourges of perverse consciences, whereby they are galled while they obey not the motions of them, and render them inexcusable and unworthy of mercy in despising the conditions God requires of them, and make the case of Sodom 'more tolerable in the day of judgment' than the condition of such men, Mat. xi. 24. We are apt to bring an unreasonable charge against God of cruelty and injustice, as though his punishments did not consist with righteousness. God therefore shows us our duty, and demands it of us, and it is confessed by us to be our duty; man is therefore deservedly punished, because he does wilfully cherish the old nature in him, the fountain of all sin; he has the truth, and he holds it in possession, but in unrighteousness, therefore the wrath of God is justly revealed from heaven against that unrighteousness of his, Rom. i. 18. God calls sinners, though he knows they will not renew themselves, as men send servants to demand the possession of a piece of ground, though they know it will not be delivered to them; but they do it that they may more conveniently bring their action against such a person that will not surrender. So upon God's command to men to be renewed, his justice is more apparent upon their refusal; as he sent Moses to Pharaoh, though he knew before that Pharaoh would not hearken to him. This punishment is only accidental to the gospel, it becomes the savour of death per per accidens, because of the unbelief of those that reject it; the gospel is designed for the salvation of men, not for their condemnation. If the corruption of man produces condemnation to himself, must God abstain from doing good to the world? There is not a man but abuses the light of the sun which shines upon him, and the mercies God gives him, and thereby brings wrath upon himself, and God knows they will do so; would we have God, therefore, to put out the light of the sun, and divest the earth of its fruitfulness? Shall God lay aside his right of commanding, and take away the preaching of the gospel, and so excellent a thing as the happy revelation of his gracious promises and exhortations, because many men by their wilfulness bring the just wrath of God upon them for their refusal? Will any man accuse our blessed Lord and Saviour, when ho comes to judgment, that he did them wrong to come and die for mankind, and cause the news and ends of his death to be published, and exhort sinners thereupon to believe in him? Surely men's consciences shall be full of convictions of their own wilfulness, and the equity of God's justice thereupon.

4. The commands and exhortations are of use to bring men to God, according to the nature of rational creatures, and also to keep them with God. Man not having lost his reason, though he has lost his rectitude, cannot be drawn to God in a rational way but by cords proper to man; for he is a creature governable only by laws, and therefore must have laws suited to his nature; and commands and exhortations are so, for the weakness brought upon men to answer them is by their own defection. God

does not bring men to him by instinct, as he brought the beasts to Adam, or the creatures into Noah's ark; such a conversion would not be reasonable, nor spiritual, nor agreeable to God, no more than the obedience of the beasts to Noah. God therefore draws men by commands, and promises, and exhortations thereupon convenient to the nature of man, accommodated to the rational capacity of the creature; for man being created after the image of God, ought to be conducted and governed after another manner then other creatures. The grace of God therefore working suitably to the nature of man, cannot be conceived by us in any other way than in this of commands and exhortations. And when men are renewed, the commands for perfect regeneration are still incumbent upon them (though they cannot attain it in this life), to stir up their hearts to an exercise of that gracious ability they have to walk in the ways of holiness, and to that end to a reliance on the grace of God. The promises are given to them to inflame them to a love of holiness, and to show them where their chief strength lies; this appears plainly to be the intent of the Spirit of God in that command and promise, Philip. ii. 12, 13, 'Work out your own salvation; for it is God that works in you to will and to do.' He writes to those already regenerate, Work out your salvation, use your gracious power, and be encouraged by the assistance God gives you. Use your own power as if there were no grace to help you in the performance; depend upon the grace of God which works in you both to will and to do, as if you had no power at all of any motion in yourselves.

So that to sum up the whole of this later discourse, the impotence of man does not excuse him.

1. Because the commands of the gospel are not difficult in themselves to be believed and obeyed. If we were commanded things that were impossible in their own nature, as to shoot an arrow as high as the sun, or leap up to the top of the highest mountain at one start, the very command carries its excuse with it in the impossibility of the thing enjoined. But the precept of regeneration and restoring to righteousness is easy to be comprehended, it is backed with clear and manifest reason, and proposed with a promise of happiness which is very suitable to the natural appetite of our souls. To command a thing simply impossible is not congruous to the wisdom, holiness, and righteousness of God; it would not be justice, but cruelty. No wise man will invite another man by any promises to do that which is simply impossible; no just judge will punish a man for not observing such a precept; no righteous and merciful person would impose such a command. But these commands of the gospel are not impossible in their own nature, but in regard of our perversity and contumacy. The command of righteousness was possible when first given, and impossible since by our own folly; impossible in our voluntary corrupted nature, and by reason of our voluntarily cherished corruption. The change is not in the nature of the law, but in the nature of the creature; and what is impossible to nature is possible to grace, and grace may be sought for the performance of them.

2. Because we have a foundation in our natures for such commands, therefore man's weakness does not excuse him. It had been unjust for God to have commanded Adam in innocence to fly, and give him no wings; this had been above Adam's natural power, he could not have done it, though he would fain have obeyed God, because his nature was destitute of all force for such a command. It would be strange if God should invite the trees or beasts to repent, because they have no foundation in their nature to entertain commands and invitations to obedience and repentance; for trees have no sense, and beasts have no reason to discern the difference between good and evil. If God did command a man that never had eyes to contemplate the sun, man might wonder, since such a man never had organs for such an action. But God addresses himself to men that have senses open to objects, and understandings to know, and wills to move, affections to embrace objects. These understandings are open to anything but that which God does command, their wills can will anything but that which God does propose. The command is proportioned to the natural faculty, and the natural faculty proportioned to the excellency of the command. We have affections, as love and desire. In the command of loving God and loving our neighbour, there is only a change of the object of our affections required; the faculties are not weak by nature, but by the viciousness of nature, which is of our own introduction. It is strange, therefore, that we should excuse ourselves, and pretend we are not to be blamed, because God's command is impossible to be observed, when the defect lies not in the want of a natural foundation, but in our own giving up ourselves to the flesh and the love of it, and in a wilful refusal of applying our faculties to their proper objects, when we can employ those faculties with all vehemence about those things which have no commerce with the gospel.

3. Because the means God gives are not simply insufficient in themselves. God does afford men beams of light, he makes clear discoveries, as it is, Rom. i. 19, 'He has showed it to them, "efanerose", 'it is manifest in them. He displays in their hearts some motions of his Spirit, produces some velleities. The standing of the world under the cries of so many hideous sins, is a daily sermon of God's kindness and patience in bearing up the pillars of it, and is a standing exhortation to repentance; as Rom. ii. 4, 'The forbearance, long-suffering, and goodness of God leads to repentance.' The object is intelligible: 'The word is near us, in our mouths, in our hearts;' it is apprehensible in itself, Rom. x. 6, 7. The revelation is as plain as the surface of the heavens, Ps. xix. 1-3, applied to the preaching of the gospel. Rom. x. 18. That men are not renewed, and turned to God, is not for want of a sufficient external revelation, but from the hardness of the heart; not from any insufficiency of the means, but the depravity

and wickedness of the soul to whom those means are offered. The commands and means of the gospel are no more weak in themselves than the law was, but weak through the flesh, by reason of the inherent corruption man has fastened in himself, Rom. viii. 3. Would not the hundredth part of any revelation of some worldly object, connatural to man's corrupt heart, be sufficient in itself to put him upon motion to it, and embraces of it? The insufficiency does both not lie in the external means, for the gospel is an act of mercy and grace; the call is an act of kindness. It is clear to man that God offers; it is clear that God will accept, if man will embrace his counsel; and shall this be said to be insufficient, because man will reject it?

4. Because this impotence in man is rather a wilfulness than a simple weakness, therefore man's pretended weakness does not excuse him from the command. It is not a weakness arising from a necessity of nature, but an enmity of will, whereby some other apparent good is beloved above God, and some creature preferred before him. There is a double impotence, *merae infirmitatis*, which is a want of power in the hand, when there is a readiness in the will to perform, or *malignitatis*, which is seated in the will and affections, whereby though a man has a power to perform, yet he cannot because he will not: he will abhor any return to God, and will not be whetted by his promise to any endeavour. A simple impotency deserves pity, for it is a rational excuse, but an obstinate perversity is so far from an excuse that it is an aggravation. The deeper the habit of obstinacy, the more inexcusable the person. What a ridiculous excuse would this be, to say to God, (1.) that I ought not to be obliged to restore myself to righteousness, and obey the command of the gospel, because I am of so perverse a disposition that I will not obey, and will not be restored; or (2.) that God is bound to restore to him that will to obey and renew himself, otherwise he is guilty of no crime. The first would be ridiculous, and both impious. What hinders any man from being regenerate under the call of the gospel, but a moral weakness, which consists in an imperious inclination to evil, and a rooted indisposition in corrupt reason and will to believe and repent? And here the Scripture lays it upon the hardness of the heart, Rom. ii. 5, and a rebellious walking after our own thoughts: Isa. lxv. 2, 'I have spread out my hands all the day unto a rebellious people, which walk in a way that was not good, after their own thoughts.' We are impotent and cannot, because we are rebellious and will not. For since man has an understanding capable to weigh arguments on both sides, and see the advantage of the good proposed, and the disadvantage of the evil tempting, if he does the evil, and refuses the good, is not the fault clearly in his will? And when by a custom in sin we ripen the power of our evil habits, we contract an impossibility of doing the good required, and casting out the evil forbidden. This does in no sort excuse us, because it is an inability contracted by ourselves. God himself threatens punishment to the Israelites, when he confesses that they could not attain to innocence: Hosea viii. 5, 'My anger is kindled against them: how long will it be ere they attain to innocence?' "lo yuchlu"; how long can they not? Purity or innocence. They had raised such an habit in them, by casting off voluntarily the thing that is good, ver. 3, that they could not divest themselves of it, which was so far from excusing them that it sharpened the anger of God against them.

5. This weakness does not excuse from obedience to this command, because God denies no man strength to perform what he commands, if he seek it at his hands. No man can plead that he would have been regenerate, and turned to God, and could not, for though we have not power to renew ourselves, yet God is ready to confer power upon us if we seek it. Where did God ever deny any man sufficient strength, that did wait upon him in serious and humble supplications, and conscientiously used the means to procure it. A man cannot indeed merit grace, or dispose himself for it, so that it must by a natural necessity come into his soul, as a form does into matter upon dispositions to it. But if a man will do what he can do, if he will put no obstacle to grace, by a course of sin, would not God, out of his infinite bounty to his creatures, and out of that general love whereby he would have all men saved, and come to the knowledge of the truth, give him special grace? Has not our Saviour made a promise in his first sermon to the multitude, that God 'will give good things to them that ask him,' with a much more than men give good gifts to their children, Mat. vii. 11. They were not only his disciples that he preached that sermon to, but the multitude, comparing it with Mat. v. 1, and Mat. vii. 28. Has not God declared, that he 'delights not in the death of a sinner,' Ezek. xxxiii. 11, and does he not out of his infinite goodness condescend to beseech us to be reconciled to him? Will not the same infinite goodness bow itself down to form a new image in them that use the means to be reconciled and conformed to him, as much as they can? Has not our blessed Saviour already given a testimony of his affection to such endeavours, in loving the young man for his outward observation of the law, Mark x. 21, who wanted but one thing only to pass him into a gracious state, the refusal whereof barred him of it? And shall not he have a choicer affection to those that strive to observe the rules he has left in his gospel? Will he not be pleased with such motions in his creatures towards their own happiness? Will he not further that wherein he delights? Think not therefore to justify yourselves at the bar of God for your sloth, because you are too weak to renew yourselves. It will not help you then. The question will then be asked, Did you ever seriously beg it, as for your lives? Did God ever desert you when you would fight against sin, when you set yourselves seriously and dependently on him for grace? God gives us talents, but by our sloth we embezzle them. It is upon that score Christ lays it, Mat. xxv. 26, 'Thou wicked and slothful

servant.' God has not promised to furnish you with more talents, when you improve not the talents you have already; non-improvement of them cuts oft all pleas men may make against God upon the account of their impotence. As there never was a renewed man, but acknowledged his regeneration as a fruit of God's grace, so there was never any man that can say, he did use his greatest industry in trading with the talents God entrusted him with, and God refused him the supply of his special grace. If you have not a new heart and a heart of flesh, ask your own hearts whether ever you did seriously inquire of God to do it for you. God never fails them that diligently seek him.

For the use of this:

1. For information.

(1.) See the strange misery of man by his fall. We cannot be the authors of strength to our own souls, since we are despoiled of that vital principle which constituted us spiritually living in the first creation. How are we sunk many degrees below other creatures, who always have, and still do answer the ends of their creation, when we, wretched we, have lost both the will and power to answer the end of ours? We can understand, will, move, but not as man in innocence could. In ourselves we are nothing, we have nothing, can bring forth nothing spiritually good and acceptable to God; a mere composition of enmity to good and propensity to evil, of weakness and wickedness, of hell and death; a fardel of impotence and conceitedness, perversity and inability, every way miserable unless infinite compassion relieve us. We have no more freedom than a chained galley slave till Christ redeem us; no more strength than a putrefied carcass till Christ raise us, an unlamented hardness, an unregarded obstinacy, an insensible palsy spread over every part, a dreadful cannot and will not triumphing in the whole soul. The heart turned into pleasure with its own wounds and chains is an amazing misery both to good men and angels, because it is so great, and yet unbewailed to see a man endued with a soul so rare, even with its crack, that the heathens thought it to be a particle of God; an understanding that can peer into heaven, fathom the earth by contemplative inquisitions, yet cannot strike up a spark of enlightened reason about everlasting happiness; that that reason, which understands a worldly interest, should be so blind, so weak, about a heavenly bliss! A short-sighted mind, that cannot cast a look so high as to spiritual things, nor rise up in one holy thought without the grace of God; a perverse will, that cannot commission one spiritual desire; a weak arm, that cannot strengthen itself to grasp and hold one spiritual gift; a dry wilderness, that cannot issue out a tear till God open the fountain of the great deep of grace to flow in upon it; a hard heart, that relents not under afflictions on earth, nor could under the flames of hell without grace! What a woeful thing is it to be miserable, and have no strength to be happy! to look into a law, and behold it wholly spiritual, and to reflect upon our souls, and behold them wholly carnal! Rom. vii. 14, to find a command of regeneration in the judgment of our own consciences, just for God to impose, good for us to receive, and an utter inability to square ourselves according to it!

(2.) See the vast power of sin. It is this that has cast its infectious roots so deep in our souls, that it is impossible for us to pluck up this degenerate plant. The first defection from God was of that nature, that it did per se, of itself, produce an inability in us, as sickness does in a body, or disjointing a member does weakness in a man; otherwise man, after he had sinned, had been found in strength, and had had a power to do good, till God by punishment had taken away that power, and inflicted a contrary weakness, which would be very absurd to affirm. Adam threw off the royal robe of righteousness; and in all those ages which are run out since, man could not find by all the inquiries of nature how to put it on again without a supernatural strength. This sin that has taken hold of us, keeps us down, that we cannot lift up our heads to divine knowledge, or reach out our hands to perform any divine precept, it is this has emptied us of our treasure, stripped us of our strength, made us as poor as Job upon the dunghill, and as feeble as the cripple at the pool; and which is worse than this, has not only deprived us of our health and strength to cure ourselves, but of our will to be healed by another; and possessed us with such a frenzy that we are friends to our madness, and enemies to those that would deliver us from it; we are all possessed with a legion of devils, that makes us cry out against Christ before we be turned to him, Mark v. 7. It is this first poison diffusing itself in the heart of Adam has made us all by nature a generation of vipers, and infected our very tongues, that we cannot, being evil, speak that which is good, that is, perfectly and spiritually good, as it is Mat. xii. 34, 'O generation of vipers, how can you, being evil, speak good things?' and poisoned our souls at the very root, that not one grape of grace can grow upon the thorn of nature. All the coin of our actions bears the impression of the evil treasure in our hearts, Luke vi. 43-45.

(3.) We may from hence see the groundlessness of any conceits rising in us, of the power and freedom of our own wills to anything spiritually good. This conceit reigns in most men's hearts naturally; it is a legacy left to our natures by the will of Adam. The not submitting our wills to the will of God, in a way of humble waiting upon him, is the source of the misery of mankind; such imaginations will creep up in our hearts, that our understandings can aspire to all knowledge, our wills spring up in grace, as naturally as a clear fountain in pure waters. The cause of such conceits is the ignorance both of the depth and largeness of the wound original sin has made in all our faculties. Paul, while a pharisee, without question was of this mind, and cried up the liberty of the will as much as he cried down the truth of the Christian religion; he was 'alive without the law once,' Rom. vii. 9. But when he takes out the lesson of the sinfulness of natural concupiscence, Rom. vii. 7, the experience of his slavery, and being sold under sin, grew up with the notion of the extent of original corruption, and he found himself a mere dead man, as may be observed in several passages in Rom. vii. Every man is born with this conceit, since we find the only peculiar nation God had in the world asserting it in the whole body of them, in the face of God, Exod. xxiv. 8. When Moses told them all the words and judgments of the Lord, all the people answered with one voice, 'All the words which the Lord has said will we do;' and ver. 7, 'All that the Lord has said will we do, and be obedient.' Not one man among them duly sensible of natural slavery, nor making any application to God for grace to keep them; but as confident of the strength of their mutable wills as if they had as much power as the first man in innocence. This vain confidence has its bitter root in the imagination of all Israel; and that it may not appear to be a sudden and rash passion, they assert it again more solemnly upon second thoughts: ver. 7, 'All that the Lord has said will we do, and be obedient.'

[1.] It is a high piece of pride. To boast of a great estate, when a man has not a farthing in his purse, is very ridiculous, or for a slave to brag of liberty, with his chains upon his hands and feet. What a vain self-reflection is it when we are bound naturally in our sins, as a slave in his shackles, with Satan's padlock upon us, till the Son make us free indeed! John viii. 36. It is the very moth of pride which ate out the beauty of Adam's garment who, whilst he would stand upon his own bottom, laid the scene of his own ruin; he affected to be his own conductor, and proved his own cut-throat; and aspiring to an independence on God, fell down into the dungeon of slavery to, and dependency upon, Satan. It is a pride like that of Adam, an invasion of God's property, an affecting to be that by ourselves which we can only be by Christ; it is an arrogance like that of the Babel builders, to think by this slime of nature to raise up a spiritual building as high as heaven. We sin over again more formally the sin of Adam, by affecting an equality with God.

[2.] It is a disparagement to God. It is an unquestionable idolatry, and never yet practised, to set up any creature as the author of the temporal good of the whole world. Is it not more to set up many thousands of free wills as the authors of the spiritual good of the creature, to make every man's will an idol? Is the robbing God of the glory of his grace less criminal than the divesting him of the glory of his outward work? Or are the works of grace in the soul more inconsiderable than those of nature? It disparages Gods grace; it makes his grace subsequent, not preventing; it makes the highest spiritual work to be the seed of man, not the seed of God. If this conceit takes place in your hearts, God is like to be without much praise from his creature. Peter will be no more beholden to God than Judas, Paul no more than Simon Magus; both had the outward revelation, and so both owe a praise to God; but what further debt of praise did Paul owe to God, if his regeneration sprang forth into being by the power of his own will, without any further contribution from God than an objective proposal? It takes off the crown of glory from the head of Christ; for though it will be acknowledged that he bruised the head of the common serpent by the power of his death, yet the destruction of the works of the serpent in our hearts, which is our immediate happiness, was wrought by the seed of free will. It would be strange that the apostle Paul should be so over-seen, to give such praise to the grace of God manifested to him, if he had not been particularly beholden to that for the turning of his heart. By this God is beholden much to the creature's will, in being a great cause of keeping up the interest of God in the world, which had no footing, notwithstanding his revelation, without the compliance of man's will, untouched by any supernatural grace. Such a conceit of man's power seems to envy God the glory of his whole grace. And such a bitter root of this, I doubt, may be one secret cause that we are so heart-tied and tongue-tied in the praises of God for his grace.

[3.] It takes away a great part of the glory of the Spirit's work in the world. Was his convincing the world of sin and righteousness only external by the objective proposals of the word, and fitting the apostles for the propagation of that convictive revelation? Was he to stand only as a spectator to behold which way the motion of free will would cast the balance? Is he to preserve grace in the heart? and is there not more need of his creating it there, than preserving it after? Is there more danger of the devil's quenching the flame kindled in the soul, than there was of its first touch upon the heart? Is he a Spirit of grace only to propose it, not to work it? The Spirit makes no verbal proposal of it, that is by man; if an inward proposal barely by applying it to the understanding, has not man as much power to do that, as to work it in his will? How can it be a well of water springing up to eternal life, if it works nothing efficaciously upon the heart? This secret pride and conceit in the heart may be a cause we make so few applications to the Spirit of God, taking little notice of him in our attempts.

[4.] It puts a bar to all evangelical duties. It makes us cleave to ourselves rather than to God, and presume upon our own strength rather than rely upon his. The heathens (as Seneca) asserted, that it was a silly thing for a man to desire that of heaven which he had power to do without it. Why should we go to him for renewing grace, when it is in our own power to renew ourselves? May it not be said to us, as it was in another case, 'Why trouble you the master?' As long as we think we can spin a righteousness out of our own bowels, we will never go to Christ for a robe of his weaving, though never so rich. And while we think we can rear a stately spiritual building by our own skill, we shall never desire the art of another workman. Our Saviour would have nothing to do with his fullness, if He stood in no need of it; and what need had we of it, if we could despatch this great business of grace ourselves? This secret imagination in the heart is one cause of the neglect of duties, especially prayer, or of a slightness and coldness in it.

[5.] This conceit endangers a man's destruction, by encouraging a delay of using the means necessary to this work in God's ordinary course. What sensualist would not delay using means for repentance, who conceits he can repent when he will, and that to will is in his own power? This makes men think they have a key to unlock heaven at their pleasure, and have the command of the treasures of grace; and therefore are afraid to attend upon evangelical means, for fear they should be put upon serious reflections too soon. The common sentiments of men are a sad evidence of this; you shall hear many acknowledge their weakness in other things, but not in this; they cannot leave such a course of sin, they cannot pray with so much affection, yet their hearts are right, they can repent and believe when they will, that is in their own power; which makes them sluggish and careless at the calls of God. But what a folly this is, let Solomon witness, who sets the fool's cap upon such confidence; 'He that trusts in his own heart is a fool,' Prov. xxviii. 26; it is to trust in a weathercock that is mutable with every wind of temptation. To depend upon our wills, is to depend upon the oldest and the most certain bankrupt in the world, that broke as soon as it was set up, many ages since, and never recovered itself. Who told you, therefore, that you can melt the stone within you at your pleasure? that you can cast the strong man out of your wills without a stronger than he? But suppose the grounds were rational, and that you had a power to cure yourselves; the consequent is very irrational, for that cause to delay it; for what man in his wits would endure a wound or deformity many years, because he can heal or beautify himself at his pleasure in a moment? Take heed therefore of such fancies of your own power to regenerate yourselves, and upon that account to neglect that which you have power to do; but imitate Ephraim with all speed, notwithstanding your cheating imagination, and cry out, 'Turn thou me, and I shall be turned,' Jer. xxxi. 18.

(4.) It informs us, that regeneration is not wrought merely by moral suasion, or only by exhortations; then it would principally be the work of the will of man. Our Saviour had a will to preach to all in Jerusalem, but he had not a will to quicken all: John v. 21, 'the Son quickens whom he will;' so that it depended upon his inward operation, not only upon his outward exhortations. It is true there is a suasion in the ear by the word, but the persuasion is in the heart by grace; the suasion in the word may cause some rational reflections as a moral cause, but no spiritual motion towards God as a physical cause. Men are not disputed or exhorted, but created into grace; the proposal of a good by the understanding is not always embraced by the will, unless it be a good suitable and connatural to those habits in the will. Where, therefore, there is no suitable habit planted in the will, rational reflections in the mind and conscience are not like to prevail much.

[1.] If it were only by suasion and exhortation, the most eloquent preaching were like to do most good. Whereas it never was God's method to found conversion upon the 'words of man's wisdom,' though 'enticing' in themselves, but upon the 'demonstration and power of the Spirit,' 1 Cor. ii. 4. The most eloquent preaching would then most fill the gospel nets. And the reports of that rhetorical prophet Isaiah would have been soon believed, which were not so, because 'the arm of the Lord was not (always) revealed with them,' Isa. liii. 1. If any words, as words, were like to have an edge to cut deep into the soul, they must be the words of our Saviour; since 'never man' (even in the judgment of some of his enemies) 'spoke as he spake.' But though 'his lips were full of grace,' Ps. xiv. 2, most of his hearers' hearts were empty of it under his ministry; not the eloquence and pressing reasons of Christ, nor the wrath of God revealed from heaven, can reclaim the heart of man, without the power of grace. The Pharisees were prouder under Christ's melting bowels, and the Jews harder under God's wrathful blows, Isa. i. 5; neither hearing nor feeling will prevail upon hardened souls.

[2.] What bare exhortations can work upon a dead man? Can a well composed oration, setting out all the advantages of life and health raise a dead man, or cure a diseased body? You may as well exhort a blind man to behold the sun, and prevail as much. No man ever yet imagined, that the strewing a dead body with flowers would raise it to life; no more can the urging a man, spiritually dead, with eloquent motives, ever make him to open his eyes and stand upon his feet. Did our Saviour come out of his grave, or could he ever have done it, by mere suasion, without the power of God to raise him? Eph. i. 19, 20. The working of mighty power is a title too high for the capacity of mere moral exhortations. A mere suasion does not confer a strength, but suppose it in a man, for he is only persuaded to use the power which he has already.

[3.] Does not daily experience testify the contrary? Have you never discoursed with some profane, loose fellow, so pressingly, that he seemed to be planet-struck at every reasoning, shaken out of his excuses for his sinful course, yet not shaken out of his sin; that you might as soon have persuaded the tide at full sea to retreat, or a lion to change his nature, as have overcome him by all your arguments. Have you not seen many at a stand in sin, by the force of some convincing reasons, return again to their vomit? Have not many tears at command in anything that concerns themselves, the loss of some estate, or some dear friend, but in the things of God, in his dishonours, as dry as the parched earth? That you may almost as soon extract water out of a rock, as repentance for sin out of their stony hearts. So that it is not the faint breath of man, or the rational considerations of the mind are able to do this work, without the mighty pleadings and powerful operations of that great Paraclete or Advocate, the Spirit, to alter the temper of the soul.

[4.] There is no likelihood that any man in the world would be renewed, if it were only by moral suasion. Satan's logic would be stronger than God's; his arguments would more suit our imagined interest, and our real enmity against God; his persuasions would find more kindred in the principles of our minds and habits of our wills to take fire by him, than the suasory allurements of God, which will meet with nothing in our hearts but contrariety to them. The deceitfulness of sin within us, and the subtilty of Satan without us, both being active as well as persuading adversaries, would fix us in our rebellion, without a contrary power, as well active as exhortative, and God would do no more towards our restoration than Satan does towards our destruction, since the devil can only propose to us, not by any physical touch incline our wills. We are wholly inclined to him in our own natures, in love with the knife that cuts our throats, and too fond of our shackles ever to knock them off. The will is so enamoured with its corrupt habit, that were this work left barely to self will, and no other power employed in it than exhortative, not one person were every likely to come unto God.

[5.] If it were wrought by suasion, the will would have the whole praise of the work. For suasion or exhortation is nothing else but the proposing arguments to the understanding, but the motion, according to those arguments, is wholly from the will, which has a power to receive them or refuse them. God, indeed, would be the first speaker, but not the first agent; God would be only the assisting cause, as all moral causes are, he would only assist the motion of the will, not cause it. The motion of the will is a physical act; if, then, the physical act be from the will, and God only the moral cause, the will will be the greater sharer in the work, fo- moral causes are in vain without a physical effect in those things they work morally upon: as all the reasoning of one man with another will be to little purpose, if there be not a physical motion of the will of that person to comply with the other's reasonings. If, therefore, the reasoning part be only from God, and physical motion from man, the most debauched wretch, under the preaching of the gospel, is as much beholden to God as the highest believer, who had both the same suasions and exhortations; for though the suasion was from God, the persuasion was from their own wills. God only made the revelation, and was afterwards but a spectator, not an actor.

(5.) Information. We may draw a conclusion hence whereby to judge of the truth of doctrines. Man cannot renew himself. Whatsoever doctrine does depress and humble man and advance the glory of God, is true, it answers the main design of the gospel, which all centres in this, that man is to be laid low, and God to be exalted as the chief cause. It pulls man from his own bottom, and transfers all the glory man would challenge into the hands of God; it lays man in the dust at God's footstool. That doctrine which crosses the main design of the gospel, and encourages pride in man, is not a spark from heaven: 'No flesh must glory in God's presence,' 1 Cor. i. 29. The doctrine of justification by works is thrown down by the apostle with this very argument as a thunderbolt: Rom. iii. 27, 'Where is boasting then? it is excluded by faith;' that is, by the doctrine of the gospel, boasting would be introduced by ascribing regeneration to nature as much as it is excluded by denying justification by works; the doctrine of the gospel would contradict itself, to usher in boasting with one hand whilst it thrust it out with the other. Our Saviour gave this rule long ago, that the glorifying God is the evidence of truth in persons: 'He that seeks his glory that sent him, the same is true,' John vii. 18. By the same reason also in things and doctrines, and indeed, Christ speaks it in relation to his doctrine, as appears, verse 16, 17. All truth gives God the pre-eminence in all gracious works; the first creation, the progress and top-stone, are the works of this great Bezaliel, this mighty artifices, both the first draught and the last line. To confound nature and grace together, is to join the creature in commission with God, and make them co-heirs in the glory which is only due to the only wise and almighty Creator.

Use 2 is for exhortation. 1. To the regenerate. If this doctrine be true,

1. Then ascribe nothing to flesh. (1.) Not to yourselves. No more praise is due to us than to gold for being melted by the fire and wrought by the workman into a vessel of honour; it is due to the skill of the artifices, not to the vessel itself. When the reparation of human nature was to be wrought by the gospel, when the crooked should be made straight, and the rough places plain, then should flesh be as grass, when the Spirit of the Lord should blow upon it; yea, the people, those that are God's peculiar ones, by reason of privileges, are grass, Isa. xl. 4, 6, 7, they should be nothing in themselves, that God might be all in all: the Spirit of God blows upon all their self-confidences. If God be the God of all grace, what share have our wills in it then? He calls, he opens the heart, he strengthens, he perfects; all the grace we have is his 'treasure,' 1 Peter v. 10. He first delivers from Egypt; preserves in the desert; conducts to a footing in Canaan. Grace triumphs in the whole work, from Dan to Beersheba, from the beginning of the work to the end. What glory can belong to us? We will, it is true, but God gives that will; we work, but God bestows and stands by that power to work; what have we then to do with the

praise? It is 'in his light we see light,' Ps. xxxvi. 9. The rays whereby we have a glimpse of him are not darted from us to him, but from him to us. The light in the air springs not from itself, but from some other body enlightening it; how can any good be ascribed to us, where there is nothing but insufficiency and defect? It is to belie the Lord, to entitle a work of omnipotence to so infirm a cause, it is worse than the pharisee, who, in the midst of his boasts of his own moral righteousness, thought a tribute of praise due to God: 'Lord, I thank thee, that I am not as other men are,' Luke xviii. 11. Shall we entitle God the author of our beings, and ourselves the creators of our spiritual beings? Is it less to have an elevation of our faculties, and an animation of them by a new virtue, than to have simply the faculties themselves? If the creature be unable of itself to move without a dependence on God in way of common providence, much more unable is it to move without dependence on God in a way of supernatural vitality. The glory of the act is as little due to man as the glory of the first habit.

Now, 1, review yourselves, consider what you were before regeneration, what after it; and then, how can you ascribe anything to yourselves?

(1.) What you were before regeneration. Was not sin as deeply rooted in you as any other, which made you as incapable to raise yourselves as the most wicked man in the world? Were you not prisoners in chains, captives under locks and bolts, when grace first set up its standard for your recovery? How thick was the darkness of your minds? how stout the perversity of your wills? how impetuous the violence of your sinful affections? Did they not all conspire together to make as stout a resistance against the work of the gospel as any others? Can you then say, that because God saw you more inclinable to grace than another, that he drew you? You were created; did you bring clay enough to compose the least particle of flesh about you? You are new created; what part of the new man was formed by your direction? Did you bring grace enough of yourselves to form one holy thought, or send out one holy desire? Did your own will single you out of that multitude of degenerate men of better natures than yours, left still in their own nothingness? Was it nothing but your own will that planted you in the nursery of the invisible church, that made you capable of a divine union? Were not other men's reasons as strong as yours? the means they enjoyed greater? their moral disposition sweeter? What was the reason their wills did not bend themselves as well as yours? What is the reason they did not hold out their hands to catch this all-necessary grace? Did this noble birth cost none any pains but yourselves? Was this goodly fabric reared by your own wills? Look on it; methinks it is a piece too comely and noble for human skill.

(2.) What are you since your regeneration? What, do you find no rebellion of the law in your members against the law of the mind? Are there not powerful allurements of the flesh? Are your thoughts always flying up to God, and hovering about him? Are you always nimble in your praise of him? or not rather lifeless many times under the breathings of the Spirit? Why are you thus? Did you first by your own force begin this noble conquest of sin? And can you not by the same power make a better progress? Did you breathe a life into yourselves when you had not a spark, and can you not blow up this spark into a greater liveliness? Surely then this work was not at first the birth of your own wills. Do you not yet find some scale and thick matter upon your understandings that you cannot pick off? some darkness in your minds, as there is some in the air after it is enlightened? Are there not obstructions in your wills? no shackles upon the executive power? Can you not remove that darkness with that great light you have? nor unlock those fetters by the strength of your habitual grace? Can then the first powerful entrance of it, the fall of the first scale from the understanding, be judged to be the work of your own hands? or the first teeming of your wills with grace to be the effect of your power? View yourselves well in both states, and you will find no ground whereon to build so much injustice towards God, and pride in yourselves, but must needs acknowledge that God and not yourselves have wrought all your works in you, Isa. xxvi. 12, not only your temporal advantages, which the church there means, but your spiritual, and much more spiritual than temporal.

To stave off any ascribing to yourselves, consider,

[2.] He that ascribes it to his own will has great reason to question whether he be regenerate or no. He may well doubt whether he understands or feels what it is, since those in Scripture who have been most experimented in it, and therefore are the most competent judges, have most highly magnified the grace of God, and most deeply vilified themselves; they have given the glory of it so entirely to God that they have not let a grain of it stick to their own fingers. Thus David often, 'Thou hast quickened me.' The apostle Paul owns his effectual call to be owing to the 'grace of God,' Gal. i. 15, and to an abundant 'grace in Christ,' 1 Tim. i. 14; he was a persecutor, but his faith and love was from the abundance of the grace of God, and that in Christ too, not from any thing in nature. Peter is not behind him in the admiration of it: 1 Peter i. 8, 'Blessed be the God and Father of our Lord Jesus Christ, who, according to his abundant mercy, has begotten us again.' And it is that the church in the times of the gospel prophesied of: Ps. c. 8, 'It is he that has made us, not we ourselves;' made us his people, as it follows, 'We are his people, and the sheep of his pasture,' 'not we ourselves.' Whenever the naughtiness of their hearts has been ready to launch out to self-praise, they have turned the tide quickly to the grace of God. When Paul had owned grace as the cause of his spiritual being, 1 Cor. xv. 10, and began to speak of his labouring more abundantly than they, he flies back in haste, as one that had gone beyond his line, 'Yet not I, but the grace of God which was with me;' another, 'Yet not I;' Gal. ii. 20, 'I live, yet not I, but Christ lives in me.' There is no mention of any in Scripture that ever in this case did sacrifice to their own net.

[3.] If a man be regenerate, such a boasting of himself is very dangerous. Though it may not rifle you of the new nature, yet by the just judgment of God, it may cloud the comfort of it. If such a man be renewed, this pride is but a prologue of some dark veil to be drawn between him and the light of God's countenance, between him and the sight of his own grace. A swelling up in pride presages a sinking down in desertion. If God be not owned by you to be the God of all grace in you, he will not own himself to be the God of all comfort to you. Grace follows humility, and some shrewd shock attends spiritual pride, it is such an idolatrous robbing God of his glory (whereof he is most jealous), and giving it to another, that he will not let it pass without a remark. The clouding of your grace will be the fruit of the smothering of his glory. For since the main intendment of the gospel is to humble, God will humble you if any grace be in you. If the Spirit of grace has breathed upon your souls to renew you, he will blow upon your grass to consume it, Isa. xl. 7, he will pull down those proud thoughts and strong holds, and cause your vain confidences to wither and come to nothing. Ascribe it not therefore to yourselves; be not so presumptuous, as, while you allow God to be the author of the being and motion of a little fly, to cry up your own wills as the chief cause of grace, a work more excellent than the material world.

2. Ascribe nothing to instruments, either men or means. It is not of the will of man, not another's will. Without the efficacious working of the Spirit, the gospel itself is but as a dead letter, the Spirit only quickens it. It is not outward teaching and blowing which of itself will kindle these sparks; an instrument cannot act without the strength of an agent to manage it; the chisel forms the stone into a statue, but according to the skill and strength of the artifices moving it. It is not the breath of man, and a few words out of his mouth, can produce so great a work as the new creation; this might be a reason why God chose so weak an instrument as man to preach the gospel, to evidence that the great work was not from the weakness of man but the power of God.

Exhortation 2. Let us be humbled under our own natural impotence and inability, and keep up this humiliation. There is danger of the pharisee's pride climbing up into the heart, even after regeneration. Renewed men have instructions to humility above other men; their sin may strike them low, because it is the growth of their own nature; their grace may keep them low, because it is no plant of their own setting; sin, because it is originally theirs; grace, because it is originally none of theirs; it is no beam of their own understanding, no stream from the fountain of their own will. If we think believingly and fruitfully of Christ at any time, we cannot but think of our own weakness, nothing in him but minds us of it; our weakness to obey the law was the cause of his coming; our weakness to satisfy God was the cause of his dying; our inability to repair and support ourselves was the cause of his fullness. His death minds us of our impotence to redeem ourselves, his grace minds us of our impotence to renew ourselves. The more we grow up in the new birth, the more deeply sensible shall we be of our impotence. Oh, let this text be written in our hearts, 'Not of the will of the flesh, nor of the will of man.'

3. Resolve nothing in your own strength. The power to believe and be renewed is a power 'given,' not inbred, Philip. i. 29; our strength is deposited, not in the cracked cabinet of our own wills, but in the treasures of Christ. Our purposes are weak without grace to strengthen them, our resolutions vanishing without grace to establish them. If we should be left to the sails of our own faculties, without the breath of the Spirit to fill them, we should lie wind-bound. The will can never in this life be so firm but the allurements of the great tempter will make inroads upon us and overset us, without the special grace of God to establish and strengthen us. As we are not to do anything for our own glory, so we are not to do anything in our own strength. As we must not be our own end, so we must not be our own principle; the power the best have is but derived, the stream must know it is but a stream still. The actual exercise of Paul's ability grew from strength in another hand, 'I can do all things through Christ strengthening me,' Philip. in. 14; all things by him, nothing by himself. When the Israelites went out with God, no sons of Anak, no walls of Jericho, nor chariots of iron could stand before them. When they trusted in themselves, nothing could be resisted by them. The devil was certainly none of the lowest rank of angels; he had a great clearness of gifts, yet he falls for cleaving to his own will and strength, not to the grace of God. And Adam, in depending upon himself, lost himself and his posterity. For us to undertake the government of ourselves is like a ship without a pilot, to be dashed soon against a rock. To lean on our own wisdom and will, is to lean on broken reeds, deceitful supports; self-confidence is the worm of grace, conceit of a spiritual fullness in ourselves is the way to an emptiness of spiritual comfort. Self-will and self-wisdom are the great idols of the soul, and some little images of them are in the hearts of the best men, which they are ready sometimes to fall down before and worship; they would oppose temptations themselves, do duties themselves by the strength of habitual grace, without regard to the strength of God, the great support of it.

4. Therefore live dependently upon God. Do you not find how apt you are to stagger at every temptation; how weak your wills are to good; how easily your purposes are broken, the thoughts of God

few and distracted, your motions heavy in divine ways? Is there not, then, need of a constant looking unto God, as they did upon the brazen serpent, for the healing of our natures, while the wound remains imperfectly cured? All bodies on the earth, though they have a principle of motion in themselves, yet dependently upon the heavenly bodies. If the motions of the heavens should cease, that all motions in the earth would cease too is the opinion of philosophers. Without dependence on the grace of God and fullness of Christ, we sink into weakness and impotency, as a beam expires into duskiness upon the clouding of the sun. It is God only can be a 'dew to Israel,' Hosea xiv. 5. Think not of bringing forth the after-fruits of grace without his influence, no more than you could plant in yourselves the first root of grace without his power: the same breath of the Spirit must blow the fire up as well as kindle it. As by our own wills we should never turn to God, so without the continuance of efficacious grace we should quickly start from God. 'As you have received Christ, so walk in him,' Col. ii. 6. You received him by faith, walk in him by faith. This is the reason of the different thrivings of one Christian above another, under the same means. One endeavours to act upon his own bottom; the other clings to the vine. Christ knew the things of God by lying in the bosom of the Father; we come to know and do the things of God by lying in the bosom of the Son. All natural effects, if taken off from the influence of their own cause, by which they live and increase, lose their power and die. The soul separate from God, by non-exercise of faith, loses its strength, become stiff and inactive. How often do we return to our wonted coldness, bring forth lazy fruits, creep like snails in the ways of God, without the spur of quickening grace! And we want it because we do not seek it; for though we be armed with the whole armour of God, helmet, shield, breastplate, yet prayer and supplication must he added as a mark of our necessary dependence: Eph. vi. 18, 'Praying always with all prayer and supplication.' Then will the Spirit endue us with a fresh vigour, confirm our languishing wills, restrain the flames of natural corruption, and excite the fear and faith of God in the heart.

2. The second branch of the-exhortation, to those yet in a natural condition.

1. Endeavour to be sensible of your natural impotence. Be deeply humbled at the feet of God, strip yourselves (as much as in you lies) of the conceitedness of reason and pride of will. Every man is born with high conceits of himself and his own power; it being a natural evil, should cost us the deeper humiliations. Consider yourselves by nature under the dominion of sin, the demerit of wrath, the curse of the law, the hatred of God, and a feebleness to help yourselves in this wretched condition. View yourselves often in the glass of the law, bring the spiritual word and the carnal heart together, and behold the beauty of the one and deformity of the other; let all the nasty corners of the heart come under the examination of that purity, and then let the carnal mind hang down at the thoughts of your inability to frame yourselves according to a spiritual law. The view of our natural condition cannot work regeneration in us, but it is some kind of preparation towards it. 'The law is a schoolmaster to drive to Christ,' Gal. iii. 24. It works not this grace, but it fires a man out of himself, shows him how much he differs from the holiness of God, and is an occasion for casting about and looking after some remedy, whereby he may be made like to God, and of earnest crying for the showers of grace. Be sensible also of your contrariety to the grace of God, our wilfulness against it is worse than our emptiness of it. God 'will teach the humble his ways,' Ps. xxv. 9. those that are sensible of their own insufficiency to guide themselves.

2. Make use of the power you have. Man (as has been sheen) has some power by those restored relics of nature. There is no plea therefore to lie snorting upon a bed of sluggishness. We must not expect a divine assistance will fly to us from heaven while we play the sluggards. Though God does rouse up some on the sudden, before and previous act of their wills, yet we must not expect God will use the same methods to all. Our own power must be stirred up and exerted as much as may be. To be faithful in a little is the way to be made ruler over much. Though the top of nature cannot merit grace, yet if nature struggles to come to the top it may find an invisible hand helping it up step by step. The damnation of most men will not be for the fault of their first parents, but for the abuse of their own power, the perverseness of their wills, and neglect of what they might have done towards the seeking of God. Though Moses had a promise of victory over Amalek, yet Joshua must fight, and the Israelites stand to their arms. God saves not men in ways encouraging their laziness. 'The sluggard desires and has nothing, but the soul of the diligent shall be made fat,' Prov. viii. 4. The sluggard has nothing but lazy wishes, not active endeavours. If it be not worth the having, why do you desire it? If it be worth the desiring, why not worth the seeking?

(1.) Avoid those sins you have power to avoid. Every sin, though never so little, does increase our weakness, as every wound does the distemper of the body. It makes us weigh down towards the centre of sin. Every grain cast into the scale makes it the more unable to rise. As a virtue which is risen to that height that it cannot degenerate into vice is most worthy of praise, so the vice that possesses the soul so deeply as to incapacitate it to the doing good, being contracted by ourselves, is the more worthy of wrath.

(2.) Use the means appointed by God. Though we are torches which cannot light ourselves, yet we may bring ourselves to the word, which may both melt and kindle us. Though the giving rain and the increasing the fruits of the earth be from God, yet no man ever held ploughing, and sowing, and pruning unnecessary. The work of grace is the work of the Spirit, who is a 'wind which blows where it lists,' John iii. 8. But may we not wait for those gales? May we not spread our sails and watch for the successful breathings? How do you know but whilst you are waiting upon God in an humble posture, God may unlock your hearts, and pour in the treasures of his grace? Acts x. 44, 'While Peter yet spake these words, the Holy Ghost fell on all them which heard the word.' It you will not harden your hearts today, God may soften your hearts today: Heb. iii. 16, 'Today, if you will hear his voice.' These are the times wherein God parleys with the soul, and inclines it to the happy surrender. Though the power is God's, as the water is the fountain's, yet he has appointed the channels of his ordinances through which to convey it: 'Ministers by whom you believed,' 1 Cor. iii. 5. The gospel begets instrumentally, God principally 1 Cor. iv. 15. God calls by the gospel, 2 Thess. ii. 14. As God is the governor of the world, yet it is by instruments and second causes, which he clasps together to bring about his own designs. He that does not use these means may fear that God will never work savingly upon him, for it is an utter refusing any acceptance of this grace, or anything tending to it. This is to be peremptory, never to do ourselves any good, or receive any from God. In despising the means, you despise the goodness of God. As God gave up the heathens to themselves, because they were 'unthankful,' Rom. i. 21, for that light of nature and means which they had, so if we use the means of the gospel with thankfulness to God, God may give himself up to us. But by neglect of them we take the larger strides to destruction, and the same dreadful sentence may be pronounced against us as against them in Ezek. xxiv. 13, 'Because I have purged thee,' that is, offered thee means whereby thou might have been purged, 'and thou was not purged, thou shalt not be purged from thy filthiness any more; but in thy filthiness thou shalt die.' The using the means afforded by God has a common illumination, and a 'taste of the heavenly gift' attending it, Heb. vi. 4.

[1.] Use the means fervently, with as much ardour as you set upon anything of worldly concern; do it with all your might, since the eternal blessedness of your soul depends upon it: Eccles. ix. 10, 'Whatsoever thy hand finds to do, do it with thy might.' Stir up your souls to hear and meditate, as David does to bless: Ps. ciii. 1, 2, 'Bless the Lord, O my soul; and all that is within me, bless his holy name.' Employ all your faculties in this useful work; bring your hearts as near to the word as you can, screw up your affections to what you meditate upon, check your hearts when they begin to rove. Consider your own particular case in anything you hear; and let the word be as a delightful picture in the view of your minds continually; let every evangelical object excite your inbred affections.

[2.] Use the means dependently. Objective proposals are not useless, because God has ordained them; though they are not always successful, unless God does influence them. The means do not work naturally, as a plaster cures a wound, or a hatchet cleaves wood; nor necessarily, as fire burns; for then they should produce the same effects in all, as fire does in combustible matter; but as God pleases to accompany them with his grace, and edge them with efficacy, they must be used with an eye to God, building with one hand, and wrestling with God with the other. Men speed best in ordinances as they strive in prayer. There are promises to plead before you come to hear: Exod. xx. 24, 'In all places where I record my name, I will come unto thee, and bless thee.' The promise was made to the whole nation of Israel, the visible church, therefore pleadable by every one of them; and fix it upon your hearts, that as the death of Christ only takes away the guilt of sin, so the grace of Christ only takes away the life of sin, and the death of nature.

[3.] Pray earnestly. Entreat God to send his grace; beg of him to issue out a divine force, and a quickening power, to enlighten your minds, incline your wills. Lie at his feet, groan, wait till this work be wrought in your soul. How do you know, but while you are looking up to God, God may come down to you? Can a man be wounded, and not cry for plasters? Can he be shipwrecked and not cry out for some vessel to relieve him? Let such a voice frequently issue from you, 'What shall I do to be saved?' Is there no balm for a wounded soul, no hope for a distressed sinner, no city of refuge for one pursued by wrath and vengeance? Do you pray for daily bread? Why do you not for special grace? Are there no rational pleas you can urge? Is there not a fullness of arguments in the word? Why do you not then use those arguments God has put into your hands? Why do you not spread his own word before him? Put him in mind how his thoughts were busy about the work of redemption, and that the regeneration you desire of him was the great end of that, and a thing pleasing to him? Why do you not reason with God, to what purpose he sent his Spirit into the world, but to do this work in the hearts of men which you are now soliciting him for; and that you come not to beg any alms of him, but what he freely offers himself? You may daily read such arguments in the word, where a revelation is made of them; you may daily plead them: if you do not, it is not your cannot, but your will not. Cry out of the blind eyes you cannot upscale, the iron sinew you cannot bend, the false heart that will not go right, and the fallen nature which cannot reach so high as a holy thought. Surely God will not be deaf to the natural prayers of his rational creatures put up to him with a natural integrity, no more than he is to the cries of animals, to the voice of the lion seeking for his prey, into whose mouth he puts, by his providence, what may satisfy it. God gives the Spirit to them that ask him; not to the idle, lazy, and peevish resister of him and his grace.

If you have power to regenerate yourselves, why do you not do it? If you have not, why do you not seek it? Is the way of heaven shut to you; or rather, do you not shut your own hearts against it? Have you sought it earnestly, and can you say God denies it you? No man can say so; there is a promise for it: James iv. 8, 'Draw near to God, and ho will draw near to you;' he speaks it to sinners, as it follows, 'Cleanse your hands, you sinners.' You can pray for other mercies, why not principally for this particular determination of your wills to God, above all other things? Lord, give me to will and to do. Never leave off praying till God has crowned your petitions with success; and be encouraged to seek to him, whose great business in the world was to destroy the works of the devil, whose principal work was the spiritual death of man. If you have such earnest desires in your souls, that you would rather have it than the whole world, and esteem it above all worldly wealth or honours, be of good comfort, some of the rubbish of nature is removed; the steams of such desires shall be welcome to God, and the Spirit's commission shall be renewed to breathe further upon your souls. Desire as vehement as hunger and thirst shall be satisfied, if our blessed Saviour's promise be true, who never deceived any, or broke his word: Mat. v. 6, 'Blessed are they that hunger and thirst after righteousness: for they shall be filled.' A fullness attends a sense of emptiness, accompanied with hungering desires. But I am afraid few people put up their petitions to God for it; that I may say, as Daniel of his nation, 'all this evil' of unrighteousness and sin is 'come upon us' by our depraved natures; 'yet made we not our prayer before the Lord our God, that we might turn from our iniquities, and understand thy truth,' Dan. ix. 13.

[4.] Nourish every motion and desire you find in your hearts towards it. Have you not sometimes motions to go to the throne of grace, and beg renewing grace of God? Do you not find such tugs and pulls in your consciences? Is there not something within you spurs you on? Kick not against it, nor resist it, no, nor smother any spark of an honest desire in your hearts; be constant observers of lessons, your natural consciences, or whatever any other principle set you. Natural notions are not so blotted, but they remain legible; would men be more inward with themselves, than abroad with the objects of sense, which draw their minds from pondering that decalogue written in their souls. There is not the most wicked man under the gospel, but has sometimes more bright irradiations in his conscience than at other times, but they are damped by a noisome sensuality; he has some velleities and heavings, some strugglings against the solicitations of unrighteousness, some assents upon the presenting of virtue; for as grace is not always so powerful in a good man as to stifle temptation, so neither is corruption so powerful in a wicked man as always to beat back those motions to good which rise up in his soul, whether he will or no. As the law of the mind is not always so sovereign in a gracious man, but that it is affronted by the law of the members, so neither is the law of the members so absolute in a wicked man, but that it is somewhat checked by the law of nature in the mind. Are there not upon hearing the word, or reflecting upon yourselves, some wishings, some inward velleities which partake of reason, and the nature of that faculty which represents the necessity of it to you? As there is some kind of weak knowledge left in us since the fall, there is also something of a weak desire. Cannot these desires be improved and represented to God? Why is not the grace of God fulfilled in you? Because you persevere not in these desires, you quench the sparks of the Spirit, and willingly give admission to Satan to chase them out. Shut not your eyes then against any light, either without or within you, which may provoke God to withdraw this grace from you. How do you know but, upon using the means, praying earnestly, observing inward motions, God may give you an actual regeneration? The neglect of these is a just reason for God to refuse you any further gift; and may take off all things which you may think to bring against him in your own defence. The use of them has been beneficial to many, and no example can ever be brought, that God has condemned any that conscientiously used the means of salvation. Therefore I say again, if any man use the means, pray earnestly for this grace, observe the motions of the Spirit in him, he will not want a superadded grace from an infinitely good, tender, and merciful God.

End of part 1 of A Discourse of the Efficient of Regeneration.

Part 2

Which were born, not of blood, nor of the will of the flesh, nor of the will of man, but of God.-- John 1:13.

Two doctrines were raised from these words.
1. That man, in all his capacities, is too weak to produce the work of regeneration in himself.
This I have despatched, and now proceed to the
2nd Doct. God alone is the prime efficient cause of regeneration.
It is subjectively in the creature, efficiently from God. Ezekiel's dry bones met not together of their own accord, Ezek. xxxvii. 5, 6, or by chance, but were gathered by God, and inspired with life; and not only the last act of life, but the whole formation of them in every part, he does particularly own as the act of his own power. And doing every part of it by degrees, they should know, by that admirable work

upon them, that he was God: 'I will cause breath to enter into you, and you shall live. And I will lay sinews upon you, and will bring flesh upon you, and cover you with skin; and you shall live, and you shall know that I am the Lord.' This work does as much discover the glory of his deity, and speaks him God in a more illustrious manner than the creation of the world. We know him to be the Lord Jehovah by his creation of the world; but a clearer knowledge of him in his power is added by his regeneration of the soul. The sinews, flesh, skin, all the preparations to grace, are from God, as all the preparations of that mass of clay for the breath of life in Adam were from the power of God, as well as the living soul itself. Most do understand it of the recovery of the Jews from the captivity of Babylon; but certainly it has a higher import, and respects the time of the gospel, and the renewing of life in the soul of all the Israel of God. (1.) Because the prophecy extends further than the two tribes captivated in Babylon; for, verse 11, the bones are said to be 'the whole house of Israel,' who despaired of ever seeing and good, complaining that their bones were dried: ver. 11, 'Our hope is lost, we are cut off for our parts.' Which could not be rationally the complaint of the Jews, who had a promise that, after seventy years' captivity, they should return, and therefore their case was not so desperate. (2.) Because, verse 14, he speaks of 'putting his Spirit into them;' meaning thereby that work he had spoken of in the former chapter, Ezek. xxxvi. 7, which certainly, being a covenant of grace, respected the times of the gospel. If it be said that it is meant of forming the church, it must also be meant of forming every member of it, since the least member of Adam was formed by God, as well as the whole body. Certainly, if renewed men, after some great falls, having still the root of habitual grace in them, cry to God, out of a sense of their own insufficiency, for the creating a clean heart, as David does, Ps. li. 10, 'Create in me a clean heart, O God, and renew a right spirit within me;' if he then, who had this root remaining, and had some sparks which presently were blown up upon Nathan's speech to him, cries out for a new creation, what need has he then of an almighty breath who has not any warm ashes of grace or any one string of a spiritual root in his soul! Whatsoever, therefore, is holy, good, and spiritual in us, we owe to the new-creating grace of God. All graces are his "charismata", his free donatives, over and above his common largeness to nature, a present from his infinite liberality.

I shall show,

I. That God is the efficient.

II. That it is necessary he should be so.

III. From what principles in God it flows.

IV. How God does it.

V. The use of it.

I. That God is the efficient.

(1.) In the first promise, Gen. iii. 15, 'I will put enmity,' &c. In which promise is included the whole work of redemption, and new creating man under another head, with another nature, which should not comply with the designs of Satan, or gratify the great enemy of God and mankind by unravelling the work of God, and subjecting himself to misery. It was necessary to our happiness that the league between Stan and us should be broken, that we should turn to God, hate the works of the devil, and join with the interest which Satan endeavoured to overthrow. And God promises that he would do it; he challenges it as his own work: 'I will put enmity;' he leaves it not to men or angels to begin hostility. Every one, therefore, that is at a true variance with Satan is 'God's workmanship, created in Christ,' by a second creation, as well as he was created to a natural life in Adam by the first creation, and 'created to good works, that he may walk in them', Eph. ii. 10. That is, is fashioned by God to walk in ways contrary to those of Satan, which is the greatest enmity we can express to the devil, who envied God a service from the holiness of Adam's nature. And Satan having made that conquest, and gained man to be his friend, it is not easy to conceive how any lower power could unfasten this knot, and set them at variance, since the devil had both wit enough to humour man and strength enough to keep him.

(2.) In the times of the gospel. No less than seven times I will he does affix to his promise of the covenant, as has been observed before, Ezek. xxxvi. 25-27. What seed was left to keep up the name of God among the Jews was of his begetting: Rom. ix. 29, 'Except the Lord of Sabaoth had left us a seed,' cited out of Isa. i. 9. Their standing was not their act, but God's: and 1 Kings xix. 18, 'I have left me seven thousand, all the knees that have not bowed to Baal.' Others were left to themselves; these were signally wrought upon by his grace. Others are but instruments; God is the principal agent in all the seed of the church scattered in the whole earth: Hosea ii. 23, 'I will sow her to me in the earth,' alluding to the name Jezreel, which signifies the seed of God. If ever the sons of Japheth 'dwell in the tents of Shem,' it must be by God's 'persuasion,' Gen. ix. 27. The word rendered enlarge signifies to allure. The Spirit of grace is of God's effusion, Zech. xii. 10; it is God's pouring out a Spirit of grace on them before their looking up to God. (Where, by the way, observe a signal testimony of the deity of Christ; 'They shall look upon me whom they have pierced;' he that pours upon them the Spirit of grace is he whom they pierced, which was the Lord Jehovah, verse 8; for where in your Bibles Lord is written in great letters, the Hebrew word there is Jehovah; the highest name of God is here attributed to Christ.) And even in the last times he will still be the only agent in it. When God speaks of the Jews' dispersion, under which they are at this day, he owns this work upon their hearts at last to be an act of his own power and of covenant mercy: Deut. xxx. 6, 'The Lord thy God will circumcise thy heart,' &c., which some of the Jews understand of the time of the Messiah. God will challenge this work as his own right to the end of the world.

2. Christ appropriates it to God, and acknowledges it to depend only upon his will. Had any other cause been in conjunction with God, our Saviour would not have deprived it of its due praise, nor with so much thankfulness and amazement admired the gracious pleasure of his Father as he did,--Mat. xi. 25, 'At that time Jesus answered and said, I thank thee, O Father, Lord of heaven and earth, because thou hast hid these things from the wise and prudent, and hast revealed them unto babes: even so, Father, for so it seemed good in thy sight,'--at that time, after he had been discoursing of the judgments upon them for their refusal of the gospel, worse than Sodom and Gomorrah. It was God's pleasure not to reveal it to them, and God's justice to punish them for refusal, because they wilfully refused it. The outward teaching was to all in the ministry of Christ, the inward revelation only to few according to the good pleasure of God. Christ was the outward teacher, but God the inward inspirer. That others are not renewed by him is not because he cannot, for he is Lord of heaven and earth, but because he will renew some and not others. Our Saviour refers it here only to the good pleasure of God; he had erred much in ascribing it to God, if he had had the assistance of any other cause. Why this part of the clay he had created was formed into the body of Adam and not another, had no other cause but his pleasure; why this part of corrupted Adam is formed into a temple, a divine image, and not another, can be ascribed to no other but the same cause. He that formed Adam in the earthly paradise, forms every believer in the church, the spiritual paradise, and neither has a co-worker nor motive without himself.

3. The Scripture everywhere appropriates it to God. They are therefore called his saints, Ps. xxxiv. 9, as being sanctified by him as well as belonging to him, 'his people,' 'the branch of his planting', 'the work of his hands,' peculiarly his, as being created for his glory, 'that I may be glorified,' Isa. lx. 21. Their fitness by grace for glory is the work of his hands. The vessels of wrath are fitted for destruction, not by God, but by themselves, Rom. ix. 22. But the vessels of mercy are prepared by him, ver. 23, 'He had before prepared unto glory.' Adam lost himself, but whosoever of his posterity are recovered are 'wrought by God for glory,' 1 Cor. v. 5. It is observable that the apostle ascribes this in the whole frame of it to God: 1 Cor. i. 30, 'But of him are you in Christ Jesus, who of God is made unto us wisdom, righteousness,' &c., because he would remove all cause of boasting in the creature. He did not only set forth Christ at first as a principle of righteousness, and redemption, and sanctification, but engrafted in him, whosoever is in him, for the enjoyment of those privileges, and made him not only in general to the world, but to us, in the particular application, a principle of sanctification as well as righteousness. Union with Christ, engrafting in him, new creation, putting into another state, are all purely the work of God. He has no sharer in it. As Christ trod the winepress alone in the work of redemption, so God engrafts men alone into this vine. As Christ was the sole worker of redemption, so is God the sole worker of regeneration. In him we are created, but solely by God's skill; Christ the vine, and believers the branches, the one planted and the other engrafted by the same husbandman, John xv. 1, 2; he only planted and dressed Christ for us, he only plants and dresses us in Christ. It is 'by his own will,' not any other, that 'he begot us,' James i. 18. 'Of his own will,' his own good pleasure was the motive, his own strength the efficient. Hence he is called 'the Father of spirits,' Heb. xii. 9, not so much (as some interpret it, and that most probably) as he is the Father of souls by creation, as by regeneration, which adds a greater strength to the apostle's argument for submission to him and patience under his strokes. He keeps in his own hand the keys of the heart, no less than the key of the womb, which was always acknowledged to be in the hands of God. It is with this prerogative of God that Jacob silences Rachel, when she so impatiently cried out for children, as if she had a resolution to kill herself if she had them not, with this, 'Am I in God's stead?' Gen. xxx. 1, 2. He only opens the womb of the soul as well as that of the body, impregnates it with grace, and brings forth the fruit of holy actions, as Philo in his allegory descants upon the place. The Jews perhaps meant no less in that saying in their Cabala, Abraham had not had Isaac if a letter of the name of God had not been added to his name; the power of God, a letter of his name, must go to regeneration. It is appropriated to none but God in Scripture: to the whole Trinity, without the conjunction of any creature, to the Father as the author, therefore called 'Our Father;' to Christ, as the pattern; to the Spirit, as the inspirer of that grace whereby we are made the sons of God. The very heathen have acknowledged this, some philosophers have affirmed, that the great virtue, wherein they placed the happiness of man, could not be had but by the favour of God, and all thought their heroes to be born of their gods.

And the Scripture affirms that,

(1.) All preparations to this work, as well as the work itself, are of God. The removing indispositions, and the putting in good inclinations, is the work of the same hand; the taking away the heart of stone, as well as the giving a heart of flesh. He removes the rubbish as well as rears the building; razes out the old stamp and imprints a new; destroys sin, which is called the old man, and restores the new by the quickening of the Spirit. The preparations of the dust of the ground to become a human body, had the same author as the divine soul wherewith he was inspired.

(2.) All the parts of the new creature are of God. Faith, which is the principal part of it, is 'the faith of the operation of God,' Col. ii. 12; not but that love and other graces are wrought by God, but in this grace, which is a constitutive part of the new creature, God comes in with a greater irradiation upon the soul, because it has not one fragment or point in nature to stand upon, carnal reason and mere moral righteousness being enemies to it, whereas all other graces are but the rectifying the passions, and setting them upon right objects. Yet all these, too, own him as the author. Our knowledge of God is a light growing from his knowledge of us; 'we know God' because we 'are known of him.' Gal. iv. 9. The elective act of our wills is but a fruit of his choice of us: John xv. 16, 'You have not chosen me, but I have chosen you;' our willing of him is a birth of his willing us, our love a spark kindled by his love to us. God first calls us my people, before any of us call him my God, Hosea ii. 23. The moon shines not upon the sun till it be first illuminated by it. God first shines upon us before we can reflect upon him; he calls us before we can speak to him in his own dialect; our coming is an effect of his drawing, and our power of coming an effect of his quickening. Every member in Adam was a fruit of his power, as well as the whole body; every line drawn in the new creature is done by his pencil as well as the whole frame.

(3.) The acts of the new creature. God does not only give us the habit of faith, but the act of faith: Philip. i. 29, 'Unto you it is given in the behalf of Christ, not only to believe, but also to suffer for his sake.' By believing is meant the act of believing, as by suffering is meant not only the power of suffering, but actual suffering; as the fruits upon the trees at the first creation were created as well as the tree which had a power to bear. The very attention of Lydia to the gospel preached by Paul was wrought by God, as well as the opening of her heart, Acts xvi. 14. Our walking in his statutes is a fruit of his grace, as well as the putting in his Spirit to enable us thereunto. The very act of motion is made by the head and heart, if there he a failing of spirits there, if any obstruction that they cannot reach the indigent part, the motion ceases. David acknowledged God his continual strength in his holy pursuits, 'My soul follows hard after thee,' Ps. lxiii. 8. But what was the cause? 'Thy right hand upholds me.' His life and power issued out from the right hand of God. The graces of God's people stand in need of the irradiations of God, like the Urim and Thummim, before any counsel could be given by them.

(4.) The continuance both of the power and acts are from God. Habitual grace is called the 'fear of the Lord' put into the soul; the continuance of it is by his constant sustentation, it is that we may not depart from him Jer. xxxii. 40, 'from upon him,' from leaning upon him, or believing in him, as the word "me'alaw" imports. If that fear put in did once depart from us, we should no longer cleave to God; we stick to him only because he ties us to himself, and cannot be continually with him unless he 'holds us by his right hand,' Ps. lxxiii. 23. The grace that is wrought, as well as the gospel which instrumentally wrought it, is 'kept by the Holy Ghost,' 2 Tim. i. 14; he begins every good work, and he performs it. He was the sole active cause in the creation of the faculties, and the principal cause in preserving them; he is the sole cause of the elevation of the faculties, and the preservation of them in that elevated state. As the virtue of the loadstone is not only the cause of the first attraction of the steel, but of its constant adhesion, therefore it is said: 1 Cor. i. 21, that 'God does establish us,' not has done, to note the continual influence of his grace upon us. It was the dropping of the two olive trees that constantly fed the lamps in the candlesticks, Zech. iv. 2, 8. Take this new birth in all the denominations of it, it is altogether ascribed to God. As it is a call out of the world, God is the herald, 2 Tim. i. 9; as it is a creation, God is the creator Eph. ii. 10; as it is a resurrection, God is the quickener, Eph. ii. 5; as it is a new birth, God is the begetter, 1 Peter i. 3; as it is a new heart, God is the framer, Ezek. xxxvi. 26; as it is a law in the heart, God is the penman, Jer. xxxi. 33; as it is a translation out of Satan's kingdom, and making us denizens of the kingdom of Christ, God is the translator, Col. i. 13; as it is a coming to Christ, God is the drawer, John vi. 44; as it is a turning to God, God is the attracter.

II. The second thing; it is necessary God should be the efficient of regeneration. He is, or none. In regard of God.

1. As he is the first cause of all things. He is the creator of the lowest worm, and the highest angel; the glimmering perfections of the least fly, as well as the more glittering eminencies of the angelical nature, are distinct beams from that fountain of light and power. Shall not he then be the cause of the divine motions of the will, as well as of the natural motions of the creatures? Every perfection in a rational creature, or any other, supposes that perfection to be somewhere essentially; every impression supposes a stamp that made it, every stream a fountain from whence it sprang, every beam a sun, or some lucid body from whence it darts. Whence should this gracious work then be derived? Not from nature, which is contrary to it; not from Satan, who is destroyed by it. It must be then from God, since it must have some stable and perfect cause. He who was the cause of all the grace in the head is also the cause of all the grace in the members. The same sun that enlightens the heavens enlightens the earth. The grace that Christ had was 'the gift of God,' John iii. 34, much more must it be his gift to us, though we had souls as capacious as his. If the head derived not his grace to himself, the members cannot; for Christ being a creature, in regard of his humanity, must necessarily be dependent; for to make any

creature independent upon God is to advance it above the degree of a creature-state, and make it God's fellow, yea, to have a godhead in itself, as being the first principle of its own being. To say any creature can move to God, without being moved by God, or live without his influence, is to make the creature independent on God in its operations; and if it be independent in its operations, it would be so consequently in its essence, besides, if it be not created by him, it may subsist without him, it stands in no need of his quickening. The believers in Scripture were very unadvised then to pray to God for his quickening and establishing grace, if he were not the enlivener and author of it. His power works in preservation as well as creation, John v. 17, and whatsoever is dependent on him in preservation is dependent on him in creation and the first framing. And if it does not depend upon him in preservation, it is not his creature, but it is a god. All creatures have a dependence upon something immediately superior to then. The moon receives her light and chief beauty from the sun, which else would be but a dusky body; the earth its influence from the heavens. In artificial things the little wheels in a watch depend upon the greater, that upon the string (spring?), that in its motion upon the hand that winds it up. The higher any creature is, the more immediately it depends upon God in its production; the waters brought forth the fish, but God himself formed man.

2. As he is the promiser of it. The divine promise is only fulfilled by a divine operation, it is necessary then for the honour of his truth to be the performer of it. All his promises concerning this matter run in that strain, I will: Hosea ii. 19, 'I will betroth thee to me for ever; I will betroth thee to me in righteousness, in judgment, in loving-kindness, and in mercy: I will even betroth thee unto me in faithfulness; and thou shalt know the Lord.' The Lord promises by this of knowing him all gracious works upon the soul, regeneration, faith, &c., for this knowledge is an effect of the covenant which God promises in that great copy of it: Jer. xxxi. 34, 'They shall all know me, from the least of them to the greatest.' It is not a simple abstracted knowledge, for so the devils know God, and Christ crucified, but such a knowledge that implies faith and love, and a new frame of soul. It is necessary his power should make good what his goodness has promised. It was not necessary any word of promise should go out of his mouth, there was no engagement upon God to do it, but it is necessary this promise should be performed; though he were free before he promised, yet he is not free after he has promised, because his truth engages him to perform it, and perform it as his own act, as much as his mercy moved him to promise it as his own act. As mercy made it, so his mercy is as pressing for the performance, and there comes in a superadded obligation from that of his truth over and above his mercy, to perform it in the same manner he promised it, and in all the circumstances of it. So that, supposing (which cannot be supposed) that his mercy should repent of making it, he would not be true if he did not perform it; besides, it consists not with his truth not to perform that by himself which he has promised by himself, nor with his wisdom to leave that to an uncertain cause at the best, and, further, a cause utterly unable (as every creature is) to produce that which he had promised to do with his own hand, as the cleansing the soul, pouring clean water upon it, pouring out a spirit of grace, writing the law in the heart, which imply his own act principally in this affair, in concurrence with the means he has ordained to that end. The performance of God's promise is as infallible as the cause that made the promise. No power can perform that for another which he promises himself to do; for the thing itself may be done by another, yet not being done by the party promising to do it, it is not truly done, and in conformity to the promise made. If it were possible then to be done by any but a divine hand, it would not be done truly, because God promises it as his own act, and therefore the working it must be his own act in conformity to his truth.

3. As he has the foreknowledge of all things. It is necessary God should foreknow everything future, and that shall come to pass. This is a perfection necessarily belonging to God; and to imagine the contrary is to frame an unworthy notion of God, and infinitely below the great creator and governor of the world. He therefore wills everything, for if he foreknew anything before he willed it in itself, or in its necessary causes, he foreknow nothing. If he did not will it, how can it come to pass? Therefore he did not foreknow that it would come to pass. If he did foreknow it, then he willed it, otherwise his foreknowledge depended upon an uncertain cause, and he might have judged that to come to pass which never might; unless the cause be determined by God, it is merely contingent. He willing therefore a work of grace in such and such persons, did foreknow that it would be wrought, because he did will that it should be, and his working is done by an act of his will: Rom. viii. 29, 'Whom he did foreknow, he did predestinate to be conformed to the image of his Son.' The foreknowledge of God being stable and infallible, and being in this case a foreknowledge of what makes highly for the glory of all his attributes, can have no dependence upon an uncertain and fallible cause, but upon a cause as stable as his foreknowledge, which is his will, himself. His foreknowledge of this is not a foreknowledge of it in any created cause, but in himself as the cause; because, as it will appear further, no created cause could accomplish it.

In regard of the subject of this new birth.

1 In regard of the subject simply considered, the heart and will of man, none can cork upon it but God, or have any intrinsic influence to cause it to exercise its vital acts. Angels, though of a very vast

power, cannot work immediately upon the heart and will of another creature, to incline and change it, by an immediate touch. All that they can do towards any moving the will, is by presenting some external objects, or stirring up the inward sensitive appetite to some passion, as anger, desire; whereby the will is inclined to will something. But the stirring up those natural affections in an unregenerate man, can never incline his will to good; for being the affections of the flesh, they are to be crucified. Angels also may enlighten the understanding, not immediately, but by presenting similitudes of sensible things, and confirming them in the fancy; but to remove one ill habit from the will or incline it to any good, is not in their power. God gave an angel power to purge the prophet's lips with a coal from the altar, Isa. vi. 6, 7, but that was done in a vision, and a symbol or sign only that his uncleanness was removed. A coal could have no virtue in it to purge spiritual pollutions from the spirit of a man. Neither can man change the will; men by allurements or threats may change, or rather suspend the action of another, as a father that threatens to disinherit his son; or a magistrate that threatens to punish a subject for his debauchery, may cause a change in the actions of such persons; but the heart stands still to the same sinful points, and may be vicious under a fair disguise. He only that made the will, can incline and 'turn it as the rivers of waters; the heart of the king is in the hands of the Lord,' Prov. xxi. 1, and so is every man's heart kept in the hands of him that created it, both cabinet and key. No man knows the heart, no, the heart itself knows not everything which is in it. God knows all the wards in the heart, and knows how to move it. If a man could turn the heart of another, it could only be in one or two points; it cannot be conceived how he should alter the whole frame of it, make it quite another thing than it was before. The spirit of man being 'the candle of the Lord,' Prov. xx. 27, not to give light to him, but lighted by him, can only when it is out be re-lighted, and, when it burns dim, be snuffed by the same hand. Or, suppose for the present he could do this, it must be with much pains and labour, many exhortations and wise management of him upon several occasions. But to do this by a word, in a trice, to put a law into the heart in a moment, and give the hidden man of the heart possession of the will, that a man knows not himself how he came to be changed, this whole work bears the mark and stamp of God in the forehead of it. Men may propose arguments to another, and he may understand them if he has a capacity, but no man can ever make another have a capacity who is naturally incapable; it is God only can make the heart capable of understanding, he only can put a new instinct into it, and make it of another bent; it is he that renews the spirit of the mind to enable it to understand what he does propose, and elevates the faculty to apprehend the reason of it.

2. In regard of the subject, extremely ill qualified. Can any question the divinity of the work, when stones are made children to Abraham; when waters of repentance are drawn out of a hard rock, Aaron's dry rod made to bud and blossom, and bring forth fruit, Num. vii. 8, when souls deeply allied to the kingdom of darkness are translated into the kingdom of light? To see habits strengthened by custom, in a consumption, and hearts filled with multitudes of idols in several shapes, casting them out with indignation, and flourishing with new springing graces, it is too great a miracle to be wrought by the hand of any creature. Could anything but the arm of the Lord change the temper of the thief upon the cross, to advance further in the space of an hour in the kingdom of God, than all the apostles had done in the three years' converse with their Master; to confess him, when one of the most eminent of them had denied him; to be more knowing in an instant, than they had been in a long time; and acknowledge his spiritual kingdom, when they even after his resurrection, and just before his ascension, expected a temporal one? Acts i. 6, 'Wilt thou at this time restore the kingdom to Israel?' If a Socrates, or a Cato, or those braver lights among the heathen, were turned to God, the interest of God in the work might upon some seeming ground be questioned; but when the leviathans in sin, drunkards, extortioners, adulterers, men guilty of the greatest contempt of God and the light of nature, in whom lust had kept a peaceable possession in its empire for many years, are thoroughly changed, who can doubt but that such must indeed be 'washed and sanctified by the Spirit of our God'? 1 Cor. vi. 11. What can this be but the will of God, since their hearts were so delightfully filled with evil, that they had no room nor love for any holy thought? It is not conceivable that where sin has made such a rout, and cut and slashed all morality in pieces, things should he set in order there, but by a power stronger both than sin and the law, from whence sin derives its strength. It is no less than a divine miracle to renew an habituated sinner.

(3.) In regard of the nature of this new birth. It is a change of nature; a nature where there was as little of spiritual good as there was of being in nothing before the creation. It is a change of stone into flesh; a heart that like a stone has a hardness and settledness of sinful parts, a strong resistance against any instrument, an incorporation of sin and lust with its nature. Where the heart and sin, self and sin, are cordially one and the same, none can change such a nature but the God of all grace, who has all grace to contest with all the power of old Adam. No man can change the nature of the meanest creature in the world; he may tame them, bring them to part with some of their wildness, but he cannot transform them. If no man can transform the lowest creature from one nature to another, much less can any but God transform man into another nature.

This nature is changed in every believer; for it is impossible a man should stand bent to Christ, with his old nature predominant in him, any more than a pebble can be attracted by a loadstone, till it put on the nature of steel. An unrighteous nature cannot act righteously, it must therefore be a God, who is above nature, that can clothe the soul with a new nature, and incline it to God and goodness in its operations. Now to see a lump of vice become a model of virtue; for one that drank in iniquity like water, to change that sinful thirst for another for righteousness; to crucify his darling flesh; to be weary of the poison he loved for the purity he hated; to embrace the gospel terms, which not his passion but his nature abhorred; to change his hating of duty to a free-will offering of it; to make him cease from a loathing the obligations of the law, to a longing to come up to the exactness of it; to count it a burden to have the thoughts at a distance from God, when before it was a burden to have one serious thought fixed on him, speaks a supernatural grace transcendently attractive and powerfully operative. Heavy elements do not ascend against their own nature, unless they be drawn by some superior force. To see a soul neighed down to the earth, to be lifted up to heaven, must point us to a greater than created strength that caused the elevation. These acts are supernatural, and cannot be done by a natural cause; that is, against the order of working in all things, for then the effect, as an effect, would be more noble than its cause.

(4.) In regard of the suddenness of it. Peter and Andrew were called when they thought of nothing but their nets; and Paul changed by a word or two, who before was not only unwilling, but rebellious. Some have gone into a church wolves, and returned lambs. This change comes upon some that never dreamt of it, and has snatched them out of the arms of hell; upon others who have resisted with all their might any motion that way, and were never greater enemies to any, than to those that would check their sinful pleasures with such admonitions, and yet these have been on the sudden surprised. What ground is there to ascribe any of this, but to a divine work? Many have dropped in unto a sermon with no intention to stay, who have felt God's hook in their souls; have leaped like fish out of their element for a while, and God has caught them in his hand. Have you never heard of some who have gone to make sport with a convincing sermon, or to satisfy lust with unclean glances, who have been made prisoners by grace before their return? This quickness of the soul in coming to Christ was promised to be the fruit of the gospel: Hosea iii. 5, 'They shall fear the Lord and his goodness,' when they should 'seek the Lord and David their king.' The word "pachad" signifies not only to fear, but to hasten; both significations may be joined together in the sense of the verse. They shall make haste to fear the Lord and his goodness; surely the power that performs it, is the same with the goodness which promised it. Thus some of the disciples have followed Christ at the first call, and moved readily to him, as iron to the loadstone. For a man that was at a great distance from God, and any affection to him, to be filled on the sudden with a warm love and zeal for him, when nothing of interest could engage him (and sometimes it has been with loss of friends, estate, yea, life too), is as great a discovery of a divine hand, as if a fly were changed into the shape and spirit of a hero; because a spiritual change is more admirable than a natural; and the more by how much the enmity, which was greater, is driven out, for a choice affection to rise up in its stead. The season when such a work is wrought is more significant of a divine force, when men have been in the heat and strength of the pursuit of their sinful pleasures, being then torn out of the embracements of lust with an outstretched arm of God.

(5.) In regard of the excellency of the new birth. Is it reasonable to think that the image of God should be wrought by any other hand than the hand of God, or the divine nature be begotten by anything but the divine Spirit? Since none but man can beget a child in his own likeness, none but God can impart to a soul the divine nature. It is not a change only into the image of God with slight colours, an image drawn as with charcoal; but a glorious image even in the rough draught, which grows up into greater beauty by the addition of brighter colours. 'Changed,' says the apostle, 2 Cor. iii. 18, 'into the same image from glory to glory;' glory in the first lineaments as well as glory in the last lines. Is it not too beautiful then, even in the first draught, to be wrought by any pencil but a divine? It is next to the formation of Christ, for it is an initial conformity to him. God is the fountain of all our good things. If 'every good and perfect gift comes from him,' James i. 17, shall not the best of beings be the author of the best of works? If believers are 'light in the Lord,' Eph. v. 8, they are no less light from him and by him who is the 'Father of lights.' It is a 'heavenly calling,' Heb. iii. 1, therefore a heavenly birth. The new heart, the spiritual house wherein God dwells, as well as in the heavens, was not made with a less power and skill than the earth, which is his footstool, or the heaven, which is his throne. If none be able to make God a footstool, much less a throne, as Jerusalem, the church, is called in the times of the gospel, Jer. iii. 17. (The embroideries and ornaments of the material tabernacle were not made by common art, but by a Bezaleel inspired by the Spirit of God, Exod. xxxi. 3); can any but himself rear up a temple for the God of heaven to dwell in? 1 Cor. iii. 9. Or is the spiritual house of God fit to be made by and but by that God that dwells in it? It was according to the image of God that we were first created; it is according to the image of Christ that we are new created, Rom. viii. 29. Who understands the image of the Son but the Father? Who knows the Father but the Son, and he to whom the Son will reveal him? The new creature, according to the copy, can only be wrought by him to whom the copy is only visible. It is for the honour of God to allow him to be the framer of all creatures in the rank of beings. Is it not a dishonour to him not to acknowledge him the framer of the new creature in the rank of spiritual beings, since the later is more excellent than the treasures of the earth or the stars of heaven, than body or soul;

since the image of God consists not so much in the substance of the soul as in a likeness to God in a holy nature? Eph. iv. 24. To be a righteous regenerate man is more excellent than to be a man; the most glorious effect, then, must have the most glorious cause. One beam of this divine image is too excellent to be the workmanship of any but a divine hand. The very first regenerate thought, to the last dropping off of impurity, is from the same hand. The first drawing us from sin, much more the stripping us of it, is more admirable than the drawing us out of nothing.

(6.) The end of regeneration manifests it to be the work of God. It is to display his goodness. Since this was the end of God in the first creation, it is much more his end in the second. What creature can display God's goodness for him, or give him the glory of it, without first receiving it? Goodness must first be communicated to us, before it can be displayed or reflected by us. The light that is reflected back upon the sun by any earthly body beams first from the sun itself. Both the subject and the end are put together in Isa. xliii. 20, 21, 'The beasts of the field shall honour me, the dragons and the owls: because I give waters in the wilderness, to give drink to my people, my chosen. This people have I formed for myself; they shall show forth my praise.' The Gentiles shall have the gospel, who are beasts of the field for wildness, dragons for the poison of their nature, owls for their blindness and darkness. The waters of the gospel shall flow to them to give drink to their souls. This people have I formed for myself. Even beasts, dragons, owls, if formed for himself, they could not be formed but by himself, who only understands what is fit for his own praise. How can such incapable subjects be formed for such high ends, without a supernatural power? So in Isa. lx. 21, 'The branch of my planting, the work of my hands, that I may be glorified.' Planted by God, that God might be glorified by them. As God only is the proper judge of what may glorify him, so he is the sole author of what is fitted to glorify him. Nothing lower than the goodness of God can instil into us such a goodness as to be made meet to praise, serve, and love him; such a holiness as may fit us to be partakers of the inheritance of the saints in light, and enjoy him for ever. As infinite wisdom formed us in Adam, and moulded us with his own hand to be a model of his perfection, so are we no less his workmanship in Christ by a second creation to good works, which, as they are ordained by the will of God, so they are wrought in us by the skill and power of God; what is ordained positively by him and for him is wrought by him. The whole world consists but of two men and their offspring the first man, Adam, the second man, Christ; both they, and all in them, created by God. It is a forming a creature for himself for his own delight. What delight can God take in anything but himself, and what is like himself? Man in his best estate is vanity. As his being is, so are his operations. Vanity, and the operations flowing from thence, are no fit object for the delight of an infinite excellency and wisdom. What pleasure can he have in those things which are not wrought by his own finger? Who knows how to dress anything savoury and pleasant to God but his own grace? Can a finite thing touch an infinite being to enjoy him without the operation of an infinite virtue? Can God delight in anything principally but himself, as he is infinitely good; or in other things but as they come nearest to that goodness? Whatsoever has a resemblance to a superior being must be brought forth into that likeness by something superior to itself.

Now since the ends of this work are so high as to fit us for his praise, his delight, and a fruition of him; since it is to bring the interest of God into the soul, set him up highest in the heart who before was trampled under our feet, enthrone him as king in the soul, cause us to oppose all that opposes him, cherish everything that is agreeable to him, this must be his work or the work of none.

(7.) The weakness of the means manifests it to be the work of God. How could it be possible that such weak means, that were used at the first plantation of the gospel, should have that transcendent success in the hearts of men without a divine power? That a doctrine attended with the cross, resisted by devils with all their subtilty, by the flesh with all its lusts, the world with all its flatteries, the wise with all their craft, the mighty with all their power, should be imprinted upon the hearts of men; a doctrine preached by mean men, without any worldly help, without learning, eloquence, craft, or human prudence, without the force, favour, or friendship of men, should get place in men's hearts without a divine inspiration, cannot well be imagined. If it be said there were miracles attending it, which wrought upon the minds of men, it is true; but what little force they had in our Saviour's time the Scripture informs us, when they were ascribed to Beelzebub, the prince of devils. Though miracles did attend it after the ascension of our Saviour, yet the apostle ascribes not so much to them as the means, as he does to the 'foolishness of preaching, ' it was that which was the 'power of God,' 1 Cor. i. 18; it was that 'whereto God saved them that believe,' 1 Cor. i. 21. But the greatest change that ever was wrought at one time was at the first descent of the Spirit, by a plain discourse of Peter, Acts ii., extolling a crucified God before those that had lately taken away his life, those that had seen him die, a doctrine which would find no footing in their reasons, filled with prejudice against him, and had expectations of a temporal kingdom by him. Must not this change be ascribed to a higher hand, which removed their rooted prejudices and vain hopes, and brought so many as three thousand over at once? If there be 'diversities of operations, it is the same God that works all in all,' 1 Cor. xii. 6. He conveys this 'treasure in earthen vessels, that the power might appear to be of God, and not of men,' 2 Cor. iv. 7. Such weak means as earthen vessels cannot work such miraculous changes. Therefore perhaps it was that the preaching of

Christ in his humiliation had so little success attending it, that nothing should be ascribed to the word itself, but to the power of God in it. To evidence that success depended on the good pleasure of God, who would not make his preaching in person so successful as that in his Spirit, which appears by Christ's thanksgiving to his Father for revealing these things to babes, and not to the wise: 'Even so, Father, for so it seemed good in thy sight,' Luke x. 21. Have you never heard of changes wrought in the spirits of men against their worldly interest, when they have been made the scorn of their friends, and a reproach to their neighbours? Can the weakness of means write a law so deep in the heart, that neither sly allurements nor blustering temptations can raze out; that a law of a day's standing in the heart should be able to mate the powers of hell, the cavils of the flesh, and discouragements from the world, when there are no unanswerable miracles now to seal the gospel, and second the proposals of it with amazement in the minds of men? The weakness of the means, and the greatness of the difficulties, speaks it not only to be the finger but the arm of God, which causes the triumphs of the foolishness of preaching. When the proposal crosses the interest of the flesh, restrains the beloved pleasure, teaches a man the necessity of the contempt of the world, and that men should exchange their pride for humility, the pleasure of sin for a life of holiness; for a man not only to cease to love his vice, but extremely to hate it; to have divine flights, when before he could not have a divine thought; to put off earthly affections for heavenly, and all this by the foolishness of preaching, it is an argument of a divine power, rather than any inherent strength in the means themselves.

(3.) The differences in the changes of men evidence this to be the work of God, and that it is from some power superior to the means which are used. As God puts a difference between men in regard of their understandings, revealing that to one man which he does not to another, so he puts a difference between men in regard of their wills, working upon some and not upon others, working upon some that have known less, and not working upon some that have known more, some embracing it, and others rejecting it. We may see,

[1.] The difference of this change in men under the same means. One is struck at a sermon, when multitudes return unshaken. Why is not the case equal in all, if it were from the power of the word? How successful is Peter's discourse, closely accusing the Jews of the murdering of their Lord and Saviour, which is the occasion of pricking three thousand hearts? Yet Stephen using the same method, and close application of the same doctrine, Acts vii. 62, had not one convert upon record. While Peter's hearers were pricked in their hearts, these gnashed with their teeth, ver. 54. The corruption of the former was drawn out by the pricking of their souls, the malice of the latter exasperated by the cut of their hearts. What reason can be rendered of so different an event from one and the same means in several hands, but the overruling pleasure of God? The reasons were the same, set off with the same human power; the hearers were many of the same nation, brought up in the reading of the prophets, full of the expectations of a Messiah; they had both reasons and natural desires for happiness, as well as the other, yet the one are turned lambs, and the others worse lions than before; the bloody fury of the one is calmed, and the mad rage of the other is increased. The grace of God wrought powerfully in the one, and lighted not upon the other. Two are grinding at the same mill of ordinances, one is taken and another is left. Man breathes into the ears, and God into what heart he pleases.

[2.] The differences in the changes of men under less means. One is changed by weaker means, another remains in his unregeneracy under means in themselves more powerful and likely; some are wrought upon by whispers, when others are stiff under thunders. The Ninevites by one single sermon from a prophet are moved to repentance; the Capernaites, by many admonitions from a greater than all the prophets, seconded with miracles, are not a jot persuaded; some remain refractory under great blasts, while others bend at lighter breathings. One man may be more acute than another, of a more apprehensive reason; yet this man remains obstinate, whilst another becomes pliable. Whence does this difference arise, but from the will of God drawing the one, and reusing the other to the conduct of his own will, since both will acknowledge what they are advised to, to be their interest, to be true in itself, necessary for their good, yet their affections and entertainment are not the same? Some of those Jews who had heard the doctrine of Christ, seen the purity of his life and the power of his miracles, admired his wisdom, yet crucified his person; they expected a Messiah, yet contemned him when he came; when the poor thief who, perhaps, had never seen one miracle, nor heard one sermon of our Saviour, believes in him, acknowledges him to be the Son of God, whom he saw condemned to the same death with himself, and dies a regenerate man under great disadvantages. A figure (says one) of all the elect, who shall only be saved by grace, and a clear testimony of an outstretched arm of grace. Those that our blessed Saviour admonished only as a doctor and teacher were unmoved, none stirred but those he wrought upon as a creator.

[3.] Difference of the success of the same means in different places. How various was the success of the apostles in several parts of their circuits! Paul finds a great door of faith opened at Corinth, and in Macedonia, and his nets empty at Athens; multitudes flocking in at one place, and few at another. He is entertained at Corinth, stoned at Lystra, Acts xiv. 19, in danger of his life at Jerusalem, while the Galatians were so affected with the gospel, that they could have 'pulled out their eyes' for him. The apostle was the same person in all places; the gospel was the same, and had a like power in itself; men had the same reasons, they were all fragments from the lump of Adam: the difference must be then from the influence of the divine Spirit, who rained down his grace in one place and not in another; on one heart, and not on another; who left darkness in Egypt, while he diffused light in Goshen.

[4.] Difference in the same person. What is the reason that a man believes at one time under the proposal of weak arguments, and not at another under stronger? It is not ex parte objecti, for that was more visible and credible in itself, when attended by strong arguments, than when accompanied with weaker. Perhaps God has stricken a man's conscience before, and he has undone that work, shaken off those convictions; he has contended with his maker, and mustered up the power of nature against the alarms of conscience; struggled like a wild bull in a net, and broke it, and blunted those darts which stuck in his soul; he has afterwards been screwed up again, and the arrow shot so deep, that with all his pulling he could not draw it out. What but a divine hand holds it in, in spite of all the former triumphs of nature? How come convictions at last to be fixed upon men, which many a time before did but flutter about the soul, and were soon chased away? And God by such a method keeps up the honour of his grace in men after regeneration, and teaches them the constant acknowledgement of his power in the whole management. Do we not daily find that the same reasonings and considerations which quicken us at one time in the ways of God stir us not at another, no more than a child can a millstone; that we are quickened by the same word at one time, under which we were dull and stupid at another; and the same truth is deliciously swallowed by us, which seemed unsavoury at another, because God edges it with a secret virtue at one time more than another? Hereby God would mind us to own him as the author of all our grace, the second grace as well as the first. Upon all these considerations this can be no other than the work of God. Can a corrupt creature elevate himself from a state of being hated by God, to a state of being delighted in by him? Satan's work none can judge it to be; the destroyer of mankind would never be the restorer; the most malicious enemy to God would never contribute to the rearing a temple to God in the soul, who has usurped God's worship in all parts of the world. Good angels could never do it, they wonder at it; the wisdom of God in thus creating all things in Jesus Christ is made known to them by it, Eph. iii. 9, 10. They never ascribed it to themselves; if they did, they could never have been good, their goodness consisting in praising of God, and giving him his due. Good men never did it; the first planters of the gospel (whereby it is wrought) always gave God the praise of it, and acknowledged both their own action, and the success, to be the effect of the grace of God, and upon every occasion admired it, Acts xi. 21, 23. It was 'the hand of the Lord' and 'the grace of God.'

III. The third general head, from what principles in God it flows, or what perfections of God are eminent in this work of regeneration. What is observable in the forming Christ in the womb of the virgin, is observable in the forming Christ in the heart of a believer: grace to choose her to be the holy vessel; sovereignty to pitch upon her rather than any other of the lineage of David; truth to his promise in forming him in the womb of a virgin, and one of the house of David; wisdom and power in the formation of him in a virgin's womb, above the power of nature; mercy bears the first sway as the motive of the decree, but in a way of sovereignty to call out some, and not others; truth to himself obliges, after sovereign mercy had made the resolution; wisdom steps in to contrive the best way to accomplish what mercy had moved, and sovereignty had decreed; holiness rises up as the pattern; and power rides out for the execution. Mercy moves, sovereignty decrees, truth obliges, wisdom counsels, holiness regulates, power executes.

1. Mercy and goodness is a principal perfection of God, illustrious in this work. 'Born not of the will of man, but of God,' of the will of his mercy. Plato thought that heroes were born "ex erotos Theon", from the love of God; divine love brings forth an heroic Christian into the world; all outward mercies are streams of God's goodness, but those are but trifles if compared with this. There is as much of God in imparting the holiness of his nature as in imputing the righteousness of his soul. We are justified by Christ, quickened by grace, saved by grace; grace is the womb of every spiritual blessing. To be delivered from places and company wherein we have occasions and temptations to sin, is an act which God owns as the fruit of his mercy: 'I brought thee out of the land of Ur of the Chaldees,' Gen. xv. 7, an idolatrous place; it is a greater fruit of his goodness to be delivered from a nature which is the seed-plot of sin. 'He heals our backslidden nature,' because he 'loves us freely.' It is therefore called grace, which is not only goodness and mercy, but goodness with a more beautiful varnish and ornamental dress.

(1.) Therefore in this take notice of the peculiarity of mercy. Such a goodness that not one fallen angel ever had, or ever shall have a mite of; neither did mercy excite one good thought in God of new polishing any of those rebellious creatures; mercy cast no eye upon them, but justice left them to their malicious obstinacy. That the rivers of living water should refuse to run in such a channel, or flow out of such a belly, to run in the heart of a man more muddy! As peculiar grace pitched upon the very flesh of Christ, to be limited to the second person, so the like grace pitches upon this or that particular soul, to be united to the body of Christ. That singular love which chose Christ for the head, chose some men in him to be his members: 'Chosen us in him,' Eph. i. 4. And the anointing which is upon the head is poured out by such a peculiarity of love upon the members, not only by an act of his power as God, but by an act of appropriated goodness, thy God, Heb. i. 9. God anoints his fellows with that holy gracious unction, as their God, not only as God; for anointing him as the head, under that particular consideration, he anoints also his fellows, his members, under the same consideration too, because he is as well their God, the God of the members, as well as the God of the head, for they are his fellows in that unction; the difference lies in the greater portion of grace given to the human nature of Christ. And the apostle Peter, 1 Peter i. 3, intimates in his thanksgiving to God, that God begot us as the Father of our Lord Jesus Christ: 'Blessed be the God and Father of our Lord Jesus Christ,' the paternal affection he bears to Christ being the ground of the regeneration of his people; the paternal affection first pitching upon Christ, then upon others in him. Indeed, it is a peculiar affection. In his mercy to the world, he acts as a rector or governor, in that relation he proposes laws, makes offers of peace, urges them in his word, strives with men by his Spirit, enduing men with reason, and deals with them as rational creatures; he uses affections and mercies, which might soften their hearts, did they not wilfully indulge themselves in their hardness. This is his rectoral mercy, or his mercy as a governor, and as much as his relation of a governor can oblige him to. If men will not change their lives, is God bound as a governor to force them to it, or not rather to punish them for it? But in regeneration there is a choicer affection, whereby, besides the relation of a governor, he puts on that of a father, and makes an inward and thorough change in some which he has chosen into the relation of children. As a father, who cannot persuade his son lying under a mortal distemper to take that physic which is necessary for saving his life, will compel him to it, open his mouth, and pour it in; but as he is a governor of his servant, he will provide it for him, and propose it to him. To do thus is kindness to his servant, though he does not manifest so peculiar an affection as he does to his son. God governs men as he is the author of nature; he renews men as he is the author of grace; he is the lawgiver and governor; it does not follow that where he is so he should be the new creator too; this is a peculiar indulgence.

(2.) As there is a peculiarity of mercy, so there is the largeness of his mercy and goodness in this work. It was his goodness to create us, but a full sea of goodness made us new creatures: 1 Peter i. 3, 'Who according to his abundant mercy has begotten us again to 'a lively hope,' "kata to polu autou eleos". His own mercy, without any other motive; much mercy, without any parsimony, not an act of ordinary goodness, but the deepest bowels of kindness, an everlasting spring of goodness, an exuberance of goodness. The choice love he bears to them in election cannot be without some real act; it is a vain love that does not operate; one great part of affection is to imitate the party beloved; but since that is unworthy of God to imitate a corrupt creature, he performs the other act of love, which is to assimilate us to himself, and bring us into a state of imitation of him, endowing us with principles of resemblance to him. It is abundant mercy to love them; it is much more goodness to render them worthy of his love, and inspire them with those qualities, as effects of his love of benevolence, which may be an occasion of his love of complacency. Worldly mercies do many times, yea, for the most part (if you view the whole globe of the earth) consist with his hatred, but this is a beam from a clear sun. At best other benefits are but the mercies of his hand, this of his heart. In those he makes men like others of a higher rank, in this like himself.

[1.] It is a goodness greater than that in creation. It is more an act of kindness to reform that which is deformed, than to form it at the beginning, because it is more to have a happy than a simple being. To repair what is decayed is a testimony of greater goodness than at first to raise it. Creation is terminated to the good of a mutable nature, regeneration is terminated to a supernatural good, and partaking of the divine nature. The creation was an emanation of his goodness, never entitled the work of his grace. Man's first uprightness was an impress of God; his second uprightness is far more pleasing to him, as being the fruit of his Son's death, wherein all his attributes are more highly glorified. It is a regeneration 'by the resurrection of Christ,' 1 Peter i. 3; that being the perfection of it, includes his death, which is the foundation of it, as the perfection of a thing includes the beginning. God pronounced all the structures of the first creation good, but not with those magnificent titles of his delighting in it, forming it for himself, that it might show forth his praise, which expressions testify a greater efflux of his goodness in this second creation. Nor did Christ ever say his delight was in that, or in that one man Adam, but in the sons of men, of apostate Adam, as to be redeemed and renewed by him after their apostasy: Prov. viii. 31, 'My delights were with the sons of men.' What sons of men? The exhortation, ver. 32, intimates it, those that are his children renewed by him that hearken to him and keep his ways. God pronounced it good, but not his treasure, his portion, his inheritance, his segullah, his house, his diadem. All those things which he made, even the noblest heaven, as well as the lowest earth, he overlooks and speaks slightly of them: Isa. lxvi. 1, 2, 'All those things has my hand made, and all those things have been,' &c., to fix his eyes, "avit", upon a contrite spirit, a renewed nature. He speaks of them as things passed away, and is intent only upon the new creation; values it above heaven and earth, and all the ceremonial worship. What is the object of his greatest estimation partakes of a greater efflux of his goodness to make it so. And the apostle Peter aggrandises this abundant mercy in regeneration, from the term, 'unto a lively hope;' not such an uncertain hope as Adam had when he was fullest of his mutable uprightness;

a living hope, "elpida dzosan", that grows up more and more into life, till it comes to an inheritance that fades not away as Adam's did. Surely there is more of bowels in the Spirit's brooding over a sinful soul, to bring forth this beautiful frame, than in brooding over the confused mass to bring forth a world.

[2.] All the grace and goodness God has is employed in it. In the creation you cannot say, all the goodness of God was displayed, as not all his power nor all his wisdom: for as to his power he might have made millions of worlds inconceivably more beautiful and more wisely contrived; for though there be no defect of wisdom and power, yet neither of those attributes were exerted to that height that they might have been. So for his goodness, he might have made millions of more angels and men than he did create, with as (and more) illustrious natures; for a man may conceive something more than God has displayed in the creation, as to the extensiveness of his perfections at least. But in this God has displayed, as it may seem, the utmost of his grace, for no man or angel can conceive a higher grace than what God shows in this, of beginning in man a likeness to himself, and perfecting it hereafter to as high a pitch as a creature is capable of. Therefore called 'unsearchable riches of Christ,' Eph. hi. 7. A further good cannot be imagined or found out than what is there displayed. Therefore the apostle Peter speaks of God as effectually calling us into his eternal glory by Christ, under the title of ' the God of all grace,' 1 Peter v. 10, which calling includes all preparation for glory. All grace does not less fit us for it, than call us to it, there is more of grace in fitting us for it than barely in calling us to it; and the call itself has more of grace in it than the giving the possession of that inheritance you are called unto. It is not so high a favour in a prince actually to set his royal bride in the throne with him, as to call her to and prepare her for so high a dignity. To prepare a soul for it by regeneration is an act of pure grace; to give it after a preparation for it, is an act of truth as well as grace; nothing obliged him to the first, his promise binds him to the latter. What if I should say, this renewing of us, and subduing our sins in us, is a greater act of grace than a bare remission! Micah vii. 18, 19, seems to favour it. To pardon us is an act of his delightful mercy; but to subdue our iniquities is an act of his most tender compassion. Mercy is there joined with pardon, and compassion with subduing And the latter expression, 'Thou wilt cast all their sins into the depths of the sea,' may refer to both those acts of grace, against the guilt and filth of sin.

[3.] The freeness of his mercy is manifest in it. It is as free as election: Eph. i. 3, 4, 'Who has blessed us with all spiritual blessings' (of which regeneration is none of the meanest), 'according as he has chosen us in him', "kathos exelexato". It is as free in the stream as it is in the fountain. Jesus Christ is as freely formed in us, as we were freely chosen in him, as freely, quoad nos, as to us, not in regard of Christ, who merited the former though not the latter. It is his own mercy, 1 Peter i. 3, 'his own will', James i. 18, not moved by any other, as we do many things by the will of others when our own are not free, in which are mixed acts. It is in regard of this freeness called grace. Supposing God would create man, and for such an end as to enjoy blessedness, he could not create him otherwise than with a universal rectitude, because, had God created him with a temper contrary to his law, he had been the author of his sin. Some therefore call not the righteousness of Adam grace, because it was a perfection due to his nature upon his creation. But there was no necessity upon God to bestow new creating grace, after he had stripped himself of the righteousness of his first creation. And also supposing God will restore man to that end from which he fell, and refit him for that blessedness, he cannot fit him otherwise than by restoring him to that righteousness, as a means of attaining that blessedness. Yet both these are free, because the original foundation of both is free. God might choose whether he would create man when he was nothing, and choose whether he would restore man when he was fallen. Yet there is more freedom in this latter than in the former, in regard of the measures of the new created righteousness, and in regard of the immutability of it, in regard also of demerit. Adam's dust, before creation, as it could merit nothing, so it had an advantage above us that it could not lie under demerit. But we, after the fall, are in a state of damnation, children of wrath, so that regeneration is not a creating us from nothing, but recovering us from a state worse than nothing. In regard that man was miserable, he was capable of mercy; but as he was a criminal, he was an object of severity. That is free mercy to renew any man by grace, when he might have damned him by justice, to work him for glory when he had wrought himself for damnation. The apostle therefore excludes all works whatsoever from any meritoriousness in this case: Titus iii. 5, 'Not by works of righteousness which we have done, but according to his mercy he saved us, by the washing of regeneration, and renewing of the Holy Ghost.' I say, he excludes all works, because not one work, as good, was in being before the renewal of the soul, for so verse 3 plainly implies, when he concludes all men, himself too, in a state incapable of doing anything that was good; the honour of his truth indeed excites him to perfect it, but his grace only, without any other motive, moves him to bestow it. All the grace you have in regeneration sprung only from this; the righteousness you are arrayed with, the flames of love in your hearts, the flights of your faith, cost you nothing, they were all the births of love. Goodness decreed all when you were nothing, grace formed all when you were worse than nothing, your faith is 'the faith of God's elect,' Titus i. 1. New creatures were chosen to faith by grace, and by the same grace was faith formed in the womb of the soul; electing grace preceded, renewing grace followed, the stream cannot be merited when the spring was free. Regeneration is an accessory to election. No man can merit the principle, therefore not the accessory.

2. As mercy and goodness, so the sovereignty of God is illustrious in this work. 'Of God,' in the text, is 'of the will of God.' The covenant runs in a royal style: 'I will put my Spirit into them; I will give a heart of flesh,' of my own free motion and good pleasure, like the patents of princes. God reserves this in his own power, to give to whom he pleases; Cameron says, that faith, which is a great constitutive part of regeneration, was not purchased meritoriously by Christ's death; and though Christ does give us faith as well as repentance, yet he does that, not as considered as a satisfier of God's justice in his death, but as God's commissioner in his exaltation, being empowered by God to give the conditions upon which they agreed together in the first compact about the work of mediation, unto all those that God had given him to satisfy for. Whether this opinion be well grounded or no, I will not determine; yet the making it depend solely upon election, and to be given as a fruit of election, that hereby we may be partakers of Christ, makes it more fully depend upon the sovereignty of God. God renews when he pleases. 'The wind blows where it lists,' John iii. 8. To some he affords means, to others not; he deals not with every nation as he dealt with Israel. In some, he works by means; to others, he gives only the means without any inward work; it is his pleasure that he works upon any one to will, his good pleasure that he gives to and one to do: Philip. ii. 13, 'of his good pleasure.' Some hear the word, others the Spirit in the word; some feel the striking of the air upon their ear, others the stamp of the Spirit upon their hearts. Who chose this rough stone to hew and polish, and let others lie in the quarry? Who frames this for a statue, a representation of himself, and leaves another upon the pavement? What does all this result from, but his sovereign pleasure?

(1.) No ultimate reason can be rendered for this distinction, but God's sovereignty. We can render an immediate reason of some actions of God: why the heavens are round, because that is the most capacious figure, and fittest for motion; why the sun is the centre of the world, as some think, because it may, at a convenient distance, enlighten the stars above, and quicken the things below; why our hearts are in the midst of our bodies, because they may more commodiously afford heat to all the members; so also, why God loved Adam, because he saw his own image in him; why he sends judgments upon the world, because of sin; why he saves believers and condemns unbelievers, because they receive the grace of Christ, those reject it. We have not recourse immediately to God's will for a reason; the nature of the things themselves affords us one, obvious to us. But no reason can be rendered of other actions of God but his good pleasure. Why he chose Abraham above other men, and delivered him from Ur of the Chaldees; why Israel above other nations, since all other men and nations descended from Adam and Noah, and they were in their natures equally corrupt with others; they were not in themselves better than others, nor other nations worse than they; so in Esau and Jacob, why the elder should serve the younger, since they both issued from the same parents, lay in the same womb, were equally depraved in their nature, had original sin equally conveyed to them by their parents: no reason can be rendered but the will of God. So, if it be asked, why men are condemned, because they do not believe. Why do they not believe? Because they will not. God has given them means and faculties. If you ask, why God did not give them grace to believe and turn their wills, no other answer can be given but because he will not. It is his free will to choose some and not others. Election is put upon his pleasure: Eph. i. 5, 'Predestinated according to the good pleasure of his will;' and the making known the mystery of his will is put upon his pleasure: Eph. i. 9, 'Having made known unto us the mystery of his will according to his good pleasure.' As God regards us absolutely, it is rather mercy than his good pleasure. Why has he changed our wills? Because he loved us, and bare good will to us in his everlasting purpose, to which he was incited by his own mercy. But if we compare ourselves with others, and ask, why he renews this man and not that, then it is rather an act of the sovereign liberty of his will, for there cannot be the result of any reason from any thing else; he pitches his compassion where and upon whom he pleases. The apostle joins mercy and this sovereignty of his will together: Rom. ix. 15, 'I will have mercy on whom I will have mercy; and I will have compassion on whom I will have compassion.' He is so absolute a sovereign, that he will give no account of these matters but his own good pleasure. Why he renews any man is merely voluntary; why he saves renewed men is just; why he justifies those that believe is justice to Christ and mercy to them; but why he bestows faith on any is merely the good pleasure of his will. The pharisees believed not, because they were not of Christ's sheep, John x. 26; that is, they were not given to Christ by the Father, as is intimated, verse 29. And the prosperity of those which are given to Christ is resolved wholly into the pleasure of God: 'The pleasure of the Lord shall prosper in his hand,' Isa. liii. 10. In all our searches into the cause of this, we must rest in his sovereign pleasure; our Saviour himself renders this only as a reason of his distinguishing mercy, wherein himself does, and therefore we must, acquiesce: Mat. xi. 27, 'Even so, Father, for so it pleased thee.'

(2.) We may well do so, because he is no debtor to any man in the way of grace. There is nothing due to man but death; that is his wages; the other is a gift: Rom. vi. 23, 'To you it is given to know the mysteries of the kingdom of heaven, to them it is not given,' Mat. xiii. 11. Who shall control him in the disposal of his own goods? 'Who shall say unto him, What dost thou?' Grace is his own treasure; if he gives the riches of it to any, it is his pleasure; if he will not bestow a mite on any man, it is no wrong; 'if any man has given to him, it shall be recompensed to him again,' Rom. xi. 35. It is not unjust with God to deny every man grace; it is not then unjust to deny a great part of men this grace: 'Who has enjoined him his way?' says Job; or, 'Who can say, Thou hast wrought iniquity?' Job xxxvi. 23. He is not to be taught by man how to govern the world, neither can any man justly blame him, if they judge aright of his actions. Though every man is bound to endeavour the conversion of others, and every good man has so much charity that he would turn all to righteousness if he could, and though the love of God is infinitely greater than man's, it cannot be argued from thence that therefore God should renew every man. This charity in man is a debt he owes to his neighbour by communion of blood, upon which the law of charity is founded, which obliges him to endeavour the happiness and welfare of his neighbour; but God is free from the engagements of any law, but the liberty of his own will; he is under no government but his own; he has none superior, none equal with him, to enjoin him his way, and to prescribe him rules and methods. If he gives any favour to man, it is his pleasure; if man improves it well, God is not indebted to him, and obliged to give him more, no more than a father is bound to give his son a new stock, because he has improved well the first he has entrusted him with; it depends only upon his pleasure.

(3.) God's proceedings in this case do wholly declare it. In the first gift of his people to Christ, he acted like a God greater than all in a way of super-eminent sovereignty: 'My Father which gave them me is greater than all', John x. 29. He acts as a potter with his clay; he softens one heart, and leaves another to its natural hardness. He converts Paul a persecutor, but none of the other pharisees who spurred him on in that fury and commissioned him to it; he snatches some from the embracements of lust, while he suffers others to run their race to hell. David, by grace, is made a man after God's own heart, and Saul left to be a man after his own will; some he changes in the heat of their pursuit of sinful pleasures, others he wounds to death by his judgments. The reason of the latter is deserved justice; the reason of the other is undeserved pleasure. He chooses the mean things of the world to be highest in his favour, and passes over those that the world esteems most excellent. 'Not many wise, not many mighty,' is his sovereign method. The amiable endowments esteemed by the men of the world have no influence upon him. He acts in this way with his own people; he gives sometimes to will, when he does not give presently to do; he distributes greater measures of grace to one than to another; he sometimes excites them by his grace, sometimes lets them lie as logs before him, that he may be owned by them to be a free agent. And further, it must needs be thus, because God does not work in regeneration as a natural agent, and put forth his strength to the utmost; as the sun shines, and the fire burns, ad extremum virium, unless a cloud interpose to hinder the one, or water quench the other, but as an arbitrary agent, who exerts his power according to his own will, and withholds it according to his pleasure. For there are two acts of his sovereign will: one whereby he does command men to do their duty, promises rewards, and threatens punishment, but the subject is to be disposed to do God's will of precept. Here comes in another act of his sovereignty, whereby he wills the disposing such and such hearts to the accepting of his grace, and does will not to give others that grace, but leave them to themselves. This we see practised by God almost in every day's experience.

3. The truth of God is apparent in this work. Truth to his own purpose: 1 Tim. i. 9, 'Who has called us with a holy calling, according to his own purpose and grace, which was given us in Jesus Christ before the world began.' Sovereignty first singles this or that man out; and truth to that firm and immutable counsel, and that resolve in his own mind, steps in to excite his holiness, wisdom, and power, to make every such person conformed to the image of his Son. It was not from any truth respecting any condition annexed to any promise he had made which he might find in the creature, for the apostle plainly excludes it, 'not according to our work'; for what motion can our work in a state of nature cause in God but that of anger and aversion arising from truth to his threatening, the condition whereof is fulfilled by us, but not one mite of good fruit that could as a condition challenge this great work at the hands of the truth of God by virtue of his promise. His truth to his threatening would have raised up thoughts of destroying men; his truth to his purpose carried on his design of effectually calling them. It is not an engagement of truth to his creature, but of truth to himself. So that if you ask why he has Peter, Paul, and others, since many better conditioned than they have rejected the gospel, the answer is, because he had so purposed in himself; and he is faithful, and cannot deny his own counsel, for that were to deny himself, and that eternal idea in his own mind: 2 Tim. ii. 13, 'He is faithful, and cannot deny himself,' in regard of his purpose, in regard of his absolute promise. Truth to his promise; his promise to his Son, for so Titus i. 2 is principally to be understood: 'In hope of eternal life, which God, that cannot lie, promised before the world began.' There was a donation of some made to Christ, and a donation of grace to Christ for them, deposited in his hands as a treasure to be dispensed to every one of them in their proper time. His truth comes in upon this double donative: a donative of grace to them in Christ, before the world began, which would be but as a useless rusty treasure, if not bestowed upon those for whom it was entrusted in his hands; a donative of some, according to this purpose, to Christ, whose death, and resurrection, and purchase, would be ineffectual, if those thus given were not in time engrafted in him, and renewed by him, to be made partakers of all that which he purchased and

preserved for them. Jesus Christ was to have a seed by covenant, a people to be conformed to his image. The issue then of forming a people for his seed, is the effect of God's truth to Christ. And consequent to this antecedent purpose in himself, and promise to Christ, he gives him an order to bring in those that were thus designed to be his sheep, which he calls his sheep by right of donation, before they were renewed: my sheep, by right of gift from my Father, mine by right of purchase at my death, mine by right of possession at their effectual call, these I must bring in; not I may, but I must; and they shall hear my voice: John x. 16, 'Other sheep I have; them also I must bring, and they shall hear my voice;' not they may, but they shall be inclined to comply with my word and call. Satan and their own lusts shall not hinder them from coming unto me, but they shall be overruled by a powerful Spirit. So that there is truth to his purpose, truth to his promise to Christ' truth to the depositum in Christ's hands, truth to his word published, that he would give a new heart. So that whatsoever heart his work is wrought in, it is a manifest effect of the truth of God to himself and his Christ. The gift of grace, in possession, is a necessary consequent of that gift of it, in purpose, before the world began.

4. The wisdom of God appears in this work. The secrets of wisdom shine forth in the great concerns of the soul in Christ, who is made wisdom principally to us in our sanctification, as well as righteousness and redemption. Wisdom in the imputation of righteousness, in the draught of sanctification, and in the perfection of it in a complete redemption; wisdom, like thread, runs through every part of the web. The new birth is the great wisdom of the creature; by this he becomes wise, since the Scripture entitles all fools without it. The inspiration of this wisdom can own no other but divine wisdom for the author. It is his own wisdom; for 'Who has been his counsellor?' Rom. xi. 34. He works all things according to the counsel of his own will, freely, wisely; a work of his will, a work of his understanding: Eph. i. 11, 12, 'Who works all things according to the counsel of his own will, that we should be to the praise of his glory,' that the glory of the Father may shine out in us. If all things are thus wrought with the choicest counsel, much more the rarest work of God in the world. If all things are wrought with counsel, because he will have a praise from them, much more that from whence he expects to gather the greatest crop of glory. The bringing us to trust in Christ is for the praise of his glory; a glory redounds to him, because there is nothing of our own in it, but all his; a farther glory redounds to him, because it is in the wisest manner. It is to the praise and the glory of his goodness in the act of his will; to the praise of the glory of his wisdom in the act of his counsel. There was a mystery of wisdom in the first secretion and singling out this or that person; a revelation of wisdom in the preparations to it, and formation of it. If there be much of his counsel in the minute passages of his providence in the lowest creatures, which are the subjects of that providence, much more must there be in the framing the soul to be a living monument of his glory. It is not a new moulding the outward case of the body, but the inward jewel wrapped up from the view of men; the spirit of the mind, which, being more excellent, requires more of skill for the new forming of it.

(1.) The nature of the new birth declares it to be an effect of his wisdom. It is a building a divine temple, a spiritual tabernacle, for his own residence: 'ye are God's building,' 1 Cor. iii. 9. Strength will not build a house without art to contrive and proportion the materials; skill is the chief requisite of an architect. The highest pieces of art come from the most excellent idea in the creature. The beautiful fabric of grace is modelled by the wisest idea in God; that which is glorious in the erection, supposes excellent skill in the contrivance. Every renewed man is a 'lively stone:' 1 Pet. ii. a, 'Ye also as lively stones,' every one of you polished and carved by the wise Creator for an everlasting statue. It is he that has 'wrought us to the self-same thing,' 2 Cor. v. 6, "katergasamenos"; polished us and curiously wrought us, who were rough stones, covered with the rubbish of sin. As a wise builder, he lays the foundation in sound habits, whereon to raise a superstructure of gracious actions. The counterpart in the heart is no less a fruit of his wisdom than the law in the tables of stone; wisdom in the first framing the law, wisdom also in the deep imprinting of it. That which enlightens the eyes, and makes wise to salvation, can be entitled to no other original cause than divine wisdom. The soul is a rational work of God. Surely, then, that which is the soul of the soul, the glory of the creature, the preparation for happiness, more pleasing to God than the brightest nature, than the natural frame of the highest soul, that which is the pleasure and delight, must be the fruit, too, of infinite wisdom. Bare effects of power are not the immediate objects of God's special delight.

(2.) The means of it declare it to be a fruit of his wisdom. Christ the exemplar has the treasures of wisdom; grace copied from it is part of those treasures. The gospel, the instrument, is 'the wisdom of God,' as well as 'the power of God,' 1 Cor. ii. 7. Divine skill framed the model, reared the building, no less sows the seed in the heart. What did partake of wisdom in the contrivance, progress, all the parts and methods of it, partakes of the same in the inward operations of it upon the soul.

(3.) The manner of it speaks it to be so. In regard of the enemies he has to deal with, there must be prudence to countermine the deep and unsearchable plots of the powers of darkness. As there is the strength of sin within, the might of Satan without, as fit subjects for his power, so there are the stratagems of Satan, the subtleties and deceits of the flesh, as a fit occasion for his almighty skill against hellish policy. In regard also of his working upon the soul, he works upon those that are so contrary to his design without imposing upon their faculties; he moves them according to their physical nature, though contrary to their moral nature; he makes us do willingly what we would not; he so tunes the strings that they speak out willingly what naturally they are most unfit for. The Spirit acts wisely in the revealing to us the knowledge of Christ, as Eph. i. 17, 'The spirit of wisdom and revelation in the knowledge of him,' which may note the manner of his acting in the revelation, which is the first work of the soul, as well as the effect it does produce, though I suppose the effect is principally meant. Some question the wisdom of God in acting so upon the will as not to lease it to its own indifference in this change. What reason is there to question his wisdom? Do not the angels in heaven admire God's wisdom as well as his grace, who has immutably fixed them to that which is good? Do they question the wisdom of God for so happy a confirmation of them against that indifference which destroyed some of their fellows by creation? But is there not an evident art in this work, to make the will willing that had no affection to this change; to fit the key so to all the wards that not one is disordered; to move us contrary to our corrupt reason, yet bring us to that pass to acknowledge we had reason to be so moved; to move our faculties one by another as wheels in a watch; to present spiritual things with such an evident light as engages our understandings to believe that which they would not believe before, and our wills to embrace that which our affections gainsay? It must therefore be a fruit of divine skill since it is a fruit of divine teaching, John vi. 45.

(4.) There is a greater wisdom in it than in the creation of the world. The higher the work rises, the more of skill appears. It is a divine art to make man to live the life of plants in his growth, the life of beasts in his sense, the life of angels in his mind; more it is then to make him live the life of God in his grace. Man in his body partakes of earth, in his soul of heaven, in his grace of the heaven of heavens, of the God of heaven. The grace in the new birth is nearer the likeness of God than the figure of men in the first birth. God therefore does more observe the numbers and measures in the second creation than he did in the first. Man was the most excellent piece in the lower creation, therefore more of art in the framing of him than in the whole celestial and elementary world. The glorious bodies of sun, moon, and stars had not such marks upon them. The nearer resemblance anything has to God, the more of wisdom as well as power is signified in the make of it.

(5.) The holiness of God is seen in this work. The day of God's power breaks not upon us in the change of our wills, without his appearance in 'the beauties of holiness,' Ps. cx. 3. The Spirit is called a spirit of holiness, not only as he is the efficient, but as he is the pattern, and like fire transforms into his own nature; for that which is born of the Spirit is spirit. The law in the tables of stone was an image; the law in the heart is an extract of God's holiness. Our first creation in a mutable state was according to his own image, Gen. i. 26. Our second creation is more exactly like him, in a gracious immutability. The holiness in Christ's human nature was an effect of the holiness of God; the holiness we have then in resemblance to Christ, must be a fruit of the same perfection. If we are renewed according to his image, it must be according to his holiness. To be merciful and just, is to have a moral image; to be holy, is to have a divine. The apostle intimates this in his exhortation, we must be holy in serving him, because he was holy in calling us: 1 Peter i. 16, 'As he which has called you is holy, so be ye holy,' &c. In this respect, God calls himself, not only a holy one, but the holy one of Israel: Isa. xliii. 15, 'I am the Lord your holy one, the creator of Israel, your king.' He is not only holy in himself, but displays his holiness in them, by an act of a new creation. By creator is not meant, his being the creator of them, as he is of all, even of wicked men and devils; but implies a peculiar relation to them, as distinguished from others. He is the creator of devils, holy in his actions towards devils, but not their holy one by any inward renovation, or consecrating them to himself, as he is the holy one of Israel. As he is a God in covenant, he is our God, therefore our God as he is a holy God, as well as he is a powerful God, communicating the one as well as the other in a covenant way, therefore the prophet Habakkuk joins them both together, 'O Lord my God, my holy one,' Hab. i. 12. His holiness is no less necessary for the felicity of his people, than his mercy and power. What happiness could his mercy move, his wisdom contrive, or his power effect, without the communication of his holiness? Mercy could not of itself fit a man for it, nor power give a man possession of it, without holiness attiring him with all those graces which prepare him for it. God, as sovereign, chose us; as merciful, pardons us; as wise, guides us; as powerful, protects us; as true, makes good his promises to us; but as holy, cleanses us from our old habits, makes us vessels of honour, filled with the savoury and delicious fruits of his Spirit, his pleasant things. The implantation of grace in the heart, is no less an effect of his holiness, than the preservation of it is, which our Saviour intimates, when in his petition for it he gives his Father rather the title of holy, than of any other attribute: John xvii. 11, 'Holy Father, keep through thy own name.'

6. The power of God appears in this work. 'Since the world began was it not heard that any man opened the eyes of one that was born blind,' John ix. 32; neither was it ever heard that any man could open the understanding of one that was born dark. Everything that pertains to life and godliness, of which regeneration is not the meanest, is the work of divine power: 2 Peter i. 3, 'According as his divine power has given to us all things that pertain to life and godliness, through the knowledge of him who has called us to glory and virtue;' glory and virtue, by a hendiadis, for a glorious virtue; and the apostle

adds, that this calling was an effect of a glorious power; it is not "eis", but "dia", through glory and virtue; the same preposition "dia", which, as joined with knowledge, is translated through; as much as to say, through a glorious virtue or power, both "agete" and virtus, signifying valour and strength in their several languages. When God hardens a man, he only withdraws his grace. But a divine virtue is necessary for the cure of our hereditary disease. There is no great force required to cut a dead man, but to raise him requires an extraordinary power. We may as well deny this work to be a new creation, a resurrection, as deny it to be an act of divine power. There is a word that calls; there is also a power to work: 1 Thes. i. 5. 'Our gospel came not unto you in word only, but also in power, and in the Holy Ghost;' that is, the power of the Holy Ghost. There was not only grace in the word, to woo, but the power of the Holy Ghost in it, to overcome the heart. There is not only an act of an almighty Spirit, but an act of his almightyness. The hand of the Lord created the world, 'the heavens are the work of his fingers,' Ps. viii. 3; but grace is the work of 'his arms,' Isa. liii. 1. It may be said of the first grace in the new birth, as it was of Reuben, Gen. xlix. 3, it is his 'might, the beginning of his strength, and the excellency of his power.' Though ministerial gifts were as excellent as Paul's, whose preaching was with demonstration and power, and who knew the readiest ways to men's hearts, if a man ever did, yet 'the excellency of the power was of God;' and when he brandished his spiritual weapons, they were only 'mighty through God,' 2 Cor. x. 4. Though the declaration was his, yet the working was Christ's, Rom. xv. 18; none of his people are willing, till the day of his power, Ps. cx. 3.

(1.) It is as great, yea, greater power, than that put forth in creation. It is as great; it is the introduction of another form, not in a way of any action or fashion, but in such a manner as was in the creation, that is, by the mighty operation of God; otherwise it could not be called a new creature though it might be called a new thing. You call not that which is made by the art or power of man, as a watch, a clock, a house, a new creature; for there is nothing of creation in them, but art and industry, setting the pieces of matter, created to their hands, together in such a form or figure. But this is called a new creature, not so much in regard of the newness of the thing, but in regard of the power that wrought it, and the manner of working it, being the same with that of creation. And being termed so, it implies the exerting an efficacious power; for creation is not brought by a cessation of action (which would be in God, if the will were only the cause of it) but the employment of an active virtue. God does not hold his hand in his bosom, but spreads it open, and applies it to an efficacious action. Since it is a new creation, it implies a creator, and a creative power, creation cannot be without both. It is a greater power expended in regeneration than in creation; more power morally in this, than physically in that. One word created the world; many words are combined for the new preparation of the heart. It is easier to make a thousand glasses, than to set together one that is dashed in pieces. It is easier with God to make a world (quoad nos, as to our conception, for all things are alike easy with God), and create thousands of men with his image, as bright as Adam's, than to bring that into form which is so miserably defaced.

[1.] First, In regard of the subject, sin has turned man into a beast, and omnipotence only can turn a bestial man into angelical and divine. There is a less distance between the least dust and the glorious God, than there is between the holy God and an impure sinner; sin and grace are more contrary to one another, than aliquid and nihil, something and nothing. A straw may with less power be made a star, than a corrupted sinner be made a saint. In creation, God was only to put in nature, here he is to 'put off' one that is strong, and to bring in another altogether strange and new, it is hard to bring a man off from his old stock, and as hard to make him nakedly to trust Christ. It is more difficult to make a man leave his sin, than to change his opinion, since men are more in love with habitual wickedness than with any opinion whatsoever. In regard of the indisposedness of the soul. There is some foundation for a natural religion, there being general notions of God and his attributes, which would administer some conclusions that he was to be feared and reverenced; and according to these notions many cheeks of conscience, which would induce men to some moral behaviour towards God. But in the setting our hearts right to God, and creating them in a mediator, there was not the least dust in nature to build upon. In the creating of Adam's body, there was some pre-existent matter, the dust of the ground, whereof his body has by a divine power made and organised; but we meet with no pre-existent matter for the formation of the soul, which made him a rational creature; that indeed was the breath of God, not engendered by any concurring cause in nature. There is no pre-existent matter in the creature, of which this image is formed, though there be a pre-existent subject to receive the impression of it; it is not the rearing anything upon the foundation of nature, but introducing a nature wholly new, which speaks almightyness. In regard of the contradiction in the subject. The stream of man's natural reason, the principles, of self, whereby he is guided, run counter to it, there is a pride of reason which will not stoop to the gospel, which in man's wisdom is counted foolishness. Man is an untamed heifer, a wild ass that snuffs up the wind, full of hatred to the ways of God, guided by gigantic lusts, which make as great a resistance as a mountain of brass; stoutness of heart, strong prejudices against the law of God, fierceness of affection, drinking iniquity like water, universal madness, resisting the spirit, hare-brained imaginations; frowardness in the will, forwardness to evil, perversity against good; can anything, less than an almighty power, make a universal cure? It is more easy to make men stoop to some victorious prince, and become his vassals, than to bring men to a submission to God and his laws, which they entertain with contempt and scorn. Nothing obeyed God's word in the creation; though it contributed not to his design, yet it could not oppose him, it could not swell against him, because it has nothing. But every sinner is rebellious, disputes God's commands, fortifies himself against his entrance, gives not up himself without a contest. This pride is hereditary, it bore sway in the heart ever since Adam's fall, and has prescription of as long a standing as the world to plead for possession. What but infinite power can fling down this pride at the foot of the cross, make the heart strike its swelling sail to Christ, and become nothing in itself, that Christ may be all life in him, and all righteousness to him? It is only possible to God to make a camel, with this bunch on its back, pass through a needle's eye; no less than divine power can bring down these armies of opposite imaginations, which have both multitude and strength (and no man knows either their number or strength), and the whole frame of contradiction against the grace of Christ. Our Saviour intimates this creative power in that thanksgiving to his Father: Matt. xi. 25, 'I thank thee, O Father, Lord of heaven and earth,' &c. Christ, in all his addresses to his Father, used attributes and titles suitable to the business he insisted on. The revelation of divine knowledge to babes, the moulding their hearts to receive it, was an act of God as he is Lord of heaven and earth, putting forth an infinite power in the forming of it. If God were the author of grace in the hearts of those babes, persons better disposed, and nearer the kingdom of heaven, as he was Lord of heaven and earth, then there must be some greater power than that of the creation of the world put forth to conquer the wise and prudent, whose wisdom and prudence stands armed in the breaches of nature to beat off the assaults of the gospel.

[2.] In regard of the opposition of the present possessors. The chasing out an armed devil, that has kept the palace in peace so long, must be by a power superior to his own, Luke xi. 21, 22. This great Goliath has his armour about him, has had long possession and dearest affections; the impulses of natural concupiscence take his part; he has his alluring baits, his pleasing proposals; the world and the flesh are linked with him in a league to hinder the restoration of the soul to Christ, and the restoration of God's image to the soul. A threefold cord is not easily broken. It must be a power superior to those three great posters in conjunction, that must bind the strong man; and casting him out, and spoiling his goods, are acts of power, Mat. xii. 29. Satan is too strong to be easily cast out, and the flesh loves him too dearly to be easily divorced from him; he is never like to lay down his arms by persuasions; though all the angels in heaven should entreat him, he would not give up one foot of his empire. Nay, though what God does propose has a greater weight of goodness, pleasure, and profit in itself, than what those three great impostors can offer, yet, since reason is weak and mightily corrupted under the conduct of sense, which has an alliance with Satan's proposals, and first sucks them in, it is not like to meet with any entertainment, as being against the interest of the flesh; and the will being backed with two such powerful seconds, as Satan and the world, to assist it in its refusals. Indeed, if he that is in the regenerate, were not greater and more powerful than he that is in the world, they would not be able to resist his allurements and subtilties, 1 John iv. 4. The triumphs of Christ at his ascension declare his power in his acquisition; with a strong hand he broke the chain of sinners, and 'led captivity captive' before he gave gifts to men, Ps. lxviii. 18. He does the like in giving grace to the heart; he rides upon his white horse in the power of almighty grace, when he conquers the enmity in the soul, as well as when he overcomes the enemies of his church, Rev. vi. 2.

(2.) It is a power as great as that which wrought in the resurrection of Christ. It is considerable how loftily the apostle sets it out: Eph. i. 19, 20, 'And what is the exceeding greatness of his power to us-ward who believe, according to the working of his mighty power, which he wrought in Christ when he raised him from the dead, and set him at his own right hand in heavenly places.' Exceeding greatness of his power, "huperthallon", with an hyperbole, according to the working or efficaciousness of his mighty power, noting the infusion of faith in the soul by a powerful impression, 'according to the working of the might or strength.' One word was not enough to signify the great power working: it is strength with a greater edge upon it; as when a man would fetch a mighty blow, he stirs up all his strength, sets his teeth on edge to summon all his spirits to assist his arm. The power of God in creation of nature is never in the whole Scripture set forth so magnificently as his power in the creation of grace is in this place. The apostle picks not out any examples of God's power in his ordinary works, or that power in lesser miracles which exceeded the power of nature, to illustrate this power by. He does not say, It is that power whereby we work miracles or speak with tongues: no; neither is it that power whereby our Saviour wrought such miracles when he was in the world. It is a more illustrious power than the giving sight to the blind, speech to the dumb, hearing to the deaf, yea, or life to a putrefied carcass, this is an extraordinary power. But yet this gracious power is higher than all this, for it is as great as that which wrought the two greatest miracles that ever were acted in the creation as great as the raising Jesus Christ perfectly dead in the grave, and having the weight of the sin of the world upon him, and as great as that power which, after the raising of him, set him in his human nature at his right hand, above principalities and powers, above the whole angelical state, as much as to say, As great as all that power which wrought the whole scene of the redemption, from the foundation-stone to the top-stone. It is such an unconquerable power, whereby God brings about all his decrees which terminated in Christ. Some say this power is not exercised in the begetting faith, but in the faithful after faith is begun. It is very strange that a less power is necessary to beget, than to preserve a thing after it is brought into being. And the same power is requisite to raise the heart of the most moral man under heaven out of the grave of corrupted nature, as well as those that are furthest in their dispositions from God. As, had not our Saviour had the weight of the sins of men upon him, had he been dead but an hour or two, lain in the grave with a little loose or light sand cast upon him, it would have required infinite power to have restored him to life. The apostle mentions this in other places, though not so highly as in this: Rom. vi. 4 'That like as Christ was raised up by the glory of the Father, even so we should walk in newness of life.' It must be understood thus. Even so we, being raised up by the glory of the Father, should walk in newness of life. And it may be partly the meaning of the apostle Peter, 1 Peter i. 3, 'Who has begotten us to a lively hope by, or through, the resurrection of Jesus Christ from the dead,' not only as the foundation of our hopes, but by a power conformable to that which raised Christ from the dead. I would only by the way note, that this infers a higher operation than merely an exhortation and suasion; for would any man say of a philosopher that had taught him morality, that he had displayed in him the exceeding greatness of his power, only upon the account of advising and counselling him to reform his manners, and live more soberly and honestly in the world? Our Saviour esteemed this one thing greater than all the other miracles he wrought, and declared himself to be the Christ more by this than by any other. When John sent to know who he was. he returns no other account than the list of his miracles: 'The blind see, the lame walk, the lepers are cleansed, the deaf hear, the dead are raised, to the poor the gospel is preached,' Luke vii. 20. That which brings up the rear as the greatest is, 'the poor "euangelidzontai", are evangelised;' it is not to be taken actively of the preaching of the gospel, but passively, that they were wrought upon by the gospel, and became gospelled people, transformed into the mould of it, else it would bear no analogy to the other miracles; the deaf hear, and the dead were raised; they had not exhortations to hear and live, but the effects were wrought in them; so those words import not only the preaching of the gospel to them, but the powerful operation of the gospel in them. This greatest miracle in the catalogue is the only miracle our Saviour has left in the world since the cessation of all the rest.

I have insisted the longer upon these perfections in God apparent in this work.

1. To stir up every renewed person to a thankful frame towards God, that he should engage his choicest attributes for the good of a poor creature. To what purpose did the apostle so long and so highly speak of the power of God in raising them from a spiritual death, but that they should acknowledge it, and admire God for it? It cannot but raise high admirations and adorations of God, to consider how mercy moved for them, sovereignty called them out, wisdom modelled them, holiness cleansed them, and power framed them.

2. To stir up deep humility. It is a plain declaration of our miserable estate by nature, and the difficulty of emerging out of it, impossible for any creature to effect. Had not God been infinitely merciful, wise, holy, true, and omnipotent, and put forth his power to free men from a slavery to sin, not a man had been able to escape out of it; and these two, admiration of God, and humiliation of self, are the two great acts of a Christian, which set all other graces on work. Mercy speaks us very miserable, wisdom declares us fools, holiness unclean, and power extremely weak.

3. How mightily will it give a ground to the exercise of faith! He that is deeply sensible of this work of holiness and power in him, cannot but trust God upon his deed, as well as before he did upon his word. As you go to the promises without you, consider also the counterpart of the promise within you, and the efficacy of that power which wrought it. You have a ground of faith within you; the power extends to every one wherein this work is wrought: 'What is the exceeding greatness of his power to us-ward who believe;' this the apostle speaks to all the believing Ephesians.

4. Therefore look much into yourselves by way of examination, to observe the actions of God's wisdom, holiness, and power within you. The want of this makes many gracious persons live disconsolately. Paul was certainly diligent in his observation, since he speaks so feelingly and experimentally of it. It is the way to answer Satan's objections, silence unbelieving thoughts, when you can trace the steps and operations of them in you; it would make you strive for an increase of this work of regeneration, that you may feel in yourselves more evidences of the holiness and power of God.

5. Those that want it may well despair of attaining it by themselves and their own strength. Divine wisdom and power are exerted in this work, and men may as well think themselves able to raise a dead man, yea, Christ from the grave, and set him at the right hand of God, as do this by their own strength. If we want an eye or a hand, all the creation cannot furnish us with either. How can any power but that which is infinite give us an eye to look to Christ within the veil, and a hand to clasp him in heaven?

6. It directs men where to seek it, and to seek it earnestly. At the hands of God, since infinite wisdom, holiness, and power, are necessary for the production of it. With earnestness, because it is so transcendent a work, has so many perfections of God shining in it, that creature-strength and wisdom is utterly unable to frame and raise it; and with hopes too, if they earnestly seek it, since God has hereby

declared himself infinitely loving, in the combination of so many attributes for the effecting of it. Plead, therefore, the glory of God in these his attributes, and if God give you a heart to seek it, it is a probable argument he will give you that grace which he has given you a heart to desire.

IV. Quest. How God does this?

1. This work is secret, and therefore difficult to be described. The effects are as obvious to a spiritual sense, as the methods of it obscure to our understandings; secret as the original of winds, sensible as the sound and bluster of them, John iii. 8. If a dead man were raised, he would not know the manner how his soul returned into the body, how it took its former place, and made up a new union, yet he would know that he lives and moves. A gracious soul knows that he was carnal, and now spiritual, blind, and that he now sees. He finds strength instead of weakness, inclinations to good instead of opposition, sweetness in the ways of God instead of bitterness. The methods of grace are obscure as those of nature: Eccles. xi. 5, 'Who knows the way of the spirit, or how the bones grow in the womb of her that is with child? even so thou knows not the works of God who makes all.' The manner of the formation of Christ in the soul is as undiscernible as the formation of a child, or the manner of Christ's conception in the womb of the virgin, both which are fearful and wonderful, as it is said of the first, Ps. cxxxix. 14, 'Who can declare his generation 9' Isa. liii. 8; that is, the generation of Christ, either in his person or in his people. We cannot give a satisfactory account of the natural motions of our souls, how one faculty commands another, how the soul governs the several parts of the body, what the nature of the action of our mind is in contemplation and reflection, how our wills move the spirits in the body, whereby the members are acted in their motion, and the functions of life performed. Much more undiscernible are the supernatural methods of the Spirit of God. We know ourselves heirs to the corruption of the first Adam by the inbeing of it, the light of the grace of the second Adam discovers itself in the soul, but the manner of the descent of either is not easily to he determined. The loadstone's attracting of iron is the best representation of this work; the soul, like that, moves sensibly, cleaves strongly to God; but wherein this virtue consists, how communicated, both in that of nature and this of spirit, dazzles the eye of reason.

2. Yet this is evident, that it is rational; that is, congruous to the essential nature of man. God does not deal with us as beasts, or as creatures destitute of sense, but as creatures of an intelligent order. Who is there that believes in Christ in such a manner as heavy things fall to the earth, or light things fly up to the air, or as beasts run at the beck of their sensual appetite, without rule or reason? If the Spirit of God wrought so upon man, this were to lay our faculties asleep, not to act them, but to act only upon them; this were to invert the natural order by creation, to raze out the foundations of virtue, and deny the creature the pleasure of his condition, who, according to such a manner of operation, could not understand his own state, no more than a brute can the harmony of music, or the pleasing variety of colours. But grace perfects our souls, possesses them with new principles, moves one faculty by another, like the motions of the wheels in a clock or watch; like the common course of providence, wherein he orders all affairs according to the dependence of them one upon another by creation, without making any inroad upon the natural rights of any creature, but preserving them entire, unless in some miraculous action. He diffuses a supernatural virtue into the soul, not to thwart it in that course of working he appointed it in the creation, but to move it agreeably to its nature as a rational being. As the sun conveys a celestial virtue upon the plants, drawing them forth by its influence according to their several natures, so the Holy Ghost introduces a supernatural principle into men, whereby they act as reasonable creatures in a higher strain. What methods our Saviour used in the first declaration of the gospel, he uses in the propagation of it in the hearts of men. The same reason that is used in writing the indenture is used in writing the counterpart. He might, by his omniscient wisdom, have found the way to the most secret corner of every man's heart, and by his power have set up what standard he pleased in every part of the castle, without proposing the gospel in the way of miracles and arguments; but he transacts all that affair in such a manner, that men might be moved in a rational way to their own happiness. He required a rational belief, as he gave rational evidences: John x. 37, 'If I do not the works of my Father, believe me not;' that is, the works that none but one empowered by God could do. God, that requires of us a reasonable service, would work upon us by a reasonable operation. God therefore works by way of a spiritual illumination of the understanding, in propounding the creature's happiness by arguments and reasons, and in a way of a spiritual impression upon the will, moving it sweetly to the embracing that happiness, and the means to it which he does propose; and indeed without this work preceding, the motion of the will could never be regular.

God does this by a double work.

1. Upon the understanding.
2. Upon the will.

1. Upon the understanding. The opening the eyes precedes the conversion from darkness to light, in God's operation as well as in the apostles' commission, Acts xxvi. 18. The first appearance of life, when God raises the soul, is in the clearness and distinctness of its knowledge of God, Hos. vi 2, 3. And the apostle, in his exhortation to the Romans, tells them the way for the transformation of their souls

was by the renewing of their minds: 'Be ye transformed by the renewing of your minds,' Rom. xii. '2. The light of the sun is seen breaking out at the dawning at the day, before the heat of the sun be felt. As the action of our sense is to sensible objects, so is that of our soul to spiritual. Our eye first sees an object before our hearts desire it, or our members move to it; so there is an apprehension of the goodness of the thing proposed, before there be any motion of our wills to it; so God begins his work in our minds, and terminates it in our wills. In regard of this, as a state of nature is set forth under the term of darkness, so a state of grace is often termed light, that being the first work in the new creation, as it was the first word of command in the old, 'Let there be light,' 2 Cor. iv. 6, Col. iii. 10, and is therefore called a renewing 'in knowledge,' or unto knowledge or acknowledgement, "anakainoumenon eis epignosin". If you consider the Scripture, you will find most of the terms whereby this is set forth to us have relation to the understanding. The gospel itself is called knowledge, Luke i. 77, wisdom, 1 Cor. i. 30. What faculty in man is appointed for the apprehending of a science to gain wisdom, but the understanding? That whereby we receive the gospel is called 'the spirit of the mind,' 'the eyes of the understanding' and 'sight,' which is put before believing: John vi. 40, 'Every one which sees the Son, and believes on him.' The work of grace is called 'revelation,' Gal. i. 16, 'illumination,' Eph. i. 18, 'translation from darkness to light,' 'opening the heart.' The action of our minds being enlightened, is called 'comprehending', Eph. iii. 18, and 'knowledge,' 2 Peter i. 2. All respect the understanding as the original wheel which God primarily sets in order, from whence he does influence secondarily all the other faculties which depend upon its guidance, God preserving hereby the order which he instituted in nature. Therefore, when the understanding savingly apprehends the deformity of sin, the will must needs hate it; when it apprehends the mercy of God, and the beauty of holiness, the will must needs love him, and the higher the degrees of this saving illumination are in the mind, the stronger and firmer are the habits and acts of grace in the will. This illuminative act of the Spirit is before, prior natura, the other of inclining the will, for the understanding is first exercised about the word, as verum, true, before the will is concerned in it as good. The understanding takes in the light of the gospel, which, by the working of the Spirit, is reflected upon the will, whereby it is changed into the image of Christ, whose gospel it is: 2 Cor. iii. 18, 'Beholding as in a glass the glory of the Lord, we are changed into the same image.' The first act is of the mind, which is the eye of the soul; where the apostle intimates, that the whole progress, as well as the first change, is wrought in this manner.

This is wrought,

1. By removing the indisposition and prejudices which naturally are in the mind. As a wise physician which orders his medicines for the removing of the principal humour. Chains of darkness must be broken, films upon the eye must be removed, which hinder the act of vision; for what the eye is to the body, that the understanding is to the soul. The darkness of ignorance is promised in the covenant to be scattered: 'They shall all know me, from the least to the greatest of them,' Jer. xxxi. 34. This being a law in the inward parts, the eye must be cleared to read it, as well as the heart cleansed to obey it. The object being spiritual, requires a spiritual disposition in the faculty for the reception of it. This is called in Scripture a giving eyes to see, and ears to hear, Deut. xxix. 4, and the revealing things not only by the word, but by the Spirit, 1 Cor. ii. 10, which, in regard of rectifying the reasons and judgments of men, is called a 'spirit of judgment,' Isa iv. 4, 'and shall have purged the blood of Jerusalem from the midst thereof; by the spirit of judgment. and the spirit of burning:' a spirit of judgment, as it is light in the understanding, removing the darkness, a spirit of burning, as it is heat in the heart, thawing the hardness. It reduces the mind into a right order, and teaches it to judge between truth and falsehood, between good and evil, the want of which is the cause of sin; whence sins are called "agnoemata", Heb. ix. 7, errors, as arising from error in judgment. Since the mind is hued with fogs, and incapable to perceive the splendour of divine truths, God acts upon the mind by an inward virtue, causing the word proposed to be mixed with an act of faith, which he begets in the soul, whereby it apprehends the excellency of that state presented to it in the gospel. As there is a manifestation of his name in the word, so there is an operation of his grace, an internal teaching by God, as well as an external by the gospel; the proposal of the word by man, the opening and fitting the heart by God: John vi. 45, 'Every man that has heard, and has learned of the Father, comes unto me'. Christ taught all by his ministry, the Father only some by his Spirit. Learning of God goes before coming to Christ, and those two acts are plainly distinguished: Isa. vi. 9, 10, 'Hear and not understand.' The lock of their minds was to be opened, as well as that of their ears; the prophet's voice could unlock the one, the Spirit only had the key of the other. Men may enlighten as moral causes, God only as the efficient cause, to root out the inward indisposition. The Sprit also removes the prejudices against Christ as undesirable, against holiness as troublesome, takes down the strength of corrupt reasonings, pulls down those idols in the mind and false notions of happiness, out-reasons men out of their inward thoughts of a happiness in sensual pleasures, pride of life, mammon of honour or wealth, which are the root of our spiritual disease, and first to be cured. In this there is a manifest difference between the working of Satan and the operation of God; he sets his battery against the affections, because the entry is there easiest; God breaks in upon the understanding, which, being the chief fort, will quickly be a means to reduce the lesser citadels. And when the work

begins in removing the blindness, it is the way to a true conversion; when it begins only in the affections, it is a prognostic of a quick starting aside. In an outward exhortation, God acts suitably to our nature, since we are endued with understanding and will; but in acting upon us within, he does remedy the vice of our nature. since our reason and will are corrupted.

(2.) It is wrought by bringing the mind and the object close together. Sight is produced in a blind man by drawing off the scales from his eyes, and the recourse of spirits to the eye necessary for sight; besides this, there must be outward light, and objects coloured by that light; and from the eye so disposed within, and the thing discovered without, arises the action of sight. So from the preparation of the understanding, and the application of the object, arises this action of spiritual vision. There is a double opening, one of the gospel, the other of the understanding; our Saviour did both, he 'opened the Scriptures,' Luke xxiv. 32, and 'opened their understandings,' ver. 45, that there might be a mutual entrance, that the word might dwell in their hearts, and their hearts have admission into the I ord. The Spirit shows the great things of the gospel to the soul: John xi. 14, "anangelei", 'He shall receive of mine, and show it unto you,' not in general, but bring them near to them, to make them view 'and know the things that are freely given to them of God,' 1 Cor. ii. 12, the benefits of the death and resurrection of Christ. He repeats them again and again, that there may be an evidence in the mind that they are the royal gifts of God. There is a knowledge, before this work of the Spirit, but as of things at a distance. Many know the things proposed in the gospel, but they know it not as a glorious gospel, nor see the wonders in this law, till the Spirit brings that and the faculty close together. As a man may discern a statue or picture at a distance, but till the eye and the objects meet close together, it cannot discern the beautiful workmanship upon them with any affection to them. Not that a man knew nothing, or knows new reasons of those things which he knew before; but there is a nearer, and therefore clearer, representation of them, which is demonstratio ostensiva, whereby he knows them in another manner than he did before. As a man may know the promises before, but they were not brought so near to him as to taste them; taste being an addition to knowledge, whereby a man knows that sensibly which before he only knew notionally. It is one thing to know a mechanical instrument, and another to know it in the operation of it, when it is applied to its proper use. It is like a man that has his understanding more cleared by seeing mathematical demonstrations, and lines drawn, than by all the rules of art in his head.

(3.) By fixing the mind upon the subject so closely presented. The Spirit settles that light and the object so in the mind, that it can no more blow it out than puff out the sparklings of a diamond, or than an artist endued with the habit of some art can divest himself of his skill. Many men have some convictions of truth, but flashy and uncertain, and which slip from their minds. But when the Spirit opens the heart, it holds the object to the mind, and the mind to the object, starts one holy thought after another about the truth it has darted in, makes the mind peer about it, and take notice of every lineament of that truth that we eye, and those thoughts lie down, rise up, and walk with us. When Lydia's heart was opened, she 'attended to the things spoken by Paul,' Acts xvi. 14, her whole heart cleaved to them. In this respect the Spirit is a remembrancer, making the soul ponder and and over again with all intenseness of mind the goodness and truth of those things in the gospel which are brought unto it, that the heart is, as Paul was, 'bound in spirit to Jerusalem,' Acts xx. 22. The thoughts of that journey did so haunt him and follow him, as the shadow does the body, that no arguments of friends, nor fear of danger, could divert him; the soul is bound by them, one consideration overtaking another, and all at work beating upon the mind. Hence consideration is put before conversion: Ezek. xviii. 28, 'Because he considers and turns away from all his transgressions.' And it is called the 'engrafted word,' fastened to the soul as a graft to the stock; when the heart is opened by the Spirit, the word is inserted in and bound to it, and at last the heart becomes one with the word, and grows up with it.

(4.) By bringing the soul to an actual reasoning and discourse upon the sight of the evidence. God convinces the judgment with reasons proper to evidence the truth and goodness of what he does propose, and that with pregnant and prevailing demonstrations, which give a competent satisfaction; therefore called the 'demonstration of the Spirit and power,' 1 Cor. ii. 4, that is, a spiritual and powerful demonstration. When the eye is opened, and the revelation made, and held close and fast to the soul with a divine demonstration, that this is the only means to elevate him to a high condition, and at last bring him to a blessed immortality, the understanding is moved to compare the force of those arguments, and consequently judges that true which before it counted false and foolishness, and comes by the help of this spiritual light to reason spiritually, and spiritually to discern the proposition made to it. It compares its natural state with the happy state offered to it, its own ignorance with that light, its own misery with that mercy. God will not have man, that is so far above a beast, do anything without reason; for this would be to do it brutishly, though the thing done were never so good, When men act as men, they follow the judgment of the best reason they can. And shall man, that was created a rational creature, be renewed without reason, when the very work is to advance him to the true state of a reasonable creature, and his reason is enlightened by the Spirit, that it may rightly judge of the demonstrative arguments it offers to him? Is there not as much reason for the guidance of the will in the highest concern, as for the conduct of it in affairs of a lower sphere? Man was first endued with reason, that he might rationally serve God; and his depraved reason is reformed, that he may rationally return to God. If, therefore, he act like a man in other things, he does not surely act like a brute in this; but the Spirit excites that reason he has enlightened to judge of those excellent things he does propose, and the strength of the arguments he backs them with, which are so clear and undeniable that they cannot be refused by a mind divested of those indispositions which drew out before a contempt of them. The change in the will being an election and choice, cannot be made without convincing and satisfying reasons which induce it to that choice, and justify the election it has made. That can hardly be called faith, when a man believes that which he does not think upon the highest reason was his duty to believe. And indeed what man is there that cannot allege some reason why he is induced to this or that act? God moves men by presenting things to the understanding under the notion of good, honest, profitable; and when the understanding is enlightened to judge of things in some measure under the same notion that God proposes them, a man's own reason cannot but upon a view of them assent unto them, and that assent is followed with a change, according to the degrees of that illumination, if it be a saving one. Upon this account that our own reason is excited to judge of the proposal, our faith can no more be said to be a human faith, or the work to proceed from our own power, than it can be said to be sensitive because it comes by hearing; for though faith depends upon hearing and reasoning, as upon natural powers, yet the light whereby the faculties are acted is wholly supernatural, and from the Spirit of God.

(5.) Hence follows a full conviction of the soul. Both the knowledge of its own misery, and the amiableness of the gospel offer, whence issues a weariness under the one and desires for the other. By this enlightening, the soul sees sin in its empire, God in his wrath, Satan in his tyranny, and the hardness of the stone within him; he sees the law accusing, sin triumphing, heaven shut and hell open, God ready to judge him, and his soul every way deplorable. He sees also in the gospel how Christ has expiated sin, answered the demands of the law, stills the clamours of conscience, satisfied the justice of God by bearing his wrath; hereupon the soul closes with Christ, and is born again. Here are heaps of sin that cannot be numbered, on the other side are riches of mercy that cannot be reckoned, there is sin to damn, here is a Christ to save; heaven and hell, sin and Christ, damnation and salvation, are presented in their proper colours, and pressed upon the understanding; which beholds all by a clear light. And thus, by the illuminative virtue of the Spirit, the soul is laid at God's foot in a sense of its misery, and then drawn into Christ's arms by a sense of his grace. This is wrought by a connective persuasion, for so the word "elegchein" signifies, John xvi. 8, which causes both a sight of sin and a sense of righteousness, and produces a full assent in the understanding.

2. The next faculty wrought upon is the will. The will is inclined, as well as the understanding enlightened, whereby spiritual things are approved with a spiritual affection, the same hand that darts light into the mind, puts heat into the will. After the act of understanding has preceded in a serious consideration, and thorough conviction, the act of the will, by virtue of the same Spirit, follows in a delightful motion to the object proposed to it; it is conducted by light, and spirited by love; the understanding hands the object to the will, as necessary to be embraced, and the arms of the will are opened to receive it, as the eyes of the mind are to behold it.

For the understanding of this, take these propositions.

Prop. 1. There seems to me to be an immediate supernatural work upon the will, as well as upon the understanding: not that the understanding is only enlightened, and the will follows the dictate of that without any further touch of the Spirit upon it; but the will, as it is the will, and therefore cannot be forced, there is need of a moral cause which may determine it according to its nature, and draw it by the cords of a man. When a master instructs a youth in his trade, he does it by arguments morally; when he holds his hand with the instrument in it, and directs the motion, he acts physically; so does the Spirit exhort us to spiritual motion, telling us inwardly which is the way, that we may walk in it, and take our wills by the hand, as it were, and lead them in the way they are to go. A nurse's tongue and exhortation is not enough to make a child to go, because of the weakness of its limbs; nor the light in the understanding sufficient to move the will, wherein there is an habitual weakness and contradiction. How did God work up the wills of the Egyptians to lend their jewels to the Israelites, but by some immediate touch. Their reason might have furnished them with many more arguments against it than it could for it. They knew the Israelites had been highly injured, and that very lately, too; that they could not but have a deep sense of their oppression, and intentions of revenge, as far as their power extended. They knew that the Israelites prepared for flight, and might more than conjecture that they intended never to return or send their jewels to them; for what need had they of so many goods barely to sacrifice in the wilderness? How were their wills thus banded against so many arguments against this action, and without any strong reasons to move them to consent to such a desire of the Israelites? How must this be but by the efficacious power of God, not forcing their wills, but taming their fierceness, softening them by a secret instinct, and exciting them to a grant of the Israelites' request? The apostle says, God 'gives to will.' If there were not a particular act upon the will, it had better been said, God gives to understand and know, and man to will and do. After the evidence set up in the understanding, there is a secret touch upon the will, opening and enlarging it to run the way that is proposed in an excellent and charming manner. As the poser of God raises every part of Christ, so the same power raises every faculty of the soul; it was also a physical power, since mere exhortation would never have effected it.

(1.) The Scripture intimates this in the terms whereby it signifies this work to us, as creation, resurrection, regeneration, new birth, all which denote some physical operation distinct in each faculty in the new creation, as there was in the first; not only the law in the mind to direct, but the heart of flesh to comply, is God's act. The fleshy heart is wrought by him, as well as the knowledge of the mind lighted by him. In generation something is removed, another thing introduced; in regeneration then of the will, there is consonant to that an eradication of corrupt habits, and an implantation of gracious ones. It is called a 'giving a heart,' a 'circumcision of the heart to love God,' Deut. xxx. 6. Love is an act of the will, though it supposes a knowledge of the amiable oldest in the understanding. If faith be principally in the will, as I think it is, as to consent; and the words leaning, resting, coming rather note an act of the will than an act of the understanding; there is then an operation of God upon the subject, viz. the will, in the implanting of it.

(2.) The will is corrupted as well as the understanding. The works of the flesh issue from both; if the corruption were only in the understanding, then that being removed, the will would be regenerated. As in a watch, if the fault be only in one wheel, that being mended, the whole frame is rectified; but if there be a flaw in all, the mending of one, though the principal one, which moves the rest, will not set every wheel right, without a particular application of art to restore them to their due frame. Was not original righteousness subjectively in the will as well as in the mind? Did not a stoutness in the will succeed in the place of that righteousness, as well as darkness in the place of light? Must not there then be a habit of mollifying grace bestowed upon the one as well as a habit of enlightening truth set up in the other; an inclination to good in the will, and an aversion from evil, as well as the knowledge of both? The corrupt proneness in the will is the cause that it is easily excited to evil by the persuasion of the devil and the world; and is there not need of an inward rectitude in the will to bias it to a free embracing and close adherence to the good proposed to it by God, that his grace may be efficacious in every part? This work is a quickening a man under a universal spiritual death; the will was dead, as well as the mind dark, which must have life instead of its deadness, as the other has light instead of its darkness; and if they be two distinct faculties, then there are two distinct acts of the Spirit, though they depend one upon another. There is no less power requisite to make us spiritually willing than to make us spiritually knowing, since the corrupt habits in our wills are rather stronger than the prejudices in our understandings; therefore there seems to be a distinct act in removing the resistance from the one as well as expelling the darkness from the other. As the Spirit takes away the wisdom that was sensual, earthly, and devilish, so it divests the will of that disposition whereby it was enamoured on that devilish wisdom of the flesh, and makes it willing to cut off the right hand and right eye, to deny sin, which is the very self, and engage in an irreconcilable quarrel against all that which engrossed its choicest affections..

(3.) If the understanding has such a power, by virtue of its illumination, without an act also of the Spirit upon the will, and a particular application of the understanding to the will, and the will to the understanding, why did not Adam's will follow his understanding? His understanding was clear, without darkness; his affections first made the rebellion; sense was the leader, and the will the follower. Eve's understanding was not silent under the temptation of Satan, her knowledge was actuated in that speech, 'God has said, You shall not eat of it, neither shall you touch it, lest you die,' Gen. iii. 3. She cites the word, her understanding must needs concur with it, unless it were corrupted and darkened before the fall. Where lay the resistance? In the affections, and the will which sided with them. Why may not the will, possessed with those evil habits, resist the understanding imperfectly restored to its primitive light, as well as Adam's will did where there was no scale or film upon the eye of his soul? And likely his affections had kept their due order, if the will had preserved its due dependence upon reason, and its sovereignty over the sensitive part. Do we not find that our wills are oftener in contradiction to the true sentiments of our understanding, and in conjunction with the affections, than in a due subordination to the one and commanding over the other? Is it not frequently seen that men of much light, knowledge, and gifts of reason, answer not the end of that illumination, and are without a will to turn to God? Besides, since corruption came in by the way of the affections, when the understanding was clear, how can regeneration of the will come in by the illumination of the understanding, without a particular operation upon the will and affections? If it be said, the will follows the dictate of the understanding, why did it not so in Adam? If we were perfectly restored, as Adam was in innocence, without the grace of God in our wills, as well as light in our understandings, we were not like to keep up in due order.

(4.) God in his other creatures gives not only a light and fancy in nature, but endues them with such principles that incline them to their motion, as connatural to them. Why then, shall we not think, since the will is an habitual power, that when the will is moved to supernatural ends, it is endued with such a supernatural habit, whereby it may be sweetly and readily moved to the chief good as its proper object? Are there not corrupt habits in the will, which the Scripture calls 'lusts,' and 'the works of the flesh,' Gal. v. 19-21, which the Spirit mortifies as well as those of the mind? Why not, then, gracious habits set up in the room of the other in this faculty as well as in the other?

(5.) If there were not a physical operation and habits in the will, what would become of infants, who cannot in that state be renewed without such a kind of working? They are not capable of moral exhortation, we cannot conceive any other way the Spirit has to work upon them, but by such a physical operation, putting habits into their wills, whereby they are renewed and sanctified; they are capable of the habit, though not of the act. We never find our Saviour spending any exhortations upon infants, but he took them in his arms and blessed them, and told us that of such is the kingdom of heaven; and if the kingdom of heaven be of such, there is some operation upon them different from this method of working only upon their understanding.

(6.) If there were not some operation of the Spirit upon our wills, regeneration and conversion would be more our work than God's. If the Spirit terminates his working only upon the understanding, and the will be moved by the understanding alone, without any conjunction of the Spirit in the work upon the will, then the Spirit does not immediately concur to the chiefest part of regeneration, but as it illuminates the mind; for the chief part of renewing grace is in the will; so it would be more our work than God's, if the moral only were his, and the physical operation only ours. It was in a less affair than this, wherein David blessed God for the people's willingness, offering so freely, acknowledging it indeed the people's act, but by God's overruling their wills, 1 Chron. xxix. 13, 14.

(7.) God is all in all in glory: 1 Cor. xv. 28, 'When Christ shall have delivered the kingdom to his Father, God then shall be all in all,' all in their understandings, all in their wills; he shall be the immediate cause of all things, and govern and dispose all things by himself, and for himself; binding the souls of all the glorified by everlasting ligatures to himself; all in all to the glorified, all light in their understanding, all love and delight in their will, objectively, efficiently. What efficacy he has in glory, shall we deny him in grace in every particular faculty?

Prop. 2. Yet this work, though immediate, is not compulsive and by force. It is a contradiction for the will to be moved unwillingly, any force upon it destroys the nature of it; if it be forced, it ceases to be will. It is not forced, because it is according to reason, and the natural motion of the creature; the understanding proposing, and the will moved to an embracing; the understanding going before with light, the will following after with love. The liberty of the will consists in following the guidance of reason; to have a liberty to go against it, is the greatest misery of the creature. That is properly constraint, when we are compelled to work contrary to the natural way of working; there is no constraint by force, but there is a kind of a constraint by love, because the Spirit accompanies this operation with so much efficacy, that instead of that sadness we should have in a thing we were forced unto, there is an unspeakable joy and contentment in the soul; it not being possible to taste so much of the love of God, to be delivered from so fearful a condemnation, to be brought to so glorious a hope, without being seized upon with much pleasure and delight. God changes the inclination of the will, but does not force it against its inclination; the will, being a rational faculty, cannot be wrought upon but rationally. Since the main work consists in faith and love, it is impossible there can be any force; no man can be forced to believe against his reason, or love against his will, or desire against his inclination. Belief is wrought by persuasion; no man can be persuaded by force. It cannot be conceived, that the will should will against the will. No man can be happy against his will, all happiness consisting in a suitableness of the object to the faculty; those things that in themselves are the greatest pleasures of the world, if they please not a man, cannot confer any happiness upon him. The Spirit never works thus, because 'where the Spirit of the Lord is, there is liberty,' 2 Cor. iii. 17; he destroys not the liberty, but reduces it to will more nobly than before. Besides, the liberty of the will does not stand in indifference to this or that thing, for then the will would lose its liberty every time it has determined itself to any one thing, because after the determination it would be no longer indifferent to the other. But the liberty of the will consists in being carried out according to the dictate of the practical judgment, and not by a blind instinct. God does not deal with us as stones and logs, or slaves, whom the whip makes to do that which they hate in their hearts; but conducts us in ways agreeable to our nature; he calls, saying, 'Seek you my face;' and inclines the will to answer, 'Thy face, Lord, I will seek,' Ps. xxvoo. 8. That God who knows how to make a will with a principle of freedom, knows how to work upon the will, without entrenching upon, or altering the essential privilege he bestowed upon it; he that formed us, as a potter does his vessel, knows very well the handles whereby he may take hold of us, without making any breach in our nature.

Prop. 3. It is free and gentle. A constraint, not by force, but love, which is not an extrinsic force, but intrinsic and pleasant to the will; he bends the creature so, that at the very instant wherein the will is savingly wrought upon, it delightfully consents to its own happiness; he draws by the cords of a man, and by a secret touch upon the will makes it willing to be drawn, and moves it upon its own hinges. It is sweet and alluring; the Spirit of grace is called 'the oil of gladness;' it is a delightful and ready motion which it causes in the will, it is a sweet efficacy, and an efficacious sweetness. At what time God does savingly work upon the will, to draw the soul from sin and the world to himself, it does with the greatest willingness, freedom, and delight follow after God, turn to him, close with him, and cleave to him, with all the heart, and with purpose never to depart from him: Cant. i. 4, 'Draw me, and we will run after thee.' Drawing signifies the efficacious power of grace; running signifies the delightful motion of grace;

the will is drawn, as if it would not come; it comes, as if it were not drawn. His grace is so sweet and so strong, that he neither wrongs the liberty of his creature, nor does prejudice his absolute power. As God moves necessary causes, necessarily; contingent causes, contingently; so he moves free agents freely, without offering violence to their natures. The Spirit glides into the heart by the sweet illapses of grace, and victoriously allures the soul: Hosea ii. 14, 'I will allure her, and speak to her heart;' not by crossing, but changing the inclination, by the all-conquering and alluring charms of love, as a man does that person whom he intends for his spouse; for to that he alludes, because in the latter part of the chapter, he speaks of the consummation of his marriage with the church: ver. 16, 'In that day thou shalt call me Ishi.' In what day? In the day that he should allure her, and speak to her heart. God puts on the deportment of a lover in changing the frame of the will. The Spirit is as one that leads the way into truth (the Spirit 'shall guide you, "hodegesei", into all truth,' John xvi. 13); not drags; he opens the heart, not by a forcible entry, but as a key that fits every ward in the lock. The attraction of the will is much like that of iron by the loadstone, which had no motion of itself till the powerful emissions of the loadstone's virtue reached it, and then it seems to move with a kind of voluntariness; there is no force used, but a delicious virtue emitted

which does, as it were, both persuade and enable it to join itself to its beloved attracter. There is a secret virtue communicated by God, which, as soon as it touches the soul, puts life and delightful motion into it, which before lay like a log. It embraces Christ as its portion, and passes a decree that it will keep his words: Ps. cxix. 67, 'Thou art my portion, O Lord. I have said that I will keep thy words.'

Prop. 4. It is insuperably victorious. What the mouth of God speaks, what his will purposes, his hand does fulfil, 1 Kings viii. 24. It is not a faint and languishing impression, but a reviving, sprightly, and victorious touch. As the demonstration of the Spirit is clear and undeniable, so the power of the Spirit is sweet and irresistible; both are joined, 1 Cor. ii. 4. An inexpressible sweetness allures the soul, and an unconquerable power draws the soul; there are clear demonstrations, charming persuasions, and invincible efficacy combined together in the work. He leaves not the will in indifference. If God were the author of faith only by putting the will into an indifference, though it be determined by its own proper liberty, why may not he also be said to be the author of unbelief, if by the same liberty of this indifference it be determined to reject the gospel? For in the same manner God is author of one motion of the will as well as of the other, if he does no more than leave the will in an aequilibrium. This irresistibleness takes not away the liberty of the will. Our Saviour's obedience was free and voluntary, yet necessary and irresistible. He could not sin in regard of the hypostatical union, yet he had a greater aversion to sin than all the angels in heaven. Is not God freely and voluntarily good, yet necessarily so? He cannot be otherwise than good, he will not be otherwise than good. So the will is irresistibly drawn, and yet does freely come to its own happiness. The soul is brought over to God, and adheres to him, not by a necessity of compulsion, but of immutability. As the angels necessarily obey God, not by compulsion, but from an immutable love. A sinner is necessarily a servant to sin, a regenerate man necessarily a servant to God; both by a kind of necessity of nature. Our main business, then, is to see what new enlightenings there are in our minds by the Spirit in the gospel, what tastes and relishes we have of divine truths, how our wills are allured to a sincere and close compliance with the proposals of God in the gospel, what vigour is in them. This is God's method, to work first upon the understanding, then upon the will. That work which begins first in the affections, without light dawning and breaking in upon the mind, and growing up by consideration and inquiries into the gospel is to be suspected, and is not like to be durable.

This is the Scripture method, and every regenerate person may find it more or less in himself.

V. The use is,

1. For instruction.

(1.) If God alone be the author and efficient of the new birth, then it does instruct us how insufficient a good education of itself is to produce this work in the soul, and how unfit to be rested on, without a further work. I doubt many may rest upon a religious education, without searching and inquiring into themselves what further work of God has been wrought upon them. God has entrusted parents with a power of instructing their children, but reserves the power of renewing grace to himself. If parents may set the object before them, God only can give them a spiritual eye to discern it; if they may inform the understanding, a divine touch only can bend the will; if they may lay the wood of spiritual lessons together, yet the fire to kindle them in the heart, and consume the lusts, must descend from heaven. Education may correct, but not extirpate the malignity of nature; good instruction, meeting with an orderly constitution, may sow the seeds of moral virtue, and restrain natural corruption, but not weed that out of our nature, or plant the root of grace, any more than the skilful management of a beast can change its natural inclination, though it may curb it. The folly bound up in the heart of a child is too strong for the wisdom of man, and is wholly to be expelled by the wisdom which comes down from heaven, set up in the heart by Christ, who is the wisdom of the Father. The little stars of precepts glittering in the mind, cannot make the young plants sprout up with their heads towards heaven, without the influence of the sun. Christ, the Sun of righteousness, fixed in the soul by the Spirit, can do more than all the stars of moral instructions in the world. Timothy had as religious instruction from his religious mother and grandmother as any in the world, both being believers, 2 Tim. i. 5, yet Paul calls him his 'own son in the faith,' 1 Tim. i. 2, as having 'begotten him in the gospel.' Those instructions did not beget him, though they might facilitate the evangelical work which was wrought by the gospel in Paul's ministry. Therefore the apostle manifestly distinguishes between instructors and fathers: 1 Cor. in 15, 'Though you have ten thousand instructors in Christ, yet have you not many fathers: for in Christ Jesus I have begotten you through the gospel.' He distinguishes their instructions from Christ, the efficient cause, and himself through the gospel, the instrumental cause. Yet such instruction is not to be neglected when children are capable; God may set home that by the gospel, which has been sucked in in younger years. Men may as well turn their backs upon the hearing the word, because it is insufficient without the operation of the almighty grace. Instruction and prayer should go hand in hand together; but take heed of resting upon a good education.

(2.) It instructs us that regeneration does not depend merely upon the word, if God alone be the efficient cause of it. It depends upon the inward efficacy of the Spirit. Had it depended upon the power of the apostles, or the outward demonstration of that word, they would have converted all that they had preached to, they would not have suffered any to have remained obstinate against the gospel: charity would have obliged them to the exercise of their power; and their power would have made their charity effectual. As God does seldom work without means, so means can never work without God. David had the law of God in his hand, but could not learn it without God's teaching; therefore he prays, Ps. lxxxvi. 11, 'Teach me thy way, O Lord: I will walk in thy truth.' And in many places of the 119th Psalm he takes notice, that all spiritual knowledge comes from God, though in the way of his precepts: ver. 98 'Thou through thy commandments hast made me wiser than mine enemies'; and ver. 104, 'Through thy precepts I get understanding.' While we use the means, our eye should be upon God. Thomas had his fingers upon our Saviour's wounds, but his thoughts upon Christ's divinity: 'My Lord, and my God.' Food maintains the body, but by virtue of the soul animating it, and enabling it to concoct that food. The Spirit of God is the soul of the gospel, and of all means, to make them efficacious; and with this power of the Spirit the weakest means can effect more than the greatest means without it, which, indeed, can produce little or nothing. Peter's sermon, Acts ii., was but short, but improved by the Spirit to the conversion of three thousand souls. Means can do nothing of themselves to change the heart. When the disciples had two ordinances representing the death of Christ, i. e. the Passover and the Lord's supper, pride, the great enemy to regeneration, put up its head above water; they quarrelled 'who should be greatest,' Luke xxii. 24.

(3.) There is no reason to confide in our own purposes and resolutions, or any strength of our own, if God alone be the efficient cause of regeneration; for it depends not upon our resolves without the grace of God. Satan fears not our vows; he knows, without grace they are but as light feathers, easily to be puffed away by him; but sparks, which, without his breath, the flood of corruption in our souls would extinguish as soon as they begin to appear. How can our resolves without grace renew us, when Peter's resolve, with his inherent grace, could not defend him? who, after his boasting, when certainly he sincerely meant what he said, fell so shamefully, that he stood in need of a new conversion. How soon do we, after a transient awakening fall to nodding in our spiritual sleep? If grace be not present with us to cure our lethargy, our purposes are as empty sails hoisted by us, the breath of the Spirit only fills with a full gale for motion. We can never 'steadfastly look into heaven, and see the glory of God,' unless we be 'full of the Holy Ghost,' Acts vii. 55. Stephen's eye would have been twinkling, had not the divine Spirit fixed it. How soon will a slight blast of a temptation shake a building, which has no other foundation but the moveable sand of our own purposes, when as slight a temptation shook the image of God out of Adam with all its brightness, who was built with God's own hand, with a power also to keep himself! Adam could not be without purposes of obedience when he heard the precept, yet with a slender temptation came tumbling to the dust, and fell as low as hell. A vain confidence in our own resolutions is so far from being a cause of this spiritual birth, that it is rather a hindrance, and part of the pride of nature, that must be demolished, and to be reckoned as one of the eldest things among these old things that are to pass away. Trust not, therefore, to yourselves; look up daily for the divine influence; lean not to your own understanding, though in part enlightened; confide not in your own wills, though in part inclined to the best things, pursue nothing in your own strength.

(4.) It is an injury to God to associate any thing with him in this work, which he challenges as his own production. Would it not be a disparagement to deny him the sole efficiency in one of the noblest works of his wisdom and holiness? That he who wrought the comely fabric of the first creation by his power and wisdom, without a co-partner, or deputing any of the highest angels to bring the world into form, should not have the honour of a work which bears the stamp of a higher wisdom and power than the whole creation! That he who contrived the models of the little creatures in the world, should leave this to the foolish contrivance of any creature! Why should we imagine that the divine image, upon whom the highest blessedness of the creature depends, should be of so little value in the judgment of God's infinite wisdom, as to be turned over from the care of so wise a workman, to the capriciousness of a light and uncertain will, more blind and mutable than Fortune the heathen goddess? It is more (we have heard) to frame so excellent a piece as the new creature is, out of the rubbish of sin, than to frame the whole celestial and elementary world out of a rude mass of matter; since there is a greater gulf to be shot between corruption and grace than between nothing and the beautiful structure of heaven and earth; and, therefore, we may less disparage him, in denying him the title of creator of the world, than that of the creator of a new heart, since he has promised by his own mouth to do it with his own hand. The apostle cannot be charged with ignorance, but knew what he said in that comprehensive thanksgiving for 'all spiritual blessings in Christ;' if all, then one of the highest, the new creation, is not intended to be left out of the roll of spiritual blessings, associating none with God, as the principal, but Christ as the Mediator, conveying this grace by his Spirit, according to the orders of the Father: 'Blessed be the God and Father of our Lord Jesus Christ, who has blessed us with all spiritual blessings in heavenly places in Christ,' Eph. i. 3.

(5.) See from hence how excellent a thing it is to be born again, if God be the sole efficient of it! Whatsoever God is the author of in his ordinary works, is excellent in its kind, they are all the effects of his will; this is an effect of his gracious will. Other generations are by the will of man, wherein the will of God concurs with them; this is solely by the will of God, without any concurrence of the will of man in the first work, called therefore by way of excellency, 'the faith of the operation of God,' Col. ii. 12, not a gift conveyed by angels, but his Spirit. A grain of grace of God's planting is more worth than millions of gold of man's getting; a more worthy gift than all the gold of Ophir, which God gives to men by their industry, who shall never see his face; but this by his own Spirit in order to glory. It is a royal gift he reserves in his own hands, to bestow upon those that were his favourites in his eternal purposes; it grows not in every man's ground, neither is it sown in every man's field. The soul is more excellent than the body, not only in respect of its nature, but in respect of its immediate author. God is called particularly, 'The Father of spirits,' not of bodies, though he is so; but in the production of bodies he acts by the hand of nature, in the production of the soul by his own hand. In that work he acts by the intervention of second causes; in this, without. serving himself of any other efficient cause but his own will. If the soul, as being the only work of God, is therefore more excellent, then certainly a new-born soul is more excellent than anything in the world, in regard God is the author of it in a more peculiar manner, by the operation of his choicest affections.

(6.) If God be the efficient of regeneration, then there is a necessity of the influence of God in all the progress of grace. It is yet imperfect, the same hand that planted it must also water and dress it. There is a tough sinew left in man's will, which makes him halt after he has the new name of Israel put upon him, a weakness of faith, a coldness of love, a faintness of zeal. What he is the creator of, is nursed by his providence; what he is the new creator of, is fostered by a succession of grace. The scripture therefore appropriates all to him: he is the God that calls us, the God that anoints us, the God that carries us, the God that establishes us, the God that keeps us, and the God that perfects us. He is the author of grace in its first issue, its fruitful sproutings, its delicious ripenings, it depends upon him in creation, preservation, augmentation, as well as natural things depend upon him in all their progressive motions, from one degree to another, as the author of nature. When nature was most unspotted, grace was necessary to preserve and fix it in that state. Adam needed the assistance of grace with the embellishments of nature. The same power that inspires us with life, inspires us with a perpetual continuation of it. If the tide that turns the stream of the river desert it, and return to its own channel, the river will return to its natural current. Our hearts will decline, our life languish, unless fed by that supernatural efficacy which did first produce it. The plants cannot grow merely from their own internal form, nor trees bring forth their pleasant fruits without the influence of rain and sun, feeding and hatching their innate spirits, and drawing them out to make a show of themselves in flowers and fruits; and when they are brought forth, they stand in need of the same rain to fill them, the same sun to ripen them.

(7.) If God be the efficient, &c., we see whither we are to have recourse in all the exigencies of the new creature, to whom, but to the author of those beginnings of eternal life! God is all, in all parts of this glorious work: 'The God of all grace, who has called us into his eternal glory, make you perfect, strengthen, establish, settle you,' &c., 1 Peter v. 10. There is need of preserving, strengthening, increasing, quickening, and perfecting grace.

These you need, and these must be sought, and will be had from the same goodness and power by which you were new born.

[1.] Preserving grace.

First, God only can give it. There is a necessity of it; as God rears it, so he only can keep it from pining away. Plants will wither if the rain do not descend; the flame will be extinguished if fuel be not added. There is as much a necessity of a constant influence to keep up this new nature, as there is of the sun to preserve the horizon from that darkness which would invade it upon the turning its face to other parts of the world. The perpetual duration of renewing grace is not essential to grace, for then Adam and the angels had stood by virtue of their grace, for nothing ever loses its essential property; but it is by an additional grace, distinct from the first grace wherein our regeneration does consist, as the preservation of the creatures in their natural beings is by an act of God, distinct from his creative act. The first grace God gives now is a bounty to his creatures, but it is further an obligation upon himself, not as it is grace, or as it is his own work, for Adam's grace which failed was brought by his fingers, inspired by his breath, but as it is a new covenant grace which alters the condition of it. God's finger wrote the law in the heart, and his breath can only blow the dust off, that would fill the engraved letters.

Secondly, God will preserve it. Job would argue with God, and ask him, 'Is it good unto thee that thou should despise the work of thine hands?' Job x. 3. Is it agreeable to his goodness and wisdom to slight and neglect the work of his own heart; not a fruit of his common liberality to the creation, but a choice fruit of his redeeming love? His common love, as he is the author of nature, preserves the old creation; much more his special love, as he is the author of the new nature, will preserve the new creation. His general goodness made the world, but his gracious goodness formed the soul; the one is more splendid than the other, therefore the effect more durable. Mercy compasses the godly about. Ps. xxxii. 10, like bulwarks that surround a city for its defence, against the assaults of spiritual enemies. A higher providence attends man than other creatures, because he is of a more noble constitution; upon the same account a higher providence must attend the new creature, as being far more noble than mere man. God embraces all creatures in his arms with a common love as creatures, he lays the new begotten ones in his bosom by a special love. His power too is to be considered. He will not want a power to preserve that which he did not want power to new create. The power being the same that raised Christ from the dead, which raised any from their natural condition, will have the same issue, since it never suffered Christ to return to the grave again, neither will it suffer any new born soul to return to a spiritual death. Every new creature is the Father's by purpose, and by actual traction; they were his before they were Christ's. The Father draws them to Christ; and the power of Christ will be as eminent to preserve them, as the power of the Father was to draw them. Why were the creatures brought, by that instinct God put into them, into Noah's ark, but to be preserved from the destroying deluge? Why did he take pains to write the law anew in the heart, if be would suffer it to be dashed out again? If he would not preserve his own work, why did he not let the soul lie wallowing in its old filthiness, and forbear the expense of those fresh colours he has new drawn his image with? It seems to be a greater power to take off all that load of sin which lay upon you, than to preserve you from having so great a burden again upon you. It is not reasonable to think that God should be at so much cost, only to restore man to Adam's mutable condition, whereby to incur a greater condemnation.

[2.] Strengthening grace. This we need, as well as preserving grace. It is God that strengthens us in the inward man; by that strengthening grace the new creature can do all things, without it nothing. Through him we are more than conquerors over principalities and powers, Rom. viii. 37, 38. Strength to mount up to heaven as an eagle, to run our race without weariness, to walk without fainting, to combat difficulties without sinking fears, is only to be had by waiting upon the Lord, who is the fountain whence all these flow, Isa. xl. 31, and by his grace confers a supernatural fortitude: Isa. xl. 31, 'But they that wait upon the Lord shall renew their strength; they shall mount up with wings as eagles they shall run, and not be weary; they shall walk, and not faint.' Look not therefore for strength in your new nature; look for it in God, in that Spirit which first renewed you, since that glorious power is imparted to strengthen you. which was at first employed to new-create you. This was the matter of the apostle's prayer for the Colossians, and this should be ours: Col. i. 9, 11, 'Strengthened with all might, according to his glorious power.' There is much weakness in us, a medley of lusts, an army of enemies, but the way is open for us to that glorious power, to endue us with a new vigour, which first seized upon us with an insuperable efficacy, our shattered and weakened sins shall not be able to resist that glorious power by which they could not stand the shock of when they were in their full strength. 'God will be a sun and a shield,' Ps. lxxxiv. 11, a sun to dispel our darkness, a shield to secure us from darts; a sun against the allurements of the world, defeating them by a charming light; a shield against the allurements of the world, overpowering them by an irresistible force; the sun that gave us life, the shield that secures our strength. The glorious power which we need in our progress lies in the same arm which wrought our deliverance, and from thence must be fetched. It is only by him that we have strength to tread down the wicked one's temptations; and those fiery darts are made as ashes under the soles of our feet, Mal. iv. 8.

[3.] We need increasing grace; and that is from God. The increase depends upon him, as well as the first planting. When we want it, he is the fountain from whence we must draw it; so did the disciples, Luke xvii. 5, 'Increase our faith,' or add to us faith, "prosthes hemin". Every new spring, fresh bud, spreading blossom, is an addition by his influence. When we have it, we must acknowledge his sole hand in it, so the apostle did when he saw the growth of the Thessalonian faith, and the abounding of their charity: 2 Thes. i. 3, 'We are bound to thank (eucharistein ofeilomen) God always for you, because that your faith grows exceedingly.' He did it by obligation: no such tie had lain upon him had God left them to increase it themselves. The new fruits you bear is from his new purging, as the first power to bear was from his planting, John xv. 2. If you would thrive, it must not be by your own, but by the increases of God; 'God gives the increase,' both in the outward administration and inward operation of the gospel, 1 Cor. iii. 7. Faith, in every assent, is conducted by that power which first settled it in the heart, and without it cannot commence any higher degree. As every spark of spiritual life is by his kindling, so every sparkling of that spark is by his blowing. Look for it at God's hands, beg of him to write that law deeper, which his fingers first engraved in your hearts. It is God's being 'a dew to Israel' makes him grow up in beauty as 'the lily and the olive tree,' in strength 'cast out his roots as the cedars of Lebanon,' Hosea xiv. 5-7. If you would grow up as calves of the stall, you must lie under the healing wings of the Sun of righteousness: Mal. iv. 2, 'Unto you that fear my name shall the Sun of righteousness arise with healing in his wings,' &c. That Sun which by his beams conveyed into you a spiritual life, can only by the same heat influence you to a taller growth. Every drop of the knowledge of his will till you come to be filled, every mite of wisdom and spiritual understanding, is to be drawn from him only, Col. i. 9, both the additions of knowledge and the deeper impressions and lively sproutings of what we know.

[4.] Quickening grace. This also we need. As our life, so the liveliness and activity of grace depends upon the divine influence; a divine motion is necessary to elevate our souls to those actions which are supernatural; our grace depends upon God in actu secundo, as well as actu primo. As God first puts a nature into creatures (in the exercise as well as the being) and then quickens them by his providential concurrence in those acts suitable to their nature, which acts are therefore natural to those creatures, so by a gracious concurrence he does quicken the new nature in the soul to the exerting of gracious operations, according to that nature he has endued it with. As he tunes the strings by his skill to fit them for a divine harmony, so he enlivens them by his touch to make what music he pleases; every heavenly prayer, every gracious groan, every start of spiritual affection, is from the Spirit tuning, quickening, assisting against infirmities and deadness. There must be a continued drawing to make a continued running. 'Draw us, and we will run after thee,' Cant. i. 4. It was the church, the gracious church, the spouse and dove of Christ, yet sensible of her own inability to quicken her pace to new communion with Christ, without fresh communications first from him. There is a bias in the soul to direct it in a right motion; there must be a hand without to put it upon that motion; Christ must 'put his hand in at the hole of the door' before a lazy soul, though gracious, will stir at his call, Cant. v. 3; or as a child, which has a principle of motion, must be assisted and quickened by the nurse before it can move a step. Grace is more prevalent to keep us from sin than excite us to holiness, yet neither can be done by it without new quickenings; our motion is in him and by him, as well as our life, spiritually as well as naturally Acts xvii. 28, 'In him we live, move, and have our being;' the old stock must have continual supply. Without Christ we can do nothing, John xv. 5; without him we cannot have grace in the plant, nor grace in the fruit. As the soul excites the spirits in the eye to an act of vision,--if they be not quickened by their governor, though things be before our eyes they see nothing,--so the Spirit of God excites, as it were, the spirits of grace to their particular acts, faith to apprehend and love to work. The goodness that made the promise guides the hand of the soul to fasten upon it: Ps. cxix. 49, 'Remember the word unto thy servant, upon which thou hast caused me to hope.' As God makes the promises, so he makes the meeting between the soul and the promise; every motion proceeds from God's touch upon the heart enlarging it, therefore our dependence must be upon God's grace: Ps. cxix. 32, 'I will run the way of thy commandments when thou shalt enlarge my heart.' I will run, not by my own strength, but by the hand of God enlarging and enlivening my heart. Indeed, if God did not give to act as well as implant the habit, he would give no more to us in the new covenant than he gave to Adam in the old, who had a power to do, but not the act of doing; his power was from God, but the act of obedience depended upon himself, and for want of actual obedience he fell. We see whence we must derive our quickenings; we want them because we expect them from the new nature in us, not from the author of that nature, and the concurrence of his grace with it, and depending upon habitual more than actual grace is the cause of our having many a slip. We are as dead lumps, notwithstanding all the grace we have, if God did not cause a free life to spring up in us by successive breathings.

[5.] Perfecting grace is only from God. He is the finisher of what he is the author of, Heb. xii. 2, and in our spiritual warfare supplies us with new recruits, till the combat end in victory, and the victory in triumph. He will come 'as the former and the latter rain,' Hosea vi. 3: as the former rain to open the womb of the earth, and the latter rain to ripen the fruits of the earth. As he has laid the foundation of mount Zion, so he will perform the whole work in it; he fulfils the work of faith with the same power wherewith he begins it, 2 Thes. i. 11. The power which caused the resurrection of Christ caused his ascension; he had his forty days upon the earth, after his resurrection, before he was taken up to glory. There is a continuance of a believer in the world after his resurrection from a spiritual death, but the same power which caused his spiritual resurrection will as surely cause his heavenly ascension. That arm that brought him out of Egypt will conduct him to the limits of Canaan, the flourishing pastures of the promised land. Grace is the first gift, glory is the latter; glory follows upon the heels of grace: 'He will give grace and glory,' Ps. lxxxiv. 11. Grace to fit for glory, and glory to reward his own grace; all grace till it ends in glory. God must be sought and depended on for this; we cannot will our perfection without grace, as we cannot will our regeneration without grace; God gives the will, the progressive as well as the initial will. Then seek only to God, depend upon him only, for the warmth of his goodness, to bring those chickens to perfection which he has gathered under his wing; his affections are not tired, it is a pure disinterested love mingled with no defects; his wisdom and power is no less able to perfect than his love is to incite him to it.

Use 2. The second use is of comfort.

Is God the author of regeneration? He that is the God of all grace is the God of all comfort too. Where he is the one, he will be the other. As he creates the soul to good works, so he creates it to heavenly consolations. When God acts as a God of justice toward sinners, he appears as a terrible God in his punishments; when he acts towards saints as a God of grace, he appears as a comforting God, he fills the one with all terrors, prepares the other for all comforts; he calls you by a new creation into his eternal glory, and sends therefore some sparkles of glory into the soul here. Are you born of God? You approach in excellency as near to Christ as a creature's capacity will admit. Christ was his natural begotten son, believers his spiritually regenerated children. Christ is 'the first born,' but 'among many brethren,' Rom. viii. 29, that Christ 'that sanctifies, and we that are sanctified, are all of one,' Heb. ii. 11, of one nature, say some, of one Father, say others; therefore 'he is not ashamed to call them brethren,' one nature does not so much make us brethren as one father. Christ was not regenerated, but generated, he stood not in need of the other, because the first generation failed not, neither could he, being God, he is the exact image of his Father's person, and so particularly of all his attributes, because he partakes of his essence. Believers are the living images of God's holiness, not partaking of all his attributes, but of that.

Particularly,

(1.) God will rejoice in his own work. If he rejoiced in the first planting of his image at the creation, he will no less rejoice in it at the restoration and with more gladness embrace the son that is returned from death to life by returning from his debauched coarse, than that son that remained with him all the while. Why does he renew the face of the earth by the mission of his Spirit, but that he may rejoice in his works? 'Thou sends forth thy Spirit, they are created: and thou renews the face of the earth. The glory of the Lord shall endure for ever: the Lord shall rejoice in his works,' Ps. civ. 30, 31. If God shall in time rejoice in the earth, wherein he had little joy after the creation of it, and soon repented of his work, he will rejoice in the noblest work, in the frame of his image, which, next to Christ, makes all other works of the lower creation pleasant to him. He 'creates Jerusalem a rejoicing, and her people a joy,' and he will rejoice in the new creation of his people, in the people he has new created, Isa lxv. 18, 19.

(2.) He will destroy all enemies to his own work. How will his love pierce into every part, and employ his poser in destroying the enemies of his work; whip buyers and sellers out of his spiritual temple, cast out all their remaining rubbish; let not his house be always a den of thieves, that shall rob God of his glory, and his temple of its beauty! That God that can raise men five thousand years ago dead as easily as one dead the last minute, can remove all the bands of corruption, though never so strong. If he has raised you from death, he will lift you up from all the remainders of death; the grave-clothes which yet remain about you, shall be in time untied, as well as the soul unloosed from the principal bands of death. Though there be in you a ' spirit that lusts to envy,' as well as a spirit that lusts to love, yet 'God gives more grace,' James iv. 5, a. Lusts will down, corruptions fall in time before his grace, darkness must hide its hated head, when that word breaks louder from his lips, 'Let there be light.' The promises of a thorough sanctification belong to you, as well as the promises of a perfect remission. If God be the teacher, no matter what the scholar is; if God be the workman, no matter what the matter is; if God be the guardian, no matter what the enemies are; nothing is too rugged for his skill, or too hard for his power.

(3.) He will order all things for the good of his own work. 'They shall not labour in vain; for they are the seed of the blessed of the Lord,' Isa. lxv. 23. He did not want grace to restore them, he will not want comforts to support them. Their very afflictions shall be ordered to preserve the work of his own heart in them; and while he prunes and cuts, he will purge away the luxuriant corruptions, that his vine may be more beautiful and delicious. And if he does chasten you sharply, it is that you may be nearer 'partakers of his holiness,' Heb. xii. 10.

Use 3. The third use is of exhortation.

1. To the renewed.

(1.) Walk humbly. Swell not big, as if your own power had procured it, let not pride spread its sails in your souls. Consider, you are creatures still, though new creatures. As God put into you whatsoever you have of natural existence, so he has put into you whatsoever you have of spiritual; you are dust still by your natural creation, though new formed by the Spirit. There is nothing of grace, no act of grace, but you receive mediately or immediately from God. You opened not your own eyes, nor thrust back the lock of your own hearts, nor can call one spark of that spiritual life you have, your own creature; it moved not at your beck, obeyed not your orders; it is when God says, Go, that it goes, and,

Do this and that, Settle upon this or that soul, and it does it. How humble should you be, since grace does nothing in any but by God's order, not your own. God works in us, we add nothing to God. The melted wax receives the stamp from the seal, but the wax adds nothing to the seal. 'What hast thou that thou hast not received?' 'If thou did receive it, why dost thou boast as if thou had not received it?' 1 Cor. iv. 7. Grace is God's communication to you, not yours to yourselves. What is received, is not your own work, but another's gift; were it desert, we had reason to boast; but being a gift, we have no reason to grow big. Lie therefore before him in your own nothingness. Renewing grace first lighted upon you when you were humble; and grace in its increase flourishes when the soul is in the same posture.

(2) Ascribe all that you are, as renewed creatures, to God. Ascribe it wholly to him; let self rub off every filing of this gold from its own fingers. 'Not unto us, not unto us, O Lord, but unto thy name be the praise,' Ps. cxv. 1. The repetition removes the glory far from themselves. If praise be comely for an upright person, it is most comely in the greatest cause that can happen to him, Ps. xxxiii. 1. Account yourselves therefore nothing, and God and grace all; and let no shootings be heard in your souls while God is rearing up the divine temple, but those of Grace! Grace! Zech. iv. 7, both in the foundation and superstructure, till he comes to the top stone. Your breathing after God is but the effect of his breathing after you; the moon has no light of herself, but what she receives from the sun; nor any creature a spark of grace, but what is derived from the Father of lights. God's purity is as the sun, your grace as a beam from that sun, not primitive in your nature, but derivative from God. Were it not from grace, Saul had never been Paul, nor Peter a penitent, nor Mary a convert, nor Zacchaeus a Christian, nor had thou ever been brought to the sweetness of a spiritual life, or advanced to the state and comforts of another world. Did you will to run till mercy moved your wills and spirited the feet of your souls? Your will, your race, was nothing; God's grace was all, Rom ix. 16. Was it not his word of command, Let there be life? Was it not his invincible power battered down the strongholds of sin? Oh seriously think, O Christian, that dry and desert heart of thine could never have been mollified and watered by rocky nature, nor virtue ever bud and blossom in that barren soil, unless the soil were mended, as well as the plant fixed, by some powerful hand. Bless God, therefore, since had it not been for him, you had never been humbled, never been renewed, never reached so high as a holy desire, or a penitential tear, but lain till this day, and for ever, bemired in fallen nature.

That you may know what reason you have to bless God with the highest praises, consider,

[1.] What your obligation is, how great! What good would your creation have done you since your fall without a new creation by the same hand? It must have rendered you miserable without this, and could never have rendered you happy but by the intervention of this. Without this you might have been his sons and daughters by creation, and devils by corruption. The heathens were God's offspring, as they were rational creatures, Acts xvii. 28, and the devil's children, as they were corrupt creatures. You might have had the image of God in a glimmering reason, without his image in a divine holiness. Was it not a greater obligation to restore that with kinder circumstances which you had wilfully thrown away, when it was in no wise due to you, than it was at first to bestow it? There was something like debt at first; supposing God would create a rational creature, integrity and innocence was naturally due to it, in regard of the holiness and wisdom of God, unless he would have been the author of the creature's sinfulness; but since that voluntary defection, the restoration was in no sort due, therefore the obligation greater. If God had created a thousand worlds, and given you the lordship of them for some millions of years, had this been such a kindness as to afford you a new nature, whereby you will be eternally happy in a likeness to God and enjoyment of him? As the work of redemption, so this of regeneration, darkens the glory of the work of creation; since more of grace, wisdom, power, holiness, are the springs of it, the obligation must be far greater; the difference is as great as between heaven and earth. Will you not bless God for making you creatures, for recovery from a fit of sickness? Is the obligation less in delivering you from a spiritual death? Is not the reason of blessing God greater for the second creation than the first, since it is the same skill adorns you with his image in the new creation, which beautified man with that image at the first?

[2.] Was there not as much unfitness in you as in the worst of men by nature? Not one good disposition grew upon nature, but all was the work of preventing grace. Could, then, the iron gates of your hearts fly open of themselves? Or could any else but a God break them open? Was not your nature carried as violently to sin as any, perhaps not into such brutish sins as others, yet more refined and devilish? If you did not launch out into the grossest sins, you owe your preservation to restraining grace. That Socrates was better and wiser than another, was from God, in the acknowledgement of a heathen, who says he was chosen to virtue, "Kata tou Theou cheirotonian", by the divine suffrage. Were your strings better? Sure they were of God's tuning. Man was not more unfit for a natural being before God created him, than the best man in the world was for a spiritual being, till God wrought him with his own finger. Was not the worst in the world naturally as fit for it as yourselves? Did any better thing dwell in your flesh than in theirs, to give grace entertainment? Did not grace at first make its way, conquering, and to conquer, and not one blow struck by you to facilitate the victory? Nay, were you not so far from having a grain of grace by nature, that there was nothing but opposition and rebellion against the Author of it? Did you not want everything to make you lovely in God's eye? Nay, did you not hate him while he had a love of benevolence towards you? And have you not reason to bless him then, that he would not disdain to look upon you, such an impure and rebellious creature? Perhaps our case was the same with hers, Hos. ii. 5, who said, 'I will go after my lovers.' She decreed to follow her idols, and was resolved not to be reclaimed; but God resolved otherwise, ver. 6, 7, who would not leave her till he had made her change her base and unworthy resolution for better: 'She shall say, I will return, &c.' And was it not a happy resolution in the divine breast, not to suffer you to run mad and furiously to hell? What an irrecoverable condition had you been in if God had not spoken a powerful word, 'Hitherto thou art gone, but no further shalt thou go!' Were you not once in your blood, and pitied by no eye, when God said, Live? And can you not wonder at the mercy of his lips, and raise your notes above an ordinary strain? Read over the records of the first work upon thy heart, and see if anything were written there with thy own finger. The very sense of thy own wretchedness was God's writing on thy heart; thou was weighed in the balances and found wanting; lighter than vanity, nothing of thy own to concur with God, but folly and misery.

[3.] If grace found thee unfit and rebellious, there could then be nothing of the least desert; and this should make you cast a wondering eye at the greatness of God's kindness. Man's voluntary defection, without any violence offered to him, had rendered him unworthy of any recovery; you did no more deserve it than the worst devil, who shall never have one line of it drawn upon him. Not one previous disposition, not one sigh or groan for it, could be discerned, much less the draught itself. Your true earnings were nothing but that death you lay under. The unloosing any band of it, or knocking off any fetter, was merely free grace. Is there not, then, reason to bless the Lord, when an undeserved power has been put forth to new create you, when a deserved power might have buried you for ever under your own ruins? Suppose you had been the most exact moralists in the world, the supernatural grace of the new birth could not be deserved by you, because nothing can be merited but by an act as excellent as the reward. No man can merit by any act a thing of a greater value than the act itself; but this grace is of another order, and far superior to any moral natural work. Indeed, upon covenant, if a man does such a thing, he shall have such a reward, the thing promised may be challenged upon the performing the condition, but cannot be said to be merited, because the act was inferior to the reward in the true value of it, but this grace could neither be merited nor challenged at God's hand upon a condition, since he had made no promise in this kind to give you a right to such a demand. It is one thing to be capable of it, another thing to have a just right. A sinner in the state of sin is capable of being changed, but not capable of having a right to that change. Well, then, you could never deserve such a mercy; and will you prize it and bless God for it?

[4] Since you did not deserve it, no, nor the proposals of it, consider what a condition you had been in had God left you to yourselves, or put your wills only into an indifference. Had it been by a mere suasion, or a naked proposition of the truth, I suppose you are so sensible of the mutability of your wills, that you might well believe you should scarce have complied with God. Your security at best had been but as good as Adam's, who had his posse but not his velle. What furious passions and devils in your souls were set against him! and had you been left to your own choice, you would not have stirred one foot to follow his chariot. If you did 'purify your souls in obeying the truth,' it was 'through the Spirit,' 1 Peter i. 22; and all the faith you have was from the same fountain, Acts xviii. 27, 'which believed through grace.' Put it to yourselves: Do you think your hearts were not so stout, that nothing but divine grace could mollify them? Do you think there would have been any heat or warmth in you unless God had kindled the flame? Can you imagine your frozen hearts would have melted but by a divine breath? It was happy for you that God would put your wills beyond an indifference, and deal with you by the same power as he dealt with Christ, not leaving him or you in a doubtful state between life and death. How happy was it for you that God would be conqueror, and surmount your resistance, tame your force, scatter your counsels, level your mountain, and bring your fierceness under the yoke; that he would not wait your choice and leisure, but make the event certain; that he had mercy on you, because he would have mercy; that he would turn the stream of your hearts by the overmastering tide of his grace, and overpower the flesh in the chief parts of your souls, and secure the rational powers of mind and will for himself! How glad may you be of the loss of that indifference that secures your happy estate for ever! Who that is in favour with a prince would not willingly have his will fixed to please him, and dread nothing more than such an indifference, whereby he might hate his prince and lose his favour?

[5.] Is there not reason you should bless God, when he has dealt thus graciously with you, and not with many others in the world, why any of you should be raised up to a spiritual life, when you see so many others near you stretched out in a spiritual death; why one upon the same bench and not another; why one should be gathered with his arm, and another left to the jaws of the devouring lion, why you should have any choice fruit grow in any of your hearts, when thorns and briers grow in every hedge? That God should have afforded you means of regeneration, and not to most others in the world, is a ground of blessing and praise, much more that he should afford you the grace of regeneration, and not to many others under the same means. He has not dealt so with every nation in giving them the means, Ps. cxlvii. 19; he has not dealt so with every person in giving them the grace. That wind that blows where it lists has left other dry bones to remain dry still, passed by others more civil and of sweeter conversations; drawn his image in one, and left others to tumble down to hell in the likeness of Adam, wherein they were born, overlooked one that was not far from the kingdom of heaven, and laid hold on another that was many leagues further from Christ. The Spirit of God only makes this distinction: he will pour out his grace in Galatia and Macedonia, and not suffer it to be known in Bithynia: Acts xvi. 6-8, 'And they essayed to go into Bithynia, but the Spirit suffered them not;' cause it to rain in one city, on one person, and not on another; call one out of the grave, and leave others under the bands of death and in the dregs of human nature. You see your calling, and you may see how distinguishing it is, 'not many wise after the flesh, not many mighty,' 1 Cor. i. 26. Can you see this and not bless the caller, the renewer? A less favour wrought so much upon David's heart that he would bless God in spite of mocks and scoffs, 2 Sam. vi. 21. Oh rich discriminating grace! Where any are peculiar monuments of grace, they should have peculiar notes of praise. What reason can others have to bless God, if such should have no hearts to bless him for so great a mercy? All are under God's will of precept, all are under his will of promise, if they perform that precept; but all are not under his will of purpose, to give them strength to perform that precept.

[6.] It is to be considered, too, with what pains and patience God wrought this work in your hearts. You may best know what ado God had with your hearts before they were thus formed according to his will. Were they not as clay to the potter, which needed much tempering before they were fit for use? Did God find that pliableness in you that the devil found? Had he a cordial welcome at the first proffer? Do you not remember resistance enough to make you for ever ashamed that ever you should put the blessed God to that toil? And yet you know not the thousandth part of that resistance God knew was lodged in your nature. Do you not remember how he met you at every turn, hedged up your perverse way with thorns, before he could be admitted to speak a word to your heart, how he answered one objection after another, whereby you would have stifled his work? Can you remember this, and not admire the mercy that took such pains with so unprofitable a heart? It is called a resurrection, but it is more. Before the resurrection of the body, one part of man lives and waits for reunion though the body be crumbled into very dust; but there is no life in you naturally: so little in you to take part with God, that even that which is the glory of man, his mind, and reason, and wisdom, were in arms against this work, as well as the sensitive and brutish part, for 'the carnal mind was enmity against God,' Rom. viii. 7. What was your language to God at first, but like that of the hellish spirit in the man in Luke iv. 34: 'What have we to do with thee?' Yet he dealt with you as the sun with the earth, which scatters the mists it sends out to choke its light, and spreads its warm wings over the face of the world. So does God, though men offend him with the steams of their sins, and uncivilly command him to depart from them, yet he leaves them not till he has made them willing that he should do them good.

[7.] The work itself requires admiration and blessing in regard of the excellency of it. It is more admirable than all the miracles of nature; the whole world can no more compare with it than a dunghill can equal the worth of a rock of diamonds; all blessings which make you happy spiritually and eternally are wrapped up in it. What can God give greater than his own nature? What are you capable of more than what he has done and will do upon that foundation? If God had only given thee knowledge, thou might have been a devil for all that; but the new nature makes you equal with angels. What man or angel could you be born of with so great advantage as to be born of God? There is no higher being to be born of. What can he do more than thus to beget you? You are new-born according to that image after which his only Son was eternally begotten; conceived by that Spirit whereby Christ was conceived in the womb of the blesses Virgin; raised by the same almighty hand whereby the great pattern of the new birth was raised from the dead. It is the highest elevation of human nature to be united to the Son of God, and to be made like to that glorious image. Greater gifts cannot be than these two, Christ to descend to partake of human nature, and the creature elevated to partake of the divine. If you will not loudly bless him for this, what can God do that shall deserve your praise, since a greater he cannot confer, more full of the spirits of his favour towards you?

[8.] May there not be some circumstances in your particular new birth that may raise your hearts to blessing and praise? Perhaps thou were 'born in a day,' as his promise is of a nation, Isa. lxvi. 7, 8, and without those racking pains which attend the new birth of many. He did not take thee by the throat, nor arrest thee with legal terrors, but breathed upon thee with a gentle wind; conceived and formed thee in a little space of time, that thou were within the prospect of heaven before thou thought thyself out of the suburbs of hell, and brought thee forth a man-child before thou didn't imagine thyself to be delivered. Was it not mercy to renew thee without worrying thee; to melt thee by a gentle fire of love, not break thee piece-meal by the hammer of wrath, that thou should scarce discern the lance from the balsam, and the wound from the plaster? Perhaps he arrested thee in a full course of sin, in some desperate career, when some plot was laid for a high piece of wickedness. It had been an act of his power had thou been brought up in some religious family, tutored in the ways of religion by a choicer education; but perhaps

God took thee from the very steams of hell, when thou had not one thought of him, and he might have let thee alone as well as he did others of thy companions. It had been admirable power to turn clear water into wine, but more to turn stinking and putrefied water into a generous wine. Do not the visible characters of mercy and power in such a case call for more praise at thy hands? Can any other cause have a pretence to put in for a share in thy acknowledgements?

[9.] You are not without many examples to move you to this acknowledgement. Our Saviour himself could not regard the centurion's faith without astonishment. He wondered at that in his humanity which he wrought himself by his divinity, Mat. viii. 10. And when Peter professes his faith in him by acknowledging him to be the Son of God, Christ presently owns his Father as the author of it: Mat. xvi. 17, 'Flesh and blood has not revealed it unto thee, but my Father which is in heaven.' Angels sang both at the first and second creation, and shouted for joy when the corner-stone thereof was laid, Job xxxviii. 6, 7. When they saw its beautiful order, they then showed themselves to be the sons of God indeed, in glorifying their Father for his incomparable works. The second creation being more glorious than the first, is not celebrated by them with fainter shootings; if God has then hallelujahs for you, it is fit he should have hallelujahs from you. If angels speak loud, it is not fit you should speak low; it is their concern, as they are God's friends and servants; your concern, as you are his workmanship, of his own carving. The saints in all ages of the church have led the way in this acknowledgement. The elders, made kings and priests on earth, in a conquest of Satan and their own hearts, crowned with a blessed grace, cast down their crowns at the feet of God Rev. ix. 11, 'For thou hast created all things, and for thy pleasure they are and were created,' both the present new creation and the old. 'Thou hast loosed my bonds,' Ps. cxvi. 16. What follows? 'I will offer to thee the sacrifice of thanksgiving.' And God's renewing David's youth like the eagle's, his changing him into a new man, says Jerome, is one argument of David's praise, Ps. ciii. 6. Add to this, heathens have acknowledged it to be the work of God, one examining the reason why Homer calls virtuous men "dious", answers. Because goodness was not a work of art, but "ergon Dios". If divining and mystical knowledge be "theiai tini epipnoiai", by divine inspiration, shall we say of virtue it is "ergon technes thentes", the work of man's art? Where do you find any like Nebuchadnezzar, gazing upon the divine formation in his own heart, and proudly crying out, 'Is not this great Babylon which I have built?' Does such language drop from a David's mouth? No; but 'thou hast quickened me.' Or from Paul? No, 'by grace I am what I am.' Every inch, every spark, every joint of the new man is from grace.

[10.] If you do not acknowledge it to God, and bless him for it, you may justly suspect you are not born of him. It is the nature of true grace to reflect back upon God, as it is of a sunbeam shining upon a wall to reflect back upon the sun. Blessing God for it, is a character of a renewed man. It is an evidence of the ruin of the contradiction of nature against God, when man can strip himself of all, and own God the prime fountain of what he is and has. If a man boast of his being the cause of a new birth in himself by any work of his own, it is a shrewd sign he is not renewed, because by such boasting he crosses the main end of the gospel, which is to stain the pride of man, and debase him to the dust from all grounds of glorying in himself. How jealous was the apostle in this case, and therefore backs his assertion again and again, that he might beat man's hands off from fingering anything of God's glory: Eph. ii. 5, 'By grace you are saved;' again, verse 8, 9, 'and that not of yourselves: it is the gift of God.' Once again, 'Not of works.' And the reason why he is thus earnest, was perpetually to discountenance self-confidence, 'lest any man should boast.' The design of God in all gospel dispensations, is to pull away the stool whereon the flesh sits to glory: 1 Cor i. 29-31, 'That no flesh should glory in his presence.' It would seem strange that the new birth, a main gospel work, should be wrought without promoting a gospel end. To have a new birth, and such a flourishing pride, opposite to the end of it, is a contradiction. If the doctrine of faith does exclude boasting, as Rom. iii. 27, boasting is 'excluded by the law of faith,' the grace of faith also will exclude it; where the new birth is wrought, pride, the great enemy to it, will surely be captivated. We are then something in and by God, when we are most nothing in ourselves.

Well, then, be much in the work of praising God, who shined into thy heart when it was dark, and sealed instruction to thee; who took away the stony heart, and introduced one of flesh in the room; who manifested a day of power in the night of your weakness. Can you, dare you, to ascribe it to yourselves? Let God then have the praise. It is our fault we are more in complaints of what we want, than acknowledgements of what we have. Oh, rob not God of his deity, pretend not yourselves partners with him in the least of the stock. The more you return the glory of his grace, the more will he return the comfort of it to you; the more you give him that glory he is so jealous of, the more he will give you that grace he is so liberal of.

(3.) A third duty for those that are renewed. Acknowledge God in all the changes you see in others. Miracles must be regarded. It is greater for the apostles to act with new hearts than to speak with new tongues; greater than to stop the sun in its course, which would set all the world upon an astonished gaze. Shall any such miraculous work be done in our view, and we stand only as stupid spectators, and not render to God that glory which is due to him for his choicest work? As the sight and consideration of the material creation kept up the notion of the being of God as creator, so the consideration of his works upon the souls of men will quicken thy sentiments of God as a new creator. One is an argument to prove the power of his essence, the other an argument of the power of his grace. Noah does not bless them first for that act of filial duty showed to his father, but blesses God as the author of that modesty Shem had shown in covering his father's nakedness: Gen. ix. 26, 'Blessed be the God of Shem.' When a great number were turned to Christ, Barnabas presently cast up his eye to the grace of God, 'he saw the grace of God,' Acts xi. 21-23. Let every Lazarus you see raised from the grave raise up your faith to a higher elevation, and dress it in a jubilee attire. When you see a new temple reared to God, own it as the Lord's doing, and let it be marvellous in your eyes.

(4.) Be content with every condition your new creator shall cast you into. Discontent at any of God's dispensations does ill become one whom God has new begotten to a glorious inheritance. What can he do more than he has done, and what he will do upon that foundation? All that he acts is to further that which he has so powerfully and mercifully begun. What son would repine at the losing a rattle, as long as he is born to a never-fading inheritance? If grace has put forth a power to new create you, it will not use that power otherwise than for your good. It may contradict your carnal desires, not your spiritual interest. Well may any man be content with the jewel that is left, though the casket be lost. All things are too light if put into the balance with the new birth: the dearest husband or wife, the sweetest children or friends, the most flourishing inheritance; study, therefore, contentment in the worst condition upon this ground; you know not how soon you may be put to practise all your skill. Do you not see the heavens gathering blackness over your heads? A new birth, that allies us to God as his children, will be of more force to settle us, than calamities can be to discompose us; for never was child so dear to an earthly, as a new created soul is to its heavenly Father.

(5.) Walk worthy of the author of it. A verbal acknowledgement will signify little without a real imitation of the virtues of him 'that has called you out of darkness into his marvellous light,' 1 Peter ii. 9. A holiness is to be expressed by you, like the holiness of that God who has renewed you. Let no devilish or brutish carriage be yoked with a divine birth, indeed it cannot; the bespotting corruption of the world will not agree with the regeneration of the soul; the stains of the flesh are inconsistent with the purity of the new nature. Belial and Christ, God and Satan, are not joint begetters; Satan's impure breathings upon you should not be admitted to mix with the breath of God. A new nature by grace must not imitate a brutish nature by sin; a soul born of God must not be fashioned according to the world. If you differ from the world in your nature by grace, differ from the world also in your carriage by holiness. It is uncomely for one born of God to be taken with the foolish, flaunting pride of the world, more than the pattern God has set him; that is, to imitate beasts, not a heavenly Father. The world is little, nothing, vanity in the eye of God; so should it be in the eye of a divinely begotten soul. Use the world as travellers an inn, to lodge, not to dwell in, to accommodate you in your journey to that Father of whom you were born. Let a heaven-born nature be attended with heavenly flights, longing for that happy state wherein nothing but the divine nature shall be seen in union, as nothing but fire is seen in melted gold.

(6.) Mourn for your imperfections. Give God his due, and grieve for your defect in paving him his own. The soul in creation comes pure out of God's hand, but it is poisoned by the flesh, and the impurity in the sensitive part of man. Though your grace be from God, yet your imperfections are from yourselves. The waters that run through sulphur and alum mines flow from the sea, but the ill taste and scent are communicated by the matter it mixes with in its passage. God is the author of your faith, but not of the weakness of your faith; the author of your love, but not of the coldness of your love; the author of your zeal, but not of the faintness of your zeal. Chide your hearts, therefore for your weakness, as Christ did his disciples for their slowness in faith. 'Rejoice with trembling,' Ps. ii. 11, rejoice in what you have, and mourn for chat you want and come short in. Reason you have, since there is too much of the power of nature remaining with our best grace, so that it may be said of it, as Lot of Zoar, What grace has enclosed is but a little one.

Exhort. 2. To those that are not born of God. You see at whose hands you are to seek it. God was the first contriver of the gospel, the first preacher of the gospel, the sole artist in any gospel operation. No man can come except the Father draw him; not some men, but no man; every man must therefore seek to this great attracter. It is a vanity of human nature, that every man loves to be "autodidaktos", his own teacher; and no less a vanity it is, that every man loves to be "autogennetos", his own begetter. Men glory in the knowledge they get without a teacher, and no less glory in any change they can hammer out without a spiritual Father. As he that scorns to be taught by another shall surely have a fool to his tutor, so he that thinks to gain spiritual life by himself, shall be sure to have death for his quickener. No man would seek life from death, or light from darkness, and the best natural man is no better. The glory of the Lord must rise upon us, before we can rise out of our death in sin: 'Arise, and shine, for thy light is come, and the glory of the Lord is risen upon thee,' Isa. lx. 1.

(1.) Seek it only at the hands of God. It is not to be had by outward rules, but divine influence; the streams of life must come from him, since with him only is the fountain of life: Ps. xxxvi. 9, 'I will give a heart of flesh;' I alone, without any other co-ordinate cause, either man or angel. He only has the key of the heart, as well as that of the womb; confide not in yourselves. Adam was a root to convey sin and death, but no root to convey spiritual life. Corruption comes by propagation from him, grace only by spiritual regeneration from God. Would any wise man seek for water in a desert, or for grace from himself, who is naturally a dry wilderness? What toad, naturally full of poison, ever made himself sweet and wholesome? As Christ was by the grace of God made partaker of our nature in his incarnation, so by the same grace only can we be made partakers of his nature by regeneration. We are naturally weeds; if ever we be flowers in God's garden, the transformation must be God's act alone.

Seek it of God. But,

[1.] In the use of means, not abating anything of thine own industry. Seek, while God offers it; hold your mouth under the fountain while it runs. Moses hewed the tables, but God wrote the law. God promised David and Gideon victory, but not with their hands in their pockets, but their arms and armies about them. Moses must fight with the arms of Israel, but pray to the God of battles and victory. We must with one hand use the directions God has given, and lift up the other in spiritual supplication for success upon them. Therefore let not the doctrine of God's being the cause of the new birth encourage your laziness and sloth. This sloth among men Chemnitius thought to be the occasion of Pelagius his error, who, seeing the laziness of Christians, thought to correct it by making them think highly of their own strength; but that was a dangerous extreme.

[2.] Yet let your eye be solely upon God in the use of them, since all the means in the world cannot do it without him. Unless God pull up the floodgates, no water of life can stream into the soul; means can no more of themselves cast out death than the disciples could cast out some devils; but Christ was able to do what they could not. All the angels in heaven and men upon earth have not been able, these almost six thousand years, to make one fly; yet all the angels and the whole frame of the world were made by God in six days. Men speak to the sense, God to the heart; they to the understanding, and God into it; men argue with the will, and God persuades it. All the clamours of the whole nation of the Jews, yea, of all the men in the world, would not have made Lazarus stir out of the grave, had not our Saviour spoken the word, 'Lazarus, come forth.' How often do the clouds of heaven drop upon men, yet they still remain as a dry chip, their stony hearts perhaps moistened with some transient flashy affections, but not mollified into flesh. Pray therefore to God, before the use of any means, Lord, breathe life so powerfully upon me, that I may walk before thee, and never find myself again in a natural winding-sheet. Let thy voice, Lord, be heard and felt by me as the voice of thy Son was by Lazarus. To use means without a seeking to God for his blessing, is to be exercised in divine institutions with an atheistic spirit. He is an atheist that expects nourishment from his meat without God's benediction, and he no less that runs to means without lifting up his heart to God, thinking to get grace conveyed by the means without God's operation.

(2.) Direction. Plead much with God from the glorious attributes he honours in this work. Lord, here is a subject for thy power to work upon. God made the heavens when there was nothing but a rude mass; he brought forth the sun, moon, and stars, with all their glory, out of the barren womb of nothing. Is thy heart worse than nothing, more contradictory to God than nothing? It is so. Assume an argument from hence: Lord, here is a subject for thy power above what was manifested in creation; there is not a more tough heart in the world than mine; lose not the opportunity of displaying the greatness of thy power, since there is scarce a heart more stout and unwieldy than mine is. Lord, bestow a vital principle upon me; thou did it to the lifeless body of Adam; thy power will be more magnified in the breathing upon a lifeless soul of a son and daughter of Adam. In the same manner plead his wisdom and holiness. Plead also the enmity thy sin has against him, the wrong it has done him, in spoiling the creation, changing the end of it, hindering thee from thy natural duty, and that it is not for the interest of his glory to let sin bear such a sway and dominion, and usurp his room in one who would fain be another man.

(3.) Be deeply sensible of the corruption of thy nature; the want of this is the cause there is so little sense in men and women of the absolute necessity of the grace of regeneration, and a change of nature. Therefore labour to see yourselves in a forlorn condition by spiritual death. Look upon your great fall as a son of Adam, a slave of Satan, and possessor of a hellish nature, and at a vast distance from God and happiness.

(4.) Grieve not the Spirit in any of his operations. Quench not the sparks of the Spirit in any previous preparations and dispositions to this new birth. Be pliable to his breathings, hoist up your sails to receive his gales; when he knocks, open thy heart as wide as may be, push it to the furthest point, that there may be no remora; let all the house be free for his triumphant entrance. Since thy strength is too weak for it, beg of him at such a season to break it open; set upon prayer at such a season, and leave not till you have prayed your spirits up and your resistance out. How ungrateful and foolish is it to grieve that Spirit, who offers to form you into a new birth, and bring the life and joy of heaven into your heart! This is the only means to recover the loss you had by the fall of Adam, and surmount all the misery of it. Seek to him; he that can gather the dust of your bodies, if blown to the further part of the world, and knit it together, can overcome the filthy and deadly noisomeness of your souls; he can make a barren wilderness to become pools of water, a lump of vanity a garden of pleasure, a heap of rubbish to sprout up a new-born sun. If you would therefore be animated with a spirit of life, you must approach the beams of the sun, and lie under the rich and enlivening influences of it.

End of part 2 of A Discourse of the Efficient of Regeneration.

A Discourse of the Word, the Instrument of Regeneration

Of his own will begot he us with the word of truth, that we should be a kind of first-fruits of his creatures.--James 1:18.

I have chosen this text to treat of the instrument of the new birth.

The apostle having advised them (verse 13, 'But let no man say when he is tempted, I am tempted of God: for God cannot be tempted to evil, neither tempts he any man') not to charge God as the author of any temptation to evil, showing it to be contrary to the nature of God, who is infinite goodness and righteousness; for as he cannot be tempted with evil, so neither can he tempt any man; and declaring the true cause and spring of all evil to be inherent in ourselves, even that lust which is riveted in our nature, which he calls our own lust, - verse 14, 'But every man is tempted, when he is drawn away of his own lust, and enticed,' - he takes occasion from thence to show the order of sin's working. Sin is first conceived by that original corruption in our nature, and formed and brought forth into action; and when it is finished, and grows into a habit, it 'brings forth death,' verse 15. To remove this error, which some in those days had sucked in out of a natural self-love that man has to excuse himself, and remove the cause of sin far from him, the apostle shows that God is the author and fountain of all the good we have: ver. 17, 'Every good gift and every perfect gift is from above, and comes down from the Father of lights, with whom is no variableness, nor shadow of change.' God being the infinite Father of lights, who has no eclipses or decreases, no shadows or mixtures of darkness, but always shines with a constant and settled brightness, of this goodness has given a great evidence, in conferring the choicest mercy upon us, even a new begetting through the gospel, and thereby the relation of children to him, that we might be consecrated to him as the first fruits and a peculiar portion. Of his own will, "bouletheis; by his mere motion, induced by no cause but the goodness in his own breast. (1.) To distinguish it from the generation of the Son, which is natural, this voluntary; of his own will, not naturally, as he begot his Son from eternity. (2.) Not necessarily, by a necessity of nature, as the sun, to which he had compared God before, does enlighten, and enliven, when matter is prepared to receive his quickening beams; but by an arbitrariness of grace. (3.) Not by any obligation from the creature; the will of God is opposed to the merit of man. The new creation answers to election; the first purpose was free, the bringing that purpose to execution is free whatsoever obligation there is, results not from the creature, but from himself, his own immutable nature, which has no variableness, nor shadow of change. "Begot us,' "apekuesen", or brought us forth, for the same word "apokuei", ver. 15, is translated 'brings forth.' 'By the word of truth', a title given to the gospel both in the Old and New Testament: in the Old, Ps. xiv. 4, 'And in thy majesty ride prosperously, because of truth,' or 'upon thy word of truth,' in the New Testament, Eph. i. 13, 'In whom you also trusted, after you heard the word of truth, the gospel of your salvation.' So 2 Cor. vi. 7, and 2 Tim. ii. 15. And it is called truth by way of excellency, as paramount to all other truth. (1.) Either, by an Hebraism, the word of truth; that is, the true word. (2.) Or rather, by way of eminency, as containing a higher truth, more excellent in itself, more advantageous for the creature, than any other divine truth; wherein the highest glory of God, the sure and everlasting happiness of the creature, is set forth; a word which he has 'magnified above all his name,' Ps. cxxxviii. 2.

And called the word of truth.

1. In regard of the author, truth itself; and the publisher, he who was 'the way, the truth, and the life.'

2. In opposition to all false doctrines, which can never be the instruments of conversion; for error to convert to truth, is the same thing as for darkness to diffuse light, or water to kindle fire.

3. In opposition to the windy and flashy conceits of men, which can no more be instrumental in the begetting a Christian, than mere wind can beget a man.

4. In opposition to the legal shadows; the gospel declares the truth of those types. Both the law and prophecy were but as a dim candle 'in a dark place,' 2 Peter i. 19, but this as a sun shining out at noonday. All other discourses did stream to this as their great ocean, wherein they were to be swallowed up. The law was the word of truth, but referred to the gospel as the great end of it. This contains the

whole and ultimate purpose of God, for saving men by Jesus Christ, and in him enriching them with all spiritual blessings, and not by the works of the law, and thus the Spirit, which enlightens and seals instruction upon our souls, is called 'the Spirit of truth,' John xiv. 17, as it is called a Spirit of holiness, as it makes us holy, a Spirit of grace, as it makes us gracious, or as it declares the grace of God. Some by the word of truth understand Christ, the essential and uncreated "logos", Word, as it is understood by some in 1 Peter i. 23, 25, 'By the Word of God, which lives and abides for ever; and this is the Word which by the gospel is preached to you.' Possibly it may be meant of Christ, who by the gospel is declared and preached to be the mediator between God and man, appointed to raise up those that are given to him. Others by the word there, mean the will of God of giving grace in Christ, which is manifest in, and expressed by, the gospel. But here it is evidently meant of the gospel, because of the inference the apostle makes: ver. 19, 'Be swift to hear;' that is, prize the word, wait upon the means with all readiness; 'slow to speak,' to utter your judgment of it, or be wise in your own conceit, whereof a readiness to speak peremptorily in divine truth is sometimes an evidence; 'slow to wrath' and passion, which hinder any profit by the word. 'That we should be a kind of first fruits of his creatures;' the chief among his creatures. The first fruits were the best of every kind to be offered to God, whereby they acknowledged God's gift of them, and desired his blessing upon them, and were given as God's peculiar right and portion. It was commanded in the law, Deut. xviii. 4. It was a custom among many of the heathens. To offer them was a token of thankfulness; not to offer them, was accounted a sign of atheism and profaneness. The new creature is God's peculiar portion taken out of mankind; and it bespeaks duty too: being consecrated to God by a new begetting, they should serve God with a new spirit, new thankfulness, new frames.

We see here,

1. The efficient of regeneration, God; 'he,' the Father of lights.
2. The impulsive or moving cause, 'his own will.'
3. The instrumental cause 'with the word of truth.'
4. The final cause, 'that we may be a kind of first fruits.'

The doctrine I am to handle is,

Doctrine. That the gospel is the instrument whereby God brings the soul forth in a new birth.

The Scripture does distinguish the efficient and instrumental cause by the prepositions "ek", or, "eks", and "dia". When we are said to be 'born of the Spirit,' it is, John iii. 5, "ek pneumatos"; 1 John iii. 9, v. 1, "ek Theou"; never "dia pneumatos", or "dia Theou:" but we are nowhere said to be born of the word, or begotten of the word, but "dia logou", by or with the word, 1 Peter i. 23; and "dia euangeliou", 1 Cor. iv. 15, I have begotten you 'through the gospel.' The preposition "ek" or "eks", usually notes the efficient or material cause; "dia", the instrumental or means by which a thing is wrought. Sin entered into the heart of Eve by the word of the devil, grace enters into the heart by the word of God; that entered by a word of error, this by a word of truth: 'Ye are clean through the word I have spoken to you, John xv. 3, whereby our Saviour means the word outwardly preached by him, for it is the word spoken by him. Not that it had this efficacy of itself, but as an instrument of their sanctification, rendering them ready to every good work. The holiness, therefore, which it begets, is called the holiness of truth, Eph. iv. 24, opposed to the "epithumiai tes apates", 'lusts of deceit,' ver. 22. Lusts grow up from error and deceit, and holiness of the new man grows up from truth. The gospel administration, in regard of the effects of it, is called 'the kingdom of God,' Mark i. 14; it erects the kingdom of God in the world and in the hearts of men, and called the regeneration: Mat. xix. 28, 'Ye which have followed me in the regeneration;' the gospel administration being a creating of 'new heavers and a new earth,' Isa. lxv. 17. This is the triumphal chariot, wherein Christ rides majestically to the conquest of hearts: Ps. xiv. 4, 'And in thy majesty ride prosperously, because of truth,' "'al dvar 'emut", a psalm the Jews themselves understand of the Messiah. The word of his truth is the support of his kingdom, whereby he awes sinners into submission. Peace from heaven, and the health of our nature, is 'the fruit of the lips,' though of God's creation, Isa. lvii. 19. It is like the dew or mist which watered the ground, and prepared the earth for the formation of Adam's body, into which God breathed afterwards a living soul, Gen. ii. 6. 7.

I. For explication, take some propositions:

1. It is not the law that is this instrument. The law, taken in general for the legal administration prescribed to the Jews, was instrumental for renewing, because there was a typical gospel in that Judaic administration: Heb. iv. 2, 'For to us was the gospel preached as well as unto them.' They were evangelised, "Euangelismenoi", as the word signifies. The Judaic administration was composed of law and gospel: the moral law, as a covenant of works; the ceremonial law, representing the covenant of grace. The law of God, or gospel among them, is said to convert the soul, Ps. xix. 7. But the law, taken as a covenant of works, was not appointed for renewing the soul, otherwise what need had there been of enacting another law for that work? And those that say the law is instrumental in conversion, or inflaming our affections to obedience, say that all the benefits by it are to be ascribed to the covenant of grace in Christ. It is true, the law considered in itself is preparatory to cast men down, and show them their distance from God and contrariety to his command; but the law without the gospel never brought

any man to Christ. Whatsoever it does in this case is not of itself, but by the mingling the gospel with it, which spirits it to such an end. Though the law did not encourage sin, yet it gave no help against it, but left the soul under the dominion of it, which is evident by the apostle's inference: Rom. vi. 14, 'Sin shall not have dominion over you; for you are not under the law, but under grace.' Hence the property of the law, which is meant by 'the letter,' 2 Cor. iii. 6, is to kill, but 'the Spirit' gives life; that leaves under the severity of justice, after sin had entered; but the spiritual administration, wherein the Spirit works, is to quicken and renew the soul, and make it able to get above the guilt and power of sin. The apostle, therefore, wholly excludes the law: Gal. iii. 2, 'Received you the Spirit by the works of the law, or by the hearing of faith?' that is, the word of faith, as the gospel is called, Rom. x. 8. By Spirit is meant, says Calvin, the grace of regeneration, as by faith is meant the doctrine of faith. I might have preached (as if the apostle had said) the works of the law till my lungs had been worn out, and the renewing Spirit would never have entered into you by that fire, but it descended upon you in the sweet gospel dew. The gospel is therefore called the 'ministration of the Spirit,' and the 'ministration of righteousness,' 2 Cor. iii. 8, 9. It is the chariot or vehiculum wherein the Spirit rides, the proclamation by which it is declared, the channel through which it is conveyed. The law discovers the righteousness of God as well as the gospel; but that demands a righteousness from the creature, the gospel confers a righteousness upon the creature; the law shows us God's righteousness in his nature, the gospel shows us God's righteousness in his nature and grace. The law is a hammer to break us, the gospel God's oil to cure us; the law makes sin live and our souls die,--Rom. vii. 9, 'When the commandment came, sin revived, and I died,--the gospel makes sin die and our souls live; the law awakens the lion, the gospel lets out his blood. At the best, the terrors of the law do chain up our furious affections, but the sweetness of gospel mercy changes them. The law prepares the matter, the gospel brings the new form. That was appointed for the rule of our walk, not for the restoration of our life. And they are the promises of mercy which are the motives to return; rebels will not submit to their prince as long as they know they shall have no quarter. Hue and cry makes the thief fly away the faster. By the 'great and precious promises;' we 'are made partakers of the divine nature,' 2 Peter i. 4. The promises of the law being conditional, belong not to us without fulfilling the condition, of which we are incapable of ourselves. The law, therefore, since the fall, is destructive, the gospel restorative, and the promises of it the cords whereby God draws us.

2. The gospel is this instrument. It is an instrument to unlock the prison doors, and take them off the hinges, strike off the fetters, and draw out the soul to a glorious liberty. It is by the voice of the archangel men shall rise in their bodies; it is by the voice of the Son of God in the word that men rise in their souls. Nothing else ever wrought such miraculous changes. To make lions become lambs, Isa. vi. 6, Hosea iv. 13; beloved idols to be cast away with indignation; to make its entrance like fire, and consume old lusts in a short time: these have been undeniable realities, which have created affection and astonishment in some enemies as well as friends. It has a more excellent instrumentality in it than other providences of God, because it is a higher manifestation. Every creature conducts us to the knowledge of God, by giving us notice of his power, wisdom, and goodness, Rom. i. 20. The declaration of his works in the world is instrumental to make men seek him, Acts xvii. 27. Every day's providence declares his patience, every shower of rain his merciful provision for mankind, Acts xiv. 17, every day's preservation of the world under a load of sin manifests his mercy. The heavens have a tongue, and the rod has a voice; the design of all is to lead men to repentance, Rom. ii. 4. If these, therefore, be some kind of instruments upon the hearts of considering men, the gospel being a discovery superior to all these, in manifesting not only a God of nature, but a God of grace, must be designed to a choicer and nobler work. The heavens and providence are instruments to instruct us, this to renew us.

It is an instrument; but,

(1.) It is not a natural instrument, to work by any natural efficacy, as food does nourish, the sun shines, or the air and water cools, or as a sharp knife cuts if it be applied to fit matter. If it were thus natural, it would not be of grace. Though the shining of the sun, or the healing by a plaster, are acts of the goodness and mercy of God, yet the Scripture calls them not by that higher title of acts of grace. If the operation were natural, the gospel would never be without its effect wherever it were preached; as the sun, wherever it shines in any land, does both enlighten and warm. Our Saviour then would have had more success, since the gospel could not have greater natural efficacy than from his lips; yet the number of his converts were probably not much above five hundred, for so many he appeared to after his resurrection, 1 Cor. xv. 6, when many thousands in that land heard his voice, and saw his miracles. Christ, who was always able to give himself success, would not, perhaps for this among many other reasons, to advance his spiritual above his corporal presence, and to prevent any thoughts of any natural virtue in the word, without the power of the Spirit working by it. Every day teaches us, that though many see the glass of the gospel, yet few see the glory of God in that gospel. Were it natural, then, that all that hear it were not renewed, would be more miraculous than that any are; as it was more a miracle that the sun should stand still in Joshua's time, against its natural course of motion, than that it moves every day in the heavens. If it were a natural instrument, it must then have life in itself, but how can the voice of a man, or the words and syllables in a book, be capable of receiving spiritual life, which they must have before they can naturally convey it to others? Were it a natural instrument, it would have the same effect upon the soul at one time as at another. But does not daily experience witness, that the word shines at some particular times upon the soul with a clearer ray than at other times, that such a soul has thought itself in another world (as it were), and that too when it has been much clouded by the weakness of the instrument declaring it? Lastly were it natural, the wisest men, men of the sharpest understandings, could not resist it, no man can hinder the sun's shining upon him, when he is under the beams of it, it would warm him whether he would or no, yet have not such been the most desperate opposers of it in all ages of the world, as well as in the times of the apostles? It is not then a natural, but a moral instrument, which will follow afterwards, when we come to consider how it works.

(2.) It is the only instrument appointed by God to this end in an ordinary way. God has made a combination between hearing and believing, Rom. x. 14, 17, so that believing comes not without hearing. The waters of the sanctuary run only through the channels of the gospel; the mines of grace are found only in the climates of the word. Why does not air nourish? Because God did not set that, but meat, apart for each an end. Though God could by his almighty power bless air to this end, yet in an ordinary way he has fixed his blessing on these natural causes of his own ordaining. God has appointed second causes for natural operations; if we would be warm, God has appointed fire and sun to warm us; he could do it immediately, by spreading a lively heat in every member, as well as he gave at first a power to fire to burn; but he uses natural instruments in natural effects, and likewise spiritual instruments in spiritual productions. God may blow in an extraordinary way upon the soul by a divine breath without any instrument, as he did immediately upon the prophets, or as he gave light to the world the three first days of the creation without a sun, but since only by the sun and stars. But God seems here to have fixed his power: Rom. i. 16, the gospel is 'the power of God to salvation;' not that his power shall always attend it, but that he will exert his power, at least ordinarily, only by it; no other organ through which the wind of the Spirit shall blow, no other sword which the Spirit shall manage but this, Eph. vi. 13. Though our Saviour prayed upon the cross for some of his greatest enemies, who had their hands embrued in his precious blood, though he was heard, yet his prayer was not answered but through Peter's ministry, to grace the first spiritual discovery of the gospel. Nothing else can have that efficacy. Had every man in Israel made a brazen serpent, and looked upon it when they had been stung, they might have looked till they had groaned their last, before they had met with any cure, because only one was of God's appointing. To a cast of an eye upon that, he had only promised his healing virtue, in that only then he had lodged his power.

(3.) It is therefore a necessary instrument.

[1.] In regard of the reasonable creature there must be some declaration. God does not ordinarily work but by means, and does not produce anything without them which may be done with them. God does not maintain the creatures by a daily creation, but by generation; he maintains that faculty of generation in them by the means of health and nourishment, and that by the means of the fruits of the earth, and does all this according to the ordinance he fixed at the creation, when he appointed every kind of creatures their proper food, and bestowed his blessing upon them, 'Increase and multiply.' So according to the method God has set of men's actions, it is necessary that this regeneration should be by some word as an instrument, for God has given understanding and will to man. We cannot understand anything, or will anything, but what is proposed to us by some external object; as our eye can see nothing but what is without us, our hand take nothing but what is without us, so it is necessary that God by the word should set before us those things which our understandings may apprehend, and our wills embrace. Now we believe things as we conceive them true, or not believe them as we conceive them false. We love, desire, delight in things, as we conceive them honest or profitable; we hate, we refuse, or grieve, as we conceive them dishonest, or troublesome, or hurtful to us; whatever we are changed by in our understandings, wills, and affections, is represented to us under some of these considerations. To make an alteration in us according to our nature of understanding, will, and affection, it is necessary there should be some declaration of things under those considerations of true, good, delightful, &c., in the highest manner, to make a choice change in every faculty of the soul, and without this a man cannot be changed as a rational creature; he will otherwise have a change he knows not why, nor to what end, nor upon what consideration, which is an inconceivable change in a rational creature.

[2.] It is necessary the revelation of this gospel we have should be made. There is a necessity of some revelation, for no man can see that which is not visible, or hear that which has no sound, or know that which is not declared. There is also a necessity of the revelation of this gospel, since faith is a great part of this work. How can any man believe that God is good in Christ, without knowing that he has so declared himself? Since the Spirit takes of Christ's, and shows it to us, there must be a revelation of Christ, and the goodness of God in Christ, before we can believe. Though the manner of this revelation may be different, and the Spirit may renew in an extraordinary manner, yet this is the instrument whereby all spiritual begettings are wrought; the manner may be by visions, dreams, by reading or hearing, yet still it is the gospel which is revealed; the matter revealed is the same, though the formal revelation or manner may be different. Paul's regeneration was by a vision, for at that vision of the light, and that voice of Christ, I suppose him to be renewed, because of that full resignation of his will to Christ, Acts ix. 6, yet the matter of the revelation was the same, that Christ was the Messiah, for so Paul understands it, in giving him the title of Lord. Though God may communicate himself without the written word to some that have it not, yet according to his appointment, not without a revelation of what is in that word.

[3.] This necessity will further appear, if we consider that it always was so. Adam and Eve were the first after the fall wherein God did constitute his church, whose regeneration and conversion were wrought by that promise of the seed of the woman made to them in paradise; God surely putting an enmity in the heart of those to whom this first promise of an enmity was made, upon which promise a sacrifice followed, which some ground on Gen. iii. 21, 'God made them coats of skins' of beasts, which the word "'od" signifies, and is never taken in Scripture otherwise than for the outward skin of a beast. And, indeed, it is not likely that 129 years should be between the promise and the first sacrifice, for some think Abel was killed by Cain in the 129th year after the creation, for it is certain 130 years after the creation Seth was born, Gen. v. 3. And this is confirmed, Heb. ix. 32, 'Neither the first testament was dedicated without blood.' The first testament was of more ancient date than the Jewish service ordained by Moses; and some ceremonies, as sacrifices, and distinction of clean and unclean beasts, were in use before, Gen. viii. 20, so that there seems to be a sacrifice representing the Messiah for the dedication of the first testament, which Adam had received from God and transmitted to Abel, whom he taught the way of sacrificing. What regeneration Adam had was by this word of the gospel. Had not Adam believed it, he would not have delivered it to Abel; and Abel had not sacrificed, unless he had been taught so by his father, or immediately by God; but most likely by his father, because God does not use extraordinary means, when ordinary will serve. And Abel was regenerate, for it is said 'by faith he offered' this sacrifice, Heb. xi. 4: and it was faith in Christ, faith in the promised seed, for all of them in that catalogue, Heb. xi., did eye Christ by faith, as well as Moses. of whom it is particularly expressed, ver. 26, that 'he esteemed the reproach of Christ greater riches than the treasures of Egypt.' Considering all this, it is evident, that the ancient restoration was by the revelation of Christ and the gospel as the only necessary means. Abraham, it is likely, had some external word in his father Terah's family, by tradition from the patriarchs, and had the revelation of the promise made to him by God, Gen. xviii. 19. And it was wrought then in an ordinary way by instruction, for, for that Abraham is commended, and no doubt but Isaac and Jacob did the same, so that all along this change of the heart was wrought by a declaration of the word of the gospel.

(4.) It seems to be the standing instrument of it to the end of the world. Some indeed think the conversion of the Jews shall not be by the declarations of the word in a way of preaching and instruction, as the Gentiles were brought in, but by a visible appearance of Christ, which they ground upon Zech. xii. 10, 'They shall look upon him whom they have pierced,' they shall see Christ in the clouds as pierced by them, and understand Paul's conversion by an extraordinary light shining round about him, and a voice from heaven, to be a type and pattern of God's manner of the future conversion of the Jews, which is intimated, 1 Tim. i. 16, that the mercy he obtained was 'a pattern for them which should hereafter believe on him to life everlasting'. Whether this be so or no, yet however the conversion is by a revelation of that which is the matter and substance of the gospel, it is the revelation of Christ himself; and if, like Paul's conversion, by a voice, as well as by sight, by instruction as well as apparition; but it seems to me to be the perpetual standing means of regeneration. The fruits of our Saviour's ascension shall endure to the end of the world, and the enduing men with gifts for the building him a spiritual house is a great end of his ascension, Ps. lxviii. 18, compared with Eph. iv. 8, 9, 'Thou hast ascended on high, thou hast led captivity captive, thou hast received gifts for men; yea, for the rebellious also, that the Lord might dwell among them.' He receives gifts upon his ascension, for the subduing and changing the hearts of the rebellious, that they may be a fit habitation for God, who dwells in them by his Spirit; these gifts being the fruit of so glorious an ascension, and a rich donative to him for the accomplishment of his undertaking in the world, and being given for the smoothing, polishing, and fitting rude stones to combine together for a temple for the Lord to dwell in (which is the reason why he keeps up the world). As long therefore as God has a temple, and any stone to polish, these gifts will remain in the ministry of the word, and be exercised in order to so great a building; and we may infer also by the way, that it is not likely that God does dwell in any, but such who are so subdued and formed by the ministry of the word, which is the fruit of Christ's ascension. It seems also to have an more ancient date, and founded upon the covenant of redemption between the Father and the Son. All that prayer in the 17th of John seems to me to run upon those articles agreed on between them. Those that were given to Christ were given to keep his word: John xvii. 6, 'Thou gave them me, and they have kept thy word.' Which word was given to Christ by God in order to be given to them: ver. 8, 'I have given them the word which thou gave me.' And in his prayer for their sanctification, her. 17, he seems to intimate that this was the ordinary method then subscribed to by both, and the settled means of sanctification; he does not only propose his desire for their sanctification, but the means, 'through thy truth,' and specifies what he means by truth, 'thy word is truth.' And what he did here pray for, for them that were then with him, he did for all that should hereafter believe, ver. 20; and though this be meant of a further sanctification of those that were already regenerate, yet it will, I think, evidently follow that if the word by agreement between the Father and the Son be the instrument of every degree of sanctification, it must be also of the first; since there can be no faith, but refers to the object believed, and the ground why it is believed, whence 'belief of the truth' is joined with the 'sanctification of the Spirit,' 2 Thes. ii. 13; besides, ver. 20, all belief for the future was to be through the word, 'through their word.' Let me add another inference from this; what an excellent argument is this to plead in prayer, before you go to hear or read the word; Lord, was not this an article of agreement between thee and thy Son? Was not this the desire of our Saviour, who knew the best means of sanctifying?

[5.] It is necessary, by God's appointment, for all the degrees of the new birth, and all the appendixes to it. When God shows his own glory for a further change, he represents the species of it in the glass of the gospel: 2 Cor. iii. 18, 'Beholding as in a glass the glory of the Lord, are changed into the same image, from glory to glory.' It is the ministration of the Spirit in all the acts of the spirit. If the Spirit quicken, it is by some gospel precept; if it comforts, it is by some gospel promise; if it startles, it is by some threatening in the word. Whatsoever working there is in a Christian's heart, it is by some word or other dropping upon it. If any temptation which assaults us be baffled, it is by the word, which is the sword of the Spirit. The life of a Christian is made up of increasing light, refreshing comforts, choicer inclinations of the heart towards God. By the same law whereby the soul is converted the heart is rejoiced, and the eyes further enlightened: Ps. xix. 7, 8, 'The law of the Lord is perfect, converting the soul, making wise the simple, rejoicing the heart, enlightening the eyes.' The Spirit makes the word not only the fire to kindle the soul, but the bellows to blow; it is first life, then liveliness to the soul. It is through the word he begets us, and through the word he quickens us: Thy word has quickened me,' Ps. cxix. 50, 93. It is by the word God gathers a church in the world; by the same word he sanctifies it to greater degrees, Eph. v. 26. It is the seed whereby we are born, the dew whereby we are refreshed. As it is the seed of our birth, so it is the milk of our growth, 1 Peter ii. 2. Faith comes by hearing, and salvation after faith by the 'foolishness of preaching,' 1 Cor. i. 21. It helps us after we have believed through grace, Acts xviii. 27. Our fruitfulness depends upon our plantation by this river's side. The influence of other ordinances depends upon it. Sacraments that nourish and increase, are not efficacious, but by virtue of the word; they have their dependence on the word, as seals upon the covenant. The word is operative without sacraments; sacraments are not operative without the influence of the word, they are only assistants to it. This quickens and increases habitual grace, as well as it was the instrument first to usher it into the heart: Eph. v. 26 'That he might sanctify and cleanse it with the washing of water by the word.' As God will have the mediation of his Son honoured in the whole progress and perfection of grace as the meritorious cause, the efficacy of the Spirit as the efficient cause, so he will have the word in every step to heaven honoured as the instrumental cause; that as Jesus Christ is all in all, as the chief, so the word may be all in all as the means. As God created the world by the word of his power, and by the word of his providence bid the creatures increase and multiply, so by the word of the gospel he lays the foundation, and rears the building, of his spiritual house.

4. As it is not a natural instrument, but the only instrument appointed by God, and therefore, upon these and upon other accounts, a necessary instrument, so it is an instrument which makes mightily for God's glory. The meaner the appearance of the instrument, the more evident the power and skill of the workman. It would be miraculous for a man to raise up another from death, by a composition of medicines syringed down the throat, but a greater miracle to raise him by speaking a word. In the new birth there is nothing sensible to man but the word, the other causes are secret; like the wind, you know not whence it comes, nor whither it goes. The instrument being weak in itself, none can claim any share with God in the glory of the work. But were there a natural strength in the means, much of the honour would be pared from God, and assumed by the creature. It is like the trumpet in the right hand of Gideon's soldiers, and a pitcher with a lamp in the left. Upon the blowing of the trumpet and the breaking of the pitcher, the enemies fled; and God would have the means but small, but three hundred of thirty-two thousand, that Israel might not vaunt, and say, Mine own arm has saved me, Judges vii. 2. It had not been so admirable for Samson to have killed so many with a sword or spear, or if the walls of Jericho had fallen flat by the force of some battering engine; but it was wonderful to see them tumble at the blast of ram's horns. Is it not the same to see strong-holds, high thoughts, Goliath-like corruptions, and spiritual death itself, fly before the voice of the word? To see a man like the Babel-builders, swelling and rearing up his vain confidences against God, to have all the former language of his soul confounded by a word; to think of other objects, speak in another strain, descend from self to dust, deny pleasure, embrace a crucified Christ; that carnal reason should be silenced, legions of devils driven out, a messy Dagon fall before an ark of wood, that has nothing in it but the rod of Aaron and the pot of manna: in such weak means is the power of God exalted, and no other cry can reasonably be heard but 'This is the Lord's doing, and it is marvellous in our eyes.' So it was more glorious for our Saviour to turn many of the Jews to him after his death than in his life, to bring them to believe by a Word, upon a person they had crucified as a malefactor, than if he had brought them to believe while he was attended

with a train of miracles. The power of his miracles might seem in their eyes to be extinct with his death, since he that delivered others did not deliver himself from the hands of his murderers. He now honours both his own words and their faith, in bringing them to believe by the preaching of men, who did not believe by the Word from his lips, attended with the seals of so many glorious miracles.

5. Consider, as it is an instrument, so but an instrument. God begets by the word; the chief operation depends upon the Spirit of God. No sword can cut without a hand to manage it, no engine batter without a force to drive it. The Word is objective in itself, operative by the power of the Spirit; instrumental in itself, efficacious by the Holy Ghost. The Word of Christ is first spirit and then life. 'The words that I speak unto you, they are spirit and they are life,' John vi. 63. The word is the chariot of the Spirit, the Spirit the guider of the word; there is a gospel comes in word, and there is a gospel comes in power, 1 Thes. i. 5. There is a publishing of the gospel, and there is the 'fullness of the blessing of the gospel,' Rom. xv. 29. 'There was the truth of God spoken by Peter and Paul, and God in that truth working in the heart: Gal. ii. 8, 'He that wrought effectually in Peter to the apostleship of the circumcision, the same was mighty in me towards the Gentiles.' The gospel in itself is like Christ's voice; the gospel with the Spirit is like Christ's power raising Lazarus; other men might have spoken the same words, but the power of rising must come from above. It is then successful when an inward unction drops with the outward dew, when the veil is taken from the heart, and the curtain from the word, and both meet together, both word and heart; when Christ kisses with the kisses of his mouth, and the man embraces it with the affections of his heart. The light in the air is the instrument by which we read, but the principle of that light is in the sun in the heavens. The word is a rod, a breath, but efficacious in smiting and slaying the old man, as it is the rod of Christ's mouth, the breath of his lips, Isa. xi. 3; a rod like that of Moses to charm us, but as it is the rod of his strength, Ps. cx. 2; a weapon, but only 'mighty through God,' 2 Cor. x. 4; a seed, but brings not forth a plant but by the influence of the sun. The word has this efficacy from the bleeding wounds and dying groans of Christ. It is by making his soul an offering for sin that he sees the travail of his soul in his new born creatures. By his blood are all the promises of grace confirmed; by his blood they are operative. The word whereby we are begotten was appointed by God, confirmed by Christ, and the Spirit which begets us was purchased by the same blood. To conclude: the word declares Christ, and the Spirit excites the heart to accept him; the word shows his excellency, and the Spirit stirs up strong cries after him; the word declares the promises, and the Spirit helps us to plead them; the word administers reasons against our reasonings, and the Spirit edges them, the word shows the way, and the Spirit enables to walk in it; the word is the seed of the Spirit, and the Spirit the quickener of the word; the word is the graft, and the Spirit the engrafter; the word is the pool of water, and the Spirit stirs it to make it healing.

II. Quest. How does the word work?

1. Objectively, as it is a declaration of God's will, as it does propose to the understanding what is to be known, in order to salvation hereafter and practice here, as it does declare the purpose of God to save only by Jesus Christ the Mediator, and by him to deliver us from sin, Satan, and whatsoever is contrary to everlasting happiness; and thus is significative of something to our minds and understandings. The Spirit gave us an eye to see, and the word is the light which discovers the object to the eye. The Spirit gives us an organ, but something must be proposed for that organ to exercise itself about, otherwise there is no use of the understanding in any rational operation; which certainly there is, for though the object is supernatural, and the inward work upon the mind supernatural, yet the proposal of the object to the mind is made in a rational manner. The word does objectively propose life and death in a way suitable to the nature of man, that he may rationally choose life: 'I have set before you life and death, blessing and cursing, therefore choose life,' Deut. xxx. 19. Both the blessings of the gospel and the curses of the law are presented in the word, that the one may be chosen, the other avoided. The word is proposed under various notions: as true, and so it is the object of the speculative understanding; as good, so it is the object of the practical understanding and will; as profitable, so it is the object of the appetite and affections. When it is received into the speculative understanding, it is a preparation to the new birth; when it is received into the practical understanding and will, it is the new birth. It discovers the wonders in God's own heart, his Son, and his promise; the Spirit demonstrates it, and gives power to embrace it. It first presents the promise and then answers the pleas the stubborn heart makes against it, yet by the same gospel, it fetches demonstrative arguments from that quiver to satisfy a cavilling understanding, and motives from thence to overcome a resisting will, it silences the fears, points to the way, excites the soul to an acceptance of Christ, all by this gospel, and so draws us, as a man draws a child, by presenting some alluring object to him. The Spirit immediately himself touches the soul, but by the word, as an instrument proposing the object, and drawing out the soul into an actual believing. The two chief parts of the word are,

(1.) The discovery of our misery by nature. The heart is ripped open, our putrefied condition in our blood evidenced, our deplorable state unfolded, and thereby the conscience awakened to sensible reflections. It dissects the heart, discovers the secret reserves, unravels the thoughts, pursues sin to its fastnesses, and pulls and brings it out, as Joshua the kings to execution: 1 Cor. xiv. 26, 'And thus are the secrets of his heart made manifest, and so falling down on his face he will worship God, and report that God is in you of a truth.' It opens sin to the very bowels, discovers the inward filth, takes off its beautiful disguise, its silken covering, and shows the running ulcer under it. It discovers the forlorn estate by nature, and the insufficiency of flesh and blood to inherit the kingdom of God. Let the word be whispered by the Spirit in the ears of a ruffling sinner, and the curtains which obscured his sin from his eye drawn open, that he may see what a nest of devils he has, what astonishment will it raise in him! How will he stand amazed at his own folly! How will he loathe that self which before he so vehemently loved!

(2.) A second discovery is of the necessity and existence of another bottom. It discovers our misery by nature, and our remedy by Christ, the plague brought upon the world by the first Adam, the cure brought to the world by the second. It proclaims a peace, concluded between God and the humbled sinner, by his Son, the great ambassador, confirmed by his blood, assured by his resurrection. It shows him the fountain of death in his sin, the fountain of life in Christ, the free streams and gracious communications of it. The promise discovers the gracious nature of God, his kindness to man, the openness of his arms to receive him, and thus bring the soul off from itself to the foot of God and the bottom of the cross. When the word like fire and the heart like tinder come close together, the heart catches the spark and burns. From the word reconciliation and peace step out and meet the soul, it finds the kisses of Christ's mouth inspiring it with life, the box of the gospel promises broke open, the window of the gospel ark opened, and the dove flying out of it into the desert heart. The word proposes things as they are in reality, and the soul knows things as it ought to know, 1 Cor. viii. 2. It understands the unavoidable necessity and the infallible excellency of the things proposed; it sees the rocks and shelves wherein the danger lies, and a compass whereby to steer, a road wherein to lie safe at anchor; whereupon he relents for his sin, is astonished at divine kindness, rejoices at the promise as before he trembled at the threatening, and has far other thoughts of God than he had before, in which act divine life is breathed into the soul.

2. The word seems to have an active force upon the will, though the manner of it be very hard to conceive. It is operative in the hand of God for sanctification. The petition of our Saviour, John xvii. 17, 'Sanctify them through thy truth, thy word is truth,' seems to intimate more than a bare objective relation to this work; it both shows us our spots and cleanses them. It is a seed. Seed, though small, is active, no part of the plant retains a greater efficacy; all the glory and strength of the plant, in its buds, blossoms, and fruit, are hidden in it. The word is this seed, which being settled in the heart by the power of the Spirit, brings forth this new creature. It is a glass that not only represents the image of God, but by the Spirit changes us into it, 2 Cor. iii. 18. A word that pierces the heart, Heb. iv. 12, ye, 'sharper than a two-edged sword, dividing asunder the soul and spirit.' It is a fire to burn. The Spirit does so edge the word that it cuts the quick, discerns the very thoughts, insinuates into the depths of the heart, and rakes up the small sands from the bottom, as a fierce wind does from the bowels of the sea. It is God's ordinance to batter down strongholds. Though it be not a natural instrument to work necessarily, yet it is likened to natural instruments, which are active under the efficiency of the agent which manages them; and this also, in the hands of the Spirit, works mighty effects. The 'sanctification of the Spirit and belief of the truth ' are joined together, one subordinate to another, 2 Thes. ii. 13. The Spirit efficiently infusing holy habits; the word objectively and actively--objectively, as outwardly proposed; actively, as inwardly engrafted;--it at least excites the new infused gracious principle, and produces our actual conversion and believing. As the pronouncing excommunication in the primitive times filled the person with terror; and no question but upon the same account the authoritative pronouncing the pardon of sin by the apostles, though only declarative, might have a mighty operation upon the soul in filling it with joy; yet both, as managed by the Spirit, concurring with his own ordinance. So that the word is mighty in operation as well as clear in representation; for an activity seems to be ascribed to it by the Scripture metaphors. The chief activity of it is seen in that likeness which it produces in the soul to itself. Seeds have an efficacious virtue to produce plants of the same kind with that whose seeds they are; so the word produces qualities in the heart like itself. The law in the heart is the law in the word transcribed in the soul; a graft which changes a crabbed stock into a sweet tree, James i. 21; like a seal it leaves a likeness and impression of itself; it works a likeness to God as he is revealed in the gospel, for we are changed into the same image. What image? The same image which we behold in that glass, 2 Cor. iii. 18; not his essential image, but the image of his glory represented in the gospel for our imitation. The word is the glory of God in a glass, and imprints the image of the glory of God in the heart. It is a softening word, and produces a mollified heart; an enlightening word, and causes an enlightened soul; a divine word, and engenders a divine nature; it is a spiritual word, and produces a spiritual frame; as it is God's will, it subdues our will; it is a sanctifying truth, and so makes a sink of sin to become the habitation of Christ. To conclude: this is certain: the promise in the word breeds principles in the heart suitable to itself; it shows God a father, and raises up principles of love and reverence; it shows Christ a mediator, and raises up principles of faith and desire. Christ in the word conceives Christ in the heart; Christ in the word, the beginning of grace, conceives Christ in the soul, the hope of glory.

III. The Use. 1. Information.

1. How admirable, then, is the power of the gospel! It is a quickening word, not a dead; a powerful word, not a weak; a sharp-edged word, not dull; a piercing word, not cutting only skin deep, Heb. iv. 12. That welcome work does it make, when a door of utterance and a door of entrance are both opened together! It has a mighty power to out-wrestle the principalities of hell, and demolish the strongholds of sin in the heart. It is a word of which it may be said, as the psalmist of the sun, Ps. xix. 6, 'His circuit is to the ends of the earth, and there is nothing hid from the heat thereof.' To part of the soul is hidden from a new birth by the warm beams of it, when directed by God to the soul. What a powerful breath is that which can make a dead man stand upon his feet and walk! If you should find your faces, by looking in a glass, transformed into an angelical beauty, would you not imagine some strange and secret virtue in that glass? How powerful is this gospel word, which changes a beast into a man, a devil into an angel, a clod of earth into a star of heaven!

(1.) It is above the power of all moral philosophy The wisdom of the heathens never equalled the gospel in such miracles; the political government of the best states never made such alterations in the hearts of men. How excellent is that gospel which has done that for the renewing of millions of souls, which all the wit and wisdom of the choicest philosophers could never effect upon one heart! All other lectures can do no more than allay the passions, not change them; bring them into an order fit for human society, not beget them for a divine fellowship; not draw them forth out of a principle of love to God, and fix them upon so high an end as the glory of God that is invisible. This is the glorious begetting by the gospel, which enables not only to moral actions, but inspires with divine principles and ends, and makes men highly delight in the ways they formerly abhorred. What are a few sprinklings of changes moral philosophy has wrought in the lives of men, to the innumerable ones the gospel has wrought, which were such undeniable realities, that they were never openly contradicted by any of the most violent persecutors of the Christian religion, and were always the most urged argument for the truth of the gospel in the ancient apologies for it? How long may we read and hear mere moral discourses, and arrive no higher than some reformation of life, with unchanged hearts: have sin beaten from the outworks, yet retain the great fort, the heart!

(2.) Above the power of the law. The natural law sees not Christ, the Mosaical law dimly shows him afar off; the gospel brings him near, to be embraced by us, and us to be divinely changed by him. The natural law makes the model and frame of a man, the Mosaical adds some colours and preparations, and the gospel conveys spirit into them. The natural law begets us for the world, the Mosaical kills us for God, and the gospel raises up to life. The natural law makes us serve God by reason, the Mosaical by fear, and the gospel by love. It is by this, and not by the law, those three graces which are the main evidences of life are settled in the soul. It begets faith, whereby we are taken off from the stock of Adam, and inserted in Christ; hope, whereby we flourish; and love, whereby we fructify. By faith, we have life; by hope, strength; by love, liveliness and activity. All these are the fruits of the gospel administration.

(3.) Its power appears in the subjects it has been instrumental to change. Souls bemired in the filthiest lusts, have been made miraculously clean; it has changed the hands of rapine into instruments of charity, hearts full of filth into vessels of purity; it has brought down proud reason to the obedience of faith, and made active lusts to die at the foot of the cross; it has struck off Satan's chains, and snatched away his captives into the liberty of God's service; it has changed the most stubborn hearts. The conversion of a great company of those Jewish priests that were most violent against it and the author of it, is ascribed to the power of the word: Acts vi. 7, 'And the word of God increased, and a great company of the priests were obedient to the faith.' How many were raised to life by Peter's sermon! More souls turned than words spoken upon record. It subdues the will, which cannot be conquered but by its own consent. Light can dart in upon the understanding whether a wan will or no, and flash in his face though he keep it in unrighteousness. Conscience will awaken and rouse them, though men use all the arts they can to still it. The will cannot be forced to any submission against its own consent; the power of the gospel is seen in the conquest of the will, and putting new inclinations into that.

(4.) The power of it is seen in the suddenness of its operation. In a moment, in the twinkling of an eye, like the change at the last resurrection: 1 Cor. xv. 51, 52, 'We shall all be changed, in a moment, at the last trumpet.' How have troops of unmastered lusts fled at the voice of the gospel trumpet, like a flock of frightened birds, and left their long-possessed mansion! How have the affections, which have sheltered so many enemies against God, been on the sudden weary of their residence, and abhorred what they loved, and loved what the moment before they abhorred! How have welcome temptations been upon this sudden change rejected, a despised Saviour dearly embraced, a furious soul tamed, a darling self crucified, and a soul open to every temptation strongly fortified against it! How frequent are the examples, in the first times of Christianity, of men that have been almost as bad as devils one day, one hour, and joyful martyrs the next; and as soon as ever they have been begotten by it, asserted the power of it in another new birth by flames!

(5.) And this has been done many times by one part, one particle of the word. One word of the gospel, a single sentence, has erected a heavenly trophy in a soul, which all the volumes of the choicest mere reason could never erect; one plain scripture has turned a face to heaven that never looked that way before, and made a man fix his eye there against his carnal interest. One plain scripture has killed a man's sins, and quickened his heart with eternal life; one word of Christ, remembered by Peter, made him weep bitterly, and two or three scriptures, pressed by the same Peter upon his hearers, pricked their hearts to the quick. How has hell flashed in the face of a sinner, out of a small cloud of a threatening, and heaven shot into the soul from one little diamond spark of a promise! A little seed of the word, like a grain of mustard seed, changed the soul from a dwarfish to a tall stature! This the experience of every eye can testify.

(6.) And this power appears in the simplicity of it. Savonarola observes, that when he neglected the preaching of the Scripture, and applied himself to discourses of philosophy, he gained little upon the hearts of people; but when he came to illustrate and explain the Scripture, the minds of people were wonderfully inflamed and excited to a serious flame; and that when he discoursed in a philosophical manner, there was a non-attention, not only of the more ignorant, but the more learned sort too; but when he preached Scripture truths, he found the minds of men mightily delighted, sting with divine truth, brought to compunction, and a reformation of their lives, which shows, says he, the power of the word, acting more vigorously than all human reason in the world. And indeed Scripture, and Scripture reason, is the wisdom of God; all other reason is the wisdom of man. God will depress man's wisdom and advance his own. It works as it is 'the word of God which lives and abides for ever', 1 Peter i. 23. To wrap a fine piece of silk about a sword, or gild a diamond, is to hinder the edge of the one, and the lustre of the other.

2. Information. The gospel is then certainly of divine authority, since in this 'God has set a tabernacle for the Sun of righteousness to move in, as the heavens are the tabernacle for the material sun, Ps. xix. 4. That word that raises the dead, must needs be the word of no less than God. Our Saviour's discovery of men's thoughts argued his deity. The word's discovery of the inward workings of the heart, and the alteration it makes there, evidences a divine stamp upon it. God would never have made a lie so successful in the world, or blessed it in making those alterations in men, so comely in the eye of moral nature, so advantageous to human society, as the principles it instils into the minds of men are. A lie would never have been blessed to be an instrument of so much virtue and truth; it would not consist with the righteousness of God's government, or his goodness and truth as governor, to bring the hearts of men into so beautiful an order by a deceitful gospel. What word ever had such trophies! What engine ever battered so many strongholds! If the lame walk by the strength of it, if the dead are raised by the power of it, if lepers are cleansed by the virtue of it, if impure souls are sanctified, dead souls enlivened, are we to question its divine authority? Should a word work such wonderful effects for so many ages, that had no stamp of divine authority upon it? Would all those witnesses be given by God to a mere imposture? Let the victories it has gained evidence the arm that wields it. What sword was used at the first conquest of the world through grace, but this of the Spirit? How soon was the devil, with all his heap of idols, fain to fly before it! How soon was the devil, with all his pack of lusts, forced to leave his habitation in the hearts of men! Is not that of divine authority that so routs the enemies of God, puts sin to flight, expels spiritual death, breaking the bands of that worst king of terrors; that had skill to find out sin in its lurking holes, and power to dispossess that, and introduce spiritual life into the soul? Can that be a thing less than divine, that restores man to his due place as a creature respecting his Creator, referring all things to his glory; that implants the love, fear, hope of God in the mind; that makes man, of a miserable corrupt creature, to become divine; that roots out the vices of hell, and stores the soul with the virtues of heaven? Can such a gospel be termed less than a divine word of truth? If there be any word that can so change the nature, and transform wolves into lambs, let it have the honour and due praise when it is found out; but whatsoever the atheism of the world is, that never felt the powerful efficacy of it, you surely that have felt it a mighty weapon to conquer the devils that once possessed you, and an instrument to new beget you when you lay in your blood, should entertain no whisper against the divine authority of it, but count it the power and wisdom of God as, indeed, it is in itself, and in its effects upon souls, Rom. i. 16. It is said there to be 'the power of God to salvation.' Upon that account the apostle was not ashamed of it; neither should we, but conclude as the same apostle says, 'If I be not an apostle, yet to you I am an apostle.' So if the gospel be not in itself the gospel of God, surely it is so to you who have been renewed.

3. Information. It shows us the reason why the gospel is so much opposed by Satan in the world. It begets those for heaven whom he had begotten for hell. It pulls down his image and sets up God's; it pulls the crown off his head, the sceptre from his hand, snatches subjects from his empire, straitens his territories, and demolishes his forts, breaks his engines, outwits his subtilty, makes his captives his conquerors, and himself, the conqueror, a captive; it pulls men 'out of the kingdom of darkness, and translates them into a kingdom of light,' Col. i. 13. And all this, as it is a word of truth, opposed to his word of deceit, whereby he has cheated mankind and deceived the nations; that we may well say of him, as the apostle of death, 'O death, where is thy sting?' 1 Cor. xv. 55. O hell, where is thy sting? O Satan,

where is thy victory? This slays Satan and revives the soul.

4. We see then how injurious they are to God, who would obstruct the progress of the gospel in the world; that, as the papists, would hinder the reading and the preaching of the word. Whose seed are they, but the seed of that dragon, that would as well hinder the new birth as devour a divine-begotten babe 'as soon as ever it were born,' Rev. xii. 4. Such would hinder the greatest and most excellent work of God upon the souls of men, would have no spiritual generations for God in the world. Such envy Christ a seed, and God a family, they would despoil him of a family on earth, though they cannot of a family in heaven. In banishing the word, they would banish the grace of God out of the world, and leave no place in a world drowned with ignorance, where this dove should set her foot. Those that would take away the seed, would not have a spiritual harvest, but reduce souls to a deplorable famine, lock them up in the grave, and keep them under the bands of a spiritual death.

5. It informs us, that the gospel shall then endure in the world, as long as God has any to beget. Men may puff at it, but they cannot extinguish it, it is a word of truth, and truth is mighty, and will prevail. It was a mighty wind wherein the Spirit came upon the apostles, to show not only the quick and speedy progress of the gospel, as upon the wings of the wind, but the mighty force of it, that men can no more silence the sound of the gospel than they can the blustering of the wind. It shall prevail in all places, where God has a seed to bring in, a people to beget. Those given to Christ shall come from far: 'from the east,' Isa. xlix. 12, 'and from the west, and from the land of Sinim' (now, I think, called Damiata, in Egypt). The word, being the instrument, shall sound everywhere, where he has sons and daughters to beget for Christ. As long as Christ does retain his royalty, 'his mouth shall be a sharp sword,' Isa. xlix. 2. That is the first thing concluded on between God and Christ, before they come to any further treaty, which is expressed in that chapter. As Christ shall be his salvation to the ends of the earth, so shall the word be the instrument of it to the end of the world: the 'polished shaft' is 'hid in his quiver.' As he is a light to the Gentiles, so the golden candlestick of this gospel wherein this light is set, shall endure in spite of men and devils. Since his promise of a seed to Christ stands sure, the word, whereby he begets a generation for him, is as sure as the promise, and shall not return void: Isa. lv. 11, 'but it shall accomplish that which he pleases, and it shall prosper in the things whereto he sent it.' Never fear then the removal of the gospel out of the world, though it be removed out of a particular place, since it is a word of truth, and an instrument ordained to so glorious an end.

6. It is a sign, then, God has some to beget, when he brings his gospel to any place. He has a pleasure to accomplish, and it shall not return unto him void. Prosperity is entailed upon it for the doing the work whereto he sent it. Since then it is appointed an instrument, in the hand of the Spirit, for a new begetting, it will be efficacious upon some souls where it comes, for the wise God would not send it, but to attain its main end upon some hearts. God never sends his word to any place, but it is received and relished by some as the savour of life. It looses the bands of spiritual death in some, and binds them harder upon obstinate sinners, to them that perish it is the savour of death. In every place the gospel was savoury to some: 2 Cor. ii. 14, 15, 'God made manifest the savour of his knowledge,' by the apostles, 'in every place.' Wherever this seed is sown, the harvest has been reaped, either more or less. It is fruitful at Corinth, for there God had much people, Acts xviii. 10. It is not fruitless at Athens, though the harvest was less; most mocked, but some believed, and but one man of learning and worldly wisdom, Acts xvii. 32, 34. When God sends John in a way of righteousness, if the Pharisees believe not, God will make a conquest of publicans and harlots: Mat. xxi. 32, 'John came to you in the way of righteousness, and you believed not: but the publicans and harlots believed him.' The net of the gospel is not cast wholly in vain, but from the time of its coming, to the time of its removal, some souls have been caught, though not of the most delicious fish, yet of the worst sort.

7. It informs us, what an excellent thing is a new birth! The end is more desirable than the means, this is the chief end of all the ordinances of God in the world. The gospel had never been revealed but for this intent, this is the 'design of the Spirit's operation in any gospel administration. All the lines of the word are to draw the lineaments of grace in the heart. This must be a noble and excellent thing, for which chiefly the oracles of God sound in the world, for which so great a light is set up in the gospel. All the love of Christ breathes in the gospel; the whole Testament is sealed by his blood; the perpetual workings of the Holy Ghost, the preaching of the word, the celebration of the sacraments, are in subservience to this end, the one to make us live, the other to make us grow. How inconceivably excellent is that, how valuable in the eye of God, how advantageous to the happiness of men, that is, the design wherein so many divine operations meet!

8. What a lamentable thing is it, that so few should be new begotten by the word of truth! How many are there among us that understand not what a new begetting and birth is, no more than Nicodemus when he discoursed with our Saviour! What a deplorable thing is it that the word should be preached, and so little regarded! that not only an hour's, but many years' discourses should pass away (as the Psalmist speaks of our lives) 'like a tale that is told!' Ps. xc. 9. How miserable is that man that has the objective cause of the new birth, without the effective! It is the word of truth. What will become of you, if you prefer a word of error before it; if you prefer the devil's killing suggestions before God's

reviving, oracles? What does the word of truth move you to, but to a new birth? Why will any man struggle against it? Every resistance of the word is a resistance of God himself. It is God hews by the prophets, Hos. vi. 5; it is God offers to beget by the word; every reluctance then against the word is a reluctance against God. The word will either bring in a new form of grace, or a new form of torment. If the working of the one be rejected, the in-working of the other cannot be avoided; it will either cut the bands of a spiritual death, or cut the sinews of our souls. That piece of timber that has not its knots cut off for the building, shall be cut in pieces for the fire. A new life waits for them that obey the gospel; an endless death for them that reject it; they that obey not the gospel, know not God, 2 Thess. i 8. And what is reserved for such, but revenging flames in another world? It would be happy for such, that they had never heard of a renewing gospel. Every gospel discourse that might have been the cause of a spiritual life, and a divine cordial, if sucked in, rejected, will be a bitter drug in that potion which shall be drunk in an eternal fever.

9. Hereby you may examine whether you are new begotten. It is the word of truth whereby God befits. In this word he opens the glory of his grace, and through this he conveys the power of his grace. The conquests of Christ were to be made by the word, and it was so settled at the first constitution of him as Mediator and Redeemer: Isa. xlix. 2, 'He has made my mouth like a sharp sword.' It was by this the hearts of men were to be conquered. And what heart is not subdued by the sword of his mouth, is not subdued by the power of his arms. Some word or other was the instrument to beget you (I speak of people grown up). The apostle's interrogation is a strong negative. There is no believing without hearing, Rom. x. 14. Hearing goes before believing; he lays it down as a certain conclusion from his former arguing: 'So then faith comes by hearing, and hearing by the word of God.' If you conclude yourselves new begotten, how came you by it? Is it by the word, or no? That is God's ordinary means. If you be not renewed by this, it is not likely you are renewed at all; no other instrument has God ordinarily appointed to this end. Afflictions may plough men for it, but the word is the only seed that renews the face of the earth. All false notions or presumptions of the new birth must be brought to this touchstone; it is a misshapen and monstrous birth, that is not by a seed of the same kind; the law in the heart has no seed of the same nature with it to engender it, but the law in the word, that word which we properly call gospel; the word of truth, not the word of philosophy, which is a word of uncertainty; God's word, not Plato's word. If a thousand beasts had been consumed by common fire, not one of them had been an holocaust, a grateful sacrifice, unless consumed by the fire of the altar which came down from heaven. Moral wisdom is not that fire, has not that eminent descent from heaven; it is not that speech from heaven whereby our Saviour is said yet to speak, Heb. sit. 26. A little spark kindled by the voice of Christ from heaven, from whence he yet speaks in the gospel, is more worth than all the bonfires in the world, kindled by the sparks of moral wisdom. Those qualifications which grow of their own accord, without the word, are like the herbs which sprout in wild places without any tillage, which are of a different kind than what are planted and watered in a garden, and overlooked by the care of man. If your dispositions you boast of were not planted by the word, how fair soever they may look, they are but a wild kind of fruit; therefore, it concerns you to look back upon yourselves, think what word it was whereby you were begotten. If no particular word can be remembered, if your regeneration were wrought insensibly in your younger years, examine what suitableness there is between the word and your souls, whether your hearts are turned into the nature of it. The measures of grace are according to the measures of the word. If you cannot remember the first glorious entrance of it, you must see for the rich dwelling of it. An inhabitant may enter into our houses unseen, but he cannot dwell there without our knowledge; the lines of the word will be seen in the heart, though the particular pencil whereby they were wrought may not be remembered.

10. It instructs ministers how to preach. It is the word of truth, the gospel, that must be the main matter of our preaching; and those things in the gospel that have the greatest tendency to the new begetting men, and working this great change in them, and driving it on to greater maturity. The instrument of conversion is not barely the letter of the word, but the sense and meaning of it, rationally impressed upon the understanding, and closely applied to the conscience. The opening the word is the life of it, and the true means of regeneration. If any man would turn his servant or child from a course of sin, would he discourse to them of the nature of the of the sun and stars, their magnitude, motions, numbers, and qualities? This would be nothing to the purpose; his way would be to show them the deformity and danger of their sin. The word of truth is God's instrument, and it should be ours; what is the end of the word, should be the end of our preaching. It was through the gospel the apostle begot the Corinthians; not that the preaching of the law is excluded, but it must be preached in order to the gospel as a preparation to it. Whatsoever in the word of truth does prepare for the new birth, produce it, cherish it, preserve it, centre in one and the same end. How careful and industrious should we be to beget children to God, that we may present them, and say, 'Here am I, and the children, which thou hast given me.' The new birth will be your joy, and crown and you will be ours, 1 Thess. ii. 19,20. Aaron's sons are called the generations of Moses, as well as Aaron, Num. iii. 1, though none of his natural sons are reckoned; Aaron's by natural generation, Moses' perhaps by a spiritual regeneration and instruction.

Use 2. Of exhortation.

1. Highly glorify God for the word of truth, which is so great an instrument. How thankful should we be for an intention, to secure our estates from consuming, houses from burning. bodies from dying! The gospel, the word of truth, does much more than this: it is an instrument to beget a soul for God; an instrument whereby God makes himself our Father, and us his children. It is but an instrument; let not the glory be given to the instrument, but to the agent. As it is an instrument, let it have part of your affections, but nothing of the glory that belongs to God; love the truth, but glorify and bless the God of truth, that has ordained it to be so excellent an instrument.

(1.) Bless God in your hearts. [1.] That ever you had the word of truth made known to you. How many millions sit in a spiritual darkness, without so much as the means of a new begetting! Millions never heard the sound of it, nor ever will. [2.] Much more that it has been successful to any of you. Have you any thing in your spirits that bears witness to the truth of it? When you read or hear it, do you find something of kin to it in your souls, and feel something within you rise up and call it blessed? How should you read and hear it, with eruptions of thankfulness to God for it, hearty embraces for it, and fervent ejaculations to God to work more in you by the power of it! Why has the word grappled with any of our souls, and not with others; arrested any of you in a course of sin, and left others to walk in their own ways, to ran down silently like the streams of a river, till swallowed up in an ocean of death? The apostle Paul heard the voice, others with him only a sound of words, Acts ix. 9, 7, xxii. 9; some have heard a sound of words, without the voice of God in it, while others have heard a divine voice in a human sound. The wind has blown upon many, God in that wind only upon few; some have received air, whilst others have received Spirit and life; some have only the body of the word, while others feel the spirit and power of it in their hearts. Shall not God be glorified for this? Had it not been for him, and his Spirit, words had been only words and wind to all as well as to some.

(2.) Glorify God in your lives. As you feel the power of it in your hearts, let others see the brightness and efficacy of it in your actions. The new born creature should principally aim at the glory of God, since the instrument whereby he is begotten was first published for the 'glory of God in the highest,' Luke ii. 14. What is produced by the efficacy of such an instrument must have the same end, viz. the glory of God in the practice of holiness. A holy gospel imprinted can never leave the heart and life unholy. A gospel coined for the glory of God, when wrought in the heart, can never suffer the soul to aim chiefly at self; but at the great end for which the gospel was first discovered. The gospel of holiness and truth in the heart will engender sincerity and holiness in the life.

2. Prize the word of truth, which works such great effects in the soul. Value that as long as you live, which is the cord whereby God has drawn any of you out of the dungeon of death. Never count that foolishness by which God has inspired you with the choicest wisdom, and never count that weakness which has made any of you of death, living; and of darkness, light; and of miserable, happy by grace. If a soul be worth a world, and therefore to he prized, how precious ought that to be which is an instrument to let a soul for the felicity of another world! How should the law of God's mouth be better to us than thousands of gold and silver! Ps. cxix. 72. How should we prize that word whereby any of us have seen the glory of God in his sanctuary, the glory of God in our souls! When corruptions are strong, it is an engine to batter them; when our hearts are hard, it is a hammer to break them; when our spirits are impostumated, it is a sword to cut them; when our hearts are cold, it is a fire to inflame them; when our souls are faint, it is a cordial to refresh them, it begins a new birth and maintains it. It is the seed from whence we spring, 1 Peter i. 23, the glass wherein we see the glory of God, 2 Cor. iii. 18. By the waters of the sanctuary, we have both meat for nourishment, and medicines for cure, from the tree that grows by its streams: Ezek. xlvii. 12, 'The fruit thereof shall be for meat, and the leaf for medicine.' Have a great regard to it, keep it in the midst of your hearts, for it is life, Prov. iv. 21, 22.

3. Pray and endeavour for the preservation and success of the word of truth. Were there a medicine that could preserve life, how chary should we be in preserving that? The gospel is the tree, whose leaves cure the nations, Rev. xxii. 2. It was a blessing God endued the creatures with, when he bid them increase and multiply, Gen. i. 22. It was an evidence that he intended to preserve the world. If the gospel get ground in the hearts of men, it is an evidence it shall continue in spite of the oppositions of men or devils.

4. Wait upon God in the word. Where there is a revelation on God's part, there must be a hearing on ours. Sit down therefore at the feet of God, and receive of his words, Dent. xxxiii. 3. (1.) Despise it not; he that contemns it never intends to be new begotten, since he slights the means of God's appointment; he that intends an end, will use all means proportionately to his desires for that end; he that contemns it never was renewed. Habitual grace being wrought by it, cannot, but in its own nature, have a great affection to it. He that loves Christ cannot but love all the methods of his operations. (2.) Despise it not because it is but an instrument: say not, because God is the chief agent, therefore you need not come to the word. Our Saviour knew that 'man did not live by bread alone, but by every word that proceeds out of the mouth of God,' Mat. iv. 4. Did he therefore neglect means for preserving his life? Because God gives the increase, should not the husbandman plough and sow? If God does not

work upon you by the means, you can have no rational hopes he will do it any other way. What though ministers can only speak to the ear? John Baptist could do no more, whose ministry was notwithstanding glorious, in being the forerunner of Christ. To neglect it, therefore, is to double-bar your hearts against the entrance of grace, and slight the truth which Christ brought down from the bosom of God.

(1.) Never did God appoint any other way but this. Miracles were never appointed but as attendants upon this. Miracles come after teachings in the great gifts to the church, 1 Cor. xii. 7-10. First, the 'manifestation of the Spirit," the word of wisdom and the word of knowledge,' then 'gifts of healing and miracles.' Miracles are ceased, as being not absolutely necessary; but the ministry of the word will last to the end of the world. By the prophets God brings souls out of a state of bondage, and by the prophets he preserves them in a state of grace: Hosea xii. 13, 'By a prophet the Lord brought Israel out of Egypt, and by a prophet was he preserved.' Miracles and the resurrection of one from the dead, was never appointed under the legal administration, but Moses and the prophets, Luke xvi. 13. These were the ordinary means, and if these did not work, miracles were inefficacious.

(2.) God never made any promise but in this way. God promised to circumcise their hearts to love him with all their soul, but in the way of hearing his voice, and observing his statutes, Deut. xxx 6, 10, 11. He meets souls only that remember him in his way, Isa. lxiv. 5. And to the preaching of the gospel only, our Saviour promised his presence to the end of the world, Mat. xxviii. 20; the promise is perpetually and immovably throughout all ages of the world fixed to this command. The promising his presence to the preaching of the gospel, implies that his presence shall be enjoyed only by attendance on the gospel. The gracious workings of the Spirit are by this, they are the words of Christ brought to remembrance by him, whereby he does so mightily operate.

(3.) No other way did God apparently work by formerly. In the time when God did especially manifest himself to his people by visions, dreams, and apparitions of angels, and in those days made revelations to them, he converted not any either from a state of nature, or from a particular fall, but by the word. Manasseh's conversion was by the word of the seers, 2 Chron. xxxiii. 18; nor was David reclaimed after his fall by an immediate vision, but by the ministry of Nathan; Peter by a look, which revived the word spoken to him, Luke xxii. 61. The angel that attended the eunuch, Acts viii. 26, made no impressions upon him, but was ordered to direct Philip thither to explain to him the mystery of the gospel; and the Spirit particularly orders him to go near the chariot, ver. 29, but makes no impression upon him but by the ministry of the word. An angel is sent to direct Philip, but Philip is sent to discover Christ. An angel is sent to Cornelius, not to preach the gospel, but to direct him where to send for a teacher, Acts x..3, 5, 6, the Spirit prepares Peter to go, verse 19, 20, and likewise prepares Cornelius for his reception; God prepares the jailer by an earthquake, but renews him not but by the ministry of Paul, Acts xvi. 26, 32. In the times of the gospel there was first to be a teaching of God's law, before a walking in his paths, Isa. iii. 3. The arm that made heaven and earth makes the new heart and new spirit, but by a word as well as them. The net of the gospel is only appointed to catch the fish, though the fish that had the tribute-money in its mouth was immediately for the service of Christ, yet he would not use his power to bring it to the shore, without Peter's casting out the net. Christ first brings souls to the net, and by the net to himself.

(4.) God has always blessed this more or less. Moses' rod in Moses his hand has brought miracles, Christ's rod in the Spirit's hand has wrought greater; the new creations have been always by it, and the after-breathings of the Spirit through it. By this he makes men righteous, holy, sincere, in a way of eminency, as the morning light which increases to a perfect day, and no longer as a morning cloud which quickly vanishes, Hosea vi. 5, which some understand of a gospel promise mixed with that discourse. How has the light of the beauty and excellency of God, flashing upon the understanding from the glass of the gospel, filled the will and affections of many with desire and love to that glory it represents, and that state it offers! The very leaves of it, the profession has healed nations, and brought human societies into order, and the fruit of it has been the cure of many a soul. Wait therefore for the falling of this fruit. Grace is a beam from the Sun of righteousness, but darted through the medium of gospel air; a pearl engendered by the blood of Christ, but only in the gospel sea. It has not been without its blessing to others, it has raised men from death to life. Is the virtue of the seed expired? or the strength of the Lord grown feeble? If ever therefore you could have the image of God in inward impressions of grace, and outward expressions of holiness, you must look for your transformation in and by the gospel. All the other knowledge in the world cannot give a man a right notion of the new birth, much less produce it. Look not after enthusiasms, nor expect it in new ways, 'to the law and to the testimony,' ways of God's appointment. The Jews could not expect an angel to bring them soundness of limbs, but by the pool; nor we the Spirit to infuse grace into us, but by the word. It is from the mercy-seat only God speaks to Israel; wisdom's gates are the places where to expect her alms, Prov. viii. 34. Wait therefore upon the word, Herein the Spirit of God travails with souls.

Quest. How shall we wait upon the Lord, so as that we may be new begotten by it?

1. Wait upon the word frequently. Be often in reading and hearing, and meditating on it. Men set

upon these works as if they were afraid they should be new born too soon, or prejudiced in their concerns and contentments in the world, as if they feared the mighty wind of the Spirit should blow away their beloved dross too fast, as if it were a matter of indifference to be like their Maker. If you had gold not thoroughly refined, would you not cast it again and again into the fire? If filth not wholly purged, would you not use the fountain again and again? Those that are in the sun are coloured and heated by it, and have things more visible; those that are much in the word, see more of the wonders, feel more of the warmth, receive deeper impressions, are endued with the grace and holiness of truth, have a purer flame in their affections for heaven. How do you know but an opportunity missed, might have been the best market? How do you know but the Spirit might have joined himself to the word, as Philip to the eunuch's chariot, while he was reading? 'While Peter yet spake those words (it is said), the Holy Ghost fell upon all them which heard the word,' Acts x. 44. What words? Even the marrow of the gospel, ver. 43, 'that through his name, whosoever believes in him shall receive remission of sins.' God may have a portion ready for us, and we go without it, because we are not ready to receive it. We must not expect a raven to bring us food upon a bed of sluggishness. Do it the rather, because you may live to see such times, wherein Bibles may be as much shut as they are now open, wherein (as in former times) you may be willing to give a large parcel of your goods for one chapter of it. We read of some that have given a load of hay for one chapter of St James. Be frequent in waiting upon the word.

2. Let your hearts be fixed upon that which is the great end of the word. New begettings are the end of the gospel. Come, then, with minds fixed upon this end, and desires for it. Regard it not as a mere sound of words, but as an instrument of the noblest operations in the soul. If this be the great work of the gospel, we ought to read and hear it, with desires to be enlivened where we are dead, quickened where we are dull, to be made new creatures where we are yet but old, taller creatures where we are yet but of a low stature; not only to have our understandings instructed, but our hearts changed; to inquire after God to behold the beauty of the Lord, Ps. xxvii. 4, that we may be transformed into it; to look for God, who is in the word of a truth, for the kingdom of God comes nigh to you in the gospel. That was that word that Christ, when he sent his disciples out first to preach, bid them speak unto men, Luke xii. Men usually get more than they come to seek. He that goes to market, intending only to lay out his money upon some trifle, returns for the most part with no better commodity. Zacchaeus got upon the tree to meet with Christ, and so noble an end wanted not an excellent success: that day came salvation into his house, Luke xix. 9. When the Jews did not mind the end of sacrifices, and regarded not the things God principally looked for in then, God slighted them, and they went without any divine operations upon their souls by them, Isa. i. 11, 18, 14. When our ends suit the gospel, then are we like to feel gospel influences. We come with wrong ends, and, therefore, return with unchanged hearts; we come for a sound, and go away with no more. One end therefore in coming should be to gain this new begetting, or increase the growth of the new creature; our ends are not else conformable to the ends of God in it; therefore, as the earth sucks in the rain, and the roots in the earth attract it unto themselves that they may bring forth fruit, so should we open our hearts to receive the showers of the word with an aim at a new birth, or a further growth. As this is finis operis, so it should be finis operantis.

3. Mind the word in the simplicity of it, and that in it which tends to that end. Some men are more taken with colours than truth, more enamoured with words than matter, fill themselves only with air, and neglect the substance. Such are like those that are pleased with the colours of the rainbow, more than with the light reflected, or the covenant of God represented by it. No man is renewed by phrases and fancies; those are only as the oil to make the nails of the sanctuary drive in the easier: in Eccles. xii. 11, 'Acceptable words,' joined with 'words of truth,' are as the ' fastening of the nails,' both 'given by one shepherd.' Words there must be to make things intelligible; illustrations to make things delightfully intelligible, but the seminal virtue lies not in the husk and skin, but in the kernel; the rest dies, but the substance of the seed lives, and brings forth fruit; separate, therefore, between the husk and the seed. The word does not work as it is elegant, but as it is divine, as it is a word of truth. Illustrations are but the ornaments of the temple, the glory of it is in the ark and mercy-seat. It is not the engraving upon the sword cuts, but the edge; nor the key, as it is gilded, opens, but as fitted to the wards. Your faith must not stand in the wisdom of men, but in the power of God, 1 Cor. ii. 5. It is the juice of the meat, and not the garnishings of the dish, that nourishes. Was it the word as a pleasant song, or as a divine seed, that changed the souls of old, made martyrs smile in the midst of flames? It was the knowledge of the excellency of the promise, and not worldly eloquence, made them with so much courage slight gibbets, stakes, executioners; they had learned the truth as it is in Jesus.

4. Mind the word as the word of truth. Take it not upon the account of persons, value it for its own sake, as it is a word of truth. It is neither Paul nor Apollos, but God that gives the increase. Value it not by men; it is no matter what the pipe is, whether gold or lead, so the water be the water of life; the word has an edge, because it is the word of God, not because it is whetted upon this or that grindstone. Some will scarce receive a truth, but from one they fancy; as if a man should be so foolish as to refuse a medicine which will preserve his life, because it is not presented to him in a glass which he has a particular esteem of. To receive or refuse any truth upon the account of the person, is a sign of carnality,

and the way to remain carnal; upon this account the apostle pronounces the Corinthians again and again carnal, 1 Cor. iii. 4. Despise not the meanest instrument. Our Saviour in his agony was comforted by an angel, much more inferior to him who was the Lord of angels, than any minister can be to a hearer. Mr Peacock, being fellow of a college, in great despair, when some minister had been discoursing with him, and prevailing nothing, offering to pray with him, No, says he; dishonour not God so much, as to pray for such a reprobate. A young scholar of his standing by, answered, Surely a reprobate could not be so tender of God's honour; which cords prevailed more to the bringing him to believe than all that the other had spoken. When men turn their backs upon the word, because the mouth does not please them, they turn their backs upon God, John xiii. 20, and perhaps upon their own mercy. When any have respect to the man more than the word, God will leave them to the operation of the man, and withdraw his own.

5. Attend upon the word with an eye to God. Look not for the new birth only from the word. It was the folly of the Jews to think to find life in the Scriptures without Christ; life in the letter, without the original of life, John v. 39, 40. 'Except the Lord build the house' (that is the temple), 'they labour in vain that build it,' Ps. cxxvii. 1. Without God all our endeavours to build a spiritual temple are like the strivings to wash a blackamore white. No believing the word, though preached a thousand times, without God's revealing his arm, Isa. liii. 1. It is not the file that makes the watch, but the artist by it. No instrument can act without the virtue of some superior agent. It is the altar that sanctifies the gold, and Christ that sanctifies the ordinances. Paul may plant by his doctrine and miracles; Apollos may water by his affectionate eloquence; but God alone can give the increase by his almighty breath. Man sows the seed, but God only can make it fructify. The richest showers cannot make the ground fruitful, but as instruments under God's blessing. It is not said the prophets did hew them, but God by his prophets, Hosea vi. 5. Then have your eyes fixed upon God. It is the word of his lips, not of man's, whereby any are snatched out of the paths of the destroyer, as well as kept from them. Man's teachings direct us to Christ; God's teachings bring us to Christ; man brings the gospel, at most, to the heart, the Spirit only brings the gospel into the heart, man puts the key in the lock, God only turns it, and opens the heart by it, man brings the word of truth, and God the truth of the word into the soul, man brings the objective word of grace, God alone the attractive grace of the word. If where there is already the new birth, the soul must be fixed on God for further openings, much more where it is not yet wrought. David had an excellent knowledge, yet cries out for the opening of his eyes to see the wonders in God's law. It is God only can knock off the fetters of a spiritual death, and open the iron gates, that the King of glory may enter with spiritual life. If any, therefore, will regard the word more than as an instrument, as a partner with God in his operation, he may justly leave you to the weakness of that, and deny the influx of his own strength.

Therefore let the word be attended with prayer.

(1.) Before you wait upon God in any ordinance, plead with him as Moses did in another case, 'To what purpose should I go, unless thy presence go with me?' What can the letter do without the Spirit, or words without that powerful wind to blow them into my heart? None can have life by the bread of the word, without the blessing of God. As man brings the graft, desire God to insert it. As God has promised gifts to his church, so he promised his own teachings: Heb. viii. 11, 'All shall know me, from the least to the greatest.' Urge God with his own promise, desire him to open his mouth, and to open your hearts; his mouth to breathe, and your hearts to receive. When men overlook God, he makes a separation between the word and his own quickening presence. The end does not necessarily arise from the means; and, therefore, in the use of them, there must be a fiducial recourse to the grace of God. In the time, too, of waiting upon God, let there be ejaculations; let your hearts be continually lifted up to God; let your expectations be from him. We should be like Jacob's ladder; though the feet stand in Bethel, the house of God, our heads should reach to heaven in all our attendances.

(2.) After you have been at the word. God is the great seer, Christ the great prophet; we should go to him for the repetition of things upon our hearts; we may have that wind afterwards by prayer, which we felt not so stiff at hearing. The operations of truth, as well as the knowledge of it, are best fetched out upon our knees by earnest prayer. How do you know but, while you are praying, the fire may descend from heaven, and transform you into a divine likeness? Thus you will make God the Alpha and Omega of his own ordinances, in your acknowledgement of him, as well as he is so in himself.

(3.) Rest not in bare hearing. Look for God in the ordinances as he is the living God, who lives in himself and gives life to men and means: Ps. xxxiv. 2, 'My soul longs for the living God,' there is a strength and glory of God to be longed for in the sanctuary; no means are to be rested in or used, but as to lead to such an end for which they are fitted. To rest in the word heard, or read, is to make that our end, which God has appointed only as the means. The word is sweet, but as it is the pipe through which God and his image, God and his grace, which is sweeter and higher than all ordinances, stream to the soul. Rejoice in the word, but only as the wise men did in the star, as it led them to Christ. The word of Christ is precious; but nothing more precious than himself, and his formation in the soul. Rest not in the word, but look through it to Christ.

6. Attend upon the word submissively. It is not the hearer, but the humble hearer, shall find the

power of the word working in him; as it is not the speaking a prayer, but the wrestling and struggling of the heart with God in prayer, receives a gracious answer. The humble are the fittest subjects for grace, those that lie upon the ground with their mouth close to the pipe. 'He gives grace to the humble.' Resign yourselves up to the word, struggle not against the battery it makes, nor the wind that blows; receive every stroke till you see the frame of the new creature. Let a silence be imposed upon the flesh, and self bowed down to the dust, while Christ the great prophet speaks. Be not peevish, not expostulate with God's sovereignty, as they did: Isa. lviii. 3, 'Wherefore have we fasted, and thou seest not? Wherefore have we afflicted our soul, and thou takes no knowledge?' Acknowledge God a free agent, submit to his sovereign pleasure. A truly humble bow to God will prevail more than all the saucy expostulations of proud flesh. In hearing the word, pick not here a part, and there a part, as suits your humour, but consider what really is God's will, and submit to it. Cornelius was of this resigning temper when the Spirit descended upon him: Acts x. 33, 'We are here present before God, to hear all things that are commanded thee of God.' An humble soul, says Kempis, by the grace of God, understands more the reasons of eternal truth in a trice, than a man that has studied many years in the schools, because he has the operations of them in his heart.

7. Receive the word with faith. I mean, not the faith which is a part of the new creature, but an assent. There is a rational belief that it is the word of truth, which is in many men that have no justifying faith. Actuate this. The believing the word to be so, to be the word of God, is the first step to the receiving advantage by it. No man will ever comply with that which he believes not to be true, or believes not himself to be concerned in. It is said by the apostle, Heb. iv. 1, 2, 'The word profited not, because it was not mixed with faith.' There was truth in the word, but no firm assent to it in their hearts. There can never be a full compliance with Christ, in order to a new birth, if there be not first an assent to the word. Where there is a defect in the first concoction, there will also be a defect in the second and third. If you do not believe with Naaman, that the waters of Jordan are appointed by God for this end, and not those of Abana and Pharpar, you will never be rid of the spiritual death, no more than he would have been of his leprosy. You never see God in his sanctuary, nor feel God in his power for want of this. Surely as this made our Saviour suspend the power of his miracles, by the same reason it makes him suspend the power of his word: Mat. xiii. 58, 'He did not many mighty works there, because of their unbelief.' If men did believe there were a place where they might enjoy all earthly delights in a higher measure, at an easier rate, how ambitious would they be of putting themselves into a state to enjoy them? If men did believe the report of the gospel, would they not be full of great undertakings for the enjoyment of the proffers of it? But the gospel, more is the pity, has not naturally that credit with men that a fiction has.

8. Observe much the motions upon your hearts while you are attending upon God. If the sails be not skilfully ordered to catch and hold, and make the best improvement of the wind that blows, much of the wind will pass beside it, and the ship lag many leagues behind, or lie wind-bound a long time before it receive a like gale. God has particular seasons: Heb. iv. 7, 'Today if you will hear his voice.' Sometimes the Spirit is more urging than at another time, and sends his motions thicker upon the heart; let those times be observed, and when there are motions on the Spirit's part, let there be compliance on yours. Catch a promise when the Spirit opens; bind yourselves to an observance of the precept when the Spirit shows it; let God's drawing be answered with the soul's running; observe what precious oil is dropped through the golden pipes upon the heart, and spill it not; take notice of what sparks light upon you, and lose not the warmth they may convey to your hearts; what beam of light breaks in, let it not be puffed out by a temptation or diversion; observe what is afforded to make your hearts burn, and your corruptions and sinful inclinations cool. Regard not so much your affections, as what touches are upon your wills. Affections may arise from a natural constitution of the body, some tempers being more easily excited to exert affections than others, yet they are not always, nor altogether, to be disregarded, nor are they always to be looked upon as ciphers; but, especially, see what influence the word has upon the understanding and will chiefly, as well as upon the affections. Judge of yourselves by the inward power and might, by the breakings in of the light, and the sprightly strain of your wills. The might of the Spirit works in the inner man, Eph. iii. 16; not in a part of the inner man, but in every faculty. See what compunction there is in your souls, what strong desires in the will. Bare affections are but like a sponge, which will by a light compression let out that water which it so easily sucked up. Men may 'receive the word with gladness' without having any root of spiritual grace, Mark iv. 16, 17. When men regard only particular affections, they usually sit down in those sparks of their own kindling, and look not after a thorough change. Or if you find such affections see whether those affections are raised rather by the truth than the dress; whether they be kindled by the consideration of those attributes of God, his mercy, goodness, wisdom, holiness, which have a great hand in the new birth, whether by the deep consideration of our Saviour's death and resurrection, the great designs of the gospel; whether the motion be orderly, first, understanding, then will, and afterwards affections. This is a genuine flame kindled by a fire which comes down from heaven, working upon all the parts of the soul. A bare work upon the affections is rather a strange and carnal fire. Observe, therefore, what tender blades bud and

shoot forth in the higher faculties of your souls.

9. Press the word much upon your hearts after hearing. How great is the neglect of this application of the word of truth! Men will spend hours in hearing, and not one minute in serious reflections, as if the word in their ears, or a receipt in their pockets, could cure the disease in the heart. This is the worm at the root of all our spiritual advantages. What is only dashed upon the fancy, or lightly coloured, may soon be washed off. The soil must be made tenacious of the seed by the harrow of meditation, which hides it in the heart, and covers it with earth; for want of being laid deep, and branded by serious meditation, the seed takes no root, because there is not much earth about it, Mark iv. 5, 6, 16. How can food nourish your body, unless it be concocted by natural heat? or spiritual food enliven you, unless concocted by meditation? The shepherds, after they had heard the news of Christ's incarnation from the mouth of the angel, reflected upon their duty, Luke ii. 14,15. Words must be kept some time upon the mind, and rolled over and over again, before they can work any sensible change, because the heart naturally has an averseness to God and his word; as the strongest physic must be in the body some time, and be wrought upon by the stomach, before it can work upon the humours. How do you know, but while you are musing, a divine fire may sparkle in your souls, and Christ rise in your hearts? Grapes must be pressed to get out the wine that will cheer the heart. Put the question to your soul, in every part you can remember, as our Saviour did to Martha, John xi. 25, 26, 'I am the resurrection and the life. Believest thou this?' There is such a thing as the new birth: believest thou this? It is necessary to be had: believest thou this? God only can work it: believest thou this? And so for every divine truth. Leave not thy soul to its vagaries, hold it on to the work, press it to give a positive answer whether it believe this or that truth. Put not yourselves off with a slight answer to the question, but examine the reasons of your belief of it. Look upon yourselves as really concerned in the word you hear, otherwise it will no more affect you than if you should tell an ambitious ma, gaping after preferment in England, of a wealthy place fallen in Spain, which will not engage his thoughts, as being out of his sphere and at too great a distance. To have a listlessness to such duties, or any spiritual duty, after hearing the word, which is the food of the soul, shows a great corruption within, as the heaviness in the body, and corrupt vapours in the mouth, show the badness of concoction.

10. Labour to have the savour of truth upon your spirits, as well as the notions of it in your heads. The kingdom of God consists not in word, but in power: the new birth consists not in a bare notion but in spiritual savour. The highest notional knowledge comes far short of experimental; the knowledge a blind man has of light and colours, by hearing a lecture upon it, is but mere ignorance to the knowledge he would have if his eyes were opened. Endeavour to have the savour of Christ's ointments, Cant. i. 8, and inward sense exercised, Heb. v. 14. The apostle distinguishes knowledge and judgement, Philip. i. 9. Knowledge is a notion in the head, judgement, or "aisthesis", is the sense or savour of it in the heart. What a miserable thing is it to spend our lives without a taste! Knowledge is but as a cloud that intercepts the beams of the sun and does not advantage the earth, unless melted into drops, and falling down into the bosom of it; let the knowledge of the word of truth drop down in a kindly shower upon your hearts, let it be a knowledge of the word heated with love.

I might have added more; bring plain hearts to the word, put off all disguises. Moses took off his veil when he went into the presence of God. Bring not flesh and blood as your counsellors; these are no friends to a new birth. And come with love; love makes the strongest impressions upon the soul.

It might here be also worth the inquiry, why so few are renewed by the word of truth in this age; why the gospel has no more powerful effect among us, as in former ages? It is a wonder to see a man begotten by the word, as it was a wonder for the woman to bring forth a man-child, Rev. xii. When our Saviour was brought into the temple, not a man but Simeon knew him; no question but many pharisees, doctors, and gentlemen were walking there, but none but Simeon knew him, to whom he was revealed, Luke ii. 22, 25, the rest looked upon him as an ordinary child. Formerly men flocked to Christ as the doves to the windows. The sword of the Spirit was never unsheathed, but it cut some hearts, the word seems now to have lost its edge and efficacy, which ought to be considered and laid to heart.

Many causes may be rendered; I will only hint a few.

(1.) Taking religion upon trust. Old customs are hardly to be parted with: 'Every man will walk in the name of his God,' Micah iv. 5. To root out false conceptions in religion, which either education, fancy, or humour have rooted, is very difficult.

(2.) A conceit of the meanness of the word, whereby there is a secret contempt of it, and so a formal and customary use of it.

(3.) A conceit of men, that they are new born already. Many think their condition good, because of their civil honesty. Though that be a very comely and commendable thing, yet security in it kills its thousands. Many, because they are free from the common pollutions of the world, and possessed with many amiable virtues, never consider how much their hearts are stored with an enmity against God. Such count their righteousness their gain, and think it a sufficient bribe for God's mercy.

(4.) A conceit that to be new born is but to change an opinion. A change of opinion may look like faith, as presumption does, but it is not faith. The devil holds some men in the chain of sublimated speculations, which hinder the working of the most spiritual and influential truths.

(5.) Pride of reason, frequency of disputes. It is a rational age, an age overgrown with reason, and the Scripture tells us, 'not many wise,' &c. The truths of God are very much turned into scepticism.

(6.) The common atheism that so much prevails among us. How should men regard a discourse of the new birth, a begetting to God, when they scarce believe there is a God at all, but their own lusts, to be like unto? How should they be wrought upon by the word of God, that scarce believe there is any God to reveal a word, and that there is no word of God?

(7.) Hardness of heart, occasioned (through the just judgment of God) by the frequency and unprofitable hearing of the word. The word is most operative when it comes first into a nation or town. When the heart is not broken by hearing the word of truth, it becomes more hardened and compact in sin. Many other reasons might be rendered, but I have held you too long upon this subject.

End of A Discourse of the Word, the Instrument of Regeneration.

A Discourse of the Cleansing Virtue of Christ's Blood

And the blood of Jesus Christ, his Son, cleanseth us from all sin. 1 John 1:7.

The apostle, in the beginning of the chapter, puts the saints to whom he writes in mind of the Gospel he had writ, wherein he had declared to them that Word of life which had been with the Father, and was manifested to the world, and which he now declares again, that they might have a fellowship with the apostles in the truth, and not with the false teachers in their errors; and for an incentive, assures them that the fellowship of those that kept the truth as it is in Jesus was with the Father and with the Son: ver. 3, 'That which we have seen and heard declare we unto you, that you also may have fellowship with us; and truly our fellowship is with the Father, and with his Son, Jesus Christ:' with the Father, as the source and spring of eternal life and happiness; with the Son, as mediator, who has opened the way to us, removed the bars, and given us an access to and a communion with the Father. For by sin we were alienated from God, our sin had caused justice to lock up the gates of paradise, and forbid such guilty and polluted offenders to approach to the pure majesty of God. The apostle, to encourage them to cleave to the gospel, proposes to them a fellowship with God by the means of Jesus Christ, his Son and our Mediator, as the chief happiness and felicity of man, and that which can only afford them a full and complete joy. And afterwards, ver. 5, 'This then is the message which we have heard of him, and declare unto you, that God is light, and in him there is no darkness at all;' he prescribes to them the means whereby they may keep up a communion with God, which he infers from the transcendent excellency of the divine nature, who is light: light, in regard of the clearness of his knowledge; light, in regard of his unstained purity, not tainted with the least spot or dust of evil, not having anything unworthy in his nature, nor doing anything unbecoming in his actions. If, therefore, our conversations be in darkness., if we wallow in the mire of any untamed, unmortified lust, what soever our evangelical professions may be, or howsoever we may fancy ourselves entered into a fellowship with the Father by the means of the mediator, it is but a lying imagination; for how can there be a communion between two natures so different, between light and darkness, purity and impurity, heaven and hell, God and the devil? But if our conversation be agreeable to gospel precepts, we have then a fellowship with him: ver. 7, 'if we walk in the light, as he is in the light, we have fellowship one with another,' i.e. God has a fellowship with us in affection and delight, and we have a fellowship with God in salvation and happiness; God gives himself to us, and we give ourselves to God. He bestows grace and pardon on us, and we resign up our hearts and affections to him. And this is a certain proof that we are interested in the expiatory virtue of the blood of Christ. Or else those latter words may be a prevention of an objection which might result from the apprehension of the relies of corruption in the best man in this life. Since God is infinitely pure light, without darkness, and we have so much darkness mixed with our best light, we must for ever despair of having any fellowship with God; the infinite distance, by reason of our indwelling corruption, will put us out of all hopes of ever attaining such a sovereign felicity. But this reply is prevented by this clause of the apostle: 'And the blood of Jesus Christ, his Son, cleanseth us from all sin.' Let not the sense of your daily infirmities animate any desponding fears. If you square your hearts and lives in all sincerity according to the gospel rule, there is a provision made for your security in the blood of Christ. God will wipe off the guilt of your defects by the virtue of that precious blood which has been shed for your reparation. The apostle here supposes remainders of sin in those that have the privilege of walking with God, and interest in the blessings of the covenant.

The blood of Jesus Christ. By this is meant the last act in the tragedy of his life, his blood being the ransom of our souls, the price of our redemption, and the expiation of our sin. The shedding his blood was the highest and most excellent part of his obedience, Philip. ii. 8, His whole life was a continual suffering, but his death was the top and complement of his obedience, for in that he manifested the greatest love to God and the highest charity to man. The expiatory sacrifices under the law were always bloody, death was to be endured for sin, and blood was the life of the creature; the blood or death of Christ is the cause of our justification.

His Son. His sonship makes his blood valuable. It is blood, and so agreeable to the law in the penalty; it is the blood of the Son of God, and therefore acceptable to the lawgiver in its value. Though it was the blood of the humanity, yet the merit of it was derived from the divinity. It is not his blood as he was the son of the virgin, but his blood as he was the Son of God, which had this sovereign virtue. It is no wonder, therefore, that it should have such a mighty efficacy to cleanse the believers in it, in all ages of the world, from such vast heaps of guilt, since it is the blood of Christ, who was God; and valuable, not so much for the greatness of the punishment whereby it was shed, as the dignity of the person from whom it flowed. One Son of God weighs more than millions of worlds of angels.

Cleanseth. Cleansing and purging are terms used in Scripture for justifying as well as sanctifying. The apostle interprets washing of both those acts: 1 Cor. vi. 11, 'But you are washed, but you are sanctified, but you are justified in the name of the Lord Jesus, and by the Spirit of our God.' The latter words are exegetical of the former; they both are the fruits of the merit of the blood of Christ. The one is the act of the Father as a judge appeased by that blood, the other the act of the Spirit as a sanctifier purchased by that blood. And so the 'washing of us in the blood of Christ,' spoken of Rev. i. 5, is to be understood of justification. Sanctification is expressed, ver. 6, by 'making us kings and priests to God,' giving us royal and holy natures, to offer up spiritual sacrifices unto God; and several times the word "chafar", which signifies to expiate, appease, is translated to sanctify, Exod. xxix. 33, 36, and to cleanse, ver. 37; and a word that signifies cleansing is sometimes put for justifying, as in the third commandment, Exod. xx. 7, 'The Lord will not hold him guiltless that takes his name in vain,' "lo yenakeh", will not cleanse or purge them. But it must be understood of cleansing from guilt, because it refers to the penalty of the law. It is here used in this sense; it is spoken to them that are sanctified and have a fellowship with God, that if they walk in the light, God will impute to them the blood of his Son for their absolution from the guilt of all their infirmities.

The blood of Christ cleanseth.

1. It has a virtue to cleanse. It does not actually cleanse all, but only those that believe. Nor does it cleanse them from new sins, but upon renewed acts of faith. There is a sufficiency in it to cleanse all, and there is an efficacy in it to cleanse those that have recourse to it. As when we say a medicine purges such a humour, we understand it of the virtue and quality of the medicine, not that it purges unless it be taken in, or otherwise applied to the distempered person.

2. The blood of Christ cleanseth, not has cleansed, or shall cleanse. This notes a continued act. There is a perpetual pleading of it for us, a continual flowing of it to us. It is a fountain set open for sin, Zech. xiii. 1. There is a constant streaming of virtue from this blood, as there is of corruption from our nature. It was shed but once, it is applied often, and the virtue of it is as durable as the person whose blood it is.

3. The blood of Christ cleanseth. The apostle joins nothing with this blood. It has the sole and the sovereign virtue. There is no need of tainted merits, unbloody sacrifices, and terrifying purgatories. The whole of cleansing is ascribed to this blood, not anything to our own righteousness or works. It admits no partner with it, not the blood of martyrs nor the intercessions of saints.

4. The blood of Christ cleanseth us from all sin. It is an universal remedy. Whatsoever has the nature of sin, sins against the law and sins against the gospel. It absolves from the guilt of sin, and shelters from the wrath of God. The distinction of venial and mortal sins has no footing here; no sin but is mortal without it, no sin so venial but needs it. This blood purges not some sort of sins, and leaves the rest to be expiated by a purgatory fire. This expression of the apostle, of all sin, is water enough to quench all the flames of purgatory that Rome has kindled; what sins are not expiated by it are left not to a temporary, but an eternal death; not to a refining, but a consuming fire. So that we see these words are an antidote against fears arising by reason of our infirmities, a cordial against faintings, an encouragement to a holy walk with God. It is a short but a full panegyric of the virtue of the blood of Christ.

1. In regard of the effect, cleansing.

2. In regard of the cause of its efficacy. It is the blood of Jesus, a saviour; the blood of Christ, one appointed, anointed by God to be a Jesus; the blood of the Son of God, of one in a special relation to the Father, as his only begotten, beloved Son.

3. In regard of the extensiveness of it, all sin. No guilt so high but it can master, no stain so deep but it can purge; being the blood of the Son of God, and therefore of infinite virtue, it has as much force to demolish mountains of guilt as level mole-hills of iniquity.

The words are a plain doctrine in themselves:

Doct. The blood of Christ has a perpetual virtue, and does actually and perfectly cleanse believers from all guilt. This blood is the expiation of our sin and the unlocking our chains, the price of our liberty and of the purity of our souls. The redemption we have through it is expressly called the forgiveness of sin, Eph. i. 7, 'In whom we have redemption through his blood, the forgiveness of sin,' - by a metonymy of the effect for the cause; remission was an act of redemption. When the apostle, Heb. x. 14, tells, 'That by one offering he has for ever perfected them that are sanctified,' he places this perfection in the remission of sin, ver. 17, 18. He did in the offering himself so transact our affairs, and settle our concerns with God, that there was no need of any other offerings to eke it out or patch it up. As the blood of the typical sacrifices purified from ceremonial, so the blood of the anti-typical offering purifies from moral uncleanness. The Scripture places remission wholly in this blood of the Redeemer. When Christ makes his will and institutes his supper, he commends this as our righteousness: Mat. xxvi. 28, 'This is my blood of the New Testament, which is shed for many for the remission of sins,' according to the title and end given it in the prophet, Zech. ix. 11. 'By this blood of the covenant the prisoners are delivered from the pit of corruption, wherein there was no water; no water to quench our thirst, no water to cleanse our souls, but mud and mire to defile them. This was the design of his death, as himself speaks: Luke xxiv. 46, 47, 'That repentance and remission of sins should be preached in his name amongst all nations.' And Peter, in his discourse at Cornelius his house, comprises in this the intent of the whole Scripture: 'To him give all the prophets witness, that through his name whosoever believes in him shall receive remission of sins,' Acts x. 43. As this was the justifying blood in the time of the prophets, so it will be the justifying blood to the end of the world. By this blood only the robes of any are made white, Rev. vii. 14; by this blood the accuser of the brethren is overcome and cast in his suit, Rev. xii. 10, 11. The maintaining of justification by this blood seems to be the great contest between the true church and the anti-Christian state.

(1.) The blood of Christ is to be considered morally in this act. The natural end of blood in the veins is a reparation of the substance of the body by a conversion of the blood into it. And the proper use of blood is not to cleanse, for it defiles and bespots anything whereon it is dropped; but morally considered, as the shedding of blood implies loss of life and punishment for a crime, so blood is an expiation of the crime, and a satisfaction to the law for the offence committed against it. As the shedding innocent blood does morally pollute a land, so the shedding the blood of the malefactor and murderer does morally cleanse a land: Numb. xxxv. 33, 'Blood defiles the land, and the land cannot be cleansed of the blood that is shed therein but by the blood of him that shed it'. Had not this blood of Christ been shed, our sins had not been pardoned, our souls had not been secured, our chains had continued, and our terrors had been increased; the strokes of justice had been felt, and the face of mercy had been veiled; we had wholly been the vassals of the one, and foreigners to the other.

(2.) The cleansing is to be doubly considered. There is a cleansing from guilt, and a cleansing from filth, both are the fruits of this blood: the guilt is removed by remission, the filth by purification. Christ does both: he cleanses us from our guilt as he is our righteousness, from our spot as he is our sanctification; for he is both to us, 1 Cor. i. 30, the one upon the account of his merit, the other by his efficacy, which he exerts by his Spirit. The proper intendment of the blood of Christ was to take off the curse of the law, and free us from our guilt; the washing off our stains is the proper work of the Spirit, upon that account signified to us by water in the prophets. The blood and water flowing from the side of Christ upon the cross were distinct, John xix. 34, 35, as appears by the great seriousness wherewith John affirms the relation: 'He that saw it bare record, and his record is true, and he knows that he saith true.' These two liquors flowed from his side distinctly, and do not mingle in their streams; and this seems to be so disposed by the providence of God, to signify that from the death of Christ there flow two sorts of benefits of a different nature, and which ought to be differently considered; viz., sanctification, represented by water destined to washing; and justification, which arises from satisfaction, represented by the blood shed for remission of sin. These both spring up from the death of Christ, yet they belong to two distinct offices of Christ. He justifies us as a surety, a sacrifice by suffering, as a priest by merit; but he sanctifies us as a king, by sending his Spirit to work efficaciously in our hearts. When we consider the blood of Christ, we consider Christ as a sacrifice; and sacrifices were called purifications, kaqarmata, not in regard of washing away the filth, but expiating the guilt of sin; yet indeed the justifying virtue of this blood is never exerted without a sanctifying virtue accompanying it. As blood and water flowed out of the side of Christ together, so blood and water flow into the heart of a sinner together. The typical blood of the covenant, when sprinkled by Moses upon the book and people, was mixed with water, Heb. ix. 19, 20, to signify that holiness, signified by water, accompanies the application of propitiation, signified by blood. All the force of sin consisted in condemnation, to which it had subjected men as it was a transgression of the law, and in conjunction therewith it had defiled the soul as it was loathsome, and filthy. Now Christ shed his blood to make an expiation of sin, and sent his Spirit to make a destruction of sin. By virtue of his death there is no condemnation for sin, Rom. viii. 1, 3; by virtue of the grace of his Spirit there is no dominion of sin. Rom. vi. 4, 14.

(3.) This cleansing from guilt may be considered as meritorious or applicative. As the blood of Christ was offered to God, this purification was meritoriously wrought; as particularly pleaded for a person, it is actually wrought; as sprinkled upon the conscience, it is sensibly wrought. The first merits the removal of guilt, the second solicits it, the third ensures it; the one was wrought upon the cross, the other is acted upon his throne, and the third pronounced in the conscience. The first is expressed, Rom. iii. 26, his blood rendered God propitious; the second, Heb. ix. 12, as he is entered into the holy of holies; the third, Heb. ix. 14, Christ justifies as a sacrifice in a way of merit; and when this is pleaded, God justifies as a judge in a way of authority. Christ laid the foundation of a discharge from all guilt upon the cross, and procures an actual discharge upon the first look of a sincere faith towards him; and when this blood is sprinkled upon the conscience, it 'purgeth it from dead works,' Heb, ix. 14, from the guilt of death we contracted by sinful works, and from the sentence of death which the law pronounced by reason of those works, that thereby we may have a liberty to appear before God, and be fit to serve him. The sprinkling the tabernacle and the vessels of the sanctuary, and the person officiating in it, was the applying of the propitiation made by the sacrifice to those things for the special consecration of them unto God. No blood was sprinkled but the blood of the victim, solemnly offered unto God upon the altar, according to his own appointment; no blood applied to the conscience can cleanse it but the blood of this great sacrifice, which is peculiarly called 'the blood of sprinkling,' as it is the blood of the covenant, Heb. xii. 24. The virtue of it conveyed as sprinkled is from the propitiation it made as shed. A not guilty is entered into the court of God when this blood is pleaded, and a not guilty inscribed upon the roll of conscience when this blood is sprinkled. It appeases God's justice and quenches wrath. As it is pleaded before his tribunal, it silences the accusations of sin; and quells tumults in a wrangling conscience, as it is sprinkled upon the soul.

2. The evidence of this truth well appears;-

(1.) From the credit it had for the expiation and cleansing of guilt, before it was actually shed, and the reliance of believers in all ages on it. The blood of Christ was applied from the foundation of the world, though it was not shed till the fullness of time. They had the benefit of the promise of redemption before the accomplishment of the sacrifice for redemption. The cleansing we have now is upon the account of the blood of Christ already shed; the cleansing they had then was upon the account of the blood of Christ in time to be shed: the one respects it as past, the other as future. We must distinguish the virtue from the work of redemption. The work was appointed in a certain time, but the virtue was not restrained to a certain time, but was communicated to believers from the foundation of the world, as well as extended to the last ages of the world.

Several considerations will clear this.

[1.] The Scripture speaks but of one person designed for this great work. John Baptist speaks of 'the Lamb of God,' pointing to one lamb appointed to 'take away the sins of the world,' John i. 29. The world is to be understood cronkkwV, for all ages, all times of the world; as the same is meant, I John ii. 2, 'He is a propitiation for our sins: and not for ours only, but also for the sins, of the whole world;' and he, and only he, is the propitiation, by once offering of himself. Not for the sins of us only that live in the dregs of time, and the declining age of the world, but of those that went before in all ages of the world, from its youth till his appearance in the flesh and expiring upon the cross. Christ is said to be the one mediator, in the same sense that God is said to be the one God: 1 Tim. ii. 5, 'For there is one God, and one mediator between God and men, the man Christ Jesus.' As there is but one creator of man, so there is but one mediator for men. As God is the God of all that died before Christ came, as well as of those that lived after, so Christ is the mediator of all that died before his coming, as well as of those that saw his day. They had Christ for their mediator, or some other; some other they could not have, because there is but one. They might as well have had another creator besides God, as another mediator besides the man Christ Jesus. In regard of the antiquity of his mediation from the foundation of the world, he is represented, when he walks as mediator in the midst of the seven golden candlesticks, with 'hair as white as wool,' a character of age, Rev. i. 14. As God is described so in regard of his eternity, Dan. vii. 9. There is but one God from eternity, but one mediator, whose mediation has the same date as the foundation of the world, and runs parallel with it; but one captain of salvation also for many sons, Heb. ii. 10, that were brought to glory. All that were brought to glory were brought into that happy state by this captain of salvation, as made perfect by sufferings; so that either none were brought to glory before the sufferings of Christ, which is not true, or they were brought to glory by virtue of the sufferings of that captain of salvation. If that one captain were not a perfect head of salvation but by shedding his blood, then those that were under his conduct from the beginning of the world could not be perfect, but upon the account of his passion. For they had no perfection but in and by their head; the same way that he was justified for them, they were justified by him.

[2.] This one mediator was set forth ever since the fall of man as the foundation of pardon and recovery. The covenant of grace commencing from the time of the fall of man, the virtue of this blood, which is the blood of the covenant, bore the same date; and, indeed, the blood of the Redeemer, as the way of procuring restoration, was signified in that first promise, which was the first dawning of the covenant of grace after that black night of obscurity the revolt of man had drawn upon the world, Gen. iii. 15. The recovery of man from that gulf of misery the head or subtle brains of the serpent had cast them into, is promised there to be by a man (for that must be signified by the seed of the woman), and some great and worthy person able for so great an undertaking, and to be effected by suffering, intimated by bruising his heel, which could not be without something of blood in the case. Satan would not cease, but express his enmity against the dissolver of his works, and the deliverer of his captives. It must also signify a deliverance from that which he was reduced to by the subtilty of the serpent, and that was sin and destruction. It could not be meant of a freedom from a bodily death, because this promise being made before, the pronouncing the sentence of a bodily death, which was not till ver. 19, was a bar to any such thought, for it had been a mockery, a falsity in God to promise Adam a redemption for that, and afterward overturn his promise by threatening that which he had promised before to redeem him from. This bruise, therefore, that the seed of the woman was to receive from the devil, at what time soever it should be inflicted, was to extend in the virtue of it to Adam, and his believing posterity that should come upon and go off the stage of the world before the revolution of that time wherein it was to be transacted; otherwise, the making of this promise to him, which should not distil any gracious dews upon him, had been to feed him with mere smoke, a thing unbecoming the Creator of the world. Besides, it was declared in types and figures. As the ceremonial uncleanness, which the legal sacrifices were appointed to purge, was an image of the moral impurity which needed expiation, so the blood of beasts, shed for the cleansing of it, was a shadow of that blood which was designed in the fullness of time for the expiation of the other. Nay, there were not only types of it, but plain prophecies concerning it. The righteousness whereby all believers are justified is witnessed in the whole current of Scripture, both by the law and the prophets, to be without the works of the law: 'Even that righteousness of God, which is by faith of Jesus Christ,' Rom. iii. 21, 22. And therefore when there was a conference between Moses and Elias on the one part, and Christ on the other, the subject of it is not anything but that of his decease, Luke ix. 31: the declaration of that being the chief intent of the types of the law, instituted by the ministry of Moses; and of the prophets, whereof Elias was the chief, though not in the publishing of the mediator, yet in the peculiar mark of the favour of God in his translation to heaven. But Isaiah is the plainest and most illustrious in the proclamations of the coming, the design and methods of the Redeemer. And particularly the pardon of sin by virtue of his suffering is discovered: Isa. xliii. 24, 25, 'Thou hast made me to serve with thy sins, then hast wearied me with thine iniquities.' Then it follows, 'I, even I, am he that blotteth out thy transgression for my own sake.' Christ is said to serve with thy sins; and Isa. liii. is a comment upon this, showing what kind of servitude it was that the Redeemer endured, and what that weariness was which he sustained for our iniquity, viz. that he was wounded, bruised, and offered up. The whole scope of the chapter proves this, for it is spent in numbering up the benefits of the Messiah, the calling of the Gentiles, and gathering a church from all parts of the world, vers. 5, 6, etc., and vers. 19, 20; and in the last part describes the chiefest benefit by the Messiah, viz. propitiation and remission of sin; and to show that pardon was wholly free, he removes all false causes of pardon, human merit, and legal sacrifices: ver. 22, 23, 'Thou hast not called upon me, thou hast not filled me with the fat of thy sacrifices;' and then publishes the merit of the Messiah, serving with, or in their sins, upon which account out of mere grace the sins of men are blotted out, ver. 24, 25; as much as to say, Not thou, Jacob, by thy duties and offerings hast merited the blotting out of thy sins. That glory is only due to me, who served with thy sins in dying and suffering, and paid the price of redemption, that by this means, without thy merit, thy sins might be wiped out; and, ver. 27, 28, he declares the rejection of the Jewish church, the giving Jacob to a curse and Israel to reproach, for their refusal of this way of redemption.

[3.] Though these promises and prophecies of the expiation and cleansing of sin were something obscure to them, and though they did not exactly know the method how it would be accomplished, yet that sin should be pardoned was fully revealed, and something of the method of it might be known unto them.

First, That sin should be pardoned was fully revealed to them, and their faith had something clear for their support. It was sufficient that he had published a time wherein and a seed whereby Satan's head should be bruised, and afterwards had proclaimed his name in text letters, to be 'a God pardoning iniquities, transgressions, and sins,' Exod. xxxiv. 6. How could Jacob without the knowledge of this say at his expiring hour that he had waited for God's salvation? Gen. xlix. 18; how could David else so earnestly have begged for a purging hyssop? how could he be confident that there was a grace to make him as white as the unspotted snow, and his bloody soul as pure as unstained wool? Ps. li. 7; how could Manasseh have with so much confidence laid himself at the feet of God in his prison, had he looked upon him only as a revenging and not a pitying God? The promise of God's being their God was often inculcated to them, assuring them thereby that the thing should be done, that nothing of pardon and the fruit of it should be wanting to them, though the manner was not declared in that promise; for the promise of God's being their God included all spiritual blessings, particularly this of cleansing from sin, without which he could not be their God in a way of grace, but their judge in a way of wrath.

Secondly, They might know something of the method and manner of it. The mercy of God was revealed, the pardon of sin assured, and sacrifices instituted among the Jews to keep up their faith in the expectation of this promised expiation; but the manner how, and the merit whereby, was not so clearly drawn out to their view, which is fully opened to us in the gospel, Eph. iii. 5. The types indeed were obscure; it is a hard matter to understand them now since the revelation of the gospel, much harder to spell them out by that moonlight before the sun was risen. Yet the believers then could not be ignorant, but there was some excellent thing wrapped up in them, that they were not appointed for any excellency they had in themselves, or any power to propitiate God and appease his anger, which God's disdainful speaking of them many times, when they rested upon their external sacrifices, might inform them of.

They might collect from thence that they all had reference to some richer blood, and were images of some nobler sacrifice, besides what the foundation promise would mind them of, that some great person in our nature was designed for the bruising the serpent's head, by suffering the bruising of his heel by the force of the serpent. They could not read that glorious and comfortable name of God, Exod. xxxiv. 6, but that clause, ver. 7, that he would 'by no means clear the guilty,' (which belongs to his name as well as the other of pardoning, and is uttered in the same breath), might startle them, and would seem to be an exception to dash out the comfort of all the foregoing titles. How they could reconcile such distant terms of a God pardoning, and yet not clearing the guilty, without a reflection upon some grand expiatory sacrifice, which might render to justice what was due for their crimes, and draw forth from mercy what was necessary for their misery, I understand not. No doubt but some of them saw something of the Messiah's work wrapped up in the typical sacrifices and ceremonies; for it is not likely that they should all be wholly ignorant of the intendment of them. It is very likely that Job, who was not a Jew, but an Edomite, and, as some think, died that year the Israelites came out of Egypt, had the knowledge of redemption by the Messiah, and why might not the Israelites also have some knowledge of it as early? No question but they had; the place in Job is remarkable: Job xix. 25, 'I know that my Redeemer lives, and that he shall stand at the latter day upon the earth.' Most, both of Protestants and papists, understand it of Christ. The word is "go'el" a Redeemer by right of affinity, as Christ was, being our brother by the assumption of our nature; and he seems to speak not only of one that was a redeemer in act, but a redeemer by office, and his appearance to be in the latter day refers to his incarnation in the latter age of the world, whom himself also should behold with his eyes at the resurrection. It is some extraordinary and remarkable thing that he would have so noted, for ver. 23, 24, he speaks: 'Oh that my words were now written! Oh that they were printed in a book, that they were graven with an iron pen, and lead in the rock for ever.' He would have it perpetually preserved and marked; and the comfort he took in the consideration of this his Redeemer to be incarnate so possesses him that it is observed that he does not utter such heavy complaints to the end of the book as he had done before. Christ was as much Job's Redeemer before his incarnation and passion as ours since; yet as to the manner how he was to redeem, the price he was to pay, there was a veil upon him, till it was cleared up by the prophets, upon a nearer approach of the dawning of the fullness of time; for though they had some revelation of the Messiah as a great person, a great priest after the order of Melchisedec, a great king, a special favourite of God, yet how was he to cleanse sin they were ignorant of. As they did not know what new doctrines he would reveal as a prophet, or what kind of kingdom he should have as a monarch, so they did not fully know what kind of sacrifice he should offer as a priest. They had some kind of knowledge, but not a distinct one.

[4.] The ancient patriarchs had faith, and were actually pardoned. They had the same spirit of faith as those had which lived in the times of the gospel, 2 Cor. iv. 13. Noah is said to be 'a just man, and perfect in his generations,' Gen. vi. 9, when he was young and when he was old; but how? 'He found grace in the eyes of the Lord,' ver. 8. He denied his own righteousness, and fled to the grace of God, which could not be exhibited to him but in Christ; for no grace without contented justice. The ground of all the comfort and joy Abraham had was the sight of the appearance of this bleeding Redeemer, though afar off, John viii. 56. To what purpose was that sight, without a benefit redounding to him from it? And that great patriarch was justified by faith in him; which the apostle discourses of, Rom. iv.; and hereupon he was called 'the father of the faithful,' as being the first express pattern of justification set down in Scripture. For he was not the father of the faithful by carnal procreation, but upon the account of religion; the father, as he was the teacher by his example, the name of fathers being given to instructors. If he were not therefore cleansed and counted righteous upon the account of his blood, he could not be set forth as a pattern of justification unto others, the pattern being written one way and the copies another. It was the sole promise of the blessed seed which was the cause of his justification, not sacrifices or circumcision. The same righteousness is imputed to the father as is to the children, and the same to the children that was to the father. He and we have the same faith, the same object of faith; and by what we are justified, by the same he was justified. It was the same blessedness he and we have, the same gospel he and we heard, Gal. iii. 8. The grace conferred upon David was from Christ: how could his sin else have been remitted, for which no sacrifice was appointed under the law? Ps. li. 16, 17, 'Thou desiredst not sacrifice, else would I give it.' Supposing the legal sacrifices were sufficient, without any relation to something else to expiate the sin for which they were appointed, how should those sins of presumption which David was guilty of be expiated, since there was no institution of any legal victim for them? Surely the Israelites were not left destitute of help in this case. And God, by providing no sacrifice for those sins, intimated that there was a nobler sacrifice yet behind. The Messiah as a priest was in David's eye, whom he calls his Lord, though he was to proceed out of his loins, Ps. cx. 1, 4. David's Lord by another right than as God, for he does distinguish him from the Father as Lord, and therefore David's Lord by another right, a right of redemption. The Jews had a sufficient account that the sacrifices of the law could not purge sin, in the sacrifice of the red heifer, Num. xix. 2, which could not expiate their sins. If it had a virtue to this purpose, why should the priest who sacrificed her and sprinkled the blood before the tabernacle, and the person that burnt her, and the person that gathered up the ashes, wash their clothes afterwards, and be unclean till the evening, ver. 7, 8, 9, who were more likely than the rest to be expiated by it? Their sins were pardoned, but impossible to be so by the blood of bulls and goats, Heb. x. 4, yet not without the interposition of a bloody sacrifice; for 'without blood there is no remission,' Heb. ix. 22, whereby the apostle proves the necessity of the sacrifice of Christ. And could sin be pardoned without a sacrifice, the apostle's argument to evince the unpardonableness of the sin against the Holy Ghost, or of those that refused the sacrifice of Christ, would be invalid, for his reason to prove it unpardonable is because there is no more sacrifice for it; all which supposes the necessity of a satisfaction to justice by blood, to open the way to the throne of grace, and put any man into the favour of God. It was this blood, therefore, shed upon the cross, whereby the transgressions under the first testament were purged, and upon the account of which the promised inheritance was received, Heb. ix. 15. Christ could not else have pronounced a blessedness upon faith without the vision of him, as he does, John xx. 29, 'Blessed are they that have believed, and have not seen,' meaning those that died in faith in the time of the law. And the apostle is express in it, that Christ 'by that one offering perfected for ever them that are sanctified,' Heb. x. 14, understanding those that were sanctified, or cleansed, or pardoned before the actual offering, as appears by the ground of this his inference, which was the insufficiency of all other sacrifices to take away sin. There was never but one God that justifies, never but one way of justification, and that by faith, as the apostle argues, Rom. iii. 30, and therefore but one cause of the justification of all them that went before, because but one object of faith, the blood of the Messiah, the Redeemer of the world. In him only all things were gathered and summed up into blessedness, Eph. i. 12, and men are blessed in him, Ps. lxxii. 17. In his merit, says the Chaldee paraphrase, understanding it of the Messiah.

[5.] And this might well be, on account of the compact between the Father, the Judge, and the Son, the Redeemer. Had he not promised the shedding of his blood, justice had dislodged the sinner from the world. All hopes of regaining paradise had been lost, without it the authority of the law had not been preserved, the sacredness of divine truth had been violated, and the rectitude of his government laid in the dust by an easy indulgence, and passing over the sin. Christ therefore stood up, and promised his soul as a sacrifice for sin. He was before Abraham was: John viii. 58, Before Abraham was, I am;' I am, I was what I am now, a Mediator; by promise, by constitution, by acceptation; and therefore 'Abraham saw my day, and was glad,' as it is before, ver. 56. I was a Lamb slain, accepted as a Lamb slain, as Mediator, upon credit. His office was of a more ancient date than his incarnation; and he was the same in the function of a Mediator before as he was after his taking our flesh, the same for them in his compact as he was for us in the performance. A man may be freed from prison upon the promise of a surety worthy of credit, though the debt be not actually paid till some time after, according to agreement; and the possession of a purchase may be delivered, though a time afterwards be set for the payment of the price. The payment of the ransom is not of absolute necessity before the deliverance of the captive. Many were delivered from their bonds by God before the payment made by Christ, but not before the payment promised by him. The blood of this sacrifice as shed reaches us though sixteen hundred years since it was poured out; but the blood of this sacrifice promised by the Redeemer, and receiving credit with God, reached Adam four thousand years before it was shed. God imparted the virtue before Christ actually merited, and freed the captive before the ransom was paid; yet upon the account of the promised merit and contracted ransom, natural causes must be before the effect, moral causes may be after the effect. The blood of Christ cleanses not as a natural, but as a moral cause. He was in this respect a 'Lamb slain from the foundation of the world,' Rev. xiii. 8: slain federally, though not actually; imputatively, though not really; sententially in the acceptation of the judge, though not executively in the enduring the passion; and therefore he was a Lamb slain from the foundation of the world efficaciously, by whose blood the ancient believers were sprinkled, as well as those of a later date.

And though some refer those words, from the foundation of the world, not to the word slain, but to the writing of the names in the book of life of the Lamb, 'whose names were written from the foundation of the world in the book of the Lamb slain,' it will not much alter the thing. The slaying of the Lamb was agreed, as well as the writing the names in the book; and it will also follow, that no man had any place in the book, but had also an interest in the Lamb slain, and the benefits he enjoyed by virtue of the register were to flow to him through the blood of the covenanting Redeemer, and their names were writ there upon the credit of the Lamb to be slain; for in him was the choice made before the foundation of the world, Eph. i. 4, and through him were the blessings of pardon given out from the foundation of the world. Had not this Lamb offered himself to be slain, man had been cast into everlasting chains as well as the devils, who had no mediator, no lamb to be slain for them. Well, then, it follows from hence, that the blood of Christ is of a full credit with God. Christ was the same to the patriarchs as to the apostles: Heb. xiii. 8, 'He was the same yesterday, today, and forever;' yesterday, to Adam, four thousand years since. Yesterday, in the Hebrew phrase, often signifies all the time past; today, now in the time of his appearance forever, to the generations that follow, not only in regard of his person and deity, but in regard of his office and benefits. It is not meant of his deity, but of his mediation, as will appear by the following verse, where the apostle designs the alienating their judgments from too high an opinion of the ceremonial rites and sacrifices. They never purged sin, but Christ was the cause of the purgation of them under the law as well as under the gospel, though he were not so distinctly known by them as by us. The blood of Christ extended to believers in all ages; he was a seed for Abraham as well as Abraham's seed: Gen. xxi. 12, 'In Isaac shall thy seed be called;' "zera' lecha", a seed for thee, it may be rendered, a seed for thy good, and eternal deliverance; not only a seed out of his loins, but a seed for his benefit. As a flash of lightning out of a cloud in the night enlightens all things both before and behind it, so the righteousness and blood of Christ is imputed not only to men that come after him, but to those that went before him. If the credit of it were so great then, the merit of it is as great now, since the actual effusion of the blood. It is therefore rightly a blood that cleanses from all sin.

(2.) This was the true and sole end of his incarnation and death. All the ends mentioned by the angel Gabriel to Daniel centre in this and refer to it: chap. ix. 24, 'To finish the transgression, make an end of sin, and make reconciliation for iniquity, and to bring in everlasting righteousness,' and thereby should all the visions and prophecies concerning the Messiah and his work be fulfilled. And to this purpose would 'the Most Holy' be 'anointed,' as the cause and foundation of all that removal of sin mentioned before. All the words which signify sin, and contain in them all sorts of sin, are here expressed, to show the completeness of the design in regard of the subject the Messiah was to remove out of the way. The word translated to finish, "chala'", signifies also to shut up or restrain; and the word translated to make an end, "chatam", signifies to seal up. Sin was to be restrained from ravaging about at pleasure like a devouring monster, or shut up and stopped from being an accuser to condemnation; and sealed up, not for confirmation of sin, but for concealment of it, as things sealed are not to be looked into but by persons authorised thereunto. It is a breach of trust, and an invasion of another's right, to do it. So God is said to cover sin, and Christ here to seal up sin by his blood, and for ever hide it from the face of God, and to make reconciliation for iniquity, or expiate it. Since it was sin only that was the cause of the enmity, and which separated us from communion with God, wherein the happiness of a creature is placed, there was a necessity, for our rescue from misery, to remove our guilt, that that which tore us might be muzzled, that that which accused us might be silenced, that that which was a bar to our happiness might be demolished, that so the misery we endured might fly from us, and the blessings we wanted might flow down to us. For this cause the Messiah was anointed, and for this end he undertook his employment on earth, to remove the obstacle which hindered our access to God. Hence we find that the covenant of grace, when spoken of in the Old Testament to be fully revealed in the latter days, contains chiefly those promises of 'blotting out transgressions, and remembering sin no more.'

[1.] This is the fundamental doctrine of the gospel. The apostle therefore, with a particular emphasis, tells them this is a thing to be known and acknowledged by all that own Christianity: I John iii. 5, 'And you know that he was manifested to take away our sins.' You know nothing of Christianity if you know not and believe not this, that Christ appeared to take away the guilt of sin by a non-imputation, and to quell the power of sin by a mortification of it; to remove the punishment it had merited, and the corruption it had established in the hearts of men. Sin therefore will perfectly be cleansed both by remission and sanctification, else Christ would fall short of the end of his manifestation. This was the doctrine the apostles were first charged to publish, both as the reason of Christ's suffering and of his resurrection, that 'remission of sins might be preached in his name among all nations,' Luke xxiv. 46, 47; remission of sin, as purchased by his death, and assured by his resurrection. The foundation of pardon was in his passion, and the manifestation of the efficacy of his passion was by his resurrection; both of them therefore were to be declared in order to this end. And though Paul was not then present at this first commission (as being one born out of due time, and summoned into the office of apostleship afterward), yet his instructions were of the same nature, and observed by him in the same order: I Cor. xv. 3, 'For I delivered unto you first of all that which I also received,' viz. first, 'How that Christ died for our sins according to the Scriptures.' Set aside this end, what attractive can there be in a crucified man, one made the derision and reproach of his nation, to cause any to believe in him? Faith particularly pitches upon the death of Christ, and particularly eyes in that passion the intent both of the sender and of him that is sent. The first thing himself published when he exercised his office was this jubilee: Luke iv. 18, 19, 'The acceptable year of the Lord,' wherein captives were to be delivered, debts to be remitted, and bonds to be cancelled. That was the main end of his coming to die, which, when done, was the sole reason of his advancement; the purging sin, and our sin, was the ground of his glorious sitting at the right hand of God, Heb. i. 3.

[2.] There could be no other end of his shedding his blood but this. Since his death is called a 'sacrifice,' Eph. v. 2; a 'propitiation,' 1 John ii. 2, Rom. iii. 25, it can be for no other end but the cleansing of sin; for this was the reason of the institution of sacrifices. Blood shed in a sacrifice way implied blood criminal, and deserving to be shed. Had he come upon the earth in a stately grandeur, to rout armies of men, batter down the walls of cities and demolish empires, the rooting out of tyranny and monsters might have been thought his design. But this was no way for the expiation of sin, but the destruction of the sinner. But coming to shed his blood, to be a sacrifice, to be the reproach of men, and to be God's servant in this office, which he was not by nature, what end can be imagined but somewhat in relation to sin, and that both to the expiation and destruction of it? For dying and shedding his blood for it was not the way to maintain sin, but to abolish it; not a means to render iniquity lovely, but odious. If this were not the issue of his death, it would be useless, his blood would be shed in vain. His death, being a punishment and by way of sacrifice, must be for some end, it could not be for anything relating to himself, or to merit anything for himself; for, being God, there could be no accession of happiness to him; he needed not to merit anything, because he wanted nothing. All merit is a desert of something which is not at present possessed, but desired to be possessed. He had not, nor could, commit any sin for which he should become a sacrifice. The Deity is incapable of unrighteousness and crime. The punishment was not therefore upon any account of his own. No crime was committed by him in his humanity that might merit the infliction of such a punishment; this was impossible, for whatsoever crime had been committed in his humanity had been the crime of his person, and so had been a spot upon his deity, united in one person with his humanity. Besides, he took human nature to suffer in it; his incarnation had an ought to suffer linked to it, so that his shedding his blood was resolved on before any crime could be committed, if it were to be supposed that in his humanity he were capable of any error or miscarriage. His blood must be shed for some other, and the punishment inflicted upon him which was merited by some other persons. It could not be for the holy angels; they were innocent, and not criminally indebted, and therefore obnoxious to no penalty. It being for the taking away of sin, the word sin excludes the good angels, who never sinned, but always obeyed God, Ps. ciii. 21; nor could it be for the evil angels, for the Scripture excludes them from any redemption, and binds them for ever in chains of darkness, to bear the punishment in their own persons. Besides that, this punishment could not properly be borne in any other nature specifically distinct from their sinning nature, as it was. It must be for the sin of men, or for nothing. And consequently the death of Christ would be an insignificant thing; but it is utterly inconsistent with the wisdom and holiness of God to appoint, and the wisdom and honour of Christ to agree, to a task for nothing and to no purpose. Now since Christ offered his life to God (which he did not owe upon his own account), a reward was due to him upon the account of justice, which must consist in remitting something which he owed, or imparting something which he wanted. No debt for himself could he be charged with, no indigence could be in his humanity upon his own account, since all happiness was due to that by virtue of its union with the deity; nothing could be bestowed upon him for himself, because he wanted nothing; nothing could be remitted to him, because he owed nothing. Since therefore he so deeply humbled himself, not for himself but for others, and that there was a merit on his part, and consequently a just retribution on God's part due, it was necessary it should be given to some others upon his account, that what they owed might be remitted, and what they wanted might be bestowed. These could be no other than men whom he came to justify, and to whom the debt owing to God might be discounted, upon the account of Christ's payment.

3. This cleansing sin is wrought solely by his own worth, as he is the Son of God. It is therefore said in the text, the blood not only of Jesus Christ, but of the Son of God. The blood of Jesus received its value from his Sonship, the eternal relation he stood in to his Father. Since sin is an infinite evil, as being committed against an infinite God, no mere creature can satisfy for it, nor can all the holy works of all the creatures be a compensation for one act of sin, because the vastest heap of all the holy actions of men and angels would never amount to an infinite goodness, which is necessary for the satisfaction of an infinite wrong. One sin, containing in it an infinite malice, is greater in the rank of evils than all good works heaped together can be in the rank of goods. But this blood was not only the blood of Jesus, a man, but the blood of that person that was the Son of God; of him who was our surety as the Son of God before he was our surety as the Son of man; who interposed as a surety four thousand years before his incarnation and shedding his blood, though he could not act the part of a surety without his incarnation and shedding his blood. Either we had no surety before he was incarnate, or else the Son of God in his own person was our surety. The shedding his blood was pursuant to that interposition he made as the Son of God in our stead before he was the Son of man; and it was truly the blood of that person who had offered himself to be our surety, and been accepted in that relation, so many ages before a created nature was assumed by him; so that, though his humanity was a creature, and was necessary as a subject wherein the satisfaction was to be performed, yet it added no worth to the satisfaction of itself. The value which his blood had was from his deity, his being the Son of God, in which condition he entered into his relation of a mediator for us. It was the same person that was the brightness of God's glory and the express image of his person; the same person that upheld all things by the word of his power, who did by himself, in that glorious person, 'purge our sins,' Heb. i. 3. The priests under the law purged the sins of the people by the sacrifices of beasts; this was an infinitely nobler victim, a beam of brightness streaming from the eternal Father while he was purging our sins in his eclipse; the express image of his person, while he was made a curse upon the cross, upholding all things by the word of his power; while he bowed his head under the weight of his sufferings, he was all this while making an atonement for our sins, whence redounded an inconceivable efficacy to his blood. The nature of man

died, but he had another nature as immortal as the person whose brightness he was, that lived to add value to his sufferings. This divine person, by his own strength and in this glorious relation, wrestled with the flames of wrath, and took hold of the tribunal of justice, and by the value of his sufferings, smoothed the face of a frowning God, assuaged the tempests of a provoked justice, and placed before the tribunal of judgment a strong and everlasting righteousness of his own composure, as a veil between the piercing eye of divine holiness and the guilty and filthy state of a sinner. So great a person, one equal with God, was necessary for the restoring his honour and sanctifying his name; so great a person was necessary for the purging the fallen creature from his guilt and filth.

4. Hence it follows that sin is perfectly cleansed by this blood. Since it expiated the sins of former ages, since it was the end of his coming, since he did what he did by his own worth, sin must be perfectly cleansed, else the end of his coming is not attained, and his worth would appear to be but of a finite value. All cleansing is the fruit of this blood: the cleansing from guilt is wrought immediately by it; the purging from filth is mediately by his Spirit, but as it was the purchase of his blood.

(1.) The blood of Christ does not perfectly cleanse us here from sin, in regard of the sense of it. Some sparks of the fiery law will sometimes flash in our consciences, and the peace of the gospel be put under a veil. The smiles of God's countenance seem to be changed into frowns, and the blood of Christ appears as if it ran low. Evidences may be blurred and guilt revived. Satan may accuse, and conscience knows not how to answer him. The sore may run fresh in the night, and the soul have not only comfort hid from it, but refuse comfort when it stands at the door. There will be startlings of unbelief, distrusts of God, and misty steams from the miry lake of nature. But it has laid a perfect foundation, and the top stone of a full sense and comfort will be laid at last. Peace shall be as an illustrious sunshine without a cloud, a triumphant breaking out of love, without any arrows of wrath sticking fast in the conscience; a sweet calm, without any whisper of a blustering tempest; the guilt of sin shall be for ever wiped out of the conscience, as well as blotted out of God's book. The accuser shall no more accuse us, either to God or ourselves; no new indictment shall be formed by him at the bar of conscience; nay, conscience itself shall be for ever purged, and sing an uninterrupted requiem, and hymn of peace, shall not hiss the least accusation of a crime. As God's justice shall read nothing for condemnation, so conscience shall read nothing for accusation. The blood of Christ will be perfect in the effects of it. As it rent the veil between God and us, it will rend the veil between conscience and us; no more frowns from the one, nor any more janglings in the other. As Christ said, when he was giving up the ghost, 'It is finished,' viz., the sense and sufferings under a guilty state, it is then a believer may say his fears are finished, when he is breathing forth his soul into the arms of his sacrificed Saviour. Iniquities shall never more appear in their guilty charge to draw blood from the soul of a penitent believer. The soul shall be without fault before the throne of God, Rev. xiv. 5.

(2.) The blood of Christ does not perfectly cleanse us here from sin, in regard of the stirrings of it. The old serpent will be sometimes stinging us, and sometimes foiling us. The righteous soul will be vexed with corruptions within it, as well as the abominations of others without it. The Canaanite is in the land, and therefore the virtue of the blood of Christ is expressed in our power of wrestling, not yet in the glory of a triumph. It does not here perfectly free us from the remainders of sin, that we may be still sensible that we are fallen creatures, and have every day fresh notices and experiments of its powerful virtue; and that his love might meet with daily valuations in a daily sense of our misery. But this blood shall perfect what it has begun, and the troubled sea of corruption, that sends forth mire and dirt, shall be totally removed. Then shall the soul be as pure as unstained wool, as spotless as the dew from the womb of the morning; no wrinkles upon the face, no bubblings up of corruption in the soul. The blood of Christ shall still the waves, and expel the filth, and crown the soul with an everlasting victory. 'The spirits of just men' are then 'made perfect,' Heb. xii. 23.

(3.) But the blood of Christ perfectly cleanses us from sin here, in regard of condemnation and punishment. Thus it blots it out of the book of God's justice; it is no more to be remembered in a way of legal and judicial sentence against the sinner. Though the nature of sin does not cease to be sinful, yet the power of sin ceases to be condemning. The sentence of the law is revoked, the right to condemn is removed, and sin is not imputed to them, 1 Cor. v. 19. Where the crime is not imputed, the punishment ought not to be inflicted. It is inconsistent with the righteousness of God to be an appeased, and yet a revenging, judge. When the cause of his anger is removed, the effects of his anger are extinguished. Where there is a cleansing from the guilt, there necessarily follows a removal of the punishment. What is the debt we owe upon sin? Is it not the debt of punishment, which is righteously exacted for the fault committed? When the blood of Christ therefore purifies any from their guilt, it rescues them from the punishment due to that guilt. Herein does the pardon of sin properly consist, in a remission of punishment. The crime cannot be remitted, but only in regard of punishment merited by it. If God should punish a man that is sprinkled with the blood of Christ, and pleaded for by the blood of Christ it would be contrary both to his justice and mercy: to his justice, because he has accepted of the satisfaction made by Christ, who paid the debt, and acquitted the criminal, when he bore his sin in his own body upon the tree; it would be contrary to his mercy, for it would be cruelty to adjudge a person to punishment, who is legally discharged, and put into the state of an innocent person, by the imputation of the righteousness of the Redeemer. Though the acts of sin are formally the same that they were, yet the state of a cleansed sinner is not legally the same that it was; for being free from the charge of the law, he is no longer obnoxious to the severity of the law. 'There is no condemnation to them that are in Christ,' Rom. viii. 1. No matter left that shall actually condemn, since Christ for sin, or as a sacrifice for sin, condemned sin in the flesh, ver. 3.

(4.) The effect of this blood shall appear perfect at the last, in the final sentence. It cleanses us initially here, completely hereafter. It cleanses us here in law. Its virtue shall be manifest by a final sentence. 'He that believes not is condemned already,' John iii. 18; condemned by the threatening, but not by the pronounced sentence. So he that believes is justified by the plea of this blood, justified in the promise of the gospel, but not yet by public sentence, which is reserved till the last day: 'After death the judgment,' Heb. ix. 27. As Christ was justified after he had presented his blood, was owned to be God's righteous servant by a public declaration in his exaltation, 1 Tim. ii. 16, so those that have an interest in this blood have a sentential justification at their dissolution, by God as a judge, and fully complete, when their persons shall be pronounced just, at the reunion of the soul and body at the resurrection. Whence this time is called the 'day of refreshment,' Acts iii. 19, when sins shall be blotted out, when God shall no more correct, and conscience shall no more reproach for guilt. Sin is cleansed now, but said to be blotted out then, because then all the parts of salvation shall be complete. Election was an act of eternity, but then it shall be declared, in the separation of them for ever from the rest of the world, to be with him in glory. Redemption was purchased by the death of Christ, offered in the gospel, and conferred upon the believer, but then it will be complete in a deliverance from all enemies, and the last enemy, death. And therefore called the 'day of redemption,' Eph. iv. 30. There shall then be an endless repose from all sorrow within, and trouble without. Sanctification is begun to be wrought here by the Spirit, but sin is not abolished; all earthly affections are not completely put off. So it will be with our justification, as it consists in pardon of sin; sins are blotted out now, but then in a more excellent, full, and visible manner. We need a daily pardon upon daily sin, but then God will absolve us once for all, from all our faults committed in our whole lives, and no more will be committed to need a pardon. There is here a secret grant passed in our consciences; there, a solemn publication of it before men and angels. Here every one receives a pardon in particular, as they come to him. As those under the law had a particular expiation by the means of the sacrifices presented by them, but in the annual day of expiation there was a general propitiation for the sins of the people, and all their iniquities together were carried into the desert, so the pardon that was granted to particular believers shall then resolve into one entire absolution of the whole body; when Christ shall pronounce them all righteous, and present them unblameable, and without spot to his Father. Justification is complete in this world, in regard that the guilt of sin shall never return, and a person counted righteous shall never be counted unrighteous; but not so complete that the sense of sin shall never return. But then neither David's murder shall rise up against him, nor Peter's denial of his master ever stare him in the face. No need of fresh looks upon the brazen serpent for cure, because there shall be no bitings by the fiery ones to grieve and trouble.

(5.) Hence, it cleanses from all sin universally. For since it was the blood of so great a person as the Son of God, it is as powerful to cleanse us from the greatest as the least. Had it been the blood of a sinful creature, it had been so far from expiation, that it would rather have been for pollution. Had it been the blood of an angel, though holy (supposing they had any to shed), yet it had been the blood of a creature, and therefore incapable of mounting to an infinite value; but since it is the blood of the Son of God, it is both the blood of a holy and of an uncreated and infinite person. Is it not therefore able to exceed all the bulk of finite sins, and to equal in dignity the infiniteness of the injury in every transgressor? The particle all is but a rational consequent upon the mention of so rich a treasure of blood. The nature of the sins, and the blackness of them, is not regarded, when this blood is set in opposition to them. God only looks what the sinners are, whether they repent and believe. He was 'delivered for our offences,' Rom. iv. 25, not for some few offences, but for all; and as he was delivered for them, so he is accepted for them. The effect, therefore, of it is a cleansing of all, both the original and additional transgressions; the omissions of that good God has righteously commanded, and the commissions of that evil he has holily prohibited. Men have different sins, according to their various dispositions or constitutions. Every man has his 'own way;' and the iniquity of all those various sins of a different stamp and a contrary nature, in regard of the acts and objects, God has 'made to meet' at the cross of Christ, and 'laid them all upon him,' Isa. liii. 6. The sins of all believing persons, in all parts, in all ages of the world, from the first moment of man's sinning, to the last sin committed on the earth. In regard of this extensive virtue, the scapegoat was a type of him; for though there were not particular sacrifices under the law, appointed for some sins, yet in that anniversary one, all the sins of the people were laid upon the head of that devoted goat, to be carried into the wilderness, Lev. xvi. 21, "'awonot", "pish'eyhem", "chato'tam". And the same several words, signifying all sorts of sins, are there used, as God uses, Exod. xxxiv. 7, when he proclaims himself a God forgiving iniquity, transgression, and sin. And the first sin we read of cleansed by this blood, after it was shed, was the most prodigious wickedness that ever was committed in the face of the sun, even the murder of the Son of God, Acts ii. 36, 38. So that, suppose a man were able to pull heaven and earth to pieces, murder all the rest of mankind, destroy the angels, those superlative parts of the creation, he would not contract so monstrous a guilt as those did in the crucifying the Son of God, whose person was infinitely superior to the whole creation. God then hereby gave an experiment of the inestimable value of Christ's blood, and the inexhaustible virtue of it. Well might the apostle say, 'The blood of Christ cleanseth us from all sin.'

III. Thing; How Christ's blood cleanses from sin. God the Father does actually and efficiently justify; Christ's blood does meritoriously justify. God the Father is considered as judge, Christ is considered as priest and sacrifice. He was a 'Priest in things pertaining to God,' Heb. ii. 17, 'to make reconciliation for the sins of the people,' He is the 'fountain set open for sin and for uncleanness,' Zech. xiii. 1. And 'forgiveness of sin' is a fruit of 'redemption through his blood,' Col. i. 14.

This is done,

1. By taking sin upon himself. God collected all the sins from all parts of the world, in all ages of the world, bound them up together, and 'laid them upon' Christ's shoulders, Isa. liii. 6, alluding to the manner of transferring the sins of the people by Aaron's laying his hands upon the head of the sacrifice; so that, as the scape-goat purged the people, Christ cleanses or justifies men by bearing their iniquities, Isa. liii. 11. Not by bearing the pollution of them inherently, but the guilt of them, or the curse which the sinner had merited; for our sins could no more be transmitted to him, in the filth and defilement of them, than the iniquities of the Israelites could be infused into the scape-goat, but only in their curse and guilt. A beast was not capable of spiritual pollution, because it wanted an intellectual nature; nor Christ, because of the excellency of his person. Christ took our sins upon him, not thereby to become sinful, but to become devoted in a judicial manner, as a curse; and, therefore, his being said to be 'made sin' in one place, ' that we might be made the righteousness of God in him,' 2 Cor. v. 21, is to be interpreted by Gal. iii. 13, wherein he is said to be 'made a curse to redeem us from the curse of the law,' i. e. a person exposed to the vengeance of God, to procure impunity for the offenders, that they might be absolved, and treated as if they had never been criminal. He is 'the Lamb of God, that takes away the sins of the world,' John i. 29, airwn: the word signifies to take up, as well as to take away. He took the guilt upon his shoulders, that he might for ever take it away from ours. As we are made righteousness in him, so he was made sin for us. Now we are not righteous before God by an inherent, but by an imputed righteousness, nor was Christ made sin by inherent, but imputed, guilt. The same way that his righteousness is communicated to us, our sin was communicated to him. Righteousness was inherent in him, but imputed to us; sin was inherent in us, but imputed to him. He received our evils to bestow his good, and submitted to our curse to impart to us his blessings; sustained the extremity of that wrath we had deserved, to confer upon us the grace he had purchased. The sin in us, which he was free from, was by divine estimation transferred upon him, as if he were guilty, that the righteousness he has, which we were destitute of, might be transferred upon us, as if we were innocent. He was made sin, as if he had sinned all the sins of men, and we are made righteousness, as if we had not sinned at all.

2. By accounting the righteousness and sufficiency of his sufferings to us. If we stand upon our own bottom, we are lost; our own rags cannot cover us, nor our own imperfections relieve us. 'The whole world lies in wickedness,' 1 John v. 19. God is a consuming fire, and we are combustible matter; the holiness of God, and the soul of the most righteous fallen creature, cannot meet without abhorrence on the part of God, and terror on the part of man. Divine holiness cannot but hate us, divine justice cannot but consume us, if we have no other righteousness than our own imperfect one, to please the one, and be a bar to the other. There is no justification by the law, but upon a perfect righteousness, and we must be justified by the performance of the law, or we can never be justified; for the law of God was not abrogated upon the fall of man: it is the authority of the lawgiver, and not the offence of the malefactor, which does abolish a law; but we cannot perform the law ourselves. Alas! 'All have sinned and come short of the glory of God,' Rom. iii. 23, of that righteousness which glorifies God; and having once broken the law, we can never be said perfectly to keep it; for if we had grace given us to perform it for the future, it nulls not the breach of it for the time past. Since the law is not abrogated, it must be exactly obeyed, the honour of it must be preserved; it cannot be observed by us, it was Christ only who kept it, and never broke it, and endured the penalty of it for us, not for himself; for the law requires obedience of a creature, but demands not punishment but upon default of obedience. The punishment was not inflicted on him for himself, but for us; the virtue of that must be transferred to us, which cannot be any other way than by imputation, or reckoning it ours, as we are one body with him. Besides, justification cannot be by any thing inherent in us, for we are ungodly before the first instant of justification, Rom. v. 5, and sinners and enemies, Rom. v. 10. Since there is nothing but unrighteousness in us, a righteousness must be fetched from something without us. If it be without us, it is not inherent in us. What righteousness is in us after justification, cannot be the cause of the justification which preceded that righteousness. The effect never precedes the cause. If the righteousness whereby we are justified be not inherent in us, but in another, how can it be our righteousness, but by some way of counting it to us? God intended Christ's suffering as the way of bearing iniquity for us, and accepted him as one that bore

our iniquities, and made this bearing iniquity the ground of the justification of many: Isa. liii. 11, 'By his knowledge shall my righteous servant justify many, for he shall bear their iniquities.' In his bearing our iniquities, there was the imputation of our sins; in our justification, there must be the imputation of his suffering. The counting another's righteousness to us is as reasonable and easy to conceive as the counting our sins to another. Without this way of reckoning it to us, we cannot conceive of the intercession of Christ, or what pleas he can use. He is an advocate by virtue of his propitiation, and his righteousness in it, 1 John ii. 1, 2. The plea, then, must be of this nature: Father, I took flesh by thy order, and suffered death according to thy pleasure; I gave my soul a ransom for many, and the shedding of my blood was a sweet-smelling sacrifice. Thou wouldst have me made a curse to free others from the curse, and to receive wounds, that others might receive health. Let those, therefore, that plead the merit of my suffering, be absolved from their guilt. I have borne their sins, their iniquities thou didst cause to meet on me, condemn them not to bear those iniquities I have borne already. To what purpose did I bear them, if they must bear them too? And to what purpose should they believe in me, if they must sink under the same condemnation with those that refuse me? How this plea can be made without accepting those sufferings for us, and counting the righteousness of them to us, is not to be understood. Some compare this way of imputation to the sun shining upon the wall, through a green or blue glass, whereby the true colour of the wall is indiscernible while the colour communicated by the glass is upon it; yet this colour is not the colour of the wall, but the colour of the glass, and inherent in the glass, only reflected upon the wall; so the righteousness whereby we are justified, and which covers our iniquities from the sight of God, is inherent in Christ, but transferred to us. The ground of this imputation is community of nature. Because he 'took not the nature of angels,' it is not reckoned to them, Heb. ii. 16, 17. If he had taken the nature of angels, it could not have been reckoned to us, because he had not been akin to us. Had he taken the nature of angels, it could no more have been imputed to us than the fall of angels can be imputed to us; which cannot be, because we have not an agreement in the same nature with them; and, next to that, the ground of it is his resurrection from the grave. Had he lain in the grave, his righteousness could not have been imputed to us, because it had not been declared sufficient in itself; and the sufficiency of the price, and the accepting it for a ransom, must precede the accounting of it to another for his deliverance. That which is the evidence of the perfection, and agreeableness of it to the judgment of God, is the ground of the imputation of it to us; but his going to the Father, whereof his resurrection was the first step, and his ascension the next, is the convincing argument the Comforter makes use of to persuade men of the fullness and exactness of it, John xvi. 10.

(1) This cleansing of us by imputing this blood to us, is by virtue of union and communion with him. The apostle before the text speaks of a fellowship with God and Christ, which implies union with Christ, and then the blood of Christ cleanses from all sin. What Christ did as a common person, is accepted for us, but the actual imputation of it to us depends upon our becoming one body with him. If we had not had a union with Adam in nature, and been seminally in him, his sin could no more have been imputed to us than the sin of the fallen angels could be counted ours; so if we have not a union with Christ, his righteousness can no more be reckoned to us than the righteousness of the standing angels can be imputed to us. We must therefore be in Christ as really as we were in Adam, though not in the same manner of reality. We were in Adam seminally, we are in Christ legally; yet so that it is counted in the judgment of God as much as if there were a seminal union. Believers are therefore called the seed of Christ, Isa. liii. 10, Ps. xxii. 30. And they are called Christ, 1 Cor. xii. 12; and 'the body of Christ,' ver. 27. It is, says one, not numerically, but legally such. If we had been in him seminally, as we were in Adam, righteousness would have been communicated to all descending from him; but God has appointed a higher way of communication by spiritual union. As those who were in Adam by natural propagation are made guilty by his transgression to condemnation, so all that are spiritually united to Christ are cleansed from their many offences to justification, Rom. v. 16. As there was a necessity of his union with us in our nature for our redemption, since he could not be the Redeemer of mankind by death, as he was the Son of God, unless he were also the Son of man, so there is a necessity of our union with him in his Spirit. As there could be no expiation without a satisfaction, no satisfaction to be made by Christ, unless there were an imputation of our sins to him; and no imputation can be supposed, unless he were united to us in our nature; so there can be no imputation of anything in him to us, unless there be a strait union, whereby he becomes our head and we his members. What does the apostle mean in that wish of being 'found in Christ,' but this union, whereby he might have a share in his righteousness? Philip. iii. 9. Not his own righteousness, but the righteousness of God communicated through or by faith. And where is our completeness, but in him? Col. ii. 10. As we are reckoned one lump and mass with him, and being joined to him, are counted one spirit with him, 1 Cor. vi. 17. Union with him goes first in order of nature before justification; we are first united to him as our sponsor, and being in him we are counted righteous. This is the apostle's assertion: 1 Cor. i. 30, 'But of him are ye in Christ Jesus, who of God is made unto us wisdom, righteousness,' etc. And so 'the righteousness of the law,' Rom. viii. 4, dikaiwma tou nomou, or the just judgment of the law, 'is fulfilled in us,' saith Cocceius. We are judged to have in him a perfect obedience, or we are judged not out of Christ as sinners, but in Christ as

his members.

(2.) This union is made by faith, and upon this account we are said to be justified by faith. This is our willingness to receive Christ upon the terms he is offered. Since a mediator is not a mediator of one, but supposes in the notion of it two parties, there must be a consent on both sides. God's consent is manifested by giving, our consent is by receiving, which is a title given to faith, John i. 12; God's consent in appointing and accepting the atonement, and ours in receiving the atonement, which is all one with 'receiving forgiveness of sin,' Rom. v. 11. God's consent in the typical administration was evident in appointing sacrifices, and the sending down fire from heaven for consuming them. The sinner's consent was to be signified by laying his hands upon the head of the sacrifice, intimating his union with that sacrifice, and so by the sacrificing of it he was counted as quitted of that guilt for which the sacrifice was offered. We must be as willing to accept of this sacrifice as Christ was to offer this sacrifice, with a willingness of the same kind; but, alas, what creature can mount to a willingness of the same degree! God might have required many sharp conditions of us, many years' troubles and sorrows, but he requires only a willingness of us to receive and acknowledge the depths of his wisdom and grace, and conform to his will in the new covenant. This makes up the marriage knot between the sinner and the Redeemer. By this the soul empties itself and clasps about a Saviour, and then Christ and the believer are counted as one person legally; therefore, Christ dwelling in us, and our having faith, are linked together as if they were the same thing, Eph. iii. 17. By God's acceptance of this blood we are rendered cleansable and justifiable. By our acceptance of it, it is actually imputed to us, and we actually justified. However, when it was shed by Christ, and received as a sweet-smelling sacrifice by God, it made us pardonable; yet actual pardon is not bestowed without believing. His blood avails none but those that he pleads it for, and he pleads it not for those that come to God, but that 'come to God by him,' Heb. vii. 25, those that plead in his name for the benefits which are the purchase of his blood. Without him, we are combustible matter before a consuming fire, and cannot approach to the throne of God with any success. This faith must go in order before cleansing or justification. The righteousness of God is only 'upon them that believe,' Rom. iii. 22. 'We have believed that we might be justified,' Gal. ii. 16. This faith is not our righteousness, nor is it ever called so, but we have a righteousness by the means of faith. By faith, or through faith, is the language of the apostle: Rom. iii. 22, 25, 'Faith in his blood,' faith reaching out to his blood, embracing his blood, sucking up his propitiating blood and pleading it. Though faith is the eye and hand of the soul, looking up and reaching out to whole Christ as offered in the promise, yet in this act of it to be freed from the guilt of sin, it grasps Christ as a sacrifice, it hangs upon him as paying a price, and takes this blood as a blood shed for the soul, and insists upon the sufficient value of it with God. Faith respects the subject wherein it is as guilty, for it is a grace divesting a man of his own righteousness, and emptying a man of his own strength and sufficiency, and accusing the soul of guilt, and therefore eyes that which stands in direct opposition to this guilt, the free grace of God accepting Christ as a propitiation. It eyes that in craving justification, which God eyes in bestowing it, which is the Redeemer's bearing iniquity, Isa. liii. 11. It has no efficacy of itself, but as it is the band of our union with Christ. The whole virtue of cleansing proceeds from Christ the object. We receive the water with our hands, but the cleansing virtue is not in our hands, but in the water, yet the water cannot cleanse us without our receiving it; our receiving it unites the water to us, and is a means whereby we are cleansed. And therefore it is observed that our justification by faith is always expressed in the passive, not in the active; as we are justified by faith, not that faith justifies us. The efficacy is in Christ's blood, the reception of it in our faith. Though we are justified by faith, yet all our peace, and all those blessings which are bundled up in peace with God, come in and through our Lord Jesus Christ, Rom. v. 1. 'Being justified by faith, we have peace with God, through our Lord Jesus Christ.'

IV. The use.

If the blood of Christ has the only and perpetual virtue, and does actually and perfectly cleanse believers from all sin, then it affords us,

1. A use of instruction.

(1) Every man, uninterested by faith in the blood of Christ, is hopeless of a freedom from guilt while he continues in that state. Without faith we are at a distance from God, by contracting in our natural state a guilt that subjected us to the curses of the law, and we remain under that wrath the state of nature put us into, till we are interested by faith in the expiating blood of the Redeemer. All the indictments that our own consciences, and, which is incomprehensibly more, the omniscience of God, can charge upon us, remain in their full force, are unanswerable by us, and we must inevitably sink under them, till the blood of Christ, apprehended by faith, cancel the bond and raze out the accusation. The blood of Christ is so far from cleansing an unbeliever from all sin, that it rather binds his sins the faster on him. Unbelief locks the sins on more strongly, so that the violations of the law stick closer to him, and the wrath of God hangs over him. Those that have no communion with Christ, have no interest in the blood of Christ; for they are such as 'have fellowship with the Father, and with his Son Jesus Christ,' to whom John in the text appropriates this privilege of being cleansed from all sin by the blood of Christ. Those that slight the blood of Christ, render themselves incapable of cleansing, because no

other sacrifice can be offered, no other blood can be presented to God of a value equal to it: 'No more sacrifice remains for sin,' Heb. x. 26. There was but one bloody sacrifice appointed for expiation, and there can be no less required of us for the enjoying the benefit of it, than the receiving the atonement, Rom. v. 11. It is not consistent with the honour of God to discharge men upon the account of the sufferings of the surety, who will persist in that sin for which the surety suffered, and make use of a Saviour to be freed from suffering, but not freed from offending. It would be contrary to the end of our Saviour's death to sprinkle that blood upon those that tread it under their feet, which was shed for the gathering together the sons of God, John xi. 52, to let the despisers of it have an equal share in the benefits of it with those that receive it. It cannot be imagined that God will ever make it a savour of life, as much to them that will not value it, as to those that do.

(2.) No freedom from the guilt of sin is to be expected from mere mercy. The figure of this was notable in the legal economy. The mercy-seat was not to be approached by the high priest without blood, Heb. ix. 7. Christ himself, typified by the high priest, expects no mercy for any of his followers, but by the merit of his blood. What reason have any then to expect remission upon the account of mere compassion, without pleading his blood? Mercy is brought to us only by the smoke of this sacrifice. The very title of justification implies not only mercy, but justice, and more justice than mercy; for justification is not upon a bare petition, but a propitiation. To be pardoned indeed implies mercy. Pardon is an act of favour, whereby the criminal is graced and gratified, but to be justified is to be discharged in a legal way, or by way of compensation. A man may be pardoned as a supplicant, but not pronounced righteous but upon the merits of his cause. He that employs mercy, acknowledges guilt, but insists not upon a righteousness. Justification or pardon is not the act of God as Creator, for then it had been mere mercy; nor as a lawgiver, according to the terms of the first covenant, for then no man after his revolted state could be justified; but as a judge, according to the laws of redemption, and that in a way of righteousness and justice, 2 Tim. iv. 8. God is not to be sought to for this concern, but in Christ; nor mere mercy implored without the Redeemer's merit, because God does not forgive our sins, or reconcile our persons to himself, but for the propitiating blood of his Son. To expect pardon only upon the account of mercy, is to honour one attribute with the denial of, or overlooking the other. Though God be merciful, yet he is just; his mercy is made known in remission, his justice manifested in justification. Forget not the great demonstration of his justice when you come to plead for mercy. Plead both in the blood of Christ, God is merciful to none out of Christ; he is merciful to none but to whom he is just: merciful to them in regard of themselves, and their own demerits; just and righteous to them in regard of the blood and merit of his Son.

(3.) There is no ground for the merits of the saints, or a cleansing purgatory. The apostle saith not you have a treasure of the merits of the departed saints; or you must expect a purgatory hereafter to cleanse you from all your sins. He mentions only the blood of Christ as fully sufficient and efficacious for this end. To set up other mediations, atonements, satisfactions, is a contempt of the wisdom of God in his ordination of this only one of his Son; of the holiness and justice of God in accepting this, as if God had mistaken himself, when he cheerfully received this as completely satisfactory to him, and answering his ends; as if, notwithstanding his full pleasure with it, it needed some addition from creatures to eke it out to a completeness. It is a dishonour to Christ, accusing him of an imperfect satisfaction, of an insufficient and infirm blood, a stripping it of its infinite value. How can that be infinite which needs a finite thing to strengthen it, and render it efficacious? He that goes to a muddy stream to wash himself, disgraces the pure fountain he has in his own dwelling. This the Romanists use in the form of absolution: 'Let the passion of our Lord Jesus Christ, the merits of the blessed virgin, and of all the saints, and whatsoever good thou hast done, and whatsoever thou hast sustained, be to thee,' i. e. accounted to thee, or accepted for thee, 'for the remission of thy sins, the increase of thy grace, and the reward of eternal life.' (Cajetan sum. p. 2. The first head, Absolution) Nor is purgatory a small disparagement to the extensive virtue of this cleansing blood. If the blood of Christ cleanses, what interpretation can common reason and sense make of it, but that the person so cleansed is exempted from any punishment for his crime? Is the blood of the Son of God of so weak an efficacy, that it needs a cleansing fire in another world to purge out the relics of guilt left behind by it in this? If there must be such a penal satisfaction, where is the uncontrollable virtue of this blood? If this blood, which is the blood of God, has not a sufficient virtue, what finite fire can lay claim to it? What in reason can be supposed to have it? And if it be perfectly purgative, what need of anything else, that can never deserve the name of satisfaction? Shall that God, who is goodness and righteousness itself, punish a man for that crime which he has remitted upon so great a compensation? If he be pardoned, with what justice can he be punished? If he be punished by the severity of fire, with what mercy, or by what merit, was he pardoned and justified? It is no friendship to the perfection of God's justice to allege that he will punish that which he has remitted, and as little right is done to the perfection of Christ's meritorious blood, to make it of a half validity, a lame propitiation, which requires something to be done or suffered by the sinner to render it complete in the sight of God. With what face could Christ tell sinners that came believingly to him in the world, that their 'faith had saved them,' and they might 'go in peace,' if a purgatory satisfaction were to be exacted of them after this life, and his own passion had been unable to make their peace?

(4.) No mere creature can cleanse from sin. No finite thing can satisfy an infinite justice; no finite thing can remit or purchase the remission of an injury against an infinite being. A finite compensation can bear no proportion to an infinite wrong. If pardon as well as regeneration be a work of omnipotence, as we have lately heard, no creature but is as unable to remove guilt from the soul as it had been unable to remove deformity from the first matter and chaos. A creature can no more cleanse a soul, than it can frame and govern a world, and redeem a captived sinner.

(5.) There is no righteousness of our own, no services we can do, sufficient for so great a concern. To depend upon any, or all of them, or anything in ourselves, is injurious to the value and worth of this blood; it is injurious also to ourselves; it is like the setting up a paper wall to keep off a dreadful fire, even that consuming one of God's justice. The apostle does more than once complain of the seducers that crept into the Galatian church, and would sow the tares of justification by the law, and their own works, so that they made the death of Christ in vain, Gal. ii. 21, and his work of no effect, Gal. v. 4; and tells them there plainly, that the expectation of a justification upon such an account was a falling from grace. If we are justified from our guilt by works, they must be works before faith or after faith; not before faith, for the corruption of nature remaining in its full force, without any amendment, any alteration, or subduing by renewing grace, will check men that understand anything of the woeful and deplorable, the weak and impotent, condition of man by nature, from such a thought; and indeed those that hold justification by works make faith in Christ necessary to the acceptance of those works. Nor do works after faith justify, for then a believer is not justified upon his believing, but upon his working after his believing; so that faith then is not the justifying grace, but a preparation to those works which justify, which is quite contrary to the strain of the great apostle in his epistles, who ascribes justification to faith in the blood of Christ, and to faith without works. It is by faith we are united to Christ as the great undertaker for us; by that we receive the atonement, and accept of the infinite satisfaction made by the Redeemer to the justice of God. The acceptance of this, and embracing this as done for us, and accepted by God for us, cannot be an act of our works, but of our faith. All works are excluded by the apostle, Rom. iv. 5, 6, without restraining them to the works of the law, as he does sometimes in other places. Faith alone is opposed to works in general, and therefore to all sorts of works; and works after grace he does plainly exclude: Eph. ii. 8, 'By grace you are saved through faith; and that not of yourselves: not of works, lest any man should boast.' What works are those? Works after regeneration; for they are those works to which they were 'created in Jesus Christ,' which indeed, saith he, 'God ordained that we should walk in them,' not that we should be saved or justified by them. And so, when he desires not to be 'found in his own righteousness, which is of the law,' Philip. iii. 8, 9, can he understand only those works and that righteousness which he had before his conversion to Christ? As though works after faith were not more conformable to the law than works before faith; but let them be works flowing from what principle soever, he renounces them all, accounts them loss for Christ, and places no confidence in them. He did not renounce the privileges of his birth, or strip himself of a love to holy works, but of the opinion of any value they had with God of themselves to justification. Whatsoever might come under the title of his own righteousness he does cast away, as to any dependence on it, or pleading of it before God. And may not his works, after his giving up his name to Christ, be called his own righteousness, as well as those in a state of nature? Though the principle was altered, yet the acts from that principle were his own acts, and his own righteousness. So Abraham was not justified by his works after believing, no more than by those before: Rom. iv. 3, 'Abraham believed God, and it was accounted to him for righteousness.' For those words, cited out of Gen. xv. 6, were spoken of Abraham, several years after his call and compliance with it by faith, and here singled out as the cause of his justification, without any concomitance of his own works flowing from that faith, or any mixture of them, or consideration of them by God in this justifying act. And David, though he was a great prophet, yet had not so distinct a knowledge of the gospel as those that live in the times of the gospel, yet under that legal administration wherein he was born, and bred, and lived all his days, had no confidence in his own works, not in those which he wrought as God's servant, out of love to him, fear of him, trust in him; he refuses all venturing his soul upon them, before the tribunal of God, when he desires God not to enter into judgment with him: Ps. cxliii. 2, 'Enter not into judgment with thy servant;' 'Answer me in thy righteousness,' ver. 1, not according to my own. Enter not into judgment with thy servant; though I be thy servant, and mine own conscience tells me I have an upright heart towards thee, yet I dare not enter into a plea with thee upon my service, or stand before thy judgment-seat in the strength of my works; and the reason he renders shows that he understood it of justification, and is inclusive of all men that ever drew breath, for it is as generally expressed as anything can be: 'For in thy sight shall no man living be justified.' Not an apostle, martyr, prophet, can stand before God when he compares his action with the rule. David was far from any confident sentiment of his own works, or the strength of the blood of legal sacrifices. How often does he aggravate his crimes, and debase the value of his services, and speak of the sacrifices, as unable to render a satisfaction to God! We see the father of the faithful, the greatest type of Christ, and he that seems the most rational among the apostles, disclaiming any justification by their own works, even by those wrought by them after they were really listed in the service of God.

And there is good reason for it.

[1.] No righteousness of man is perfect, and therefore no righteousness of man is justifying. Whatsoever works do justify, must be, in the extent of them, and all the circumstances, fully conformed unto that precept that enjoins them. What man has a righteousness commensurate with the rule of the law, whereby his works are to be tried? Again, every man, the moment before his justification, is ungodly, Rom. iv. 5. He is in that state just before his justification. If he be justified by his own works, he is then justified by ungodly works, and then a contradiction will follow, that a man is justified by his merit of condemnation, and pronounced righteous upon the account of his unrighteousness. It is as much as to say, a man shall be justified by his sinfulness, and be judged an observer of the law by his transgressing it.

First, The mixture of one sinful act among a multitude of good works, renders a man imperfect, and consequently incapable of justification by them. Suppose a man had only one sin, and all his other works clear without a flaw, the law could not pronounce him righteous, because he fell short of that universal and perpetual rectitude which the law requires in all things: Gal. iii. 10, 'Cursed is he that continueth not in all things which are written in the book of the law, to do them.' If he fails but in one thing, and that but once in his whole life, and that but in the omission of any one circumstance it requires, be sinks under the curse. But since a man never performed in his whole life a duty entirely exact, with what face can he expect a justification from that law, which he never observed with that exactness due to it in any one action that ever he did? Works are debts; unless a debt be fully paid, a man cannot be said to be a righteous person. If a man owes a thousand pound, and pays nine hundred ninety-nine pound nineteen shillings, and pays not that one shilling, which is as much due as the whole, he is unrighteous in withholding that, and the bond may be put in suit against him for that if the creditor please. What man ever paid the full debt of works he owed to God by virtue of the law? How far is any man from paying all the parts of his debt but one only? Suppose we had not only a perfect work, but many perfect works, all perfect works but one the works might justify themselves, but not justify the person that has a stain upon him in the account of the law. But the case is more deplorable for if God will contend with man, he 'cannot answer him one of a thousand,' Job ix. 2, 3. Some of the Jews interpret it thus: that the arguments and pleas men can bring from their own works, for their defence before his tribunal, are so weak and trifling, that God in scorn would not vouchsafe to give a reply to one plea of theirs among a thousand. But rather it is to be understood, that man cannot render one little reason among a thousand pleas for his own justification, on any one of a thousand of those charges God can bring against him.

Secondly, There is not one act a man does, but there is matter of condemnation in it. As the Scripture excepts every man from doing good, as considered in his natural corruption, Rom. iii. 12, so it excepts every man from doing any one pure good action: Eccles. vii. 20, 'There is not a just man upon earth, that doeth good, and sins not,' i. e. he does not do any good work without a mixture of sin; and therefore the Scripture pronounces a man's 'own righteousness as filthy rags,' Isa. lxiv. 6. Righteousness in the whole extent of it, whatsoever he does that is righteous in a way of eminency, is but a filthy rag, it is but a shred, and that filthy too. And to think it is able to purge the soul from sin, is as much as to think to wash away one mud by another. That which is condemning cannot be justifying, that which falls short of the holiness of the law cannot free us from the condemning sentence of the law. But there is nothing that a man does but is defective, if compared with the law, which requires an exactness of obedience in every act, without any stain. It requires perfection in the person, and perfection in every service; it allows no blemish, nor pronounces a man righteous, where it does not find a completeness both for parts and time. It is so far therefore from justifying, that it must needs condemn. 'For the righteousness of the law must be fulfilled in every one of us,' Rom. viii. 4. Whatsoever plea we can raise from our own works, will represent us guilty, and that can never be the matter of our absolution, which has sufficient matter of condemnation in it. Tainted work is never able to maintain its standing before the infinite holiness of God.

Thirdly, All the works after grace fall short of the perfection required in them by the law. I do not say they fall altogether short of the perfection required in them by the gospel, i. e. fall short of that integrity and sincerity which is our evangelical perfection; but they fall short of that perfection which is required by the law. There is no grace in any renewed man in this life in that perfect degree it ought to be. Corruption of nature remains in every man, with regeneration of nature. It is true there is a new principle put in, but not so powerful as to abolish that principle which possessed us before, though it does overmaster it. There is a 'flesh lusting against the spirit,' as well as a 'spirit lusting against the flesh,' Gal. v. 17. And Paul, that was renewed as much as any man we ever knew renewed, had a flesh that served the law of sin, with a mind that served the law of God, Rom. vii. 25. No grace is wrought to its full growth. There is staggering in our faith, and coldness in our love, and hardness in our melting;

and therefore it was a good speech of Luther's, We can never be saved, if God does not turn his eyes from our virtues as well as our sins. How can that, the unrighteousness whereof was our burden before the throne of God, be our righteousness before him? How can that heal us, which stands in need of cure, and renders us sick? Who can bring a clean thing out of an unclean? Or the highest righteousness out of an unclean newness, and an imperfect regeneration? If our duties after grace be so corrupt that they need something to render them acceptable, and accepted in the sight of God, they can never be of that worth as to render our persons righteous; for that which needs something to make itself valid, can never make any other thing valid. If our duties want a pardon, and something to cover the defects, and wipe off the blemishes of them, they can never, upon any bottom of their own, plead themselves to be a sufficient righteousness for a guilty sinner, guilty in the acting that which is pleaded as a righteousness. No flesh can be justified in the sight of God, and nothing that comes from flesh can be our righteousness. The best man being in part flesh, all his works are in part fleshly. Where the nature is wholly corrupt, the fruit cannot be good; where the nature is in part corrupt, the fruit of the new nature must be tinctured by the steams of the old, and therefore is too defective to bottom our happiness upon.

And consider but these two things:

First, Men's own consciences cannot but accuse them of coming short of the glory of God, in everything they do. Can any man upon earth say he ever did a perfect action, that he dares venture his soul upon it, in the presence of God? There is no man's conscience but must needs accuse him of sin: 1 John i. 8, 'He that saith he has no sin, has nothing of the truth in him;' and what man's conscience ever bore that testimony to him, that he was perfect in all his works? Does it not rather witness that be has numberless times violated the divine precepts? Who can say he did perfectly exert an act of faith, so entire, fixed, steady, as might suit the divine holiness, or that his love had such an intense flame in any service he presented to God? No man yet, upon serious consideration, did ever judge any one of big works perfect before God. He must have very mean thoughts of the holiness of God, or be very inconsiderate of his own actions, and not dive into all the matter and circumstances of them, if he so judged. Indeed, Paul says, he knew nothing by himself, i. e. of unfaithfulness in declaring the mysteries of God, as to the matter and substance of them, yet would he not venture his justification upon that bottom, 1 Cor. iv. 4. A self-justification in this would be a self-condemnation: Job ix. 20, 'If I justify myself, my own mouth shall condemn me: if I say, I am perfect, it shall also prove me perverse.'

Secondly, But, suppose there be no accusations of conscience, durst we stand to God's trial of our works? The omniscience of God pierces further than our knowledge; for 'who can understand the errors of his ways?' Ps. xix. 12. If any action might be perfect in our account, shall we therefore think it so in the account of God's unspotted holiness, who is greater than our hearts, and knows more than our hearts? 'Who can stand before so holy a God?' 1 Sam. vi. 20. Job, therefore, chap. ix. 21, would not know his own soul, though he were perfect, he would not approve or boast of himself in the presence of God; for he might be ignorant of something in his own spirit which never yet reached his notice, but was not unknown to God, that knew all things; he would despise his life, i. e. overlook all his upright course, and bury it in silence, when he comes to appear before God.

Fourthly, Since, therefore, all our own righteousness is of this hue, it would be contrary to the justice and holiness of God to justify a man for imperfect works. His judgment is always according to truth, Rom. ii. 2. If he should judge and accept that for a perfect righteousness which is notoriously imperfect in itself, it would imply a defect in the understanding of the judge, whereby he is changed, and judges that to be exact holiness now which he judged not so before. But certainly, if it be an imperfect righteousness, the infinite understanding of God can never imagine it perfect, and the holiness of God would never deceive itself in accepting that as perfect which is not in its own nature so. If imperfect works of grace can justify now, what reason can be rendered for the strictness God required of the first man in the first covenant, and his severe dealing with him upon the transgression of it? The best reason, and most becoming the majesty of God, is the holiness of his nature, which is as infinite now as when he made the first covenant. If that holiness can now content itself with an imperfect righteousness, and pronounce us justified persons without a full conformity to the law, it might take a little further step, and pronounce us righteous without any conformity at all to it. If he could deny his holiness and truth in one thing, he might upon the same account deny it in all, and so lay it aside by degrees till it came to nothing. If we rightly understand the infiniteness of God's holiness, we cannot conceive that anything imperfect can justify us before so exact and strict a tribunal, where sits the omniscience of God to see, the holiness of God to hate, and the justice of God to punish, every defect and deviation from his law.

[2.] The design of God was to justify us in such a way as to strip us of all matter of glorying in ourselves, and therefore it is not by any righteousness of our own. This the apostle in many places asserts, Rom. iii. 26, 27. He justifies by the law of faith, to exclude boasting, which would not have been excluded by the law of works; and Eph. ii. 9, 'Not of works, lest any man should boast.' He had before spoken of salvation or justification by grace, ver. 5; and to strike men's bands off from resting on anything in themselves, and put our own righteousness out of countenance, he repeats it again, ver. 8, 'By grace ye are saved, and that not of yourselves; not of works,' because God will have all boasting excluded. The apostle's argument holds as strong against the works of grace as those of nature, the works after the receiving of the gospel as those of the law; it would else be invalid, for if we were justified by our own works, wrought by us after the grace of redemption communicated to us, it would but little more exclude boasting than the works of Adam wrought by him in the rectitude of his nature, which was the gift of God to him. The natural principle of his actions, as well as the gracious principle of a believer's, were bestowed on them by God. That was an act of God's goodness, this of his grace. And they are our works by grace, as well as the acts of Adam in innocence would have been his works by nature. For though the works of grace are wrought from a principle implanted by the Spirit of God, yet they are not the works of that Spirit, no more than Adam's works could be said to be the works of God, because they were from a principle implanted in him by God. The works would have been Adam's, by the concurrence of God as Creator, and those works are a believer's by the concurrence of God as Redeemer. And if we were justified by them, there would be as well matter of boasting as there would have been in Adam had he stood and been efficiently justified or pronounced righteous upon his innocent works. God hates any glorying before him. The Pharisee, therefore, that displayed his righteousness in the temple before God, with some kind of reflection upon his own worth, Luke xviii. 10-12, with some kind of exaltation of himself and contempt of the publican, went away unjustified, though he did thankfully acknowledge his eminency in morality above the publican to stream to him from the goodness of God. And no good man in Scripture ever pleaded his own works in prayer to God for his justification, though sometimes they have appealed to God concerning their integrity in a particular action. Daniel disowns his own righteousness, Dan. ix. 18; and the famous cardinal and champion of the Romish church, upon his deathbed, would rely on the merits of Christ, though he had disputed for the merit of works. So sensible are men of the little matter they have to glory of in themselves, when they are ready to stand before the tribunal of God. God in justification will have the entire glory of his grace to himself; but if any work of ours, though never so gracious, were the cause but in part of our justification, we had whereof to glory. If we divided it between Christ and ourselves, Christ would have but half the glory, and the other half would be due to us.

To conclude, no man can be justified but by a covenant of grace, and by the righteousness of God, not his own; since all men have been under the corruption of original sin, no man has arrived to happiness by any righteousness of his own. Every man being a sinner is under the curse of the law, and being accursed by it, cannot be justified by it. The law does not frown and smile upon a man at one and the same time. It proposes no recompense but to those that entirely observe it, and denounces a curse upon those that in the least do violate it; it accuses, does not justify, and fills the conscience with darkness and despair, not with comfort and peace.

6. We are therefore justified by a righteousness imputed to us. 'The blood of Christ cleanseth us from all sin.' It is not inherent in us, but in the veins of Christ; it is not physically or corporally applied to us, but juridical, in a judicial way, and therefore imputed to us, and that for justification. Hence we are said to be justified by his blood, Rom. v. 9. If justified by his blood, then meritoriously; the merit of that blood must then be imputed to us, and we upon the account of it pronounced righteous by God, since this blood was never inherent in us. Hence forgiveness of sins and justification is often ascribed unto it, Rom. iii. 23-25, Col. i. 14. As our iniquities were charged upon him, so his righteousness is derived to us. Our iniquities were never inherent in him, but imputed to him; so his blood never was inherent in us, but imputed to us for the satisfaction of the law, and so for our justification from the penalty and curse of it. If it were our righteousness that were imputed to us, it would be an imputation of debt, not of grace, Rom. iv. 4. It cannot be inherent righteousness, because it is a righteousness imputed without works, ver. 6; but no inherent righteousness is without works. Again, ver. 5, the object of justification is an ungodly person, one that has no righteousness of his own. But since there must be a complete righteousness to justify him, it must be the righteousness of another, for being ungodly, it cannot be his own. It is therefore by the righteousness of one man, Christ: Rom. v. 19, 'As we are made sinners by one man's disobedience, so we are made righteous by one man's obedience.' Our being made sinners by one man's disobedience, was no personal act of our own, but a personal act of Adam's; so we are made righteous, not by a personal obedience of our own, but by the perpetual obedience of Christ, which cannot be of advantage to us, unless some way or other counted to us.

Use 2; of comfort. The comfort of a a believer has a strong and lasting foundation in the blood of Christ. All our sins met upon Christ as they did upon the scape-goat, and were carried away with the streams of his blood. A cleansing blood was not the language of the first covenant. It required blood to be poured out in a way of revenge, not to be poured out and applied for the pardon of others. What can relieve us, if this blood, shed by a holy Saviour, and accepted by a righteous judge, cannot? This blood has removed the curse, purchased our liberty, and may therefore calm every believing conscience. What expression can be more stored with comfort than this, 'The blood of Jesus Christ his Son cleanseth us from all sin.'

1. The title is cheering. 'The blood of Jesus Christ his Son.' The titles of the blood of God, and the righteousness of God, are enough to answer all objections, and testify a virtue in it as incomprehensible

as that of his Godhead, which elevated it to an infinite value. What wounds are so deep that they cannot be healed by the sovereign balsam of so rich a blood? What sins are too great to be expiated, and what diseases too desperate to be cured, by the blood of him that created the world? How great is that blood, that must have more of value, since it is the blood of the Son of God, than all sins can have of guilt, since they are the sins of the sons of men! The blood of Christ is as much above the guilt of our sins, as the excellency of his person is above the meanness of ours.

2. And who can fathom the comfort that is in the extensiveness of the object? All sin. As we are not limited in the Lord's prayer to pray for the forgiveness of some debts only, and not for others, but pray for the forgiving of trespasses indefinitely, so there is no stint set to the virtue of this cleansing blood. All transgressions to it are like a grain of sand, or the drop of a bucket to the ocean, no more seen or distinguished when it is swallowed up by that mass of waters. It is a 'plenteous redemption,' since it redeems Israel, and all the Israel of God, from all their iniquities, Ps. cxxx. 7, 8. His blood can cleanse as many sins as his Godhead can create worlds, and those are numberless; since there is no limits to his power there can be none to his blood. Though our sins have weakened the law, and made it unable to save us, yet they cannot weaken the omnipotent satisfaction of the Redeemer. The multitude of sins in the sinner enhance the vastness of the payment made by the surety. Let not any believing soul be dejected, or any soul that would cordially believe and resign himself up to the conduct of Christ. That blood that has cleansed so many from sin, and from such multitudes of sins, in their several capacities, can cleanse you from all your sins, were they as great as all those jointly that have been cleansed by it from the beginning of the world. For what hindrance is there but that it can do the same in one person that it has done in many? When we look upon the multitude of our sins, our pride and vain imaginations, our omissions of service, our carelessness in the ways of God, there cannot but be a hanging down the head, till we lift up our eyes to the cross and see all balanced by the blood of the Son of God, which cannot be overtopped by the guilt of a believing person.

3. And does not the word cleanse deserve a particular consideration? What does that note but,

(1.) Perfection. It cleanses their guilt so that it 'shall not be found,' Jer. l. 20. What can justice demand more of us, more of our Saviour, than what has been already paid? The everlasting death of a believing sinner cannot be challenged by it, since the blood of a redeeming Saviour has been shed for it. It were injustice to put the creature upon an imperfect satisfaction, since the surety has given a complete one; and injustice to punish him that is no longer guilty of a crime in the judgment of the law of redemption, since by faith he relies upon the blood of the Redeemer. Justice can no more condemn any that are objects of mercy by receiving the blood of the second covenant, than mere mercy can save any one that remains an object of revenging justice under the first covenant. By this means we do not stand before God only as innocent persons, but as those that have fulfilled the law, both as to precept and penalty, Rom. viii. 4.

(2.) Continuance of justification; the present tense implies a continued act. Christ's blood is never lost and congealed, as the blood of the legal sacrifices. His blood is called a 'new way,' Heb. x. 19, 20, prosjatoV; the word rendered new signifies a thing newly slain or sacrificed. His blood is as new and fresh for the work it was appointed to as when it was shed upon the cross, as full of vigour as if it had been shed but this moment; it is a blood that was not drunk up by the earth, but gathered up again into his body to be a living, pleading, cleansing blood in the presence of God for ever. He did not leave his body and blood putrefying in the grave, the sacrifice had then ceased and corrupted, it had not been of everlasting efficacy, as now it is. The justification of a believer stands upon as certain terms as the justification of Christ himself before God. His was upon the account of shedding his blood, ours upon the account of embracing his blood. He was justified by God after his bleeding, Isa. l. 6, 8, and brought in triumph, and sending a challenge to any to condemn him, since God had justified him, ver. 9; which words the apostle alludes to, Rom. viii. 33, 34, to show the unrepeatableness of justification, and applies them to believers, though they were spoken by Christ in his own case. Christ was justified by his resurrection: 1 Tim. iii. 16, 'Justified in the Spirit,' which is no other than what Peter expresses by being 'quickened in the Spirit,' 1 Peter iii. 18. As Christ was justified by his resurrection from all the sins which met upon him on the cross, and that for ever, so are believers cleansed from all their guilt, and that for ever, by virtue of this blood. The meritorious plea of this blood continuing for ever, is not without the perpetual act of the righteous Judge justifying those for whom it is pleaded.

Hence will follow security at the last judgment. His blood cleanses from all sin here, and his voice shall absolve from all sin hereafter. He that has been a propitiation for your guilt, and an advocate against your accusers, shall never as a judge condemn you for your sins. He does not indeed judge as a priest, but as a king; but his kingly power is but subservient to his priestly office, since he was more solemnly confirmed in that, viz. by an oath, than in the other; and therefore his royal authority shall never ruin any whom his priestly sacrifice has restored to their lost inheritance. Let no believing soul therefore despond, let him draw this blood over his fears to stifle them, as God has done over his sins to cancel them, and drown them in this same ocean into which God has hurled his transgressions.

Use 3; of exhortation.

Have recourse only to this blood upon all occasions, since it only is able to cleanse us from all our guilt. We have treasured up wrath, and wounded conscience; nothing can pacify a severe wrath, and calm a tempestuous conscience, but this blood. Had we but the guilt of one sin upon us, we stood in need of an expiation by it as well as if we had ten thousand. Every infinite wrong must have an infinite satisfaction. Entertain no disparaging and little thoughts of this blood, which the Scripture pronounces of so plenteous, unsearchable, and great a virtue. It was God's intent to cleanse sin by it, when he agreed with the Redeemer about shedding his blood: Isa. liii. 11, 'My righteous servant shall justify many, for he shall bear their iniquities.' It was set out by him to this end, when it was shed. Zech. xiii. 1, 'In that day a fountain shall be opened for the house of David,' the stronger spirits, and men most according to God's heart, 'and for the inhabitants of Jerusalem,' the weaker sort; for all a fountain to fill every private cistern. Make not the covenant of God with his Son in vain; slight not his grace by refusing to drink of his open fountain. The glory of purging iniquity was reserved by God for this blood, it is committed to no other; the blood of bulls and goats never had, never could, have the honour of so great a work. It is the glorious title of his blood to cleanse from all sins, as it is the honourable signification of his name Jesus to save from all sins. We cannot please God more than by coming to him for the pardon of our sins, upon the account of this blood he has so delighted to honour. If we do not, we deny it the glory of its cleansing virtue; we undervalue the efficacy of it, and would have it without any subject to exercise its power on. We need not fear to approach to it, since God has manifested it highly acceptable to him, and available for us. The unsearchable riches of it should more encourage us than the greatness of our guilt discourage our address. Have recourse to it by faith, resting on the power of this blood, as the means appointed by God, and intended by Christ, for the expiation of sin. Faith as accepting Christ as a king does not justify, but faith as accepting Christ as a priest and sacrifice, as shedding his blood, for we must accept him in that office wherein he made the atonement; and that was not as he was a prophet or a king, but as he was a priest and a sacrifice; and therefore it is called, 'faith in his blood,' Rom. iii. 25, though indeed a faith in his blood is not without receiving him as a king, and submitting to his precepts, as well as relying on his sacrifice. He that receives the blood of Christ, as well as he that names the name of Christ, must depart from iniquity, and avoid those things which break the covenant. Mingle not any thing with his satisfaction; let no muddy waters of your own be mixed with this gospel wine. If we look for a justification by anything else, we forfeit all right of justification by him: Gal. v. 2, 'Behold, I Paul say unto you, that if you be circumcised, Christ shall profit you nothing;' take it for a certain truth, for I as an apostle speak it, that if you have an opinion that you shall be justified by circumcision, or anything of the law, or of your own works, or would make them partakers with Christ in this matter, Christ shall profit you nothing, you had as good never have had a Christ made known to you, for any virtue you are like to derive from him. As none died with him to expiate your guilt, so he will suffer none to be joined with him in justifying your persons. Christ bears this blood only in his hand, when he pleads for us; we should carry this blood only in our hearts when we plead for ourselves. It is not his blood only as shed does justify, but his blood pleaded in the court of heaven by himself, and pleaded before the throne of God by the believing sinner; without it we have no more plea than the apostate angels have, whom God has cast out of his favour for ever. And since we contract guilt every day, let us daily apply the medicine. The pleas of this blood are renewed according to the necessity of our persons. As often as an Israelite had been bitten by the fiery serpents, he must have looked up to the brazen one, if he would not have been destitute of a cure; and we, upon every sting of conscience, must look up to him who has been lifted up upon the cross for our remedy. This blood is appointed for sins after conversion, for those, that walk in the light. Since the fountain is open every day, and we contract guilt every day, let not a day pass without fresh applications of this blood upon any defects in our walking with him; since, 'if we walk in the light,' and are industrious to observe the will of God, 'the blood of Jesus Christ his Son cleanseth us from all sin.'